PEARSON CUSTOM SOCIOLOGY

Formerly published as Intersections, Crossroads & Inequalities

EDITORS

KATHLEEN A. TIEMANN
University of North Dakota
Introduction to Sociology, Social Problems & Issues, Inequalities & Diversity

RALPH B. MCNEAL, JR.
University of Connecticut
Introduction to Sociology

BETSY LUCAL
Indiana University South Bend
Inequalities & Diversity

MORTEN G. ENDER
United States Military Academy, West Point
Inequalities & Diversity

COMPILED BY:

Custom Copy for Triton College
Contemporary Society
An Introduction to Social Science
Perry & Perry

PEARSON

ISBN 10: 1-256-56852-X
ISBN 13: 978-1-256-56852-0

Table of Contents

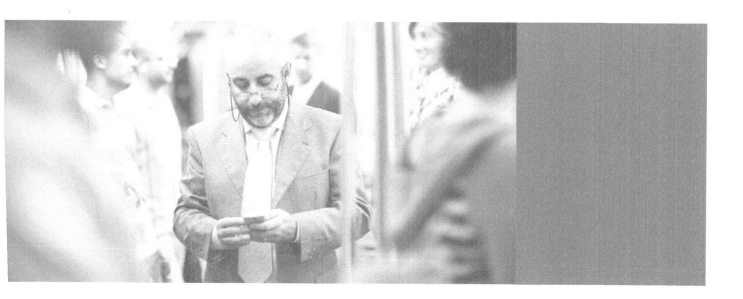

Through the Lens of Science

IN THIS CHAPTER, YOU WILL LEARN

- *of the existence of the external world, which we inherit, and the social world, which we create;*
- *that the analysis of the social world with the tools of science is a fairly recent innovation;*
- *the basic differences between the social and the natural sciences;*
- *which disciplines constitute the social sciences;*
- *the elements and steps of the scientific method; and*
- *the various research methods used in the social sciences.*

Life on our planet has undergone tremendous and dramatic changes since its beginning, both in the natural world into which we are born and the social world we have created and in which we live. What do we mean by the natural and the social worlds? Clearly, at birth all living things enter a physical world that is not of their own making. Plants and animals either adapt to this ready-made environment or die out. They cannot change the nature of their habitat, for on planet Earth all living organisms exist in an environment shaped by forces and governed by laws that are only partially and imperfectly understood and only minimally amenable to change or control. Early humans did not understand this world, so they attributed many phenomena to spirits and supernatural beings. Today, the natural world is studied by the methods of science in such disciplines as biology, physics, chemistry, ecology, and so on. These disciplines are the so-called natural or exact sciences and are not within the realm of our inquiry in this text.

Each newly born human being, however, also enters a social world that has been shaped by those born previously and is continually reshaped by each new generation. The existence of this social world, although taken for granted by the majority of people, is of seminal importance to humans. It is what distinguishes them from other animals. Animals, aside from certain biological adaptations to new environments or climates (adaptations that sometimes lead to their extinction), retain an essentially unchanged lifestyle from the moment of their

From Chapter 1 of *Contemporary Society: An Introduction to Social Science,* Thirteenth Edition. John A. Perry, Erna K. Perry. Copyright © 2012 by Pearson Education, Inc. All rights reserved.

emergence. Humans, on the other hand, have manipulated their social world to the point of affecting their lifestyles dramatically. This social world was not always well understood either, but in the past 200 years, disciplines have originated with the goal of examining it with the same scientific methodology that the exact sciences use. These disciplines are collectively called the social sciences.

The social sciences were born in a period of turmoil, when new ideas and beliefs were causing conflict and fragmentation in European societies. They represented an attempt to make sense of a reality that had become too difficult to grasp with the old tools. They offered the hope that the social world—the way people live—could also be examined in a dispassionate, objective way that would yield specific rules of behavior for people to follow to improve their individual and collective lives. Perhaps the expectations for the social sciences were too high: despite efforts, few grand theories have been developed or secrets of social life uncovered. Nonetheless, the social sciences and their methodology remain effective—and probably unique—tools for rationally examining our social world. Today, if one needed a reason for studying the social sciences, it would be sufficient to note that the autocratic government of Iran is trying to forbid the study of social sciences at their universities because they "promote doubts and uncertainty" (Slackman, 2009). Doubts and uncertainty are the conditions that lead people to seek the truth.

The Social Sciences

The purpose of the social sciences is to study systematically all aspects of the human condition and of human behavior, using a methodology borrowed from the physical sciences wherever possible. This insistence on systematic and methodical study is what distinguishes the social sciences from philosophy, art, and literature, which also comment and reflect on all facets of the human condition. In fact, insights into the nature of human behavior and the characteristics of societies have been expressed by artists, poets, and philosophers since time immemorial. Artists, poets, and philosophers avail themselves of such tools as intuition, imagination, authority, tradition, rational thought, and common sense, tools available to all of us and which we still use every day.

Unfortunately, however, these tools have a major shortcoming: They are not always accurate and thorough, and they are often colored by individual or societal prejudices. For instance, for centuries people believed that the earth was flat, and thus, one could fall off its edge. That was a reasonable deduction if one used only one's senses: The earth does look flat when we look only as far as our eyes reach. It was also accepted knowledge that the earth was the center of the universe and the sun went around it, and that too was a logical conclusion if all one did was look with the naked eye. However, when instruments were invented that could measure and see beyond the human senses, the knowledge that until then had been accepted as truth needed to be modified, and that did not happen without a fight. The Polish astronomer Nicolaus Copernicus (1473–1543) and the Italian astronomer Galileo Galilei (1564–1642) were ostracized and nearly lost their lives when they tried to convince their compatriots that it was the earth that circled the sun, not the other way around, thus challenging the ancient wisdom of such authorities as Aristotle and the Catholic Church. These astronomers had not trusted their senses alone, but attempted to arrive at the truth by using a new tool of inquiry: science.

Technology marches on! Social scientists have another tool at their disposal—the ubiquitous computer—to help them in researching how people interact even in the remotest societies.

Galileo Galilei, an Italian astronomer and mathematician, built one of the earliest telescopes, which he is showing in this drawing. Having looked at the night sky with this new tool, he theorized that it was the earth that moved around the sun and not the other way around, as was commonly believed in his time. Today, the social sciences also attempt to dispel some widely held, but incorrect, beliefs.

The Social World Seen through the Lens of Science

Science may be briefly defined as a method using a system of rational inquiry dependent on the empirical testing of facts. It is this method, rather than a particular body of content, that gives scientists a unique way of looking at things. The purpose of the scientific method is to obtain evidence that is verifiable and subject to replication and to make no judgment about even the most seemingly obvious "facts" until original suppositions are overwhelmingly supported by proof.

The social sciences emerged when some social philosophers determined to use the scientific method to study specific aspects of human behavior in the social world. Initially, social philosophy differed little from philosophy in general, but certain ideas prevalent in the eighteenth century, during the era commonly called the Enlightenment, led to the division of social philosophy into a number of separate disciplines. This historical period was characterized by an increase in people's faith in the power of reason. Scholars and philosophers became convinced that just as universal laws of nature had been discovered by natural scientists through the use of the scientific method, similar laws would become apparent if human behavior could be examined by the same approach. Once the principles of social life were uncovered, they theorized, a more perfect society could be attained.

As usually happens, the need for a new approach to the analysis of human social behavior was prompted by dramatic societal changes. The conditions brought about by the Industrial Revolution and the movement of people to cities encouraged thinkers to seek solutions to the many new problems faced by individuals in these changed societies. With the rise of industry, in fact, two new social classes emerged: the owners of manufacturing machinery and the industrial workers who operated it. There were vast discrepancies in the standards of living between these two social classes, with the workers laboring for long hours in difficult conditions and suffering frequent layoffs. As people kept moving to cities in search of factory jobs, cities became places in which conditions of overcrowding and lack of hygiene were rampant. Soon, cities became breeding grounds of poverty and crime. The early social scientists attempted to address these problems by applying the scientific method to human behavior, in this way giving rise to the social sciences. These include cultural anthropology, economics, geography (including demography and ecology), political science, psychology, sociology, and those dimensions of history that go beyond the strictly narrative recounting of events.

What do the social sciences study today? Following are some examples of what contemporary social science examines. An economist at Georgetown University is one of four authors of a report that concludes that childhood poverty costs the United States about $500 billion a year because poor children become less productive adults, earn less money, commit more crimes, and have more health problems that are paid for by taxpayers. Consequently, the authors suggest that the United States would be well served to invest significant resources to poverty reduction (Eckholm, 2007, A15).

For years, numerous economists have been producing studies attempting to explain the working of the economy. Following the meltdown of the American and world economies, many have also tried to explain the reasons for it, especially regarding the subprime mortgage crisis that has precipitated foreclosures and the loss of homes for so many Americans—unfortunately, too late to prevent such losses. Unemployment and the loss of jobs in specific industries or segments of the economy are also issues probed by economists.

Sociologists at Northwestern University's Institute for Policy Research attempted to find out the income level of students attending a four-year university and those attending a two-year school to find out which kinds of students graduate from these schools and which drop out; whether more students at public schools or private schools commit to graduate, and why (Stephan, Rosenbaum, and Person, 2010).

Sociologists and demographers at several universities in California noted that elderly immigrants often live in conditions of isolation, even though they might have immigrated to provide their children a better life. Their young children assimilate and accommodate themselves to American society, but their parents and grandparents cannot. They generally do not speak English, and many do not drive. Consequently, they are depressed, in addition to feeling rejected by their own children. When this research was made public, social agencies began offering help (Brown, 2009).

Stanford University psychologists and economists designed a study to find out which part of the brain is active when a person decides to spend money at a shopping mall, and what produces the urge to buy (Tierney, 2007, D1). A Columbia University sociologist tries to decode social interactions to discover why people give themselves reasons for actions and attitudes (Gladwell, 2006, 80).

Criminologists study conditions leading to criminal behavior, recidivism rates, the effect of prison on inmates, and many other issues. Psychiatrists and psychologists have been helpful to victims of a variety of crimes, particularly rapes and kidnappings, aiding in their readjustment to society.

Archaeologists continually find fossils that tell us about changes in the natural world. They also discover remains of past societies that have left no written records, enabling us to see the important progression of culture.

Finally, the social sciences are increasingly combining with the exact sciences to discover findings in the areas of medicine and climate, findings that eventually affect and possibly benefit people and societies. The disciplines of social cognitive neuroscience study the way genes influence behavior—using biological information—and vice versa, how social behavior affects biology—in the form of genetic changes.

Box 1   Consilience

Scientific knowledge has expanded so rapidly that today any layperson knows much more about how things work than a nineteenth-century physician did. Harvard naturalist Edward O. Wilson believes that such expansion of knowledge is due to the scientific method. Moreover, Wilson argues in his book, *Consilience: The Unity of Knowledge*, that human behavior and human affairs can only be interpreted through biology and the other natural sciences. He maintains that social scientists, by ignoring the natural sciences, have handicapped their efforts at expanding the knowledge of their own disciplines. The reason for the success of the natural sciences, according to Wilson, is consilience, by which the author means a linking of insights from a number of different disciplines into a system of explanation that is coherent. As an example, modern medicine is based on the knowledge gathered from molecular and cell biology, which in turn are based on genetics, which ultimately obey the laws of physics. The social sciences, on the other hand, often seem to operate as if they inhabited a separate

(Continued)

Box 1 Consilience (*Continued*)

universe. Wilson insists that to gain self-awareness, "we must accept that human life is a physical phenomenon, generated and sustained by the same principles as bugs, trees and fishes" (Cowley, 1998, 59).

These ideas are not new. In a preceding book, *Sociobiology: The New Synthesis,* Wilson posited that certain tendencies in human behavior—status seeking, altruism, nepotism—have a biological basis. A number of critics on the left, however, panned the book, accusing its author of social Darwinism (because life is competitive, winners are superior and rise to the top, and losers are inferior and eventually disappear). Nonetheless, the author continued to elaborate on sociobiology, and today a number of psychologists and sociologists are beginning to test his idea that human behavior has a biological component. For example, psychologists and neuroscientists have shown that the mind—a social concept—is the product of the brain—a physical organ. Because the brains of contemporary humans have evolved in the process of natural selection, certain aptitudes, biases, and abilities of humans that affect their behavior exist because they facilitated survival in some previous environment. In fact, studies have shown that people everywhere have an innate ability to acquire language, to recognize faces and the meaning of facial expressions, and that they avoid incest. It turns out that many of these abilities are located in specific areas of the brain, which neuroscientists are now tracing. Neuroscientists are also beginning to understand what dreams are, and here too they have found that certain areas of the brain are responsible for them. In the same way, Wilson believes that some day, using the combination of natural and social sciences, social scientists will find the reasons for war, inflation, and religion. They could settle the question of which social arrangements best accommodate the universal features of human nature, or which environmental conditions bring out the best or the worst in human beings.

Ultimately, Wilson hopes that through consilience, humans, who have become the greatest destroyers of life, will come to realize how dependent they are on other earthbound organisms. In Wilson's own words, "Most of the issues that vex humanity daily—ethnic conflict, arms escalation, overpopulation, abortion, environmental destruction, and endemic poverty, to cite several

of the most persistent—can be solved only by integrating knowledge from the natural sciences with that from the social sciences and the humanities. Only fluency across the boundaries will provide a clear view of the world as it really is, not as it appears through the lens of ideology and religious dogma, or as a myopic response solely to immediate need. . . . A balanced perspective cannot be acquired by studying disciplines in pieces; the consilience among them must be pursued" (Wilson, 1998, 62).

Wilson's ideas are being followed by other scientists. As noted earlier, some economists are beginning to use some tools of physics to study markets and other economic phenomena. These so-called econophysicists point out that incomes and wealth behave very much like atoms. The distribution pattern of upper-middle-class incomes (approximately $150,000) in the United States, in fact, follows a pattern called "exponential," which is the same pattern of the energy of atoms in gases that are at thermal equilibrium. This pattern is also one that is used by many other random systems. The incomes of the wealthiest 3 percent follow what is called in physics a *power law:* a very long distance between their high income and the income of the next layer. Most other developed nations follow a similar pattern of income distribution. Therefore, the econophysicists say, even though individuals have a will and governments try to redistribute wealth, neither will succeed because "large, complex systems have their own statistical logic that trumps individual, and state, decisions" (Shea, 2005, 67).

Behavioral economists, teamed with psychologists, have also developed a "Tightwad–Spendthrift" scale intended to predict whether a person will spend a lot of money on things they do not necessarily need or forgo the purchase and keep the cash. They positioned volunteers in an MRI machine, gave them an amount of money they could spend, and showed them images of a variety of objects. When a subject saw something of interest, one specific area of the brain lit up, showing activity there. If the object held no interest for the volunteer, another area of the brain became active. It was thus possible for the researchers to see, before the volunteers made their decision, whether they were going to buy the object or not (Tierney, 2007, D1 and D6).

The Scientific Method

In defining the social sciences, the key to remember is that they study data *systematically* and *methodically*. In other words, they use the scientific method. This method uses both qualitative and quantitative approaches, the one describing, defining, and concerned with meanings, the other focusing on counting and measuring phenomena.

Because the social world is subjected to scientific scrutiny, the knowledge that has accumulated about how humans live in their world is organized according to definite concepts, theories, and research and not according to random, subjective, and possibly biased observation. However, these disciplines cannot employ exactly the same methodology as the natural or physical sciences. They do share with all sciences the use of the scientific method. The basic technique of the scientific method is a special kind of observation called *scientific observation*. This kind of observation differs from simply looking around. Those of us who have the use of our vision look at things all the time, but we seldom arrive at scientific conclusions. We obtain evidence from our senses, but for such evidence to be reliable, it must first be confirmed by the scientific method. That is, scientific observation must proceed *systematically*. Scientists must select and define a problem and then make an organized plan for collecting data. Scientific observation must be *accurate and precise*. In collecting data, scientists must subject them to careful checking, rechecking, and cross-checking, as well as to careful measurement. Scientific observation should take place under *controlled conditions*, although that is frequently impossible. Researchers should be able to make particular features of the environment remain constant, so that when other features change, they can be sure which specific cause is determining which effect. This requirement is difficult to achieve in the social sciences because research on people cannot always be performed in a laboratory. Control is difficult, even in the natural sciences, because many phenomena can only be observed at a distance. Finally, scientific observation must be made by a *trained observer*. Only such a person knows which data are relevant and which are only peripherally important. The vocabulary of science includes concepts, theories, and research.

Concepts

Concepts are generalized, abstract ideas that symbolize whole categories of people, objects, and processes. They are ways of classifying things that are in the same category. For instance, the concept of "chair" includes all those objects made for people to sit on, although there is an infinite variety of such objects, from gilded Louis XIV antiques to the chrome-and-vinyl kitchen variety. Concepts are used to simplify the way people think and communicate. Society, nation, art, education, and voting are only some examples of concepts.

Concepts are used by social scientists to generalize about some aspects of human interaction. They are guidelines that direct the interpretation and analysis of reality. Concepts are the technical vocabulary of the social sciences, and they have precise meanings that may differ considerably from the generally understood versions.

Theories

Theories are sets of concepts and generalizations so arranged that they explain and predict possible relationships among phenomena. In the social sciences, theories are formulations of principles of behavior through which scientists try to increase their knowledge of human interaction. Theories are founded on observation and analysis using the vocabulary of concepts. Without theories, the accumulation of knowledge would be impossible, just as the formulation of theories would be impossible without concepts.

A theory does not have the force of a law. A law is an explanation of unchanging relationships among events. According to the law of gravity, an object always falls in the same direction under given conditions. The social sciences have no laws because they deal with people rather than with inanimate objects, and people have intelligence and will that are not subject to unchangeable laws. Theories are always open to change and even to total rejection if new evidence is presented to challenge them. Finally, when people speak of "theory" in casual conversation, they mean nothing more than a guess. In scientific terminology, a theory carries much more weight because it is based on supporting evidence.

Research

Research tests and bolsters, or refutes, theories. Research may be defined as systematic scientific inquiry conducted under controlled conditions in which data are carefully observed for the purpose of determining the relationship between one factor (for example, income) and one or more other factors (for example, child-rearing techniques).

Variables. The factors whose relationship social scientists try to uncover are called **variables**. These are characteristics that differ (vary) in each individual case—from person to person, from group to group, from time to time, from place to place, and from situation to situation. In explaining what variables are, one social scientist adds, "A variable is a name for something that is thought to influence (or be influenced by) a particular state of being in something else . . . in addition, [it is] a special kind of concept that contains within it a notion of degree or differentiation" (Hoover & Donovan, 1995, 21–22). Age, education, income, religion, and political affiliation are some of the most frequently used variables in social scientific research. Social scientists use measurements, usually of a statistical nature, to determine the value of a variable in a specific case.

Variables, then, are concepts that vary, and they are used in the social sciences to uncover how change in one phenomenon can explain change in another one. Variables are of two kinds: *independent* or *dependent*. **Independent** variables are those that exert influence on **dependent** variables. The relationship between variables may be one of *cause and effect,* in which case the independent variable is the cause, and the dependent variable receives its effect. The relationship between variables may also be one of *correlation,* meaning that two or more variables are simply related in some way. Correlation and causation are distinct phenomena and should not be confused. *Correlation* occurs purely by chance and the variables change together, whereas in *causation,* one phenomenon is responsible for another. Sometimes the correlation among two or more variables turns out to be *spurious,* meaning that it is false— that in reality the association is caused by another factor that scientists have not even considered and did not intend to measure. It is, therefore, imperative that scientific research be carefully controlled. Variables must be clearly stated and must be measurable; the relationship between variables must be equally clear and measurable; and the pursuant hypothesis (that the variables are related) must be testable (Hoover & Donovan, 1995, 35).

Steps of the Scientific Method

The steps in the scientific method, illustrated in Figure 1, may be summarized as follows.

Selecting and Defining a Topic. First, an investigator must have a clearly defined idea of what should be investigated. A topic for investigation is usually prompted by curiosity; thus, it tends to be in the form of a question. For instance, are children of first-generation immigrants more successful in attaining upward mobility than children of native-born citizens? The researcher should also specify whether a causal relationship is suspected (one variable causing the occurrence of another). Because it is difficult to prove causal relationships and distinguish cause from effect, researchers are often satisfied with proving that a correlation between two or more phenomena exists.

Reviewing the Literature. After selecting the topic, the researcher must review all the existing literature on the subject to ensure that it has not already been investigated. If it has, the researcher might have to alter the topic, perhaps focusing on a facet of it that has not been

The Steps of the Scientific Method

FIGURE 1   Science includes the method by which information is obtained. Scientists in all scientific disciplines, therefore, must follow the steps of the scientific method with rigor and objectivity.

investigated previously. A review of the literature is an important step in the scientific method. It connects new research with old, allows the accumulation of ideas, and directs scientists to the right variables to pursue. Libraries are now equipped with computerized systems that make the job of reviewing books and articles much less time consuming than it was in the past.

Forming a Hypothesis.   The **hypothesis** is a tentative statement of the selected topic that is subject to testing and verification. The hypothesis must, in clearly expressed terms, predict a relationship between two or more variables. Hypotheses may be based on a researcher's mere hunch or educated guess; for instance, a researcher may speculate that religion influences the way a person votes. The remaining steps of the scientific method may prove the hypothesis valid (yes, religion affects voting behavior), may cause it to be reformulated (yes, but only if the voter is in a specific age bracket), or may contradict it altogether (no, religion has nothing to do with voting behavior). A hypothesis may also derive from commonsense deductions, curiosity, or traditional wisdom; it may emerge from existing theories and previous research; or it may originate from a review of the literature on an issue that interests a researcher.

Developing a Research Design (Collecting, Classifying, and Analyzing Data). The research plan that is developed after the hypothesis is stated must specify from what group(s) and in what manner data are to be collected. Decisions must also be made about how best to obtain the data (direct observation, questionnaires, interviews, or a combination of research methods).

After data have been systematically collected, the researcher must classify, organize, and record them. Data must also be made public so that others may have access to both the findings and the procedures. In most scientific disciplines, including the social sciences, computers are used to classify and organize data.

The data are then analyzed. In this step, the researcher subjects the previously classified data to various statistical methods to see whether relationships are substantial or so small that they may be due to chance. Statistical computation determines whether the data support the hypothesis.

Verifying. Because most research is subject to error—of which the researcher may or may not be aware—another important step in the scientific method is verification. This step consists of repeating the research project (replication) and may be done either by the scientist who conducted the original research or by another scientist. For research to be considered successful, it must be capable of being repeated by another scientist with the same results.

Generalizing. Finally, conclusions must be drawn from the analysis of data. Do the data substantiate the original hypothesis? Do they refute it? Are alterations to the hypothesis in order? A cautious researcher tends to make undergeneralizations, which may keep his or her research from being useful to others. An overconfident researcher tends to make overgeneralizations, which may lead to false hypotheses and wrong conclusions.

Conclusions are usually summarized in reports, sometimes published in professional journals or as monographs. The researcher attempts to relate the conclusions to existing theories or current research and makes suggestions about the necessity of altering some accepted theoretical assumptions or the need for new hypotheses that have emerged from the research.

The scientific method uses primarily the quantitative approach, which is the approach favored by many social scientists because it is objective and uses mathematical models to reach testable answers. This approach has become much more frequent with the advent of computer technology, which facilitates measurements.

The **qualitative research** approach also consists of collecting data, analyzing and interpreting them, and reaching specific conclusions. However, this method is much more subjective because it depends on the observations of the scientist. Moreover, whereas the **quantitative research** approach measures and counts, looking for explanations of phenomena, the qualitative approach defines and describes phenomena, looking for a deeper understanding. Certain issues lend themselves better to one approach, other issues to the other approach.

The Scientific Spirit: Skepticism, Objectivity, Relativity

Underlying the scientific method is an attitude best described as the *scientific spirit*. The most important principle of the scientific spirit is that scientists approach everything with great *doubt and skepticism,* taking nothing for granted. This attitude must be displayed even with regard to their own findings, which are always subject to change after further analysis.

Another principle is that of *objectivity*. Scientists must try to rid themselves completely of personal attitudes, desires, beliefs, values, and tendencies when confronting data intended to support a finding. They must try to be totally dispassionate, allowing no individual biases to affect their judgment. Of course, such a degree of objectivity is only an ideal to which scientists aspire; no human can be objective all the time. The issue of objectivity has been especially polemical in the social sciences, which deal with the relationships and behavior of people.

Closely related to objectivity is the third principle of the scientific spirit: **ethical neutrality**. According to this principle, scientists must not make value judgments about their findings; they must not pronounce their conclusions to be good or bad, right or wrong. They must be concerned only with whether the findings are true or false.

Finally, scientific conclusions must never be considered final, absolute, or universal truths. Rather, they should be considered as *relative* to the time and place in which they are obtained and always subject to change or revision.

The Social Science Disciplines

The boundaries among the social sciences are artificial in the sense that they all study the same thing: human behavior in the social environment. Each discipline, however, focuses on specific facets of that world and behavior, in effect allowing social scientists to specialize. Social scientists are aware of the overlapping nature of their disciplines, and they often borrow from one another. The differences, in short, are a matter of emphasis.

Anthropology

Anthropology combines a natural science—biology—and information gathered from the social sciences to uncover the relationships between human biological traits and traits acquired socially, that is, by living in groups. The discipline is divided into *physical anthropology,* which is concerned principally with human biological origins and the variations in the human species, and *cultural anthropology,* which has traditionally dealt with the study and comparative analysis of preliterate societies.

Physical anthropologists deal with traits that appear in specific populations and with characteristics that populations develop as a result of adaptation to particular environments. The variety of "racial" groupings among human populations is a subject of research for anthropologists, as are fossil studies and research on living primates. In addition, physical anthropologists use *genetics*, the science that analyzes heredity, in an attempt to uncover how the genes of living organisms determine the characteristics of their offspring. Genetics is particularly useful to social scientists as they try to untangle the complex issue of how much of human behavior is learned and how much is inherited. Another way of putting it is that physical anthropology is divided into three branches that frequently overlap: *paleoanthropology,* meaning the study of fossils, of human and of related species; *primatology,* or the study of primates; and *genetics,* or the study of modern human variability and adaptability.

Cultural anthropology concerns itself with all facets of human culture: kinship forms, linguistics, material artifacts, economic structures, music, and folklore. In addition, cultural anthropologists today are likely to include the study of subgroups within contemporary societies and apply their methodology to new settings. An examination of the gay and lesbian community in a large metropolitan area, for instance, or a description of the lifestyles of prostitutes or the homeless are examples of studies that could be carried out by cultural anthropologists.

AP Photo/Gustavo Ercole

Anthropological research includes much dirty work as researchers dig and sift through many layers to find the fossils that provide clues to the history of the human race.

Anthropologists have developed a gamut of theories, some of which are discussed in the text. They are also trying to use the discipline to understand other cultures, in the short term even for military purposes. For instance, marines in Afghanistan are using anthropology to win the hearts and minds of tribal elders, who are easy targets for joining the Taliban. One of the researchers embedded with the marines maintains that they are using the social sciences to save the lives of Afghans and American soldiers.

Anthropology also includes the field of *archeology*, which is concerned with unearthing fossilized bones and artifacts of humans and other species to furnish dates and historical data about past societies, both those that left no written records and those whose records may have been lost or are incomplete. Anthropological concepts are used to describe the physical development of humans as well as to delineate their chief feature, culture. A recent excavation in Syria, for instance, indicated to scholars that preurban societies that existed in the upper Euphrates River region already had social stratification, with high-ranking elites in leadership positions, that there was a shift from village life to specialized craft production that depended on trade, that there was some kind of industrial site with large kilns for firing pottery and making copper tools. The researchers conclude that the seed of urban civilization had been planted there well before 4000 years BC (Wilford, 2010).

Economics

The economy is a human institution, that is, an ingrained habit through which people have attempted to facilitate their survival in the face of scarcity of resources. Economics is the discipline that studies the systems that societies construct to help them in this endeavor. Economists attempt to understand the activities of people in the production, distribution, and consumption of goods and services necessary to sustain life. They examine the value of work, of natural resources, and of money as a medium of exchange; they define the concepts of supply and demand, savings and investments, cost and price, and economic fluctuations; and they describe the principles used by political systems to justify their methods of distribution of goods and services.

Economics attempts to explain some social processes (such as "who gets what and why"), the origins of some social problems (such as poverty), the importance of work as a source of identity, occupational status, increases or decreases in the standard of living, the effects of rising expectations, and so on.

Economists, too, have availed themselves of a number of theories—classical, neoclassical, Keynesian, monetarist, and others—that will be addressed. A number of Web sites offer clear descriptions of both the theories and the scholars who espoused them (see **mysearchlab.com**).

Geography

Geography is primarily a natural science concerned with the planet we inhabit, that is, the land, bodies of water, mountains, valleys, types of vegetation, and animal habitats. These subjects are in the area of physical geography, which draws most of its knowledge from the disciplines of astronomy, botany, ecology, geochemistry, geology, meteorology, oceanography, and so on. However, geography is also concerned with the ways in which people use the natural environment: why they settle in some locations rather than others, which types of land are good for agriculture and which for mining, what routes of transportation people choose to follow and why, and where people establish their industrial centers. These matters are in the realm of human/cultural geography and depend on information obtained from such social sciences as anthropology, history, political science, psychology, sociology, urban studies, and so on. Of special importance to the social sciences are several disciplines that are offshoots of geography. *Demography* is the study of populations, including increases and decreases in size, composition, age grouping, and future trends. *Ecology* is the science that studies the relationship between all living organisms and their natural environment. It includes *biodiversity*, or the study of the variety and interdependence of species. Geography and its related fields are clearly described online; many links to geographical issues may be found at the National Geographic Web site.

History

History is not universally considered a social science because its primary objective is to record human events for future generations. In fact, historians often cannot use the scientific method. The discipline, however, does attempt to study systematically a sequence of related events—or a number of such sequences—for the purpose of learning about, verifying, and establishing meaningful relationships among them. Because history provides a context in which to study human relationships systematically, it may be considered a social science. Historical facts are interspersed in discussions of every facet of the social sciences because it is impossible to interpret the present and speculate about the future without reference to the past. The **www.history.com** Web site offers numerous links to historical information, as well as offering history in the making.

Political Science

The chief concern of political science is the study of power. The discipline probes the need for an institution to maintain order, make decisions, and provide for defense. It also analyzes the forms the institution takes and the processes that emerge. The discipline includes such concepts as the state, politics, power, and ideology. Historically, political science has had a strong philosophical, legal, and administrative orientation. More recently, the discipline has taken a turn toward the social sciences in that it is concerned with the effect of government and its processes on individuals and groups in society. An important part of political science is *international relations,* which tries to uncover patterns of behavior among the nations of the world. The University of Michigan Web site contains a wealth of resources on the subject, and googling "political science" will result in thousands of informative links.

Psychology

Psychology focuses on the forces that shape and motivate individuals, forming their minds and personalities. The discipline, especially in its medical form, *psychiatry,* draws on the natural sciences for information concerning the physical structure of humans, their nervous system, their physical development and maturation, and other physical processes. It draws on the social sciences for input in the areas of behavior that originate from social interaction. Because psychology deals with human beings, who are complex mixtures of biological and social elements, the discipline is wide ranging and the most experimental of the social sciences. Psychologists must be familiar with human biology as well as with social processes and their effects. For instance, in trying to explain the human capacity to blush, psychologists must understand how the body undergoes certain biologically caused organic changes—blood rushes into the veins and capillaries of our face and chest area. They also must be aware of the social pressures that trigger these changes—someone stares at us, or compliments us, or, on the contrary, scolds us in front of someone whose respect we crave. The embarrassment we feel is expressed by blushing.

Social psychologists specialize in studying socialization, emotions, memory, perception, and intelligence. They also examine such issues as language acquisition, motivation, learning, adjustment and maladjustment, the effects of heredity and environment, problem solving, and others. The Encyclopedia of Psychology online offers more than 2,000 links on psychological subjects.

Sociology

Sociology is the newest of the social sciences, having emerged long after the other social science disciplines were already established. Contemporary sociology may be defined as the systematic and scientific study of human social relationships and of all the social systems that such relationships engender. In more popular terms, sociology is said to be the study of human groups in interaction, or the scientific study of human society and human group behavior. Although psychology also analyzes human behavior, its focus is the individual. The focus of sociology, on the other hand, is the individual in interaction with others or as he or she moves in the social environment.

The climate for a science to study human groups did not arise until nearly the middle of the nineteenth century, when the French philosopher Auguste Comte coined the name "sociology" in his *Positive Philosophy* (1838). In this treatise, Comte repudiated authority and speculation in favor of systematic observation and classification as the bases of all scientific inquiry. He was followed most notably by the French social philosopher Emile Durkheim. Durkheim demonstrated the use of scientific methodology in the new discipline by outlining how he studied suicide by planning a research design, collecting masses of data on suicide rates in a number of societies, and using the data to derive a theory suggesting that social factors—conditions of upheaval in society and the extent of integration of people in the social order—affect even such personal choices as committing suicide (*Suicide,* 1897).

The patient on a couch and the therapist sitting behind him or her with a notebook has been a symbol of psychology ever since Sigmund Freud used it. It has also been ridiculed and used as a source of humor by comedians. However, psychologists use many other situations to help patients.

Today, sociology studies an enormous variety of subjects, in particular human groups of every stripe, organizations, and institutions. The discipline looks at the environment, religion, politics, the economy, deviance, criminality, change, demography, industry, technology, medicine, urban and rural areas, and so on. It focuses especially on the organization of complex industrial societies, such as the United States, analyzing data and events through a number of theoretical models, the foremost of which are functionalism, conflict theory, and symbolic interactionism. In addition, research is undertaken within the framework of newer theories, such as feminism, exchange theory, and postmodernism. Most of the social sciences share some of these theoretical approaches. The Web site of the Sage Publishing Company offers a list of the 50 most frequently read articles in sociology.

Research Methods in the Social Sciences

In the search for meaningful facts to test and bolster their hypotheses, leading to valid theories, social scientists use a number of research methods (Table 1).

These methods may be *historical*—that is, they may include a perusal of documents such as public records, newspapers, legal codes, court records, minutes of various committees, and annual reports of corporations; they may be comparative and *cross-cultural,* in which comparisons of different societies—or specific segments of them—are made for the purpose of tracing cultural patterns to determine either their universality or their uniqueness (these methods are especially used in anthropology); these methods are predominantly qualitative. The predominantly quantitative methods are *mathematical,* based on complicated calculations using mathematical and statistical principles to express ideas. In fact, the mathematical and

TABLE 1 Common Methods of Social Science Research

Method	Subject of Research	Procedure	Used for	Criticism
Sample survey	Statistically valid sample of a population.	Collect data; have sample fill out questionnaires; conduct personal interviews; obtain factual information; probe attitudes; establish relationships among variables.	Establishing facts.	Not always 100% accurate in reflecting attitudes and opinions.
Case study	Total behavior of a particular unit of people.	Gain confidence of members; obtain biographies of members; learn each member's views; establish hypothesis or relationships that can be tested by other means.	Studying a particular unit (family, gang, ethnic group) in depth or several units for comparison.	Most useful when events under consideration are rare; often cannot be used as a basis for generalization; expensive and difficult to compute quantitatively.
Participant observation	Members of a specific group.	Researchers take part in life of group members, sometimes without revealing their identities.	Studying all or some aspects of a group's culture from the inside out.	Depends on personality of researcher; researchers may be biased; researcher may try to overgeneralize.
Experiment	In the laboratory, people volunteer or are paid to be subjects. In the field, researcher studies an existing group.	Subjects undergo a number of tests, and their responses are recorded. Researchers control or hold constant one variable and systematically observe or measure the results.	Establishing facts that cannot be established in any other way.	Very expensive if many people are involved; physical safety and dignity of people must be considered; people change their behavior when they know they are being observed.

quantitative approaches in the social sciences have been gaining ground. In the last several decades, the computer has become a staple in social scientific research. Frequently, a combination of methods as well as sources is used: public and private documents are analyzed, the artistic output of a specific historical period is scrutinized, the literature is studied, and statistical information—birth and death rates, for instance—is compiled. Most social scientists shy away from research methods that are subject to personal interpretation. They prefer methods that appear to be more objective, that is, in which personal biases are kept out as much as possible. This does not mean that descriptive, subjectively interpreted work is not being produced, nor that such work lacks meaning. The research methods most commonly used by social scientists today are as follows. A comprehensive bibliography of research methods in all the social sciences can be found online.

Sample Survey

The **sample survey** research design consists of two separate features, the sample and the survey. The researcher decides to study a specific group, which is called the **population**, a statistical concept referring to the totality of the phenomenon under investigation. For example, the population might consist of middle-aged professionals, newly registered voters, or college students enrolled in four-year private schools. Because it is impossible to study every individual who is a member of the chosen population, researchers select a statistically valid sample. There are procedures that allow researchers to select such a sample. Only if the sample is truly representative of the total population can generalizations about the results of research be made.

The next step is to survey the sample population. Surveying involves collecting data by means of questionnaires, personal interviews, statistical information, or probing of attitudes. Most important, relationships among variables are analyzed. If a broad spectrum of the population is being surveyed at a specific point in time, the study is called **cross-sectional.** Preelection polls are a familiar example. Major magazines and news organizations are constantly polling people to probe their attitudes on current events.

If the survey continues over a longer period, engaging in contrasts and comparisons, it is referred to as a **longitudinal study.**

The sample survey is a useful research design, yielding accurate results for some investigative questions but not for others. It is comparatively easy to establish factual information with the sample survey technique, but there is a greater margin for error in surveying attitudes and opinions.

Case Study

The **case study** research design is especially helpful when it is necessary to study a particular unit in depth or to study several units for purposes of comparison. The unit may be a person, a family, a group of residents of a retirement community, employees of a particular corporation, members of a religious movement, and so on. The researcher must obtain a complete, detailed account of the behavior of the unit under consideration. In the case study, the entire population of the unit is surveyed.

Case studies are most valuable not so much because of their accuracy, but because they often suggest hypotheses that can then be tested by other methods. They are most valuable when the unit being analyzed is relatively rare, such as a group of brainwashed prisoners of war or a group of converts to an authoritarian religion. The basics of developing case studies, although these are directed at commercial enterprises, are described online.

Participant Observation

Somewhere between the case study and the sample survey techniques, we find a method called **participant observation.** Here the researcher tries to take part in the lives of the group members being studied. The researcher associates with group members as closely as possible and attempts to share in their experiences and lifestyles, sometimes without revealing his or her purpose. A number of sociologists and anthropologists have used this technique, developed by anthropologists to study preliterate cultures, to analyze ethnic and black street-corner cultures.

The participant observation technique has its shortcomings. Much depends on the personality of the researcher, who must develop trust in, and friendship with, the subjects. Thus, there is the danger of the researcher becoming too involved with the subjects and thereby losing objectivity, as well as the danger of overgeneralizing in the belief that the findings obtained from the group studied are true of all similar groups. At the same time, this method, like the case study, has given researchers many useful insights that can be tested and verified later by more quantitative techniques. Explanations and examples of participant observation may be found online. Box 2 describes one of the most recent examples of participant observation, unusual in that it follows a number of families in their everyday lives.

Box 2   An Example of Participant Observation

The scientific method rarely lends itself to the study of such private lives as those of family groups. Nonetheless, researchers at the University of California recruited 32 local families and from 2002 to 2005 videotaped their every waking moment at home. This voyeuristic kind of study, usually employed by anthropologists to observe foreign and exotic societies, was used because the American family today tends to consist of two breadwinners, a change from previous times when the father was the breadwinner and the mother stayed home to care for the children. The researchers wanted to study a "new sociological species: the dual-earner, multiple-child, middle-class American household" (Carey, 2010, A1).

The researchers chose a diverse group of families: two black, one Latino, one Japanese, some ethnically mixed couples, and two households with gay male parents. Such families, in which both parents worked, have existed for a long period of time, especially among low-income households. But although they were 36 percent of the population in 1975, in 2008 the percentage had jumped to 46 percent, and they have begun to occur at higher income levels.

How invasive was the study? Very, although eventually family members got used to being observed, and they relaxed. However, one researcher followed family members with a laptop computer, registering their location and activity every ten minutes. Four times a day members had to spit into a vial because researchers wanted to measure the levels of the stress hormone cortisol in the saliva. The reason for this procedure was that they wanted to know the part that biology plays in the frustration that occurs in family members. In fact, it turned out that when wives engaged in talking with their husbands about the day's events, the level of cortisol declined, but it declined much more slowly for the husbands.

What else did this extensive study show? First, that there was a lot of stress in these families; that mothers still did most of the housework; that husbands and wives were together only 10 percent of their waking time; that families had to engage in continual negotiations about who would do what and when; that couples who experienced the least stress tended to have rigid divisions of labor—wives did certain things, husbands did other things, and the two did not interfere with one another (by the way, the children did only 3 percent of the work around the house, and it didn't matter whether they received an allowance or not). After their regular workday, parents had to assume the roles of teachers, of personal trainers, of camp directors, of planners for their children's play dates and weekend family time. And they still managed to spend a good amount of time with their children: 34 percent for mothers and 25 percent for fathers. Half the fathers, however, managed to spend time with at least one child engaging in outdoor activities.

The conclusion that the researchers reached from the study was that it takes an enormous amount of coordination to manage these kinds of families. It reminded them of a theater production, one for which no rehearsal was available (Carey, 2010, 17).

The Experiment

The experimental method is used in all scientific disciplines. In the social sciences, the **experiment** may take place either in a laboratory or in the field. In the laboratory experiment, people are recruited to serve as subjects who can be volunteers or paid by the researcher. The scientist conducts a number of tests and records the subjects' responses. In the field experiment, the researcher goes out among the people instead of bringing them to the laboratory. In both the field and the laboratory, one variable is controlled (by setting up control groups), and the results are systematically observed and measured. Every scientific experiment consists of (1) keeping all variables constant except one, (2) changing that one variable, and (3) discovering what happens.

Obviously, experimentation under controlled conditions is not possible in all social science disciplines and is also subject to shortcomings. Wide-ranging experiments in which thousands of people are involved are very expensive and difficult to organize. The physical safety and the dignity of people must be safeguarded. It is impossible to force people to act as subjects in an experiment, and the ethics of tricking them into acting as experimental subjects are certainly questionable. Finally, when people are aware that they are the subjects of an experiment, their behavior tends to change from the usual. This tendency can ruin the experiment and make results invalid. Experiments on people are most reliable when the subjects are not aware of the true goals of the experiment but do know that some type of experiment is being conducted. Nevertheless, even harmless deception sometimes leads to intellectual dishonesty in interpreting results, and so the technique is not widely used. An example of an experiment designed to uncover whether monetary incentives would increase students' achievement in school can be found at: **http://www.edlabs.harvard.edu/pdf/studentincentives.pdf.**

Statistical Analysis

By whatever method data are gathered by social scientists, one of the most favored manners of analyzing them is with statistics. **Statistics** are methods in the form of numbers used to process the information obtained by research. Statistics simplify the communication of information and help researchers make decisions about the meaning of their research. Statistics that communicate information in a clear manner are called *descriptive* statistics. Descriptive statistics convey the *central tendency*—what is typical—of a group of numbers by calculating the mean, the median, and the mode.

The **mean** is obtained by adding all the figures and dividing them by the number of cases. This is what an instructor does when she reports on the average exam grade obtained by students. If the mean is 95, it is assumed that the central tendency of that particular population (class of students) is to study very hard. Central tendency can also be measured by the **median,** which is the number in the middle of the distribution of scores (so that roughly half the students would have higher scores than the median, and half would have lower scores). Although it is the least frequently used measurement, central tendency can be measured with the **mode,** the number that appears most frequently in a group of numbers—in this case, the one single score obtained by the largest number of students.

Statistics are also *inferential,* providing techniques researchers use to decide whether they can make valid statements about a specific population based on a particular sample of it. Statistical tests exist that allow researchers to calculate percentage statements of probability; the higher the percentage of probability, the more assurance that what was true of a sample is true of the population at large. General guidelines for choosing the correct form of statistical analysis may be found online.

The Scientific Method in the Social Sciences

In summary, none of the research methods available to social scientists is 100 percent effective or error proof. Conducting research is difficult in all sciences, but in the social sciences the difficulty is compounded by the problems of subjectivity, logistics, and the unpredictability of human behavior, and by the great number of variables that must be controlled.

As a result, social scientists often use whatever technique seems to best fit the needs of their research designs. The *historical* or *impressionistic* study, which consists of describing and analyzing observations according to informal but coherent and purposeful guidelines, is still popular. The *demographic* method is also used with good results. This is the method used by the Census Bureau to report population and urbanization trends. Demographers, sociologists, and economists all look at demographic facts and come to some conclusions on what they indicate. A few pages of an historical study of American violence—"Strain of Violence," by Richard Maxwell Brown—may be viewed online (Google Books, Historical Studies of American Violence and Vigilantism).

It should be stressed again that despite the use of the scientific method, social scientists have more difficulty obtaining verifiable data than do physical scientists. Examining fossil remains in the laboratory is very different from examining people as they relate to one another. Not only do people not lend themselves to many of the experiments that can be performed on the inert fossil, but they also evoke a reaction from the researcher, which the fossil does not. Researchers cannot help reacting to people—they find an individual likable or disagreeable, good-looking or ugly, intelligent or dense—whereas in analyzing a fossil such judgments do not even enter the researchers' minds. Much as they wish to further objectivity, the conclusions of social scientists may be tinged by bias. In the social sciences, then, there are no absolute conclusions and no absolutely objective interpretations.

The Chapter in Brief

Social science disciplines evolved from social philosophy to study scientifically how people behave in the social world that is of their own making (as opposed to the physical world into which they are born). The disciplines are fairly new, although their subject matter has occupied philosophers for thousands of years. What is really new about the social sciences is that they attempt to use the scientific method to formulate generalizations and theories about human behavior in society.

The social sciences use the scientific method as a tool for theory building. The scientific method implies that researchers do their work with a set of attitudes that includes doubt, objectivity, and ethical neutrality. The scientific method also involves a specific technique based on precise and systematic observation and recording of data. This technique includes the selection and definition of problems and a plan for the collection of data; a statement of hypothesis; the actual collection of data, their classification, analysis, and verification (replication); and generalization. Controlled conditions and trained observers are also essential. The scientific method uses concepts (abstract ways of classifying things that are similar), theories (sets of concepts arranged so as to explain and predict possible and probable relationships among phenomena), and research (which tests and bolsters theories or refutes them).

Social scientific research includes the following methods: the sample survey, the case study, participant observation, and field and laboratory experiments. In addition, the historical or impressionistic methods and the demographic method are used.

The scientific method, although it is vastly superior to gathering information by superficial observation, insight, or other traditional methods, is especially difficult to apply in the social science disciplines because of the need for objectivity, skepticism, and ethical neutrality.

Terms to Remember

case study A method of research consisting of a detailed, long-term investigation of a single social unit.

concept A generalized idea about people, objects, or processes that are related to one another; an abstract way of classifying things that are similar.

cross-section A survey of a broad spectrum of a population at a specific point in time.

dependent variable The concept affected by the independent variable.

ethical neutrality An attitude of the scientific method in the social sciences, requiring that scientists not pass moral judgment on their findings.

experiment A method of research in which the researcher controls and manipulates variables in one group to test the effects of an independent variable on a dependent variable.

hypothesis A tentative statement, in clearly defined terms, predicting a relationship between variables.

independent variable   The concept that affects the dependent variable.

longitudinal study   A survey that continues over a long period, engaging in contrasts and comparisons.

mean   The figure obtained by adding all of the figures and dividing them by the number of cases.

median   The number in the middle of the distribution of figures.

mode   The number that appears most frequently in a group of numbers.

qualitative research   A method that collects and analyzes data by describing and defining phenomena to find meanings; may be subjective.

quantitative research   Uses mathematical, statistically valid, and strictly objective measurements of phenomena seeking explanations.

participant observation   A method of research in which researchers try to take part in the lives of the members of the group under analysis, sometimes without revealing their purposes.

population   In the social sciences, a statistical concept referring to the totality of phenomena under investigation (e.g., all college students enrolled in four-year private universities).

research   An aspect of scientific methodology that bolsters and complements theories. In the social sciences, four fundamental formats are used: the sample survey, the case study, the experiment, and participant observation.

sample survey   A method of research consisting of an attempt to determine the occurrence of a particular act or opinion in a particular sample of people.

statistics   Methods in the form of numbers used to process information obtained by research.

theory   A set of concepts arranged so as to explain and/or predict possible and probable relationships.

variables   Factors whose relationships researchers try to uncover; characteristics that differ (vary) in each individual case.

Suggested Readings

Babbie, Earl. 2007. *The Practice of Social Research,* 10th ed. Belmont, CA: Wadsworth. How research in the social sciences is done—a comprehensive and readable text.

Berg, Bruce L. 2009. *Qualitative Research Methods for the Social Sciences,* 7th ed. Boston: Allyn & Bacon. A clear explanation of this methodology.

Best, Joel. 2001. *Damned Lies and Statistics: Untangling Numbers from the Media, Politicians, and Activists.* Berkeley: University of California Press. This book suggests how statistics can be misused by politicians, administrators, the media, and other activists for their own agendas.

Ericksen, Julia A. 1999. *Kiss and Tell: Surveying Sex in the Twentieth Century.* Cambridge, MA: Harvard University Press. An evaluation of the methodology used by social scientists in the many surveys of human sexuality.

Hoover, Kenneth, and Todd Donovan. 1995. *The Elements of Social Scientific Thinking,* 6th ed. New York: St. Martin's Press. A concise introduction to the vocabulary, concepts, and methods of the social sciences. Mainly jargon-free, this small book leads students through the complex path of social scientific thinking.

Ross, Dorothy. 1991. *The Origins of American Social Science.* Cambridge, NY: Cambridge University Press. A historical look at the development of the social sciences in the United States.

Tilly, Charles. 2006. *Why?* Princeton, NJ: Princeton University Press. A Columbia University scholar attempts to decode the structure of social interactions. Why do we give the reasons we do to explain our behavior? According to the author, people rely on four categories of reasons: conventions, stories, codes, and technical accounts. An interesting sociological argument.

In the Beginning . . .

From Chapter 2 of *Contemporary Society: An Introduction to Social Science,* Thirteenth Edition.
John A. Perry, Erna K. Perry. Copyright © 2012 by Pearson Education, Inc. All rights reserved.

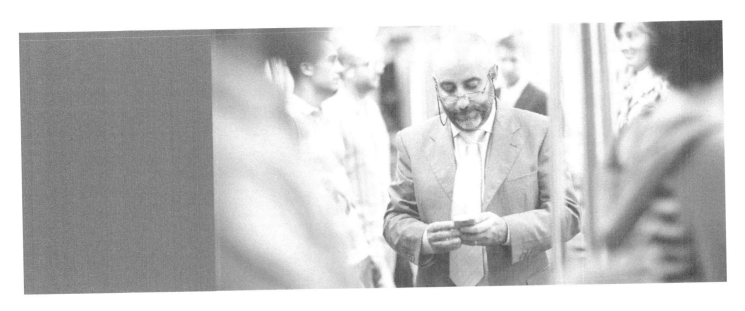

In the Beginning . . .

" In the beginning God created the heaven and the earth. And the earth was without form, and void; and darkness was upon the face of the deep. And the Spirit of God moved upon the face of the waters." So begins the Judeo-Christian Biblical account of the creation of the earth. The narrative goes on to recount how God made its first inhabitants, fashioning them out of clay and breathing life into them. Those brought up in Western societies, or at least within the Judeo-Christian religious tradition, are familiar with this introduction to Genesis and comfortable with it. The narrative is appealing because it presents the events of creation in terms that all can understand. Other societies, with different cultures and in other regions, have similar explanations of the origin of the world and of life.

The physical sciences tell a different story, one that is more difficult for people to grasp. According to astrophysicists who study the early universe, the earth, which is our home, is a fairly small and insignificant planet in the Milky Way galaxy. In turn, the Milky Way is only a minor galaxy in a universe that is unthinkable in its vastness. The exact age of the universe is still being studied—by looking at the oldest stars or by measuring the rate of expansion—but scientists at the National Aeronautics and Space Administration (NASA), using its Wilkinson Microwave Anisotropy Probe (WMAP), pegged the age of the universe at 13.7 billion years (NASA/Goddard Space Flight Center, 2010; see also the Web site on **mysearchlab.com**). This research is part of cosmology, the study of the origin and evolution of the universe, a pioneering science that holds the promise for scientists to converge toward facts, despite limits.

Current thinking, supported by the discoveries of NASA's Cosmic Background Explorer (COBE) satellite, paints a scenario in which the universe begins with a primeval explosion, commonly called the *big bang* (this is where cosmology begins its quest; before this moment the forces involved lie beyond known physics). The explosion was the result of a submicroscopic, infinitely dense, and unimaginably hot knot of pure energy that flew outward in all directions, eventually giving rise to radiation and matter. Gravity then drew the matter to denser regions that, over billions of years, became galaxies, stars, planets, and everything that exists, including life. The evidence supporting the theory includes observations that the universe is expanding; the detection of electromagnetic radiation, called microwaves, presumably left over from the initial explosion; and the relative abundance of chemical elements in the universe. The COBE satellite recorded minute temperature variations in the blanket of radiation, which were interpreted as remains from the big bang, and the discovery of those fluctuations helped explain how the seemingly homogeneous fabric of the early universe had arranged itself into the clusters of galaxies and giant voids of space that are known today. The NASA/WMAP team suggests that the big bang and inflation theories appear to be supported by its new portrait of the cosmos. They add that the contents of the universe include 4 percent atoms, 22 percent an unknown type of dark matter, and 74 percent a mysterious dark energy, which acts as a sort of antigravity (NASA/WMAP Science Team).

A graphic illustration of the big bang theory would show the expansion of the universe from less than the size of an atom to about the size of a grapefruit, an event that occurred in less than a trillionth of a second after the big bang and was dominated by a single superforce. Then, as the universe cooled and expanded, the original force broke into four forces that are observable today: gravity, electromagnetism, and the weak and strong nuclear forces, which work inside the atom (Broad, 2003, D4). Over the next 13.7 or so billion years, gravity created galaxy-like structures, stars formed in the galaxies, and the universe continued to expand. It is still unknown whether the cosmos will expand forever or whether gravity will eventually slow and reverse the expansion, causing the universe to collapse. The information gained from the COBE satellite seems to indicate that the universe is at critical density, that is, it will continue to expand, but ever more slowly, so that eventually its growth will be hardly perceptible. A new NASA satellite, called the Microwave Anisotropy Probe, or MAP, as mentioned earlier, will study the various kinds of matter in the universe. (For more on this fascinating subject and what MAP is doing right now, check out the NASA Web site at **http://www.nasa.gov**).

The Beginnings of Life

The study of the origins of the universe is in the province of the physical sciences, particularly in astrophysics, a discipline that is continually expanding as scientists probe ever deeper into space. We offer here only a superficial overview of the subject. Social scientists, on the other hand, are interested in the social world, which humans have created and continue to create. Yet, to understand life, particularly human life, as well as the structures that humans have erected to simplify their existence on earth, we should be aware of the physical framework

Scala/Art Resource, NY

Frederick R. McConnaughey/Photo Researchers, Inc.

Two views of how life began.

within which the earth and humans exist. Therefore, it is important to clarify our physical nature and the kind of natural environment we have traditionally inhabited. It is the biological makeup of humans, in fact, and the experiences of the species that have made the present-day culture-bearing, symbol-using social animal possible.

No one model, or theory, describes the origins of life on Earth with certainty. Scientists have suggested that some essential components of life could have been created by the inter-action of simple chemicals that were in existence in the "primordial soup" that was the Earth after having been bombarded by a rain of meteors. Current models also posit that the components of molecules and cells needed for life were present in the early environment of Earth. Experiments have shown that organic molecules could have originated spontaneously from inorganic forms. More detailed information about the origins of life may be obtained by accessing the Web site recommended on the **mysearchlab.com** and by "Googling" the phrase "origins of life." The point is that fossilized imprints of a thriving microbial com-munity have been found between layers of rock that were estimated to be 3.5 billion years old. This means that life was already established a billion years after the formation of the planet, a much faster evolution than had been previously believed. Therefore, life appar-ently originated on a planet still racked by volcanic eruptions and constantly menaced by comets and asteroids. Some researchers even believe that life did not begin only once; rather, it tried to come into existence several times before it finally "took" and spread all over the planet (Nash, 1993, 70).

Eventually, protoplasm, simple one-celled microorganisms that were neither plants nor animals, somehow acquired the ability to reproduce themselves. Like some bacteria we know today, these organisms floated in the waters, living on minerals and other substances that were present there. Gradually, some of these organisms developed the ability to make chlorophyll.

Using this substance in combination with carbon dioxide and sunlight, the organisms were able to build their own organic substances. They survived so well that eventually they became plants. Other organisms, which had not developed chlorophyll, began feeding on the plants and eventually emerged as animals.

Ultimately, some pioneers did venture out of the safety of the sea to try to survive in the rocky, bare, and harsh environment of dry land. This is thought to have happened about one billion years ago, although researchers have discovered microbes that lived near volcanic vents formed 3.2 billion years ago (Wade, 2000, D1). One of the earliest creatures to try this adventure is believed to have been an arthropod, a predecessor of crabs, lobsters, and insects. The scorpion-like creature eventually became half terrestrial and half aquatic. Another such creature was a kind of salamander, whose fossil remains (in the shape of an arm bone) indicate to researchers that it had been a transitional species between fish and amphibian. Originally a fish, its fins became adapted as arms, which at some point became strong enough to allow the fish to lift its head out of the water and, eventually, to push itself out of the water altogether. This, according to the researchers, would have happened 365 million years ago. Without plants, however, the dry land was indeed inhospitable. It was not until some plants also abandoned their homes in the sea, learning to survive in the coastal lowlands that were frequently flooded and drained, that life on the dry continents became possible. In a way, dry land became a testing ground for life. A large number of plants and animals came into being: some adapted to existing conditions and lived; others could not and perished. Plants developed through a succession of mosses, ferns, and seed plants. Terrestrial animals included huge reptiles, flying birds, and small mammals.

The Emergence of the Theory of Evolution

By what processes did simple one-celled organisms become immensely complex animals and plants? We know that the processes occurred extremely slowly, in a span of time so great that it is difficult for us to grasp. During this span, a large number of species appeared and later became extinct, and many social mechanisms that developed as an aid to survival also disappeared without a trace. However, scientists have been able to reconstruct the milestones: The appearance of primates among mammals, leading eventually, through apes and **hominids,** to modern humans; the emergence of cultural traits, contributing to the development of agriculture; and, within the past 5,000 years, the emergence of urban societies and the concept of the state.

The reconstruction of events so far in the past has been painful and painstaking. It began only when scientists, basing their studies on scientific theories and using the scientific method, took advantage of the fossil record to support the hypotheses these theories suggested.

Curiosity about the vast variety of animal species in existence, as well as the diversity in the physical appearance of the human species, led thinkers long ago to speculate that both animals and humans had undergone changes to adapt to different environments. The ancient Greeks and Romans thought so, but as the societies of the West embraced Christianity, they tended to discount any explanation that went against the teachings of the Bible. Working within Biblical limits, scholars contented themselves with classifying and describing. For instance, the Swedish naturalist Karl Von Linné (Carolus Linnaeus, 1707–1778) classified plants and animals according to their similarities and arranged them in hierarchical categories, with *Homo sapiens* (humans) at the top and invertebrates such as worms at the bottom.

Another naturalist, the French Baron Georges Cuvier (1769–1832), compared the structures of one animal with those of another, thus giving origin to a major field of biology, comparative anatomy. When confronted with the mineralized bones and teeth of animals that were not currently living, Cuvier had to admit that these were the fossil remains of extinct species. This belief, however, went against the religious beliefs of the West. A strict interpretation of the Bible had maintained that God created humans and all other living creatures that were inferior to humans at the same time, and none of these had changed since the moment of creation. One reason people believed in static, immutable creation was that the political and social orders of Europe were static and appeared unchangeable at this time, too.

The seventeenth and eighteenth centuries saw an increase in critical thinking and relatively free inquiry, and the nineteenth century brought dramatic changes of a social and cultural nature because of the Industrial Revolution. The rising middle class, whose members were generally well educated, were unwilling to accept the idea that the status quo was the only proper condition of a society. The climate was favorable to the notion of change. In France, a country torn by a revolution that saw the monarchy supplanted by a republic, scholars began to speculate openly that living organisms were probably subject to changes that were passed on to succeeding generations. They based this idea on the visible changes that forces of elements such as rain, wind, sun, and tides wrought on the appearance of the earth. Thus, Baron Jean Baptiste de Lamarck (1744–1829) wrote that it was obvious that animals were not fixed in appearance but changed in response to certain requirements of their environment. Furthermore, those changes were passed on to the offspring, which were then better suited to life in their environment. (By the way, the reason why so many aristocrats wrote on the subject was that anthropology was considered a gentleman's hobby because people could see no practical use from pursuing information about the origins of species.) Their claims were reinforced by findings of fossils, including some of species no longer living, which were being discovered at about that time during excavations for industrial purposes. However, although they speculated, they could not produce sufficient evidence to make their case.

Detlev van Ravensway/Photo Researchers, Inc.

An illustration of Earth, as seen from space, with the Milky Way galaxy underneath it. Earth is a small planet, but miraculously, it contains all the right ingredients to create and sustain life.

A Revolution in Thought: Darwin and His Theory

In 1830, a Scottish geologist, Charles Lyell (1797–1875), published a book, *Principles of Geology*, in which he maintained that natural forces operating in a uniform manner had transformed the topography of the world into its present appearance. In other words, the earth was continually being altered by the forces of wind, rain, and temperature as well as by the flooding of rivers and volcanic eruptions. These changes, he thought, occurred very slowly, so the planet had to be very old—many millions of years old, and not the few thousand years that the Bible and the Christian establishment attributed to it.

Lyell's book came into the hands of amateur naturalist Charles Darwin (1809–1882), who was able to observe the flora and fauna, as well as the peoples of various continents, during his tenure as a ship's naturalist during a five-year voyage. That voyage, on a ship called the H.M.S. *Beagle,* which surveyed the coasts of South America, Australia and Asia, and the South Seas, led him to develop a revolutionary theory. In 1859, Darwin published his famous *On the Origin of Species* (preceded by a preliminary paper that Darwin presented with a young colleague, A. R. Wallace). In it, Darwin maintained that species are not immutable, as was previously thought; on the contrary, species belonging to the same category are lineal descendants of some other species likely to be extinct. Darwin also posited that the changes occurred as a reaction to environment. Most important, Darwin offered proof by describing the *mechanism* of evolutionary change: namely, natural selection.

Natural Selection

Natural selection is a process that, in simplified form, works this way: Some individuals, out of the total population of a particular territory, are born with a random feature—let us say, a thumb that can be opposed to the rest of the fingers on the hand. These individuals do better in an environment in which they have to grasp objects than individuals who lack this feature. Thus, they survive longer and have a chance to reproduce, passing the feature on to some of their descendants. Individuals who lack the opposable thumb are less likely to survive long enough to reproduce. Eventually they disappear altogether from the population.

Darwin deduced the process of *natural selection* from his observations that among both plants and animals more offspring in each generation are born than can possibly survive. In nature, there is competition for living space, resources, and mates. Some individuals are more successful in competing than others because of specific traits that they possess in a particular environment. This fact is usually referred to as "survival of the fittest," but this phrase may be misleading. A "fit" organism is one that survives and reproduces in a particular environment at a particular time. When the environment changes, as it frequently does, a new trait may be required, and organisms possessing the new trait will become the "fittest." In this way, the natural environment selects which genes are preferable, and those genes become more frequent in a given population, at least until there is a change in the environment.

A frequent example of how natural selection works is the explanation for the long necks of giraffes. Among the entire giraffe population at a certain period of time, individual giraffes were born with necks of varying proportions. The giraffes with longer necks were able to reach higher into the trees and, thus, were better fed and healthier. As a result, they lived longer and had more offspring, some of which inherited the trait for long necks. Gradually, there came to be more long-necked giraffes than short-necked giraffes, until finally the whole giraffe population had longer necks than the giraffes of previous times. Had the environment in which the giraffes lived changed to one in which plants grew in the form of grass and shrubs only, the long necks would have become liabilities. The giraffes that by chance were born with a short neck would then have had the advantage and would have eventually become the norm.

The Role of Heredity

Some points of the natural selection process puzzled Darwin, however. One was how the beneficial trait was transmitted if individuals possessing it mated with others who did not possess it. In Darwin's time, it was believed that offspring inherited a blend of their parents' traits, but there was not sufficient evidence to support the idea.

An answer to this puzzle came through the work of an Augustinian monk, Gregor Mendel (1822–1884), who had been crossbreeding plants. Mendel concluded from his experiments that traits are not blended, nor do they disappear completely. Rather, some traits are dominant and tend to be expressed; others are recessive and tend to remain hidden. A recessive trait, hidden by a dominant trait, may disappear for a generation but may reappear in a later generation.

Mendel's work remained obscure until the beginning of the twentieth century, when the combination of Darwinian evolutionary theory and Mendelian genetics, now termed the *modern synthesis*, was validated by a number of researchers. The latter were able to prove mathematically that even minute differences in the ability to survive and produce offspring could result, in a long enough span of time, in substantial change. Their work laid the groundwork for contemporary evolutionary theory, which is best understood in the context of genetics.

Genetics

The relatively new science of **genetics** is divided into three subfields: chromosomal or Mendelian genetics, concerned with how chromosomes transmit genes across generations; cytogenetics, which focuses on biochemical and cellular events; and population genetics, which deals with natural selection and other reasons for genetic variation and changes in populations. To understand how humans evolved and why they exhibit such a wide variety of physical traits, we must become acquainted with some of the mechanisms of heredity.

Population Genetics: Factors for Change

The structural traits of plant and animal—what the plant and animal will look and be like—are transmitted by hereditary units called **genes.** Genes contain a blueprint with instructions to the reproductive system about how a specific plant or animal should appear and function: what color eyes, hair, and skin it should have; what height and body type it should be; and whether it should have four legs and a tail or two legs, two hands, and no tail. This blueprint, or code, is dependent on the arrangement of the DNA molecules, which make up the content of genes. **DNA** stands for deoxyribonucleic acid and is the basic building block of all life. Each type of gene has a DNA of a slightly different chemical structure, and this is what determines the inheritance of specific traits. In turn, each organism has a different kind and number of genes, varying from a very small number for simple organisms, such as viruses, to a very large number for complex organisms, such as humans.

Genes, each containing a section of DNA with an identifiable structure or function, are arranged in a linear order and packaged in units called **chromosomes.** Humans normally have 46 chromosomes arranged in matching pairs. Each individual inherits one set of 23 chromosomes from its mother and another set of 23 from its father. Chromosomes are located in the nucleus of every cell.

Lisa F. Young/Shutterstock

Each newborn inherits 46 chromosomes: 23 from its mother and 23 from its father. As a result, each person resembles each parent, but is not a copy of either. In this photo it is easy to see the resemblance of grandmother, mother, and child.

The Human Genome Project. Scientists have in the recent past uncovered the order, or sequence, of the human genetic code. The cracking of the genetic code of human life has been called a pinnacle of human self-knowledge because, in effect, scientists have deciphered the hereditary set of instructions that defines the human organism. This is the script by which, millions of times, an egg meets a sperm, and the resulting individual is born with all its parts in place, ready to function in the myriad ways in which a human being functions.

The script consists of more than three billion base pairs—the rungs between the strands of the double helix of the DNA. The bases are adenine (A), cytosine (C), guanine (G), and thymine (T). In the future, scientists hope to locate all genes and uncover their function. This would lead to practical applications in the area of health. The sequencing, in fact, is expected to revolutionize the practice of medicine. The knowledge gathered from the sequencing of the genome is already being used to direct the communication system of the body to act in specific ways: for instance, ordering cells to repair damaged tissue or fight off invaders. Eventually, scientists expect to develop a variety of diagnostic tools and treatments that may be tailored to individual patients. They also hope that the sequencing will be helpful in taking advantage of the body's ability to self-repair.

Gene Frequency. Within each inbreeding population—a group of individuals who breed with one another because they live in the same general territory—genes occur in specific proportions. That is, such a population might contain individuals with 30 percent of gene X, 20 percent of gene Y, and 50 percent of gene Z. This condition is called **gene frequency.** As long as gene frequency remains constant, the population will have a specific appearance. If gene frequency changes—if the proportion of a given gene increases or decreases—the population is undergoing **evolution.** Eventually, changes will occur in some aspect of the population's appearance or structure.

Mutation. How does gene frequency change? Normally, the DNA is a stable structure not subject to change. On occasion, however, a slight change in DNA does occur; then the information content of the gene is changed, and the change is transmitted to later generations. Permanent change in genetic material is called **mutation.** Mutation is rare (mutant genes have been calculated to run from a low of about five mutations per million sex cells to a high of about 100 per million, in the human population), but it is constant, and it is the source of the variations characteristic of humans. Sometimes mutations produce obvious abnormalities, such as Down syndrome, but the large majority of them produce more subtle effects (Haviland, 1995, 63). Scientists have speculated that some forms of mutation are caused by radiation, certain chemicals, and heat, but it is likely that we are ignorant of many other causes.

It should be stressed that what happens when an offspring is born with the inherited genes from its father and mother—which make the offspring appear distinct from either parent—is *not* mutation: It is a reshuffling of existing genes. Mutation is a random, chance occurrence that sometimes has positive results, enhancing an organism's chance of survival, and at other times has harmful consequences, causing disease or malformation. A harmful mutation that leads to the organism's death has no consequences for the process of evolution. A positive mutation contributes to the genetic variation within a population (the reason for differences in skin coloration, for instance) and is a necessary condition for natural selection.

As an example, geneticists have recently speculated that a mutation in a gene that occurred around 2.4 million years ago was probably responsible for reshaping the human face. The mutation took place in a gene responsible for developing strong jaw muscles for chewing and biting. Other primates, like chimpanzees and macaques, still have such strong jaws, as well as the gene responsible for producing them. In humans, however, a mutation inactivated this gene. As a result, human jaws became smaller, less protruding, and weaker. At the same time, this led to the development of a larger brain. Jaw muscles apparently limit the growth of the skull, so smaller jaw muscles left more space in the skull to be filled by the brain.

Genetic Drift. In addition to mutation, the balance of a gene pool may be upset by genetic drift. (A **gene pool** consists of all the genetic material available to a specific population to be inherited by the next generation.) **Genetic drift** is the effect of chance events on the gene pool of small populations. In particular, it affects small populations that are isolated for several generations. In these circumstances, a random trait will tend to become so common in the span of a few generations that the group will begin to look distinct from the original group.

Gene Flow. On the other hand, some breeding populations exchange genes with members of different gene pools (members of some societies are required to choose mates from a different population group). **Gene flow** is the term that denotes the movement of genes from one genetic pool to another. Gene flow results in hybridization (the offspring look different in some respects from either parent). It is theorized that such matings result in *hybrid vigor*, or offspring that are better specimens than either parent. (Modern Hawaiians, a hybrid population that is a mixture of Polynesian, European, and Asian populations, are noted for their size, good health, and general vigor.) One effect of gene flow has been the establishment, in the last 400 years, of a new **phenotype** (the physical, or outward, appearance of an organism, as opposed to the **genotype,** which is the actual genetic composition of an organism) in Central and South America. This phenotype was formed when the gene pool of the native populations mixed with genes of the Spanish colonists as well as with those of the Africans whom they imported as slaves.

Speciation. The ultimate form of variation is the evolution of one species into another. The development of a new species, or *speciation,* occurs when two or more groups of an original species become isolated from one another and, in time, by adapting to their separate environments, develop such profound genetic changes that they can no longer breed with one another. (Only members of the same species can exchange genes through reproduction. Members of different species can mate, even reproduce, but the offspring will either die or be infertile.) Speciation was used by Darwin to explain the fact that humans, monkeys, and apes descended from a common primate ancestor.

It should be pointed out here that the variations among humans we call races are not separate species but slight variants of a single species. Differences in appearance are due to gene flow, genetic drift, and migration. It is clear that some human groups do not interbreed because of geographic and cultural reasons, but all human groups *can* interbreed.

Natural Selection and Adaptation.   The processes we have enumerated produce changes in gene pools and, thus, changes in specific populations, but change in itself is not necessarily advantageous to the population. Changes must fit a specific environment, or be adapted to it. **Adaptation** is a process that intervenes to ensure that organisms achieve an adjustment to their environment that is beneficial, and it does so through the process of natural selection. As we saw earlier, **natural selection** is the name given to the evolutionary process in which certain factors present in the environment of a specific location exert pressure in such a way that they select some individuals for survival and reproduction of the next generation, whereas others are not so favored. Natural selection, then, is not a random process but one that leads to an organism's adaptation to the environment. The process may take the form of **directional selection,** in which change in gene frequencies is promoted (because an adaptation to a new environment is needed), or it may take the form of **stabilizing selection,** in which natural selection promotes the status quo rather than change (because change would be detrimental to the organism's adaptation to its environment).

A number of important conclusions can be drawn from this simplified review of the theory of evolution. First, human evolution is not just a matter of highly complex biochemical events carried on by the DNA genetic code; it also involves cultural patterns of behavior such as occur in mating practices, migrations, isolation, wars, and so on. Second, by providing two sources of genetic material (from the mother and the father), the sexual reproduction system ensures the existence of a balanced range of variation in genetic traits. Offspring resemble their parents and ancestors in many ways but are never identical copies of them. Third, the processes of natural selection and adaptation through mutation, genetic drift, and gene flow are responsible for constantly changing the genetic composition of a population through a progressive weeding out of some characteristics while passing on others. Finally, it should not be assumed that every feature of every population is the result of adaptation and selection. Some of the visible differences among populations may be due to accidental genetic drift.

The Long Trek: Human Evolution

The long evolutionary journey of humans begins with the appearance of mammals. These initially small, insignificant animals made their appearance on earth during the Paleocene epoch, or 65 to 55 million years ago (Table 1; see also Web sites dealing with the geological history of the earth.) They fed at night on plants, insects, eggs, and worms (they were flesh eaters) to stay out of the way of the gigantic reptiles that dominated life during the day. Night feeding accustomed them to being active in cooler temperatures and eventually led to their developing warm blood. In turn, with warm blood they could survive in a wider range of climates and temperatures than could the cold-blooded reptiles. This ability became invaluable when great

TABLE 1 Major Milestones in the Evolution of Mammals

Years, in Millions	Periods	Epochs	Life Forms
345	Carboniferous		
			Earliest reptiles
280	Permian		
			Reptiles with mammal-like traits
230	Triassic		
180	Jurassic		Earliest mammals
135	Cretaceous		
65		Paleocene	Earliest primates or primate-like mammals
55		Eocene	
			Earliest monkey-ape ancestors
34		Oligocene	
23		Miocene	
5		Pliocene	Earliest hominids
2		Pleistocene	

changes in the geology of the earth resulted in a cooler and drier climate and the disappearance of swamplands; the large reptiles could not adapt and eventually disappeared, but the small mammals adjusted and survived.

One order of mammals, the **primates,** appeared during the Eocene epoch, about 55 to 50 million years ago and took to the trees in the forests that covered most of the earth. Primates are an order of mammals to which monkeys, apes, and humans belong (Table 2; for further details, see the Web sites recommended for this chapter at **mysearchlab.com**). They gradually developed brains, sense organs, limbs, and reproductive systems (at which point they are called prosimians), and their adaptation to the environment and living conditions of the forest prepared them for the next evolutionary step.

This highly successful group of tree dwellers began, about 35 million years ago, to evolve first into monkeys, larger in size than their predecessors and fond of plants, and a little later into apes. The apes were still larger than their forebears and more adept at hanging from branches with three limbs while picking fruit with the fourth. Eventually, some apes came down from the trees to attempt survival on the ground. The reason for this change of environment was probably climatic: The earth was changing once more, with forests giving way to open woodlands and later to grassy savannas.

These apes are referred to as **hominoids,** that is, they belong to the superfamily *hominoidea* (Table 2). Of those, the *ramapithecines* were more terrestrial and adapted to the open country. Because they also had a rather humanlike appearance, some scholars assumed that their fossil remains, named **Ramapithecus,** were those of **hominids,** that is, that they belonged to the family *hominidae,* to which only humans belong. This view is no longer held today.

TABLE 2 The Place of Humans in the Animal Kingdom

Kingdom	Animalia	Consists of living creatures with a limited growth period and the ability to move. Includes animals from amoebas to mammals.
Phylum	Chordata	Beings with an internal stiff structure, such as a spinal cord.
Subphylum	Vertebrata	Animals from the phylum Chordata with a segmented spinal column.
Class	Mammalia	Animals with these features: warm blood, hair, sweat glands, four-chambered heart, breasts for feeding the young, diaphragm for breathing.
Subclass	Eutheria	Placental mammals who bear their young after a full-term pregnancy.
Order	Primates	Placental mammals with grasping hands, two breasts on the chest, a small number of offspring per birth, long pregnancies, and long periods of infancy. Monkeys, apes, and humans are primates that share good vision and a bony eye socket.
Suborder	Anthropoidea	Includes monkeys, apes, and humans.
Superfamily	Hominoidea	Primates defined by dental traits. Includes apes and humans.
Family	Hominidae	Modern humans and their closest ancestors, *Australopithecus* and *Homo erectus*.
Genus	Homo	Includes *Homo erectus*, Neanderthals, and modern humans.
Species	Sapiens	Neanderthals and modern humans.
Variety	Sapiens	All modern humans, i.e., all living races.

(A Web site on **mysearchlab.com** presents perhaps more than you want to know about primate evolution, but it is interesting.)

Split between Chimpanzee and Human Lines

Hominids differed from other primates in that they were bipeds (they walked on two feet), and they had large brains, smaller and nonprotruding faces, and smaller teeth arranged in a curve on the jaws. Based on molecular analysis, it appears that the split between hominoid and hominid occurred between 7 and 5 million years ago (Relethford, 2000, 312). However, a more recent finding of fossils in Spain points to an ape species dating to about 13 million years ago. Paleontologists believe that this species may have been the last common ancestor of all living great apes, including humans (Wilford, 2004, A8).

The evolution of hominids from the time of the split to the appearance of *Homo sapiens*, the scientific name of modern humans, is the subject matter of physical anthropology, paleontology, and archaeology. A great number of scientists have been involved in research in this area, and the fossil record has often been corrected when new fossil finds occur. This fascinating subject has been exhaustively presented in a number of Web sites. Modern humans may have developed independently in various parts of the world from successive hominid and *Homo* ancestors. In fact, the issue of whether *Homo sapiens* has a single African origin or a multiregional origin has not yet been resolved. The latest fossil research seems to indicate that for at least three million years of recorded history the human line was confined to Africa, that it consisted of at least two major subdivisions, and that eventually the line dispersed throughout the globe. (Follow the work of paleontologists, anthropologists, and archaeologists on Web sites provided at **mysearchlab.com**.)

As noted, the evolutionary line of development from hominids to modern humans is in the realm of prehistory, and thus our view of it is based on speculation and educated guesswork about fossilized remains. All that seems to be apparent is that 10 million years ago, the world was full of apes, whereas 5 million years ago, records show that hominids appeared (Gee, 2002). For example, in 2009 a number of researchers announced that they had found the partial fossilized skeleton of a hominid female that they dated at 4.4 million years old (Mangels, 2009, Shreeve, 2009, Wilford, 2009). She is believed to be part of an ancient prehuman species called *Ardipithecus ramidus*, found in a region of contemporary Ethiopia. This species still lived preponderantly in trees (their big toe was suited for grasping branches), but they were capable of walking upright—they did not knuckle-walk like chimps or gorillas. They also had strong thumbs and flexible fingers, presaging later human skills of tool use. As to why these hominids began to walk upright, some researchers speculate that it was because it freed the arms of male hominids to bring meat and edible plants to the females in exchange for sexual access to them. In fact, apes and chimps fight for such access, even today. But these hominids began to form temporary relationships with females for the purpose of reproduction, avoiding the necessity to fight for the privilege of mating.

The importance of this find is that this hominid seems to have been more modern than scholars believed, and that it differed both from apes and from later humans. In addition, she predates "Lucy," a fossilized skeleton of a female dated at 3.4 million years ago and belonging to the hominid group called *Australopithecus afarensis*. She had been considered the earliest precursor of *Homo sapiens*.

Paleoanthropologists now think that modern humans did not evolve in a straight line from their apelike precursors. Rather, it seems more likely that more than one group of hominids lived side by side. For instance, there is evidence that several hominids (*Australopithecus robustus*, or "robust southern ape"), *Australopithecus boisei*, and *Australopithecus africanus*, related to the other australopithecus but smaller—barely 4 feet tall—coexisted by exploiting different resources. By approximately one million years ago, only one type of hominid remained, giving scientists reason to believe that something happened to destroy their coexistence. In short, researchers who once believed that only one hominid species existed at one time now tend to believe that the human family tree looks more like a bush, with many branches pointing in different directions. This belief is fueled by more refined analyses of fossils and a number of new discoveries.

Newer findings have concluded that the differences between chimps and humans lie most especially in the genetic activity of their respective brains. In fact, whereas scientists have long been aware that chimp DNA is 98.7 percent identical to human DNA, what they could not determine was the origin of the differences. At first, researchers focused on language, which is the defining difference between the two species. However, research showed that the area in the left hemisphere that mediates language was equally large in both chimp and human brains. When they began to probe differences on the genetic level, however, researchers found that human and chimp genes show very different patterns of activity in operating brain cells. ". . . the gene activity levels in the evolution of human brain genes have been five times faster

Box 1   Evolution and Its Discontents

Evolutionary scientists are still facing a bitter controversy. People who follow a literal interpretation of the Bible do not accept the theory of evolution, and parents in a number of states have lobbied school districts not to teach it or to teach a variant of the Biblical explanation alongside it. Scientists, on the other hand, are so convinced of its veracity that they want the word theory deleted altogether. They have probed the fossil record, deciphered genomes, and scrutinized the details of plant and animal development. In addition, they have experimented in laboratories and are able to confirm almost everything that Darwin postulated. For instance, one researcher at Stanford University has been able to demonstrate natural selection in action. He found that in a hot environment, butterflies that have a metabolic gene that confers tolerance to high temperatures reproduce at higher rates than butterflies that lack that gene. Eventually, all butterflies in the hot environment had that gene; butterflies that functioned better at lower temperatures disappeared from that environment.

Moreover, paleontologists working in the hills of Pakistan have recovered fossils that illustrate, step by step, how a hairy, doglike creature wandered off into the sea and eventually took the form of the first whales. Other issues that bedevil scientists include the question of whether evolutionary change occurs slowly or whether it can occur rapidly, and whether there are consequences of the change. For instance, they are speculating that sometimes catastrophes occur that change the environment dramatically and wipe out entire species. Any survivors that are able to adapt to the new environment may give rise to a new species altogether. This is what is thought to have happened when an asteroid impact with the earth killed off the dinosaurs some 65 million years ago. The mammals that had coexisted with the dinosaurs for about 150 million years were small, ratlike creatures. When the dinosaurs disappeared, however, they had the opportunity to evolve new features, which eventually led to the development of more complex mammals, including humans (Hayden, 2002, 43–50).

Evolution did not end with the development of *Homo sapiens,* but continues to the present day. Findings based on decoding human DNA conclude that people have continued to evolve ever since they left their ancestral homeland some 50,000 years ago. The processes of change have been through genetic drift and natural selection. In fact, there are many examples in which natural selection has changed people to adapt to new diseases, climates, diets, and maybe even behavior.

What is interesting, too, is the genes that change are local, that is, they affect populations of specific areas. For instance, lactose tolerance, or the ability to digest milk and its products in adulthood, developed in populations of northern Europe—who are herders of cattle—some 5,000 years ago. In other populations, lactose intolerance sets in after weaning, but because milk products have such nutritional value, northern Europeans adapted to being able to digest milk. About 3,000 years ago, the populations of Kenya and Tanzania also developed lactose tolerance, independent of northern Europe. This genetic mutation allowed people who carried it to leave 10 times more children, which of course was a great selective advantage. Similar occurrences have been studied in various regions, showing certain evidence that people develop local mutations to adapt to local challenges (Wade, 2007).

The latest evidence of evolution acting as an instrument of adaptation has been found by a team of biologists in China. They compared the genes of the Han Chinese (the dominant ethnic group in China) and those of Tibetans who live at altitudes of 13,000 feet, breathing air that has 40 percent less oxygen, yet do not suffer from mountain sickness. The researchers found that about 30 genes had undergone evolutionary change in the Tibetans to allow them to survive on the high plateau. The biologists from the Beijing Genomics Institute maintain that the Han and the Tibetans split apart only 3,000 years ago, which makes this one of the most recent cases of evolutionary change found thus far (Wade, 2010b).

Finally, a frequent dream of scientists is to be able to create life in the laboratory. It is not a new idea: We all have seen movies about the Frankenstein monster created from body parts and brought to life by an electric charge. But contemporary scientists are trying to approximate the creation of the first living thing, as it may have occurred in reality, in a thimble-size test tube. They believe that a molecule that has evolved in their lab with the capacity of reproducing may have been the precursor of the current ribonucleic acid (RNA). In turn, the RNA, together with the DNA, carries the genetic code in all living creatures. Although the scientists do not know what causes the transition from nonliving to living, they do know that at some point the distinction between the two blurs and disappears. Should they succeed in creating a "living" molecule, then the question to be tackled next will be whether life was a unique one-time event, or whether it results from a common chemical process, making the creation of life continuous.

Experiments such as these are becoming widespread, so that the discipline of biology is continually expanding. The genomes of more than 300 species have been decoded, with more in the works, and new scientific findings seem to be appearing on a daily basis. In fact, many science writers are beginning to refer to biology as the new science of "evo devo." This name, which sounds like the name of a band, is

(Continued)

Box 1 Evolution and Its Discontents (*Continued*)

the shortened form of *evolutionary developmental biology*, the term for a discipline that offers a new way of looking at how life evolved. Evo devo contends that organisms undergo two types of changes through time. One change occurs during the lifetime of an animal, the other in the historical evolution of a species, and the two types of changes are connected.

The idea that evolution and development are related had occurred to scientists before. Even before Darwin's work, scientists opined that the development of an organism from a single cell—the ovum—into an embryo and finally into a living individual echoes the history of life. We know that, as an embryo develops, rudimentary forms of a former being appear, only to disappear when a new, better mechanism develops. The embryo develops gills, for instance, but they soon give way to lungs, which work better when the individual must breathe in the air and not in water. The appearance of the gills during the embryo's development indicates to scientists that an ancestral form of the individual lived in water at some point in the distant past.

Evolutionary developmental biology has begun to explain more exactly the processes that turn a formless egg into a complex adult. The explanations revolve around the manner in which DNA builds organisms. As is noted in the text, DNA's function is to command cells to make proteins, and specific stretches of DNA, called genes, make specific proteins. In short, a distinct sequence of DNA tells a cell to build a distinct kind of protein, which yields a distinct organ. Not all genes are expressed, however, and species look different because they use the same bits and pieces of DNA in different combinations. Living beings still must adapt to their environment through natural selection, but the adaptation does not occur through the creation of new genes. Rather, it occurs by genetic "switching," that is, by combining existing genes, with some alterations, in different ways. Thus, a small number of primitive genes has yielded, through the millennia, wings and fins, arms and legs.

The evo-devo discipline, in other words, supports the Darwinian and the Mendelian theories of genetics, which posit that all life forms on the planet derive from one or a few common ancestors (Carroll, 2005).

than that of the chimp brain genes. This finding fits well with other evidence suggesting that an explosive evolutionary development took place, at least in the human lineage, after the comparatively recent split between the common ancestors of chimps and people some five million years ago . . ." (Wade, 2002, A18).

Modern Humans: The Road to *Homo Sapiens*

New studies based on genetic and archeological data support the hypothesis that behaviorally fully modern humans originated in sub-Saharan Africa. These humans had made important cultural improvements: They had language, some type of boats or rafts, and more sophisticated stone implements. At this point, they began to move out of Africa, reaching Europe and Asia between 65,000 and 25,000 years ago and probably closer to 45,000 to 35,000 years ago for Europe (Wilford, 2007a, 1–3). The researchers believe that these humans had become meat eaters and were searching for a wider area in which to hunt animals (Wilford, 2000, 1, A28).

Remains in England and Germany point to close precursors of modern humans as having appeared some 300,000 to 250,000 years ago. Definite fossils of *Homo sapiens sapiens* (the species label for modern humans) date back only 75,000 years, but in early 2005 researchers uncovered evidence that bones found in Ethiopia's Lake Turkana are roughly 195,000 years old. The best known of these are the fossil remains of the **Neanderthals,** of whom some inhabited Western Europe as recently as 36,000 years ago (the classic Neanderthals), while others were found in Asia, Africa, and Europe. It is from the Neanderthals that we derive the stereotype of the "caveman," for they had thick skulls, heavy brow ridges, broad noses,

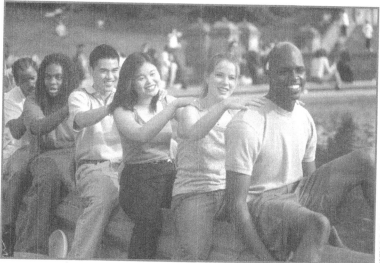

The United States is a heterogeneous society now, containing people from all over the globe.
The differences in the outward appearance of people, however, derive from their former
genetic isolation and from the effects of genetic drift and gene flow.

low foreheads, and not much chin. These features, as well as a short, stocky, and muscular body build, may have been adaptations to the glacial climate of Western Europe at the time. Neanderthals used much more sophisticated tools than their predecessors, lived in fairly settled communities, used caves for shelter, and buried their dead with ceremonies and flowers, indicating the development of ritual and the possibility that they believed in an afterlife. They probably used a primitive type of language to communicate with one another. Archeologists and anthropologists at Duke University have recently probed the brains of humans and compared them with casts of brains from ancient human fossil skulls. This analysis has convinced them that vocal capabilities like those of modern humans could have evolved more than 400,000 years ago. This would mean that earlier species, even before the appearance of the Neanderthals, had the use of speech (Wilford, 1998a, A1, A17, 4).

Scientists do not agree whether or not the Neanderthals are the ancestors or precursors of modern humans. On the one hand, genetic material (DNA) from the bones of a 30,000-year-old Neanderthal seems to indicate that Neanderthals did not interbreed with modern humans, even though the two species may have coexisted. The test, in fact, prompted the scientists who performed it to say that Neanderthals "diverged away from our line quite early on, and this reinforces the ideas that they are a separate species from modern humans" (Wade, 1997, A14). On the other hand, paleontologists have recently examined the 24,500-year-old skeleton of a young boy discovered in Portugal, and their conclusion was that he was a hybrid. This discovery has prompted scientists to hypothesize that Neanderthals and modern humans coexisted for thousands of years, and moreover, that they cohabited and interbred with modern humans. They suspect that Neanderthals and *Homo sapiens* were not two separate species or subspecies, but two groups that thought of each other as appropriate mates. "They intermixed, interbred and produced offspring," as one paleoanthropologist states (Wilford, 1999, A1, A21). This discovery may undermine the out-of-Africa hypothesis of modern human origins and bolster the multiregional continuity theory, discussed earlier. The fact remains that Neanderthals stopped flourishing and seem to have disappeared abruptly around 28,000 years ago (Wade, 2000, A16).

The next fossil remains, found at a site in south central France and dating from about 35,000 to 30,000 years ago, are those of **Cro-Magnon** humans. These are definitely classified as belonging to *Homo sapiens sapiens*. The Cro-Magnon were tall and light-boned and had high foreheads, smaller faces and jaws, definite chins, and slight or no ridges over the eyes and in the back of the head. They were also hunters and gatherers, but they must have been more efficient at providing a constant food supply because their numbers seem to have increased. The beautiful paintings they left on the walls of their caves indicate a certain sensitivity to their surroundings and an early attempt at art, perhaps in the service of religious beliefs. According to population geneticists, today's Basques of France and Spain are very likely the most direct descendants of the Cro-Magnon people, the first really modern humans (Subramanian, 1995, 55).

The Cro-Magnons and other groups of *Homo sapiens* were well established in the Old World (Europe, Africa, and Asia) from 40,000 BC to 12,000–8,000 BC. Some of the *Homo sapiens* appear to have arrived in the New World about 40,000 years ago, during the Ice Age, probably via a land bridge across the Bering Strait. However, the earliest hard evidence of a human presence in this hemisphere goes back only 14,000 years (Rincon, 2004). We share most of our physical features with these distant ancestors. Their activities bring us to the last period of prehistory, which ends with the invention of agriculture. A large number of Web sites deal with the subject in much more detail; see them on **mysearchlab.com**.

Agriculture: Cultivation and Domestication

During what is called the Neolithic, or New Stone Age, which began about 12,000 to 10,000 years ago, a transition from foraging for food to domesticating plants and animals occurred. This slow transition eventually transformed hunting, gathering, and fishing peoples to food producers, representing a dramatic change in the manner of subsistence and the economy. Actual farming was preceded by the domestication of plants and animals, an evolutionary process in which humans, intentionally or unintentionally, alter the genetic makeup of certain plants or animals, so that the latter are finally unable to survive or reproduce without human intervention.

Domestication was certainly facilitated by the ending of the Ice Age. The retreating glaciers left the planet warmer and wetter, favoring the spread of vegetation, including such grasses as wild wheat and barley. This type of vegetation attracted herds of animals, which in turn attracted hunters and gatherers, who found a ready supply of food and so may have abandoned their nomadic ways.

The domestication of certain plants changed them from wild to cultivated and resulted in larger size of the edible parts. It also led to a reduction, or a total loss, of the means of seed dispersal and of protective devices—such as thorns, husks, or toxins—events that were advantageous to humans. Domestication resulted in a better-tasting plant and a more secure source of food.

Domestication eventually led to agriculture—the deliberate growing of food—which is thought to have appeared in several areas independently, although perhaps not at the same time. The world's very first farmers were probably inhabitants of the Near East, in the region called the Fertile Crescent (Figure 1), a 2,000-mile arc that includes parts of Israel, Lebanon, Jordan, Syria, southern Turkey, Iraq, all the way to the head of the Persian Gulf. Among the chief crops were wheat, barley, legumes, grapes, melons, dates, pistachios, and almonds. The

The Fertile Crescent

FIGURE 1 This 2,000-mile-long area extending from modern Israel and Jordan to Iran and the Persian Gulf is called the Fertile Crescent. It is considered to be the birthplace of agriculture.

first domesticated animals—sheep, goats, pigs, and cattle—also appeared in this region (Wilford, 1997, B9). Some of these crops spread from the Fertile Crescent across Europe and Asia between 7000 BC and 2500 BC, but it was several thousand more years before maize or corn became a cultivated crop in the Americas. This was because there was no native wild wheat or barley here, and the domestication of maize requires a more sophisticated biological reorganization. (Read about the origins of agriculture on the Web site suggested at **mysearchlab.com**).

The Fertile Crescent was an area in which natural living conditions were very favorable, and it soon attracted large concentrations of people. Eventually, the region became so overpopulated that some people were forced to leave and retreat to locations where food was less abundant. To supplement their more meager supplies of plants, these emigrants transplanted some of the seeds of the wild wheat and barley near seasonal streams, where they flourished. In this manner, agriculture spread to other areas.

With agriculture came permanent settlements as well as surpluses. Here begins the dichotomy of human nature: When a definite advantage to survival emerges, a disadvantage also appears almost concurrently. One of the results of surpluses, in fact, was warfare, as some groups tried to appropriate the surpluses of others. Populations grew at phenomenal rates, and cities came into being, requiring the development of ever more sophisticated social structures. Eventually, writing appeared, and the recorded portion of the history of humanity began.

The Evolution of Human Nature

Long before recorded history, our ancestors were honing what we commonly call "human nature." That is, they were evolving customs and habits that aided survival in specific environments and, at the same time, differentiated them from other animals. This differentiation usually had *biological origins* but *social consequences*.

Biological Foundations

Even at the hominid stage, certain evolutionary developments in the physiology of humans became the precursors of some of the social structures that were to come into existence. For example, walking on two legs may have developed because it was easier for the hominids to see both predators and prey as they walked in the tall grass of the savanna. Walking upright also freed two of the limbs for carrying things, food and their young, from one place to another. Having the use of hands may also have led to the use of tools for digging roots or transporting objects.

In turn, thinking about how to use tools and improve chances for survival led to enlargement of the brain. A bigger-brained infant that had to pass through the birth canal of an upright-walking female had to be born small in body, thus still immature. Such an infant had to remain dependent on its mother for a long time, and a mother saddled with a helpless infant was herself not a very effective provider. Hence, a division of labor according to sex became a necessity for survival. Females were able to forage for plants and roots even with an infant in their arms, but both depended on males for occasional meat, the product of the hunt. The distinctively human habit of food sharing, as well as the institution of the family, may be traced to these beginnings.

Many other social processes and constructs resulted from mechanisms of biological adaptation. Human females lost their **estrus** (periodic sexual receptivity) and began to be sexually receptive all the time. This helped them forge stronger bonds with specific males, lessened competition among males for females (each male and female could form a pair), and benefited the children, who had the protection of two adults. Rudimentary moral systems based on reciprocal altruism ("do unto others as you would have them do unto you") came into being, as did the incest taboo, designed to force individuals to choose their sexual partners outside their own family or troop, thus minimizing hostilities among troops. Feelings such as gratitude, sympathy, and friendship may have emerged, as well as guilt, shame, and moral indignation, all necessary social tools for keeping groups together and making the individual loyal to the group.

When groups had grown to fairly large size and complexity, some type of organization was needed. It is a characteristic of most primates that they organize themselves into troops, choosing leaders and hierarchies of dominance. Humans followed this tendency, and soon there were tribal unions and confederations of various sorts. In a group setting, more rules have to be developed and followed, and thus remembered. Natural selection would favor the individuals who learned best and remembered longest, as well as those who could inhibit violent impulses.

Progress in social organization and the development of social systems were greatly enhanced by the discovery of fire. The domestication of fire allowed humans to wander farther into colder climates, to keep predators away from campsites, and to inhabit caves, all elements helpful to survival. Fire also encouraged the cooking of food, and the softer food reshaped the contours of the human face. Fire may have promoted personality changes, leading to sociability, an increase in conversation, and thus the further development of language. Finally, fire probably played a distinct role in advancing religious practices.

In the period following the advent of big game hunting, the discovery of fire, and the invention of agriculture, early humans began to resemble modern people to an extraordinary extent. These humans had already evolved a considerable culture, as well as many of the patterns of behavior by which we live today. From then until the present, the social world, with its complexities and contradictions, has been the subject of evolution. Whether evolution explains human nature is the subject of discussions among a number of contemporary scientists.

The Chapter in Brief

According to scientific research, the universe is around 13.7 billion years old. The currently dominant theory assumes that it began with a gigantic explosion (the "big bang") that was the result of a submicroscopic, infinitely dense and unimaginably hot knot of pure energy that flew outward in all directions, eventually giving rise to radiation and matter. The force of gravity then drew the matter to denser regions, which, over billions of years, became galaxies, stars, planets, and everything that exists in the universe. The universe is still expanding, although we do not know whether expansion will continue forever or whether eventually it will reverse and collapse.

Life is thought to have originated in the form of microorganisms capable of surviving in an extremely hot environment, and later in the oceans, where simple one-celled organisms developed and acquired the ability to reproduce. Growing in complexity, these organisms eventually gave rise to plants and animals. When plants could survive on dry land, the environment was ready to house living things such as huge reptiles, flying birds, and small mammals. Mammals were the most insignificant of the animals, but they were adaptable and survived great climatic changes. One order of mammals, the primates, took to a life in the trees of the thick forests that were covering the earth and began an evolutionary process that culminated in the emergence of humans.

Evolution functions through a process of natural selection in which individuals who possess a feature that is successful in a given environment multiply, and those who lack that feature eventually die out.

The study of genetics has clarified how this process works. Mendel found that inherited traits are either dominant or recessive. Traits are never blended, nor do they disappear completely. The dominant ones are expressed, and the recessive ones may wait several generations before reappearing. Variation in species is caused by mutation, gene flow, genetic drift, and migration.

Evolutionary adaptations prompted by climatic changes led the tree-dwelling primates to come down from the trees, become bipedal, and hunt small game. Between 6 and 4 million years ago, primates began to diverge into precursors of modern monkeys and apes, and ancestors of humans. It is believed that a number of prehumans, or hominids, coexisted at one time, but by 1 million years ago, only one, *Homo erectus,* seems to have survived. In the interval between *Homo erectus* and the appearance of *Homo sapiens,* "wise man," such social phenomena as big game hunting, rudimentary families and troops, a division of labor between males and females, and the fundamentals of a moral system appeared. Technology was greatly improved by the discovery and taming of fire. The Neanderthals and the Cro-Magnon were two species that preceded somewhat the emergence of modern humans, the latter being almost indistinguishable from them. The appearance of agriculture some 8,000 years ago closed the long period of human prehistory. Agriculture brought with it a population explosion, the establishment of permanent settlements and cities, warfare, and writing, with which the recorded portion of human history begins.

Terms to Remember

adaptation   A process that intervenes to ensure that organisms achieve an adjustment to their environment that is beneficial.

Australopithecus   A prehuman who lived from about 4.5 million to 1 million years ago. Some researchers maintain that this type of prehuman is not a direct ancestor of modern humans, but rather is a contemporary of an upright-walking, meat-eating, large-brained species that survived; others insist that *Australopithecus* is on the human ancestral line.

chromosomes   Carriers of genes, or the hereditary blueprints of organisms. Each human inherits a set of 23 chromosomes from each parent.

Cro-Magnon   The closest predecessors or perhaps contemporaries of modern humans, who lived about 35,000 years ago. They were expert toolmakers and artists, and they lived in tribes that displayed evidence of rules and kinship systems.

directional selection   Change in gene frequencies is promoted because an adaptation to a new environment is needed.

DNA   Deoxyribonucleic acid. A complex biochemical substance that is the basic building block of life. It determines the inheritance of specific traits.

estrus   Period of sexual receptivity and ability to conceive.

evolution   A theory that explains change in living organisms and variation within species. Evolution functions according to processes of natural selection, mutation, genetic drift, gene flow, and speciation.

gene flow   The movement of genes from one gene pool to another. It results in new combinations of genes in the offspring.

gene frequency   The proportion in which the various genes occur in an inbreeding population.

gene pool   All the genetic material available to a population to be inherited by the next generation.

genes   Hereditary units that transmit an individual's traits. They are contained in the chromosomes and made up of DNA.

genetic drift   The fluctuations in frequencies of specific traits in a small, isolated population, so that visible differences between an isolated population and the population from which it broke away become obvious.

genetics   The science of heredity.

genotype   The actual genetic composition of an organism, which is not necessarily expressed.

hominids   Prehuman creatures who walked on two feet.

hominoids   Apes that came down from the trees to attempt survival on the ground. They belong to the primate superfamily *hominoidea*.

Homo erectus   The upright hominid thought to be a direct ancestor of modern humans.

Homo sapiens   A species whose fossils date back 75,000 years (or perhaps 195,000 years) and includes Neanderthals. The species label for modern humans is *Homo sapiens sapiens*, whose fossils date back 30,000 years and include Cro-Magnon.

mutation   A permanent change in genetic material.

natural selection   A process of evolution in which random traits are tested for their survival value; the successful traits are passed on, whereas organisms possessing less successful traits eventually become extinct.

Neanderthal   A subspecies of *Homo sapiens* (but some consider them hominids) whose fossil remains date from 70,000 to 35,000 years ago. They are known to have buried their dead.

phenotype   The physical, or outward, appearance of an organism.

primates   An order of mammals to which monkeys, apes, and humans belong.

Ramapithecus   A hominoid having hominid-like features, dated between 14 and 8 million years ago.

stabilizing selection   When natural selection promotes the status quo rather than change, because change would be detrimental to the organism's adaptation to its environment.

Suggested Readings

Angier, Natalie. 2007. *The Canon: A Whirly-gig Tour of the Beautiful Basics of Science.* New York: Houghton Mifflin. A frequent contributor to the *New York Times* Science pages, the author intends to remedy Americans' ignorance of the basics of science.

Boaz, Noel T. 1997. *Eco Homo: How the Human Being Emerged from the Cataclysmic History of the Earth.* New York: Basic Books. The author maintains that human evolution was spurred by changes in climate, a claim not universally accepted. The human–chimp split, bipedalism, and the development of culture are written about interestingly.

Brace, C. Loring. 2000. *Evolution in an Anthropological View.* Walnut Creek, CA: AltaMira Press. An anthropologist who has spent more than 35 years working in the area of evolution presents an intelligent and very informative look on the principal issues in evolution.

Cavalli-Sforza, Luigi Luca. 2001. *Genes, People, and Languages.* Berkeley: University of California Press. A well-known geneticist describes the migrations of our forebears for the last several hundred thousand years. A provocotive survey of human evolution.

Fagan, Brian M. 2007. *World Prehistory: A Brief Introduction.* 7th ed. New York: Prentice Hall. For those who find this subject interesting, another worldwide look at the findings of archaeologists that reveal some aspects of our prehistoric past.

Haviland, William A. et al. 2009. *The Essence of Anthropology.* Belmont, CA: Wadsworth. An anthropology text, in paperback, that includes all the basic divisions of anthropology and presents the concepts and terminology relevant to each with engaging and student-friendly examples.

Scarre, Chris. 2009. *The Human Past: World Prehistory and the Development of Human Societies.* London: Thames & Hudson. A fascinating and readable narrative of the origins of human societies.

Stringer, Christopher, and Robin McKie. 1997. *African Exodus: The Origins of Modern Humanity.* New York: A John Macrae Book/Henry Holt & Company. The authors argue for an "out of Africa" theory, that is, that hominids emerged in Africa about a million years ago and spread to the Middle and Far East.

Wells, Spencer. 2003. *The Journey of Man: A Genetic Odyssey.* Princeton, NJ: Princeton University Press. The author is a geneticist who used DNA to identify genetic markers that record the spread of humans around the world. Small mutations in the Y chromosome are passed on from father to son, so that descendants of a single individual can be traced through many generations. Also a PBS documentary.

Culture: Product and Guide to Life in Society

From Chapter 3 of *Contemporary Society: An Introduction to Social Science,* Thirteenth Edition.
John A. Perry, Erna K. Perry. Copyright © 2012 by Pearson Education, Inc. All rights reserved.

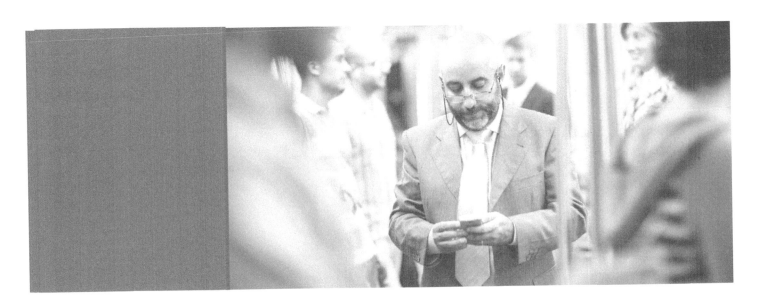

Culture: Product and Guide to Life in Society

IN THIS CHAPTER, YOU WILL LEARN

- *what makes humans unique;*
- *the importance of symbols, especially language;*
- *the importance of shared meanings;*
- *why culture is responsible for human progress and the social evolution of societies;*
- *what is the content of culture;*
- *why norms are vital to societies;*
- *the difference between the attitudes of ethnocentrism and cultural relativity; and*
- *of the existence of subcultures and countercultures.*

Though all modern humans belong to the same species, *Homo sapiens sapiens,* and are all the result of the same physical evolutionary development, it is obvious to any observer that they differ from individual to individual. The physical differences are slight: Some groups have dark skin or hair, some have blue eyes and light hair, some have prominent cheekbones and almond-shaped eyes. All, however, are recognizably members of the group called "humans," both in their physical appearance and especially in their genetic makeup. A group of population geneticists summarized the variation among humans at the level of their chromosomes in this way: With the exception of genes for surface traits such as skin coloration and height, all humans are remarkably alike. In fact, the variation from individual to individual is so much greater than the differences among groups that it makes no sense to speak of "races" at the genetic level. "What the eye sees as racial differences—between Europeans and Africans, for example—are mainly adaptations to climate as humans moved from one continent to another" (Subramanian, 1995, 54). Anthropologists who use genetics in their research also support this finding, noting that external differences are genetically inconsequential. They are small variations that evolved in response to the environment. For instance, the fair skin of northern Europeans, a result of a change in just one gene, may have developed to better absorb sunlight in areas where it was rare, and to synthesize vitamin D (Shute, 2001, 40).

The differences among humans are much more apparent in the languages they speak, the gods they worship, the governments to which they profess loyalty, and the traditions they follow. These differences are often quite dramatic, and their causes have aroused curiosity and interest. When they occur within groups that occupy the same or contiguous territory, they are also often a source of conflict.

In a very basic sense, the differences arise from the fact that people are scattered in different parts of the planet, where they live in groups of all sorts, the largest of which are called societies. Within these societies, people mate with partners much like themselves, until through the centuries, specific biological traits become characteristic of the group—straight, blond hair and blue eyes, for instance, or dark, curly hair and brown eyes. Similarly, because they interact most frequently with members of the same group—their society—the people of each group come to share similar values, beliefs, and patterns of behavior: in short, they come to share a *culture*.

Culture is extremely important to people and becomes so much a part of individual personality and group characteristics that it has often been mistaken for having a biological origin. The fact is that people who live in groups, close to one another, end up looking and eventually thinking very much alike, whereas those farther removed develop slight or great differences in appearance, customs, languages, religions, and lifestyles. In heterogeneous societies, in which members have been drawn from a variety of locations, different groups may be characterized by distinct traits.

Many women in Muslim countries subscribe to an extreme cultural interpretation of Islam, which exhorts them to maintain a modest appearance, sometimes to the point of being totally covered.

It cannot be stressed enough, however, that despite the variety we encounter among the peoples of the world and in our own midst, all humans share more qualities than they differ on. In part, the similarities derive from our biological nature, as pointed out by the research of geneticists. No matter how widely we travel in the world, we observe that all people must eat, although what they eat and when and how they eat may vary tremendously from place to place. All people must sleep, though some do it in beds with thick mattresses and others on thin mats or on bare floors. All people build some sort of shelter for themselves, though some weave their homes out of palm fronds and mud, others from lumber and bricks, and still others, with the help of objects available in their environment, from blocks of ice to sheets of tin. All people classify themselves according to some sort of kinship system, although in some places first cousins are considered the best source of marriage partners, and in other places they are taboo for such a purpose. All people develop some kind of social system, with rules for behavior, values, attitudes, customs, and traditions, and all make decisions for survival according to some type of economic system. In short, though people are infinitely different, they are also infinitely alike. If people's common humanity unites them, the differences in cultures tend to divide them. In a society in which a number of cultural groups coexist, therefore, tensions are common. In such societies (and most industrial and postindustrial societies are heterogeneous), people are being pulled in myriad directions, and they do not follow a monolithic set of values, beliefs, behavior guides, and traditions.

Culture: Concept and Importance

The term *culture* is one of the most important concepts in the social sciences, for culture is the most easily observed and most distinctive product of our group way of life. Although it may be a source of division, it is also what makes us uniquely human. As a term, *culture* is often misunderstood and misused. In everyday conversation, people tend to refer to well-educated persons with good manners or to those who attend concerts of classical music and art exhibits as being cultured. In reality, every individual who was brought up in a social group is cultured because culture is what results whenever a group of people lives together for any period of time. It becomes the way of life of a people, and whoever learns that way of life absorbs the culture of the group.

Culture is the *product* of a social group—and the group that is generally considered today is society, the largest group in which people live. It should be stressed, however, that society and culture are two aspects of the same phenomenon; the two are interrelated and interdependent. Society, culture, and the individual form a triangle within which human life is acted out from beginning to end. Culture cannot exist apart from society because it is its product, and it is inconceivable that a society would fail to produce a culture.

What is more, humans cannot exist outside a social group for very long, at least not until they are self-reliant, when exposure to the group's culture has already taken place. An individual who has not undergone such exposure can hardly be called human. Quite a few instances of infants isolated from human interaction exist. In all cases, these "feral" ("savage; wild-animal-like") individuals either die in childhood or survive as animal-like creatures, without the ability to walk or communicate in a human way. They are not truly human, for they fail to learn how to act as humans do. An individual, then, is dependent on his or her social group for physical survival and for learning how to be human. What individuals learn is precisely the culture of the society into which they are born and more specifically of the social group to which they belong.

Culture is not only an outgrowth of interaction, but it also becomes itself a pattern for further interaction. The relationship of culture to society may be better understood in a theatrical context. Society may be compared to a group of actors who play roles befitting their characters according to the position they occupy in the play. The script used by the actors is comparable to culture. Just as a script is written by a playwright for actors to perform, so culture has been established by generations of humans for their descendants to live by, but the creation of culture is a much less deliberate act than the creation of a play. However, just as a playwright edits the script, changing some roles and expanding others, so, too, each generation adds, deletes, changes, and modifies some parts of culture.

Biological Predispositions to Culture

Although biology is responsible for our ability to speak and symbolize—and thus, indirectly, for our ability to create culture—it is also very limiting. In many respects the human biological makeup has made it difficult for people to survive on earth. Because humans cannot breathe in water, vast parts of the earth are uninhabitable to them. Because they have a thin layer of skin with very little hair on it, they need protection from the elements. Because they lack the claws and fangs and poisons of many animals, they must develop other means to defend themselves.

These biological shortcomings are more than made up for, however, by the qualities humans *do* possess. These include (1) a grasping hand with a thumb that can be opposed to the other four fingers, enabling them to handle the most delicate of objects; (2) an upright posture, freeing the forelimbs to handle and carry objects; (3) stereoscopic (two-eyed, with overlapping fields) vision, enabling them to focus far or near; (4) highly complicated vocal equipment, making it possible for them to speak; and (5) an extremely well-developed brain, part of a complex nervous system that coordinates the functioning of the whole human machine.

It is this biological equipment that has made it possible for humans to create culture. In turn, culture has been a tool for adapting to the environment in those instances where physical qualities were lacking. And the fact that language made it possible to communicate information made the process that much easier and faster.

The Birth of Culture

No doubt there was evidence of culture even among small groups of hominids able to communicate with one another. Anthropologists generally maintain that ever since *Homo erectus*—that is, between 100,000 and 40,000 years ago—cultural evolution has been more important than biological evolution. In other words, human populations began to depend on the development of appropriate tools, food production, clothes, shelter, and weapons to counter certain environmental problems, rather than depending on the alteration of their genetic makeup through natural selection to reach the same goal. This was not, of course, a conscious choice, but rather the result of interaction based on the human ability to communicate. It may be said, then, that human groups began to rely on brainpower, or their cognitive capacity, for survival. What is meant by brainpower is not limited to intelligence but includes other skills: the ability to learn, to form concepts, to be creative, self-aware, and reliable, to be able to evaluate oneself and others, to perform under stress, and so on.

The first evidence of an explosion of culture, usually termed the Middle/Upper Paleolithic transition, included the following major developments (thought to have originated between 40,000 and 30,000 years ago):

1. Change in stone-working technology from flakes to blades, including the technique of attaching blades to handles
2. Widespread manufacture and use of tools and weapons made from bone, antler, and ivory, including the techniques of grinding and polishing
3. Appearance of ornamentation of the body by means of jewelry made of pierced teeth, as well as beads and perforated shells
4. The first representational art forms, such as engravings on bone and stone, as well as ivory sculptures
5. Reliance on a specific animal, such as reindeer in Western Europe, for food
6. A shift from living in small, dispersed groups to a pattern of several large groups occupying large sites in addition to many smaller sites
7. Higher population densities and expansion in previously uninhabited zones, such as Australia and the Americas
8. During the Upper Paleolithic period, rapid and continuous technological change and innovation, as well as the first evidence of variation in forms of artifacts from region to region (Jolly and White, 1995, 368)

Anthropologists are still debating the reasons for the occurrences outlined here. Many suggest that they resulted from climatic changes and from the appearance of language as a form of symbolic communication. Others believe that language had been present prior to the emergence of *Homo sapiens,* at least in a rudimentary form. There is agreement that for the first time all elements of what we call culture were present: language, art, religion, technology, and so on.

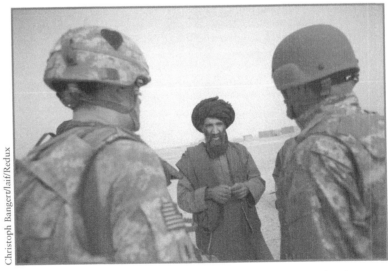

Language is the most important element of culture. Because it reflects a specific culture, communication across cultures is often difficult. For example, speaking through a translator, American soldiers have had to question natives of several Muslim countries. Although words may be translated literally, there is no doubt that their meaning and the way they are spoken will often be misunderstood, creating problems for people of both cultures.

Another dramatic change in human cultures occurred around 10,000 years ago as a result of the end of the last glacial era. Areas that had been covered by ice became available for human settlement; grasslands changed into deciduous forests; and rivers and seas were teeming with aquatic life. These changes in the physical environment required changes in the way of life of people. As some of the large animals that had been objects of the hunt became extinct, people turned to hunting smaller animals and depending more on seafood and other local resources. Finally, this is the time in which the domestication of plants and animals, and ultimately agriculture, emerged, evoking yet again dramatic changes in culture: a sedentary lifestyle; population increases that may have forced people to move to new areas bringing their culture with them; the beginning of trade; increased manufacture and use of pottery, indicating a settled way of life in agricultural villages; the building of permanent housing; and the weaving of textiles. An agricultural way of life marks the beginning of civilization. New archeological discoveries on the border between Syria and Turkey have yielded clay tablets with cuneiform writing, indicating that an early urban civilization and literacy were present more than 5,000 years ago in the region (Wilford, 1993, B7). A description and slides of early urban civilizations may be seen at a number of Web sites suggested at **mysearchlab.com**.

The agricultural era, rendered more sophisticated by the founding of numerous cities, and eventually states, endured for a very long time. It was supplanted only around the middle of the eighteenth century by a system called industrialism. That system is only now being pushed aside by one based on artificial, computer-driven intelligence.

Cultural Evolution and Sociobiology

Darwin's theory of evolution, was enormously influential not only in the biological sciences but also in the social sciences. A number of social thinkers began to adapt Darwin's ideas to the social world, speculating, for instance, that the reason humans, dispersed in a variety of environments, have nonetheless remained similar in appearance is due to the fact that they evolved through culture rather than biological adaptation. This view came to be called *cultural evolution* because it maintained that the most successful cultural adaptations were handed down to the next generation, while the least successful disappeared. An English social philosopher, Herbert Spencer (1873), coined the phrase "survival of the fittest," by which he meant that those who were most successful at adapting in a particular society—those who prospered—had the best chances of surviving the longest and passing on the successful traits to their children. These ideas, known later as *social Darwinism,* include the notion of progress—from primitive to civilized, from chaos to order, etc.—and were ultimately interpreted to mean that Western societies, having become the wealthiest and most powerful in the world with their adoption of capitalism and adaptation to the industrial system, were superior to all others. This interpretation was rejected by later social scientists, who concluded that cultural evolution did not result from superior individuals but rather from other social factors.

The idea that some human behaviors depend on biology and not strictly on culture has continued to reappear, however. The discipline of *sociobiology,* a term coined by the Harvard biologist Edward O. Wilson (1980), attempts to apply genetic factors to social behavior. Such factors exist in relation to animals, but it is a matter of controversy whether they also exist in human societies. For instance, sociobiologists maintain that some human behaviors, particularly aggression, homosexuality, and even religious feelings, are genetically programmed and not simply learned through socialization. Although a number of studies have claimed to have found genes responsible for certain behaviors (especially in the case of homosexuality), it is safe to say that behavior is the result of the interaction between culture and biology. Several Web sites discuss sociobiology in greater detail—see **mysearchlab.com.**

What, Then, Is Culture?

We have been speaking of culture, its origin and importance, without actually ever defining it. **Culture** is everything that humans make, use, learn, know, and believe. It is how they behave and what they share with each other and transmit to each new generation in the attempt to deal with the demands their common life makes on them. Culture is something that humans create and have done so for thousands of years. It is what each generation inherits from the preceding one and to which each generation adds its own touch. It is uniquely human (though this is subject to argument, because studies of nonhuman primates indicate that they too are capable of some forms of communication and the use of simple tools). It includes all the accumulated knowledge, beliefs, ideas, values, and goals, as well as all the material objects that groups of people have ever invented or used. Culture is learned during the process of socialization—learning to be human—through *symbolic interaction,* that is, language and gestures with which we communicate. Culture evolved to allow humans to adapt to their various environments without waiting for genetic alterations. Culture provides each individual with ways of satisfying biological and emotional needs in the best manner possible, without having to personally do so by trial and error. Although each society develops a culture that is distinct from other cultures—because it is a response to a specific environment—all cultures share similarities because they are reactions to universal human needs. Cultures, just like the groups that create them, are in a constant state of flux.

Box 1   Culture as an Evolutionary Force

We tend to think of evolution as having occurred in the past, a force that has made us as we are today in response to natural phenomena to which we had to adapt. However, scientists are discovering that for the last 20,000 years, people have been shaping their own evolution. That is, they have been adapting not only to their environments, to forces outside themselves, but also to their culture, or to what they have learned, including specific behaviors and the technologies they have invented. This fact came as a surprise to researchers who had considered culture a force that shielded people from the forces of nature—knowing how to make clothes, or build housing blunts the effect of cold, for instance. Once this cultural change takes place, however, one no longer has to adapt to a cold climate.

Covered and sheltered, people leave more progeny—that is, they are more successful in surviving and survival occurs faster than if they had depended on natural selection alone. In short, genes and culture evolve together, and sometimes culture changes genetic structure. This is clear in the fact that many populations who could not digest dairy products as adults became lactose tolerant when they changed from hunting and gathering to cattle rearing. Their genetic structure changed because being able to digest dairy products as adults and not just as babies was of such nutritional benefit to them. In sum, it appears that gene-culture coevolution is the dominant mode of human evolution, and in that the rate of cultural change is speeding up, human evolution may be accelerating as well (Wade, 2010a).

The Symbolic Nature of Culture

The most important quality of culture is its symbolic nature. Humans are called the "culture-bearing" animals because of their ability to create and use symbols. One reason animals other than humans lack a rich culture is that they lack this ability.

Animals communicate through a system of **signals** that are biologically determined and genetically transmitted responses to outside stimuli. Animals yelp in response to pain, run in response to fear, and kill in response to hunger. Of course, animals can also be taught to act in ways that are not instinctual: dogs can be taught to sit, to stay in one place, to stand on their hind legs, to come close, and to fetch the paper. However, a dog so trained will not be able to teach its newborn puppy to behave similarly; a human will have to perform this training (although some types of learned behavior are apparently passed on by some animals). Human parents, on the other hand, teach their offspring by showing them or telling them, that is, by using symbols. The advantage of this system is clear: If you can tell your child how to do something that will aid in his or her survival—or comfort—then your child does not have to waste time finding out this information by trial and error. In short, the wheel does not have to be reinvented in each generation; instead, people can refine and build on the inventions of their forebears and, therefore, have time to think about new inventions.

The Necessity of Sharing Symbols

Because we communicate through symbols, we can teach our children and have, in fact, taught them through an endless chain of generations. **Symbols** are arbitrary signs that can be used in an abstract manner and whose meanings are communally agreed on, that is, shared by the group. All English-speaking people, for instance, agree that the sound of the word *bread* stands for a type of food made with the basic ingredients of flour, water, and yeast. The word *bread* is not the object bread; it only symbolizes, or stands for, the food. The point is that the sound means nothing to someone who does not understand English, nor does it mean anything to someone in a society in which there is no such food. Symbols must be understood and shared by members of a society, or they are meaningless. Consequently, symbols vary from culture to culture. In Japan, one bows to be polite; in the United States, bowing is an expression of inferiority or submission, so it is not done except perhaps in church. To an American, a baseball bat is something used in a popular sport; to an inhabitant of the Amazon who has no access to television, it is a piece of wood, a thick tree branch shaped in such a way that it can be used to hit someone or something. Every American child knows what the red, white, and blue cloth means when it flutters in the wind in front of a school or federal building. If, however, someone were to visit from a society in which there was no state, unaware of the symbolism inherent in a flag, the object would simply be perceived as a piece of multicolored fabric. A historical look at a variety of symbols may be found at a Web site, and its links are noted on **mysearchlab.com**.

Language: The Most Important System of Symbols

Language is the most effective system of symbols used by humans, but it is not the only one. Gestures—including body language of which people may not be consciously aware—music, and the visual arts are other symbol systems used to communicate. These too must be shared with members of one's social group; otherwise, they are misunderstood or not understood at all. For instance, in the United States we nod our heads when we mean yes and shake it from side to side when we mean no, but in other societies the reverse is true or some other symbolic system prevails.

Different societies also vary in the use of space in communication. In North America and northern Europe, people stand about three feet away from one another when conversing, particularly if they are strangers or mere acquaintances. South Americans stand much closer to one another in similar circumstances. Thus, a North American might consider a South American pushy or fresh for standing so close, whereas the South American might think the North American cold and unfriendly for standing so far away.

In language, symbols are employed to name things, individuals, and categories. The fact that every object and even intangible abstractions have a name seems natural and common-place to us, but to someone who has not been taught the shared symbols, it is not necessarily so apparent. Helen Keller, blind and deaf from shortly after birth, describes the moment when she realized that everything had a name as a revelation that literally began life anew for her:

> Suddenly I felt a misty consciousness of something forgotten—a thrill of returning thought; and somehow the mystery of language was revealed to me. I knew then that "w-a-t-e-r" meant the wonderful cool something that was flowing over my hand. That living word awakened my soul; gave it light, hope, joy, set it free! (Keller, 1903)

Language plays a particularly important role in the development and transmission of culture. There cannot be a flourishing culture without language because language makes possible a wide range of communication, which in turn allows people to engage in coordinated group activities that help them to survive. Historically, language facilitated cooperation in hunting ventures. Successful hunting meant fairly constant food supplies, which led to the establishment of permanent communities (cities and nations) and a more efficient division of labor.

Although it is itself the most significant invention or product of culture, language is the foundation on which culture is erected and by which it is transmitted. The social life of humans is dramatically affected by language. Their range of knowledge is infinitely expanded because it is not necessary for each individual to experience events personally. Instead, countless experiences can be told to countless people, countless times.

Language goes far beyond the signal systems that other animals use. It allows humans to create the dimensions of time and space so that events that occurred long ago (history, tradition) and far away (geography) may be related. With language, it is possible to project what might happen, or what a person wishes would happen, in the future. One can share individual thoughts and feelings, as well as information. Although the words of each language stand for, or symbolize, real objects or activities or events, they can also be made to symbolize abstractions and feelings, such as loyalty or love. Language can even be used to express things people have not experienced, such as God, as long as people agree that God can be experienced. People invent words to express everything that emerges in their culture and find new words to fit new cultural patterns as they appear. There were no such words as "group-ies" or "hippies" before the 1960s, expressions such as "user friendly" before the late 1970s, "videos" and "cyberspace" before the 1980s, "the Internet" and "Web site" before the 1990s, or "texting" before 2000, and words such as "obesogenic" in the twenty-first century, an era in which obesity has become endemic in the West.

Because of language, knowledge spreads and accumulates. Knowledge accumulation is greatly speeded up and expanded when writing is added to the spoken word, but even in societies in which writing has not been invented, special individuals are designated to preserve and pass on orally certain kinds of knowledge deemed necessary or desirable for the members of the society to know. Again, transmitting culture means that each generation does not need to rediscover things; each new generation can build on the experiences of previous generations. In fact, it is significant that cultures survive the societies in which they originate. Ancient Greece and Imperial Rome ceased to exist thousands of years ago, yet their cultures have left profound marks on all of Western civilization. The literature and art of the ancient Greeks and Romans are still read and admired today. Language, then, is a most important social tool, and it is expanding in ways we could not foresee: For instance, many people are now using Twitter. A word unknown to adults until quite recently, Twitter refers to a social networking and microblogging service used through the Internet. People use tweets—text-based posts of up to 140 characters that appear on an individual's profile and are directed at subscribers, who are called followers—to communicate. As an example, the *New York Times* columnist Paul Krugman reports that he has 377,254 followers and 819 tweets. And Twitter is not the only such service: there is also Facebook—"Facebook helps you connect and share with the people in your life," as their ad claims. New services based on the same idea seem to be springing up on a daily basis.

Does Language Create Reality?

Because of the interrelationship of language and culture, some social scientists have maintained that the very structure of language shapes people's reactions and attitudes toward reality. As an example, they cite the fact that in some languages there is no way to express the idea of past or future because the societies in which the languages developed did not focus on any time but the present. In the native language of the Sioux tribe of Native Americans, for instance, the idea of being late or of waiting cannot be expressed. For them these ideas did not exist; they viewed the world from the perspective of the present. The Hopi did not differentiate between the past and the present; their verbs did not express the idea of time. In fact, there is no word for time in the Hopi language. Instead, they used verbs to express a report, an expectation, and a general statement. In other languages, certain phenomena can be expressed with an infinite number of nuances. Filipinos have 92 different ways of describing rice, a staple of their diet. In English, we recognize a distinction between the words "fear" and "shame," but to some Australian Aborigines, the two words are one and can also mean shyness, embarrassment, or respect. The Chinese say that their language is simply not a language for lovers: the expressions "I love you," and "kiss" sound so foreign and formal in Chinese that those who know English use that language to express their feelings in their intimate relations rather than using their native tongue. Chinese also has no equivalents of "dear," or "sweetie," or "honey," so that in dubbing American movies, rough approximations have to be coined that prompt explosions of giggles in viewers. The reason such words are lacking in Chinese is that Chinese culture is one in which people are reluctant to express emotions openly, and the Chinese are restrained and shy when it comes to expressing love. Dating was for years prohibited in high school and discouraged in college, and to kiss in public or in the view of others is still considered shameful, although these customs are giving way in the wake of China's embrace of the free market. The Chinese language too has more words describing rice than love (Kristof, 1991). Finally, in the fictional work *1984* by George Orwell, the newly created language Newspeak did not contain a word for freedom. Consequently, people could not think about or desire freedom. Think of the consequences of such an absence!

Two anthropologists who became linguistic experts, Edward Sapir and his student and later colleague Benjamin L. Whorf, wrote that languages are not simply a matter of attaching labels to things and thoughts (Sapir, 1960; Whorf, 1956). On the contrary, languages are a reflection of people's thoughts, feelings, and actions, and in turn they shape the way people think, feel, and act. In short, it is our language that tells us what is real and true; it is our language that shows us how to interpret the external world. We can know the world only as far as our language permits it—if there is no word for something, that something does not exist for us (this is known as the Sapir–Whorf hypothesis). That is why every language has some words or expressions that have no counterpart in another language, making the work of a translator very difficult. Sapir concluded that, in effect, members of different societies may be said to live in "distinct worlds, not merely the same world with different labels attached" (Sapir, 1949, 162). In short, the Sapir–Whorf hypothesis maintains that the structure of a language strongly determines how speakers of that language think and how they perceive the world.

A more recent study by Peter Gordon of Columbia University supports the Sapir–Whorf hypothesis. The researcher studied an isolated Amazon tribe whose members—only 200 people—do not count beyond the number two. Anything larger than two is referred to as "many." The researcher wanted to know whether this limits their perception of larger amounts. In a test in which they were asked to match small groups of items according to how many there were, they performed well when there were only two or three items but always answered incorrectly when there were more than three objects to match. The conclusion of the researcher was that language indeed affects perceptions of reality, although he added the caveat that his study may reflect only a unique situation (Graham, 2004). Indeed, the Sapir–Whorf hypothesis should not be interpreted as meaning that language restricts or limits a person's perception of reality forever. The fact is that language and culture give rise to each other: Language changes in response to changes in the content of culture, but at the same time, it is an important factor in shaping cultural content.

The Content of Culture

A society's culture is taken for granted by the people who make up that society. They believe their culture is the only "right" one and that things are done, were always done, and ought to be done as they are in their society. That is the reason for the "culture shock" people experience when they first encounter a society in which things are done differently than in their own. People generally accept their culture because they have been socialized to accept it—they have grown up with it and have not been encouraged to examine it dispassionately. When culture is analyzed, it becomes clear that it consists of a large number of elements.

Material Culture

First, a good portion of culture is visible and tangible because it consists of the huge number of products conceived and manufactured by humans. All material objects, from the primitive stone axe of our prehistoric ancestors to the complex computer on which these words are being written, belong to the category of material culture. Material objects are created to fill a shared need of the society. They come into being when one individual has an idea that is seized on by others, who may add to, modify, and change the idea and put it to use.

The automobile, for instance, was the foremost symbol of industrial society, just as the computer is of contemporary postindustrial society. The automobile was the result of an idea that took hold and continued to be developed throughout countless generations of people. No doubt, an ancient human honed a stone into a circular shape or found one ready-made and noticed how rapidly it rolled down an incline. Someone else, faced with the necessity of dragging a heavy boulder, thought of the possibility of having the round stone—wheel—do most of the backbreaking labor of moving it. Later, after animals had been domesticated, other ingenious (or lazy?) individuals experimented with attaching wheels to a cart, placing heavy objects inside, and letting oxen or horses pull it, again easing the hard work of agriculture and speeding up the transportation of people and things. Much later still, when the steam engine and the internal combustion engine were invented, wheels were attached to these machines, and people could ride in comfort and speed in boats, on railroad trains, and finally in automobiles. The originators of the automobile industry, then, simply applied the finishing touches to an idea born of the human brain and produced by human hands many thousands of years ago. Incidentally, the knowledge needed to put elements of material culture together to obtain new products is a function of **technology**, a practical application of knowledge. Technology includes material objects and the rules and procedures that govern them. Thus, it spans material and nonmaterial culture.

Nonmaterial Culture

The other component of culture consists of abstractions that include knowledge, beliefs, values, and rules for behavior. This part of culture is the nonmaterial part, but the material and nonmaterial parts are not distinct entities. For instance, for the automobile to be built, not only did raw materials have to exist but also ideas about the necessity for rapid and comfortable transportation. Finally, the knowledge of how to make the different parts of the vehicle work had to be present. Social scientists, as may be expected, are concerned chiefly with the nonmaterial aspects of culture because most of human life is shaped by and carried out in the context of beliefs, values, and behavioral rules.

The Components of Nonmaterial Culture: Cognitive and Normative

Nonmaterial culture consists of cognitive and normative components (Figure 1). The cognitive component includes the definitions that people give to everything that exists, or to everything they think exists. More specifically, it includes *knowledge, beliefs,* and *technology* (in the sense of knowledge of procedures for completing tasks). The normative component consists of *values, norms* (further divided into folkways, mores, and laws), *institutions,* and *sanctions.* The normative component is, if possible, an even more important feature of culture because it includes rules for behavior, and human societies could not exist if people did not follow rules.

The Normative System

The **normative system** deals primarily with *rules* (norms) that specify what ought, or ought not, to be. Norms "designate any standard or rule that states what human beings should or should not think, say, or do under given circumstances" (Blake & Davis, 1964, 456). Norms, however, are derived from values.

Values. *Values* are abstract evaluations that certain kinds of behaviors, actions, or systems are good, right, moral, beautiful, or ethical—and, therefore, that these items are desirable. For instance, the sociologist Robin Williams (1970) has listed some of the following values as recognized in American society: equal opportunity, achievement and success, activity and hard work, efficiency and practicality, progress, science, material comfort, morality, freedom, democracy, humanitarianism, individualism, external conformity, in-group superiority, and patriotism. He could have added other characteristics valued by Americans: optimism, sociability, honesty, and romantic love. Decades later, these values are just as valid, although there has been a slight

Component of Nonmaterial Culture

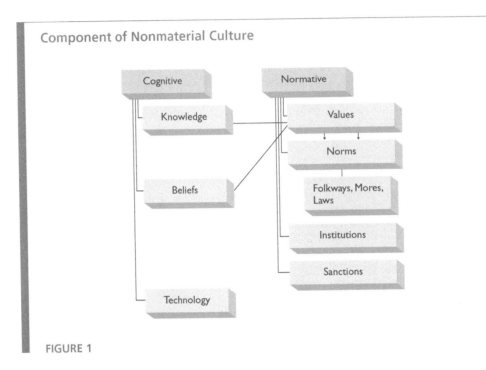

FIGURE 1

change of emphasis. Americans value freedom over equality, self-reliance over government intervention, and education for the sake of upward mobility over education for the sake of expanding one's knowledge and understanding. Some American values, moreover, may be in the process of change: Although many Americans are materialistic, some express a willingness to stop the race toward material acquisition to spend more time with their families or in the service of society.

Values are not often spelled out specifically but rather can be inferred from the way people behave. When we see superthin young women modeling clothes, and magazine after magazine displaying diets and exercise programs on their covers, we may safely guess that thinness is a value in our society. Moreover, values are often contradictory. To achieve success in business, some individuals may consider it necessary to forgo some elements of honesty or morality. We value individualism but also require a degree of conformity. Our belief in equality does not preclude our feeling superior to groups who differ from us in race or religion or from attempting to obtain advantages for the group to which we belong.

Values are also often in a state of flux, although some of our values have remained stable throughout our existence as a society. One often hears the accusation that Americans have lost their work ethic—that the "me" generation of the 1960s and 1970s, unlike their predecessors, was interested in fulfilling the self. On the other hand, the value of monogamous sexual relationships seems to be regaining some of its former preeminence after a period of "sexual revolution." The so-called family values, that is, a strong belief in marriage, fidelity, and bearing and raising children within the family circle, are being strongly espoused by certain segments of our society. Of course, because we are a highly heterogeneous society nowadays, not all segments of American society subscribe to the same values, which itself is a matter of much controversy. A good example is provided by the proposition that homosexual couples should be allowed to marry. Although one portion of the population favors this idea (and some states have adopted it), another portion is so strongly opposed that it has been recommending a constitutional amendment to forbid it.

Norms. Norms, which have been defined as rules or standards prescribing how one ought to act, think, or even feel on given occasions, cover a wide range of circumstances. They dictate conduct in both formal and informal situations as well as in significant and less significant ones. They cover everything from when, how, and with whom to shake hands to when it is permissible and when it is forbidden to kill another person.

Norms are internalized by the individual, becoming part of that individual's personality and belief system. So thoroughly are most norms internalized by most people that they are obeyed not simply out of fear of punishment but because people believe that norms represent the "right" or correct way to act. Breaking norms produces guilt feelings in most people. In short, the cultural norms that originate in each society are essentially a set of *behavioral expectations,* a system that tells a member of a society how that society expects the individual to behave in a wide range of circumstances. A comparison of norms and values may be found at a Web site noted at **mysearchlab.com.**

All cultural components are intimately interrelated. The normative system provides rules and standards of behavior, based on values, but these derive from the cognitive component of culture. We can say, then, that *beliefs* are what most people *think* is true about the reality of the world around them, whereas *values* are what most people think is *good and right. Norms* are how most people think they and others *should* behave, and how they in fact *do* behave most of the time. Norms are reflections of values, which in turn are reflections of beliefs.

The Jewish Museum, NY/Art Resource, NY

The normative system of culture consists mainly of rules of behavior that societies have established for the good of their members. If these rules are couched in religious terms—God says you must do this and refrain from doing that—they are much more likely to be followed, particularly by the believers. In Judeo-Christian societies, the Ten Commandments, which the Old Testament in the Bible says were given to Moses by God, are still widely observed.

Imperfect Agreement. The various components of culture are never in perfect agreement. Especially in heterogeneous societies, people accept conflicting norms, values, and beliefs. For instance, although Americans maintain that they believe in the equality of all people, they also believe in the value of competition, which leads to the success of some and the failure of others and, as a consequence, to inequality of income and lifestyles. Individualism is another important value in American society, having gained a foothold when the early settlers thought of the New World as a place where the individual could get ahead on his or her own initiative, without the shackles of class and status that prevailed in the Old World. Since then, individualism in one form or another has persisted as an important value of American culture. Critics charge that individualism, in the sense of an obsession with the self, has harmed public life and the public good (by which is meant the good of the society), but others believe they are seeing a reversal of this untrammeled individualism in the number of people who express a need for coherence and meaning in their lives, as well as commitment to others rather than sheer personal achievement.

Social Integration. When norms, values, and beliefs are in agreement, the society in which that culture exists is considered to be well integrated. *Social integration* is never total, but a degree of cultural integration is a must. The United States is an example of a society that is only *loosely* integrated. For instance, there is a wide array of beliefs on almost every issue: abortion, gay marriage, the death penalty, affirmative action, drug testing, and so on. A loose form of integration is true of all urban industrial and postindustrial societies, particularly those that consist of more than one cultural group.

On the opposite end of the continuum we find *closely* integrated societies, such as that of Japan. Japan will probably not continue to remain so closely integrated for very long, but for the moment, having been isolated for many centuries and having cultivated a homogeneous citizenry, the Japanese agree on most of the important values and beliefs of their society, displaying the characteristics of an extremely well-integrated social order.

Categories of Norms: Folkways, Mores, Taboos, and Laws

Norms are classified by social scientists according to their importance and functions. One category of norms consists of **folkways**, which are norms that specify expected behavior in *everyday* situations.

Norms that guide human behavior in areas of life that are considered of extreme importance are called **mores**. (*Mores* is a Latin word, the plural of *mos*, meaning custom.) Mores define for people whether a specific act is right or wrong, or its morality or immorality. A person who consistently violates some folkway, such as by becoming drunk at a dinner party, may be excluded by the hostess in the future, but a person who violates mores, such as killing another dinner guest, is punished in the name of society (that is, by some legal action). The violation of mores is considered a crime against the whole society. Mores that are expressed in negative terms ("thou shalt not") and that deal with acts considered extremely repellent to the social group are categorized as **taboos.** In most societies, taboos include incest and cannibalism.

Taboos are deeply etched in the conscience of most members of a society. Some people are physically incapable of performing an act that is forbidden so strongly, but other influences on the personality may weaken the hold of taboos and mores in general. To prevent this, or to clarify and strengthen the effect of mores and taboos, societies pass laws that prohibit specific acts under penalty of imprisonment and even death. **Laws** are formal codes of behavior that are binding on the whole society. They specify both the behavior that is considered deviant and the punishment appropriate for each kind of deviation. The punishment is meted out by official representatives of the society.

Laws are particularly necessary in a complex, heterogeneous society that is experiencing rapid social change because many norms are not clear enough for so many different groups of people to understand or accept. In simpler societies that have stronger kinship ties, a smaller number of norms is sufficient to prevent much deviation. Unlike norms, laws are not internalized by the individual (they do not become part of his or her personality) but are learned and obeyed by a majority of people because they are based on rational ideas that are understood and accepted by most. The more closely laws reinforce mores that are universally accepted in a society, the more successful the laws are.

An advantage of laws over folkways and mores is that they can be repealed or modified if they do not work. Folkways and mores, on the other hand, tend to persist as habits and customs long after their usefulness in society has passed. That is one reason why laws are sometimes passed in a society with the hope that the folkways and mores will eventually follow.

The Need for Social Control

Do normative systems have a purpose in societies? Most emphatically, they do. Every group must ensure that its members conform to most of its expectations most of the time. If they do not, anarchy and disorder prevail, and the business of the group, the reason for which it was formed, cannot go on. This is especially true if the group in question is society, because the business of society concerns the health and welfare of a large number of people. Consider what would happen if we could not trust other drivers on the road to stop at a red light. Rush-hour traffic, bad as it is when most drivers obey the rules of the road, would be a total nightmare, leaving in its wake many dead or maimed every day. Society, therefore, must have ways of exerting a certain amount of control over its members to make them obey at least the rules that are vital to the survival of the group.

A society exerts this **social control** in a number of ways. The ultimate form of control is physical force. Physical force is at the core of political power and authority. A person who represents such power and authority may use physical force against an individual who breaks the law. Thus, a police officer may knock to the ground an alleged perpetrator of a crime who is trying to escape and may even shoot if the individual does not heed the officer's request to halt. However, a society that depends on force alone to exert social control is a harsh one, characterized by much conflict or oppression.

More frequently, societies depend on more subtle methods of social control. Social control can be exerted by economic pressure: The need to get and keep a job has most workers toeing the line as far as company regulations are concerned. Occupational pressures have the effect of making a majority of individuals perform their duties appropriately in or out of their place of work; a minister, priest, or rabbi, therefore, is not likely to be seen at the corner tavern on Saturday night, though some of the parishioners may spend their time this way. A thoughtful discussion of social control from a psychological perspective, as well as a description of an unusual form of social control, are described in articles at Web sites recommended by **mysearchlab.com**.

Sanctions. Perhaps the most effective pressures exerted by societies come in the form of **sanctions.** Sanctions may be either negative or positive, official or unofficial. *Negative sanctions* consist of punishment, whereas *positive sanctions* represent rewards. For instance, being named to the Supreme Court after a distinguished career in law is an official positive sanction; it is a reward offered in the name of the whole society. Being told by an instructor that one's paper shows brilliant insights is an unofficial positive sanction; it is a reward received within a small group. A person who is jailed as a result of breaking a federal, state, or local law receives an official negative sanction; the individual is punished in the name of society. The theater patron who is asked to leave because of noisy, rude behavior receives an unofficial negative sanction; the individual is being punished, but more informally because the infraction is less severe and damages a small group, not the society as a whole.

Surprisingly, the unofficial sanctions, those that appear to be less severe, have the most impact on individuals. The reason for this is that we value members of our primary groups, our family and friends, more than we do the official representatives of the larger society, even though the latter have more power to affect our lives negatively. In other words, we would rather get a speeding ticket from a police officer than be told by our father that we are a lousy driver.

In the final analysis, social control through the enforcement of norms works because individuals are so anxious to be accepted by the group. Researchers have found that, even in group discussions, individuals tend eventually to change their minds to conform to the consensus of opinions expressed by other individuals. In a group of 20, if 15 argue one point and 5 argue the opposite point, chances are good that in time the 5 opponents will come to agree with the majority. In society, too, people yearn for acceptance; thus, many more are conformists than nonconformists.

Overt and Covert, Real and Ideal Norms

Before leaving a discussion of norms, a few more points should be noted. First, although the norms of their culture are firmly embedded in the personality of most individuals, this is not true of each and every individual. A minority of people in every society always ignores some of the norms, but no one who ignores or rejects all social norms can continue to live in a social group. Second, in every society some norms emerge that are not officially accepted as proper behavior but that are widely practiced by people anyway. So it is possible to speak of an *overt* culture, which describes the officially accepted patterns of behavior, and of a *covert* culture, according to which some people actually behave. For instance, a person who publicly subscribes to a high moral system of sexual behavior may be found to engage in promiscuous sexual behavior privately.

The fact is that we can recognize in each society an *ideal* culture, consisting of the formal, approved folkways, mores, and laws, and the real culture, consisting of what people actually do and how they really behave. Although this situation may be considered hypocritical, the existence of the ideal culture provides a model of behavior toward which people may aspire.

Traits, Complexes, and Institutions

For purposes of analysis, culture is further classified into traits, complexes, and institutions. **Culture traits** are the smallest element, or unit, of culture. In material culture, every single object that people in a society use is a trait. In nonmaterial culture, every single idea, symbol, or belief existing in a society is a trait. A nail, a brick, and a house are all traits of material culture; saluting the flag (denoting patriotism), kissing (a symbol of affection), voting (a belief in a particular political system), and praying (faith in a transcendent life) are all traits of nonmaterial culture.

A number of related traits that accumulate around an activity form a **culture complex.** Football is a culture complex consisting of material traits (the pigskin itself, uniforms, helmets, a field, etc.) and nonmaterial traits (the ability of the players, a set of rules, a belief in winning, team spirit, etc.). All areas of human life display numerous culture complexes. A fuller description of culture may be found at several Web sites reported at **mysearchlab.com.**

When a number of culture complexes cluster around a central human activity, an institution emerges. **Institutions** are formal systems of beliefs and behavior composed of interrelated norms and culture complexes. In the preceding example, sport is the institution of which football is a culture complex.

Pivotal Institutions

What is important about institutions is that they emerge around some fundamental human *need* that must be filled for the individual to survive and the society to prosper. The five basic (or pivotal) institutions, which arose from the five most fundamental human needs, are the *family* (need to replenish society with new members, regulate sex, and care for the helpless newborn); the *economy* (need to procure food, shelter, and clothing); *government* (need to maintain peace and order); *education* (need to transmit culture and train new generations); and *religion* (need to overcome fear of the unknown and find explanations of the meaning of life).

These five basic institutions are common to all societies. However, the forms they assume and the traits and complexes they display differ from society to society. Each of the pivotal institutions of American society will be discussed in some detail. For now, it is well to note that institutions are cultural instruments designed to show people how to behave in such a way as to benefit them and the society and fulfill their biological needs in the best possible manner. Cultural institutions are entrenched so well in societal members that they come to believe that their needs cannot be fulfilled in any other way. In fact, those who fail to behave according to the precepts of one institution or another are ostracized and often believe themselves to be failures in life. The high rates of remarriage after divorce prove that individuals are ready to try and try again to succeed in the cultural institution of marriage.

Ethnocentrism and Cultural Relativity

Statements to the effect that "there is no place like home" are echoed by members of every society about their own country or region. And though most of us may be Americans, many of us belong to groups that are distinct from one another by reason of race, or ethnic origin, or religion; within these groups, we refer to ourselves as "us" and to the others as "them." The reason for such feelings is that we feel comfortable in the place in which we were born and brought up and among people much like us. So comfortable, in fact, that whatever we internalize from the culture of a specific place and group seems right and proper to us. The other side of the coin, of course, is that the customs of other places and groups seem to us wrong and inferior. Western travelers to some Asian countries in which dogs are considered a perfectly normal part of the diet are shocked and nauseated to see skinned bodies of what they consider pets hanging in the markets. However, an Indian traveler to a Western European or North American country would be similarly sickened to see a side of beef hanging in a butcher shop because cows are considered sacred animals and are allowed to wander freely in India. It is easy, and natural, for such travelers to express their disgust with the "barbaric" habits of the country they are visiting. In doing so, they are displaying **ethnocentrism,** a belief that one's own society is superior to others based on judging other societies with the standards of one's own. This attitude, though often irrational, reflects our cultural indoctrination that all customs that differ from our own are somehow abnormal—strange at best, uncivilized at worst. An ethnographic analysis of ethnocentrism is described in a Web site found on **mysearchlab.com**.

As noted, all societies and, for that matter, all groups display a certain amount of ethnocentrism; in moderation, ethnocentrism has the positive effect of promoting unity and loyalty within the group that exhibits it. In excess, however, ethnocentrism leads to conflict with groups that are dissimilar, or, when one group is more powerful than another, to oppression and sometimes to genocide. This was the case in Nazi Germany when the government determined to annihilate groups it considered inferior: Jews, Gypsies, homosexuals, the mentally and physically impaired, and others. Quite recently it happend in the former Yugoslavia, in which Serbs who are Orthodox, Croats who are Roman Catholic, and Kosovans and Albanians, most of whom are Muslims, have engaged in "ethnically" cleansing their respective regions of each other. In Rwanda, the Hutu and the Tutsis committed genocidal acts against each other. And in Arab societies, the followers of the two different strains of Islam, Sunni and Shia, also engage in hostilities and violence. In short, tribalism is still deeply embedded in people, despite the fact that most societies long ago abandoned tribal life in favor of divisions according to political states. There is even evidence of consumer ethnocentrism when some individuals refuse to buy products manufactured in other societies.

To counter the negative effects of ethnocentrism, anthropologists, aware that the early practitioners of the discipline were especially guilty of it, have suggested that the concept of **cultural relativity** be popularized. Proponents of *cultural relativity* assert that cultures must be analyzed on their own terms, in the context of their own societal setting. No society has the right to use its own values and norms to judge the traits of another society. In this view, there are no universal norms or moral absolutes when it comes to cultures: Cultures are neither better nor worse, only different. This does not mean that in looking at other cultures we agree with or approve of certain behaviors, or that we discard our own cultural or moral values. It merely means that other cultures should be approached with attitudes of tolerance, respect, and understanding.

Box 2 A Cultural Custom Americans Never Heard Of

In the northern, rural part of Albania, a 78-year-old woman tells of her life, which she spent as a man. At 20, she cut off her hair, put on her father's baggy pants, began carrying a hunting rifle, and promised to forsake marriage, children, and sex.

Her reason was that around sixty years ago, women in Albania had as much value as animals. The tradition, followed by the northern tribes of Albania for more than 500 years, prescribed a code of conduct that was very restrictive for women: Their role was to take care of the home and children, period. A woman's life was worth half of that of a man, and the value of a virgin was 12 oxen.

The notion of perpetual virginity and living as a man was born of necessity: If a patriarch died without a male heir, the women in the household were powerless; they could not move freely, could not own property, and could not carry a weapon in an area where wars and death were common. Sometimes living as a man was the only way a woman could avoid an arranged marriage.

Although some sworn virgins retained a feminine name, in all other ways they became men. Even in the present, and even living in an urban setting, in the capital, the old woman is treated as a man: She lords over her family of nieces and nephews who serve her alcoholic drinks. She tells of having worked in construction and having prayed in the mosque with the men. She was responsible for avenging her father's murder. Another such woman became a senior army officer. The women speak of their lives in glowing terms: They enjoyed being taken for a man, they could go wherever they wanted to, no one would swear at them because they could beat them up. They could not do "women's work" such as cooking, ironing, cleaning. They were never scared. Those who still live as men don't even know how to do "women's talk." And they all bemoan the condition of contemporary Albanian women, who have rights almost equal to those of men (Bilefsky, 2008).

Cultural Differences and Universals

When early explorers, missionaries, and adventurers first came in contact with foreign societies, they of course judged them according to their own ethnocentric standards. In some of the more exotic societies, they could not help experiencing what we now call "culture shock." They explained the dissimilarities of foreign cultures by speculating that they were due to racial, geographic, and even religious causes. However, although all these influences have a bearing on the course of cultural development—obviously, the natural environment influences culture in the sense that no igloos can be built in the Amazonian jungle, nor palm huts become the customary dwellings of Alaskans—no one reason can be found to explain perfectly what makes one culture dissimilar from another.

As striking as some differences appear to be, cultures have many more similarities than differences. Pivotal institutions, as already stated, are present in all societies. Further, many norms, values, and beliefs are also unexpectedly similar. All people enjoy adorning themselves, whether with a ring through the nose, on an earlobe, or on a finger; all people have some food taboos, whether it is against eating cows or pigs or dogs. All people have some form of music and dancing and some form of art or handicraft.

Social anthropologist George P. Murdock (1965) compiled a long list of elements that are common to all known cultures. The list includes such widely different elements as play, hospitality, and weather control. Similarities common to all cultures are called **cultural universals**. They are general themes on which each culture develops its own variations. The conclusion we draw from the fact that so many cultural universals exist is that we truly share common human bonds.

Over time, cultures undergo change. Change may be fast and dramatic or slow and imperceptible.

Box 3 Differences in Culture: An Obstacle to World Harmony

Differences in culture are often so profound that people cannot understand one another—and not just because they do not speak each other's language. A contemporary example is that of Afghanistan, a nation that has undergone many years of war against powers that wanted to control it, and later was ruled by a sect that follows a strict and rigid interpretation of Islam. In addition, their natural terrain is very rough, with high mountains that are often impassable. It follows that many residents are isolated in hard-to-reach locations and live by ancient tribal laws. One of these tribal traditions is that women are treated as inferior beings. They must be totally covered when they are in the presence of a male who is not a member of their family; they must remain in the house unless it is absolutely impossible, and they must do what the male relatives—fathers, husbands, brothers—tell them to do. Very frequently these males basically sell them as wives to other males, no matter how young the brides-to-be are (often only 12 or 14), and no matter how they feel about the generally older men they are being married to.

With the presence of NATO forces in their country, these women have come in touch with Western women serving in the military. The cultural shock the Afghan women experience is dramatic. They have never seen women who walk around uncovered, in fatigues, carrying weapons, who talk to men, shake hands with them, and even give them orders.

In these isolated villages there is no health care, particularly not for women. As the United States is attempting to convince the Afghanis to come into the twenty-first century—in the sense of abandoning tribal governments in favor of a central government—women Marines have been trying to engage the Afghani women in a dialogue by helping them with simple health-care issues.

Such a dialogue has been extremely difficult. There are language problems because the Afghani women will not allow an interpreter—generally a man—into their homes. He has to wait outside the house, behind a wall, and wait to translate. Moreover, the women usually do not believe that the American women are really women. They sometimes try to touch them in private places to make sure they are really women. Finally, although male medical officers are better trained, "Some of these women would rather die than be touched by a male," said one female Marine, who was trying to help a group of Afghani women. They had to diagnose by proxy (Bumiller, 2010).

Subcultures and Countercultures

Variation and uniformity, as noted earlier, are characteristic not only of societies but also of groups within each society. This is especially true of contemporary technologically advanced societies, which tend to be heterogeneous (made up of dissimilar groups) not only because they attract people from all over the world to their superior economies but also because many societies have been created as political units by uniting a number of separate ethnic groups.

Subcultures. In the United States, the native inhabitants and the original settlers who came from England have been augmented, through the centuries, by numerous people from all over the globe. Today, groups exist on the basis of the members' race, ethnicity or country of origin, religion, and numerous other distinguishing features. Even in more homogeneous societies, people form groups based on the region in which they live (Northerners or Southerners), their occupation (musicians, circus acrobats, doctors, lawyers), their social class (WASPS or Yuppies, middle class or working class), their religion (Roman Catholics, Muslims, Protestants, Jews), their sexual preference (gay persons, transvestites, bisexuals), or even their age (teenagers, golden-agers). Sociologists refer to these subdivisions, these groups within the larger group of the society, as **subcultures.**

© Chris George/CORBIS

Adorning oneself is a cultural universal, that is, in every culture people adorn themselves. In American society, and in Western societies in general, tattoos and nose piercings are not a type of adornment used in the mainstream. However, they are common in subcultural or countercultural groups as shown in this photo of men at a tattoo convention in England.

Subcultures have distinctive features that set them apart from the general culture of the society, yet they retain the principal features of that culture. (The word *subculture* never implies any inferiority to the larger culture—it refers only to its being a segment of that larger culture.) Teenagers are a good example of a subculture. They certainly identify with the goals and values of the larger societal culture and are guided by this culture's normative patterns. At the same time, many of their interests and some aspects of their behavior are peculiar to their age group: Teenagers seem to have a special language, a distinctive manner of dress, a taste for special kinds of music, and a fondness for specific foods and forms of recreation.

Teenagers are a temporary subculture; that is, as people grow older, they abandon it. Some subcultures are much more permanent, however. Although the United States was at one time considered a melting pot—or at least it was the alleged goal of the society to become a melting pot—in reality a large number of subcultural groups based on race and ethnicity exist among us. Whereas historically such groups preferred to be absorbed into the mainstream culture, the last several decades have seen a reversal, with most members of subcultural groups choosing to maintain a degree of cultural distinctiveness. This desire has produced some controversy, particularly when such groups are vocal in their refusal to blend into the mainstream and when their traditions clash with the laws of the society. One instance of subcultural goals clashing with mainstream values and laws is represented by the Amish, who are concentrated principally in the rural areas of Pennsylvania and Ohio. The religious beliefs of the Amish include a refusal to embrace modern technology of any kind, and they deem eight years of education sufficient for their members. All states, however, have laws requiring their residents to remain in school until they are 16 years old. Which should have preeminence, the law of the state or the religious freedom of the subcultural group?

Countercultures. Sometimes groups that emerge in a society have a faddish quality, in the sense that they come and go rather quickly. A **counterculture** differs from a subculture in that it is a group within the larger society whose members adopt a value system and goals that are in *direct opposition* to those of the wider societal culture. In the twentieth century, the United States witnessed the emergence of the "beatniks" in the 1950s, and of the "hippies" a generation later. These groups shared many goals that differed from those of the wider society, chief among them antimaterialism, rejection of conventional morality in the areas of sex, drug use, and the need to work. The hippies and "flower children" also stood in opposition to the Vietnam War and were fierce supporters of individual freedom as opposed to the norms superimposed, in their view, by the "establishment." A lengthy period of economic recession, among other things, put an end to all but a small residue of countercultural lifestyles. Many of the countercultural ideas, however, were absorbed by the mainstream culture, just as its outward symbols—the long hair, the colorful unisex attire, and the music—had been. It may be argued that the very success of the counterculture spelled its doom, but its real goals were never achieved.

A rejection of conventional norms and folkways is also displayed by "punkers," identified by their colorful if bizarre hairstyles and clothing, and "bikers," such as the Hell's Angels, whose lifestyle apparently centers around motorcycles, alcohol, and drugs.

Some criminal groups are countercultural, although not all are; most criminals accept the goals of their society and reject only the means of attaining them. A gang of delinquent youths is usually considered countercultural because its set of values and standards of behavior are distinct from, or run counter to, those of the wider culture. Members of organized crime, however, or criminals who engage in theft and fraud, are not countercultural; for them, crime is simply a shortcut to attaining the material success that others must work for (or inherit).

Almost every historical period, as well as most societies, has had its counterculture, although in some periods societies were too rigid to tolerate a counterculture and suppressed any attempts at nonconformity. Today, we have become much more tolerant of nonconforming lifestyles, although, of course, when such lifestyles endanger the lives or property of the majority, they must be proscribed. Terrorist groups and paramilitary groups proclaiming their hatred for the federal government, or for specific minority groups (the "Skinheads"), crop up periodically, with such tragic outcomes as the bombing, with enormous loss of life, of the Oklahoma City Federal Building. The attacks perpetrated by al Qaeda and similar groups against Western targets are the work of a global terrorist group that may be described as countercultural in a global, rather than a societal, sense.

The Chapter in Brief

The most important product of the interaction that occurs in groups, especially in societies, is culture. Culture may be superficially defined as the way of life of a specific people, but it is much more than this. At the very least, it acts as a guide for further social interaction—it is a blueprint for living. The most basic element of culture is language, a system of symbols that allows people to accumulate knowledge and transmit it without relying on personal experience. The sharing of symbols is a much more effective tool for survival than are the genetically inherited signals with which animals other than humans cope with life and communicate with each other.

Culture has both material content (tangible products and objects) and nonmaterial content (ideas, values, knowledge, beliefs, rules for behavior, and institutions). Much of a society's nonmaterial culture is made up of norms; rules of behavior that are learned and shared by each member of the society through interaction. Norms include folkways, mores, taboos, and laws.

The structure of culture consists of traits (the smallest unit of culture), culture complexes (a number of related traits), and institutions. Institutions are formal systems of beliefs and behavior, composed of interrelated norms and culture complexes. Institutions primarily focus on and help fill universal human needs. Five basic (pivotal) institutions are common to all human societies: the family, the economy, education, government, and religion.

The culture of each society is both different from and similar to the culture of other societies. To members of a specific society, a foreign culture may appear irrational or silly, but that impression is biased because the culture is judged by the standards of those who are doing the judging (ethnocentrism). It is more just to use cultural relativity to judge foreign cultures, because then each culture is analyzed in its own societal context and on the basis of how well it fills its members' needs.

Cultural differences among societies are partly the result of geographic and other factors, of which little is yet known. The similar characteristics displayed by cultures arise because all cultures must help to fulfill universal human needs, both biological and emotional. Characteristics common to all cultures are called cultural universals.

Because societies are made up of various groups, culture also varies within single societies. Groups within a society may be differentiated on the basis of geographic location, social class, occupation, race, ethnicity, religion, and so on. Such groups may produce a distinctive culture, including a separate language or jargon, customs, traditions, and rituals. If the principal values of such a group are the same as those of the general culture of the society, the group is called a subculture. If the principal values are in direct opposition to those of the larger culture, the group is called a counterculture.

Terms to Remember

counterculture   A group that possesses a value system and goals that are in direct opposition to those of the larger society.

cultural relativity   An attitude of judging each culture on its own terms and in the context of its own societal setting.

cultural universals   Similarities common to all cultures (example: the existence of pivotal institutions).

culture   The way of life of people in a society. The totality of what is learned and shared by the members of a society through their interactions. The product of social interaction and a guide for further interaction. Culture includes material and nonmaterial aspects.

culture complex   A number of related traits that accumulate around a specific human activity.

culture trait   The smallest element or unit of culture. In material culture, it is any single object. In nonmaterial culture, it is any single idea, symbol, or belief.

ethnocentrism   The attitude that one's own culture is right and that cultural patterns different from it are wrong.

folkways   Norms that direct behavior in everyday situations; customary and habitual ways of acting.

institution   A number of culture complexes clustering around a central human activity.

laws   Formal codes of behavior. Laws are binding on the whole society; they outline behavior that deviates from the norm and define prescriptions for punishing it.

mores   Norms that direct behavior considered either extremely harmful or extremely helpful to society.

They define the rightness or wrongness of an act, its morality or immorality. Violation of mores is punished by society.

normative system   A system of rules regulating human behavior.

norms   Behavioral standards that dictate conduct in both informal and formal situations; a set of behavioral expectations.

sanctions   Rewards (positive) or punishments (negative) directed at individuals or groups by either legal and formal organizations (official) or the people with whom one interacts (unofficial) to encourage or discourage specific types of behavior.

signals   Biologically determined and genetically transmitted responses to outside stimuli.

social control   The process by which order is maintained within society through obedience to norms—folkways, mores, taboos, and laws.

subculture   A group that has distinctive features that set it apart from the culture of the larger society but still retains the general values of mainstream society.

symbols   Genetically independent responses to stimuli in the form of representations: a word or image standing for an object or a feeling. Symbols are learned and can be changed, modified, combined, and recombined in an infinite number of ways. Language, music, and art are common symbol systems.

taboos   Mores stated in negative terms. They center on acts considered extremely repellent to the social group.

Suggested Readings

Barber, Benjamin R. 1995. *Jihad vs. McWorld: How Globalism and Tribalism Are Reshaping the World*. New York: Random House. The author analyzes the cultures of the capitalist West and those of local, traditional cultures, noting that they are in conflict. Conflict is particularly evident between global capitalism and some of the fundamentalist Islamic cultures.

Bellah, Robert N., Richard Madsen, William M. Sullivan, Ann Swidler, and Steven M. Tipton. 1986. *Habits of the Heart: Individualism and Commitment in American Life*. New York: Harper & Row. An examination of American culture, focusing on the conflict between the values of individualism and achievement on the one hand and a desire for close relationships and community on the other.

Brown, Donald E. 1991. *Human Universals*. New York: McGraw-Hill. A survey of anthropological literature focusing on cultural universals found in human groups.

Chagnon, Napoleon A. 1983. *Yanomamo: The Fierce People*. 3rd ed. New York: Holt, Rinehart and Winston. A fascinating account of a culture truly unfamiliar to Americans, as well as of the methods of research involved in this anthropological project.

DeVita, Philip B., and James D. Armstrong, eds. 1998. *Distant Mirrors: America as a Foreign Culture*. 2nd ed. Belmont, CA: West/Wadsworth. American culture as seen by scholars from Europe, Africa, Asia, and Latin America.

Mortenson, Greg and David Oliver Relin. 2006. *Three Cups of Tea*. New York: Penguin. A failed mountain climber finds himself in a remote village between Afghanistan and Pakistan where he is received and cared for with unexpected hospitality. As there are no schools in this poor village, the author decides to find funds and begins to establish schools in this forsaken region. In the meantime, he describes a culture few Westerners are familiar with.

Weinstein, Deena. 2000. *The Music and Its Culture*. Cambridge, MA: Da Capo. An examination of the subculture formed by those engaged in "heavy metal" music.

Zellner, William M. 1995. *Countercultures: A Sociological Analysis*. New York: St. Martin's. The Unification Church, the Church of Scientology, Satanists, skinheads, survivalists, and the Ku Klux Klan examined as examples of countercultural groups.

Group Interaction:
From Two to Millions

IN THIS CHAPTER, YOU WILL LEARN

- *that humans are group animals who survive and become true human beings as a result of being members of groups;*
- *that within each group, individuals are assigned statuses and carry out roles, a condition that makes each group a social system;*
- *that a social system has structure, which gives life a pattern of predictability;*
- *that of the multitude of groups, primary groups are those most important to the individual;*
- *that the largest group to which people belong is society;*
- *that there has been a trend away from the small, traditional societies of the past (Gemeinschafts) to the large associational societies of the present (Gesellschafts);*
- *that the interaction that occurs within all social groups is based on the processes of cooperation, competition, exchange, and conflict; and*
- *that the way to manage life in large, complex societies is through the establishment of formal organizations that depend on bureaucracy to function.*

"United we stand, divided we fall," "In unity there is strength," "E pluribus, unum." All these sayings attempt to bring home an ancient truth that has become a cliché by virtue of so much repetition: people are *social* animals. Being a social animal means that humans do not live in isolation. From the moment of birth as fragile, helpless creatures, humans depend on others, at first for sheer survival and later for protection, companionship, affection, reproduction, and economic survival—in short, for everything.

From Chapter 4 of *Contemporary Society: An Introduction to Social Science,* Thirteenth Edition. John A. Perry, Erna K. Perry. Copyright © 2012 by Pearson Education, Inc. All rights reserved.

A group way of life is not only a necessity for humans but also an advantage in the difficult task of survival. It is much easier to exist in a family group than alone: The newest born is fed and protected, and all eat better when two or three adults work to provide for the group instead of each individual working alone. It is also easier to defend one's home or belongings (or territory from predators) in a group setting; thus, there is much truth in the sayings about the importance of the group.

Despite all its advantages, a group way of life lends itself to disorder and chaos because whenever people live in close proximity to one another, there is a potential for conflict. Individuals differ in temperament, in likes and dislikes, in goals and desires. When the groups that live in close quarters are many, the problems of coexistence multiply. Therefore, a group way of life requires the development of some sort of **organization,** or system, to ensure a fairly smooth coexistence. Individuals must know what is expected of them and, in turn, what they can expect of others. They must agree on their duties and responsibilities to the group, and what the group members owe them. They must know what to expect from the behavior of group members, and how they themselves should behave toward them. They must ensure that no social encounter is a complete surprise in terms of what members of the group say and do, but on the contrary, that the encounter be predictable to a great extent. Otherwise, groups cannot function adequately.

An organizational system does, in fact, develop within groups, though we are not consciously aware of it. It emerges thanks to the repeated interaction of individuals with other individuals, and of groups with other groups. The system is structured because people behave according to the statuses they hold in each group and to the roles those statuses oblige them to play. Moreover, it is obvious that interaction takes place in the framework of specific social processes. Social life, in short, is organized into a system with its own definite structure.

The presence of a system does not guarantee harmony, but it does guarantee a certain amount of predictability. This makes our group way of life much easier.

How Is the Social System Organized and Structured?

Social scientists who analyze group life do so at two levels: the interpersonal or **microsocial** level and the group or **macrosocial** level. On the microsocial level, they focus on the way individuals relate to one another based on the position that each holds in relation to the other: husband to wife, father to daughter, teacher to student, employer to employee, and so forth. On the macrosocial level, they examine relationships between and among groups that make up the largest group, society, and focus on the values and rules for behavior that emerge when people live in a society. The social system that emerges from such interactions is, of course, an abstraction, a model that illustrates how social relationships work. It is important to remember that every group, whether it consists of only two people or many millions of people, is basically a **social system.** As is characteristic of systems, each part is connected to, and dependent on, every other part. It follows that the way each individual in a group behaves influences every other individual in the group. This interconnectedness and interdependence eventually result in shared patterns of behavior that members come to expect of each other.

The orderly and fairly predictable patterns of interaction that emerge in a social system give that social system structure. **Social structure,** also referred to as **social organization,** is the foundation underlying the network of organized relationships among the component parts of a social system. It is the patterned and recurring way in which individuals and groups interact.

Social structure should not be viewed as a fixed set of rules. Rather, it is a dynamic process in which stable and predictable patterns are continually redefined and altered to fit the changing conditions of each situation. The members of a musical band are an example of a group that exhibits a social system with a structure and organization. These members meet every afternoon, Monday through Thursday, from 1:00 to 3:00, for the purpose of rehearsing a program they will perform Thursday through Saturday nights at a downtown hall. The musicians are there for a specific goal, and to achieve that goal they behave according to regular and predictable patterns. Most come in carrying their instruments; they take their assigned seats; they tune their instruments; they stop chatting when their lead musician appears; they begin to play when he or she gives them a signal. Each member of this social system knows what to do, and each expects the other members to know what to do and to do it. As long as they do this, the social system of the band is stable and enduring, and the group can function. If one or more members begins to be consistently late for rehearsals, or some members fail to bring their instruments; if they continue to talk when they should be playing; if they question the leader's right to tell them how to play a passage; if they take out sandwiches and begin eating in the middle of a number—if any of these things should happen with any frequency, the organization of this system will inevitably be destroyed, and the group will eventually have to disband because it can no longer function as a group with a specific purpose. As you know, many bands have in fact broken up and ceased to exist or have been reconstituted with other members because the original system had become unworkable.

Elements of Social Structure: Statuses and Roles

In the earlier example, the social structure became ineffective because some members failed to follow the norms, did not behave according to their **statuses,** and did not perform their expected **roles** in the situation of the rehearsal. In their simplest definition, *norms* are rules for behavior, *status* is a position in a social group, and *role* is the carrying out of the status. People have such statuses as mother in a family group, teacher in an occupational group, or plumber in a work group. The dynamic aspect of that status, or what the mother, the teacher, and the plumber *do,* is the role. The theatrical term *role* is very appropriate. It may be said, in fact, that each individual is handed a script by society. Individuals are like actors who perform assigned roles throughout their lives. When we say that society assigns roles, we are of course speaking figuratively. We are not really handed a script, but we are born with some statuses, and we acquire others because of what we do or fail to do. Statuses are ranked; that is, they are value-rated according to the prevailing values of the group. In American society, the teacher has a higher status than the plumber, and both have a lower status than a famous musician.

A person who occupies a specific status is expected to behave in a way befitting that status. We do not expect the plumber to give us a lecture on the English literature of the Middle Ages, nor do we expect the teacher to fix our leaky faucet. (Of course, the teacher may in fact be able to fix faucets, just as the plumber may be an expert in literature.) When you enter a classroom at the beginning of a term, you expect one individual, man or woman, to come and stand in front of the class, write his or her name on the board, and proceed to tell you what textbook to buy, how many exams you will take, how many papers you will write, and how many times you will be allowed to be absent. You assume that this person is an instructor—even though you have no absolute proof—and so you find it natural to follow his or her instructions. If a child came into your classroom and attempted to give you similar instructions, you would be outraged, and rightly so. Similarly, if you go for a job interview, you recognize that the interviewer has a right to ask you fairly personal questions about your past performance or about your salary requirements, questions that you would not tolerate from a stranger you had just met while waiting for a commuter train. Or, should you find yourself in the emergency room of a hospital, you would find it natural to address the woman with the stethoscope as "Doctor," even though she might call you John, and to remove your clothes and let yourself be examined. Because you are the patient and she the doctor, you do not address her as Jane, nor do you expect to give her orders. As a student, a prospective employee, and a patient, you accept as a given the behavior of your instructor, your future employer, and your doctor in certain situations; in other situations, or with people of different statuses, you would not abide it.

Statuses and roles evolve from the need of each group to perform its tasks efficiently. In a society, a great many functions must be performed each day if the society is to operate well. Food must be grown or produced and made available for consumption, shelter must be built, the sick must be healed, children must be educated, and so on. In time and through experience, it has become clear that efficiency is much improved when tasks are allocated to particular individuals who specialize in performing them. Such an allocation of tasks is what we call *division of labor*, which is the origin of most, though not all, statuses (some statuses are allocated on the basis of gender or age).

Statuses and the roles that grow from them are not static. They are continually subject to change, growth, and replacement. Change within each group and change in society, as well as daily interaction, constantly redefine statuses and roles. Additional discussions and examples of statuses and roles, as well as lecture notes that may help to illuminate some of these sociological concepts, are found at **mysearchlab.com**.

Statuses: Ascribed and Achieved

Some statuses and their roles are ours at birth; that is, we cannot avoid having them. A child is born either male or female; it is either white, African, Asian, Hispanic, or a mixture of these; its parents are either working class, middle class, or upper class—or somewhere along the social class continuum—and they may claim allegiance to a given ethnic group and/or religion. These statuses of the newborn child are **ascribed** to it; they are not attained through any individual effort or merit or fault. *Ascribed* statuses are involuntary, being based on gender, age, race, ethnic background, and the social position and religious affiliation of one's family.

Most other statuses, however, are **achieved** by individuals through their own effort and choice, or conversely, through lack of effort, apathy, or poor choices. We become college graduates, wives, or bank managers because we want to, and we put some effort into it, or we remain unemployed or end up in prison because we failed to obtain a skill or made unwise decisions.

In preindustrial societies, ascribed status is more prevalent than achieved status. For instance, in feudal Europe, society was divided into estates—a kind of permanent and rigid social class—and mobility from one estate into another was almost impossible to achieve. In India, too, until recent times, people were divided into castes based on occupation. In such societies, the scope of individual choice is small. Even with ability, talent, or hard work, individuals cannot rise above the occupation and social class of their parents (however, India is fast becoming an industrial society and its stratification system is becoming much more flexible). In industrial societies, on the other hand, there is a commitment to individualism and personal achievement. Freedom of choice is jealously defended, and the accomplishments of the individual are ardently applauded. As a result, achieved status is valued, although the ascribed status that comes from belonging to a family that has enjoyed a high status for a few generations is also highly valued.

Societies and their cultures do not change at the same pace. India, for instance, is still largely preindustrial and agricultural. Statuses in such a society are mostly ascribed, that is, people are born into a particular status, such as these women planting rice in a flooded rice paddy.

The status of women in India has undergone a dramatic change since that country began to industrialize its economy.

In most postindustrial societies, and especially in the United States, the past several decades have seen much upheaval as a result of people's dissatisfaction with their ascribed statuses and the consequent roles they have been forced to fulfill. Thus, women, homosexuals, and racial and ethnic minorities have fought to change certain discriminatory practices to which they were subjected as a result of their ascribed statuses. Although the problematic aspects of their roles have not been eliminated entirely, progress has been made in that direction.

The Multiplicity of Statuses and Roles

As must be quite obvious by now, each person has many statuses and performs many roles in a lifetime. The CEO of Hot Dogs, Incorporated, is best known by his status of corporation president, which becomes his *master status*, but he also has the added statuses of son, husband, father, brother, lawyer, regent of the state university, member of a country club, elder in the Presbyterian church, and fund-raiser for the Republican Party. On an occasional basis, he also occupies the statuses of patient (when he sees his doctor), client (when he visits his stockbroker), customer (when he goes shopping), and driver (when he drives his car).

Not all these statuses are equally important. The importance of the statuses is determined by the values of the group that is involved in ranking them. On a macrosocial level, the individual described would be ranked as having a high status because of his position as a corporation president. On a microsocial level, however, he may be ranked low by his wife and children, in whom he takes little interest. His status may be ranked equal with that of the other elders in the church, though the volunteers in the Republican Party may consider him an upstart.

Clearly, if there is a multiplicity of statuses, there is an equally large number of roles that people must perform. No one performs all roles well. The corporation president in this example must be good at performing his master role, or he would not remain in his position for very long. As was noted, however, he may leave much to be desired in his roles of husband and father. Generally, people select the roles they consider most important and perform these roles best. There is a relationship between a person's self-image and the role he or she chooses to perform best. The chief executive in the example may see himself as a great American business leader and consequently performs his role of CEO well, whereas he may feel that he was forced to marry because of pressure from his pregnant girlfriend and her family, and so performs the role of husband and father badly.

Real and Ideal Roles

Groups frequently prepare their members to fill roles they then never have the opportunity to fill, or they teach their young ideal patterns of behavior that are seldom or never really followed. In Sunday school, for instance, children learn that people should love their neighbor and turn the other cheek, but their football coach tells them to "murder" the opposing team and take revenge for a previous loss. Such contradictory teachings do not necessarily constitute hypocrisy. Ideal patterns of behavior serve a necessary function by acting as a brake on real patterns that may decline to an undesirably low level.

Conflict, Strain, and Confusion in Roles

When the real differs substantially from the ideal, however, confusion follows. Young people are disillusioned when they come in contact with the "real" world; they feel betrayed. In some instances, the disparity may have positive results, as individuals resolve to bring the real more in line with the ideal and work to reach a social goal; in other instances, stresses and strains result from the discrepancy.

Rapid social change, on the other hand, contributes to a situation in which future lifestyles are unpredictable, and thus it is impossible to prepare for them. In industrial societies, many tasks are performed outside the home, and children grow up without knowing exactly what their parents do when they "go to work." Some roles, then, are not learned at all, or are learned improperly in childhood, and have to be picked up as one goes along. Again, these problems do not arise in preindustrial or emerging societies, but in postindustrial, technological societies they are very common.

Strain. Often, playing one's role well produces strain. For instance, a supervisor must uphold discipline to ensure that a work group reaches its goals. In the process, however, the supervisor may have to be severe, even unfriendly, or drive workers too hard, and so become disliked by the subordinates. The alternative is to be a "good guy" and be well liked at the expense of attaining group goals. A leader must constantly weigh his or her behavior in terms of the role of leading.

Role strain can also occur when entrenched statuses become altered as a result of changes in the social system. Women traditionally occupied the statuses of wives, mothers, and homemakers, which were considered undemanding tasks requiring little intellectual acumen or talent, and they were consequently ranked low. Men, on the other hand, held the statuses of providers, which, although ranked according to the prestige and financial rewards their particular job brought, were generally considered to require superior capabilities. As a result, all the positions of real power in society were held by men. As women achieved more education, however, they began to compete with men in the labor market. In turn, as they became financially independent, their roles within the family strengthened. Many men were not able to adjust to their changed roles, and conflicts between marital partners frequently led to divorce. Divorced women were forced to compete for jobs as a matter of survival, theirs and the children of the failed marriage (angry fathers frequently shirk their financial responsibilities toward their children). The consequent shift in statuses and roles that follows social change, then, has created a situation that necessitates adjustment both within the family institution and in the society at large. As we are constantly reminded by the media and politicians, the institution of the family has been in a period of crisis for several decades. Eventually, people will learn to adjust to new roles, or adapt old roles to new circumstances, but the transitional period is very difficult for both individuals and the society.

Conflict. Having to fulfill multiple roles can produce **conflict**. A corporation president's role demands spending an unusually large proportion of time on business connected with the corporation. To be a good spouse and parent, however, enough time should also be spent in family activities, so that intimate interaction can take place. Each individual must choose which of these roles should take precedence, and the difficult decision is sure to create conflicts for individuals, frequently leading to the breakup of families.

Box 1 War: The Ultimate Group Conflict

History, both of our country and of the world in general, is replete with wars. Reading it, one would be justified in saying that conflict among groups is the oldest of social processes. When groups fight over territory or over hunting grounds, as they did in the past, it is somewhat understandable: Group members were fighting for survival. But when groups in the same society fight one another, the matter becomes much more critical: Civil wars pose brother against brother. Unfortunately, civil wars in one guise or another dominate the news as rival groups in a number of societies fight each other. Whether it is the sects of Islam, Sunni and Shia, who engage daily in violent acts in Iraq, or radical Islamists in a number of Arab or Muslim countries, or tribal leaders who disagree with the central government in Afghanistan or Somalia, the end result is a dramatic loss of life. War, of course, is the ultimate step in the social process of conflict. But what exactly brings a society to be divided by such extreme conflict?

Common sense suggests that it is the presence of a number of groups that differ from one another culturally or physically that causes violence between and among them. A study by two political scientists from Stanford University, however, points out that the presence of various groups is not the only or the predominant cause of civil wars (*civil war* is defined as internal conflict in which at least 1,000 deaths per side occur). James D. Fearon and David D. Laitin analyzed 127 civil wars that broke out between the end of World War II and the end of the

(Continued)

Box 1   War: The Ultimate Group Conflict (*Continued*)

twentieth century. Their findings are that civil wars break out in countries that are politically unstable and poor and that have a large population and a rough terrain. The fact that they are multiethnic, multiracial, or multireligious may be one reason for conflict, but it is not the main reason. The main reason is that in such countries it is easy to organize an insurgency. Insurgent groups rise up to fight the government for control or to separate from it.

The researchers report that in the time frame they examined, civil wars have broken out at a rate of 2.3 per year, and that by 1992, more than one-quarter of the states in the world were experiencing civil war, of which two-thirds had an ethnic

rivalry cause, one-half had secessionist goals, and the rest were provoked by rebels who wanted control of the government. These civil wars saw a minimum of 16 million people killed. Many civil wars, moreover, last a long time when insurgents are able to finance them by profits from the sale of arms, drugs, or diamonds.

The researchers' findings may be reassuring to countries such as the United States and others containing many ethnic and religious groups but with stable political systems and good economies. But it foreshadows many years of conflict for countries such as Iraq, which has neither (Fearon & Laitin, 2002).

Confusion.   Finally, roles may create confusion, particularly when a person in a specific status must suddenly abandon the corresponding role and embrace a new one. An accountant pushed out of employment because of mandatory retirement, for instance, may feel a loss of identity and may refuse to accept the role of retiree, particularly if interests always revolved around the job, and he or she cannot fill the hours of leisure. College-educated women, especially those on the threshold of promising careers, may also experience confusion if an unplanned pregnancy pushes them into the roles of mothers and full-time housekeepers.

Roles that are performed poorly according to societal judgments may cause individuals not only confusion and strain but also mental illness, maladjustment, or a condition of constant frustration. For many reasons—sometimes simply by chance—people fail in the roles for which they have been prepared. In a highly competitive economic system, people frequently fail in their professions and businesses. The high incidence of divorce shows that large numbers of people fail in their marital roles. It is obvious, however, that most people cannot fill all roles equally well, and sometimes a person may fail in one role while succeeding in a conflicting one. Gender confusion in children is explored in a number of Web sites on the Internet.

Groups

As noted in the preceding section, all social interactions take place according to an abstract social system in which individuals have specific statuses and play the roles associated with those statuses. The interactions, of course, take place within groups. In turn, groups are not what they seem to be.

The word **group** is commonly understood to mean a number of people congregated at the same time in the same place. However, 15 students cramming for an exam in a student lounge are not necessarily a group in the sociological sense. Twenty commuters on the morning train into Manhattan are not necessarily a group, either. These people, who are merely in the same place at the same time, are **aggregates**, not groups.

Many people also share a certain characteristic: they may have red hair in common, for instance, or may have been born on the Fourth of July. These people do not make up a group either; instead, they form a **category.**

Suppose, however, that 3 of the 15 students cramming in the student lounge have been studying there since the beginning of the school year. Suppose, further, that they have an English class together, and they eat lunch at the same time. Because they are human and, therefore, social beings, these students, after the first exchange of greetings, begin to sit together in English class and in the cafeteria and stop to chat every time they pass each other in the hall. Of an aggregate of 15, then, 3 have formed a group. By the same token, if all the redheads in the United States who were born on the Fourth of July of 1945 decided to organize a club, if they corresponded regularly and met periodically, they too would have ceased to be a category and would have become a group.

For a number of people to constitute a group, these conditions must be met:

1. Symbolic interaction among the members should be taking place. (**Symbolic interaction** is communication by means of speech, gestures, writing, or even music. Members are aware of one another, respond to one another, and behave in such a way that they influence one another.) Group members expect interaction to continue indefinitely, but many groups form and disperse within short periods of time.
2. There should be recognition by each member that he or she is part of the group and recognition by the group that each person is a member. Group membership gives members a feeling of identity.
3. A certain amount of agreement or consensus among the members about the rules of behavior, values, and goals they share should exist.
4. The group should have structure; that is, members should be aware of their statuses, roles, rules of behavior, duties, and obligations, as well as the privileges that result from group membership.

In other words, what constitutes a group is a matter of degree; it depends on how much members interact with one another, how strongly they feel their "we-ness," and to what extent group norms affect their behavior.

Groups are extraordinary in number and diversity. In size, groups may vary from two to several hundred million or even a billion—from a couple to a whole society. In fact, there are more groups in a society than there are individuals because each person is a member of more than one group at any one time. The factors that are considered in classifying groups are size and special characteristics. The creation of the Internet has added even more groups; just try to google the word "groups"!

Group Size

The smallest of groups consists of two members and is called a **dyad.** The dyad is the most elementary social unit and is a very fragile one: The unit ceases to exist as a group when one of the members withdraws (Simmel, 1905/1956). The **triad,** or group consisting of three members, is a more stable social unit because one of the members may withdraw without destroying the group. Thus, triads are considered more important to the structure of societies (Caplow, 1968). Interaction within small groups, as exemplified in an airplane cockpit, is explored at a Web site noted at **mysearchlab.com.**

Size in general has a definite impact on members. With each additional member, the number of possible relationships increases and with it the probability of new coalitions forming. Rapid increases in membership may also prove disruptive: If there are more than 10 or 12 persons

AP Photo/Kevork Djansezian

These seniors playing bridge do make up a group because symbolic interaction is taking place. Each person recognizes that he or she is a member of the group, they agree on how to play, and each is aware of his or her status, of rules of behavior, of their duties and obligations, as well as of the privileges of belonging to the group.

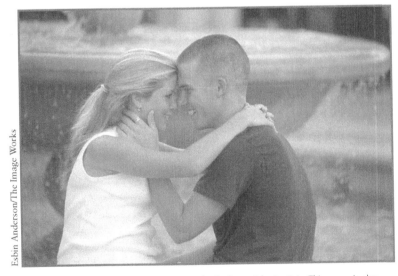

Esbin Anderson/The Image Works

Even two people are considered a group—a dyad—by social scientists. This group is also organized according to a social system, and because it consists of two young lovers, it is a primary group.

in a group, a leader becomes necessary to ensure that each member contributes equally to the group. The addition of new members tends to be discouraged by the original members who feel comfortable with the status quo.

Small groups—families, close friends, a clique within a large organization, a committee formed to solve a problem—share common characteristics. Relations among members tend to be face-to-face, and members generally hold similar values. The small group is quite durable, as members identify with it and are loyal to it. Small groups are influential in the impact they make on the behavior of their members, and they are more accepting of democratic leadership than are large groups.

Large groups, of course, display the opposite features. Above all, they tend to be highly organized. The largest group to which people belong is society, but large groups also include formal organizations (such as corporations) and their bureaucracies, which are discussed later in the text.

Primary and Secondary Groups

A very important classification of groups is that into primary and secondary groups. The term **primary group** was coined by Charles Horton Cooley, who designated as primary groups those in which members engage in intimate interaction and cooperation of the sort that is basic to the development of an individual's personality (Cooley, 1909/1910). Additional characteristics that distinguish primary from other groups include (1) relatively small size, (2) physical nearness of members, (3) intense interaction among members, and (4) group stability and relatively long duration. The family is the foremost example of a primary group.

If primary groups were put at one end of an ideal continuum (a conceptual model representing a hypothetical ideal type to which reality may be compared in analyzing phenomena), the opposite end would be occupied by secondary groups. **Secondary groups** tend to be large, and people's interaction within them is formal, role-based, utilitarian, specialized, and temporary. The transaction that takes place between a salesperson and a customer, no matter how friendly, is of a secondary nature (unless the two happen also to be personal friends). Of course, many secondary relationships eventually develop into primary ones, as when people who were just acquaintances discover they have a hobby in common and start to see each other on a regular basis, and occasionally a primary relationship slides into a secondary one, as when two good friends quarrel and from then on exchange only icy greetings when seeing each other.

Primary groups are universal and are of tremendous importance to individuals. It may even be said that they are necessary to the well-being of most people. It is easy to break the spirit of a person who is totally removed from primary relationships. Such a person's mental health may be severely affected. That is why isolation is often used as a method of brainwashing or torture. If primary relationships are lacking in what we would generally consider a "natural" primary group—the family, for instance—people go out of their way to create such relationships in other groups. The frequency of gangs created by teenaged youths to take the place of a broken or nonexistent family is one example of the need for primary groups. Even so, not all primary relationships are of a harmonious nature, nor are they always satisfying to the individual. They may involve a large amount of conflict or the enforcement of conformity, which stifles individuality.

Urban postindustrial societies such as the United States have increasingly become characterized by secondary relationships. Many of the functions that at one time were performed by primary groups are now carried out by secondary groups. For example, in the past, the sick were cared for by the family at home rather than by paid nurses and doctors in a hospital. Doctors and the hospital staff are much more capable of healing than members of the family and their home remedies. They undoubtedly help cure many more people than families did in the past, but they cannot have the same feelings for their patients, nor their patients for them; hence, the alienation and impersonality that is experienced by many people confined to hospitals and nursing homes. This is not to say that primary-type relations do not flourish in secondary-type groups. The fact that people live in neighborhoods, some of which are based on national origin (Chinatown, Little Italy, Spanish Harlem, Little Vietnam) has long been acknowledged as a source of community, even in the largely anonymous urban environment. In fact, such neighborhoods have been characterized as "urban villages," meaning that, for all practical purposes, people live in them as if they were small villages. Moreover, even when they do not live in close-knit communities, urban residents can easily find a number of people with whom they are compatible, simply because a city, with its large number and variety of people, offers a wide choice of friends and acquaintances. People do not need to be neighbors of place; they become neighbors of taste (they come together because they have talents or interests in common). In an often-quoted description of New York, the author E. B. White maintained that many a New Yorker spends a lifetime within the confines of an area smaller than a country village, and that such a person feels ill at ease even a few blocks from his familiar corner (White, 1949). A clear definition of primary and secondary groups may be found at several Web sites that discuss groups. See **mysearchlab.com.**

Box 2   **The Making of Groups**

As noted in the text, a large sophisticated society such as ours has an innumerable number of groups. And new groups are being constantly formed. For instance, a group of immigrants from Bhutan, a small country in the Himalayan foothills, were recently resettled in the Bronx, New York. The reason for the resettlement was that these were people of Nepali origin—and/or their descendants—who had first immigrated into Bhutan. Bhutan expelled them, maintaining that they were illegal immigrants, and they were lodged in seven refugee camps in Nepal, cared for by aid agencies. The International Rescue Committee had the task of resettling around 170 Bhutanese in New York, after the United States agreed to resettle around 60,000 of them in this country.

These were people who came from a farming background. They came from rural plains, most had never lived in homes as we know them, had never had indoor plumbing or even electricity. Imagine such people being suddenly placed into the mayhem of New York—with its traffic, its myriad languages (including English, which the Bhutanese do not speak) its stores, its crime. The only way they can survive is to stick together—to form a group. And that is what they did.

Eight families, numbering about 40 people, were given apartments in one building, a five-story walkup with dirty stairs and weeds in the courtyard, in the Bronx. They are a minority in the building, but they depend on each other to overcome the obstacles of their new world. They drop in on one another, they share meals, they get information about jobs or classes, or they just hang out to pass the time. They say that this is the way it was in their refugee camps, where neighbors and relatives walked from hut to hut to interact with each other.

An important change in their culture is that the young now must take care of the old. First, the young learn English faster and tend to get jobs sooner. They are the ones to enroll young children in school, to accompany parents to doctors and immigration offices. They protect them from criminal elements. They are the ones who support their families. As one of the Bhutanese commented, he was afraid he would suffer from cultural shock in this new country, but when he walked into this building and saw women who looked like his mother and men who looked like his father, he knew he would be all right (Semple, 2009).

Additional Classification of Groups

In addition to their size and primary or secondary nature, groups are classified according to other features. **In-groups** and **out-groups** are based on the distinction between *us* and *them*, probably one of the oldest distinctions people have made and one with which we can all identify, whether we belong to the Avondale Country Club or the Purple Sharks. **Reference groups** provide us with standards we use to evaluate our own status against that of others. They serve as points of comparison and affect people's values, goals, attitudes, and behavior. **Membership groups** are either formal or informal organizations to which individuals belong; for instance, the YWCA is a formal membership group, whereas one's friends from high school constitute an informal membership group. Finally, some groups are of a *voluntary* and some of an *involuntary* nature. A person's family (which cannot be chosen) and a branch of the armed services into which a person is inducted during a war are examples of involuntary groups. Conversely, there are thousands of groups, ranging from fraternities to political parties, from fan clubs to bridge clubs, that individuals may join entirely of their own free will or for reasons of social and economic expediency. Such groups are voluntary.

Society

Society is defined as the largest group of people inhabiting a specific territory and sharing a common way of life (culture). The people in a society share this common way of life as a result of interacting on a regular, continuous basis and because they have acquired patterns of behavior on which all more or less agree. Society differs from many other large groups because within this group people can live a total, common life, whereas in smaller groups a person lives only one facet of her or his life. In short, society is not an organization limited to a specific purpose, as is, for example, the American Medical Association. Rather, it is the most self-sufficient group, and its independence is based on the techniques developed for fulfilling the needs of its members.

Classification of Societies

Throughout history, societies have assumed a number of different forms. One way of classifying societies is according to their chief mode of subsistence (Lenski, 1970/1987, 18–142). Another type of classification is according to basic patterns of social organization.

Classification According to Chief Mode of Subsistence

In classifying societies according to the way they provide their members with food, shelter, and clothing, we find that the most commonly occurring types include the following.

The *hunting and gathering society* is one of the earliest and least technologically complex forms of society. It is characterized by a small (around 40 individuals), nomadic population, uncomplicated technology, little division of labor or specialization, and particular stress on the importance of kinship ties.

For most of the approximately 2 million years of human existence on the planet, people have lived in hunting and gathering societies. Hunters and gatherers are nomadic by necessity: They must forever search for better hunting grounds and new areas where naturally occurring fruits and vegetation are more abundant. As a result, they cannot accumulate belongings, as everything each person owns must be carried to the new food source. A few small hunting

Our earliest ancestors existed in hunting and gathering societies. Most of the world has since moved on to other types of societies; however, a small number of hunting and gathering societies still exist. These are Borra Indians from a village along the Amazon River in Peru.

and gathering societies still exist in the rain forest of Brazil as well as in the Philippines and in Central America (Headland & Reid, 1989). More information about such societies is available at several Web sites suggested on **mysearchlab.com.**

The *pastoral,* also called the *herding, society* has tended to develop in areas ill suited to the cultivation of land but containing animals amenable to domestication and use as food sources. This subsistence strategy leads to a more secure food supply and a possible surplus of animals. A surplus raises the standard of living of all, resulting in larger populations, but it also leads to ranking people according to their possessions, leading to social classes, conflict, and warfare. Pastoral societies still exist, at least as parts of industrial or industrializing societies. Descriptions of pastoral societies may be found on the Internet.

The *horticultural society* appeared when people discovered how to cultivate grains, and the *agrarian society* was firmly established with the invention of the plow at around 3000 BC. In the horticultural society, small garden plots are cleared with digging sticks and gradually with sticks tied to stones, bison shoulder blades, and much later to metal objects, eventually resulting in a hoe. Although hoe gardening produces surplus food, the amount is minimal, and the soil becomes depleted very rapidly, forcing people continually to cultivate new gardens. Once the use of the plow becomes established, however, large areas of land can be cultivated. Interesting descriptions of horticultural societies are also available on the Internet.

In both the horticultural and agrarian societies, ever greater surpluses are produced, and a settled lifestyle predominates. Some of the side effects of the shift from horticulture to agriculture are negative: People become differentiated, principally into landholders and landless peasants, and a bureaucracy develops to oversee an increasingly complex economy. Finally, some societies are predominantly *fishing* and *maritime societies* because of their location on rivers and seas. A historical review of fishing and maritime societies in the South American continent is found on the Internet.

Industrial Societies

The most revolutionary change in the form of societies, however, comes with the emergence of the *industrial society*. Most societies in the world today are already industrial, trying to become industrial, or postindustrial. Industrial societies are characterized by (1) urbanization, or growth of cities at the expense of rural areas; (2) massive mechanization and automation, or the substitution of machines for human labor and intelligence; (3) a complex bureaucracy, or organization into formal groups for greater efficiency; (4) separation of institutional forms, that is, the development of schools, hospitals, stores, and factories to perform functions formerly filled by the family; and (5) the substitution of impersonal, secondary relations for primary relationships. The transition from agrarian to industrial societies has been accompanied by disorganization and disruption. The *Dictionary of Sociology* online expands on the concept of industrial societies.

Increasingly, a form of society that has been described as *postindustrial* is emerging. Although the first technological revolution of 200 years ago brought steam-powered transportation and factory machine production, the second technological revolution, which occurred 100 years ago, spread electricity and chemistry, permitting the production of synthetics and plastics. The third technological revolution, which is still underway, has joined computers and telecommunications to produce television imagery, voice telephone, digital computer data, and facsimile transmission (Bell, 1987). These products, and many more that are further expansions of them (cell phones, smartphones, GPS systems, etc.), are changing contemporary societies. Societies, in fact, have become not simply geographic places but global networks accessible with the push of a button. Power in postindustrial societies belongs to those who have the ability to respond speedily and flexibly to new information; thus, the old organizational structures are in the process of being dismantled, and new ones will have to be instituted. These new organizational structures are more fully explored, but it is instructive to point out that, of course, such a transformation is disruptive to social organization. First of all, the statuses of certain individuals must be permanently altered, and new statuses are often acquired at the cost of great sacrifice. Transitional periods between different economic systems are always conflict producing and painful, as the many victims of "downsizing," outsourcing, and layoffs can testify. Changes in social structure associated with the transition to a postindustrial society are briefly explored by an academic scholar online; see **mysearchlab.com.**

Classification According to Social Organization

Another important classification of societies, and manner of analysis, is according to their basic patterns of social organization. In small, homogeneous societies, members interact with one another on an informal, personal, face-to-face basis, and behavior is dictated by tradition. This kind of society is called a **Gemeinschaft,** which is roughly translated from German as a "communal or traditional society." In societies that are large and heterogeneous, such as modern industrial societies, relationships among members are impersonal, formal, functional, and specialized. Furthermore, they are often contractual (dealings are spelled out in legal contracts rather than by word of mouth or tradition). This society is called a **Gesellschaft,** or "associational society" (Tönnies, 1887/1957). It is obvious that Gemeinschafts are characterized by primary relationships, whereas Gesellschafts more commonly display secondary relationships.

In the modern world, there has been an easily observable shift from Gemeinschaft to Gesellschaft societies. The large size of societies and the complexities of a technological economy require secondary groups, which are dedicated to efficiency rather than sentiment. A much more expanded discussion of these terms may be found on the Internet.

Interaction and Social Processes

Societies, and the various kinds of groups that exist within them, are not static entities. They are in constant flux, undergoing change and modification. Interaction among the members of a group and among the many groups is continually taking place. *Interaction* refers to behavior or action that is symbolic; that is, words and gestures that have meaning. It is also behavior that is directed toward others, in the sense that each person is aware of how others will probably respond, and is reciprocal, in the sense that each person is conscious of and responsive to the actions and reactions of others.

Although interaction is not governed by rigid rules, it is not haphazard, either. Interactive behavior is repeated sufficiently often that it creates a pattern capable of predicting future behavior when similar situations arise. Following behavioral patterns established by others long ago is a way of simplifying our lives.

A number of key patterns of interaction are present and at work whenever interaction takes place. They have been called the "microelements of the social bond, or the molecular cement of society" (Nisbet, 1970, p. 50). These patterns of interaction are the **social processes**.

Social interaction, whether it occurs on a primary or a secondary group level, involves a great many social processes. We focus on four primary social processes: exchange, cooperation, competition, and conflict. All other processes, which include accommodation, assimilation, and coercion, are really combinations of, or derivations from, the primary processes.

Exchange is a transaction in which one of two individuals—or groups, or societies—does something for the other with the expectation of receiving something of equal value in return. If you take notes for an absent fellow student, you expect him or her to take good notes for you when you are absent. When the doctor clears up your skin infection, you are expected to pay the bill. When you are hired to work for a corporation, it is expected that you will receive a salary in exchange for your labor. In short, exchange is a pervasive process in groups of all sizes, and it is generally found in the context of the norm of *reciprocity*, which requires that you do something in return for what someone has done for you. When social exchanges are fair and equal, the social structure of the group tends to be solid, but when exchanges are perceived as one-sided, eventually the social structure suffers, leading to a disintegration of the group involved.

Cooperation is a primary social process involving two or more persons or groups working jointly in a common enterprise for a shared goal. It is often considered the most basic of the social processes because without it, life would be difficult, if not impossible.

Competition is a form of interaction that occurs when two or more individuals try to take possession of the same scarce object, whether it be tangible, such as a precious gem, or intangible, such as someone's love. Competition is a basic process because most living organisms must compete for limited resources necessary to their survival; plants, for instance, compete for sunlight, water, and nutrients. Animals, including humans, compete for food, shelter, and sexual gratification. But whereas plants and animals limit their competitiveness to things needed for survival, people also compete for things that they have learned to need but that are not necessary for survival.

Conflict is diametrically opposed to cooperation; that is, conflict is a hostile struggle between two or more persons or groups for an object or value that each prizes. Conflict is also the process in which opposing parties attempt to injure, harm, or destroy one another to achieve a specific goal. Like cooperation and competition, conflict is also present in most facets of life. It was believed at one time that conflict was a universal characteristic of humans, but the discovery of societies in which conflict is kept at an absolute minimum largely disproved

Ruth Fremson/The New York Times/Redux

The social process with the most horrific results is war. Not only does war kill and maim those whom one group defines as "the enemy," but it often kills and maims members of one's own group. This photo illustrates what war has done to one American soldier.
Source: Ruth Fremson/The New York Times

this belief. Examples and further discussions of social processes and social interaction in the form of computer-mediated communication systems are discussed on the Internet.

It should be clear that although the four foremost social processes are discussed separately, in reality they are not so distinct, and they often occur in the same interactive situation. Two opposing teams cooperate when setting dates for games, but they compete for victory. Moreover, the members of each team cooperate among themselves, but also compete in trying to achieve the greatest number of points, or being the best player. Cooperation sometimes deteriorates into conflict, and history has shown many instances of conflict evolving into cooperation.

To recapitulate, human life is lived in a large variety of groups. People interact within these groups, and groups interact with one another according to social processes, the most important of which are exchange, cooperation, competition, and conflict. Interaction, in turn, crystallizes into distinct patterns of behavior that give each group structure and organization.

Formal Organizations

Organization, in the sense of "order," is characteristic of most enterprises in which humans participate. Communication in the form of speech is organization of sounds. Music is organization of tones. Teams are organized players. All human interaction, in fact, acquires some structure (organization) because of constant repetition. In urban, industrial societies characterized by large numbers of anonymous individuals with only loose loyalties to the state and to each other, organization is of the essence. We have seen that the coming of the information society was preceded by the transition to secondary groups that are prevalent in Gesellschaft-type societies. These types of societies contain a maximum number of formal organizations, groups in which a system of organization, or organization seen as a process, is brought to its highest point.

Formal organizations are associations that are deliberately brought into existence to enable people who do not know each other to carry on complicated relationships for the purpose of attaining specific *goals*. It is through these formal organizations that most necessary activities are carried out in large, complex societies. For example, the business of governing is carried out by a network of formal organizations called "the government." Educating each new generation is the task of formal organizations called "schools." Production, distribution, and trade occur through countless formal organizations called "corporations."

Formal Organizations and Institutions Distinguished

An important distinction must be made between formal organizations and institutions. An **institution** is a procedure, an established way of doing things, a pattern of behavior, a deeply ingrained societal custom that becomes part of the social structure. Institutions are *not* groups of people. One cannot join an institution; one can merely do things in an institutionalized way. When two people marry, they carry out a human activity—establishing a paired relationship for the purpose of propagating the species—in an institutionalized way. If a couple simply live together, they carry out that activity in a noninstitutionalized way.

On the other hand, formal organizations *are* groups of people. One may join formal organizations or have dealings with their members or employees. When speaking of government as an institution, what is meant is the regular and established way in which political decisions are made, laws are enacted, and order is maintained in society. When speaking of a particular government (such as the government of the United States), what is meant is the formal organization consisting of large numbers of highly structured and hierarchically ranked people who are elected, appointed, or hired to carry out the activities involved in the governing process (Figure 1). Similarly, although education is an institution, a process attempting to prepare individuals for life in society, the University of Michigan, for example, is a formal organization. The economy is an institution, but the Bank of America is a formal organization. Religion is an institution, but the Roman Catholic Church is a formal organization (in fact, each diocese, even each church, is a formal organization.)

Characteristics of Formal Organizations

Formal organizations display the following characteristics. First, they have a *formal structure;* that is, goals and how to carry them out are stated formally in policy guidelines, constitutions, and other bylaws. They include a body of officers, whose relations with one another and with other members of the organization are specified in writing.

Second, formal organizations are meant to be relatively *permanent*. Some of them, especially those established for profit making, may prove to be temporary, but the expectation is that the formal organization will last as long as it performs the tasks it set for itself.

Third, authority is organized in a *hierarchical order,* giving rise to a bureaucracy. The leadership of the organization is assumed by individuals, who are ranked from high to low. The high-ranking individuals make decisions and give the orders, and each lower rank executes them.

Fourth, formal organizations have a *formal program*. Those who are part of the organization use the program as a guide to attain their goals. Relationships among individuals in the organization are systematic and complex, following bureaucratic principles (see later discussion) and the guidelines specified in the program.

Organizational Chart of the U.S. Department of the Navy

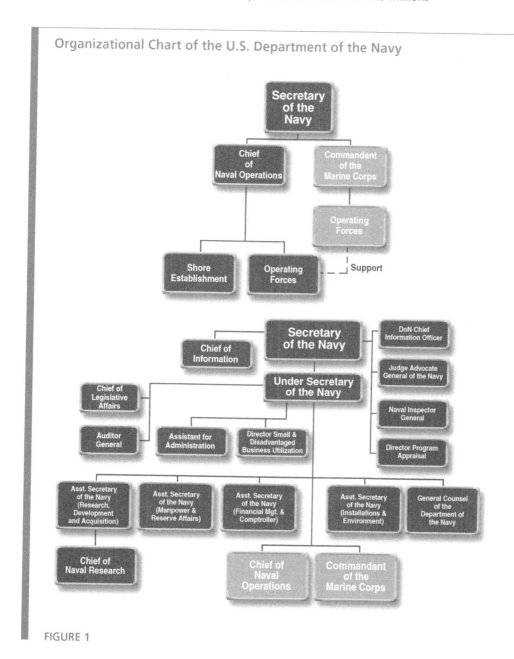

FIGURE 1

Types of Formal Organizations

Formal organizations are of all types: private and public, local or national or global, voluntary and involuntary, focusing on special interests or on universal needs. One distinction among them is made on the basis of how control is exerted over people, or how members relate to the organization. Sociologists identify three types of formal organizations on this basis: normative, coercive, and utilitarian (Etzioni, 1975).

Normative Organizations. Some formal organizations are joined by choice because individuals feel that their goals are worthwhile. These formal organizations are called *voluntary associations*. They consist of members who are spare-time volunteers, although most also have a core of full-time, paid, professional employees. Examples of voluntary associations are church organizations (i.e., sisterhoods), professional groups such as the American Medical Association, and recreational associations such as the American Contract Bridge League.

Americans are known as "joiners," and there are a great many voluntary associations. In reality, however, only a minority of people are active in voluntary organizations. The latter are usually urban residents in their middle years, married and with children, socially and economically upwardly mobile or already at a high socioeconomic level, residentially stable, and well educated.

Voluntary associations bring together people whose particular interests are not shared by the whole society; for instance, not everyone agrees that a woman should be able to obtain an abortion in the United States, but a good number of people do agree that she should. The supporters of legal abortion are better able to work for the cause effectively when they organize into a voluntary association. They may even be able to convince an indifferent or hostile majority of the value of their goal. Thus, voluntary associations are often testing grounds for social programs that are still too controversial to be handled by institutional organizations. They also provide a channel through which the private citizen can share in the decision-making process of society. This facet is particularly important to interest groups, political parties, and social movements, all important voluntary organizations that are examined.

Coercive Organizations. Organizations that people are compelled to join with the threat of force include prisons, mental hospitals, and the military when there is a draft. Naturally, members of these organizations do not join voluntarily and have no commitment to them. In the United States, the military services have become voluntary associations, but during previous wars they had been coercive. Prisons, hospitals, and the military are illustrative of an extreme type of coercive organization, the **total institution,** which isolates inmates from the rest of society, providing an all-encompassing social environment in which special norms and distinctive physical features prevail. The goal of coercive organizations is to change the attitudes and behavior of the inmate or patient—in particular, to change an individual's sense of self, or personality (Goffman, 1961).

Utilitarian Organizations. People join some formal organizations out of necessity to gain material benefits. For instance, if they want a job, they may have to become employees of a corporation. Businesses of all types, and all the various industries, are examples of utilitarian organizations. Utilitarian organizations do not coerce their members as coercive organizations do, but they do not offer them as much personal freedom as normative organizations. In short, people join utilitarian organizations because they have to make a living, and not because they especially enjoy participating in them. As a result, particularly at the lower end of the organization, workers are not too committed to the goals of the organization: They do what they must to get paid. Examples of formal organizations and comparisons to institutions and other groups may be found on a Web site suggested by **mysearchlab.com.**

Bureaucracy

All formal organizations, when they attain a certain size, are administered according to the principles of bureaucracy. **Bureaucracy** is a hierarchical system (or an organizational model) for rationally coordinating the work of many individuals through a division of labor and a chain of authority. In other words, a bureaucracy is a system for organizing a group of people in a pyramid fashion. The purpose is to administer large-scale organizations in the most efficient and intelligent manner. It is an attempt to obtain the desired goals by the best possible means.

In its ideal form, as set forth by Max Weber, a pure bureaucracy *ought* to be characterized by (1) specialization, or division of labor; (2) a chain of command, or a hierarchy of authority; (3) a body of rules covering both rights and duties of all members at all ranks; (4) another set of rules outlining procedures for carrying out all tasks; (5) impersonality in the relationships among members; (6) selection based on merit and job tenure (seniority); and (7) the norm of efficiency (Weber, 1925/1947, 334).

Weber believed that a bureaucratic form of organization made social life more "rational" because it was a system in which goals could be attained efficiently and with a minimum of conflict among people. In a bureaucracy, individual personalities do not matter to the organization because each position consists of activities that remain the same, no matter who fills the position. This formality gives the organization stability, predictability, and continuity. Bureaucratic organization works equally well for private and public associations—in fact, for all kinds of associations designed to serve people.

Weber knew that bureaucracy would not work as well in reality as in the ideal form he described, and it does not. The worst thing that can be said about bureaucracy is that although it is supposed to serve people, it often frustrates them instead. Bureaucracies are resistant to change, and bureaucrats somehow start to believe that rules are ends in themselves. Blind loyalty to rules results in the familiar "red tape" phenomenon, as well as in the stifling of personal initiative on the part of bureaucrats. Bureaucrats often want to "pass the buck" because it is easier to shift the responsibility for decision making to someone higher in the hierarchy—then that person can be blamed if the decision turns out to be wrong. Bureaucracies also have a nasty habit of becoming devoted to their own welfare and perpetuation simply because employees want to hang on to their jobs.

Dynamic Quality

Despite its several failures, bureaucracy has a certain *dynamic* quality that enables it to respond to changing conditions in society. In some respects, in fact, bureaucracies may be instrumental in promoting innovation in a society. Blau and Meyer (1971, 105) suggest that the ideas of scientists alone could not lead to the inventions that in turn trigger social change. In today's complex societies, bureaucratic machinery is needed to translate the ideas of scientists into products and to furnish scientists with laboratories and environments in which they can collaborate on new developments. The authors conclude that the "deliberate introduction of a social innovation ... depends on bureaucratic methods of administration."

Informal Side of Bureaucracy

Finally, alongside the formal and structured side of bureaucracy exists an informal side made up of networks of personal relationships that develop among employees. These networks are occasionally responsible for getting things done through the influence of individuals instead of the regular channels of authority. Sometimes the informal structure, in getting around the rules of the formal structure, actually defies the purpose of the formal bureaucratic organizations. In the long run, however, it may help to reach the goals of the formal organization.

The *New World Encyclopedia* has a good discussion of bureaucracy online. See the address on **mysearchlab.com.**

The Chapter in Brief

People are group animals who spend the best parts of their lives in groups of one kind or another. Life in groups acquires a certain pattern through repetition; each group is a social system with a structure and an organization. The structure consists of shared and repeated patterns of behavior that emerge as a result of the interaction of group members. People interact by using a number of social processes and by relating to others from the standpoint of their own position (status) in the group while carrying out the behavior befitting that position (role). Some positions (statuses) within the group are ascribed; that is, people have no control over them (such as gender, age, race, or ethnic origin). Other statuses are achieved as a result of personal effort or merit or lack of it.

Because of the multiplicity of statuses that each person holds in a large variety of groups, people are faced with role confusion, conflict, and strain, as well as failure. In general, people attempt to fill the role attendant on their master status best.

A group is defined by (1) symbolic interaction among the members; (2) members' awareness of membership; (3) members' awareness of the roles, duties, obligations, and privileges resulting from group membership; and (4) members' agreement on shared values.

Groups are classified into dyads (groups consisting of two individuals) and triads (groups consisting of three individuals), which are the basic social units, and according to their size. Groups are also classified by whether they are primary or secondary, in-groups or out-groups, reference groups, formal or informal groups, and voluntary or involuntary groups. Of these, the most important classification is that into primary and secondary groups. Primary groups engage in intimate, intense, informal, and spontaneous interaction on a personal and total basis; secondary groups tend to be large, temporary, formal, utilitarian, and specialized. Although primary relationships are very satisfying and important to the individual, industrial societies are increasingly characterized by secondary groups.

The largest group to which people belong is society. Societies are classified according to either their chief mode of subsistence (hunting and gathering, pastoral or herding, horticultural, agrarian, fishing or maritime, and industrial) or their basic patterns of social organization (traditional or communal—Gemeinschaft; modern industrial or associational—Gesellschaft). Gemeinschaft societies are relatively small, with a homogeneous membership; behavior is dictated by tradition; and members interact on an informal, face-to-face basis. Gesellschaft societies tend to be large and heterogeneous, and relationships among members are impersonal, formal, functional, contractual, and specialized. The trend historically has been a transition from a Gemeinschaft to a Gesellschaft type of society.

The reciprocal relationships that occur within and among groups are called interactions. Interaction takes place through a number of social processes, the most basic of which are exchange, cooperation, competition, and conflict. Whatever the type of relationship—primary or secondary—one or more of these social processes is at work.

All human activities are somewhat organized and structured. In complex societies, organization is on a large scale; that is, groups of people who are not personally related must carry on complicated relationships to attain some specific goals. Most of the activities of modern societies are performed in these groups, which are called formal organizations or associations. Some of these organizations are normative, or voluntary; others are coercive, such as prisons, mental hospitals, and the military, and still others are utilitarian, such as business companies. Formal organizations have a formal structure, a degree of permanence, a hierarchical order of authority, and fixed relationships among members. Most are highly organized in an administrative pattern termed a bureaucracy.

Bureaucracy is a hierarchical arrangement based on division of labor and a chain of authority for the purpose of rationally coordinating the work of many individuals. Bureaucracy in its ideal, or pure, form seldom corresponds to its real functioning: It tends to resist change, its rules become rigid and ends and means become confused, it stifles personal initiative, and it makes employees indecisive. At the same time, bureaucracy is dynamic enough to respond to change and promote innovation in society.

Terms to Remember

achieved status A position attained through individual effort or merit.

aggregate A number of people who are in the same place at the same time, but who do not interact with one another.

ascribed status An inherited position—one that is not attained through individual effort or merit.

bureaucracy The hierarchical system of administration prevailing within a formal organization. The hierarchy depends on job specialization, a set of rules and standards to promote uniformity, and an attitude of impersonal impartiality.

category (referring to people) A number of people who have some characteristics in common but who do not interact with one another.

competition A social process (form of interaction) that occurs when two or more individuals try to obtain possession of the same scarce object or intangible value using rules and limits.

conflict A social process (interaction) consisting of a hostile struggle in which two or more persons engage for an object or value that each prizes, possibly to the point of destruction.

cooperation A basic social process (interaction) involving two or more individuals or groups working jointly in a common enterprise for a shared goal.

dyad The smallest type of group, consisting of two members.

exchange A social process (interaction) consisting of a transaction in which one of two individuals—or groups or societies—does something for the other with the expectation of receiving something of equal value in return.

formal organizations Large-scale associations of people in which most of the activities of complex societies are handled. They are highly organized groups displaying a formal structure, a body of officers, the expectation of permanence, and a hierarchical organization of authority (bureaucracy).

Gemeinschaft A small, homogeneous, communal, and traditional society. Relationships among members are personal, informal, and face-to-face, and behavior is dictated by tradition.

Gesellschaft A large, heterogeneous society, typified by the modern industrial state. Relationships among members tend to be impersonal, formal, contractual, functional, and specialized. Also called an associational society.

group A number of people who engage in symbolic interaction; who are mutually aware of and influence one another; who recognize their membership in the group and are in turn recognized as members by the group; who are aware of the roles, duties, obligations, and privileges of membership; and who agree to a point about the behavioral guidelines, values, and goals they share.

in-group Group to which the individual belongs and which confers on the individual a social identity.

institution A procedure, a pattern of behavior, a deeply ingrained societal custom that becomes part of the social structure. Institutions are <u>not</u> groups of people.

macrosocial The level at which social scientists analyze interaction between and among groups.

microsocial The focus of analysis is on interaction of individuals to each other.

membership group Formal or informal organizations to which individuals belong.

organization A formal process that deliberately brings into existence a group of people to perform tasks directed at achieving a specific goal. It allows people who are unacquainted with each other to cooperate effectively on complex projects.

out-group Group to which others belong, excluding the individual defining group membership.

primary group A relatively small group of people who live physically near one another and who interact intensely. Characteristics include stability, relatively long duration, informal and spontaneous interaction, and individual, personal, and total types of dealings.

reference group A group providing individuals with standards against which to measure themselves.

role The carrying out of a status. A way of behaving that befits a status and is transmittable as well as fairly predictable.

secondary group   A group that is in general larger and of shorter duration than a primary group. Interaction among members is formal, role-based, utilitarian, specialized, and temporary.

social organization   The network of patterned human behavior that is the product of interaction and, at the same time, guides interaction.

social processes   Key patterns of interaction common to all human societies (cooperation, competition, exchange, and conflict).

social structure   The content of the social system, consisting of statuses, roles, groups, norms, and institutions.

social system   A conceptual model of social relationships in which each part is interdependent and interconnected to every other part.

society   The largest social group. An interrelated network of social relationships that exists within the boundaries of the largest social system.

status   A ranked position in a social group. Statuses are rated according to their importance in a social group.

symbolic interaction   Communication through speech, gestures, writing, or even music.

total institution   An extreme type of coercive organization that isolates individuals from the rest of society, providing an all-encompassing social environment in which special norms and distinctive physical features prevail, with the goal of changing the individual's attitudes, behaviors, and personality.

triad   A group consisting of three individuals. A more stable social unit than a dyad.

Suggested Readings

Hall, Richard H. 1991. *Organizations: Structures, Processes, and Outcomes.* Englewood Cliffs, NJ: Prentice Hall. An overview of how sociologists analyze the various types of organizations.

Janis, Irving L. 1989. *Crucial Decisions: Leadership in Policymaking and Crisis Management.* New York: Free Press. The author originated the expression "groupthink," meaning an individual's diminished capacity for critical thinking because of the conforming influence of the group.

Kafka, Franz. 1925, 1926, 1999. *The Trial* and *The Castle.* New York: Schocken (paperback). These two novels by the Czech-German (Jewish) novelist are dramatic examples of how bureaucracy can be incomprehensible and absurd, and how it can alienate people in societies that were becoming more and more of a Gesellschaft in which secondary interactions prevailed.

Kephart, William M. 1991. *Extraordinary Groups: An Examination of Unconventional Life-Styles.* New York: St. Martin's Press. A collection of essays about groups that are unconventional and out of the mainstream, such as self-help groups, unusual occupational groups, and ethnic groups.

Kottak, Conrad P. 1999. *Assault on Paradise: Social Change in a Brazilian Village.* 3rd ed. New York: McGraw-Hill. The transition from a Gemeinschaft to a Gesellschaft type of society is described by an anthropologist who records the transformation of a fishing village into a tourist attraction.

Lenski, Gerhard, Jean Lenski, and Patrick Nolan. 2001. *Human Society: An Introduction to Macrosociology,* 9th ed. New York: McGraw-Hill. A detailed account, from a sociological perspective, of different types of societies and the role technology plays in each of them.

Putnam, Robert D. 2000. *Bowling Alone: The Collapse and Revival of American Community.* New York: Simon and Schuster. The author maintains that participation in voluntary organizations has been declining in American society, which has resulted in a consequent decline in shared cultural values.

Woolsey Biggart, Nicole. 1989. *Charismatic Capitalism: Direct Selling Organizations in America.* Chicago: University of Chicago Press. Some organizations, for instance, Amway and Mary Kay Cosmetics, foster a type of bureaucracy based on emotional intensity among its members in the hope of motivating them to excel in sales.

Zollinger, Janet Giele and Elke Holst. 2003. *Changing Life Patterns in Western Industrial Societies.* New York: Elsevier. This book analyzes the changes in life patterns that followed and continue to follow the advent of industrial societies. The authors describe the trends across a number of countries and speculate on the direction of future change.

Becoming a Person: The Birth of Personality

IN THIS CHAPTER, YOU WILL LEARN

- *that human infants must learn how to become human beings;*
- *that personality is based on a delicate interplay of heredity and environment;*
- *that the acquisition of personality occurs through the process of socialization;*
- *the various theories of socialization;*
- *who are the agents of socialization;*
- *that socialization occurs throughout a person's life; and*
- *that one has to become resocialized to each new role in life.*

If one were to look into a hospital nursery almost anywhere in the world, the picture would be similar: rows of cribs or baskets containing infants of indeterminate gender, some of whom are squirming and crying while others are sleeping peacefully. A closer look will reveal differences in appearance, but at first glance, all the babies look very much alike. Should one meet the same babies 20 years later, the differences among them would no doubt be dramatically obvious: Not only would these individuals be distinctive in looks but also, if engaged in conversation, they would display a variety of attitudes, opinions, beliefs, and values. Moreover, they would differ in the manner in which they expressed them.

The infants met in the hospital have been subjected to two unavoidable processes. One is *maturation*, or the physical development of the body, which proceeds at approximately the same rate for everyone. The other is **socialization,** or the process of becoming human, learning societal norms and values while developing a personality unique to each individual.

You may ask at this point whether it is necessary to *become* human, whether in fact people are not *born* human. The answer, based on a large number of instances of social isolation, seems to be that, indeed, one must learn from others to become human. That is, the infant is basically a creature capable of a few bodily functions but little more. Infants who have been

From Chapter 5 of *Contemporary Society: An Introduction to Social Science,* Thirteenth Edition. John A. Perry, Erna K. Perry. Copyright © 2012 by Pearson Education, Inc. All rights reserved.

left alone without any human companionship, even if their biological needs are attended to, either die or fail to develop normally. It is only in the process of relating to others of our species and learning from them that we become unique individuals with distinctive personalities who fit into a particular social structure.

Personality

It is frequently said of a person that he or she either has a nice personality or no personality at all. The first description is only partial and vague, and the second one is impossible, for every person has a personality. People tend to use the term *personality* imprecisely.

Personality may be defined as a complex and dynamic system that includes all of an individual's fairly consistent behavioral and emotional traits—actions, habits, attitudes, beliefs, values, goals, and so on. It is, of course, an abstract term. It is *dynamic* because personality continually changes and adjusts to events that affect the person or in accordance with how the person perceives these events. Personality may also be seen as a *circular* system: Although the roles people fill in society affect their personalities, personalities also influence the way roles are seen and accomplished. Finally, personalities are *distinctive* because each individual is born with a specific set of inherited traits and potentials and then has experiences that are exclusively his or her own. Even identical twins, with the same biological heredity, may display personality differences based on different life experiences.

Personality: A Social Product on a Biological Basis

The study of personality has involved a number of scientists—psychologists, sociologists, anthropologists, and ethologists (scientists who study animal behavior in natural surroundings). Much of the research concerns, first, the issue of what proportion of personality is made up of *inherited traits* and what proportion consists of *learned behavior*—are people predominantly biological or predominantly cultural creatures? Unfortunately, no easy answer

These babies may differ in weight or hair color, but there is not much one can say about their character or personalities. Those traits will emerge after a process of socialization.

Diane Macdonald/Photolibrary

can be given. Research to date seems to indicate that personality development occurs as a consequence of the interplay of biological inheritance, physical environment, culture, group experience, and personal experience.

The biological inheritance that all humans share is one that, in some respects, predisposes them toward accepting learning from others, in the process of which they acquire a personality. Humans lack strong **instincts**; thus, to a great extent they must *learn* how to act to their best advantage. (Although they lack instincts, humans do have biological drives, such as self-preservation, hunger, thirst, and the need for sex. Some also add the drive toward exploration, experimentation, and analysis. These drives are perceived as tensions or discomforts in the organism that must be relieved. How best to relieve the discomfort is the function of culture, which represents the accumulated learning of countless preceding generations of people.)

Biology is also responsible for the universal human need for social and physical contact, which humans share with a number of animals and which may be interpreted as a need to receive and give love. As noted earlier, it has been shown repeatedly that infants deprived of loving human contact—those institutionalized because of being orphaned, those isolated because of being illegitimate or having been born to mothers with mental illness, or those simply badly neglected—do not develop normally, either physically or mentally. Some fail to thrive and die in infancy. Others grow up to be mentally or otherwise damaged (Spitz, 1964). Although the reasons are not clearly understood, it seems that absence of body contact and stimulation in infancy inhibits the development of higher learning functions. In this need, humans are not alone: Our close biological cousins, members of the ape family, show a need for similar closeness and body contact. In a well-known experiment involving rhesus monkeys, researchers found that rhesus infants, when separated from their biological mothers, preferred a soft and cuddly "mother" made of terrycloth, even though "she" did not feed them, to a surrogate mother made of wire from which they did receive food. The infants ran to the soft "mother" in times of stress and preferred to spend most of their time near "her" (Harlow, 1966). In the wild, many animals engage in grooming behavior, which is thought to be an expression of bonding and the need to share an activity with others—to interact socially. Articles exploring the importance of touching as studied by recent scholars may be found on the Internet.

Photo Researchers, Inc.

In a classic experiment, rhesus monkeys who were fed by a wire "mother" substitute ran to embrace the soft, terrycloth "mother" when frightened or anxious.

One such study supports the idea that parent–infant bonding has a biological basis and has a profound impact on later development. A team of researchers reports that in a group of mice, those individuals who lack a gene that allows them to obtain relief from pain also have difficulty establishing bonds with their mothers. In the first few days after birth, mice are very vulnerable, and when separated from their mothers, they cry out in distress. Apparently, cries for help cement mother–child attachment. Such attachment is fundamental to survival, but the mice lacking the specific gene do not engage in the attachment behavior. "The study provides strong evidence that the same brain chemicals that control physical pain also regulate the psychological ache of loss and separation" (Carey, 2004, D7).

Box 1 The Isolated and/or Feral Child

People have long been fascinated with the question of how children who are not socialized by the example of other humans turn out. Myths and legends abound about human babies left to be suckled by a she-wolf (Romulus and Remus, the founders of the city of Rome), about little boys abandoned in the jungle to be raised by apes (Tarzan), about the "wild boy of Aveyron," found in a forest in France and believed to have survived without human contact (this last story is based on a true event). It is said that even King James of England isolated some babies to see if they would grow up speaking Hebrew, the language of the Bible. He must have been sorely disappointed. The so-called feral children—thought to have been raised by animals—or those isolated from most human contact fail to develop into full human beings.

The first reliable information about such children in the twentieth century comes from the work of sociologist Kingsley Davis (1940–1947), who studied a six-year-old born illegitimately to a mildly retarded woman. The child, Anna, had been discovered living in pitiful conditions in the attic of her grandfather's house. The child's mother had kept her alive physically but had neglected her in every other way. When found, she was sitting with her arms tied above her head to prevent any movement. Davis found her frail and emaciated to the point of being unable to use her arms and legs. She did not smile, laugh, speak, or show any emotion, as if she were unaware of the world around her. Eventually, after much intensive therapy, she learned to walk, to feed herself, to play with toys, and to respond with something approaching human emotion. However, it was obvious that she would never catch up to children her age: She did not begin to use language before her tenth birthday, and she died soon thereafter.

Another case that came to Davis's attention also involved an illegitimate child, known as Isabelle, who had been kept isolated under very similar conditions, but with a deaf-mute mother. This six-year-old displayed some of the same symptoms as Anna: She could not speak, walked only with great difficulty, and seemed more animal-like than human. When she was first tested, psychologists concluded that she was retarded and probably uneducable. However, they worked intensively with her, and she soon began to thrive. By the age of 8, she had attained the development of a normal 6-year-old, and at 14 she was attending sixth grade. Davis concluded that social isolation is extremely damaging, that it hinders development even in cases where later socialization is undertaken intensively, and consequently that the socialization process is necessary for becoming fully human.

The latest known instance of social isolation that took place in the United States involved a girl, born to a psychotic father and a blind mother, who was kept strapped to a potty chair in a secluded room from the ages of 2 to 11. Genie, as she is called by researchers, was in a similarly emaciated physical condition, and although she outwardly looked normal, she tested as having the mental development of a one-year-old. She knew a few words, which she babbled, but she had absolutely no social skills, continually spitting and masturbating in public. Researchers were at first unsure whether her retardation was due to prenatal physical causes or resulted from her isolation. In time and under constant guidance, Genie learned many more words than the average retarded person acquires. However, she never mastered the complexities of grammar, which the normal child acquires as a matter of course by imitation. The researchers concluded that Genie had missed the critical period in her development when she was ready to learn language and, thus, would probably never totally master it. In fact, though she seemed to exhibit traits pointing to a high intelligence in some areas, her language skills never went beyond those of a third grader. Genie is still alive, but she has never become a fully social being who is able to interact with others and show human emotions. Those in charge of her case conclude that the absence of parental love has damaged her so that she is unable to express her feelings and thoughts and live a full life (Rymer, 1993; see also http://www.feralchildren.com).

The biological fact that human infants are born helpless and must depend on adults for sheer survival also predisposes them to accept learning from adults and leads to the formation of strong bonds between them. Finally, the biologically based potential for learning and using symbol systems makes it possible and probable that humans accept the culture into which they are born. In turn, the capacity for language is what makes the creation of culture and social structure possible.

Heredity and Environment or Nature v. Nurture

In addition to having these general effects on humans as a species, biology also affects people as individuals, accounting for some of their uniqueness in appearance and personality. Just as each individual inherits from each parent specific genes that determine whether the individual is short or tall, has blue or brown eyes, and has straight or curly hair, so too heredity determines many personality characteristics, including intelligence, sociability, timidity, and basic temperament (Herbert, 1982; Horn et al., 1976; Juel-Nielson, 1980). Other personality traits, such as leadership abilities, control of impulses, attitudes, and interests, however, depend to a much greater extent on the environment in which a person is raised. These two factors, heredity and environment, are so interrelated as they act on the personality that it is impossible to measure exactly the influence of either. All that can be said with certainty is that whether a person's full potential is developed depends on that person's social experience or the environment in which life is spent.

Social scientists have pondered the mystery of why siblings, who share 50 percent of their genes, can at times be so dissimilar. Two professors of human development have stated in their book, *Separate Lives: Why Siblings Are So Different,* that siblings are also 50 percent different genetically. Those differences, when measured by tests of personality, attitude, belief, and temperament, explain why the same environment is perceived differently by siblings, despite sharing the same parents, social class, and most daily experiences. These idiosyncratic responses mold characters in different directions. For example, a child who is genetically shy reacts differently to having a social butterfly for a mother than his or her outgoing sister. The research reported by these writers has been replicated in studies of thousands of children in Sweden, England, and Colorado (Dunn & Plomin, 1990).

Biological inheritance determines personality in another way also. People respond to certain physical traits in a particular way—favorably to some, negatively to others—and their reaction influences an individual's personality. A fat person is considered beautiful in some societies and, thus, develops a positive self-image, which in turn may result in a self-confident, pleasant, outgoing personality. In the United States, on the other hand, fatness is not considered a positive attribute. As a consequence, such a person may have a low self-image and be withdrawn, shy, self-conscious, and unpleasant in interaction with others (though this unpleasantness may be in self-defense). In short, it is not biological inheritance per se that necessarily affects personality; rather, it is the way a society and culture interpret biologically inherited traits that has a bearing on an individual's personality.

As to the physical environment, although it is not true that personality types correspond to climatic or geographic areas, as was once believed, it is true that certain conditions caused by the physical environment may influence some dominant personality traits. One example from the not-too-distant past concerns the Ik. These inhabitants of a region of Uganda lost their traditional hunting grounds because of the country's political partition. They then began to suffer profound deprivation to the point of starvation. A previously friendly and outgoing people, the Ik became incredibly selfish and greedy, lacking compassion toward the old, whom they encouraged to die, and taking the last morsel away from their own children so that they themselves might eat (Turnbull, 1973).

Culture too has a definite impact on personality, in the sense that every society subjects its members to unique experiences that differ from those of members of other societies. Because of this commonality of social experiences, most members of a specific society share a particular configuration of personality traits. This so-called *modal* personality is thought to be representative of that society. People speak of the Latin lover, the hard-drinking Irish, the "keep-a-stiff-upper-lip" British, the punctual German, and the arrogant French. Although these descriptions of personality types have become stereotypes that do a disservice to their respective societies, it remains true that each society, by virtue of its dominant values and beliefs, develops one or more personality types that reflect the society's culture. In a complex, heterogeneous society, moreover, there may be as many personality types as there are subcultures; witness the "Southern belle" and "urban cowboy" familiar to Americans, in addition to stereotypical portraits of minority groups. Ultimately, however, even in the most conforming of societies, human personality retains a great amount of individuality.

In the 1970s and under the influence of the feminist movement it was popular to state that babies are blank slates and that the environment in which they were raised taught them masculine or feminine roles and affected much of their behavior in other areas. Today, researchers are not so sure. Investigators have found that biology plays a very important role in personality formation. For instance, a study of "virtual twins," that is, children raised in the same home but not biologically related, found that there were marked differences in personality traits between the siblings. (A situation of virtual twins emerges when parents adopt or agree to raise a child from infancy and then have their own biological child.) The author of the study on virtual twins, professor Nancy Segal, has concluded that such children have much less in common in terms of intelligence, behavior, and decision-making ways than either fraternal or identical twins, even those who have been raised apart (Kershaw, 2008). Virtual twins may be very similar at a young age and act as biological twins do, but in the long term the shared environment does not have a lasting impact. An interesting article on this subject may be accessed online: the address is found on **mysearchlab.com.**

Becoming Human: Socialization

A just-born infant is completely unaware of self. The infant at this point is a living bundle of drives that create tensions demanding to be satisfied. Most theorists agree that the infant does not know that it is human or even that it exists. In fact, the creature cannot distinguish between itself and other objects in its environment. It is only when others act toward the infant in a manner that is distinct from the way they act toward other people and objects that the infant begins to recognize that he or she is a separate entity. This awareness of one's distinctiveness, or separateness, of having borders between oneself and others, is the first step in the emergence of the self—and it occurs as a result of interaction with others.

The emergence of self, in turn, is a first step in socialization. Socialization is the process that teaches individuals how to become functioning human beings who must fit into a number of groups and be productive members of a society. Sociologists maintain that a distinctive personality is acquired during the process of socialization.

Goals and Functions of Socialization

From the point of view of society, socialization has specific goals. First, it teaches the basics of life in the society. Second, it transmits skills that are important to survival in the society. Third, it instills in new members of society a desire to work toward some goals that the society considers important. Fourth, it teaches members how to fulfill social roles, for only if a majority of people does so can the social system continue to exist. Finally, it provides each individual with an identity because people need to know who they are so they may act accordingly.

The process of socialization is not limited to infants and children. Rather, it continues throughout an individual's lifetime, as there are always new roles to be learned and new circumstances to which to adjust. However, socialization is different for children and for adults. Children must, first of all, learn how to regulate their biological drives in socially acceptable ways. They must learn to develop values that are in accordance with the aims of their society. They must develop a self-image. Adults, on the other hand, must primarily learn new roles as they enter the labor force or as they change their statuses—as they get married or become parents or grandparents. The experience of socialization is also different for the two groups. Children tend to be emotionally involved with those who socialize them, which makes the process much more effective. Adults are usually socialized voluntarily, but the involvement with their socializers is secondary in nature. They deal with professors or supervisors instead of mothers and fathers. This type of socialization is less effective and easier to resist, and the results are more superficial.

Socialization occurs on both a conscious and an unconscious level. Children are deliberately taught certain behaviors, attitudes, and values, but others are picked up unconsciously, from overheard conversations or observed actions of adults. Behavior, attitudes, and values picked up unconsciously are usually much more difficult to shed.

Finally, socialization must take into consideration the feelings, or emotions, that humans display. Three of the most fundamental of human emotions are love, anger, and anxiety.

Love is needed to ensure normal development. Unloved children become unloving adults, who may display psychological disturbances. Rejecting parents who deny their children love, respect, and self-esteem risk causing serious maladjustment and stunted development in their children.

Ariel Skelley/Photolibrary

The socialization process, which turns bundles of flesh and blood into human beings, begins when a significant other interacts with the newborn. This mother smiling at her baby is engaged in this process.

Anger is the reaction to deprivation and frustration. One of the chief aims of socialization is to channel anger in such a way that it does not result in aggression. Parents who are unable to direct their children's anger often put up with temper tantrums, which are the child's way of attempting to control others in a destructive and disruptive form, and they may leave themselves open to antisocial behavior throughout their offspring's adolescence.

Anxiety, unlike anger, is not a definite, sharply defined emotion. Rather, it is a diffuse state of mind in which the individual feels uneasy but is not aware of exactly why. In this respect, anxiety differs from fear, which is a response to a definite threat. Anxiety has been considered the hallmark of modern Western societies; in fact, some of our values are very anxiety producing.

If socialization is to be successful, these emotions must be manipulated so that they do not become destructive to individuals or to society. The process of socialization functions to the advantage of both society and the individual. Society profits because each new generation learns how to behave as a member of it, and the individual profits because he or she acquires a self and a unique personality in the bargain.

Theories of Socialization

Exactly how the self emerges during socialization has been the subject of numerous theories, both in sociology and in psychology. The most widely accepted theories from the sociological perspective are those of the "looking-glass self" and symbolic interactionism. Psychologists, on the other hand, have viewed the acquisition of personality in the process of becoming human from the perspective of the unconscious, the rational, the moral, and the transitional self.

The Looking-Glass Self: Cooley

Charles Horton Cooley (1864–1929) and his colleague, George Herbert Mead (1863–1931), were two American sociologists who formulated the original interactionist theories based on the finding that the self is the result of a learning process that occurs when individuals interact with those around them. Cooley speculated that the development of a socially defined self begins in the early stages of life. In interaction with their immediate family and later with peer groups, maturing individuals learn that they are distinct from others and that their needs are satisfied because they are loved. Essentially, they learn how they stand in particular relationships to others and how others feel about them. Each individual senses the opinions of others from their reactions to him or her. Cooley called this process the **looking-glass self** because it resembles looking into an imaginary mirror that reflects back to the looker his or her image as others see it (the others, of course, are society in general; thus, society is internalized by the individual). If the reflected image is good (as society says it should be), the person is satisfied. If the image is bad, the person feels ashamed and dissatisfied with himself or herself. Further explanations of the theory may be found online.

The Self in Society: Mead

The theory that social, and particularly symbolic, interaction is the basis of the emergence of self and personality was further developed in the work of George Herbert Mead. Many complex ideas are embodied in **symbolic interactionism,** but they all center around the inter-relationship of **mind** (the abstract whole of a person's ideas), **self** (the individual's self-concept or self-awareness), and society.

Symbolic interaction is the first prerequisite for personality formation, according to Mead. Such interaction is at first nonverbal—the infant cries, and the parents respond to it. This sets the stage for more meaningful communication through language. Once language is present, mind and self can emerge, and actions can be replaced by ideas. Mind and self are social products because individuals internalize, or make their own, the attitudes of those around them through language. Thus, individuals become capable of thinking about themselves as they think about others: They become objects to themselves. They begin to realize the distinctions among I, me, and you, and they begin to treat themselves as they treat others. This enables them to learn to control their own behavior and direct it into meaningful channels. People become self-critical because others are critical of them. In this manner, society begins to control individuals.

This uniquely human quality of being able to get outside oneself and view oneself as others do is possible because of the human ability to take on various roles. Role-playing is learned by children in the course of play. At first, the others whose roles children take are members of their family and of their peer group or, as Mead called them, the **significant others**. Later, individuals learn to take the role of society as a whole or, in Mead's terms, to take into account the **generalized other**. The change from taking the role of significant others to taking the role of the generalized other is complete when the child, in considering some action, no longer thinks, "Mommy says I must not do it," but rather, "It's not right to do it." At that point, the child has internalized—made a part of herself or himself—the folkways, mores, values, and other norms of society, thereby acquiring a conscience.

Although the self that emerges as a result of internalizing the attitudes of others is principally of a social nature, it has another more creative and spontaneous element. Mead called this element the *I*, positing that it emerged before the social element, which he called the *me*. The I is the subjective, acting, natural, uninhibited part of the self. The me, in contrast, is the objective representative of cultural and societal expectations that have been made part of personality by the individual. The I is unique to each individual; the me is conventional in that it is shared with others. Summaries and analyses of Mead's work may be found on several Web sites.

The Self and the Unconscious: Freud

The best-known personality theorist—and widely regarded as the founder of modern psychology—is Sigmund Freud (1856–1939). Freud attempted to explain the structure of personality in the light of biological drives. The theories that he and some of his followers espoused, called psychodynamic theories, used a sophisticated definition of the word *instinct*. They also assumed that culture and society had a definite effect on human behavior.

Freud's **psychoanalytic theory** presupposed the existence of unconscious, as well as conscious, processes. The unconscious processes resulted from repression of painful experiences and revealed themselves in dreams or in analysis. Freud also speculated about the existence of the **libido**, an instinctual drive toward pleasure whose representative within the personality was the **id**. Social learning, according to Freud, caused the development of the **ego**, a part of the personality that functioned to restrain the primitive, irrational actions of the id. Finally, the **superego** emerged as a result of having internalized the values and norms of one's culture. The superego operated subconsciously, whereas the ego functioned on a conscious level.

Freud also insisted that personality developed according to a fixed number of **psychosexual stages** in the period from infancy to adolescence. Each stage represented the individual's attempts to gratify the libido at different periods of physical maturation. The success of the ego and superego in channeling the energy of the id into socially approved activities depended on how well an individual has resolved the conflicts at every stage. The stages are

1. *Oral*, in the first year of life
2. *Anal*, in the second and third years
3. *Phallic*, or *Oedipal*, in the third through fifth years
4. *Latency*, from age five to the beginning of adolescence
5. *Genital*, during puberty and into adulthood

Freud further maintained that dysfunctions of personality—that is, behaviors that society labeled abnormal or deviant—were caused by lack of harmony between the id, the ego, and the

Box 2 The Impact of Freud on Psychology

Sigmund Freud is considered a giant in the discipline of psychology. Although today the discipline has taken other directions, the impact of his theories has been widespread. Freud's essential idea was that by observing patients' symptoms, their cause could be discovered by searching their unconscious. Of course, even today most therapies attempt to do the same, that is, discover the cause of problems with the hope of overcoming them.

In addition to the theories mentioned in the text, theories and therapies based on Freud's thought include some of the following.

An early collaborator of Freud's was Carl Jung, responsible for the so-called analytical psychology. Jung broke away from Freud because he disagreed with him concerning the importance of early sexuality. Jung classified people as introverts or extroverts and posited that the unconscious is not present only in individuals, but that all humanity exhibits similar fears, thoughts, and behaviors, which he called a collective unconscious. It is this collective unconscious that influences personality.

Discounting the function of the unconscious was B. F. Skinner's *operant conditioning,* a therapy based on his predecessor, John Watson, who preferred an empirical method of overcoming psychological problems. Skinner focused on observable behaviors and posited that behavior changed as a result of responses to stimuli (that is why this approach is also called the stimulus-response theory) backed up by reinforcements.

Quite well known to most of us is group therapy, which utilizes the shared experiences of the group and is used in such rehabilitating institutions as Alcoholics Anonymous. Groups are also the focus of the interpersonal psychotherapy of Harry Stack Sullivan, who focused more on the social and cognitive aspects of personality and developed a method of guiding and supporting patients. Finally, groups are also the crux of the social psychoanalysis of Karen Horney and the psychoanalytic feminism of Nancy Chodorow, both of whom focused on gender as determinant of personality. Horney responded to Freud's notion that women have "penis envy," while Chodorow bases personality on gender identity (see http://www.answers.com/topic/feminism-and-psychoanalysis).

Cognitive therapy is an effort to change a person's troubling or self-destructive behavior by manipulating the content of his or her thoughts. This therapy is the prevalent one today and is used mostly in trying to deal with depression and posttraumatic stress disorder but also for a number of other mental illnesses and problems. It is sometimes combined with behavioral therapy in an attempt to change negative thoughts or behavior. It was developed by Aaron Beck and is still run by the therapist and his daughter from the Beck Institute for Cognitive Therapy and Research.

As popular as this therapy is, psychology marches on. A former collaborator of Aaron Beck's, Steven Hayes, is proposing that persons afflicted with depression, anxiety, panic attacks, and so on not try to change their negative thoughts but accept them. Hayes believes that suffering is a part of life, that happiness is not normal, and that rather than changing one's thoughts, one ought to examine them dispassionately, or "disidentify" from them, so they no longer control one's behavior. The name given to this therapy is *acceptance and commitment therapy* (ACT), and it is currently the most divisive therapy in the discipline. The adherents are termed third-wave psychologists; the second wave are the cognitive psychologists, who turned away from the first wave, or the behaviorism of B. F. Skinner.

superego. The disharmony created anxiety, and anxiety in turn led to the development of defense mechanisms. Defense mechanisms are the frequently unconscious actions that individuals use to ward off anxiety. Some of the more common ones include repression, regression, projection, and displacement. These mechanisms hide from individuals their real motives and goals and thus protect them from loss of self-esteem. However, overreliance on defense mechanisms can cause individuals to show disturbed behavior of varying intensity. It is such overreliance, as well as other forms of "abnormal" behavior, that Freud set out to cure with the therapy he called *psychoanalysis*, which is designed to delve into a person's subconscious to uncover causes of specific behaviors.

Freud's influence has extended far beyond the field of psychology, and his theories have given us valuable insights into human personality. Today, however, psychoanalytic theory is accepted by most behavioral scientists only with reservations. The most serious criticism involves the importance Freud assigned to the early years of life. He maintained, in fact, that personality was fixed by the age of 5 and difficult to change without psychoanalysis. More contemporary theories tend to stress that personality development does not stop after infancy, childhood, or even puberty but, on the contrary, is a never-ending process, changing to respond to changing demands.

Virtually thousands of Web sites deal with Sigmund Freud the person and Freud's works as the "father of psychoanalysis." Many contain a number of links to the psychosexual stages as well. A number of videos are even available online that are discussions of, lectures about, or critiques of Freud, some of which are extremely interesting. Find them all on **mysearchlab.com**.

The Transitional Self: Erikson

Freudian thought has given origin to numerous theories that have enlarged and modified some of its basic assumptions. Among the neo-Freudians, Erik Erikson (1968) contended that human personality development takes place in eight psychosocial stages that closely parallel Freud's psychosexual stages. Erikson's stages, however, encompass the entire life of the individual and, thus, are more compatible with contemporary thought.

Erikson maintained that at each of the eight developmental stages, the individual is faced with an identity crisis in which the self must try to redefine itself. (Erikson's eight stages are infancy, early childhood, play age, school age, adolescence, young adulthood, adulthood or middle age, and maturity.) If the individual is successful in redefining the self, that is, if the challenges presented by a new stage of the life cycle are conquered—he or she is able to progress to the next stage, thereby achieving increasing maturity. If the individual is unable to satisfy the new demands of a particular stage, psychological problems may develop, preventing the person from progressing to the next stage and from reaching a higher level of maturity. For instance, at the stage of adolescence, the individual is faced with rapid physical growth and sexual maturity and must learn to fill new roles related to a future occupation, as well as to a functioning sexuality. Young people at this stage are plagued by role confusion and absence of a definite identity. According to Erikson, this is why young people tend to overidentify with cliques and popular culture and why they "fall in love" so often. What they call and perceive as "love" for another person is in reality an attempt to project their own image on another and see it reflected back and thus clarified (Erikson, 1963, 262). Successful young individuals eventually come to know who they are and what they want to do. Those who have not resolved these questions remain at a loss, not knowing what kind of person they are or what they should do in life. Socialization, then, never ends, according to Erikson, and the self must constantly meet new crises and learn new roles until death.

Developmental Theories: Piaget

Developmentalism, whose chief proponent was the late Swiss psychologist Jean Piaget (1896–1980), stresses the importance of individual interpretations of situations according to moral values and intellectual skills. Intellectual and moral development can proceed only in stages, however. In turn, these stages can develop only according to an individual's physical maturation. For instance, Piaget insisted that a child of 3 could not understand the concept of speed, and no amount of conditioning would make the child understand it.

Piaget designated the stages of cognitive development as:

1. The sensory-motor stage, from birth to 2 years, in which children cannot understand societal rules
2. The preoperational stage, from 2 to 7 years, in which rules are learned but not questioned, although they may be disobeyed
3. The concrete-operational stage, from age 7 to 11, in the course of which such concepts as numbers, weight, cause and effect, and other cognitive skills needed for everyday life are mastered
4. The formal-operational stage, from age 11 to 16, in which the capacity for rational and abstract thinking is fully developed and education becomes the best vehicle for exploring the mind

Developmentalists also assert that people are essentially active organisms, who are capable of judging, interpreting, defining, and creating their own behavior, provided they have reached a specific stage of physical maturation. Thus, although it will prove fruitless to force a child of 5 to reason abstractly, there is no reason why an adolescent of 14 or 15 cannot do so to the same extent as an older adult.

Moral Development: Kohlberg

Expanding on Piaget's ideas that children's intellectual development proceeds in stages, American psychologist Lawrence Kohlberg (1963, 1981) theorizes that their moral development, their sense of what is right and wrong, proceeds similarly. Moreover, he posits that children's sense of morality develops from within themselves rather than being superimposed by society. He arrived at this conclusion by doing research in a number of countries and noting that even though societies differ on the specifics of what is considered right and wrong, the same basic values are taught in every society. In short, morality seems to be a cultural universal: Although certain foods may be forbidden in one society but allowed in another, such values as concern for others (empathy) and desire for equality and reciprocity (justice) appear to exist in all societies. Individuals do not all have equally developed systems of moral values because they are at different levels of maturity.

Kohlberg claims that there are three levels of moral development, each more complex than the preceding. All children reach every level as they mature, but not all children absorb it, so not all progress to the next level equally equipped. Young children define right and wrong in terms of obedience and disobedience to authority, their concern being the consequences of an act and not the intention behind it; they have a *preconventional* morality. Adolescents adopt a morality based on socially approved values, trusting in a higher authority to define right and wrong; they are at a *conventional* level of development. Some, but not all, adults reach a *postconventional* level, in which the existence of conflicting values is acknowledged and the attempt is made to resolve the conflict in a rational manner or according to what are perceived as higher principles. An individual at this level may consider breaking the law if the law is perceived as unjust.

Kohlberg has been criticized on several counts. First, the fact that an individual recognizes that an act is immoral does not prevent the individual from committing the act. Second, Kohlberg has been accused of focusing on the way men and boys perceive ethics and justice; had he included women and girls, he might have obtained a different view. And finally, Kohlberg's assumption that his theory is applicable to all cultures has been questioned; in particular, the postconventional stage is thought to be more characteristic of liberal, technologically advanced, democratic societies than of authoritarian, agrarian, or undemocratic ones (Gilligan, 1982; Snarey, 1987).

Everything you ever wanted to know about personality development is available in links online. See **mysearchlab.com.**

Agents of Socialization

Specific people, groups, and organizations are chiefly responsible for transforming a raw bundle of tissues and nerves into a functioning human being, knowledgeable in the ways of society, competent in enough skills to survive and sometimes to thrive and excel in the society, and with features and traits familiar to others, yet still recognizably unique.

The Family

The foremost socializers are the people who raise newborns. Barring unusual circumstances, in most societies these people are generally the infant's parents. Thus, most socialization occurs within the family.

The role of the family in socialization is crucial. First, the family influences the child in its earliest stage of development, when the child is most receptive. It meets all the child's needs, both physical and emotional. It is a constant influence because most people maintain family relationships from infancy into adulthood. The family is also a primary group, and the personal and emotional ties are conducive to effective socialization. The family, finally, provides the new individual with his or her first identity, as the infant is born into a particular racial group, religion, and social class.

Although parents try to teach, guide, influence, and control the behavior of their children, the latter are not mere clay in parental hands. Socialization, in fact, is reciprocal. The way infants look and act has a bearing on how parents feel and act toward them. And even the most helpless infant can initiate interaction simply by crying. Infants who obtain a positive response to the crying—who are picked up, cuddled, and comforted—receive a different view of the world and their position in it than infants whose crying is ignored.

James Marshall/The Image Works

The father plays a very important role in socializing a child.

Parental behavior varies in each family. It also has been shown to vary according to social class and even to race and ethnicity (Harrison et al., 1990; Kohn, 1977; Starrels, 1992). For instance, in African-American families and among Afro-Caribbean immigrants, child rearing appears to be the responsibility of a wider range of relatives than it is among white families. In addition, because of the changing nature of the family, many children are being reared by single parents or in households that combine children from previous marriages or by same-sex parents. As a result, socialization experiences are varied.

The School

Second to the family, the school acts as a powerful agent of socialization. It is the first formal agency charged with the task of socializing children and represents the first link to the wider society. In school, children must learn not only basic skills needed in the society but also the hidden curriculum of how to cope successfully in a competitive environment. American schools have often been hotbeds of controversy (school prayer, the decline in standards), probably because they are recognized as being such important socializing agents.

Day Care Centers

Many children are becoming acquainted with a type of school much earlier than children did in the past. Day care centers have become necessities as increasing numbers of women have joined the workforce. Such centers are by no means sufficiently numerous to meet demand, nor are they free from controversy. Many Americans are against them on the basis that a child's own mother is the best socializing agent for the child. That has not always been found to be true: Many women are, in fact, better mothers when their lives are focused on things other than house and family exclusively. In addition, research has shown that when children from stable families attend high-quality day care centers (in which the ratio of staff to children is one to three for infants and no higher than one to six for toddlers), their intellectual development is neither helped nor hindered to any great extent, though their ability to interact with others is increased (Belsky & Steinberg, 1978).

One of the researchers of this study, however, has changed his mind on the effects of child care. In the largest long-term study of child care in the United States, the results indicated that children who spend most of their time (30 hours per week) in child care are three times as likely to exhibit behavioral problems as aggressiveness, disobedience, and defiance as those who were cared for primarily by their mothers (Stolberg, 2001, A18). Dr. Jay Belsky, a principal investigator in this research study, said that these children scored higher on such things as "[getting in] fights, cruelty, bullying, meanness as well as talking too much" and demanding that their needs be tended to immediately (Stolberg, 2001, A18). However, the study has been controversial, as other researchers have come to different conclusions.

The National Institute of Child Health and Human Development is carrying on an ongoing study of early child care and youth development. Its findings, summarized year by year, may be found on their Web site, **http://www.nichd.nih.gov/research/supported/seccyd.cfm**. Its findings regarding child care, however, are frequently politicized. From a conservative point of view, findings would be skewed to show that day care is detrimental to children. From a more liberal point of view, day care allows mothers to pursue careers that might be considered more fulfilling than being strictly mothers and housekeepers, and most important, in most American families, it is a financial necessity for a mother to work, especially in homes where the mother is the chief, or the only, wage earner. Other studies have come to a somewhat similar conclusion: Quality is critical. In other words, if the day care center or the adult caregiver treats the child with affection, with care, with attention, such a child will thrive. The child might even do better than peers in vocabulary in later school years and will be readier to socialize with other children.

Schools are also used as socialization agents for the labor market. In that function, they are expected to teach manners, respect for authority, and the development of basic social skills. At the same time, schools manage to stress certain cultural values (such as competition) and disseminate the idea that the society of which students are a part is superior to others. This is the *hidden curriculum* that schools impart above and beyond basic skills. Of course, how well schools perform any of their responsibilities has become a controversial point.

The Peer Group

Of increasing importance in American society, where school-age children spend more time with their friends than they do with their parents, is the peer group. Socialization within the peer group takes place informally and unintentionally, that is, most effectively. In addition, activities within the peer group tend to be strictly pleasurable, unlike those in school and in the family, which involve work as well as fun. Membership is voluntary, again unlike the situation in the family or school, and members treat each other as equals without having to answer to those higher in authority. All these factors explain the attraction of the peer group and its great influence on the individual. Finally, the peer group offers a source of identification: Adolescents especially turn to their peers to learn what kinds of people they are.

According to one theory, peers are *the* most influential shapers of a young person's personality (Harris, 1999). The author of this theory maintains that, contrary to the current notions in psychology, parents really matter very little. The type of person we become

Susan Woog-Wagner/Photo Researchers

The peer group is second only to the family as the most effective socializer of children.

is determined by two things: (1) our genetic inheritance and (2) the kinds of peers with whom we associate outside the home. The theory demolishes almost every tenet of the child development discipline inasmuch as it is based on existing research used in a new way. For instance, a number of comprehensive studies, particularly those by behavioral geneticists, have shown that about 50 percent of the personality differences among people is attributable to genes, which means that the other 50 percent is due to one's environment. When researchers try to find causal links between a child's social environment created by parents and how that child eventually turns out, however, they cannot find them. On the contrary, according to a large and rigorous study, when adopted children and their adoptive parents were closely followed for several years and given extensive personality and intelligence tests, the results showed that the adopted children had very little in common with the adoptive parents. In fact, they were no more similar to one another than if the children had been compared with strangers off the street (Gladwell, 1998, 57). A control group of 250 parents and their biological children, subjected to the same tests, on the other hand, showed that the children were fairly close to their parents in intellectual ability and other aspects of personality. This particular study concluded that the only reason we resemble our parents is that we share their genes, and there is no similarity when there is no genetic inheritance. Additional readings about peer groups, about the nature of the adolescent subculture, and how it may contribute to the creation of cliques (and even gangs) is discussed on several Web sites that are noted at **mysearchlab.com.** A reading adapted from the *Education Encyclopedia* also deals extensively with adolescent peer groups and may be found at the same location.

Nature versus Nurture

The "nature versus nurture" question has been answered by maintaining that personality consists of both, though in unknown quantities. According to one theory, however, researchers have been looking in the wrong places. Nurture is not so much a function of the home, but of the neighborhood, the school, and the people with whom the growing child associates. The author provides more examples: It is true that children who are treated with affection turn out to be nice people who treat others with kindness, and those who are beaten and mistreated at home turn out to be people who are cruel and unpleasant to others. But is the reason for such an effect the behavior of the parents, or the temperament of the child who induces the parent to treat him or her one way or another? In other words, is it not possible that a parent feels like hugging a child that is well behaved and nice and finds it more difficult to hug one that is nasty and frequently misbehaves? This proposition—that a child's temperament evokes the style of parenting—has also been thoroughly tested by behavioral geneticists. Contrary to all predictions, one study showed that although differential parental treatment relates to differences in adolescent adjustment, the negativity of parents does not cause the negative adjustment in their children: It merely reflects it (Gladwell, 1998, 58). Parents are hostile because their children are hostile.

The other point made by the author of the peer-important theory is that children behave differently among their peers, in the outside world, than they do at home. Although admittedly a parent's behavior toward a child influences how the child behaves in the presence of the parent, or in the context of home, this behavior does not necessarily carry over outside the home. Again, a number of studies purport to prove this point. The importance of the peer group was illustrated by a study done by a sociologist who asked a number of students to write an autobiographical sketch describing the event in their lives that made them most unhappy. More than a third of the respondents described something that a peer did to them, and only 9 percent attributed the hostile act to their parents. The author concludes that whatever our parents do to us is overshadowed by what our peers do to us (Gladwell, 1998, 59). In short, this theory "calls for neighborhoods, peers, and children themselves to share the blame—and the credit—for how children turn out" (Gladwell, 1998, 62).

Another study begun by Harvard psychologist Jerome Kagan that followed babies for 20 years also showed that nature has much to do with personality. In this study, babies that reacted with calm to changes in their environment, to new faces, new objects, and new sounds, remained calm into their adult years. On the other hand, babies that were distressed by novelty, showing their distress by flailing their legs, arching their backs, and crying, grow into anxious adults. No matter how positive their living conditions are, they are always preparing for doom. Professor Kagan maintains that some people (he suggests 15 to 20 percent of newborns) are wired to worry, that is, born predisposed to be anxious (Marantz-Henig, 2009). However, for some individuals the anxiety can be submerged or alleviated by a "benign" environment, although for others it always exists below the surface. Googling "nature vs. nurture" will produce a treasure trove of discussions, articles, lectures, and so on. One Web site that examines the issue from a number of points of view may be found on **mysearchlab.com.**

The Media

One of the most powerful sources of socialization, equaling the socializing influence of the peer group and in many instances surpassing that of school and family, is the influence of the *mass media*. Newspapers, magazines, radio, and most especially the Internet and television have infiltrated every American home to the point where characters from the innumerable TV shows and games are much more familiar to people, especially to children, than any other heroes or villains past or present. The amount of time spent watching television and the quality of the

Box 3 Humans: The Social Animals

We have seen that children brought up in isolation, whether they are abandoned by parents and survive in forests with the aid of animals or are neglected and raised with little human contact, do not fare well. Even when they are rescued and taught to behave as humans behave, they never quite catch on. From observation of feral, isolated, or neglected children, scientists have deduced that there is a physical reason for the inability of these individuals to join the human race. With progress in disciplines that study the brain, answers are slowly emerging.

One study followed adopted children who had been neglected as infants in foreign orphanages. Even two or three years after adoption, these children produce two important hormones in different patterns from children who have been raised in a loving environment. These hormones are oxytocin and vasopressin, small proteins produced by the pituitary gland. Researchers have discovered that these hormones, in addition to having physical functions in the body, affect social behavior. In particular, they promote positive interactions with other persons, especially the social bonds between mother and child and sexual bonds between men and women.

In children who have developed positive relationships with their mothers, oxytocin levels increase after about a half hour of physical interaction with her. Previously neglected children, however, do not show this rise. In addition, when in need of comforting, children with a secure parental bond seek out a parent, whereas the formerly neglected children run to the nearest adult. The adopted children, unfortunately, also have difficulties in forming and maintaining relationships even in adulthood.

The researchers speculate that there is a period during the first two years of life in which strong relationships are developed between infant and caregiver, and when this occurs, later relationships are easier to attain. The oxytocin acts as a kind of reward. It provides a positive feedback about social interactions. Possibly, this development occurs during a critical window of time, and the neglected children may have missed it.

As the discipline of neuroscience progresses, scientists are able to unravel the molecular pathways that allow individuals to feel, think, dream, and so on. It is becoming clear, for instance, that our brains are wired to connect with one another; therefore, one person's mood affects another's. This happens even among strangers (that is why it is probably true that if you smile, the whole world smiles with you). But it is especially true between people who are close to each other. In his book entitled *Social Intelligence*, Daniel Goleman maintains that the brain itself is social and that we connect with others all the time, sensing moods and feelings and reacting to them. He also notes that oxytocin is secreted during positive interactions, whereas cortisol is secreted during stressful occasions. The first hormone boosts the immune system, whereas the latter interferes with some immune cell functions.

Goleman speculates that throughout human history people lived in extended families, including young and old members, and this fact is responsible for our need for others and for the manner in which others affect our own personalities. Despite being born with a distinct temperament, our connections with others can temper and shape our personalities in other directions—anger-prone individuals, say, can spend time with mellower, calmer individuals and absorb less-aggressive behavior. This, in fact, is the essence of what the author means by "social intelligence." Social intelligence, or the ability to experience others, leads to empathy (feeling what the other person feels), which is the antidote to cruelty. We are wired for kindness because survival is much more dependent on helping one another than on killing one another (Goleman, 2006). As it refers to socialization, then, perhaps parents need to heed what psychologist Carl Rogers said about 50 years ago: that we need not just to love our children, but to love them unconditionally. That is, we should love them for who they are, not for what they do. A difficult, but not impossible task.

entertainment presented (centering on sex and violence) have been blamed for inciting criminal and delinquent behavior, as well as for the decreasing level of taste and general knowledge of the population. However, no simple cause-and-effect relationships have ever been unfailingly established, although definite factors point to the negative influence of television and the Internet as socializing agents.

Television does not reproduce reality as most of us experience it but selects specific areas, themes, topics, and interpretations for presentation. Even in a newscast, not everything that occurred on a certain day is reported; only news items of a certain level of importance and/or judged to have wide appeal are selected. Thus, children may derive a false idea of what the world and our life in it is all about. Television also popularizes norms that may be prevalent only among a small number of people, again giving the young and unsophisticated a wrong impression of how the majority of people in the society live (Bierman, 1990; Donnerstein, Slaby, & Eron, 1993). Even the incidental learning—what the audience unintentionally learns as a side effect of entertainment—may lead to distortions and stereotyping. Television, however, has been shown to be a very effective teaching tool; in fact, its very effectiveness has many thinking persons frightened.

The computer, and especially the Internet, are causing controversy as well because they too have enormous educational potential alongside possibly deleterious effects. At the moment, children who have access to the Internet can find hard-core pornographic material not intended for them, at the same time that they can garner an encyclopedic amount of information with the click of a mouse.

Occupational Groups

The role of occupational groups or organizations as socializing agents cannot be ignored. The experience provided by such groups is termed *specialized* or *occupational* socialization, and it consists, basically, of training to fit a particular occupational role: that of clergyman or labor-union public relations official or corporate executive. The successfully socialized individual eventually displays personality traits that reflect the needs of the occupational role: conformity, cooperation, team orientation, and so on.

Reverse Socialization

In urban, industrial societies, the younger generation often transmits knowledge and skills to the older generation—a turnaround from what took place in the older, traditional, agricultural societies. In the United States, for instance, this is often the case in immigrant families, in which the children who were born here understand and feel more at ease in American culture and often find themselves explaining the way things are done to their parents and grandparents. When social change is very rapid, the same thing can happen even to the native born: Young children may know more than their middle-aged parents about the functioning of digital cameras or computer software or the way certain mind-expanding drugs work.

Resocialization

Personality development continues throughout a person's life. Because life is a succession of changes in which people constantly assume new statuses, it is necessary for people to keep learning new roles. Some changes are so profound that they require almost total **resocialization,** a radical alteration of formerly held values and behavior. This process of role transition—shedding old roles in favor of new ones—may be quite dramatic. Resocialization in general refers to situations in which entirely new sets of norms and values must be learned—and old ones forgotten—because people are suddenly thrust into different cultures or subcultures, are isolated from their former primary groups, become handicapped as a result of an accident or illness, or embrace a new religion or political ideology. Some situations requiring resocialization are entered into voluntarily; most are not. In either case, a radical redefinition of one's self-concept and a rethinking of values and beliefs are usually in order.

The most dramatic instances of resocialization occur when individuals are forced, either by an organization or by representatives of society, to alter their former identity. This may happen when a foreign power "brainwashes" prisoners of war to inculcate the superiority of their own political system. It also happens when society, to protect itself, isolates certain individuals and denies them freedom of movement by containing them in prisons or mental hospitals.

Prisons and long-term hospitals, as well as all branches of the military service, convents and monasteries, prisoner-of-war or refugee camps, and similar places, are called **total institutions**. In total institutions, individuals live in groups that are cut off from the rest of society for a period of time, residing and working in a controlled, rigidly structured environment. Total institutions attempt to resocialize their inmates to give them totally new identities and behavior patterns: Former criminals are expected to become productive citizens, drug addicts are expected to become drug free, and converts to a cult are expected to develop blind loyalty to their new religion. Definitions and examples of the various stages of socialization may be found on the Internet.

Socialization through the Life Cycle

Other changes, less dramatic but no less important, require an adjustment of socialization to accommodate new values and modes of behavior. Certain periods of the life cycle—such as adolescence and old age—and specific crises—such as divorce, death of a spouse, loss of a job, or becoming disabled—also force the individual to submit to resocialization to become reintegrated into the social system and continue to live a productive life.

Childhood

Childhood is defined as roughly the first 12 years of life. Not until societies became industrialized was childhood perceived as a separate stage. The concern of parents was for the survival of children (infant mortality rates were very high), and children who survived were considered little adults, with the same duties and responsibilities. Today, in technologically advanced societies, children are expected to enjoy freedom from adult responsibilities. They dress differently from adults and are socialized to behave differently. Of late, however, it has been noted that strong pressures exist to have children grow up faster. The media expose children to graphic violence and sex as well as other problems—financial and marital—that were previously considered totally out of their sphere. In addition, the increasing number of working mothers and latchkey children forces the latter to degrees of independence and responsibility unheard of a generation ago.

Adolescence

The years of puberty and adolescence were similarly never considered a separate stage of life until societies became industrialized. Until then, children barely past infancy were forced into menial labor on farms, in mines, onboard ships, and as apprentices to artisans. The lives of children were not carefree, unless they belonged to the upper classes. This situation changed in the United States with the introduction of child labor laws and compulsory education, which kept children out of the labor force until they turned 16. The need for an ever more skilled labor force has also extended the period of adolescence in this century by encouraging greater numbers of young people to attend college.

Adolescence has been characterized as a stage of life rife with emotional and social turmoil. The adolescent is said to be in limbo, neither child nor adult. The search for identity is exacerbated by physical changes and contradictory messages from socializing agents. Adolescents reach sexual maturity and become capable of reproduction. However, they are strongly urged to refrain from such activity by adults, who realize that they lack the psychological maturity—not to mention the financial means—to support a family (pregnancy being a frequent outcome of sexual activity). Similarly, adolescents are expected to become increasingly self-reliant and responsible, but they lack the skills to obtain jobs that would make them financially independent of their parents. There is, therefore, much anxiety, conflict, and bewilderment on the part of adolescents regarding the nature of their new roles: They are asked to abandon their roles of children, but they are not allowed to acquire the roles of adults. The result may be rebelliousness toward authority, running away from home, dropping out of school, or withdrawing into moody silence. The last decade has also seen a marked increase in suicide in this age group.

Adulthood

Adulthood, too, has had to be redefined as a stage of life in industrial societies. Whereas in agrarian societies most of a person's life was spent as an adult—since children began to work as soon as they could fend for themselves, and the old worked until they died—technology and medicine have wrought so many changes that adulthood has a number of steps.

Erik Erikson divides adulthood into three stages: *young adulthood,* in which the individual must resolve the dilemma of committing to another person or remaining self-absorbed (intimacy versus isolation); *middle age,* in which one must decide whether to establish and guide the future generation or fail to meet the need to be needed (generativity versus stagnation); and *old age,* in which one either accepts in a mature way how one has lived one's life or is disillusioned with life and afraid of death (ego integrity versus despair).

For a majority of individuals, the years of young adulthood are spent in forming a family, learning parenting, and solidifying career goals. All these events can be very trying. Intimate relationships require adjustments that some individuals are unable or unwilling to make. People are generally not taught the parenting role, and the arrival of a child can be perceived as traumatic to unprepared parents. Careers often demand people make sacrifices—such as leaving the area of the country where one was born or having to travel extensively—and are particularly difficult for women, who have to make choices concerning the roles they want to fill. The situation is made even more difficult when choices are not available, and young mothers must work for financial reasons.

Later adulthood, after the age of 40, is often marked by crises. Men can feel trapped in jobs or careers they never really liked. Marriages can begin to feel stale. Mothers who raised children may suddenly feel unneeded, and job opportunities are scarcer for those over age 40. Both sexes must begin to accept their physical decline, a difficult proposition in a society that prizes youth and attractiveness. These factors are responsible for the widely recognized **midlife crisis** that impels many to divorce or to make radical changes of occupation. At this point, too, old roles must be unlearned and new ones learned. Society offers little support for these older adults in crisis; thus, the crisis sometimes becomes catastrophic. Divorced women of this age group are hit particularly hard: Their income is drastically lowered, and their chances of remarriage are slim.

New research into this phase of life refutes the notions delineated here, however. Sociologist John Clausen, in a study of a group of 300 people who passed through middle age and did not encounter any "crisis," concludes that there are many turning points in people's lives, but most of them come before the middle years. Most people specify marriage, divorce, a death in the family, or career choices as turning points, and success or failure in high school as predictive of future stability (competence in high school was credited for nearly half the stability of men over the next 40 years of their lives and one-third of the stability of women).

In addition, it turns out that some individuals have a number of crises, and others have very few. The crisis-prone individuals frequently were divorced long before age 40 and changed jobs frequently (Irving, 1990).

Old Age

Old age is defined as beginning at 65 and is, of course, the stage that culminates in death. As life expectancy increases, an ever-larger number of Americans live well past this age; in fact, the percentage of 65-year-olds in this society has risen threefold since the beginning of the last century, and now seniors surpass teens in number. (Currently, 75 percent live past age 65, and the oldest old—those 85 and over—are the most rapidly growing group. The elderly population will double between now and 2050 to 80 million and by 2030 one in five Americans will be elderly; U.S. Bureau of the Census, 2008.) Nonetheless, the elderly in an industrial society do not enjoy the respect and influence that they do in traditional societies. Moreover, rather than leaving old roles for new, the elderly must abandon former roles that gave them a social identity and provided meaningful activities and prepare for the ultimate role: facing death. Because this prospect is anything but pleasant, and because many elderly people are also burdened by lack of funds and physical and mental deterioration, the resocialization process is not smooth. Many elderly people are left feeling dejected, useless, and confused as their principal obligation becomes that of disengaging from former social roles. Though more support groups are springing up to help the elderly and the dying to cope, this stage of the life cycle continues to be the most problematic.

Some Conclusions

The socialization process clearly does not always work perfectly: Some individuals fail to be properly socialized, or perhaps the socialization process is not strong enough to overcome certain temperamental anomalies. Yet, societies cannot exist in chaotic circumstances. They must have a degree of order. In turn, order in society is promoted by adhering to norms and fulfilling roles, thereby making the social system work smoothly. And, of course, roles and norms are learned in the process of socialization. Is it a failure of socialization that some individuals refuse to follow common norms? Is it an inborn defect in some individuals? In attempting to answer such questions, we broach the subject of deviance and deviants.

The theories of personality formation represent only the major directions in which social scientists have sought answers to the basic questions regarding what makes people become what they are and the roles played by nature or nurture. The discipline of psychology has produced many theories in an attempt to answer these questions. Theories stressing self-concept and self-actualization, for instance, emphasize what we can become instead of what we are and how individuals can improve their self-concept and therefore fulfill their potential, instead of dwelling on how they got to be the way they are. Carl Rogers (1961) and Abraham Maslow (1968) are two American psychologists associated with these theories. The school of Gestalt psychology, founded by German theorist Max Wertheimer (1880–1943), maintains that behavior has to be viewed as a whole, rather than being reduced to parts that can be examined (in German, Gestalt means "whole" or "entire figure"). The individual perceives reality as a whole, and that whole is more than the sum of its parts. Gestalt psychologists stress not only that behavior must be considered in its entirety but also that behavior depends on how the individual perceives the situation.

The existence of these and many more theories that have not been mentioned should suggest the complexity of the subject as well as the absence of definite answers to the puzzle of human personality. Each theory emphasizes a different aspect of the individual and consequently reaches somewhat different conclusions. Clearly, however, people do not mature into productive human beings unless they interact with others, and the quality of such interaction is of utmost importance.

The Chapter in Brief

Personality is an abstract term denoting a dynamic system that includes all of an individual's behavioral and emotional traits—attitudes, values, beliefs, habits, goals, actions, and so forth. Personality develops on the basis of certain biological factors common to all humans as well as according to a unique genetic heredity. On this basis are superimposed a unique physical environment; socialization into a shared culture; common, or group, experiences; and unique, or individual, experiences.

Biology plays an important role in personality formation. Each individual is born with specific inherited physical and temperamental traits to which others in the society react. All humans are also born with certain biological drives and needs that they must learn to satisfy in socially approved ways. Socialization is the process in which they learn to do so. In the bargain, people develop a self and a personality.

Humans are predisposed toward accepting socialization by biology. They need to be physically touched and loved by others. They are totally helpless as infants, needing the ministrations of others for sheer survival. Socialization is a process that is advantageous to both the individual and society. As to how socialization occurs, from a sociological perspective Cooley maintains that it is a process in which others supply a mirror image of the individual, who then judges himself or herself accordingly. Mead also insists on the need for symbolic interaction with others and on the necessity of learning a variety of roles and seeing how complementary they are.

Other theorists view personality formation from other perspectives. Freud stresses the importance of the psychosexual stages of development from infancy to adolescence and the resolution of the struggle between the id, the ego, and the superego. Piaget speculates that intellectual and moral development

proceeds in stages according to the individual's physical maturation. Kohlberg focuses on moral development.

The principal agents of socialization include the family, the school, the peer group, and, increasingly, the mass media. In traditional societies, the family is the most important socializing agent. In technologically advanced societies, the peer group usurps this function, particularly during adolescence. The danger of the mass media as socializing agents is that they present an unrealistic and selective view of the world.

Socialization is a continuing process as individuals learn to fulfill new roles befitting new statuses acquired at different times of the life cycle. In some cases, the new roles require that old patterns of behavior and the old identity be completely abandoned. This process is called resocialization and is used most frequently when the individual enters a total institution such as the military services, a prison, or a mental hospital.

Resocialization is at work at every stage of the life cycle. In adolescence, the individual must relinquish childish roles and acquire adult ones, though society is ambiguous about the identity of the adolescent. Hence, the rebellious and nonconformist behavior of adolescents and their clinging to a youth subculture. Adulthood generally consists of three stages, but it is being suggested that with the lengthening of human life, this stage is in the process of change.

Some theories eschew explanations. Rogers and Maslow are concerned with acquiring a positive self-concept and attaining self-actualization, regardless of how or why a specific personality developed. Gestalt theorists stress the totality of behavior and individual perceptions of reality as they affect personality.

Terms to Remember

developmentalism A school of thought in modern psychology whose chief exponent was Jean Piaget. Developmentalists hold that personality development proceeds in stages that are dependent on physical maturation (sensory-motor, preoperational, and concrete- and formal-operational).

ego (Freud) A part of the personality that functions on a conscious level. It attempts to force the id to satisfy its instinctual needs in socially acceptable ways.

generalized other (Mead) The individual's perception or awareness of social norms; learning to take the role of all others with whom one interacts or of society as a whole.

id (Freud) The representative of the libido in the personality, existing on an unconscious level and making up the primitive, irrational part of the personality.

instincts Genetically transmitted, universal, complex patterns of behavior.

libido (Freud) The instinctual drive toward pleasure, which is the motivating energy behind human behavior.

looking-glass self (Cooley) The process of personality formation in which an individual's self-image emerges as a result of perceiving the observed attitudes of others.

midlife crisis What many people in middle adulthood experience when they reflect on their personal and occupational roles and find them wanting.

mind (Mead) The abstract whole of a person's ideas.

personality A complex and dynamic system that includes all of an individual's behavioral and emotional traits, attitudes, values, beliefs, habits, goals, and so on.

psychoanalytic theory A theory of personality developed by Sigmund Freud. It assumes the existence of unconscious as well as conscious processes within each individual.

psychosexual stages (Freud) The manner in which individuals attempt to gratify the force of the libido at different periods of physical maturation. The phases are oral, anal, phallic (or Oedipal), latent, and genital.

resocialization A process in which the individual's existing self-concept and identity are erased in favor of a new personality or are altered to fit new roles.

self (Mead) The individual's self-conception or self-awareness.

significant others (Mead) Important people in an individual's life whose roles are initially imitated.

socialization The learning process by which a biological organism learns to become a human being, acquires a personality with self and identity, and absorbs the culture of its society.

superego (Freud) A final element of personality, existing largely on an unconscious level and functioning to impose inhibition and morality on the id.

symbolic interactionism A school of thought founded by George Herbert Mead whose theories center around the interrelationship of mind, self, and society and include the belief that society and the individual give rise to each other through symbolic interaction.

total institution An organization or a place of residence in which inmates live isolated from others and where their freedom is restricted in the attempt to resocialize them with new identities and behavior patterns.

Suggested Readings

Adler, Patricia A., and Peter Adler, eds. 1986–1989. *Sociological Studies of Child Development: A Research Annual*. 3 vols. Greenwich, CT: JAI Press. A number of essays focusing on child development from a sociological perspective.

Arana, Marie. 2001. *American Chica: Two Worlds, One Childhood*. New York: Random House. A common experience for immigrants is growing up in two cultures, in which socialization expectations are sometimes contradictory. This book portrays such a socialization experience.

Craig, Grace. 1995. *Human Development*. 7th ed. Englewood Cliffs, NJ: Prentice Hall. A textbook in human development embracing the entire life course.

Dennis, Everette, ed. 1996. *Children and the Media*. Rutgers, NJ: Transaction. Readings in this anthology examine such issues as how the media treat children as news, the content of educational programming, and how the media deal with issues that affect children.

Gilligan, Carol. 1982. *In a Different Voice: Psychological Theory and Women's Development*. Cambridge, MA: Harvard University Press. A colleague of Lawrence Kohlberg analyzes moral development during the process of socialization, focusing on differences between males and females.

Harris, Judith. 1998. *The Nurture Assumption*. The author presents a radical new theory, discounting the influence of family and positing that heredity and experiences outside the home shape personality.

Kenny, Lorraine Delia. 2000. *Daughters of Suburbia: Growing Up White, Middle Class, and Female*. Brunswick, NJ: Rutgers University Press. A study of teenage girls from suburban Long Island focuses on a seldom-explored population: the average American young woman.

Sheehy, Gail. 1995. *New Passages: Mapping Your Life Across Time*. New York: Random House. The arrival of the Second Adulthood stage of life is celebrated by this author, who had examined the stages of the life cycle in a previous book.

Deviance and Criminality: The Need for Social Control

From Chapter 6 of *Contemporary Society: An Introduction to Social Science,* Thirteenth Edition. John A. Perry, Erna K. Perry. Copyright © 2012 by Pearson Education, Inc. All rights reserved.

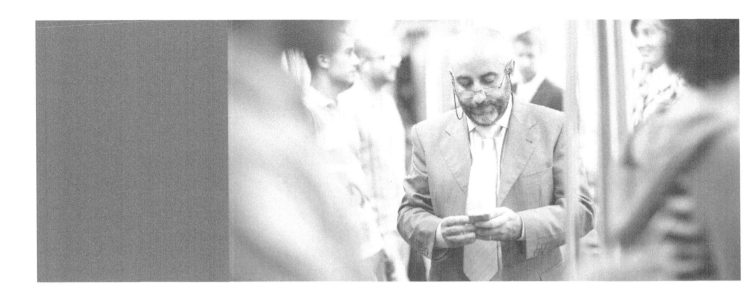

Deviance and Criminality:
The Need for Social Control

IN THIS CHAPTER, YOU WILL LEARN

- *what is meant by the term deviance;*
- *the functions and relative nature of deviance;*
- *the various explanations of deviance furnished by the social sciences;*
- *the nature, extent, and classification of crime; and*
- *the inadequacies of the criminal justice system.*

The media overwhelm us daily with the horrible deeds of some people. A baby is found strangled and thrown into a garbage bin; a man confesses to having killed and dismembered a large number of young men; another individual goes on a killing spree in a small-town restaurant. A battered wife shoots her husband dead with his hunting rifle; a stepfather stabs his teenage stepdaughter to prevent her from testifying at his rape trial, at which he stands accused of having molested her since she was a little girl. There is no need to go on with examples; every newspaper in the country, every local television newscast, every radio news program includes a number of such events every day, and many, many more, so that a reader or viewer or listener some days feels overcome with revulsion at the world. Why do some people commit such atrocious acts? What should society do to keep such persons from doing further harm? What can be done to prevent such acts from ever happening?

These questions have been asked a great many times, and neither theologians, nor philosophers, nor scientists have been able to answer them satisfactorily, though each has tried. The presence of "evil"—the term applied by religion and philosophy to acts deemed damaging to others and to the social group as a whole—was acknowledged long ago and has been experienced in all societies of the world. The extent and frequency of "evil," however, is not the same everywhere. Nor is the effect or the result of "evil" the same everywhere (the result of evil that science *can* discuss is crime). In societies that are homogeneous and well integrated, such as Japan or Finland, although crime exists, it does so to a much lesser extent than in multiethnic, heterogeneous societies. The reason is that a great majority of Japanese and Finns hold the same values, follow the same norms, honor the same traditions, and aim for the same goals. Moreover, in Japan the social group is more important than the individual, and individual wishes and desires are always subjugated to the needs of the group. Finally, the idea of individual freedom and individual rights—on which our entire political system is predicated—has a very short tradition in Japan. Finland, too, is a relatively classless society, in which people are convinced that the state is benevolent, and they display a trust in its civic institutions. As a consequence, street crime is low and law enforcement officials receive support from a majority of the public.

When the United States was a society of English settlers, originating from the same places in Europe and bound together by an authoritarian religion, it is quite possible that crime was less frequent, but certainly not altogether absent. Today, however, the United States has become very heterogeneous, consisting of people from all parts of the globe, with all sorts of traditions and norms. The United States that evolved from the generations of settlers' descendants has given Americans a common character, and there are still values and issues that unite us. But there are also as many issues that divide us. We are divided racially, religiously, linguistically, politically, and on a great many other bases. The information explosion and its wide diffusion to the masses have overwhelmed us, so that many of us are not quite sure what to believe. These factors, and many more, of course, have rendered our social cement—what holds us together—brittle, and when the social bond is broken, when the society is fragmented, it is easier to act without considering how it affects one's neighbor.

Of course, even with the abundance of acts that are against law and morality, we must realize that only a small portion of the population is involved. The majority is still law abiding. Driving down the street, most of us still stop for a red light and then proceed on green. That we do this regularly is symbolic of two important aspects of life in society: one, that people in a society share common norms; and two, that people (or at least most people) obey those norms and, most important, they trust others to obey them. In this case, the common norm is the command (transmitted by a symbol, the traffic light) to stop on red and proceed on green. The norm is so well ingrained in most people that they stop on red even when the streets are deserted and they are not being observed by another living soul. And the shared expectation is the trust exhibited by those motorists who proceed with the green light, as well as by pedestrians who cross the street when the signal says "Walk." Both are certain that motorists who have the red light will unfailingly stop. When this trust is betrayed and a motorist fails to stop at a red light, the predictable result is that either a collision occurs or a pedestrian is hit. In either case, the orderly flow of cars and people is disrupted, giving way to temporary chaos.

Deviance

The word **deviance** has an immediately negative connotation. That is, we think "bad" when we hear "deviant." However, that is an erroneous perception of the word, for the term refers simply to a departure from social norms or behavior that does not conform to social norms. In this definition, Joan of Arc was certainly deviant, for it was surely against the social norms of the time for women to lead armies into battle. Yet she has come down through history not as a villain but as a heroine and a saint (even though the French refer to her as *la fou* or "the crazy one").

"Departure from social norms," then, is too broad a definition of deviance. There are many gradations of social norms, and while a violation of a folkway may be informally sanctioned, it would make little sense to call the violator a deviant. To make matters even more confusing, even in instances of universally held mores, deviance is relative. Thus, killing is a universal taboo, prohibited by both secular governments and religions. Yet there are exceptions to the proscription: In time of war, as self-defense, or in defense of one's family, killing is not only allowed but ordered and encouraged, and people receive medals and commendations for it.

Other types of departure from social norms also do not fit our perception of deviance. Some individuals are able to do calculus at 6 and graduate from college at 14. Mozart was writing splendid music before he was out of his teens. Such people are statistical rarities whom we admire; they are not deviants. On the other hand, individuals who may also be statistically rare because of defects or disabilities—people afflicted with dwarfism or those born with obvious malformations or physical and mental abnormalities—tend to be considered deviant. Thus, it is the departure from social norms that is *perceived negatively* by a majority of people that defines deviance.

The same act sometimes may be considered deviant or not, depending on who performs it. A small child might find a gun and discharge it at a passerby, killing him, but we would hardly call the child a murderer. White-collar crimes are also punished less harshly because they do not involve violence. In addition, social class also plays a role: A banker who is found to have embezzled funds may be imprisoned but tends to receive a lighter sentence than had the act been committed by an unemployed drifter.

Distinctions must also be made between *nonconforming* behavior, which may be prompted by ideological convictions, and *aberrant* behavior engaged in for personal gain, out of greed, or because of mental illness. A person who is arrested for protesting against the International Monetary Fund is not in the same category of deviance as the one arrested for shooting an elderly man to steal his Social Security check.

The Relative Nature of Deviance

The preceding discussion should have made it amply clear that deviance can neither be easily defined nor pointed out with assurance. Of course, in the past—and in some cases even today—people tended to subscribe to much more absolutist views. They believed that social norms were clear-cut, and thus, certain types of behavior were obviously deviant. Moralists among the population still cling to the idea that deviants are immoral, antisocial, or sinners.

Social scientists, and those who prefer a scientific approach to human behavior, admit the ambiguity of the term and stress its *relativity.* Deviance is relative, as noted earlier, because it varies according to the circumstances, time, place, age, mental health of the individual, and even according to the social status of both the deviant and the person who does the defining. The relative nature of deviance is particularly apparent in societies such as that of the United States, which is extremely heterogeneous, made up of large numbers of subcultural, and occasionally countercultural, groups.

The terms *deviant* and *deviance* are used here in preference to *normal* and *abnormal,* which tend to be value laden (that is, one makes an even harsher value judgment when one defines a person as "abnormal"). However, the terms are, for all practical purposes, interchangeable. Defining normality and abnormality presents the same problems as defining deviance and the lack of it. In the social sciences, sociologists prefer to speak of deviance rather than abnormality, whereas psychologists use the other term. Similarly, sociologists tend to see deviant behavior as a failure of socialization, or of factors in the environment, whereas psychologists incline toward

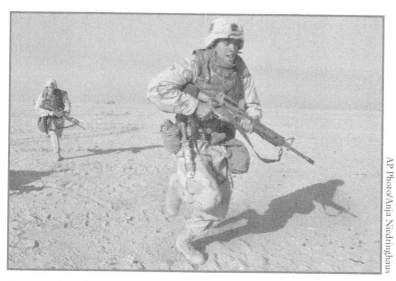

Killing is forbidden in all societies, by secular laws and religious tenets. However, there are exceptions: in time of war, soldiers are permitted, even ordered, to kill those they consider the enemy. In addition, the state and its government can use death as punishment for a capital crime in societies in which the death penalty is not prohibited by law.

the medical view, which speculates that societies, like individuals, are healthy, and deviance is evidence of disease. Both views are discussed here.

Functions of Deviance

It seems odd to attribute functions to deviance, yet it appears that it is not entirely disruptive to society. It has been said, in fact, that if there were no deviants, societies would have to invent them. To begin with, deviants become examples of the kind of person *not* to be, and their behavior a model of behavior that is *not* condoned by society. Thus, deviants help define the boundaries of permissible behavior. The example of deviants and the punishment that is meted out to them reaffirm the existing norms of the group, serving as a warning not to stray from the straight and narrow. Group cohesion is enhanced as members reassert the values of the group and are reassured in the conviction that they are worth preserving. As paradoxical as it seems, deviance may add to the stability of society. As a well-known sociologist has said, in controlled quantities deviance is an important condition for stability in society (Erikson, 1964).

Another important function of deviance is its contribution to social change. The learning of new norms and the abandonment of some old ones become imperative in all societies. Some of these new norms may actually emerge from the deviant activities of a minority of people. The first individual who challenges the status quo is usually considered deviant, as is the one who attempts to do something in a new way. For example, women who picketed the White House and staged demonstrations in an attempt to gain the right to vote at the beginning of the twentieth century were no doubt considered deviant, yet had they not acted in this deviant manner, the women of the current generation probably would still not be able to vote.

Explaining Deviance

It has often been said that good and evil are two sides of the same coin, existing equally in all humans. Because what is considered "good" is understood by most to ultimately benefit the individual and group, acting in conformity with group norms is not generally questioned. What is questioned is why some individuals break the rules. Thus, attempts to explain deviance have existed from the earliest times, couched in the idiom and philosophy of the times. Most religions approach deviance as sin, or the breaking of God's commandments. In modern times, psychologists search for the reasons for deviance within the individual. Sociologists look for explanations in the interaction of people.

The treatment of deviants depends on how deviance is explained. Throughout history, people who behaved in a manner other than that prescribed have been accused of being witches or of being possessed by the devil. To free them of their affliction, they were regularly hanged, burned, or put to death in other horrible ways. Even when, in fifteenth-century Europe, the idea appeared that perhaps such people were ill, they were still beaten, locked away, chained, and treated like subhumans. The English word *bedlam*, meaning confusion and uproar, comes from the name of a well-known "madhouse" in England.

Early Biological Explanations

Explanations of a more scientific nature have been offered from the points of view of biology, psychology, and sociology. The instinctive fear inspired by someone who looks threatening was given expression in the theories of the Italian criminologist Cesare Lombroso (1911), who held that some individuals become deviant because of inborn and genetically transmitted traits. Lombroso was convinced that his ideas could be supported by scientific research: He described and measured traits that he attributed to a "criminal" type, such as a jutting jaw, red hair, a sparse beard, and insensitivity to pain. Despite the initial popularity of Lombroso's theories, it later became apparent that these traits appeared almost as frequently among the noncriminal population as among the criminal population.

In the United States, psychologist William Sheldon revived a version of the theory by claiming that body structure was related to personality. Sheldon classified people into **endomorphs,** with soft, round bodies and a social, easygoing, and self-indulgent personality; **mesomorphs,** with muscular, agile bodies and a restless, energetic, and insensitive personality; and **ectomorphs,** with thin and delicate bodies and an introspective, sensitive, nervous, and artistic personality (1940, 1949). In a later study, Sheldon concluded that mesomorphs were disproportionately represented among a sample of delinquent boys, a finding that was subsequently expanded in another research project by behavioral scientists Sheldon Glueck and Eleanor Glueck (1956). The latter, however, were careful to add that body type *in addition* to other traits and experiences probably predisposed certain people to deviance.

This is a very important qualification. In fact, it is very probable that it is not the body type per se that predisposes one to specific behavior. Rather, it is how others react to a person's body type, and how that individual comes to perceive himself or herself, that may cause specific kinds of behavior. A short person, called "Shorty" in a ridiculing and denigrating way, may well acquire a poor self-image and may choose to strike back in ways that may be termed deviant. On the other hand, it is unlikely that a thin, fragile youth would be invited to join a juvenile gang, or that an overweight person would become a cat burglar. Thus, body type is only very indirectly responsible for behavior.

Another biological explanation of deviance focuses on sex chromosomes. In a normal male, these consist of an X and a Y, whereas a normal female has two X chromosomes. Some persons are born with more than their share of chromosomes, however: XXY, XYY, and so on. In a study of male patients who had an XYY chromosome configuration, it was shown that the latter were taller than average males, tended to be mildly retarded, and appeared more often in criminal than in noncriminal groups (Owen, 1972). Here, too, however, it is possible that the deviance is caused more by being an extremely tall, ungainly looking male than by the extra chromosome; at any rate, the theory came into disfavor. Research on the topic of possible genetic causes in violence and aggression continues to generate controversy. On the one hand, criminality is such a complex form of behavior that to assign a single, biological cause to it is extremely shortsighted. On the other, some researchers maintain that such traits as impulsiveness and the inability to defer gratification—which may, if unchecked, lead to criminal behavior—are essentially genetically transmitted and so could possibly be tracked in affected individuals. A study conducted by a psychologist that compared more than 14,000 adopted men to their biological fathers found there was a correlation: The biological fathers of adopted men who had convictions for theft were also likely to have had similar convictions (Goleman, 1992, B5, B8). This research, however, did not find any direct inherited tendency for violence.

Box 1 Why Are Humans Killers?

A widely believed "fact," even among scientists, is that only humans kill members of their own species. However, two anthropologists report in a book that they observed a number of chimpanzees travel, on purpose, to the border of their range, enter neighboring territory, attack and kill a male from that territory, and then return home (Wrangham & Peterson, 1996). Although this was the first recorded instance of such behavior, it was not the only one. As a result of improved observation techniques, students of primate behavior began to notice that killing others of their own species was part of a pattern of ape behavior. Such behavior includes raids in which victims are murdered, females are battered and raped, and infants are killed.

The recording of the observed violence was important not only because it debunked the myth that only humans kill one another but also because chimpanzees happen to be the species closest biologically to humans. DNA analysis has shown that chimps are closer to humans than they are to gorillas, leading to speculation that the common ancestor to both humans and chimpanzees existed as recently as 5 million years ago (Lehmann-Haupt, 1996, B6). In addition, anthropologists have recently shown that a system of male-initiated territorial aggression is widespread and consistent throughout human civilization. This system includes lethal raids into neighboring territory in which males look for vulnerable victims to attack and kill. Therefore, despite descriptions of utopian societies, violence is *not* an invention of Western civilization. Rather, the two anthropologists conclude, humans are killers universally.

Why this is so is a question to which the scientists do not know the answer. Some form of violence may be beneficial to the group and may convey advantages to future generations, but other forms appear to be senseless. The anthropologists stress the importance of culture as a way for humans to overcome the instinctual baggage they may have inherited. However, they point out that nature (biology) and nurture (culture) are not two distinct elements: Chimps put a lot of thought into apparently instinctive behavior, and some apparently rational human behavior is dictated, or impelled, by biological drives. In their opinion, it is pride, in the sense of achievement of high status, that motivates both humans and chimps.

Humans, then, find themselves in an evolutionary bind. On the one hand, the lust for high status and the taste for meat helped us evolve into humans. On the other, we are burdened with the instinct for violence to attain them. It is a classic dilemma, one that will be overcome only with a rigorous application of human intelligence.

Jim Noelker/The Image Works

Those who are deviant as a result of psychological dysfunctions have never fared well among the rest of societal members. Mental hospitals tend to be very depressing places.

Personality Disorders That May Cause Deviant Behavior

A major form of disorder that may result in deviant behavior is caused by a malfunction in the brain, that is, a disease. Such a malfunction may be organic, acute, or chronic in form. Another is mental retardation, which may result from poor prenatal care, from the mother having contracted rubella during pregnancy, or from a genetic cause (as in Down syndrome, in which the individual has 47 chromosomes instead of 46). These mental disorders are physical in origin and are not necessarily considered examples of deviance. However, emotional disturbances and deviant behavior may develop either from the symptoms (in the form of disturbed thinking processes) or from the way people react to the symptoms.

Another form of disorder is **psychosomatic,** meaning that the individual suffers physical symptoms of disease that do not arise from a physical cause. The physical symptoms result from emotional tension or anxiety and can take the form of colitis, migraine headaches, gastritis, asthma, skin disorders, ulcers, hypertension, anorexia, and impotence or frigidity. Although people who suffer psychosomatic disorders are often not taken seriously, it is important to stress that the symptoms are in every way as real as if there were an organic cause. In addition, as our medical knowledge increases, physical causes are often found for these symptoms.

Neuroses, also called *anxiety disorders*, are considered to be mild **personality disorders** that do not prevent the affected individual from functioning in society. Nonetheless, they may be debilitating for the neurotic person and for those around him or her.

Almost all of us have neurotic tendencies, and neuroses have been so widely discussed in the popular press that we are at least familiar with them. The most common ones include *anxiety reaction* (feeling anxious without reason), *phobias* (unreasonable fear of heights, the dark, tunnels, bridges, enclosed places, open places, snakes, or bugs), *depression* (feeling that life is not worth living), *obsessive-compulsive reaction* (being unable to stop fixed ideas from occurring or repeating certain activities without being able to stop), *hypochondria* (believing oneself ill or always about to acquire a disease), and *dissociative reaction* (amnesia and multiple personality, both of which are attempts to repress an idea or experience). Most of these disturbances rarely require institutionalization, but some do require treatment. In severe cases of depression, phobia, and dissociation, institutionalization may be prescribed. In less severe cases, treatment is provided on an outpatient basis. Going to one's analyst, or "shrink," has become a cliché in some circles, particularly among well-to-do professionals. The rest of the population copes as well as it can with the occasional disruptions caused by their neuroses.

Next in severity are the personality disorders that result in well-ingrained maladaptive behavior. Persons suffering from these personality disorders include **sociopaths** (who engage in antisocial behavior without anxiety or remorse), sexual deviants (transvestites, necrophiliacs, bestialists, and pederasts, the last being the most dangerous to others because they use children to obtain sexual gratification), and addicts.

Finally, **psychoses** are serious mental disorders that cause those affected to be hospitalized because of their inability to function in society. The three major psychoses are schizophrenia, paranoia, and manic-depression or bipolar disorder.

Schizophrenia is a label applied to people for whom there seems to be no other label. Schizophrenics vary in the intensity of their disturbance. Some are totally withdrawn, unable to interact with other people. Others can function in society but are severely limited in certain areas. All, however, fail to function at the level of their capabilities. The disturbance appears to run in families, but it is not known precisely whether it is inherited or is a genetic predisposition that expresses itself in a specific environment. If the cause of onset is diagnosed correctly and institutionalization is brief, treatment has been known to be possible and effective.

True **paranoia** (which exhibits links to schizophrenia) is rare, but paranoid tendencies are frequent. Persons who are paranoid feel that the world is against them and that people around them spy on them and intend to do them harm. Some also believe themselves to be great and famous personages ("delusions of grandeur") and attribute their persecution by those around them to envy.

Any of the preceding forms of psychosis may cause the affected person to hallucinate. Such a person may be certain of hearing voices where there are none, which is a wrong perception of reality, or may have delusions about themselves or others, which is a misinterpretation of reality. Some live for years in an imagined world. In short, for them the distinction between the real and the imagined becomes so blurred that they fail to distinguish one from the other.

Anxiety and severe depression, on the one hand, and unprovoked happiness or euphoria, on the other, characterize *manic-depression*, formally called **bipolar disorder**. These mood swings can occur from one moment to the next. People with bipolar disorder represent a threat mainly to themselves: In their depressed states they may attempt suicide, whereas in their manic states they may take on tasks beyond their capacity. Fortunately, drugs are available that stabilize this psychosis fairly well.

Treatment of Personality Disorders

There have been dramatic improvements in the treatment of mental disorders in this century, as people have become more aware of the nature of these disorders and as medicine and the disciplines of psychology have attained more knowledge. However, a great many of those afflicted by mental disorders are not being helped, either because treatment is not within their means or because it is ineffective. The following are the major forms of treatment:

1. **Psychotherapy.** This includes psychoanalysis, group therapy, family therapy, transactional analysis, and various other forms of analysis. All these forms have in common the fact that nothing physical goes on, nor are drugs given. The therapies are simply verbal exchanges between patient or patients and therapist.
2. **Behavior therapy.** Based on the principle of conditioning, this kind of therapy stresses the modification of behavior through rewards and punishment.
3. **Psychopharmacology.** Sometimes used in conjunction with other therapies, this form uses drugs and chemicals to treat symptoms of mental disorders.
4. **Hypnotherapy.** This treatment uses hypnosis—subconscious suggestions—to deal with mental disorders.
5. **Electroconvulsive shock therapy.** This type of treatment, which is very painful and can cause loss of memory and learning disabilities, has been popularized in the movies and in literature because unethical therapists have used it to punish patients. However, it has lost much credibility and is not used as frequently as in previous years. It consists of subjecting patients to severe jolts of electricity to the cranial area. The method works by suppressing neuron activity, and it has been effective in some cases of severely depressed patients.

In the 1930s and 1940s, *psychosurgery* in the form of frontal lobotomy was hailed as a method for treating severe mental disorders, but it often left patients totally dysfunctional and at other times increased aggressive behavior. As a result, the operation is no longer performed for psychological disorders.

Psychological Explanations of Deviant Behavior

Psychological explanations of deviance have become very popular in this century as a result of Sigmund Freud's work. Freud assumed that people are born with tendencies toward aggression and sexuality, drives that are potentially destructive and thus must be inhibited. Inhibition occurs through the development of the ego, which directs people to solve physical needs in socially approved ways, and of the superego, a kind of conscience that prohibits behavior that the individual has learned to consider wrong.

In the Freudian scheme, deviant behavior occurs when the superego is not sufficiently developed to be able to impose its will on the other component of the personality, the id, which is uncivilized and primitive. Deviance may also be the result of an overdeveloped superego, in which case people act in a deviant way to bring punishment on themselves for the drives they feel they should never have experienced, even if they inhibited them successfully.

Psychological theories resemble biological theories and follow a medical model in that they assume deviance is caused by mental defects, abnormality, or illness. But they are more sophisticated in that they recognize that one cannot separate the cause from its effect. There is little doubt that mental illness may cause behavior easily perceived as deviant. But mental illness is also used as the rationalization for deviant behavior. Alcoholism, drug addiction, child abuse, and crimes committed for reasons other than greed or financial gain are often attributed to mental illness. In fact, the judicial system uses this rationalization to exonerate certain criminals from punishment.

Sociological Explanations of Deviance

As is becoming clear, not all deviants are mentally ill, nor are all mentally ill persons deviant. The psychological theories and their variants—that deviance is caused by aggression triggered by constant and profound frustration, or that it originates in unconscious processes having to do with an improperly developed superego or conscience, or that it is a form of disease or birth defect—are very difficult to test empirically. They fail to take into account the relative nature of deviance and the role played by social interpretations of deviance. They focus too exclusively on the act—deviance—and the actor—the deviant—and not enough on the stage—society—on which the actor performs. At least, this is so in the opinion of sociologists.

There is no single-factor explanation for human behavior. It is always the result of a variety of factors, some of a genetic and some of a social nature. Sociologists, who focus on human interaction, maintain that all human behavior, including deviant behavior, is a product of the type of social organization in which people live, of the social structures they erect, and of the social processes in which they are involved. The focus here is not only on the act and the actor, then, but also on the set, the scenery, the script, and the audience.

Social Integration and Anomie: A Functionalist View

One of the earliest attempts to explain deviance from a sociological perspective was put forth in the work of Emile Durkheim (1897/1951/1966). This nineteenth-century social philosopher introduced the concept of **anomie**, which he defined as a condition of normlessness that pervades individuals when the established rules of behavior are no longer valid, are conflicting, or are weak. Such conditions develop in times of crisis or rapid social change. At such times, people are confused because old norms that formerly gave structure to their lives are no longer effective. Individuals in such societies are said to be loosely integrated culturally and socially because they fail to agree on norms and values and are consequently confused about behavior. Obviously, in these circumstances, individuals are vulnerable to deviance. A great disparity in crime rates is noted when we compare the crime rates of homogeneous and highly culturally integrated societies—for instance, Finland—and those of heterogeneous and loosely integrated ones, such as the United States.

A society with a high degree of anomie is in danger of falling apart because the cement that holds it together loses its ability to bond people. People no longer share goals and values. They do not agree on what constitutes right and wrong. They do not impart similar values to their children—in fact, many do not impart any values at all, leaving children to grow up directionless. One of the results of such neglect is the increase in violent behavior on the part of the young, particularly in violent action that seems to have no provocation and that makes little sense.

The high rates of crime in the inner cities, for instance, may be attributed to anomie, coupled by the pervasive presence of drugs and their high profitability, as well as the ease of obtaining guns in our society. Additional causes that have been suggested include poverty, social tension, and hopelessness, conditions that have afflicted inner cities for many generations. The tendency to form gangs to take the place of dysfunctional or nonexistent families and a street ethic that requires young men to act tough to prove their manhood are also cited as causes of violence.

Merton's Classification of Deviant Behavior

The concept of anomie has been expanded by Robert Merton (1938, 1968), who has applied anomie theory to a variety of forms of deviant behavior. Merton sees deviant behavior as the consequence of a lack of balance in the social system, as a gap between what the society sets up as goals for its members and the means that it puts at their disposal for reaching them. This gap produces strains that can result in deviant behavior.

An obvious example may be found in American society, which sets up as one of its most important goals the achievement of success, usually translated into economic terms as the attainment of wealth. The socially accepted ways of satisfying that goal are either to be born into a wealthy family or to obtain the type of education or skills that will guarantee employment in a profitable enterprise where one can, by dint of hard work and innovative thinking (or just plain good luck), rise to the top.

Obviously, the first way is strictly up to chance, and only a very small percentage of families in the society are in a high social class. The second way of attaining success is also difficult. Higher education is expensive and requires intellectual ability that is not universal. And even the best education and training do not guarantee success. Consequently, a substantial segment of the population who wants to be successful is denied access to success through the acceptable ways. Such people may experience anomie and, in frustration, may turn to various forms of deviance—socially unacceptable means—to achieve the desired societal goals that they have internalized (see Table 1).

Merton's classification of behavior is based on people's acceptance or rejection of either the cultural goals or the means of achieving them. Merton's theory is quite general, but it has been very influential and has given origin to many more specific theories. Albert Cohen (1955), for instance, asserts that gangs are usually made up of lower-class youths to whom the middle-class means of achieving success are not available. Youth gang members achieve success among their peers by deviating from society's norms to follow gang norms.

Criminologists Cloward and Ohlin (1960) also use anomie theory to suggest that gangs supply their members with a respectable status that they cannot obtain through socially approved means. The researchers classify juvenile gangs into three subcultural groups: the criminal, interested in material benefits; the conflict, involved in territorial squabbles; and the realist, using alcohol and drugs to bind its members together. In all three types, the members feel that they are achieving success despite what others in the society think of them.

TABLE 1   Robert Merton's Theory of Deviance

Mode of adaptation	Cultural goals	Institutionalized means	Deviant?	Examples
Conformists				
	Accept	Accept	No	Study and attain professional status
Deviants				
Innovators	Accept	Reject	Yes	Gang member, member of organized crime, embezzler, bank robber
Ritualists	Reject	Accept	Yes	Low-level bureaucrat, missionary, government worker, worker with the poor (individuals not interested in money or power)
Retreatists	Reject	Reject	Maybe	Drug addict, dropout, alcoholic, street person
Rebels	Reject/Accept	Reject/Accept	Yes	Revolutionary, terrorist

The anomie theory, however, does not explain *all* forms of deviance. It focuses on society as the source of deviance, rather than on the individual. It assumes that there is an agreement on values in the society that does not exist, in reality, to quite the extent Merton implied.

Cultural Transmission (Differential Association): Interactionist Perspective

The **cultural transmission** theory, also called the **differential association** theory, is a kind of learning theory, as it is based on the proposition that deviance is learned through symbolic interaction, much as all other human behavior. Again, as is true of learning in general, the learning of deviance occurs most effectively in small, intimate primary groups such as the family, the peer group, and the neighborhood. The individual interacting with people who are themselves deviant learns deviant techniques and rationalizations for deviant acts, as well as conceptions of law, property, and human rights from a deviant perspective.

According to Edwin Sutherland (1949, 1961), the following factors influence an individual's becoming deviant:

1. The intensity of association with others—whether they are friends and relatives or merely acquaintances.
2. The age at which interaction takes place—children and adolescents are more impressionable than older individuals.
3. The frequency of association—the more one associates with deviants, the more one is influenced by them.
4. The duration of contact—the longer the association with deviants, the better the chance of acquiring deviant tendencies.
5. The number of contacts—the more deviants an individual knows, the better the chance of becoming deviant in turn.

Becoming deviant, however, is not simply a matter of having "bad companions." Rather, it is a matter of the choices an individual makes in response to his or her needs.

One implication of this theory is that a society with a number of subcultures (a heterogeneous society) has higher rates of deviance because people do not share the same values, norms, and goals. Members of subcultures may also feel a greater loyalty to their own group than to the majority group or dominant culture, whereas members of the dominant culture may perceive some subcultural values and norms as deviant.

The focus of the cultural transmission theory, that deviance is learned, is important. However, it overlooks the possibility that some forms of deviance may be learned not only from people but also from ideas. Some individuals may join such groups as the American Nazi Party after reading works by authors who espouse the Nazi ideology. On the other hand, people such as lawyers and social workers who have frequent dealings with deviants seldom learn deviant behavior from their clients, or at least they seldom act on it. And finally, it is also known that knowledge gained from associating with nondeviants can be used in a deviant way. A pharmacist who sells drugs illegally for gain is engaging in deviant behavior that he or she did not learn from deviants. Thus, the theory explains only partially why some people learn deviance and others do not, and it does not touch on the reasons for specific behaviors being defined as deviant.

Labeling Theory

A different conception of what constitutes deviant behavior and how people are defined as being deviant is represented by the **labeling** theory. This approach places an emphasis on the process by which an individual is labeled as deviant and on how the individual is treated as a consequence of having been so labeled, rather than on the behavior of the person. Some of the questions asked by labeling theorists are: How does the group come to define a specific individual as deviant? How do the members of the group modify their reactions and interactions with an individual defined as deviant? What are the effects of the changed behavior of group members on the deviant individual?

Howard Becker (1963), a sociologist who was instrumental in developing the labeling theory, maintains that all of us are guilty of deviant behavior at one time or another. This *primary deviance* is temporary, unimportant, prompted by curiosity, and easily concealed. Examples of primary deviance are a junior executive who pads an expense account somewhat, a guest who takes a towel from a hotel room, or a youth who has one homosexual experience or tries an illegal drug. Such behavior is usually not discovered by others, and the perpetrators do not consider themselves deviant.

In some circumstances, however, the act is discovered, perhaps by parents, friends, employers or employees, school administrators, teachers, or the police. The perpetrators are then on the way to becoming labeled as deviants. They are accused, sermonized, and often punished in what Becker calls a "degradation ceremony." They are made to feel that they are morally inferior to their accusers and are called by such unflattering labels as "nuts," "weirdos," "queers," and so on. Other people, in response to these labels, react to the labeled individuals as if they were in reality what the labels indicate. Eventually, the labeled individuals come to accept these labels, altering their self-concepts to fit the reaction of others to themselves, and they begin to act them out. Now their behavior is *secondary deviance* and becomes habitual.

At this point, after being labeled as deviants and accepting the label, the offenders' lives take a new turn. They are stigmatized (pointed out, isolated, avoided) by nondeviants and forced to seek the company of other deviants, which reinforces their behavior. Lacking a way out, they are well on their way to a deviant career, inasmuch as being deviant becomes their master status. The labeled person's life becomes a self-fulfilling prophecy. This is in keeping

Crimes against persons are often dramatic. This photo of the young man who shot a congresswoman and killed nine others at a political meeting has become a symbol of a criminal action whose motivation is difficult to understand. None of the theories of deviance seem to fit his action.

with the view that socialization is a process in which the self emerges and is characterized by the reflected reactions of others: the symbolic-interactionist perspective.

The labeling theory has been helpful to students of deviance because it shows that only certain people or actions are selected for labeling as deviant, but the theory has its shortcomings. Labeling is not always involved: Many persons who are never discovered nevertheless continue to act in a deviant fashion. Are they any less deviant because others do not know about their deviance? The theory also overlooks the fact that some deviants may actually be jolted out of their behavior by the labeling process and as a consequence may be moved to change their behavior to conform to norms (Liazos, 1972). Further examples of the labeling theory, as well as an overview of the theories mentioned here may be found online.

Crime: Deviance That Hurts

Most people equate deviance with crime, but of course the two are not the same, as the foregoing discussion should have made clear. Everyone is deviant to some extent or other, at one time or another, but not everyone is a criminal. Criminals represent only a small minority of people in society, but the acts they perpetrate are very damaging, so that crime and criminals are very much on the public's mind.

In most contemporary societies, informal social control is not sufficient to contain deviance. Therefore, formal social controls must be instituted. One type of formal social control is the enactment of statutes, or laws, that define the actions that are prohibited to members because they are too destructive to the society. The prohibited actions are termed crimes and are punished by the society through its judicial system.

Crime, then, is any action that violates the law. Laws, in turn, are passed at a variety of governmental levels: local, state, and federal. Laws differ from the unwritten societal norms in that (1) they are put into effect by political authority, (2) they are specific rules instead of informal understandings, (3) they are applied uniformly, (4) they carry specific punitive sanctions, and (5) they are administered through official agencies of the society.

Even though crimes and punishments are specifically defined, they too are relative, varying in kinds and extent. One distinction is made between criminal behavior on the part of adults as opposed to juveniles under 18 years of age. The distinction is based on the belief that minors are not yet fully socialized (but if they commit an especially serious crime, juveniles may be treated as adults by the criminal justice system). Another distinction is between the so-called index crimes and actions that are considered crimes by the legal codes but not by a majority of people. The **index crimes** involve the violation of mores and include murder (including homicide, voluntary manslaughter, and involuntary manslaughter), rape, robbery, aggravated assault, burglary, larceny, arson, and auto theft. Crimes that most people ignore range from the regional prohibition to serve alcohol by the glass, although one can buy bottles, to the 55-mile-per-hour speed limit, which was a federal law for a few years and was observed only when a police car was in sight.

Classification of Crimes

Criminal behavior ranges over a very wide spectrum and is perpetrated by individuals belonging to a large variety of groups. Most crimes fit into one of the following categories.

Crimes against Persons. These crimes almost always involve violence and the use or threat of force to injure victims and are, therefore, the ones most feared by people. Violent crimes include murder and nonnegligent homicide, forcible rape, robbery, and aggravated assault.

Crimes against Property. These crimes do not involve the threat of force or injury to victims; rather, the goal of perpetrators is to gain possession of, or to destroy, property by unlawful means. Property crime includes burglary, larceny-theft, motor vehicle theft, and arson.

Juvenile Delinquency. This refers to violations of the law by minors. In the last decade, we have witnessed a number of violent crimes perpetrated by ever-younger persons. Not only have there been several instances of teens killing teachers and fellow students, but 10- and 12-year-olds have brutally murdered younger children. Juveniles have also been engaged in criminal behavior as members of gangs.

Hate Crimes. The FBI reports crimes committed on the basis of race, religion, ethnicity, disability, and sexual orientation.

As we have seen, most sociologists tend to assign social factors to the causes for crime. Their research shows that children who become juvenile delinquents tend to have experienced harsh and erratic discipline three to four times more often than children who do not become delinquent. Such children tend to have, on average, a verbal IQ eight points lower than the norm because of prenatal factors, such as a mother who abuses drugs and alcohol during pregnancy, a fact known to damage the central nervous system of the fetus, or because they were exposed to high levels of lead from peeling paint and auto fumes. The latter factors are known to lower IQ and impair concentration, predisposing children to hyperactivity, a pattern predictive of crime in adolescence. When they arrive in first grade, such children are unprepared to learn. "They are more aggressive than other kids, have conduct problems, and low reading achievement, a pattern that solidifies by third grade, at which point these youngsters get marked as problems and put in special education classes. As early as third grade, they are stigmatized, and at a social disadvantage" (Goleman, 1992, B5, B8). The labeling theory, in this case, may explain their criminal proclivities. Subsequently, they may prefer to associate with others like themselves (differential association theory), or they may use illegal means to reach the societal goals that become impossible to reach by legal means (anomie theory).

Because of the increase in senseless, savage murders resulting from the easy availability of guns, juvenile crime has been subjected to additional scrutiny. It appears that whereas in the past unimportant conflicts used to be settled with a fistfight, today they are settled with firepower, which often results in death. Over and over, however, research shows that lessons in cruelty start at home and are simply facilitated by the presence of weapons. In *Kids Who Kill,* psychologist Charles Ewing reports that many young people who commit seemingly motiveless crimes have themselves been sexually or physically abused, even though they seldom admit to having once been a victim. It seems that to abuse another human being, a youngster has to have been abused first. Abuse, neglect, instability, and a sense that no one cares are almost certain to create individuals who focus on their own immediate gratification, no matter who suffers as a result. The ease with which guns are available in our society helps to transform anger and frustration into murder and mayhem. According to a lobbying organization called Handgun Control, in 1996 handguns were used to murder only 2 people in New Zealand, 15 in Japan, 30 in Great Britain, 106 in Canada, 213 in Germany, and 9,390 in the United States (Herbert, 1999, A31). The point has been made repeatedly that if young people could not obtain guns, they would use their fists or other less lethal weapons to express their feelings and avoid the frequent massacres at American schools that we have sadly witnessed. (For additional facts on guns as they affect murder rates, as well as estimates of firearm crime and international comparisons, see the Internet.)

Social Order Crimes or Crimes against Morality

Criminal acts such as gambling, prostitution, illegal drug use, vagrancy, and public drunkenness do not impose physical suffering on others but offend the moral sensibilities of the majority. These crimes are often referred to as *victimless crimes* because no other person is allegedly hurt. However, it is obvious that such crimes make victims of the perpetrators and, very often, their families. Drunken drivers can become killers, and alcoholics frequently expose their families to poverty as a result of losing jobs or to physical abuse while intoxicated. Drug addicts can rob, burglarize, and kill in pursuit of their next fix, and they certainly get in trouble with the law if they also sell drugs. Women who abuse drugs while pregnant make victims of their babies, who are often born addicted or with physical and behavioral problems. Prostitutes subject themselves to dangerous situations, can easily acquire venereal diseases, including AIDS, and are likely to experience a lifestyle in which drug and alcohol abuse are rampant, leading to self-destruction. Family life for such women is rare, and if they have children, they are forced to live in an unhealthy environment.

White-Collar Crime. Criminal acts committed by respectable persons, often of high status, in the performance of their occupational roles are listed as white-collar crimes. The FBI categorizes these crimes as illegal acts that are characterized by deceit, concealment, or violation of trust but that are not dependent on force or threat of force. The acts include false advertising, copyright infringement, swindling, stock manipulation, price fixing, tax evasion, embezzlement, forgery, and fraud. These acts are committed by individuals and/or organizations to obtain money, property, or services; to avoid payment of taxes or money owed; to prevent a loss of money or services; or to secure a personal or business advantage. Such crimes are tolerated more than others because they seldom involve violence and are not committed by seasoned criminals. However, in sheer numbers of dollars, white-collar crime costs society three times more per year than the four other major categories of property crimes. In recent years, the American public has been made aware of corporate crime with the examples of Enron, Adelphia, and several of the major financial institutions, but there are thousands of cases involving health care fraud, government fraud (e.g., contractors overcharging government agencies for work, services, or manufactured items), financial institution fraud (e.g., bank managers or employees embezzling, check fraud, counterfeiting, credit card theft), antitrust cases, price fixing, money laundering, environmental degradation, and Internet fraud, to mention just a few. Several years ago Bernard Madoff was responsible for a Ponzi scheme of gigantic proportions. In this scheme, a large number of people invested with what they thought was a financial institution that was returning generous interest rates because of wise investment strategies. Instead, Mr. Madoff did no investing: He paid old investors with money he obtained from new investors, eventually leading the early investors to lose their investment altogether. Because so many investors lost their life's savings while Mr. Madoff lived a life of luxury on their money, he received a life sentence, unusual in a white-collar crime case.

Organized Crime. The criminal activity of groups of individuals who are organized to maximize efficiency and minimize the danger of apprehension and punishment is collectively called organized crime. Organized crime is in the business of satisfying human wants that are prohibited by the ideal norms of society and by the legal codes: Members provide houses of prostitution and call-girl services, direct illegal gambling establishments, furnish drugs, manufacture and distribute pornographic materials, and make loans to high-risk borrowers at steep interest rates.

White-collar crime does not evoke the same repulsion as other crimes because it seldom involves violence. Nonetheless, this type of crime costs the society and specific members of it not only in terms of lost money, but also because of the trampling of ethics and fair play.

Crime Statistics: How Much Crime, and Who Commits It?

Crime statistics are compiled annually by the Federal Bureau of Investigation and published as the *Uniform Crime Reports* (UCR). However, the crimes reported by the FBI are limited to 29 categories and focus only on the eight index crimes. These numbers are compiled from crimes reported to police departments throughout the nation. It is thought that the actual crime rate is two to three times higher than what is reported because many crimes are never detected and the less serious crimes may even go unreported.

Another way of reporting crimes is the National Crime Victimization Survey (NCVS). The survey has been used since 1972 and was redesigned and reimplemented in 1993. It contains questions for crime victims; therefore, it does not count homicides but includes simple assaults and domestic violence as well as rapes, robberies, and aggravated assaults that have been reported to police.

Crime seems to undergo periodic increases and decreases. For instance, after an eight-year period of crime decreases, it dramatically increased in 2001, especially in a number of cities. Then, from 2007 to the present, violent crimes, property crimes, and arsons have been declining. Violent crime fell by 1.9 percent nationally in 2008 from the preceding year, which meant that there were 454.5 violent crimes per 100,000 inhabitants (see Crime in the United States 2008, Uniform Crime Reports). However, murder and manslaughter rose in midsized cities with populations 50,000 to 100,000 as well as in some smaller cities.

Forcible rapes were up in the Northeast, in addition to burglaries and larceny-theft, and rapes increased in cities with populations of one million-plus. These figures change every year, of course. See Figures 1 to 3 and Tables 2 and 3 to see the numbers of crimes, the victims, and the perpetrators for 2009.

Crime Rates Continue to Decline

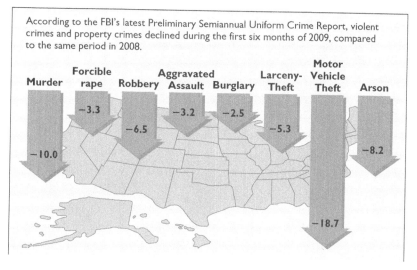

According to the FBI's latest Preliminary Semiannual Uniform Crime Report, violent crimes and property crimes declined during the first six months of 2009, compared to the same period in 2008.

Murder −10.0
Forcible rape −3.3
Robbery −6.5
Aggravated Assault −3.2
Burglary −2.5
Larceny-Theft −5.3
Motor Vehicle Theft −18.7
Arson −8.2

FIGURE 1
Source: From http://www.fbi.gov/page2/dec09/crime_stats_122109.html

Homicide Victimization Rate

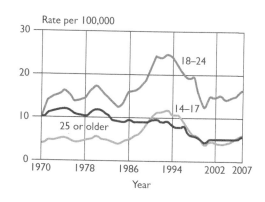

Rate per 100,000

18–24
14–17
25 or older

FIGURE 2
Source: From FBI, The Uniform Crime Reports (UCR) http://bjs.ojp.usdoj.gov/content/glance/homage.cfm

Violent Crime Rates by Gender of Victim

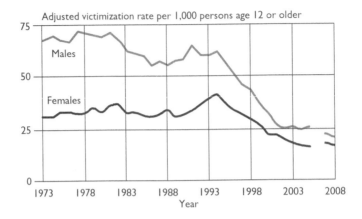

FIGURE 3

Sources: Rape, robbery, and assault data are from the **National Crime Victimization Survey** (NCVS). Ongoing since 1972 with a redesign in 1993, this survey of households interviews about 134,000 persons age 12 and older in 77,200 households each year about their victimizations from crime. The homicide data are collected by the **FBI's Uniform Crime Reports** (UCR) from reports from law enforcement agencies. **http://bjs.ojp.usdoj.gov/content/glance/vsx2.cfm**

Most of the crime is committed by young males in their late teens and early twenties. Some violence is random, other occurs among people who know each other, and some happens between gangs (Police Executive Research Forum, 2006).

Although males are disproportionately represented as perpetrators of violent crime, the female crime rate has recently been inching upward. Partly, this may be an unfortunate side effect of a more egalitarian atmosphere in the society. A more dramatic reason for the increase, however, seems to be women's growing dependence on drugs, particularly crack. This dependence leads to involvement in criminal activities to provide for their needs. The rates for men and women, therefore, are getting closer. Noteworthy, too, is the fact that the victims of violent crimes committed by women are principally other women, whereas males victimize both males and females in almost equal numbers.

The Bureau of Justice Statistics, an agency of the U.S. Department of Justice, periodically publishes a variety of statistics on crime. Their Web sites are available on the Internet.

The Criminal Justice System

Although deviance performs some useful functions in society, crime cannot be ignored. Every society has felt the need to protect itself from violent deviants, as well as to punish those who have committed deviant acts. Unfortunately, the judicial system, comprising the institutions that have arisen to deal with the dispensation of justice, is anything but ideal.

TABLE 2 Preliminary Annual UCR Showing Declines (Percent Change by Population Group)

Population group	Number of agencies	Population	Violent crime	Murder	Forcible rape	Robbery	Aggravated assault	Property crime	Burglary	Larceny-theft	Motor vehicle theft	Arson
Total	13,237	265,670,842	−5.5	−7.2	−3.1	−8.1	−4.2	−4.9	−1.7	−4.2	−17.2	−10.4
Cities:												
1,000,000 and over	10	25,873,144	−6.9	−11.2	−1.2	−9.7	−4.6	−7.9	−5.7	−5.5	−21.1	−12.8
500,000 to 999,999	24	16,653,305	−7.5	−11.7	−1.3	−9.6	−6.3	−4.8	−1.9	−2.8	−18.5	−4.4
250,000 to 499,999	41	14,221,382	−6.2	−8.0	−0.9	−7.1	−6.0	−4.6	−1.5	−2.9	−17.3	−12.4
100,000 to 249,999	198	29,419,083	−6.1	−6.2	−4.3	−10.3	−3.5	−3.7	−0.3	−2.9	−15.5	−10.4
50,000 to 99,999	413	28,340,331	−4.3	−6.0	−4.0	−5.0	−4.0	−4.9	−1.4	−4.3	−17.0	−8.7
25,000 to 49,999	723	24,856,909	−4.7	+5.3	−5.2	−3.9	−5.1	−3.1	−2.5	−2.1	−15.6	−6.7
10,000 to 24,999	1,577	24,916,580	−2.2	−2.2	−1.1	−6.3	−0.9	−4.2	−1.1	−4.2	−14.2	−13.2
Under 10,000	6,600	21,083,558	−4.9	−9.6	−7.3	−5.3	−4.5	−3.9	−2.0	−3.8	−14.3	−11.3
Counties:												
Metropolitan[1]	1,462	56,659,715	−4.0	−6.8	−3.7	−6.7	−3.0	−5.8	−1.1	−5.9	−16.9	−12.7
Nonmetropolitan[2]	2,189	23,646,835	−3.0	+1.8	+0.3	−0.7	−3.7	−6.7	+0.5	−9.5	−14.6	−7.9

[1]Includes crimes reported to sheriffs' departments, county police departments, and state police within Metropolitan Statistical Areas.
[2]Includes crimes reported to sheriffs' departments, county police departments, and state police outside Metropolitan Statistical Areas.

Source: U.S. Department of Justice—Federal Bureau of Investigation *Preliminary Annual Uniform Crime Report, January–December 2009*, http://www.fbi.gov/ucr/prelimsem2009/table_1.html

TABLE 3   Hate Crime Statistics 2008 (Incidents, Offenses, Victims, and Known Offenders by Bias Motivation, 2008)

Bias motivation	Incidents	Offenses	Victims[1]	Known offenders[2]
Total	7,783	9,168	9,691	6,927
Single-Bias Incidents	7,780	9,160	9,683	6,921
Race:	3,992	4,704	4,934	3,723
Anti-White	716	812	829	811
Anti-Black	2,876	3,413	3,596	2,596
Anti-American Indian/Alaskan Native	54	59	63	61
Anti-Asian/Pacific Islander	137	162	170	140
Anti-Multiple Races, Group	209	258	276	115
Religion:	1,519	1,606	1,732	632
Anti-Jewish	1,013	1,055	1,145	353
Anti-Catholic	75	75	89	35
Anti-Protestant	56	60	62	34
Anti-Islamic	105	123	130	85
Anti-Other Religion	191	212	222	90
Anti-Multiple Religions, Group	65	67	70	33
Anti-Atheism/Agnosticism/etc.	14	14	14	2
Sexual Orientation:	1,297	1,617	1,706	1,460
Anti-Male Homosexual	776	948	981	921
Anti-Female Homosexual	154	194	198	156
Anti-Homosexual	307	415	466	336
Anti-Heterosexual	33	33	34	25
Anti-Bisexual	27	27	27	22
Ethnicity/National Origin:	894	1,148	1,226	1,034
Anti-Hispanic	561	735	792	711
Anti-Other Ethnicity/National Origin	333	413	434	323
Disability:	78	85	85	72
Anti-Physical	22	28	28	26
Anti-Mental	56	57	57	46
Multiple-Bias Incidents[3]	3	8	8	6

[1] The term *victim* may refer to a person, business, institution, or society as a whole
[2] The term *known offender* does not imply that the identity of the suspect is known, but only that an attribute of the suspect has been identified, which distinguishes him/her from an unknown offender
[3] In a *multiple-bias incident*, two conditions must be met (a) more than one offense type must occur in the incident and (b) at least two offense types must be motivated by different biases

Source: U.S. Department of Justice—Federal Bureau of Investigation November 2009 *Hate Crime Statistics, 2008*, http://www.fbi.gov/ucr/hc2008/data/table_01.html

These institutions consist of the police, the courts, and the prisons. In the United States, as in most societies, all three tend to be fraught with problems, so that only seldom is the intent of justice served.

The dilemma faced by a democratic society is how to protect the innocent, punish the guilty, and still respect each individual's rights. Preventing crime and effecting swift punishment of crime would be simpler if law enforcement could restrict people's movements, tap their phones, and search their homes at will. But in so doing, the freedom and privacy of many innocent people would be violated. To prevent such abuse, the writers of the U.S. Constitution provided a number of safeguards, such as allowing citizens the right to be presumed innocent until proved guilty, the right not to incriminate themselves, and other rights. Law enforcers are restricted in their ability to search homes and question suspects. Such procedures protect citizens, but they enfeeble the criminal justice system, which cannot act as decisively as it could in a repressive or totalitarian political system.

As a result of its perceived ineffectiveness, the criminal justice system is universally criticized by victims, on the grounds that it coddles criminals, and by the perpetrators, on the grounds that police treat suspects brutally, courts convict unjustly, and prisons are barbaric places.

Is the criticism justified? It is true that a large percentage of serious offenders are never apprehended. Large numbers of criminals are never punished, and, of those arrested, better than half manage to get off free because busy dockets force many charges to be dropped. The vast majority of those who are convicted receive reduced penalties as a result of plea bargaining, a procedure in which defendants agree to plead guilty to lesser charges. The result is that only about 5 percent of all perpetrators of serious crimes ever serve time, and of those, nearly 80 percent are released early on parole. White-collar criminals are seldom punished to the full extent of the law because their financial status allows them to hire the best legal advisers, who are able to manipulate the loopholes in the legal process to their advantage.

In the meantime, the cost of fighting crime is constantly increasing. In 2008, the latest year for which figures are available, the cost for police, prisons, and courts had risen to $185 billion, an increase by a large percentage from the previous decade. The increase is largely due to increases in prison inmate populations in state and federal prisons. The number of people in some form of correctional supervision jumped to over 7.2 million in 2009, up from 488,000 in 1985. The rise in inmate population was the result, at least partly, of decisions by the public and politicians to become more punitive. More offenders had been sentenced to prison terms and for longer periods of time. The punitive legislation was passed when state budgets were growing. Today, as states are facing deficits, it has become imperative to change punishment policies. After sharp increases in the 1980s and 1990s, the incarceration rate has grown at a slower pace and has declined slightly. The Bureau of Justice Statistics offers a comprehensive list of facts and statistical information relevant to types of crimes and imprisonment figures: Check out **www.ojp.usdoj.gov**, Key Facts At A Glance.

Among democratic nations, the United States has emerged as the nation with the highest imprisonment rate. Even with the slower rate of imprisonment, our prisons are bulging because we also jail more people for lesser crimes than do other Western industrial nations. The length of sentence is also high compared to terms of imprisonment in other nations: Murder in the United States may be punished by life imprisonment or execution; in Sweden, imprisonment is of much shorter duration, and the death penalty was abolished in the 1970s. Nonetheless, it appears that a lower rate of imprisonment, particularly for minorities, has occurred in the past couple of years. As noted, the Bureau of Justice Statistics offers a trove of information about the numbers, gender, minority status, and so on, on their Web site.

Box 2 Dropping Out of School: A Prescription for Jail

A Northeastern University study tracked census and government data to see the effect of dropping out of high school on young males. Not surprisingly, the effects are dramatic. One in 10 young male high school dropouts is in jail or juvenile detention, compared with 1 in 35 high school graduates. The effect is even worse for African-American males: their rate is 1 in 4 incarcerated or institutionalized, compared with 14 white, Asian, or Hispanic males.

The dropout rate—a high 6.2 million high school dropouts—seems to be driving the prison population upward, and that creates a drag on the economic competitiveness of the United States. The cost to the nation, according to the researchers in this study, is $292,000 over the working life of each high school dropout. This sum takes into account lost tax revenues—dropouts earn less and pay fewer taxes—as well as the cost of food stamps and other social aids for unemployed or incarcerated dropouts. The unemployment rates,

in fact, for dropouts are sky high: 54 percent of dropouts ages 16 to 24 were jobless in 2007, as opposed to 32 percent (also very high) for high school graduates of the same age. Because of the recession, it is certain that the rates have increased since 2008.

Female dropouts do not fare well either. They are nine times more likely to have become single mothers than high school graduates who go on to college. The high rate of out-of-wedlock children is also partly a result of male dropouts—because the latter are jobless and cannot afford to marry and provide a home.,

Finally, the changes in the American economy add to the difficulties of high school dropouts. Thirty years ago, a high school dropout could get a job in a steel plant or an auto plant and make a good enough living to provide for a family. Today, such jobs have vanished, leaving very little opportunities for individuals without skills (Dillon, 2009).

Recidivism

Neither the fact nor the length of imprisonment seems to deter crime. (Arrest seems to deter it, however. According to one study, arrested offenders are less likely to commit a crime at a future date than are offenders who are released by police without being arrested [Smith and Gartin 1989].) Prisons are termed "crime schools," where inmates learn how to be better criminals. Rates of recidivism—the repetition of criminal offenses—are high. Conversely, one of the reasons for a temporary decline in the crime rate has been attributed to an increase in incarceration.

A recent study, however, maintains that harsher prison conditions lead criminals to offend again. The study, which tracked almost a thousand inmates who had been released from federal prisons in 1987, found that those who were in a low-security lockup rather than in a minimum-security facility ended up back in prison twice as often as those in the easier form of imprisonment. Harsh prison conditions, in short, do not seem to deter offenders from breaking the law again (Chen, 2007). Again, the Bureau of Justice Statistics has information regarding rates of recidivism for various types of inmates.

What Price Punishment?

Critics of the American justice system maintain that we are spending too much money on a vast network of prisons, instead of spending it to solve the problems of the urban poor, which might prevent many from becoming criminals and consequently prisoners. Many states, for instance, spend $30,000 or more a year to house a prisoner, which does not include the cost of new prison construction. It seems logical to argue that if such amounts were spent on children from underprivileged backgrounds, many fewer homeless, parentless, and unsupervised children would drift into crime. In fact, the argument continues, prisons have become far better places for some individuals than the outside world is: Prisons provide housing that is often far superior to the tenements or homeless shelters where some inmates grew up. Inmates receive three meals a day; decent medical care, especially for victims of AIDS; drug and alcohol detoxification programs; remedial education; and job training. In addition, as inmates soon discover, many of their friends and relatives are in prison, too, so that they find themselves surrounded by a large social network on the inside.

Imprisonment is contemporary society's form of punishment. Punishment is thought to fulfill a number of functions in society: It is imposed for retribution, so presumably the offender suffers as the victim has suffered ("an eye for an eye"). It is used as a deterrent, in the hope of instilling fear of punishment in the offender. It is done for rehabilitation, under the assumption that if offenders see the damage they have done, they will not repeat their crimes. Finally, it offers societal protection, because imprisoned offenders are unable to commit crimes.

Whether imprisonment does what it is supposed to do is a hotly debated issue. Every society has wrestled with it, but none have resolved the problem, even with the help of the social sciences. Although punishment of a criminal makes the noncriminals in a society feel better—in the sense that it reaffirms the norms by which the society lives—imprisonment has seldom worked, either as a deterrent or as a form of rehabilitation. Even the societal protection function is temporary. Societies will have to continue to search for a solution in their political and economic systems, whose inequalities and competitiveness may impel some individuals to crime. And individuals may have to search within themselves for the causes of the dark side of the personality that allow them to harm others as well as themselves.

The Death Penalty

The ultimate punishment, of course is death. Through much of human history, death—by crucifixion, hanging, axing, guillotine, or firearms—was the accepted punishment for whatever infraction those in power considered punishable. Most Western societies have abolished the death penalty, but the United States reinstated it in 1976. Currently, 38 states have capital punishment and 12 do not. Whether to execute those accused of heinous crimes is a controversial subject, and the population at large is greatly divided. A Gallup poll in 2003 revealed that support for capital punishment was at its lowest level in 25 years; still, 64 percent supported it, and only 32 percent were against it. When respondents were given the sentencing option of life without parole, those in favor of the death penalty decreased to 53 percent, those who preferred life without parole totaled 44 percent, and 3 percent expressed no opinion. In 2006, the same poll found that two in three Americans favored the death penalty for convicted criminals: 67 percent were for it and 28 percent against it (Gallup Poll, May and October 2003 and October 2006).

The rationalization for keeping the death penalty is that it acts as a deterrent to crimes so heinous that life imprisonment is insufficient. However, criminologists have found that this is not a valid rationale. A survey of 67 heads of professional criminological organizations determined that 83 percent did not believe the death penalty was a deterrent, whereas only 11.9 percent thought that it was (Radelet & Akers, 1996). The professionals differ from the general public: 51 percent of respondents in a Gallup Poll in 1991 thought the death penalty was a deterrent, and 41 percent thought that it was not. It is important to observe, however, that in the last 20 years, the homicide rate in death-penalty states has been 48 percent to 101 percent higher than in non-death-penalty states (Bonner & Fassenden, 2000, A1).

Regardless of whether capital punishment is or is not a deterrent, the problem with imposing it is that frequently the wrong person is accused, indicted, and prosecuted for a crime, and if such a person is executed, that represents the ultimate injustice: killing an innocent. As it is, between 1973 and 1995, two-thirds of death penalty cases were overturned on appeal, because of incompetent counsel or information withheld by prosecutors or police or for other reasons.

In addition, improved DNA technology is able to prove the innocence of some inmates. Finally, it remains to be determined whether persons afflicted with mental illness or retardation or who are juveniles should be treated in the same way as those behaving in full consciousness of their actions. Figures 4 and 5 show the numbers on death row and the number of executions.

Prisoners on Death Row by Race

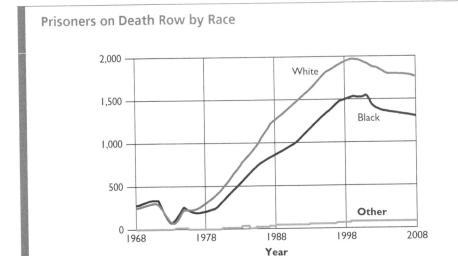

FIGURE 4
Source: *Capital Punishment, 2008—Statistical Tables,* http://bjs.ojp.usdoj.gov/content/glance/drrace.cfm

Executions

FIGURE 5
Source: *Capital Punishment, 2008—Statistical Tables,* http://bjs.ojp.usdoj.gov/content/glance/exe.cfm

The Chapter in Brief

Life in society requires a sufficient degree of order to allow peaceful coexistence. By performing the roles that go with their statuses and by obeying most of the norms of the society, individuals ensure that the social system works.

Norms and roles are learned through socialization, but the latter is never perfect, nor are informal controls adequate to maintain social order in large societies. Deviance refers to behavior or traits that conflict with significant social norms and expectations and are judged negatively by a large number of people. Deviance is relative to time and place, to who commits the deviant act, and even to who does the defining. Moreover, there are kinds and degrees of deviance.

Deviance performs some useful functions in society: it strengthens nondeviants' faith in the value of conforming to social norms; it contributes to social stability; and it often heralds positive social change. On the other hand, large-scale deviance is damaging to the social order, and when it goes unpunished, it tends to demoralize those who conform to social norms.

Explanations of why some people conform and others deviate from social norms have been offered by theorists from the perspectives of biology, psychology, and sociology.

Biological theories attribute deviance to certain physical traits or body types. Psychological theories attribute it to mental or physical disorders, whereas Freudians blame it on the imperfect development of the superego. Mental disorders include brain disorders or mental retardation, which are physical (organic) in origin but may become emotional disturbances. In addition, mental disorders may be psychosomatic (unrelated to a physical cause) or may consist of neuroses such as phobias, amnesia, obsessive-compulsive reaction, and dissociative reaction. A more severe kind of personality disorder consists of maladaptive behavior such as that exemplified by the sociopath (who engages in antisocial behavior without anxiety or remorse) or the sexual deviant. Finally, the most severe forms of mental illness are psychoses: schizophrenia, paranoia, bipolar disorder, and hallucinations.

Treatment of personality disorders and mental illness includes psychotherapy, behavior therapy, psychopharmacology, electroshock therapy, and hypnotherapy.

Sociological theories include the anomie theory (when there is a lack of balance in the social system and values are insecure, the individual responds with such deviance as innovation, ritualism, retreatism, or rebellion); the differential association (cultural transmission) theory (all behavior is learned in interaction with others in small, intimate primary groups); and labeling theory (which stresses the process by which individuals are labeled as deviant and their treatment as a result of that label). Labeling theory has a conflict perspective in that deviants are seen as victims as well as perpetrators. None of the theories can be accepted uncritically; all contribute to the explanation of deviance, but they do not explain its existence in absolute terms.

One form of deviance that is extremely damaging to individuals and society is crime. A crime is an action that has been defined by law as wrong because of its destructive nature. As such, it is prohibited to members of society, and those who disregard the prohibition are punished. The chief categories of crime are juvenile delinquency, social-order (victimless) crime, white-collar crime, organized crime, and crimes against person and property—the most threatening and frightening category. Statistics on crime are compiled annually by the FBI and published as the *Uniform Crime Reports*. The stress is on the eight index crimes consisting of murder, rape, robbery, aggravated assault, arson, burglary, larceny, and auto theft. These statistics reveal that those who commit crimes are largely under 21, males, urban residents, and African Americans, but because only the unsuccessful criminals are arrested and most crimes go unsolved, undetected, or unreported, these statistics cannot be considered totally valid.

The United States is one of the most punitive societies: The number of inmates in our prisons and jails is very high, and 38 states allow the death penalty. The crime rate has declined in recent years, but is inching upward again. The constantly increasing cost of maintaining prisons and jails, police, and courts may force legislators to pass more lenient imprisonment laws.

Terms to Remember

anomie   Durkheim's term for a condition of normlessness. Merton used anomie to explain deviance, which he thought occurred when cultural goals cannot be achieved through legal institutional means.

bipolar disorder   A psychosis characterized by extreme swings in emotion from deep depression to a high degree of excitement.

cultural transmission (or differential association)   Theory of deviance (Sutherland, Miller) based on the proposition that all human behavior, including deviant behavior, is learned through symbolic interaction, especially in primary groups.

deviance   Norm-violating behavior beyond the society's limits of tolerance.

differential association   See *cultural transmission*.

ectomorph   In Sheldon's typology (biological theory of deviance), a thin and delicate body type whose personality tends to be introspective, sensitive, nervous, and artistic.

electroconvulsive shock therapy   A treatment of severe mental disorders (particularly depression) through the application of severe electric shock. It is a painful procedure and is sometimes abused.

endomorph   In Sheldon's typology, a round and soft body type whose personality is social, easygoing, and self-indulgent.

index crimes   The eight crimes whose rates are reported annually by the FBI: murder, rape, robbery, aggravated assault, burglary, arson, larceny, and auto theft.

labeling   A sociological theory of deviance that explains deviant behavior as a reaction to the group's expectations of someone who has once been decreed as deviant.

mesomorph   In Sheldon's typology, a muscular and agile body type with a restless, energetic, and insensitive personality.

neurosis   A mild personality disorder; an inefficient, partly disruptive way of dealing with personal problems, but seldom troublesome enough to require institutionalization. Neuroses include amnesia, phobias, obsessive ideas or repetitive actions, and repression of thoughts or experiences.

paranoia   A psychosis characterized by the feeling of being persecuted or of being an important personage (delusions of grandeur).

personality disorders   Mental disorders that lie somewhere between the neuroses and the psychoses in severity. They include sociopathy, sexual deviance, and addiction.

psychosis   A serious mental disorder in which there is loss of contact with reality. Requires institutionalization when individuals become incapable of functioning in society. Psychoses include schizophrenia, paranoia, and bipolar disorder.

psychosomatic disorders   Physical ailments developed as a result of emotional tension or anxiety.

psychotherapy   A treatment for psychoses and mental disturbances that includes analysis, group therapy, family therapy, and others, centering around verbal exchanges.

schizophrenia   A label for a psychosis that varies in severity from inability to relate to others to total withdrawal from reality.

sociopath   A person suffering from a personality disturbance in which antisocial behavior does not elicit remorse.

Suggested Readings

Adler, Freda, and William S. Laufer, eds. 1994. *The Legacy of Anomie: Advances in Criminological Theory*. Vol. 6. New Brunswick, NJ: Transaction Books. A collection of essays focusing on the anomie theory, with its roots in the thought of Emile Durkheim and its development by Robert Merton, noting its continued importance in our attempts to understand deviance.

Arendt, Hannah. 2003. *Responsibility and Judgment*. New York: Schocken Books. An examination of ethical behavior under dictatorship, by the author best known for her notion that evil is banal, a notion she came to when examining the life and final days of Adolph Eichmann, a Nazi killer of hundreds, who turned out to be a dull bureaucrat.

Campbell, Anne. 1991. *The Girls in the Gang.* 2nd ed. Cambridge, MA: Basil Blackwell. What makes individuals, and especially females, join criminal gangs? This is the question pursued in this insightful account of young women in a New York street gang.

Cole, David. 1999. *No Equal Justice: Race and Class in the American Criminal Justice System.* New York: The New Press. A law professor writes about the role of race and social class in the arrest and conviction rates in the United States.

Currie, Elliott. 1998. *Crime and Punishment in America.* New York: Henry Holt. A sociologist discusses the increase in the prison population and offers policy alternatives for managing violence in the society.

Falk, Gerhard. 1990. *Murder: An Analysis of Its Forms, Conditions, and Causes.* Jefferson, NC: McFarland. An overview of violence in the United States, including discussions of public policy, social diversity, punishment, as well as the use of drugs, as these factors combine to result in our high murder rate.

Gonnerman, Jennifer. 2004. *Growing Up in the Visiting Room.* New York: Farrar, Straus & Giroux. The book traces the life in prison of a woman whose four children spend much of their childhood and young years with an imprisoned mother during visiting hours. By the time the woman is pardoned, her extended family has been effectively destroyed. The cycle repeats itself when her own children are imprisoned.

Reiman, Jeffrey. 2002. *The Rich Get Richer and the Poor Get Prison?* 7th ed. Needham Heights, MA: Allyn and Bacon. A conflict perspective on the criminal justice system, focusing on the racial and class inequalities that, according to the author, lie at the bottom of the problems created by crime in the United States.

The Great Divide: Ranking and Stratification

From Chapter 7 of *Contemporary Society: An Introduction to Social Science,* Thirteenth Edition. John A. Perry, Erna K. Perry. Copyright © 2012 by Pearson Education, Inc. All rights reserved.

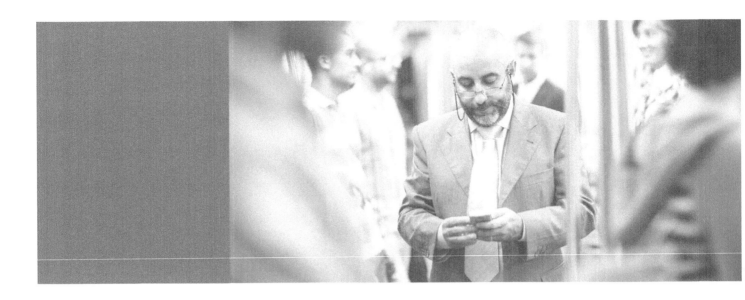

The Great Divide: Ranking and Stratification

IN THIS CHAPTER, YOU WILL LEARN THAT

- *people are differentiated by gender and age in all societies; in societies that produce a surplus they are also differentiated by the amount of wealth, prestige, and power they hold;*
- *the importance of such differentiation lies in the social meanings that are attached to it;*
- *ranking inherently results in inequality because it implies that some persons are superior to others because of the desirable attributes or commodities they possess;*
- *a stratified system results where scarce goods are distributed unequally;*
- *the theoretical explanations for inequality follow a conservative or liberal tradition;*
- *social scientists have developed several models of stratification systems;*
- *there are various ways of determining social class;*
- *the consequences of social class and the factors involved in social mobility affect human lives; and*
- *poverty seems to be a stubborn side effect of inequality.*

Governments proclaim that their citizens are all equal before the law. Religions stress that all people are "God's children." Scientists assert that all humankind is descended from a common stock. Humanitarians lobby for legislation to equalize the lifestyles of all members of society, while communist governments maintained—before their almost universal collapse—that they had already attained such equality. Philanthropists donate money for the same purpose—or to lessen their guilt for having so much more than others. In short, the idea that all humans are, or should be, equal is a frequent theme, at least in the cultures of Western societies. And yet, perhaps the very insistence on this theme reflects the reality that people are anything but equal.

We note that similar-looking babies in hospital nurseries are socialized into quite different adults. Not only appearance, but also differences in gender, age, skin color, manner of dress and speech, and many other attributes characterize individuals. These differences are easily visible. More important are the differences that affect people's lives dramatically, among which are the amounts of wealth, status, and power that individuals possess.

Differences are characteristic of all life forms. In human societies, however, the way the differences are interpreted is immensely important. That is, what counts are the *social meanings* people give both to chance biological facts and to cultural traits. These are judged as being either more or less desirable. Consequently, they are ranked, and ranking produces inequality. In other words, because some traits are valued more highly than others, people who lack those traits are not considered equal to those who have them. By the same token, because many resources are scarce and hard to obtain in most societies, those who have less of these scarce resources are considered unequal to those who have more of them.

Social Differentiation, Ranking, and Stratification

The physical world is full of examples of inequality. The fact that it is common knowledge that "the bigger fish eats the smaller fish" indicates that inequality is taken for granted in nature: Some individuals in each group have an advantage in the task of survival. Social scientists are not concerned with that type of inequality.

Of concern is the fact that all human societies practice *social differentiation*. People everywhere are categorized according to some trait (sex, age, race, ethnic background, religion) and according to how much of the scarce resources (wealth, power, prestige) they possess. Further, as noted earlier, people are ranked on the basis of having or lacking some of the listed attributes. Ranking involves a value judgment; in effect, the society establishes that it is better to be one thing than another, to have more of some things than less. Eventually, ranking results in stratification, a condition in which categories of people in a society are treated unequally.

All groups, human as well as animal, eventually develop a social hierarchy, or dominance order. The reason for this is to provide an orderly method of access to and distribution of resources. In a way, it is a method of preventing continuous fighting over scarce—and, therefore, especially desired—resources.

In simple societies, there is social differentiation based on sex and age. Sometimes, as a reward for special talents, some individuals or groups are given greater amounts of prestige, influence, and wealth. For example, nomadic hunting and gathering groups have very few possessions. At most, they have a few bows and arrows, primitive knives, and some utensils made of shells, animal skins, or animal organs. When the hunt is successful, every member of the tribe is given a fair share of the kill, and they all gorge themselves. When no animal has been killed, everyone goes hungry. Hoarding, especially of meat, is impossible because without methods of preserving it, meat spoils. As a result, no individual or family has an opportunity to accumulate more food than another. From an economic point of view, all members of such groups are equal, though they are differentiated according to sex and age: Men and women, young and old, have different statuses and perform different roles. In addition, the most talented hunters, those who exhibit special skills in magic, and the elderly, who have some knowledge resulting from experience, all have higher positions in the tribe. They are given more respect and honor; in effect, their words and decisions carry more weight than those of the lesser-endowed individuals. They may receive an extra ration of meat or drier shelter. Even in these simple societies, then, there is inequality in the sense that some individuals get more than others. However, the inequality is limited to single individuals, who are rewarded or punished for their own actions, and not to whole categories of people. This is an important distinction from the way inequality occurs in more complex societies.

Stratification

The more complex societies are, the more unequally they tend to distribute their scarce goods. The unequal distribution of scarce resources leads to **social stratification**, meaning that the society is divided into a number of strata, or layers. Stratified societies use a system of ranking according to

1. *Wealth,* or how much of the societal resources a person owns
2. *Prestige,* or the degree of honor a person's position in society evokes
3. *Power,* or the degree to which a person can direct others as a result of the preceding factors

Wealth, which includes *income* and *property,* is an element of *social class,* whereas *prestige* is an element of *status.* In turn, class, status, and power are the so-called *dimensions* of stratification. That is, stratification systems are analyzed by looking at each of these phenomena.

Stratification occurs in every society that has produced a surplus. A society that produces no surplus gives little opportunity to acquire wealth or prestige and the power based on them. Thus, stratification is intimately related to economics because the layering of people into social levels boils down to attempts to answer the question: Who gets what, and why? (That is, how shall the scarce resources in the society be distributed and for what reason?) Different societies answer these questions differently, according to their economic systems. Consequently, their stratification systems vary.

Theoretical Views on Stratification

Stratification systems essentially separate people into haves and have-nots. When attempting to analyze why stratification emerges, most social thinkers have concluded that some social inequality is inevitable. The *classical conservative* position is that inequality is part of the law of nature. It holds that people are basically selfish and greedy. Social institutions must curb this greed and selfishness or the society will not function smoothly. The curbing is done by institutions; however, institutions also promote inequality. Inequality is the price societies must pay to ensure peace and order. Later, the so-called social Darwinists proposed that because the resources of society were scarce and people had to compete for them, only the strongest, the most intelligent, or those most willing to work, would acquire most of the good things in life. This situation would result in inequality, but at the same time it would ensure that only the worthiest people in a society rose to positions of power and privilege. Ultimately, this would benefit society, for such people would provide enlightened leadership.

In the *classical liberal* view, humans are considered essentially good rather than selfish and greedy. It is society and its institutions that corrupt people because each individual or group must struggle for a share of the scarce goods and services that the society offers. The struggle becomes divisive and ends with the dominance of one group over others. The dominant group is able to exploit the others and, once in a position of power, to impose its will on the remainder of society. Inequality and stratification are then unavoidable.

Structural-Functionalist Perspective

The intellectual descendants of the conservative viewpoint are represented by the *structural-functionalist* school of thought in sociology. Functionalists stress the needs of the society rather than those of the individual, reasoning that the needs of individuals can be satisfied only within the society. The existence of every society depends on the regular performance of specific tasks that are difficult and require special intelligence, talent, and training. Societies must institute systems of rewards with which to lure the most talented, the most intelligent, and the best-trained individuals to perform these tasks. The positions most essential to the welfare of a society, and positions for which there are few qualified personnel, must be the ones that are most highly rewarded (Davis & Moore, 1945). It may be argued that collecting garbage is almost as vital to the health of a society as practicing medicine because uncollected garbage is a threat to public health, but collecting garbage requires little training or talent; therefore, many individuals are capable of performing this function. Practicing medicine, on the other hand,

© Bettmann/Corbis

Scenes like this were frequent in the major cities of the United States and Britain in the nineteenth and early twentieth centuries when capitalism reigned unobstructed. Moral repugnance at the extremes of wealth and poverty fueled the acceptance of more liberal ideas.

requires a long period of study and training. Not all individuals are capable of undergoing the discipline of such training; therefore, there are fewer potential doctors than potential garbage collectors, and consequently doctors should be much better rewarded.

In addition, functional theorists stress the need for order, stability, and balance in society. Even though it produces some social inequality, they maintain, a system of stratification has a stabilizing influence on society. It prevents conflicts from erupting and disrupting the orderly functioning of the society. (Structural-functionalism is also called the *equilibrium theory* because of its emphasis on harmony and balance.) Finally, functionalists conclude that inequality is built into the social system because not all types of work are equally necessary for, and thus valued by, the society.

Criticism of structural-functionalism centers around the facts that (1) what is an essential function is subject to interpretation (is a professional football player or an entertainer essential?) and (2) stratification systems prevent some talented people from developing their talents, while some untalented people receive rewards despite their limitations.

Conflict Perspective

The intellectual descendants of the classical liberal view are today's conflict theorists. They argue that inequality is the product of the conflicts and dissensions that originate in people's desire for power. The possession of scarce resources gives the possessor power. Groups struggle with one another to obtain power, and the group that emerges victorious tries to impose a stratification system on the society by enrolling some institutions—religion, education, the political system—to legitimize it. Thus, stratification systems are mechanisms of coercion.

The best-known conflict theorist was Karl Marx. He stated that all of history was a record of class struggles caused by the unequal distribution of rewards in societies. All societies are stratified, according to Marx, because in every society one group tries to protect its economic interests at the expense of other groups. Further, the institution of private ownership of the means of production leads to the modern division of societies into social classes. These classes are in conflict with one another because the owners (*bourgeoisie*) have, and want to keep, a monopoly of power over the nonowners (*proletariat*). The owners obtain and maintain power both by force and by instilling a value system and ideology in the masses that legitimize their power. Once they are in control and with a system of stratification in operation, the system is perpetuated through various institutions. The family transmits either wealth, opportunity for education, and prestige, or poverty and lack of opportunity, from one generation to another. Schools, too, prepare some individuals for leadership roles and others for menial occupations. Religions help people accept values that justify the status quo and encourage the poor to seek their reward in an afterlife, or direct the faithful toward a spiritual quest, offering solace from pain.

A criticism of **conflict theory of stratification,** and of Marxism in particular, is that it neglects to address two important issues: first, that people are naturally unequal in the amount of talent and intelligence they have and the amount of work they are willing to do; and second, that to a great extent the existence of inequality is a motivating force for people. The more hard-working, talented, and intelligent people will tend to rise to the top in any economic system, and the existence of inequality will motivate people to try to get to the top.

The functionalist and the conflict theories of stratification are not mutually exclusive. There is evidence that societies exhibit stability and consensus as well as conflict and dissension. The two theories suggest two different ways of looking at stratification systems of societies, but they do not offer definitive answers about the causes of stratification, nor do they provide methods for doing away with inequality.

Dimensions of Stratification: Class, Status, and Power

The basis of all stratification systems, as was noted, is ranking of people according to their possession of things that are scarce and, therefore, highly prized. These scarce resources are popularly categorized as wealth, prestige, and power, or, in more sociological terms, *class*, *status*, and *power*. It is according to these dimensions that people are assigned a rank in society and relegated to a stratum with others who are ranked similarly.

Class

Although discussions of social class figure prominently in the media and the term is commonly used in conversation, most people would have difficulty defining the term with accuracy. Americans, in fact, have an especially mistaken conception of social class: They volunteer the information that most of them belong to the middle class, and they appear only slightly aware of the vast differences in lifestyles of different groups of people.

Definitions of Class: Marx and Weber. As noted earlier, Karl Marx viewed the division of society into classes as determined by the relationship of a group in society to the *means of production*. Groups that own a large proportion of the society's wealth—particularly the tools and capital necessary to produce that wealth—have control over groups that own little of either. The groups lacking capital must sell their labor to survive. Thus, Marx's approach to stratification and his concept of class are essentially *economic* in nature.

Arguing that the Marxist view was too simplistic and that class was only one dimension of stratification, the early sociologist Max Weber (1864–1920) proposed a threefold approach to the phenomenon and added the concept of life chances to his definition of class (Gerth & Mills, 1946). Weber defined class objectively as consisting of groups of people who had similar lifestyles dictated by their economic position in society, that is, by the goods they possessed and their opportunities for increasing their income. Modern social scientists refer to money, goods, and services as *property*.

Life Chances. Property is not the only determinant of class, according to Weber: equally important are a person's life chances. **Life chances**, in Weber's view, are the opportunities that each individual has of fulfilling his or her potential in life. A person's life chances are determined by his or her position within the stratification system. The higher that position is, the more access there is to scarce resources and thus the more positive are the life chances of the individual. The lower the position, the less access there is to scarce resources and the more negative are the life chances.

Today, the Weberian concept of class tends to predominate. **Social class** is defined as "an aggregation of persons in a society who stand in a similar position with respect to some form of power, privilege, or prestige" (Lenski, 1966, 74–75). In other words, some people, because of a similarity in occupations, income, education, and lifestyles, set themselves apart from the rest of the population. In time, they become sufficiently differentiated from others and unified—sometimes unknowingly—among themselves to constitute a separate social level or stratum—a social class.

Status

Status is the degree of social esteem that an individual or group enjoys in society. In the Weberian sense, status means prestige rather than simply a position within the social system. The most important element of status is that it is a ranked position—high, middle, low—determined

Peter Hvizdak/The Image Works

The notion of life chances is exemplified by students who attend private secondary schools. The structure, discipline, and the superior education they provide—as well as the network of friendships they encourage—lead almost universally to occupations that ensure entrance into the upper classes.

by how the role attached to the status is valued. For instance, because the role of physician, particularly that of a specialist in a difficult field, is highly valued in our society, that position has a high status in the United States.

There is frequently overlap between class and status, but the overlap does not always, or necessarily, occur. Some people may have high incomes and lack status; conversely, some may have high status and lack a substantial income. Status is very important to most people, and the desire to obtain high status is learned as part of socialization. The concern for status "influences almost every kind of decision, from the choice of a car to the choice of a spouse. Fear of the loss of status, or honor, is one of the few motives that can make men lay down their lives on the field of battle" (Lenski, 1966, 37–38).

Most people are quite adept at judging each other's status. In the United States, status tends to depend primarily on occupation (achieved status is more frequent than ascribed status). The reason is that occupations are good indicators of income and particularly of education. In all surveys where respondents have been asked to rank a variety of occupations, the occupations requiring graduate-school training have been ranked highest. Although high-ranking occupations generally carry with them high incomes, this is not always the case: It is true for specialized physicians, some attorneys, and many corporate executives, but it is not true for college professors and research scientists.

Additional determinants of status are being born into a highly respected family ("old money"), living in the "right" kind of neighborhood, attending private preparatory schools and Ivy League universities, belonging to exclusive country clubs, and being members of the "right" church denominations. The factors that influence **social status**, then, include occupation and source of income, race, education, sex, age, religion, and ethnic origin.

Status Inconsistency. One would be justified in assuming that characteristics directly opposed to those associated with high social status indicate low status. However, in studying industrial societies, sociologists have become aware of the phenomenon of *status inconsistency*. A person may have amassed immense wealth, but if it is derived from organized crime and the person lacks the education and most of the other traits of high status, that person is status inconsistent. Conversely, a person may lack any visible means of support because of having gambled away the family fortune but may retain a high status because of the past glory attached to the family name.

Findings that people are subject to status inconsistency have led to theories speculating that such people will tend to suffer more frustration and dissatisfaction than those whose status is consistent (Lenski, 1966). Persons who are ranked higher on one variable of status than another—women doctors, for instance, or minority baseball stars—try to stress the higher-ranked variable and deemphasize the lower-ranked. Unfortunately, others will judge them by their *master status*, which is the status that society considers the most important of several alternatives. The woman doctor will be seen as a woman first and may be mistaken for a nurse. The athlete who has made it to star status may be admired for his athletic prowess and his high income, but he may be ignored by some people as a guest or friend. People who suffer from status inconsistency, particularly those who are denied *high* status, take out their frustrations by turning away from upper-status groups, at least in terms of political action or philosophy (Cohn, 1958; G. Marx, 1967).

Power

The third important dimension of stratification—some consider it the most important dimension—is power. **Power** is defined as the ability to carry out one's wishes despite resistance. It is the ability to get other people to do what one wants them to do, with or without their consent. Stratification based on power is, in Weber's view, essentially political rather than economic. In fact, Weber used the term *political class* or *party* to mean an elite, a group that is more powerful than other groups in society. Power is exercised in all social systems, from the simplest to the most complex.

As applied to stratification, power can be divided into personal power and social power. *Personal power* is the freedom of individuals to direct their own lives in a way they themselves choose, without much interference. Such freedom often goes with great wealth. *Social power* is the ability to make decisions that affect entire communities or even the whole society. Social power may be exercised legitimately, with the consent of the members of society. In this case, it is called **authority**. Parents, teachers, and the government all represent different levels of authority. Social power may also be exercised illegitimately, that is, without the official approval of society. Organized crime, for instance, exercises power illegitimately.

Power is such an important dimension of stratification because it affects the manner in which society's goods and services are distributed. It is deeply interwoven with the other dimensions, class and status. High-status individuals have little trouble attaining positions of power, either in government, the professions, or corporate and banking circles. In turn, those in positions of power can control decision making in such a way that events are favorable to them. In traditional, nonindustrial societies, power is often held by a small elite, whereas the majority of people are relatively powerless. In industrial societies, however, power is spread among many people, largely as a result of universal suffrage and the generally better living standard of the majority of the population. The dominance of power in the post-Communist Chinese society is discussed on a Web site mentioned on **mysearchlab.com.**

Box 1 Class, Status, and Power in America

If we compared the income of ordinary Americans to the income of some Americans, we would see great disparities. For instance, compare your net worth or salary or that of your family to that of some CEOs and celebrities, as reported by *Forbes* magazine for the year 2010:

1. Bill Gates, CEO of Microsoft Corporation: net worth $54 billion
2. Warren Buffet, stock market investor: net worth $45 billion
3. Lawrence Ellison, CEO of Oracle Corporation: net worth $27 billion
4. Christy Walton, one of the inheritors of the Walmart fortune: $24 billion
5. Charles Koch, source of wealth in manufacturing, energy, and inheritance: $21.5 billion

There are more than 40 pages of billionaires. Among celebrities, most of whom are mere millionaires:

1. Oprah Winfrey, $315 million
2. Beyonce Knowles, $87 million
3. James Cameron, $210
4. Lady Gaga, $62
5. Tiger Woods, $105 million

In which social class would you place each of these persons? Why? Are any of them status inconsistent? Do they possess power? Social or political? Are the two connected? Moreover, it is self-evident that the income of the celebrities and of the heads of corporations is vastly greater than the income of the majority of Americans. Is this right? Do these celebrities deserve to earn so much more than you and your family? Do they improve society's quality of life? Do they affect your life personally? Would you be any worse off if they did not exist?

The functionalist theorists would answer that yes, these people deserve their high incomes because they have special talents, and we reward them because they entertain us or they provide us with products we need or want. The conflict theorists would assert that such an unequal distribution of resources is patently unjust and that the high-income celebrities and CEOs are a part of a social class in a stratification system that is dangerous because it is immensely helpful in exercising stock options. Even some rank-and-file workers in technology companies have earned enough to enable them to join the affluent. By abolishing taxes on many stock dividends and capital gains, in addition to other benefits for the affluent such as eliminating the estate tax, the gap becomes larger still.

One would expect that the increasing inequality among social classes would lead to political instability and protest movements. This has not occurred in the United States, and according to one economics commentator, it will not occur because Americans care less about inequality than about opportunity. Obviously, there has been opportunity in the society, as the many newly minted multimillionaires can attest. To support this claim, the author reports on a study by Harvard University and the London School of Economics that measured personal happiness from the mid-1970s to the mid-1990s, a period of rising inequality in both the United States and Europe. The study revealed that Americans considered themselves "pretty happy" to "very happy" in much higher proportions than Europeans (economic inequality is higher in European countries to begin with, and increased even more in that period, but European governments have tried much harder to reduce it). The researchers concluded that the United States is a more mobile society than the societies of Europe, and there are more opportunities to move up or down the stratification ladder. Therefore, "Americans don't get so upset by rising inequality because they don't feel it dooms them," whereas Europeans are much more fatalistic about their place on the economic ladder (Samuelson, 2001, 45).

Systems of Stratification

Historically, societies have exhibited a variety of stratification systems. A **stratification system** is the overlapping manner in which societal members are ranked into classes, status groups, and hierarchies of power. To distinguish among them, social scientists use models, abstract conceptions that they place on an ideal continuum. At one extreme of the continuum is the closed, or caste, stratification system. The middle is represented by the estate system. At the other extreme is the open, or class, system. The stratification system of each society fits somewhere along this ideal continuum.

The Closed Society: Caste

Whether a society has an open or a closed stratification system is determined by the way its members obtain wealth, prestige, and privilege (the Weberian class, status, and power). In a **closed, or caste, stratification system,** class, status, and power are ascribed, that is, determined strictly on the basis of family inheritance rather than on individual effort or merit. In a closed society, the individual is born into a specific social stratum, called a *caste,* and has no opportunity to move in or out of it.

Classical India offers a good example of a closed society. The caste system that flourished in India for many centuries was distinguished by the fact that people were divided into a number of castes, representing areas of service to society and ranked in order of their importance to it. Some ranking also resulted from struggles for power or conquest by other groups. Religion and tradition forbade members of one caste to intermarry or interact in any way with members of other castes. Each caste was restricted in occupation, and the status of each individual was ascribed, so that a person inherited a specific social position and was unable to change it, regardless of effort or achievement. (Only a limited number of people, particularly if they exhibited extraordinary military prowess, were able to attain a higher caste, although disobeying certain norms could plunge a person into a lower one.) The caste system has been legally abolished in modern India, which has been deeply influenced by Western democratic thought, but many Indians, particularly those living in rural areas, still follow some elements of the caste system that for so long had been justified by religion and traditional mores. A discussion of the lingering remains of the caste system may be found on the Internet.

The Estate System

The estate system was the economic and social system of feudal Europe and, in different forms, has characterized a number of nations in Asia. As in the caste system, in the **estate system of stratification,** social positions were also ranked according to their functions; however, in theory, all the estates were considered to be equal in importance. The three main estates were the nobility, the church, and the peasants, and within each estate there was a stratified hierarchy of positions.

Supported by religion and tradition, the estate system permitted quite a bit more mobility among social strata than did the caste system. Because only eldest sons could inherit the title and possessions of a noble family, the remaining sons had to enter either the military or the clergy. Occasionally, serfs who had distinguished themselves were freed and given land, and some peasants were allowed to enter the lower ranks of the priesthood.

The remnants of the estate system are still visible in some modern societies that retain a landed gentry and inherited titles of nobility. Also, some elements of the system may be recognized as having existed on the plantations of the American South a century ago, although slavery falls more within the caste spectrum on the continuum. As noted, the estate system was the dominant stratification system in Europe in the Middle Ages; it is also referred to as feudalism.

The Open Society: Class System

Modern industrial and postindustrial societies such as the United States most nearly approximate the model of an open society. **Open, or class, societies** have these characteristics in common: (1) classes exist but are not institutionalized as in the caste and estate systems; (2) class lines are unclear, so people do not display excessive class consciousness, but inequality stemming from class divisions is apparent; (3) status is usually achieved, but there is evidence to indicate that status tends to be ascribed to the lowest and the highest social classes; (4) social mobility is possible and occurs frequently.

Open, or class, systems work best in industrial societies that have market economies because these offer more opportunities for achieving wealth and status than do societies with centralized economies. In government-controlled economies, people may not have the opportunity to choose their jobs and maximize advantages.

Social mobility—essentially, changing class membership—is possible and encouraged in open systems; however, it is not evenly distributed in the society. Limitations based on racial, ethnic, regional, educational, and even religious factors restrict mobility. However, the individual is still permitted much more leeway for social as well as physical movement than in closed systems.

Class systems in all societies have certain characteristics in common. The rise of social classes is almost always accompanied by the development of central political institutions, foremost among which is the state. Even the so-called classless societies that espoused a communist or socialist ideology—all of which had strong states before their downfall—also had a class system. Moreover, the more surplus a society produces, the more stratified it is and the more complex its class system is. Even though in technologically advanced societies the large surplus that is produced filters down to all social classes and starvation-level poverty exists to only a very small extent, class inequalities remain flagrant. Finally, power and wealth appear to be the most important elements of class systems, with prestige playing a less important role.

In contemporary industrial societies, power and wealth are closely interconnected in both capitalist and socialist economies. In capitalist countries, the wealthy are more likely to come to power, and in socialist nations the powerful are likely to become wealthy. However, the stratification systems of both kinds of economies are strikingly similar. Societies that have a long tradition of feudal-like stratification, although they have become open in the industrial era, retain strong class boundaries.

Determining Social Class: Occupational Prestige and Socioeconomic Status

Social scientists disagree not only about the number of social classes in existence but also about the standards that determine who belongs in which class. The categories used by researchers to pigeonhole people into social classes are arbitrary and artificial.

Historically, a number of approaches have been used to determine social class. Today, however, most researchers use one of two. In the *occupational prestige* approach, researchers ask people which occupations and sources of income are the most prestigious. This approach depends on a large sample, usually on a national scale. The occupational prestige approach has proved to be the best index of social class in the United States because of its practicality. Occupation determines the amount of money that is earned, which in turn determines, in many cases, the amount of power wielded and the prestige held. But money alone does not determine social class. Some occupations are rated very high even though the monetary rewards are relatively low, and vice versa.

A more common methodological device is based on an index that combines a number of dimensions relevant to stratification. One such index measures socioeconomic status (SES). Such an index shows at a glance the position of individuals in the social and economic pecking order. The development of such an index is possible despite instances of status inconsistency because of the related nature of the dimensions of stratification in American society.

Social Classes in the United States

As noted earlier in the chapter, people are not generally aware of social classes in the United States. That is, they are not class conscious in the Marxian sense of working for the self-interest of their class, and they tend to characterize themselves as belonging to the "middle class." In fact, social classes are very fluid in our society, first, because we lack a traditional landed aristocracy, and second, because social mobility allows people to change social class. Still, there is no question that people live different lives according to their social class; and so, despite the difficulty of assigning people to specific classes according to a rigid system, some descriptive technique is necessary.

There are a large number of models of class structure, beginning with the Marxist model, which divided people into the bourgeoisie (owners of the means of production) and the proletariat (workers). Usually, however, the American class structure is divided into five or six layers, consisting (more or less) of the following percentages: upper-upper, 1.4 percent; lower-upper, 1.6 percent; upper-middle, 10 percent; lower-middle, 28 percent; upper-lower, 34 percent; and lower-lower, 25 percent. The population may also be divided into quintiles, or fifths, as the Census Bureau does (Table 1).

The Upper Classes

The upper-upper class consists almost exclusively of people who belong to it as a result of ascribed status, that is, inherited, "old" wealth. Possessing vast fortunes accumulated through several generations, and added to through shrewd investments, this group lives an exclusive lifestyle few Americans can even imagine. Members of this social class generally reside in elite neighborhoods, in mansions often filled with first-rate art, in addition to owning additional vacation homes here and abroad; they send their children to private preparatory schools (which they themselves also attended) and Ivy League universities, where they pursue liberal arts degrees rather than specifically vocational courses of study. Conscious of their privileged situation, most engage in philanthropic endeavors, volunteering time and donating money to hospitals, charitable and artistic organizations, and other "worthy" causes. In this way they establish themselves as the "elite" of the cities in which they live. Eventually they come to know members of the political establishment, from governors to members of Congress, from Supreme Court justices to the president of the United States. Needless to say, such acquaintances add not only prestige but also power.

The lower-uppers, often disposing of similar or even greater income, differ in that the income tends to have been earned. These are mostly "self-made" individuals, whether their current wealth comes from talents—sports, show business, television, movies or from shrewd business transactions. Some may have inherited some wealth or have received a fine education, whereas others may come from very modest backgrounds. A perfect example is Bill Gates, the son of professional and well-to-do parents, a self-described "technie nerd" who purveyed an interest in computers into the Microsoft Corporation, a company that has made its founder a multibillionaire.

TABLE 1   Income Limits for Each Fifth and Top 5 Percent of All Households: 1990–2008 (Households as of March of the following year. Income in current and 2008 CPI-U-RS adjusted dollars [29])

Year	Number (thousands)	Upper limit of each fifth (dollars)				Lower limit of top 5 percent
		Lowest	Second	Third	Fourth	
CURRENT DOLLARS						
2000 (30)	108,209	17,920	33,000	52,174	81,766	145,220
1999 (29)	106,434	17,136	31,920	50,384	79,232	142,000
1998	103,874	16,116	30,408	48,337	75,000	132,199
1997	102,528	15,400	29,200	46,000	71,500	126,550
1996	101,018	14,768	27,760	44,006	68,015	119,540
1995 (25)	99,627	14,400	26,914	42,002	65,124	113,000
1994 (24)	98,990	13,426	25,200	40,100	62,841	109,821
1993 (23)	97,107	12,967	24,679	38,793	60,300	104,639
1992 (22)	96,426	12,600	24,140	37,900	58,007	99,020
1991	95,669	12,591	24,000	37,070	56,759	96,400
1990	94,312	12,500	23,662	36,200	55,205	94,748

Source: http://www.census.gov/hhes/www/income/data/historical/inequality/h02AR.xls

These two groups receive a lion's share of the income produced in the United States. For instance, in 2008, of all American households (divided into fifths, or quintiles, meaning that each fifth is equivalent to 20 percent), the highest fifth received 50.0 percent of the aggregate income of the United States; the next fifth received 23.3 percent; the middle fifth received 14.7 percent; the second to the lowest fifth received 8.6 percent; and the lowest fifth received 3.4 percent. To put it in perspective, the lowest quintile had incomes of $20,712 or less, the second lowest quintile had incomes of $20,713 to $39,000, the third quintile had incomes of $39,001 to $62,725, the fourth quintile had incomes of $62,726 to $100,240, and the highest quintile had incomes of $100,241 or more. As for the top 5 percent, they received 20.9 percent (U.S. Bureau of the Census, 2008). (A distinction should be made between income, which is earned yearly, and wealth, which includes all of an individuals's accumulated possessions. Although there is considerable inequality in incomes, the inequality in wealth is still more dramatic: In 2007, the top 1 percent held nearly $3.3 trillion more wealth than the entire bottom 90 percent, according to the Federal Reserve Survey of Consumer Finances data. However, even these figures do not reflect the reality of the wealth of America's richest families because they do not include the *Forbes* magazine list of the 400 richest Americans. These 400 held over $1.5 trillion in wealth, or 2 percent of the nation's total wealth.)

Although the income of the lower-uppers is often astronomical—some CEOs and TV and movie personalities earn as much in a day as the average American worker does in a year and sometimes in a lifetime—they are still disdained by the upper-uppers as the "new rich," who find it necessary to engage in conspicuous consumption to show the world they have "arrived." The upper-uppers, on the other hand, do not have to prove anything to anyone, having always lived in privilege. Therefore, they tend to be much more discreet and understated in their lifestyles. It is the lower-uppers, however, who are taken as role models by most Americans because it is their kind of success stories that make up the "American dream" and are a popular cultural goal.

The Middle Class

Between one-half and three-quarters of the American population fits into the middle class (and many more think they are middle class when they actually are not). The Congressional Research Service pegs middle-class incomes at between $19,000 and $91,000—a rather wide range—while the Brookings Institution bases its estimates on the median household income, ranging between $24,000 to $96,000. This category, then, must also be subdivided into an upper-middle, middle-middle, and lower-middle classification. In addition, because it includes such a wide spectrum of Americans, it is difficult to specify boundaries between these subdivisions.

In general, it may be said that the upper-middle class consists of highly educated professionals—doctors, lawyers, stockbrokers, accountants, and so on—and owners of family businesses. Such persons tend to make comfortable incomes, live mostly in the suburbs, actively participate in community affairs, try to expose their children to enriching experiences, and attempt to give them a good education. The group also includes young urban professionals, so-called yuppies, who are better educated than their parents and, being single or recently married, prefer to live within the city limits to take advantage of cultural and recreational opportunities. Their yearly income varies from around $150,000 and up (slightly lower in small cities and rural areas), and their assets are thought to be between $368,000 and $5 million. They represent approximately 17 percent of the population.

The middle-middle class (and the lower-middle, depending on income) consists of small shop owners; the lesser professionals, such as public school teachers; and a variety of white-collar employees, from sales clerks to bank tellers, from nurses to office workers, and so on. Their incomes are lower than those of the upper-middle class, and families usually depend on more than one paycheck.

Judging from polls, most people believe they are upper-middle or middle class: in 2008, 53 percent said so, whereas only 6 percent put themselves in the lower class, and 2 percent put themselves in the upper class (**http://pewsocialtrends.org/assets/pdf/MC-Middle-class-report.pdf**). The household earnings necessary to live as a middle class, according to those who define themselves as middle class, were around $52,285. (The Pew poll on the middle class is very interesting and can be found at **http://pewsocialtrends.org/pubs/706/middle-classpoll**. It is titled "Inside the Middle Class: Bad Times Hit the Good Life.")

The middle class has been stereotyped, ever since it appeared following the Industrial Revolution in Europe, as consisting of people with a narrow range of ideas who follow conforming lifestyles. In the United States, they were thought to inhabit the suburbs, where they lived in identical houses with two-car garages, and the husband commuted to work while the wife chauffeured the children to a variety of activities. They were thought to be family centered on the surface and conventionally religious. When sociologists began to investigate the suburbs with empirical studies, however, they found that they contained a wide variety of people with differing values and economic realities. In short, it is still difficult to define who, exactly, is "middle class," but we know that because this social class is so large and diverse, it is also very influential as a cultural symbol.

In the last decade, both in the United States and in other industrial nations, we have seen the emergence and coming to the fore of a professional middle class whose power derives from the members' high level of education, their reasonably high incomes, and their overlapping social and family ties to the high and middle levels of the business community. This class, sometimes termed the "New Class," is especially important because it tends to generate most of the ideas that eventually find their way into the cultural mainstream (Ehrenreich, 1989, 6). This professional middle class consists of journalists, academics, writers, and media commentators—in other words, persons in possession of skills important in an information society.

The Working Class

The working class comprises approximately one-third of the population and may include members of the lower-middle class. It consists of people who work in skilled or semiskilled occupations, such as craftsmen, foremen, lower-level managers, nonretail sales representatives (representing around 30 percent of the population), or unskilled blue-collar occupations, such as retail sales, service workers, and low-paid manual workers (representing about 13 percent of the population). The incomes of such workers range between $25,000 and $35,000 a year (up to $50,000 in large cities) and generally fall below those of the middle classes. Some "pink collar" workers—secretaries, office workers, sales clerks, restaurant workers—who earn modest weekly wages can also be counted as members of the working class, although many of them prefer to think of themselves as middle class. Table 2 shows the percentage distribution of incomes.

The working class is undergoing dramatic changes in the United States as a result of globalization and the shift of manufacturing to countries where labor is cheaper. But even in more stable times, this social class has always been subject to layoffs and temporary employment, so that working people's financial situation has always been precarious. With a household income often derived from minimum wage jobs, two or more people must work. Despite a periodically booming economy, most young working-class families cannot afford to buy a house, even though their parents were able to buy one years ago in a modest neighborhood. In addition to economic problems, working-class people also tend to have jobs that are menial, repetitive, and unchallenging, so that they obtain little satisfaction in performing them. Most working-class children cannot afford college—although

TABLE 2 Share of Aggregate Income Received by Each Fifth and Top 5 Percent of Households, All Races: 1990–2008
(Households as of March of the following year)

Year	Number (thousands)	Shares of aggregate income					
		Lowest fifth	Second fifth	Third fifth	Fourth fifth	Highest fifth	Top 5 percent
2000 (30)	108,209	3.6	8.9	14.8	23.0	49.8	22.1
1999 (29)	106,434	3.6	8.9	14.9	23.2	49.4	21.5
1998	103,874	3.6	9.0	15.0	23.2	49.2	21.4
1997	102,528	3.6	8.9	15.0	23.2	49.4	21.7
1996	101,018	3.6	9.0	15.1	23.3	49.0	21.4
1995 (25)	99,627	3.7	9.1	15.2	23.3	48.7	21.0
1994 (24)	98,990	3.6	8.9	15.0	23.4	49.1	21.2
1993 (23)	97,107	3.6	9.0	15.1	23.5	48.9	21.0
1992 (22)	96,426	3.8	9.4	15.8	24.2	46.9	18.6
1991	95,669	3.8	9.6	15.9	24.2	46.5	18.1
1990	94,312	3.8	9.6	15.9	24.0	46.6	18.5
1980	82,368	4.2	10.2	16.8	24.7	44.1	16.5

Source: http://www.census.gov/hhes/www/income/data/historical/inequality/h02AR.xls

approximately one-third of this group do manage to obtain a college degree—and so are forced into jobs immediately after high school. Of course, lacking skills, the jobs that are available to them are few and low paying.

This social class is diverse in its ethnic and racial composition, but proximity has not resulted in solidarity. Rather, the various ethnic and racial groups see one another as competing for jobs, especially in transitional times such as we are experiencing now, when many manufacturing jobs are disappearing and heavy industry is using robots and computers instead of human brawn.

The Poor

The U.S. government defines *poverty* as the level of income at which a person is incapable of providing such basics as food, clothing, and shelter. The Census Bureau listed 14.3 percent of Americans, representing approximately 43.6 million people, as living below the poverty line in 2009 (Table 2). This was the highest poverty rate since 1994. The rate increased for non-Hispanic Whites from 8.6 percent to 9.4 percent, for blacks from 24.7 percent to 25.8 percent, and for Hispanics from 23.2 percent to 25.3 percent between 2008 and 2009. The rate also increased for children under 18 years of age, from 19 percent to 20.7 percent and for people aged 18 to 64 from 11.7 percent to 12.9 percent, but it decreased for people aged 65 and older from 9.7 percent to 8.9 percent in the same time frame (U.S. Census Bureau, Poverty, Last Revised September 16, 2010; see also Table 3).

The measurement of poverty was instituted in 1964. It called for establishing a range of income levels according to factors such as family size, sex and age of the family head, number of children under 18, and urban or farm residence. Every year, revisions of price levels are based on changes in the consumer price index. Records show that the poverty rate varied between 11.1 percent and 14.2 percent from 1967 to 1981. It then peaked at 15.2 percent in 1983, declined to 12.8 percent in 1989, and rose each year after 1989 until the decline beginning in the mid-1990s. An alternative method of reporting poverty shows even higher figures because the earlier manner of measurement did not factor in rising medical care, transportation, child care, or geographical variation in living costs. Under the rubric "Poverty," the U.S. bureau of the Census has a multitude of information about poverty in the United States.

The recession that hit the United States in the first four years of the new century pushed the poverty rate upward again, and the economic meltdown of the 2007–2010 period pushed it even higher. Table 4 shows the numbers and percentages of people and families in poverty in 2008 according to various characteristics.

Poverty in this society is the condition of having less income than the average person; thus, we are not dealing with *absolute deprivation*, or not having enough income to provide the barest necessities for survival. We are dealing with *relative deprivation*, a condition in which people are deprived in comparison to others in their society at a particular time and place. From that point of view, some commentators have maintained that the poor in the United States have actually made progress in the last three decades, judging from their consumption spending and use of major modern household conveniences.

Poverty occurs more frequently among some groups than others. It is chronic, for instance, in families with a female householder in which no husband is present. This phenomenon is referred to as the *feminization of poverty*. As a result of the increase in illegitimate births and greater rates of dissolution of marital and nonmarital unions, single parenthood is no longer rare. Since the mid-1980s, the poverty growth rate for children under 6 years of age has been several percentage points higher than that of any other age group and much higher than the overall poverty rate. In 2008, for instance, the poverty rate for related children under 6 was

TABLE 3   Mean Household Income Received by Each Fifth and Top 5 Percent, All Races: 1990–2008
(Households as of March of the following year. Income in current and 2008 CPI-U-RS adjusted dollars [29])

Year	Lowest fifth	Second fifth	Third fifth	Fourth fifth	Highest fifth	Top 5 percent
Current Dollars						
2008	11,656	29,517	50,132	79,760	171,057	294,709
2007	11,551	29,442	49,968	79,111	167,971	287,191
2006	11,352	28,777	48,223	76,329	168,170	297,405
2005	10,655	27,357	46,301	72,825	159,583	281,155
2004 (35)	10,244	26,212	44,411	70,026	151,438	263,896
2003	9,996	25,678	43,588	68,994	147,078	253,239
2002	9,990	25,400	42,802	67,326	143,743	251,010
2001	10,136	25,468	42,629	66,839	145,970	260,464
2000 (30)	10,157	25,361	42,233	65,653	142,269	252,400
1999 (29)	9,915	24,345	40,750	63,423	135,250	235,077
1998	9,223	23,288	38,967	60,266	127,529	222,283
1997	8,839	22,098	37,177	57,582	122,764	215,436
1996	8,595	21,097	35,486	54,922	115,514	201,220
1995 (25)	8,345	20,397	34,106	52,429	109,411	188,828
1994 (24)	7,714	19,224	32,385	50,395	105,945	183,044
1993 (23)	7,359	18,656	31,272	48,599	101,253	173,784
1992 (22)	7,256	18,181	30,631	47,021	91,110	144,608
1991	7,226	18,150	30,148	45,957	88,127	137,530
1990	7,166	18,030	29,781	44,901	87,137	138,756

Source: http://www.census.gov/hhes/www/income/data/historical/inequality/h03AR.xls

21.3 percent, or 5.3 million. Of those, 2.5 million, or 10.1 percent, lived in extreme poverty. The number of children under 18 who lived in poverty was 17.9 million. This represents a poverty rate of 47.8 percent (U.S. Bureau of the Census, CPS Data 2006–2008). A study by the National Center for Children in Poverty concluded that the United States has the highest rate of young-child poverty of any Western industrialized nation (Sengupta, 2001, WK3). This situation has been exacerbated by the growing income gap between the affluent and the poor in this country, as well as by the federal welfare law passed in 1996 requiring a proportion of those on public welfare rolls to find jobs. Of 18 industrialized nations studied, American poor children received the least help (Bradsher, 1995b, A7).

Poverty in itself is a burden, but it is especially damaging to children. According to a new study of children's brains, the brain functions of low-income 9- and 10-year olds show damage similar to that from a stroke. These children perform below children in higher socioeconomic

TABLE 4 Poverty Status in the Past 12 Months of Families

Subject	All families		Married-couple families		Female householder, no husband present	
	Total	Percent below poverty level	Total	Percent below poverty level	Total	Percent below poverty level
Families	74,870,525	9.6%	55,706,062	4.6%	14,008,560	28.2%
With related children under 18 years	37,984,023	14.9%	25,425,019	6.4%	9,618,813	36.5%
RACE AND HISPANIC OR LATINO ORIGIN						
Families with a householder who is—						
One race	73,886,007	9.6%	55,076,323	4.6%	13,745,231	28.2%
White	58,017,001	7.2%	46,111,291	3.9%	8,382,922	23.8%
Black or African American	8,409,136	21.2%	3,756,225	6.9%	3,859,485	35.3%
American Indian and Alaska Native	542,211	20.9%	318,016	10.8%	164,376	39.4%
Asian	3,098,045	8.0%	2,521,364	6.2%	375,837	18.8%
Native Hawaiian and Other Pacific Islander	95,248	13.4%	63,890	8.6%	22,390	27.6%
Some other race	3,724,366	20.0%	2,305,537	13.0%	940,221	39.2%
Two or more races	984,518	14.0%	629,739	5.8%	263,329	32.6%
Hispanic or Latino origin (of any race)	9,513,114	18.9%	6,146,629	12.6%	2,266,140	37.5%
White alone, not Hispanic or Latino	52,586,817	6.1%	42,465,375	3.1%	7,177,733	21.7%
Householder worked	57,138,781	7.1%	42,530,753	3.1%	10,345,823	22.5%
Householder worked full-time, year-round in the past 12 months	39,844,372	3.2%	30,440,660	1.8%	6,313,182	9.6%
Householder 65 years and over	12,267,532	5.2%	9,976,718	3.9%	1,798,546	11.3%
Family Received—						
Supplemental Security Income (SSI) and/or cash public assistance income in the past 12 months	4,178,990	33.7%	1,962,707	18.2%	1,851,998	51.2%
Social Security Income in the past 12 months	17,958,322	6.6%	13,868,880	4.1%	3,058,492	16.4%

(Continued)

TABLE 4 (*Continued*)

Subject	All families		Married-couple families		Female householder, no husband present	
	Total	Percent below poverty level	Total	Percent below poverty level	Total	Percent below poverty level
EDUCATIONAL ATTAINMENT OF HOUSEHOLDER						
Less than high school graduate	10,043,635	24.3%	6,340,012	15.2%	2,606,929	47.1%
High school graduate (includes equivalency)	20,584,883	11.8%	14,484,488	5.6%	4,345,066	31.7%
Some college, associate's degree	22,141,325	8.1%	15,977,682	3.2%	4,735,632	24.1%
Bachelor's degree or higher	22,100,682	2.4%	18,903,880	1.5%	2,320,933	8.9%
NUMBER OF RELATED CHILDREN UNDER 18 YEARS						
No child	36,886,502	4.2%	30,281,043	3.1%	4,389,747	10.1%
1 or 2 children	30,090,887	12.4%	19,828,206	4.7%	7,747,680	31.3%
3 or 4 children	7,219,779	22.8%	5,148,132	11.3%	1,682,619	56.6%
5 or more children	673,357	41.1%	448,681	26.9%	188,514	74.2%
NUMBER OF PEOPLE IN FAMILY						
2 people	33,890,997	7.5%	24,368,610	3.4%	6,630,517	21.2%
3 or 4 people	31,032,583	10.2%	23,088,832	4.0%	6,066,041	32.4%
5 or 6 people	8,679,670	14.1%	7,249,958	9.0%	1,108,401	44.8%
7 or more people	1,267,275	22.4%	998,662	17.7%	203,601	45.8%
NUMBER OF WORKERS IN FAMILY						
No workers	9,657,896	23.8%	7,163,031	10.5%	2,039,446	65.5%
1 worker	23,628,034	16.1%	13,154,260	8.7%	7,744,958	29.3%
2 workers	32,777,092	3.0%	27,915,016	2.1%	3,336,363	9.3%
3 or more workers	8,807,503	1.6%	7,473,755	1.2%	887,793	5.0%
INCOME DEFICIT						
Mean income deficit for families (dollars)	8,213	(X)	7,255	(X)	8,958	(X)
PERCENT IMPUTED						
Poverty status for families	26.5%	(X)	(X)	(X)	(X)	(X)

Source: U.S. Census Bureau, 2006–2008 American Community Survey. http://factfinder.census.gov/servlet/STTable?_bm=y&-geo_id=01000US&-qr_name=
ACS_2008_3YR_G00_S1702&-ds_name=ACS_2008_3YR_G00.

strata on tests of intelligence and academic achievement as a result of their prefrontal cortex being disrupted. As for the reasons for this dysfunction, the researchers suggest that these children experience greater levels of stress and have a lack of access to stimulating materials and experiences, resulting in faulty language development and affecting their ability to plan, remember details, and focus on specifics in school (Kishiyama et al., 2009, pp. 1106–1115).

Although it is difficult to believe that such a situation exists in the wealthiest country in the world, more than 49 million Americans—one in seven—struggled to get enough to eat in 2008. This was the highest number in 14 years and was an increase from the preceding year, when 36.2 million experienced similar struggles. In addition, about one-third of Americans went hungry on occasion, a situation that worsened as a result of the recession of 2007–2009 (Abbot & Doering, 2009). The recession, especially the building bubble bust, has also produced some spectacular falls in income for many individuals: In just one example, a woman who had managed to rise from the Bronx projects to earning a six-figure income in real estate was forced, by 2010, to support herself and her daughter on nothing but food stamps (DeParle & Gebeloff, 2010).

The elderly, people over 65, made up about 9.7 percent of those who lived below the poverty level in 2008. As their numbers increase, however, fewer of them remain in poverty. The current percentage, for instance, is considerably lower than the 35.2 percent who lived in poverty in 1959. Finally, and contrary to the stereotype, not all the poor are concentrated in inner cities: Only around 17.7 percent of them lived in large central cities, whereas about 9 percent lived outside central cities. In addition, approximately 15.1 percent lived in nonmetropolitan, rural areas, where employment is difficult to obtain. A number of tables detailing numbers, percentages, and characteristics of the poor may be found on the Census Bureau Web site.

The Ghetto Poor

Sociologist William J. Wilson has written about the existence of the "truly disadvantaged," a class consisting of approximately 10 percent of those who are officially poor (some commentators have called this segment of the population an *underclass*, but this term has negative connotations). This social class lives a subsistence lifestyle with government help. Its members have severe health problems or are seriously lacking in any salable skills. Unemployment and single-parent homes are the two major problems faced by this group. Unemployment has resulted from the exodus of unskilled and semiskilled jobs from the central cities to the suburbs and partly from the disappearance of such jobs altogether in favor of jobs that require more education and technological know-how (the restructuring of the economy and of American capitalism). This structural change has given rise to a persistent and in some cases permanent type of poverty, from which individuals, cut off from the rest of society, are seldom able to escape.

The Homeless

Another segment of the poor that has become much more visible than in the past consists of the homeless. The phenomenon began in the 1970s, continued through a recessionary period in the early 1980s and, contrary to those who considered it a temporary problem, goes on today, especially as a result of the recession whose effects are still going on. Homelessness is a deeply disturbing situation to most Americans because it raises a variety of questions, among them: What is an individual's responsibility to his or her fellow human being, and what has gone wrong with American economic and social institutions to allow this condition to exist?

It is difficult to estimate the number of homeless in the United States because, of course, they live on the streets or in train stations or in shelters whose inhabitants change daily.

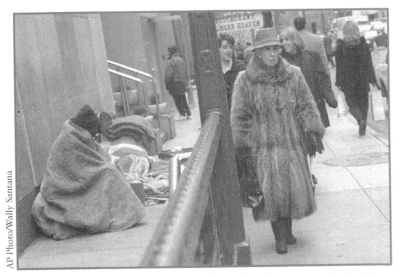

AP Photo/Wally Santana

In the past decade, class distinctions in the United States have become very evident, as the growing number of moguls—entrepreneurs in technology and financial areas—have left the rest of the population in the dust, so to speak. Here, simply a symbol of affluence versus life on the streets.

A more recent approximation of their number comes from a report by the Department of Housing and Urban Development. According to this report, presented to Congress, about 664,000 people nationwide were homeless on any given night in January 2008. Approximately 1.6 million homeless people used shelters or transitional housing programs at least once between October 2007 and September 2008. The number of homeless people in families increased by 9 percent to 516,700 in that period, probably as a result of the problems in the economy. Urban areas contain most homeless persons: one of five people homeless on a single night in January was located in Los Angeles, New York, and Detroit. However, the proportion of sheltered homeless people in suburban and rural areas increased dramatically, from 23 percent in 2007 to 32 percent in 2008. The report also noted that that more of the homeless using shelters in 2008 had had other forms of housing the year before, suggesting again that the economy had caused their homelessness.

The characteristics of this group have also changed in recent years: Where once there were elderly alcoholics or disturbed or eccentric "bag ladies," today there are many young mothers with children and whole young families whose heads have lost jobs; where once there were wage earners out on their luck, today there are dropouts with few skills, no experience, and few prospects for the future. The problems these new homeless exhibit are of such a nature that they initiate a never-ending cycle: They include mental instability, drug and alcohol use, unemployment, lack of education and job skills, alienation from family and friends, behavior problems, personal neglect, and disregard for personal responsibility. Many had depended on public assistance and are homeless as a result of the erosion of federal subsidies; others became homeless when state mental hospitals began discharging inmates in the 1970s following a movement whose adherents argued that the mentally ill should not be locked up unless they broke specific laws. Unemployment, decreasing demand for unskilled and day labor, the increase of women with children and no husband, and alcohol and drug abuse are additional factors leading toward homelessness.

The situation of homeless veterans is particularly difficult. The majority of them—and it is estimated that 131,000 veterans are homeless on any given night—are Vietnam veterans, but an increasing number are returnees from Iraq and Afghanistan. They suffer from post-traumatic stress disorder (PTSD), as well as from traumatic brain injuries. Their condition is made worse by the recession with its high rate of joblessness, as well as the lack of affordable housing around the nation (Smits and Kane, 2009). More information is available at several Web sites named on **mysearchlab.com.**

The composition of the homeless, according to the report presented to Congress, is as follows: Most are men over 30 and members of minorities, 40 percent are white non-Hispanic, 20 percent are children, and 33 are homeless together with another person. An earlier report noted that single men made up 51 percent of the homeless population, families with children 30 percent, single women 17 percent, and unaccompanied minors 2 percent. The racial and ethnic composition is estimated at 42 percent African American, 39 percent white, 13 percent Hispanic, 4 percent Native American, and 2 percent Asian (U.S. Conference of Mayors, 2006).

Social Class and Its Consequences

The concept of life chances, particularly the fact that they differ according to social class, was noted in the earlier discussion of Weber's views on social class. Not only do life chances differ, however; there are marked differences in lifestyles, encompassing such characteristics as family life, child rearing, education, personal values, consumption, leisure activities, political outlook, religion, and health. The bottom line is, of course, that the consequences of different positions in the stratification system make for a great deal of inequality. These differences in lifestyle are described next in very general terms; they are not to be understood as fitting every individual in the social class described.

Family Life

Because people tend to marry partners of their own social class, clear patterns eventually emerge. From the point of view of marriage stability, there are fewer divorces among the upper classes. The higher divorce rate among the lower classes may be caused by the frustration and anxiety that economic problems and unemployment create. At the same time, upper-class people are preoccupied with maintaining a strong family, because that is the chief medium of transmission of property. In lower-class families, marriages are much more patriarchal with respect to sex roles. Women tend to interact to a greater extent with female relatives and men with male friends than in the higher social classes. The lower classes, finally, have a high percentage of female-headed families.

Child Rearing

Middle- and upper-class child-rearing practices stress independence of action and behavior, according to principles of right and wrong. Parents in these social classes tend to use temporary withdrawal of love rather than physical punishment for social control. As a result, although children in the middle and upper classes may be prone to guilt feelings, they tend to become more independent, self-directed, and achievement oriented than individuals in the lower social classes. Parents in the latter tend to emphasize obedience to rules and staying out of trouble and tend to punish infringements more harshly. Each social class is preparing its offspring to follow in its occupational footsteps.

Education

The different socialization experiences lead middle- and upper-class children to be more successful academically, a fact reinforced by values that stress such achievement. This academic advantage tends to further upward social mobility, whereas children in the lower classes, lacking models and valuing higher education less, are hampered in upward mobility. In terms of income alone, the differences between those with only eight years of education and those with five or more years of college are striking.

Religion

The upper and upper-middle classes tend to be overwhelmingly Protestant, and there is a close correspondence between the various Protestant denominations and social class. The higher social classes identify more closely with denominations that offer subdued rituals, such as the Episcopalians, Congregationalists, Presbyterians, and Methodists. The lower social classes appear to be more comfortable with denominations that offer colorful rites, such as those found in the Baptist church and in fundamentalist and revivalist sects.

Politics

Although there are regional and, of course, individual differences, in general terms it appears that being a registered voter, voting regularly in elections, and taking an interest in civil and political affairs are activities engaged in more frequently the higher one's social class. Party affiliation is similarly correlated: The more privileged people tend to support the Republican Party, in part because the latter has symbolized a free-market, unregulated economy in which it is easier for the wealthy to protect their income. The less advantaged, on the other hand, particularly if they are also urban dwellers, favor the Democratic Party, which has historically fought for the rights of the working class. According to The Pew Research Center for the People and the Press, 38 percent of people in the upper quintile vote for Republicans and only 27 percent vote for Democrats. Conversely, 42 percent of the lower-income quintile votes Democratic, whereas only 20 percent votes Republican (August 2, 2005). The affluent are more liberal on social issues such as abortion, gay and lesbian rights, feminist issues, affirmative action, and so on. Those of lower social standing tend to be liberal on economic issues that favor them, such as job security, guarantees of full employment, and so on, but conservative on other social issues, a fact that often leads them to vote Republican, even though such a vote may be against their economic interest.

Health

Because health care is neither free nor cheap in the United States, as it is in many other industrial societies, it follows that those with a higher income can purchase more health and medical care than those with a lower income. Studies have shown that the incidence of disease among the higher social classes is smaller than among the lower classes for that reason. A substantial segment of the population is not covered by any form of health insurance because of the expense involved; yet, it is only such insurance that allows middle-income people to obtain adequate care. According to the Census Bureau, 47 million Americans were uninsured in 2006, which represents an all-time high. However, future trends appear to be even worse: The number of uninsured is projected to increase to 52 million by 2010 according to a paper published on the Health Affairs Web site (Gilmer & Kronick, 2009). In fact, several news outlets reported in March 2011 that the number of uninsured Americans had grown to 52 million in 2010. Disease, neglect, accidents, and violence are causes of death for poor children in their first year of life to a much greater extent than for children in higher social classes. The Health Reform Bill passed, after much controversy, in 2010 should help matters, but to what degree is still unknown. Finally, even life expectancy is higher at the higher social levels.

Research in the area of public health, moreover, indicates that status, in and of itself, determines to a great extent how healthy a person is. In other words, it is not just wealth, good nutrition, higher education, quality of medical care, and good genes that make a person healthier than others who lack those attributes, but simply the status of being in a high social class. "Your position in the hierarchy very much relates to how much control you have over your life and your opportunities for full social engagements" (Cohen, 2004, A17).

Both the incidence and treatment of mental illness are much higher for lower-class persons than for the upper classes. In particular, lower-class patients are much more likely to be treated with tranquilizing drugs and to be hospitalized in state institutions for longer periods. Upper-class patients tend to be treated by private therapists with various types of psychotherapy and spend only brief periods in private mental clinics. Some studies also indicate a high degree of mental impairment among persons in the poorest social classes.

Arrest and Conviction

The rates of arrest and conviction are higher for lower-class individuals, many of them minorities, than for members of the upper and middle classes. The harsher treatment by the criminal justice system is partially due to the types of crimes committed by lower-class persons—robbery, burglary, larceny, and auto theft—as opposed to those committed by middle- and upper-class persons—forgery, tax evasion, fraud, and embezzlement. The latter crimes are not considered to be as "wrong" as the former because violence is seldom involved. Finally, persons of a higher social class can generally afford a better legal defense. The so-called dream team put together to defend O. J. Simpson could not possibly be afforded by anyone who was not superrich: It is estimated that the defendant in this case spent approximately $6 million by

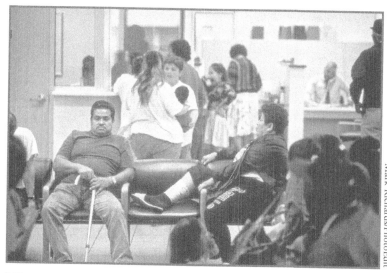

Mark Richards/PhotoEdit

With approximately 50 million Americans without health insurance, emergency departments of most hospitals are crowded and chaotic as they must deal with people who have nowhere else to go in a medical emergency.

the end of the trial. Most (80 to 90 percent) of all felony defendants in the United States are too poor to hire their own lawyers and are represented by court-appointed attorneys (Gleick, 1995, 42). Such attorneys are remunerated on sliding scales depending on local jurisdictions. Payment can vary from $1,000 to defend a death-penalty case to $53,000. Obviously, the sort of defense a defendant obtains varies from location to location. In justice as in everything else, one tends to get what one pays for. Finally, victims of crime tend also to be overwhelmingly poor and/or members of minority groups.

Values

Research has shown that, in general, middle- and upper-class people have feelings of control over their lives, whereas persons in the lower class tend to be fatalistic, believing that luck and forces beyond their control govern their lives. The higher social classes engage in long-range planning and postpone present pleasures for future goals (deferred gratification) to a greater extent than do people from the lower social classes, probably because the latter have a much less bright future to look forward to. The higher social classes also display a more liberal attitude toward sexual behavior and religious beliefs than the lower classes. The working class, in particular, is intolerant of nonconformist behavior. The values and attitudes of the higher social classes tend to set the standard for the society.

Social Mobility

One of the principal differences between open and closed societies is that there is social mobility in open societies and none or very little in closed societies. The term *social mobility* refers to an individual's ability to change social class membership, status, life chances, and lifestyles by moving up (or down) the ladder represented by the stratification system of a society.

Social scientists also distinguish between *vertical mobility,* which occurs in an upward or downward direction, and *horizontal mobility,* which occurs when there is a change of status without a consequent change of class. For instance, vertical mobility may be exemplified by a high school teacher who is promoted to principal (upward mobility), or the principal who proves ineffective as an administrator and is demoted back into the classroom (downward mobility). A school superintendent who takes a job as an executive of an insurance company at approximately the same salary is horizontally mobile. Usually, a certain amount of horizontal mobility is necessary to maximize chances for vertical mobility.

The Upwardly Mobile: Who Are They?

Various factors are responsible for vertical mobility, some dependent on personality traits, others on social circumstances. From studies on upward mobility, a profile of the upwardly mobile individual has emerged. Such an individual is (1) an urban resident; (2) an only child or one of two children; (3) influenced by ambitious parents, particularly a mother; (4) likely to acquire more education than his or her parents; (5) one who marries later and tends to marry a partner of higher status; and (6) one who waits to establish a family and limits its size to no more than two children.

Individuals who are upwardly mobile in comparison to their parents, or to the preceding generation, are displaying *intergenerational mobility*. If they also do better than their peers of the same generation, they are exhibiting *intragenerational mobility*.

Social Mobility in the United States

The United States has long been known as the land of opportunity, and a myth persists that any individual, no matter what his or her origin, can rise to become a leader of the country, or at least someone in possession of wealth and prestige. At the very least, people expect to get well-paying jobs, own their own homes, and be able to send their children to college. This is, in fact, what is meant by the "American Dream" and by such phrases as "from rags to riches" and "a Horatio Alger story." The notion that hard work, thrift, ambition, and willpower are sufficient to ensure a person's rise in the stratification system has been part of the American ethic from the very inception of the nation.

How much truth is there in this notion? How does mobility in the United States compare with mobility in other industrial nations? After gathering opinion-poll studies from a number of industrial nations, researchers found a great amount of social mobility in all the industrialized democracies, refuting the idea that the United States is unique in the openness of its stratification system (Grusky & Hauser, 1984, 35; Kerckhoff, Campbell, & Winfield-Laird, 1985; Lipset & Bendix, 1959). All the researchers concluded, first, that much of the mobility occurred because in technological societies a great value is put on efficiency. The inefficient offspring of even upper-class parents are replaced by more talented persons from lower social classes. Second, mobility is caused by industrialization itself, which has resulted in the creation of more high-status occupations to replace the largely blue-collar, lower-status occupations of a more agrarian system. This type of mobility is called **structural mobility**. Lipset and Bendix found that although the United States did not have an unusual amount of mobility, it did display more of the kind of mobility in which people may rise, but also fall, through individual merit.

Studies measuring long-distance mobility, that is, the rise of individuals from the very bottom to the very top of the stratification system in one generation, found that Americans do have a high rate of this kind of mobility. In the 1960s, a well-known study showed that a large percentage (37 percent) of the men in white-collar jobs had fathers with a blue-collar job, but an individual's own level of education was more responsible for upward social mobility than was the father's occupation. At the time, the researchers concluded that an individual's chances of occupational upward mobility were greatly influenced by the amount of education, the nature of the person's first job, and the occupation of the father. Structural mobility, however, was the factor most responsible for upward mobility (Blau & Duncan, 1967, 152–161). A later study substantiated that among the American business elite, only 1 in 10 of the top executives came from a wealthy home, and more than one-third had made it from humble origins (Lipset, 1976).

A particularly telling finding regarding mobility and the subject of inequality in general was that there is almost as much economic inequality among brothers raised in the same homes as among the population in general (Jencks et al., 1972). Inequality seems to be newly created within each generation, even among people who begin life in similar circumstances.

On the whole, it may be said that there is more upward mobility than downward mobility in the United States, though it occurs in the middle segments of the population rather than from bottom to top (Hauser & Featherman, 1977). Despite the changes in the occupational structure of the society, the total amount of social mobility has hardly been altered in the past decades. However, the global restructuring taking place currently may ultimately lead to different conclusions. Even though there are still possibilities of great jumps up the economic ladder, most Americans do not move a great many rungs either up or down in their lifetimes.

In trying to increase social equality, the government can intervene by passing antidiscrimination laws, affirmative-action legislation, training programs, and other government programs. Over and above the impact of life chances, however, individual factors also play a part in a person's mobility: ability, work habits, deferring gratification, and, finally, sheer luck.

The trend toward widening income inequality and the fact that social mobility has been stagnant and uneven since the 1970s are indications, to some social commentators, that the country is becoming increasingly stratified. Research that compared the personal finances of 5,000 households (based on a survey conducted every year since the late 1960s) has indicated that the poor are more likely to remain poor and the affluent to remain affluent (Bradsher, 1995a, 4). For instance, in 2006 the top 1 percent of households had seen an increase of 50 percent more income than the bottom 40 percent. Moreover, the top 20 percent of families received 55.7 percent of U.S. income, the next 20 percent received 19.5 percent, the mid 20 percent received 13.2 percent, and the bottom 20 percent received 3.9 percent (**http://www.toomuchonline.org/inequality.html**). Most disturbing is the fact that the lowest quintile has seen its meager earnings decrease. The wages for most Americans did not improve between 1979 and 1998: In fact, the median male wage in 2000 was below the 1979 level, despite the fact that productivity increased by 44.5 percent (**http://www.consortiumnews.com/2009/070409a.html**). The chances of this segment attaining a middle-class income have been declining, especially so in the deep recession that began in 2007. In addition to stagnating incomes, many workers lost their jobs altogether, and the bursting of the housing bubble led many to lose their homes as well. In short, although mobility, and especially upward mobility, is still a very real possibility for some in our society, a number of trends cast a shadow over the continuing existence of the American dream. A large proportion of workers must work at two or more jobs. Seasonal unemployment and low-paying jobs result in a substantial number of earners bringing home less than a living wage. This means that many young people wait to marry and continue to live with their parents, even after college. This downward structural mobility engenders pessimism in many that they may be sliding down from the middle class—the American dream turned upside down.

Global Inequality

The existence of inequality as a constant feature of human societies was once accepted as a given. Although the world has gradually embraced an ideology that finds gross inequities unfair, it has not found a means of eliminating them. On the contrary, it would appear that inequality persists not only within societies but also especially among societies. On a global basis, for instance, the so-called Third World, which houses 80 percent of the world's 6.6 billion people and accounts for 60 percent of the planet's land area, faces poverty that is far more severe and more extensive than people in the First World can imagine. (The First World consists of industrial nations with predominantly market economies; the Second World consists of industrial societies that are undergoing transformations from generally socialist economies; and the Third World consists of societies that are primarily agrarian.) In the Third World, the majority of the people are poor, meaning that hunger, unsafe housing, and disease are everyday experiences for most. The definition of hunger refers to caloric intake below that necessary to prevent serious health risks and stunted growth in children. Around the world, deficient and inadequate diets, as well as unsafe water supplies, are the destiny of hundreds of millions of people. In sharp contrast, consumption of goods and services in industrial and developing nations is soaring.

The United Nations Food and Agriculture Organization has declared in 2009 that more than 1.2 billion people across the globe are starving. That is one in six human beings, mainly due to regional wars, global financial crises, and rising energy prices and food costs. During its Hunger Summit held in 2009, the following points emerged: The largest number of hungry people—642 million malnourished inhabitants—live in developing Asia-Pacific countries; 265 million live in sub-Saharan Africa; 53 million live in Latin America; 42 million in the Middle East and North Africa; and 15 million in industrial countries.

The issue of global inequality will be dealt with in the context of international relations; however, a few examples of inequality are helpful here. In 2001, private consumption in the United States was $24,436 per capita (meaning per person). In Canada, another industrial country, it was $16,727. In Azerbaijan, on the other hand, a developing country, private consumption expenditure per capita was $1,825, and in Ukraine it was $2,368. In 2000, 81.9 percent of the population of Ethiopia consumed less than $1 per day, as did 49.1 percent in Madagascar and 36 percent in Bangladesh, all Third World countries. In the poor nations, the average household consumes 20 percent less than it did 25 years ago. The reason for this, in part, is that in many poor countries of South Asia and Africa, populations

Box 2 World Hunger: Are We Our Brothers' Keepers?

The United States and most other industrial nations face an epidemic of obesity. People spend millions of dollars on diet books, diet foods, liposuction, tummy tucks, trying to avoid carbs or fat. The situation in developing or Third World countries is starkly and dramatically different. In those countries, just getting enough calories to live another day is a constant struggle. In Malawi, for instance, children stand on the side of the road selling skewers of roasted mice. In Mozambique, people eat grasshoppers before the grasshoppers can eat their crops. In Liberia, during their civil war, every animal in the national zoo was eaten, with the exception of a one-eyed lion. No cats or dogs could be seen anywhere in the streets of the capital. But at least these foods provide some protein.

In the 1990s in Angola, World Food Program workers described how people would take old wood and leather furniture, boil the leather for many hours to soften it and remove the tanning toxins, and then boil it to make soup. Apparently, furniture or leather were eaten in many previous famines as well.

Another "coping mechanism" for hunger is strapping flat stones to one's stomach to avoid strong hunger pangs. In Somalia, people "eat" camel skin. In many African countries, people dig up anthills and termite mounds to recover the small grains that the insects have gathered. In Bangladesh, people who are hungry enough will eat a type of lentil that is known to destroy the nervous system. In Chad and West Africa, people eat plants that are known to be poisonous but are made edible by long pounding and soaking. Plants such as seaweed, tree bark, and grass, all of which have little nutritional value, are eaten in North Korea. The skins and bones of dead animals that even vultures won't touch anymore are boiled for "soup."

The final staple of the very poor around the world, and as close to the United States as Haiti, is dirt. In Zambia, street markets sell balls of edible clay. In Angola, "black salt" is sprinkled on cold food to make it more palatable. And in Haiti, biscuits called "argile," or clay, are a common snack to appease desperate hunger: They are made with clay and margarine or butter and are flavored with salt, pepper, and bouillon cubes. You can buy them for a penny apiece (McNeill, 2004, Section 4, 1, 12).

Given this scenario, what is the responsibility of the wealthy nations? We still have problems of poverty in our own country, so should we be expected to help the poor in other countries? As a matter of fact, the United States and most other wealthy nations donate large amounts in foreign aid. But somehow, the foreign aid never reaches the needy, and many social programs fail to make a dent in poverty. In fact, when one plots the billions of dollars in development aid that has been given to nations in Africa and plots the continent's GDP per capita for the same period, it becomes apparent that the GDP has not risen despite a rise in aid. A young economist at MIT is attempting to reverse this reality by using a new economic process to see whether specific programs are effective and should be tried. This economist and colleagues have founded a Poverty Action Lab, which follows a theory of "pragmatic idealism." This means that one must first believe that something can be done about poverty, and not all economists agree that it can, and then do it. To determine whether a specific program to alleviate poverty will work, these economists subject social policy to randomized control trials, a process they borrowed from medical research to test the efficacy of a drug. For instance, to lessen the chance of contracting malaria, is it better to give away free nets, or to sell the nets for a penny a piece, because people tend to value something they have to buy more than something they get for free? Two very similar groups are divided; one group is given the nets free, the other has to buy them, though at a very cheap price. At the end of a period of time, the results will show which is the better policy: The group that used more nets valued them more. Therefore, this is the policy that works best. In the case of Kenya, it was the group that was given the nets free that used most of them and cut down on the number who contracted malaria. If only all social programs could be measured in this way, we could finally attack the problem of global poverty with some hope of success (Parker-Pope, 2010).

are growing fast and living longer. Large families, in addition, deplete natural resources and household purchasing power. Richer nations are reducing population growth and have smaller families, so they can increase consumption. Here are some examples:

- Americans spend more on cosmetics (about $8 billion per year) than it is estimated it would cost to provide basic education ($6 billion) or water and sanitation ($9 billion) to the more than 2 billion people who are without them.
- Americans throw away 7 million cars a year and 2 million plastic bottles every hour.
- Total private consumption in high-income countries amounts to 81.5 percent, whereas in low-income countries it is 3.6 percent.
- The richest fifth of people consume 45 percent of all meat and fish, whereas the poorest fifth consume 5 percent.
- The richest fifth have nearly 74 percent more telephone lines; the poorest fifth have 1.5 percent.
- The richest countries own 87 percent of the world's vehicles; the poorest own less than 1 percent.
- The richest countries use 58 percent of total energy; the poorest countries use less than 4 percent.

Of course, asking the rich to consume less would not lead to the poor having more. Globally, some poor countries misuse public resources, spend disproportionately on military goods, or allow the wealthy to avoid paying taxes. Because 8 billion of the world's projected 9.5 billion people will be living in poor countries by 2050, it is imperative that a different pattern of consumption be found. The Human Development Report 2003, which compiled some of the aforementioned figures, suggests that poor countries adopt modern, efficient technologies, thus leapfrogging some of the mistakes that industrial nations have made. Ranking nations according to the life they provide for their people, the organization listed Canada, France, Norway, the United States, Iceland, Finland, the Netherlands, Japan, New Zealand, and Sweden as the top 10 of the 174 nations surveyed. The bottom 10 nations included Sierra Leone, Niger, Burkina Faso, Mali, Burundi, Ethiopia, Eritrea, Guinea, Mozambique, and Gambia. The report concluded that the world is facing an acute development crisis, with many poor nations suffering severe and continuing socioeconomic reversals (Human Development Report, 2006.)

The Chapter in Brief

Stratification is a phenomenon present in all societies that have produced a surplus. It is the process by which members of a society rank themselves and one another in hierarchies (from low to high) with respect to the amount of desirable goods they possess and the prestige and power they enjoy.

All systems of ranking are based on differences among people. Differences based on age and sex are present in all human groups, but in more complex societies, people are differentiated as a category and ranked on the basis of not only biological but also social characteristics.

Ranking has led to the existence of inequality. Inequality has been explained by a number of theories: Functionalists maintain that inequality works to the advantage of societies because rewarding the performance of some tasks higher than others ensures that difficult tasks get done. Conflict theorists assert that inequality is the result of conflict among groups in society that struggle for power. The victors in the struggle impose their values on the rest of society. In a synthesis of the two theories, Lenski states that although inequality is inevitable, it tends to lessen as a society becomes more productive. However, government intervention is needed to break the advantage of some groups over others.

All stratification systems exhibit differentiation, ranking, and institutionalization. The most important dimensions of stratification systems are class, status, and power. A social class is an aggregation of persons in a society who stand in a similar position with respect to power, privilege, or prestige. Status is a ranked position of an individual in relation to other individuals in the social system. Power is the ability of one person or group to control the actions of other persons or groups, with or without the consent of the latter.

Stratification systems may be measured on an ideal continuum. On one end, the closed, or caste, system displays social inequalities that are institutionalized and rigid. In the middle, the estate system is less rigid, allowing some mobility. At the other end, the open system, typical of modern industrial societies, consists of a number of social classes and allows social mobility, although not to the same extent for all. Mobility is restricted by life chances—the opportunity to become a complete human being and reap the satisfactions of society—which differ according to social class.

Upward mobility in industrial societies is aided by urban residence, by coming from a small family,

by having ambitious parents, by higher education, by late marriage, preferably to a mate from a higher social class, and by having no more than two children. Much of the mobility in the United States is structural mobility; that is, it is caused by industrial and technological change that upgrades jobs. Otherwise, there is more horizontal (across the job continuum) than vertical (up or down the job continuum) mobility, although talent, education, work habits, and luck sometimes lead to spectacular upward mobility.

Poverty is a tragic side effect of inequality. In the affluent societies, poverty is understood in terms of relative deprivation, of having less than one's peers. Women, children, minorities, and elderly tend to be poor in greater proportions than other segments of the population. In recent years, the gap between the rich and the poor has widened in the United States, causing fears that stratification may become more rigid.

Globally, too, the inequality between the First World and Third World nations, where most people go hungry and live on about $1 a day, is becoming difficult to ignore. As these societies are also populous and politically unstable, they may present a danger to the more affluent.

Terms to Remember

authority Social power exercised with the consent of others. Parents, teachers, and the government represent different levels of authority.

closed, or caste, stratification system A system in which class, status, and power are ascribed, mobility is highly restricted, and the social system is rigid.

conflict theory of stratification A theory of stratification according to which the natural conditions of society are constant change and conflict resulting from class struggles. Inequality is the product of such conflict, as one group is victorious over others and asserts itself over the rest of society.

estate system of stratification The prevailing system of feudal Europe, consisting of three estates of functional importance to the society. The estates were hierarchically arranged and permitted a limited amount of social mobility.

functionalist theory of stratification A theory in which social inequality is viewed as inevitable because

society must use rewards to ensure that essential tasks are performed. The natural conditions of society are thought to be order and stability (equilibrium).

life chances The opportunity of each individual to fulfill his or her potential as a human being. Life chances differ according to social class.

open, or class, society A society in which the stratification system allows for social mobility and in which a person's status is achieved rather than being ascribed on the basis of birth. Open systems are characteristic of industrial societies.

power A dimension of stratification consisting of the ability of one person or group to control the actions of others with or without the latter's consent.

social class A dimension of stratification consisting of an aggregate of persons in a society who stand in a similar position with regard to some form of power, privilege, or prestige.

social mobility An individual's ability to change his or her social class membership by moving up (or down) the stratification system. Upward or downward mobility is vertical, whereas mobility that results in a change of status without a consequent change of class is horizontal.

social status A dimension of stratification consisting of an individual's ranked position within the social system, the rank being determined mainly by the individual's occupational role.

social stratification (ranking) A process existing in all but the simplest societies whereby members rank one another and themselves hierarchically with respect to the amount of desirables (wealth, prestige, power) they possess.

stratification system The overlapping manner in which members of society are ranked according to classes, status groups, and hierarchies of power. Analyzed on a continuum from closed to open.

structural mobility Upward mobility caused by industrial and technological change that pushes skilled workers into higher-status occupations.

Suggested Readings

Kushnick, Louis, and James Jennings, eds. 1999. *A New Introduction to Poverty: The Role of Race, Power, and Politics.* New York: New York University Press. A compendium of articles that examines the causes and characteristics of poverty in the United States and the reasons for its persistence.

Liebow, Elliot. 1995. *Tell Them Who I Am: The Lives of Homeless Women.* New York: Penguin Books. A participant observation study of women in a homeless shelter in Washington, DC. This study puts a human face on the anonymous "bag ladies" we see on the streets of our cities.

Riesman, David. 1993. *Abundance for What?* New Brunswick, NJ: Transaction Books. A question we seldom ask is discussed by a noted sociologist.

Schwarz, John E. 1997. *The American Dream in Question.* New York: W. W. Norton. As unskilled jobs disappear, the author maintains, the American dream becomes more and more elusive.

Shipler, David K. 2004. *The Working Poor: Invisible in America.* New York: Alfred A. Knopf. A powerful book that illustrates the plight of the 35 million Americans who live in poverty, although most of them work full time. The author examines the lives of these forgotten Americans who live in the shadow of prosperity and for whom the American dream is out of reach, despite their willingness to work hard toward it.

Wilson, William Julius. 1997. *When Work Disappears: The World of the New Urban Poor.* New York: Knopf. This sociologist expands his views on the unfortunate consequences following the disappearance of unskilled jobs in inner cities: the flight of the middle class, the decline of inner-city businesses, and the plight of a working class left without work.

Minority Status:
Race and Ethnicity

IN THIS CHAPTER, YOU WILL LEARN

- *the definitions of minority based on race and ethnicity;*
- *how the majority has dealt with minorities in its midst;*
- *the causes and effects of prejudice and discrimination;*
- *some characteristics of the principal minorities in the United States; and*
- *that the United States is likely to become a different, racially mixed, multicultural society in the future.*

Humans have lived on this planet for many thousands, and in other forms millions, of years and have developed sophisticated and technologically advanced civilizations, but in some respects they have remained very uncivilized. Perhaps they are still following a biological imperative, which makes them suspicious of strangers and inimical to others who are not part of their group. Whatever the reasons, it is clear that even in the twenty-first century, deep hatreds still divide us.

We speak of being interconnected in a global village. In fact, governments do interact with one another in terms of politics and economics: We are allies and trading partners, and the rapidity of communication possible today allows us to keep in touch with the far corners of the planet instantly. This interaction is also responsible for cultural diffusion, a process that has allowed every society to become acquainted with the products, if not the culture, of every other society. Interaction is not really such a new phenomenon: For thousands of years interbreeding has occurred on a large scale, so that no "pure" stock exists anywhere in the world (with the possible exception of small groups that may exist in inaccessible locations). On the whole, however, it seems that people have chosen to stress their differences rather than their similarities. As a result, much of human history has been primarily a record of struggles and conflicts, of conquests and oppression, even of genocide, with one group of people pitted against another.

Differentiating people according to specific variables is a universal cultural trait. In all societies, men are treated differently from women, children differently from adults, the elderly

From Chapter 8 of *Contemporary Society: An Introduction to Social Science*, Thirteenth Edition. John A. Perry, Erna K. Perry. Copyright © 2012 by Pearson Education, Inc. All rights reserved.

differently from the young. The poor are treated differently from the rich, and the powerful differently from the powerless. As we all know, people of one skin color are also treated differently from people of another. With the rise of the nation–state, another reason for differentiation came into being: Groups of people who differ in culture or religion are suddenly forced to owe allegiance to the same state and to live side by side. As a result of immigration, colonization, or conquest, most nations have become plural societies consisting of a majority group and groups that differ from it because of culture, appearance, or religion—the so-called minorities. Occasionally, majority and minorities coexist in peace. More often, coexistence is marred by conflict. As examples, one need only mention Northern Ireland, the Middle East, South Africa, Rwanda, Darfur, or the Balkan countries of the former Yugoslavia. To a lesser extent, the United States also has problems of coexistence.

Majority–Minorities Relations: Defining the Terms

When two or more groups share the same territory but one of them has more power than the others, that group is considered the majority, and the other groups are termed minorities. In other words, the terms *majority* and *minorities* do not imply any numerical value; that is, a majority is not necessarily larger in number than any of the minority groups. On the contrary, although this is not true in the United States, in many instances one or more minorities are superior in number to the dominant majority (South Africa was a glaring example before the end of apartheid).

Minorities in the modern sense originated with the development of the nation–state. "Both the spread of dominance over formerly separate groups and the common desire to create a homogeneous nation (leading to attempts to repress cultural variation) have created the minority–majority situation" (Simpson & Yinger, 1972, 16). From the dawn of history and through many thousands of years, people lived in tribes, small groups consisting of several families. Tribalism is deeply embedded in the human psyche, and even today people view the world from a "tribal" perspective, expecting the society to which they belong to consist of their own physical and cultural type (Wagley & Harris, 1958, 241–242).

Because it does not depend on numbers, minority status refers to that category of people who "possess imperfect access to positions of equal power and to the corollary categories of prestige and privilege in the society" (Yetman & Steele, 1971, 4). Minority status, then, is conferred not on individuals but on whole categories of people who lack the kind of power that the majority group holds in a society on the basis of the ascribed statuses of race, ethnicity, and religion (and, to a different extent, on those of gender and sexual orientation, age, and disability).

By contrast, the majority, or dominant group, although it may be numerically smaller, controls the important sectors of social life, influencing the culture of the society in such vital areas as language, ideology, and even standards of beauty and worth. By definition, the majority controls access to positions of wealth, prestige, and power. Minorities find access more difficult the more they differ in looks and customs from the majority and the fewer skills, talents, and the less education they have at their disposal. Mobility within the stratification system, then, has varied accordingly for the different minorities.

Common Characteristics of Minorities

People who are considered to belong to a **minority group** share some common features. First, they are recognizable by virtue of possessing visible ascribed traits: appearance, language, accent, or last name. Second, because they possess these traits, they are subject to differential treatment. Third, their self-image and identity are centered around their minority-group membership. And finally, they are aware that they share a common identity with others in the group (Wagley & Harris, 1958, 10).

Minority status is most commonly assigned to a group because of that group's ethnic origin, religion, or race (as noted earlier, there are additional reasons, but these three are the most frequent and basic). **Ethnicity** refers to a group's distinctiveness on social and cultural grounds that differ from those of the majority because of national background. Most immigrants who share with others a common language, culture, traditions, history, and ancestry, and are recognized as such by the rest of society, are ethnic minorities. Among those who have been in the United States for several generations, some retain and some have given up the language, customs, and sometimes even the surnames of their country of origin. However, as long as a majority of them feel bonds of solidarity with others who came from the same background, they are considered to be members of an ethnic group.

Religion is a set of beliefs and rituals dealing with the sacred. People of the same religion share their beliefs and rituals and derive a sense of identity from their religious membership. In the United States, Catholics and Jews, differing in religion from the Protestants who made up the original group of settlers and who eventually became the majority, have been subject to differential treatment in the past. Minority status based on religion has lessened in importance in the past half-century.

The most difficult factor to define is race. **Race** was a concept scientists used in the past to describe biological differences occurring in the human species. Contemporary scholars would like to do away with this term altogether because it does not describe a scientific reality. The American Anthropological Association has issued a statement that although the term *race* was used to classify people into categories called races according to visible differences in appearance, the expansion of knowledge in this century has clearly shown that "human populations are not unambiguous, clearly demarcated, biologically distinct groups. . . . [DNA evidence] indicates that most physical variation, about 94%, lies *within* so-called racial groups" (Statement on "Race," American Anthropological Association, 1996, 569–570). There are no "pure" human groupings left anywhere because of the overlapping of genes in neighboring populations. "The continued sharing of genetic materials has maintained all of humankind as a single species." Therefore, the classification of people into races is artificial and does not correspond to clear and definite distinctions among humans. Neither does it correspond to national, religious, linguistic, cultural, and geographic boundaries, although isolation in the past may have been responsible for the existence of different gene pools. No social traits or behaviors of population groups have any connection with inherited racial traits. Finally, there is no scientific support for the idea that differences in personality, temperament, character, or intelligence are based on race. The Anthropological Association concludes: "Given what we know about the capacity of normal humans to achieve and function within any culture, we conclude that present-day inequalities between so-called 'racial' groups are not consequences of their biological inheritance but products of historical and contemporary social, economic, educational, and political circumstances" (see the complete statement on the Internet: **http://www.aaanet.org**).

The Making of Pluralist Society

One of the fundamental problems facing nations such as the United States has been how to make a functioning social unit, a society, out of the many disparate groups that have periodically come to its shores in search of a better future. A solution of sorts has, in fact, been achieved, for a majority of Americans do share sufficient common values and norms to maintain social stability. But the process has taken place by trial and error, and the results remain imperfect.

Ideologies Regarding the Treatment of Minorities

At different times in American history, different ideologies have prevailed regarding how minorities ought to be treated.

Anglo-Conformity. The first of these, **Anglo-conformity**, represented an attempt to super-impose WASP (White Anglo-Saxon Protestant) values on all immigrants. Thus, it was expected that the language, institutions, and cultural patterns of the United States (which in turn were based on an English model) would be learned and absorbed by all newcomers.

The Melting Pot. During the nineteenth century, the idea took hold that immigrants could make important contributions to the society. As a result, it was thought that the United States could mix, both biologically and culturally, all the various stocks within it (the **melting pot theory**), ultimately giving origin to an individual who would be the "New American."

Although the educational system and the mass media have succeeded in molding second- and third-generation immigrants into Americans who accept most of the values and institutions of the society (they tend to be, in fact, some of the most ardent patriots), in other ways ethnic minorities have remained resistant to melting. Even when their ethnic background was no longer a focus of identity for second- and third-generation immigrants, their religion was. Sociologists found that marriage followed religious lines: British, German, and Scandinavian Protestants intermarried, creating a Protestant pool; Irish, Italian, and Polish Catholics intermarried, creating a Catholic pool; and Jews married other Jews of whatever national origin, creating a Jewish pool (Kennedy, 1944; Archdeacon, 1983). Although there was a melting down of ethnicity, then, the United States was becoming a triple melting pot. This realization paved the way for the ideology of pluralism. As for the racial minorities, they hardly "melted down" at all.

© Corbis

The immigration issue that bedevils current legislators is not new: Our country is made up of immigrants from many parts of the world, looking to better their lives.

Cultural Pluralism.   The ideology of **cultural pluralism,** the most widely accepted today, stresses the desirability of each ethnic group's retention of its cultural distinctiveness, but still within the boundaries of the wider American culture. In other words, the first commitment of every person is, ideally, to the good of the United States, but beyond that, in matters such as food, family, religious rituals, community associations, and so on, individuals retain, if they so desire, their ethnic ties. It is thought that people can, in this manner, contribute much more to the society, somewhat in the fashion of a dish that tastes much better than the variety of separate ingredients that make it up.

The decade of the 1960s saw a revival of ethnic feelings as it became apparent that success and upward mobility in the society were extremely difficult for some ethnic and most racial groups to achieve. African Americans, Hispanics, and Native Americans became active in protest movements to end their unequal access to opportunities and, in the process, seemed to rediscover their ancestry and use it as a springboard for political action. Activity in political organizations seems to have generated feelings of solidarity that were lacking before among many ethnic group members.

Multiculturalism.   The contemporary prevailing ideology is couched in the policy of multiculturalism. This policy began as an educational program that tried to focus attention on the cultural diversity existing in American society. It also made an attempt at promoting the equality of all cultural traditions. It differs from cultural pluralism in that it makes a concerted effort to take into consideration the point of view of minorities, rather than defining the society as primarily a descendant of white Europeans. Its insistence on celebrating our diversity, rather than our unity as a nation, has caused much controversy and is not universally accepted.

Majority and Minorities: Processes of Coexistence

Cultural pluralism is not a goal in every society or in every historical era. Dominant majorities have treated the minorities in their midst in a number of ways, and minorities have reacted variously to their condition. Some of the processes with which societies attempt to deal with their minorities span the following continuum.

Segregation is an attempt to isolate a minority from the majority. South Africa, until quite recently, offered one example of segregation. In that society, the dominant group had forced minorities that were numerically superior into a condition of inferiority, restricting their freedom of movement and isolating them either on rural reservations or in urban enclaves. Segregation was also rampant in the United States, particularly in the South, prior to a number of Supreme Court decisions that made the segregation of public facilities illegal.

Accommodation is a situation in which a minority is conscious of the norms and values of the majority, accepts and adapts to them, but chooses to retain its own ethnic norms and values. Thus, it does not fully participate in the host culture but remains culturally, and sometimes linguistically, distinct. The Cuban community in Miami, as well as some Muslim communities, are good examples of minorities that have chosen accommodation.

Acculturation, or cultural assimilation, occurs when a minority group accepts and makes its own the norms and values of the host culture, often giving up a native language and traditions. Despite this, such groups are often still refused consideration as equals.

Assimilation is a process by which minorities absorb completely the culture of the majority and enter into its mainstream. Generally, in the United States, the minorities that were most like the majority in looks and culture were assimilated most rapidly. Those most unlike the majority failed to be assimilated, and some no longer want to be. An interesting article written in 1951 about the course of assimilation in the United States, entitled "The Emerging Hyphen," may be found in *Harper's Magazine* archives. The Internet address is found on **mysearchlab.com.**

Amalgamation takes place when all distinctions between majority and minorities are erased. In amalgamation, members of different ethnic and racial groups intermarry, so that eventually their offspring form a new and distinct ethnic, cultural, or racial group. Brazil is considered an example of a society that has adopted amalgamation, although the process is far from perfect and does not reach throughout the entire society. In the United States, amalgamation has not taken place, but perhaps things are beginning to change. Interracial marriage, once taboo and against the law in some states, is now occurring at an increasingly rapid rate.

Although pluralism and multiculturalism are the current ideals in democratic societies, the other policies—and worse kinds of treatment—are hardly unknown. Continued subjugation was for many years the policy of South Africa, one that only now is being slowly remedied. Expulsion has been practiced by Uganda, which expelled more than 40,000 Asians during Idi Amin's tenure, and Vietnam forced out close to a million ethnic Chinese. It has been practiced most recently in the former Yugoslavia, where several ethnic groups have cleansed their territories of each other. Extermination, too, despite murder being a taboo

National Archives photo no. 111-SC-204745

Genocide is not an uncommon method of eliminating a group with whom one does not want to share a territory. The Jews have been a minority group in many societies and have often suffered from persecution and discrimination. During World War II, however, their total annihilation became the goal of the Nazi regime. This image shows what the liberators found when they entered one of the Nazi concentration camps.

in all societies, has many antecedents. Europeans who settled the New World are guilty of exterminating, both directly and indirectly, the majority of the native populations in North and South America. In the twentieth century, in addition to the systematic annihilation of European Jews, Gypsies, and Slavs by Nazi Germany, we have also witnessed the genocide of approximately two million Cambodians by the Pol Pot regime, as well as the massacre of Tutsis by Hutus, two ethnic groups residing in Rwanda. The twenty-first century is witnessing more ethnic cleansing in the Darfur region of Sudan.

In the Way: Obstacles to Pluralism

Not all relations between groups that coexist in the same society are conflict producing, but many are. It is human nature to want to remain "top dog." Thus, majorities employ a variety of mechanisms to keep minorities from displacing them from their dominant positions in the social system. Most of these are no longer legal in contemporary societies, nor are they necessarily conscious efforts. Among them, the most destructive are prejudice, discrimination, and what is still referred to as racism.

Prejudice

Prejudice derives from the word *prejudgment*, which implies that a person makes up his or her mind about something without any real knowledge about it. Prejudgment is often a useful tool, even though it is based on stereotypes and hearsay, because it is sometimes necessary to depend on someone else's word or act on superficial impressions. But prejudice goes beyond prejudgment in the sense that a prejudiced person refuses to change even when confronted by unassailable evidence.

Prejudice leans heavily on stereotyping. In **stereotyping**, common, uniform characteristics are assigned to an entire category of people, without any allowance for individual differences. African Americans, for instance, have been stereotyped as athletically and musically superior to whites. In essence, a stereotype develops when the traits and behavior of some individuals are considered to be typical of the whole group, or a superficial aspect of a group's behavior is taken as that group's total behavior, without any attempt to explain its causes.

Scapegoating is another mechanism that fuels prejudice. *Scapegoating*, derived from the Biblical practice of offering a goat as sacrifice in exchange for God's forgiveness of one's sins, is a term that refers to the tendency of frustrated individuals to respond with aggression. If the source of frustration cannot be attacked directly, then a third party may become the object of aggression. In troubled times—high unemployment, high crime rates, inflation—some group can always be found to take the blame.

Why Are We Prejudiced?

Because prejudice is an obvious cause of hostilities among groups, it has been the subject of much research. Research by psychologists seems to point to feelings of anger rapidly seeking a target, particularly if that target happens to be of a different social group, sex, or ethnicity. This finding, added to previous research, suggests that prejudice may have evolutionary roots. It may have developed as a quick, crude way for early humans to protect themselves from danger. Anger is a signal that some level of threat or hostility exists in the environment, and logic indicates that the threat probably comes from someone not in one's same social group, because members of the same social group generally reinforce and protect each other (Wartik, 2004, D5).

Early sociological research seemed to indicate that prejudice was due to the isolation of groups from one another. However, the example of the South, where whites and blacks lived in close proximity and often on intimate terms (though always in a master–servant relationship), did not support this theory. In his book, *The Nature of Prejudice,* social psychologist Gordon Allport (1954) proposed a theory of contact. According to this theory, when two groups of equal status have contact with each other, prejudice decreases; however, if status inequality exists and one group is dominant over the other, prejudice remains the same or actually increases. In fact, in the South of today, a decrease in prejudice has been noted; at the same time, Southern blacks have risen in the stratification system, and with the elimination of the "separate but equal" public facilities, blacks and whites of the same social class are brought closer together. Allport, however, had to qualify his findings: It seems that even when status is equal between two groups, if there is also competition, prejudice becomes more intense. Conversely, if the groups cooperate to achieve some common goals, prejudice declines.

Another influential theory, focusing on prejudice as a personality trait, was based on a now-classic study by T. W. Adorno et al. (1950), in which a high correlation between the development of prejudice and a type of personality called *authoritarian* was found. People with that type of personality are oversocialized to accept only the norms and values of their own group, rejecting all others. They become very anxious when confronted with different norms and values and convince themselves that people who differ from them are somehow inferior, subhuman, or sinful. Other features of an authoritarian personality include submission to authority, admiration of power and toughness, conventionality, condescension toward inferiors, insensitivity to relationships with others, and a deep-rooted and partly subconscious sense of insecurity. In such persons, prejudice is merely part of a total outlook on life in which situations and problems are perceived in terms of absolutes—good or bad, right or wrong—and in which people are either heroes or villains.

© David G. Houser/CORBIS

Institutional discrimination was flagrant in South Africa during the period of apartheid, when a majority of black Africans were oppressed by a minority of white colonial rulers.

Discrimination

Whereas prejudice is an attitude or a feeling, **discrimination** consists of actions taken as a result of prejudicial feelings; for instance, the belief that all Latinos are violent is a prejudice, but the organization of a committee to prevent them from moving into a neighborhood is discrimination.

Prejudice and discrimination usually go hand in hand, but they can also occur independent of each other. A person may, as an example, continue to believe that Latinos are violent. If, nonetheless, that person, being a law-abiding citizen, allows Latino families to move into the neighborhood without harassment or interference of any sort, the person is exhibiting prejudice without discrimination. On the other hand, a person may not harbor prejudicial feelings about Latinos at all; but if, to retain the friendship of neighbors, the person signs a petition to keep a Latino family from buying property on their street, that person is discriminating without being prejudiced. In general, however, prejudice and discrimination are mutually reinforcing.

Discrimination is against the law in the United States. However, because it is so closely interrelated with prejudice, certain kinds of discrimination are still prevalent to a degree in the society. Discrimination is viewed as being of two types: attitudinal and institutional. **Attitudinal discrimination** refers to behavior that is prompted by the personal prejudice of a member of a majority or in response to the prejudice of others. **Institutional discrimination** refers to the system of inequalities existing within a society, apart from the prejudices of individuals. In *The Declining Significance of Race* (1978) and *The Truly Disadvantaged* (1987), William J. Wilson speculated that whereas in the past attitudinal discrimination was to blame for the unequal status of African Americans, today the fault is attributable largely to factors that have little to do with race and much to do with changes in the economy. Specifically, the shift from manufacturing to a service economy that has polarized the labor market into low-wage and high-wage sectors, technological innovations that require a highly skilled labor force, and the relocation of manufacturing industries out of the central cities—or out of the country altogether—are primarily responsible for blocking economic opportunities to African Americans. Even if all racial prejudice were eliminated, a good portion of African Americans would remain unemployed or underemployed and would fail to thrive.

Time after time, every group that has been at the bottom of the stratification system has encountered virulent prejudice and discrimination coupled with gloomy predictions that the group was too inferior to ever rise out of their low status. And yet, time after time, once such groups improved their occupational position and achieved an economic status comparable to that of the majority, prejudice against them diminished. As to the mechanisms of upward mobility, Stark (1985) suggests that they include geographic concentration, internal economic development and specialization, and finally, development of a middle class. Upward mobility is slowed for groups that lack a substantial middle class, and until a middle class develops, prejudice and discrimination tend to persist. A British psychologist writes in *Psychology Today* that diversity is good for us; find it on the Internet by accessing it from **mysearchlab.com**.

Racism

Prejudice and discrimination are the chief components of an attitude that is commonly called **racism**. Although racism is popularly understood as hatred of members of certain racial groups, in the language of the social sciences it used to have a more precise meaning. It referred to the ideology that some racial groups are superior to others based on a recognizable trait, such as skin color, and that this belief justified discrimination against the group deemed inferior. Related to this belief was the idea that both the physical and behavioral traits of racial groups are inherited biologically. Racism is, of course, related to the concept of race, which, as we

Box 1 Love Thy Neighbor?

Every religion enjoins its followers to love others, be they brothers and sisters, or simply neighbors. But this is precisely the one tenet that most people ignore, witness the many wars and conflicts that have occurred throughout history. Racism, in the old sense of hating someone of a different race, is one illustration of such hatred. When we speak of racism, Americans immediately think of the black–white relations in our own country. But enmity between groups need not occur only between groups that differ in skin color; it can occur between groups that differ in culture or ethnicity. A prime example is that of Rwanda, a country that had been colonized by Belgium, and that, following its independence, began having problems between its two main ethnic groups, the Hutus and the Tutsis. These two groups lived in peace before being colonized: The colonizers, perhaps believing in "divide and conquer," separated the groups, giving the Tutsis more privileges because they looked a bit more "white." Of course, this created resentment among the Hutus, who eventually came to power after independence and began a campaign of revenge against the Tutsis. This campaign came to a head in 1994, when the Hutu president was killed in a plane that was shot down. Hutu officials blamed the Tutsis for his death and incited the Hutu population to kill, rape, and destroy the Tutsis in their midst. In the space of 100 days, an estimated million Tutsis were killed and thousands escaped to neighboring countries.

By 2010, attempts at reconciliation were still problematic. The government has tried to overcome the effects of the genocide, but according to a news article, it is failing. A New York Times reporter maintains that even sixteen years after the Rwandan genocide, ethnicity is still a dominant part of growing up for the young people who will be responsible for the nation's future (Kron, 2010). The government has focused its attempts to build a postethnic society on university students. However, the government has become more repressive with the passage of time, and the effort at creating a society in which ethnic differences are ignored has turned into arrests and jail against individuals who say anything against such efforts. And even though Hutus and Tutsis have equal rights under the new regime, the two groups are still divided. In universities, students may sleep in the same dormitories and make friendships according to their interests, but on campuses life and friendships follow language and rarely cross the borders of ethnicity. By language is meant the fact that Tutsis—having returned from English-speaking countries where they were refugees, speak English (the current president is an English-speaking Tutsi), and the Hutus speak French, inherited from their Belgian colonizers.

In short, despite efforts to overcome ethnic differences that divide the two groups, the task is so difficult that it is felt such differences are only papered over, and the cult of nationalism—of people feeling themselves Rwandan first, rather than Hutu or Tutsi—has so far not shown any success.

saw earlier, is no longer recognized as valid. Still, the concept, as well as the term, persists, and not just in the United States. All societies, throughout the ages, have practiced one form or another of racism, which is just another version of **ethnocentrism**. This ability of one group to feel superior to others has functioned historically to provide a rationale for a social order based on the domination of one group over another, that is, "to use beliefs in genetic superiority–inferiority as a means of justifying domination and exploitation of one racial group by another" (Yetman, 1985, 14).

As an ideology, racism originated in Darwin's theory of evolution, particularly its concept of the survival of the fittest (although Darwin himself never intended to give it this social meaning). This theory was applied to human groups (social Darwinism) and used to rationalize the colonization of a number of nations by Europeans. The latter were considered the most highly evolved and civilized of peoples because of the development of self-rule and representative government among them.

Today, racism as an ideology has declined all over the world, and very few people in the United States would admit to subscribing to racist beliefs. The ideology, however, has been replaced by some stubborn forms of institutional racism and by a number of myths that each group believes about the other. The term remains in our vocabulary, although most people mistakenly attribute it to discriminatory actions or prejudicial feelings or simply as an expression of negative sentiments.

Racial Minorities

The four visible **racial minority** groups in the United States consist of Native Americans, African Americans, some Latinos, and Asian Americans (Table 1; note that the total population of the United States today has increased to over 300 million). With the exception of Asian Americans, racial minorities have had a different history than the more recently arrived ethnic minorities. The way the United States will look in 2050 is briefly explored on a Web site noted at **mysearchlab.com.**

Native Americans

The original inhabitants of the North American continent had been living here for more than 20,000 years—though they themselves had been immigrants of sorts: They are thought to have crossed the Bering Strait when it was a land bridge connecting Alaska to Asia. They were displaced by the European settlers, who were more advanced technologically and who took advantage of the natives' lack of unity and tribal loyalties. The number of Native Americans was greatly reduced through diseases brought by the white settlers as well as through the constant warfare waged against them.

Because the settlers believed their culture was superior to that of the American Indians (so named because Columbus was searching for an alternate route to the Indies when he landed on Hispaniola), they were able to rationalize the seizure of land and to ignore any treaties or agreements between themselves and the native populations. After the United States became an independent nation, the government forcefully removed Indians from desirable

TABLE 1 Annual Estimates of the Resident Population by Sex, Race, and Hispanic Origin for the United States, July 1, 2009

Sex, Race, and Hispanic Origin	Population Estimates	
	July 1, 2009	July 1, 2008
BOTH SEXES	307,006,550	304,374,846
One Race	301,683,044	299,216,154
White	244,298,393	242,685,070
Black	39,641,060	39,204,596
AIAN	3,151,284	3,095,246
Asian	14,013,954	13,665,386
NHPI	578,353	565,856
Two or More Races	5,323,506	5,158,692
Race alone or in combination:		
White	248,919,247	247,156,135
Black	41,804,073	41,276,843

(Continued)

TABLE 1 (*Continued*)

Sex, Race, and Hispanic Origin	Population Estimates	
	July 1, 2009	July 1, 2008
AIAN	4,960,643	4,876,973
Asian	15,989,876	15,578,098
NHPI	1,137,473	1,112,202
NOT HISPANIC	**258,587,226**	**257,396,278**
One Race	254,028,184	252,968,697
White	199,851,240	199,529,117
Black	37,681,544	37,318,578
AIAN	2,360,807	2,332,222
Asian	13,686,083	13,348,969
NHPI	448,510	439,811
Two or More Races	4,559,042	4,427,581
Race alone or in combination:		
White	203,799,820	203,357,392
Black	39,494,653	39,057,548
AIAN	3,873,681	3,828,788
Asian	15,437,231	15,047,180
NHPI	917,824	900,070
HISPANIC	**48,419,324**	**46,978,568**
One Race	47,654,860	46,247,457
White	44,447,153	43,155,953
Black	1,959,516	1,886,018
AIAN	790,477	763,024
Asian	327,871	316,417
NHPI	129,843	126,045
Two or More Races	764,464	731,111
Race alone or in combination:		
White	45,119,427	43,798,743
Black	2,309,420	2,219,295
AIAN	1,086,962	1,048,185
Asian	552,645	530,918
NHPI	219,649	212,132

Note: AIAN stands for American Indian/Alaska Native and NHPI stands for Native Hawaiian/Pacific Islander.

Source: U.S. Census Bureau, Population Division, Release Date: June 2010.

land and pushed them onto reservations, where they remained isolated from mainstream society. The land on which reservations are located is managed in trust by the Bureau of Indian Affairs (BIA), an agency that has historically been more interested in conservation than economic development. Ranked as the most inefficient of 90 federal agencies, the BIA has a sorry record of waste, corruption, and red tape. Hence, conditions on reservations have been characterized by economic backwardness, inadequate education, substandard housing, and inferior health care.

As of 2008, there were 4.9 million Native Americans in the United States, including Alaska natives, most of them in the western states of California, Oklahoma, Arizona, and New Mexico and Alaska. The Census Bureau estimates that by 2050 they will be 8.6 million. Many have now left the reservations and live in urban areas (although about 38 percent remain on reservations). However, they are the most disadvantaged of all minority groups: Almost one-third live below the poverty level, and they have alarmingly high unemployment rates. High mortality rates from alcohol-related causes and high suicide rates are also indications of the substandard conditions in which many Native Americans still live. In many tribes, life expectancy is only 45 years, and they have the lowest per capita income of any minority group in the United States. The poverty rate in 2008 was 24.2 percent, and 31.7 percent had no health insurance. The Pine Ridge Reservation in South Dakota is home to the Oglala branch of the Sioux, the descendants of such famous war heroes as Crazy Horse and Red Cloud. Unfortunately, its 16,000 inhabitants are experiencing the most profound poverty in the United States. Fewer than 3 in 10 adults have jobs, nearly all of which are in government agencies. They are ravaged by isolation, disease, political infighting, and the inability to find jobs, leading to dependence on welfare and ultimately to depression and alcoholism. In a vicious circle that often plagues minorities, lack of skills and distance or isolation from jobs leads to unemployment, and the dependence on welfare develops habits not conducive to getting and keeping jobs. However, 25 percent of Native Americans and Alaskans over 16 worked in managerial and professional occupations, and another 25 percent in service occupations. In addition, in 2008, 76 percent had finished high school, and their median income was $37,815.

The problems of Native Americans have been complicated by tribalism—many think of themselves as primarily Navajo or Cherokee, and so on because there is no uniform Native American culture or language. (Native Americans are divided into approximately 500 tribal groups, and around 50 of their original languages are still spoken.) Only in the past several decades has a new militancy become evident, as witnessed by an increase in political activity through the American Indian Movement. This has resulted in the return of some lands as well as in an effort to develop economic self-sufficiency. Following the lessons of the civil rights movements, Native Americans are beginning to use the judicial system, so that more litigation on their behalf has been initiated in the past 20 years than in the previous 200.

Asian Americans

The two largest Asian minorities living in the United States used to be the Chinese and the Japanese, before the large-scale Asian immigration that began in the 1970s. Today, Asian Americans constitute a large, highly diverse, and overwhelmingly foreign-born population. Chinese and Filipinos make up the largest Asian contingents, followed by Japanese, Indians, Koreans, and Vietnamese (see Table 2). These groups are culturally, religiously, and linguistically different from each other as well as from the dominant majority, but are generally classified together in the public mind. The total number of Asians in the United States is over 15.5 million, or 5 percent of the U.S. population. This represents an increase from 1980, when

TABLE 2 Percentages of Minority Population

White persons, percent, 2008 (a)	79.8%
Black persons, percent, 2008 (a)	12.8%
American Indian and Alaska Native persons, percent, 2008 (a)	1.0%
Asian persons, percent, 2008 (a)	4.5%
Native Hawaiian and Other Pacific Islander, percent, 2008 (a)	0.2%
Persons reporting two or more races, percent, 2008	1.7%
Persons of Hispanic or Latino origin, percent, 2008 (b)	15.4%
White persons not Hispanic, percent, 2008	65.6%

Source: http://quickfacts.census.gov/qfd/states/00000.html

they were 1.5 percent of the population. The new immigrants display a wide variety of cultural forms, differing in social class and skills (Rodriguez, 1998, 21). However, they are becoming a group to be reckoned with in terms of their economic success and civic-mindedness.

In general, Asian Americans have been financially successful, exhibiting the highest median family income of any minority group ($70,069 in 2008), the lowest divorce rates (3 percent) and teenage pregnancy rates (6 percent), and the lowest unemployment rates (3.5 percent). Their poverty rate was 11.8 percent, although a percentage live on welfare, particularly those originating in Southeast Asia who immigrated after the Vietnam War. (Thus, the medium income of Asian Indians was $90,528 in 2008, whereas that of Vietnamese Americans was $55,667.) In California, which is the residence of almost 40 percent of the Asian population in America, Asians have a higher level of college degrees than whites, and they outperform them in both education and income within one generation. The proportion of Asians with a bachelor's degree or higher is 50 percent. Even more striking, 16 percent of Asian and Pacific Islanders 25 years old and over have advanced degrees (master's, Ph.D., M.D., or J.D.), whereas the corresponding rate for all adults in this age group is 9 percent.

Chinese. Today there are approximately 3.62 million Americans of Chinese descent living in the United States, most of them in California and Hawaii. As a group, they have been upwardly mobile and are characterized by rising professionalization and being highly represented in medicine, engineering, and scientific research. Partly as a result of their high socioeconomic status, it has been easier for the Chinese to amalgamate, if they chose, as evidenced by their relatively high rates of intermarriage.

Japanese. The Japanese began to arrive at the beginning of the twentieth century and, like the Chinese before them, were subject to the same discriminatory practices, being considered part of the "yellow peril" that threatened to engulf white culture. Their real problems, however, peaked during World War II, when they were labeled as security risks and potential traitors. They were interned in detention camps, their property confiscated or sold.

At present, there are 1.30 million Japanese Americans who make up 6.9 percent of all Asians in the United States. The generation born in the United States, known as the Nisei, were socialized to value education and conformity to the norms of the dominant majority. As a result, third-generation Japanese Americans rank highest among all nonwhite groups in education and income. They have experienced high rates of upward mobility and a shift from jobs in small ethnic businesses to executive positions in the corporate hierarchy. This trend has also resulted in a great amount of amalgamation (40 percent have non-Japanese spouses), particularly among the best educated and most economically successful. Interracial and inter-ethnic marriage increases with each generation. Whereas only 13 percent of foreign-born Asians marry non-Asians, 34 percent of second-generation and 54 percent of third-generation Asian Americans do (Rodriguez, 2003, 96).

Other Asians.   More recent immigrants of Asian background to the United States include Filipinos, Asian Indians, Koreans, Vietnamese, Cambodians, and Laotians, the last three as a result of the conflict in Indochina in which the United States became embroiled (see Table 2). Although resentment against these groups has been sharp, particularly in areas where they are highly concentrated (during the 1992 Los Angeles riots, most of the hostility of black Americans was directed at Korean merchants whose businesses were located in black areas), many are economically upwardly mobile and appear to be entering the mainstream with greater ease than their predecessors. They are sometimes called the "model minority" because they are statistically more prosperous, more educated, and less prone to engage in criminal activities, succumb to drugs, or be unemployed than Americans in general.

African Americans

As of 2009 African Americans represented 12.3 percent of the total population of the nation, or nearly 40 million. They have been here longer than any other nonwhite group: By 1776, the year of American independence, nearly all African Americans were native-born. However, the entrance of blacks into the mainstream of American society has been complicated by their special problems and made more difficult by economic causes.

As is well known, African Americans originally did not come to this country voluntarily in search of a better future but rather were forced into slavery by greedy Africans and Europeans and sold to the colonists of North and South America as a form of cheap labor. As slaves in a foreign land, cut off from their native culture, they found themselves in a particularly vulnerable position. The culture that eventually emerged among the slaves incorporated some of the negative perceptions toward them exhibited by the dominant majority. And although other immigrants could always go back to their native land if things did not work out here, no such outlet was open to Africans.

Some historians have challenged the common view of slavery as a debilitating institution, responsible for splitting families or breeding slaves for the market. On the contrary, the fact that a social structure developed despite slavery could be considered a measure of black achievement. The black family that developed during slavery was a strong and enduring institution in a stable nuclear form and with a Victorian morality (Fogel & Engerman, 1974). Researchers have shown that black family life was vital during slavery, pointing out that the single-parent black household is primarily a phenomenon of recent decades and not a holdover from slave days (Gutman, 1976).

Because they have been until recently the largest minority group, African Americans represent the greatest threat to the majority in competing for jobs. This was especially true in the past, when restrictions on immigration left blacks as the only source of cheap labor and had them competing with a large pool of unskilled white workers. Size, of course, is also a powerful political tool; after barriers to voting were removed, African Americans took advantage of their strength, as witnessed by the increasing numbers who hold elected office around the country.

Even though the deep prejudice and open discrimination against blacks made their upward mobility and integration into the society difficult, the principal obstacle seems to have been economic in nature. Until World War II, the great majority of African Americans lived in the rural South, a region that until recently suffered from backwardness and poverty. Education, housing, and health care were substandard in the rural South for both blacks and whites because the Southern states could not tax their citizens enough to support these services.

The advent of World War II brought a need for workers in the defense industries, which were located chiefly in the urban North. Trainloads of poor African Americans began leaving the South in search of the better pay that industrial work offered. However, these African Americans had been subsistence farmers or farm laborers. They lacked education and technical skills and were not acquainted with the nature of urban life. According to Stark (1985), these traits made them comparable to immigrants from foreign cultures. From this perspective, they compare quite favorably with other ethnic and racial minorities, who improved their economic situation and thus began their entry into mainstream society in about two or three generations. Unfortunately, beginning with the 1970s, industrial and manufacturing jobs that had been an avenue of upward mobility for many previous generations of immigrants began to dry up in American cities, leaving a proportion of African Americans subject to unemployment and underemployment (Sowell, 1983).

Despite this, conditions continued to improve for African Americans in the following years. First, although in the 1940s whites had favored the separation of the two races, by the mid-1990s a majority declared that blacks were their neighbors and that they had close friends among them. Blacks had begun to make substantial progress even before the civil rights movement and affirmative action were put into effect. By the mid-1990s, 40 percent of African Americans were squarely in the middle class (today, the tiny minority that had existed mainly within the boundaries of the black community has grown much larger); a third lived in suburbs, and a high proportion (59 percent of women and 32 percent of men) were in middle-class occupations. The past several decades have seen sharp increases in the number of black lawyers, doctors, and engineers, and the earnings of black government workers, pharmacists, mathematicians, designers, and engineers approximate, and on occasion surpass, those of their white counterparts. In fact, 26 percent of blacks age 16 and older work in management, professional, and related occupations.

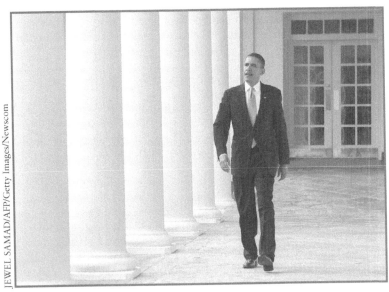

African Americans have made great strides in the past several decades. Barack Obama was elected president of the United States in 2008.

Among other changes that occurred in the decade of the 1990s, the number of black office-holders increased from 1,469 in 1970 to 8,406 in 1995. Today, of the 435 representatives in the House, 41 are African American men and women; and black mayors were elected in a vast number of American cities. College attendance, which is closely related to economic achievement, increased from only 7.2 percent in 1960 to 37.5 percent by 1995 (however, completion of four or more years of college in 1998 stood at 14.7 percent for African Americans, compared to 24.4 for the entire country). By 2008, 80 percent of African Americans aged 25 to 29 had a high school diploma, 23 percent had a bachelor's degree, and 1.1 million had an advanced degree (the Bureau of Labor Statistics produces an overview of African Americans in the labor force every February in honor of African American History Month.)

The income gap between whites and blacks has similarly narrowed; nonetheless, inequalities are still obvious. In 2002, ethnic and racial categories were redefined by the Census Bureau, allowing members to choose their own ethnic or racial makeup, so a single comparison of income and poverty is difficult to make. The annual median income of households that reported only black or black in combination with one or more other races in 2009 was $32,584 whereas the real median household income nationally was $54,2920. The poverty rate was 25.8 percent, in contrast to the official national poverty rate of 13.5 percent. At the same time, as noted earlier, 28 percent of blacks 16 and older worked in technical, sales, and administrative support jobs and managerial and professional specialty jobs. There were approximately 44,000 employed black physicians, 80,000 postsecondary teachers, 52,000 chief executives, 91,000 engineers, and 48,300 lawyers. Finally, 44 percent of all blacks owned their own homes (66.9 percent of whites did) (**http://www.factfinder.census.gov**). However, black unemployment, always high, rose to 17.2 percent in 2010 (but declined to 15.7 percent in January 2011), as a result of the recession; 19.5 percent of African American had no health insurance, compared to 10.4 percent of non-Hispanic whites; and African Americans suffer from HIV/AIDS, heart disease, stroke, cancer, diabetes, and homicide to greater degrees than other Americans (U.S. Department of Health and Human Services; CDC, 2007).

Another indication of the lessening of differences between the races is the dramatic change in the social and political attitudes about race. A survey by the Pew Research Center released in the fall of 2007 found that Americans of both races have become much more personally tolerant. For instance, the idea of blacks and whites dating is now widely accepted: In 1980, only half of the American public agreed that it was all right for blacks and whites to date each other; in 2007, 83 percent agreed. As for interracial marriage, 22 percent of all American adults state that they have a close relative who is married to someone of a different race. This is in contrast to 1970 when fewer than 1 percent of all married couples consisted of spouses of different races (Pew Research Center, 2007).

Another survey by the Gallup Organization showed similar conclusions. Most progress has been achieved in interracial relationships and the neighborhoods in which both races reside: 70 percent of whites, 80 percent of blacks, and 77 percent of Hispanics say they generally approve of interracial marriage. Compared to the 4 percent of whites who approved of such marriages in 1958, that represents gigantic progress. However, there are vast gulfs between the different races' perceptions of how minorities are treated. Although only 38 percent of blacks agree that they are treated "very fairly" or "somewhat fairly" (and one-third say that members of their race are treated "very unfairly"), 76 percent of white respondents believe that they are treated fairly. Generational differences show up in this survey as well, although in a different light: Young Americans (ages 18–29) are more likely than older respondents, especially the 65-plus segment, to favor the retention of distinctive cultures. Harvard sociologist William Julius Wilson suggests that such an attitude is a positive thing; it shows an acceptance of multiculturalism, an idea young people have acquired in school (Goodheart, 2004, 37–41, 75).

The year 2004 marked the fiftieth anniversary of *Brown v. Board of Education*, the Supreme Court ruling stating that segregated schools are unconstitutional. This was one of the most important decisions of the twentieth century and the origin of the entire civil rights movement. Unfortunately, integrated schools have not been the successes their supporters envisioned. Forced integration following the ruling began a movement of whites out of city neighborhoods into suburban areas and pushed many white students into private schools. Affirmative action, attempting to attain "diversity," has been quite successful in integrating higher education. Busing small children to public elementary and high schools, however, proved unsatisfactory to both whites and African Americans, and many cities began to ask the courts to overturn the Supreme Court decision. As the schools gave up the attempt to integrate, many schools became segregated again. Today, approximately 70 percent of black students attend schools in which racial minorities are a majority, and a third are in schools that are 90 to 100 percent minority. The ironic thing is that, in many instances, black families sue school districts that insist on keeping an integrated student body. For these families, the benefits of integration are not worth the burdens it imposes on them.

Although there is agreement that African Americans have progressed a great deal in attaining a status nearly equal to others in mainstream society, academic and demographic sources provide evidence for the existence of two African-American communities. One is made up of middle-class and affluent blacks who have flourished as a result of the increased opportunities that came with the civil rights movement. The other consists of poor, mainly urban blacks, who remain socially and economically isolated from the American mainstream.

Hispanic Americans

The more than 48.4 million Hispanic Americans represent about 16 percent of the U.S. population and are growing five times faster as a group than the rest of the American population (U.S. Bureau of the Census, 2010; Facts for Features. Hispanic Heritage Month. September 15–October 15). Hispanics overlap the categories of racial and ethnic minorities inasmuch as some Hispanics are black, others are South American Indians, and still others are white. (Incidentally, Hispanic is a name used by U.S. agencies for bureaucratic convenience. Some Spanish-speaking individuals prefer to be called Latinos because the name refers to an indigenous culture, that of Latin America, rather than depending solely on the culture of Spain.) They have overtaken African Americans as this country's largest minority group. The majority of Hispanics live in New Mexico, California, and Texas. Other states containing Hispanic populations of one million or more are New York, Florida, Illinois, Arizona, and New Jersey.

Latino neighborhoods, even though statistically poor, seem to be thriving, with lots of small stores, markets, and motels, whereas poor neighborhoods in many central cities are visibly declining. The reason is that Latinos have kept their communities intact, shopping at Latino stores, consulting Latino doctors, reading Latino newspapers, listening to Latino radio, and watching Latino TV stations. This strong sense of community will serve Latinos well in their quest for political representation and other rights in the face of hostility from other groups with whom they share their living space.

Latinos do not constitute a unified community, however, nor do they possess a common culture. This group is fragmented because members came at different times and from different places. In fact, Latinos range over a wide racial spectrum as well because they are the descendants of the original Spanish settlers of the New World and native populations of Central and South America, as well as the Caribbean. They are, however, bound together by their common

Spanish language, by their Spanish surnames, and by their Roman Catholic religion. The three major subdivisions are Mexican Americans or Chicanos (approximately 66 percent), Puerto Ricans (9 percent), and Cubans (3.5 percent). Other Spanish-speaking groups include natives of Central and South American countries.

About 24 percent of Hispanics work in service occupations and 18 percent in managerial and professional occupations. The real median household income of Hispanics in 2008 was $37,913, and the poverty rate was 23.2 percent that same year. Around 30.7 percent lacked health insurance. A large percentage—78 percent—speak Spanish at home. As for education, 62 percent of those 25 years old and over had at least a high school diploma, 13 percent in the same age group had a bachelor's degree, and about 1,000,000 persons 18 and over had an advanced degree. About 46 percent of Hispanics own their own home. Mexican Americans tend to have the largest families, and Cubans have the smallest.

Many Mexican Americans are actually native to the United States, having occupied the Southwest before the American colonization and annexation of Mexican land occurred. Others have continued to enter across the Mexican border in search of better jobs. Although the opportunities may be better for them in the United States than in Mexico, Mexicans have not been as upwardly mobile as some other immigrant groups. They are highly urbanized and are generally employed in low-wage service or manufacturing jobs in which employers are attempting to keep labor costs down and unions out. In southern California, they make up almost half the population when all the illegals are counted in. By the year 2050, it is estimated that Latinos will constitute 24 percent of the nation's total population. The state of Arizona has recently passed legislation that allows police officers to check the documents of any individual who appears to be an illegal alien. The law was meant to keep drug smugglers and other criminals from crossing over from Mexico into Arizona. However, the law has been criticized because it could lead to racial profiling and other discriminatory actions against persons who simply look Hispanic.

Although Puerto Rico has had the status of an "associated free state" of the United States since 1898, when the territory was ceded to the United States by Spain, Puerto Ricans did not begin to arrive in large numbers until the 1950s. (Puerto Rico became a Commonwealth in 1952.) Today, almost four million Puerto Ricans reside in the United States, concentrated mainly in the cities of the eastern seaboard, particularly New York, and in the large cities of the Midwest.

As a group, Puerto Ricans are culturally and racially distinct from Mexicans, being a blend of predominantly black and Spanish cultures. Puerto Ricans are economically one of the most disadvantaged ethnic groups in the United States, with a median family income half the national average and a high percentage (23 percent) living in poverty. On every health indicator, Puerto Ricans fare worse than either Mexican Americans or Cubans; infant mortality is 50 percent higher than among Mexican Americans and nearly three times that of Cubans. Moreover, the secondary effects of poverty—family breakups, single parenthood, apathy, unemployment—afflict Puerto Ricans to a greater degree than they do other Hispanics. Attempts are under way to channel the energy of the new generation into political activism to improve the group's welfare in this country. Currently, there are three members of Congress of Puerto Rican extraction.

Most Cubans came to the United States following Fidel Castro's rise to power. They differ substantially from other Spanish-speaking groups; overall they are much older and better educated. The reason is that the first wave to enter this country consisted of professionals running away from the communist regime in Cuba. They were able to use their skills, experience, and expertise in the economy almost immediately following their arrival. Their success is reflected in their income, which is higher than that of other Spanish-speaking groups. A later wave of immigrants, who arrived in 1980, does not appear to be equally skilled.

Most Cubans are concentrated in Miami, Florida (whose metropolitan population of nearly five million is approximately 60 percent Hispanic), where their financial success and high numbers have given them political clout sufficient to elect a number of Cuban-born officials. Unfortunately, this polyethnic city, rather than a model for a pluralistic society, is one of the country's most divided cities in terms of the endless complexities of racial and immigrant politics. Much more information may be garnered from Web sites that deal with the subject.

Ethnic and Religious Minorities

Looking a generation or two into the past, a majority of American families can find an ancestor who was born "in the old country." Therefore, the ethnic experience is familiar to a great number of Americans.

When one refers to "ethnics," the understanding is that one is speaking of the descendants of the waves of immigrants from southern and eastern Europe who arrived in the early years of the century. A number of sociological research projects have attempted to probe the depth of feeling such ethnics have retained for their ancestors' countries of origin. The consensus is that, in the battle of the culture of the old country and the lifestyle of the new, the new has won hands down. A random sampling of ethnics found that only 2 percent of them ever had help in business from others who shared their ethnicity, only 4 percent experienced discrimination on the basis of their ethnic background, only 1 percent ate ethnic food on a daily basis, almost none were fluent in the language of their ancestors, only 2 percent belonged to ethnic lodges or social clubs, and only 11 percent lived in neighborhoods that had a significant concentration of similar ethnics. The great majority had intermarried, rarely participated in cultural events pertaining to their ethnic group, and considered themselves in actual behavior to be fully American (Alba, 1990). The conclusion reached by this researcher is that ethnicity is more of a symbol than a real identity for most Americans. In addition, whereas earlier ethnicity had an exclusive quality—you were either Jewish or Irish Catholic— today it is inclusive—you can be European-American regardless of where exactly you came from. The fundamental change here is that white Americans think of themselves in terms of sameness rather than difference, of universal rather than particular origins.

The United States continues to be a nation of immigrants. The Census Bureau estimates that 12.5 million legal permanent residents were living in the United States on January 1, 2009, In addition, there are uncounted millions of illegal immigrants. In fact, immigration has been a chief instrument of growth for states that otherwise would have lost population—such as New York—or whose population growth would have been much smaller—such as California, or even Indiana. Many experts believe that the next decades will bring an equal or greater stream of immigrants, leading to a still different picture of American society.

White Ethnics: Catholics

Of the three factors affecting minority status, religion has been the least destructive in this society. The United States, founded as it was primarily by English and other western European settlers, remained a relatively homogeneous Protestant society until around 1820, when new waves of immigrants from Europe arrived. Even then, because most of the immigrants were also Protestants, they were fairly well absorbed into the WASP majority. Between 1860 and 1920, however, immigrants hailed from central, eastern, and southern Europe and differed not only in language but also in religion.

The descendants of these immigrants have, since the 1970s, been dubbed as the "white ethnics." White ethnics, who prize both their American citizenship and their ethnic origins, are predominantly Catholics and represent about 25 percent of the American population. The Protestant majority viewed Catholics with great suspicion until the middle of the twentieth century, attributing their loyalty to the Pope as a form of betrayal of the democratic ideology. Nonetheless, individual Catholics and Catholic families have fared well, as exemplified by the election of a Catholic president, John F. Kennedy, in 1960.

A stratification hierarchy is visible among Catholics, with the Irish and other northern Europeans at the top, the eastern Europeans in the middle, and the Hispanic groups at the bottom. However, these internal divisions have been much lessened as the anti-Catholic feelings in the society have been reduced. Similarly, the differences between Catholics and Protestants in family size, income, education, and occupation are gradually disappearing. The current generation of Catholics is the most educated and prosperous in the history of the Church in the United States. The Church has also been absorbing large waves of non-European immigrants (Davidson, 2004).

At one time, white ethnics were distinguished by living in cultural enclaves (Little Italy, Slavic Village, etc.), in which it was easier to retain a native tongue and customs. Later generations have become dispersed in the suburbs, and with dispersion came a loss of ethnic traditions. Religion, however, tends to remain. As a result, Catholicism provides a means of attaining identity and of forming primary group relationships. It appears that the Catholic Church is losing some of its adherents as a result of revelations of sexual molestation of young people by some Catholic priests and the efforts of the church hierarchy to hide these crimes rather than attempting to eliminate them and punish the perpetrators.

Jewish Americans

Jewish Americans—of whom there are approximately some 6.5 million in the United States—are ethnic in the sense that they share cultural traits and religious beliefs that are distinct from the mainstream Christian society. However, although they may be affiliated with the Orthodox, Conservative, or Reform branch of Judaism, only 46 percent of American Jewish adults belong to a synagogue. Many adult Jews are not very active in religious affairs: Judaism represents mainly a source of identification for them.

The Jewish people are a classic example of a minority persecuted throughout the ages and throughout the world. In the United States, prejudice and discrimination against Jews were rampant in the first half of the twentieth century, as they were denied access to particular neighborhoods, schools, and social clubs. However, anti-Semitism never acquired the virulent proportions in the United States that it did in some other countries. In Germany, during World War II, the destruction of the Jewish minority became a government priority, and by the end of the war 6 million Jews had been killed in Europe, an example of genocide that, it is hoped, will never be repeated.

In general, Jews have been very successful in the educational and economic spheres, being highly represented among college graduates (55 percent of adult Jewish Americans have a bachelors' degree, and 25 percent have a graduate degree). Many have attained high-earning positions—60 percent of all employed Jews are in one of the three highest status job categories: professional/technical, management, and executive. As a result of their high education levels and high-status jobs, their household income is also high. About 34 percent of Jewish households report incomes of over $75,000 (compared to 17 percent of all U.S. households), 24 percent have an income under $25,000, while the 2005 median household income was $46,242. Only 5 percent of Jewish households (and 9 percent of Jews 65 years old and over) report incomes that fall below the federal poverty line (**http://www.ujc.org**).

Box 2 Immigration and Its Discontents

America is a land of immigrants—even its original inhabitants, the Native Americans that the English settlers encountered, had come from elsewhere thousands of years before. Nonetheless, the issue of immigration has never been resolved to the satisfaction of all Americans. Should our borders be open to all, at all times? Should only some people be allowed entry, at only some times? Should numbers be restricted by countries of origin? All these questions have been asked and answered at different times in our history.

Today, immigration remains a divisive issue that the government is attempting to resolve. Because such a large number of people are trying to come here, a segment of the population believes that they take away jobs that should go to Americans. In addition, the complaint is that those who come in illegally are still benefiting from health care and schooling, paid for by tax dollars that American citizens must pay. On the other hand, to deny entry entirely seems unethical because we have all been immigrants at one time or another.

The issue is essentially an economic one, but economists disagree about the effect of immigration. Some economists maintain that because the largest contingent of immigrants is poorly educated Mexicans, they tend to hurt the poorest Americans, who depend on manual labor. This idea—that job seekers from abroad mean fewer opportunities and lower wages for native workers—is controversial in labor economics. The reason is that although the premise seems logical, there is another way of looking at it. In fact, supply-side economists maintain that a greater number of immigrants also increases the demand for goods and services, thus adding jobs and profits to the national economy.

Immigration policy, however, has never been based on economics, but more often had a racist or ethnocentric basis. The exclusionary acts directed at Chinese immigrants in the nineteenth and early twentieth centuries, as well as at immigrants from eastern and southern Europe, had some economic basis, but mostly they were a result of Americans' dislike for people who were different from them in culture or appearance.

In 1965, with the Immigration and Nationality Act, quotas were ended and substituted with a priority based on family reunification; that is, a person could enter this country if a relative was already here. Today, the proportion of foreign born is 12 percent of the population, and a large number enter the country illegally. It is the latter problem that makes it imperative to arrive at a logical and fair immigration policy, and therein lies the difficulty. Two bills are pending in Congress; the House bill would require employers to employ only legal workers and levy heavy penalties if they employed illegals. It also expects the government to build hundreds of miles of fencing on the U.S. southern border. The Senate bill would allow illegals who are already here to remain and provide them with the ability to attain legal status. It would also allow employers to bring in guest workers as long as they pay them as they would native workers. It remains to be seen what an immigration policy will ultimately look like because so far it has not yet been written into law.

Economists also believe that the country would be well served if we let in more immigrants with advanced degrees because we are already very dependent on foreigners to fill occupations in such areas as scientific research and nursing. These high earners would actually raise the national income. But they also maintain that unskilled immigrants do not take away jobs from unskilled Americans; the latter will not take jobs such as hotel chambermaids or lettuce pickers. Nonetheless, Americans who are unskilled do have to compete with unskilled immigrants. And this brings us to the ultimate problem: how to increase the skills and cognition of our youth so that they will not need to compete with unskilled immigrants. (An in-depth view of some of the issues discussed may be found in Roger Lowenstein, "The Immigration Equation." *The New York Times Magazine*, July 9, 2006, 36–71.)

Another way of looking at immigration is in how it affects the countries from which the immigrants originate. For instance, the largest number of immigrants to the United States come from Mexico. It is to our advantage that our neighbors to the south live comfortably and not in dire poverty, for it is the latter condition that sends them north in droves. According to one reporter, such immigration has left many Mexican towns almost empty, particularly of young men. However, California-style homes are going up in these communities, built by the money the immigrants send home and awaiting their eventual return. In the meantime, remittances to Mexico exceed $20 billion a year, and in 2003, they had become the country's second largest source of income, ahead of tourism and foreign investment.

Although the money that enters Mexico from the paychecks of immigrants is a boon to the country and to its impoverished residents, it also creates problems. First, as most young men leave, the towns are populated by women and children, a condition that is not beneficial to the family unit. Second, this money reduces the incentive to work to the locals left behind and fuels inflation, making it harder for those who have no relatives in the United States to survive in dignity. Finally, although the men leave with the intention of returning, most do not. The crackdown on illegal immigration makes visits to Mexico and back dangerous, and the fewer the visits, the more familial ties weaken. In short, although the flow of labor across borders appears to benefit both economies, it is not without a more somber side (Quirk, 2007, 26).

Their economic success has made them targets of some Americans, whose envy has blinded them to the true reason for Jewish success and who allow unscrupulous public figures to mislead them with ancient and spurious conspiracy theories. As a result, 68.5 percent of hate crimes were committed against Jews in 2005 (World Net Daily, 2006).

Intermarriage rates among Jews are quite high, a fact that worries many leaders inasmuch as it portends the end of ethnic solidarity. As late as 1965, 89 percent of Jews married other Jews, but since 1996, 54 percent of Jews who married have intermarried, and two-thirds of the children of all intermarried parents are not being raised Jewish. The current intermarriage rate stands at between 52 and 43 percent, depending on how intermarriage is measured. There remains strong opposition to out-marriage among Jewish people, and Orthodox and many Conservative congregations do not reach out to intermarried families, thus losing them. Moreover, because the children seldom grow up Jewish in a mixed marriage, the number of Jewish Americans is subject to attrition. It is probably because of the high rates of intermarriage, coupled with a fairly low birth rate, that the Jewish population in America has declined from nearly 4 percent following World War II to 1.8 percent today. Some commentators maintain that a kind of "reverse ethnic assimilation" is taking place, with a number of Yiddish expressions having entered everyday speech. As anti-Semitism becomes less sharp, group cohesion also tends to disappear. Nonetheless, as a reaction to the perceived loss of Jewish traditions and ethnic loyalty, a trend toward the Orthodox lifestyle is also being observed (Safire, 1995, A11).

The New Face of America

The makeup of the U.S. population is destined to change dramatically in the years ahead. Although the initial waves of immigrants stopped after the first two decades of the twentieth century, immigration resumed in 1965, and the more liberalized immigration laws, combined with favorable economic and political factors, have pushed immigration up (approximately 400,000 new immigrants have entered the country every year since 1986, not including illegal aliens, whose number is estimated at more than 7 million and perhaps as many as 11 million). Moreover, the ethnic composition of the immigrants differs from that of earlier waves: Only a small percentage are of European ancestry, the majority are Mexican and Latin Americans, and almost half originate in various parts of Asia. As a consequence, demographers predict that by the year 2050, the white population will be about 72.1 percent of the total population of about 439,010 million. Blacks will make up about 15 percent, with about 65.7 million; Hispanics about 30 percent, with 132.8 million, and Asians about 9.2 percent with 40.6 million (U.S. Bureau of the Census, Population Projections Program, 2008).

Despite increasing multiculturalism, the issue of immigration remains thorny, to the point of driving a generational divide between the older and younger generations. The legislation passed by the state of Arizona, allowing the police to stop persons they suspect of being illegals, is supported by older Americans 45 to 64 years old, who say immigration should be decreased. On the other hand, 24 percent of those under 45 do not think so. The reason appears to be that the younger generation grew up with many children of immigrants, and they see the situation as normal. They "watched Sesame Street with Hispanic characters, many of them sat in classrooms that were a virtual United Nations, and now they marry across ethnic lines in record numbers" (Preston, 2010).

With the passing of time, in fact, each generation has become more racially and ethnically mixed than the preceding one. This is one reason that the Census Bureau had to add such categories as "Race alone or in combination with one or more other races." A study by the Population Research Center, therefore, projects that the black intermarriage rate will increase so dramatically that by the year 2100, 37 percent of African Americans will claim mixed ancestry, more than 40 percent of Asian Americans will be similarly mixed, and the number of Latinos who will claim mixed ancestry will be more than twice the number claiming a single race or ethnicity (Rodriguez, 2003, 95). America, then, will have a new face.

The Chapter in Brief

Conflict seems to be an integral part of group life, especially when it involves a number of groups of dissimilar culture or appearance sharing the same territory. In such a situation, a majority–minorities relationship develops, in which minorities are denied equal access to the rewards of society. The status of minority is usually applied to groups that differ from the dominant group in appearance and/or culture, and sometimes also in religion, gender, age, and in being afflicted with disabilities.

The United States has minorities in its midst based on all these factors. Racial minorities have been the victims of the now discounted ideology of racism as well as of prejudice and discrimination. Racism is based on a faulty conception of the term *race,* whereby the cultural traits and the behavior of a group are thought to be genetically inherited. Actually, scientists used the word *race* to make very broad distinctions among populations that have inbred and interbred, and they no longer use the term.

In contrast to race, ethnicity refers to a group's distinctive social factors such as language, religion, values, beliefs, and food habits. Ethnic groups are subcultures within the larger society. Such groups are maintained by common national origin or history, by a strong in-group feeling, and by the belief in a shared destiny.

Most minorities have been subject to prejudice and discrimination. Prejudice is holding unproved beliefs about a group and retaining them even in the face of facts that prove the opposite. Discrimination is acting on such beliefs by denying members of a minority equal access to the sources of wealth, power, and privilege. Of the various kinds of discrimination, the institutional type is the most difficult to eliminate. However, it appears that as the socioeconomic status of each minority approaches equality with that of the dominant group, prejudice and discrimination against that minority disappear. The only situation in which conflict between groups is exacerbated is when the minority competes for scarce jobs. Equality of status tends to lead to cooperation among groups.

Dominant groups deal with their minorities in a variety of ways. The ideologies of Anglo-conformity—becoming like the original English Protestant settlers in language, values, and beliefs—and of the melting pot—becoming amalgamated into a new breed of American—have given way to the ideal of cultural pluralism. In a truly pluralistic society, various racial, religious, and ethnic groups retain their culture but coexist in harmony with the majority and enjoy equal access to the rewards of the society.

The United States, having long been a haven for immigrants from other nations, is aspiring to become a fully pluralistic society. For the time being, while some of its minorities have been absorbed into the mainstream, others remain distinct and still subject to prejudice and discrimination. Among the latter groups are African Americans, Hispanics, and Native Americans. The racially distinct Asian Americans (Chinese, Japanese) have achieved upward social mobility through education and professionalization.

The group described as white ethnics includes the descendants of nineteenth-century immigrants. These groups were sufficiently different from the WASPs making up the dominant group that they suffered considerable discrimination. Today, many no longer live in ethnic enclaves, and the younger, college-educated generation has entered the mainstream. The older generation is represented in large numbers in the lower and working classes.

Among the religious minorities, Catholics and Jews were subject to prejudice and discrimination at the turn of the twentieth century and in its first several decades. The feelings of hostility may have been directed toward their ethnic origin—eastern and southern European—as much as toward their religions. In any event, both groups have done well socioeconomically, being represented among the highest earners and in the ranks of professionals.

Terms to Remember

accommodation A situation in which a minority is conscious of the norms and values of the majority, accepts and adapts to them, but chooses to retain its own, thus failing to participate fully in the host culture.

acculturation The process of adopting the culture, including the language and customs, of the host country.

amalgamation The result of intermarriage between distinct racial, ethnic, and cultural groups, resulting in the erasure of differences between majority and minority groups.

Anglo-conformity The attitude, once held by the majority group, that the institutions, language, and cultural patterns of England should be maintained and that WASP values be superimposed on immigrants.

assimilation A process in which a minority group is absorbed into, or becomes part of, the dominant group in a society.

attitudinal discrimination Negative behavior against a particular group—or individual members of that group—prompted by personal prejudice.

cultural pluralism An ideal condition in which the cultural distinctiveness of each ethnic, racial, and religious minority group would be maintained, but individual members would still owe allegiance to the mainstream society.

discrimination Actions taken as a result of prejudicial feelings.

ethnicity A group's distinctive social, rather than biological, traits.

ethnic minority A group that differs culturally from the dominant group.

ethnocentrism The attitude that one's own culture is right and that cultural patterns different from it are wrong.

institutional discrimination A system of inequalities existing in a society apart from individual prejudice.

Prejudice exists on a societal level; in effect, it is a norm of the society.

melting pot theory The belief that it is possible and desirable to culturally and biologically fuse all the various racial and ethnic groups in society.

minority group Any group in society that is kept from attaining the rewards of society on the basis of culture, race, religion, sex, or age. A category of people who possess imperfect access to positions of equal power, prestige, and privilege in the society.

prejudice Prejudgment of an individual or group based on stereotypes and hearsay rather than on fact or evidence, and the inability or unwillingness to change that judgment even when confronted with evidence to the contrary.

race An arbitrary manner of subdividing the species *Homo sapiens sapiens* based on differences in the frequency with which some genes occur among populations.

racial minority A group within a society that differs biologically from the dominant group in such features as skin color, hair texture, eye slant, and head shape and dimensions.

racism An ideology, prevalent in the past but now discounted, that some racial groups are inferior to others, that they display not only physical but also behavioral differences, and that both are inherited and undesirable.

scapegoating A mechanism that fuels prejudice, a term referring to the tendency of frustraded individuals to repond with aggression toward a specific target population.

segregation An attempt to isolate a minority from the majority.

stereotyping A type of prejudice in which common, uniform characterstics are assigned to an entire category of people without allowing for individual differences.

Suggested Readings

Bonilla-Silva, Eduardo. 2009 (paperback edition). *Racism without Racists: Color-Blind Racism and the Persistence of Racial Inequality in America*. Lanham, MD: Rowman and Littlefield. The condition of racism in postracist America, with a chapter on the election of Barack Obama, a fact that the author does not consider a breakthrough.

Feagin, Joe R. 2010. *Racist America*, 2nd ed. New York: Routledge. An updated version of this text, which points out the constant outcroppings of racism in the current era.

Harvey-Wingfield, Adia, and Joe R. Feagin. 2009. *Yes We Can? White Racial Framing and the 2008 Presidential Campaign*. New York: Routledge. A sociological analysis of the historic presidential election of the first African-American president.

Huntington, Samuel P. 2004. *Who Are We?* New York: Simon & Schuster. The author, a historian, paints a bleak picture of the future of American society, whose culture will be negatively affected by massive Latino immigration and consequent bilingualism. This is not a message most of us like to hear, but in a free society all points of view deserve a hearing.

Kotkin, Joel. 1993. *Tribes: How Race, Religion, and Identity Determine Success in the New Global Economy*. New York: Random House. The author speculates that certain ethnic affiliations—Jews, Japanese, British, Chinese, and Asian Indians—promote economic success because of the values of these ethnic cultures. Interesting, though subject to criticism.

Law, Ian. 2009. *Racism and Ethnicity: Global Debates, Dilemmas, Directions*. Boston, Pearson. A textbook that covers the history, theories, and debates held about racism and ethnicity in a global context.

McWhorter, John. 2003. *Authentically Black: Essays for the Black Silent Majority*. New York: Gotham Books. An African-American linguistics professor whose ideas run counter to many assumptions maintained by the black establishment.

Pollard, Kevin M., and William P. O'Hare. 1999. *America's Racial and Ethnic Minorities: Population Bulletin 54*. A short compendium of contemporary racial and ethnic groups offers an excellent overview. It also discusses the changing definitions of race, namely the fact that the Census Bureau allows people to select more than one race, if they are bi- or multiracial.

Schaefer, Richard T. 2010. *Racial and Ethnic Groups*. 12th ed. New York: Prentice Hall. A global look at minority–majority relations. It also discusses women's subordinate role in many societies.

Scott, Daryl Michael. 1997. *Contempt and Pity: Social Policy and the Image of the Damaged Black Psyche, 1880–1996*. Chapel Hill, NC: University of North Carolina Press. An important book that tries to answer the question, "What are African Americans like?" Deals with questions of moral equality, racial conservatism, lack of self-esteem, and so on, as these are presented by the social sciences.

Waters, Mary C. 1990. *Ethnic Options: Choosing Identities in America*. Berkeley, CA: University of California Press. Irish, Polish, and Italian Catholics speak about the nature of their ethnic identities.

Young-Bruehl, Elisabeth. 1996. *The Anatomy of Prejudices*. Cambridge, MA: Harvard University Press. Although ethnocentrism is commonly considered the cause of prejudice and bigotry, this author offers an analysis based on psychological concepts linking racism, anti-Semitism, and sexism to a "hysterical," "obsessional," and "narcissistic" character, respectively.

Minority Status: Age, Gender, and Sexuality

IN THIS CHAPTER, YOU WILL LEARN

- that people are also treated unequally on the basis of such ascribed characteristics as age, gender, and sexuality;
- that the United States is becoming a society with an increasing proportion of elderly people;
- of the existence and meaning of ageism;
- that women are still treated unequally;
- how we acquire gender roles;
- why sexism is an ideology that is detrimental to both men and women; and
- that sexual orientation is also subject to differential treatment.

Societies differentiate among their members not only according to wealth, power, and status, not only according to race, ethnicity, and religion, but also according to age, gender, and sexual orientation. In every society, each age group and each gender is assigned different duties, responsibilities, privileges, and roles. Some of this differentiation is a result of common sense. In the United States, young people cannot drive before they are 16, they cannot vote before they are 18, and they cannot run for the Senate before they are 30. These age restrictions have been set by law on the basis of the belief that people are too immature to engage in these activities at younger ages. On a more informal basis, a person in his seventies would hardly be expected to work on the construction of a 30-story office building, nor has it been thought fit, throughout human history, to have women in charge of protecting societies by going to war. Women's biological role in reproduction made them too precious to be allowed to be killed in war. Similarly, prohibitions against homosexuality can also be thought of as based on a societal fear that not enough new members will be produced if sex is not strictly heterosexual. In other words, to a certain degree, age, gender, and sexuality differentiation is based on what works best for society. Still, differentiation and the consequent stratification always imply inequality, and it is this factor that this chapter examines.

The Aging Society

The elderly—people aged 65 and older—constituted about 13 percent of the American population in the year 2008. This figure—38.9 million—is expected to rise to 88.5 million by 2050, when one in five people will be age 65 or older. The "old old" segment of the population—people 85 years and over—is growing at an even faster rate. In 2008, they accounted for 5.7 million Americans, but projections show this figure increasing rapidly beginning in 2011, when the baby boomers begin to move into this age group. The Census Bureau projects that this population could grow to nearly 21 million by 2050. Finally, in November 2009 there were about 104,754 persons age 100 or older, and their number is also projected to grow quickly, provided that the dramatic gains in longevity continue (by 2050, the projected number of centenarians in the United States will be 601,000) (Table 1). The problems of the elderly, then, are everyone's concern. On the other hand, because of advances in medicine, health care, and nutrition, the elderly are really becoming "younger" in the sense not only that they can expect to live much longer than previous generations but also that they can do so in reasonably good health.

Age is an ascribed characteristic according to which we are assigned a status. Unlike gender, however, which is a permanent status, age is transitional: We are constantly getting older, thus our chronological age and the consequent statuses change. At each stage of the transition, we must be socialized to age-appropriate behavior, and our relationship relative to the dimensions of stratification (how we fit into the stratification system) continually shifts.

We view aging and the elderly as problematic because our society is unable or unwilling to provide some of its members with satisfactory roles at certain ages. The reason is that industrial and postindustrial societies have tended to devalue the roles of the elderly, whereas the agrarian and other preindustrial societies assign honorable and prestigious roles to them. (Not all of them, however. The Tiwi of North Australia used to treat their old quite brutally, going so far as to bury alive—with only their heads uncovered—old women who could not care for themselves and leaving them to starve to death.)

Theoretical Framework

Social gerontologists—scientists who study the aging process as it affects the individual and society—examine aging from the perspective of a number of theoretical frameworks. Among the best known, **disengagement theory** posits that there is a reciprocal process of withdrawal occurring between an aging individual and society. An elderly person willingly withdraws from society because of awareness of his or her diminished capacities and impending death. And society withdraws from the aging person to allow a younger person to occupy his or her former statuses. The society's stability is thus maintained, and social roles are passed peacefully from one generation to the next. **Modernization theory** assumes that the status of older people declines as the society of which they are a part becomes more modern. Industrial and postindustrial societies like the United States stress youth and the importance of highly skilled occupations for which the elderly are not prepared. Hence, the elderly lose status.

Activity theory, the direct opposite of disengagement theory, maintains that the elderly person who remains active, replacing old roles with new ones that also require interaction with others, is best adjusted and most ready to accept the physical changes that lead eventually to death.

TABLE 1   Population by Age and Sex: 2008
(Numbers in thousands. Civilian noninstitutionalized population[a])

Age	Both sexes		Male		Female	
	Number	Percent	Number	Percent	Number	Percent
All ages	299,106	100.0	146,855	100.0	152,250	100.0
Under 55 years	229,014	76.6	115,014	78.3	113,999	74.9
55 to 59 years	18,371	6.1	8,929	6.1	9,442	6.2
60 to 64 years	14,931	5.0	7,150	4.9	7,781	5.1
65 to 69 years	11,165	3.7	5,238	3.6	5,928	3.9
70 to 74 years	8,423	2.8	3,740	2.5	4,683	3.1
75 to 79 years	7,353	2.5	3,200	2.2	4,154	2.7
80 to 84 years	5,559	1.9	2,106	1.4	3,453	2.3
85 years and over	4,289	1.4	1,479	1.0	2,810	1.8
Under 55 years	229,014	76.6	115,014	78.3	113,999	74.9
55 years and over	70,092	23.4	31,841	21.7	38,251	25.1
Under 60 years	247,385	82.7	123,943	84.4	123,441	81.1
60 years and over	51,721	17.3	22,912	15.6	28,809	18.9
Under 62 years	254,326	85.0	127,292	86.7	127,034	83.4
62 years and over	44,780	15.0	19,563	13.3	25,216	16.6
Under 65 years	262,316	87.7	131,093	89.3	131,222	86.2
65 years and over	36,790	12.3	15,762	10.7	21,028	13.8
Under 75 years	281,904	94.2	140,071	95.4	141,833	93.2
75 years and over	17,202	5.8	6,785	4.6	10,417	6.8

[a]Plus armed forces living off post or with their families on post.

Source: U.S. Census Bureau, Current Population Survey, Annual Social and Economic Supplement, Internet release date: June 2009.

Disagreeing with both disengagement and activity theories, the **conflict perspective** focuses on the disadvantaged elderly and stresses political and economic factors that impinge on them and force them into a condition of dependence. An extension of the conflict view is **exchange theory,** in which the elderly are seen as being in a subservient position in American society. They lack the social and material resources that would make them valuable to others; therefore, they lose status (Dowd, 1980a, 1980b).

A Growing Minority.   Social scientists also look at the elderly as a minority group because they have unequal access to the rewards of society and experience prejudice and discrimination. Moreover, a definite ideology directed against them, ageism, is easily discerned in the society. Specialists in gerontology use all these elements to examine the conditions of the elderly in society (see some of the characteristics of the elderly in Table 2).

TABLE 2   Persons 65 Years Old and Over—Characteristics by Sex: 2008

Characteristic	Total 2008	Male 2008	Female 2008
Total (million)	36.8	15.8	21.0
PERCENT DISTRIBUTION			
Marital status:			
Never married	4.1	4.2	4.0
Married	57.0	74.5	43.9
Spouse present	54.6	71.9	41.7
Spouse absent	2.4	2.6	2.3
Widowed	29.8	13.8	41.9
Divorced	9.1	7.5	10.2
Educational attainment:			
Less than ninth grade	11.2	11.3	11.1
Completed 9th to 12th grade, but no high school diploma	11.4	10.8	11.8
High school graduate	36.9	32.0	40.5
Some college or associate's degree	20.1	19.2	20.8
Bachelor's or advanced degree	20.5	26.7	15.8
Labor force participation:[a]			
Employed	16.1	20.5	12.7
Unemployed	0.7	1.0	0.5
Not in labor force	83.2	78.5	86.7
Percent below poverty level[b]	9.7	6.6	12.0

[As of March, except as noted (29.6 represents 29,600,000). Covers civilian noninstitutional population. Excludes members of Armed Forces except those living off post or with their families on post.
[a]Annual averages of monthly figures. Source: U.S. Bureau of Labor Statistics. Employment and Earnings, January issues. See footnote 2, Table 574.
[b]Poverty status based on income in preceding year.

Source: Except as noted. U.S. Census Bureau, *Current Population Reports,* P20-546, and earlier reports; "Educational Attainment'; <http://www.census.gov/population/www/socdemo/educ-attn.html>; "Families and Living Arrangements" <http://www.census.gov/population/www/socdemo/hh-fam.html>; and "Detailed Poverty Tabulations from the CPS", <http://www.census.gov/hhes/www/poverty/detailedpovtabs.html>.

Ageism

The ideology of **ageism,** whose existence can be readily picked up in even casual conversation, asserts, essentially, that the young are superior to the old. It provides the justification for prejudice and discrimination against the elderly in economic, political, and social areas.

One need not go far to uncover evidence of prejudice and discrimination against the elderly in society. First, the elderly are highly visible: They are wrinkled, their hair is white or they are bald, and many walk haltingly with canes or stooped over. Like most minorities, they are stereotyped: as senile, unproductive, poor, lonely, living in nursing homes and institutions, having no interest in or capacity for sex, being set in their ways and unable to change, and feeling miserable (Palmore, 1977). Although these stereotypes have some basis in fact, they can be proved to be mostly false.

Health. *Senescence,* or the process of growing old, consists of *primary aging,* a biological process that starts early in life and affects all body systems, and *secondary aging,* which results not from natural aging alone but also from disease, abuse, and/or disuse (Horn & Meer, 1987, 81). Primary aging affects all persons, and speed, strength, endurance, perception, and sensation eventually decline. However, these difficulties develop gradually and usually do not affect functioning until the eighties. Nonetheless, most older persons have at least one chronic condition, and many have multiple conditions. Compared to the young, the elderly are less likely to suffer from acute or short-term diseases, such as the common cold and infectious diseases, but are more likely to suffer from chronic or long-term diseases, such as hypertension, heart disease, arthritis, cancer, or emphysema. As noted, the latter pose serious problems principally to those in their eighties. In addition, more than half the older population report having at least one disability. Disabilities may be physical or nonphysical, and many are minor, but they increase in severity with age. About 80 percent of the elderly report at least one chronic health condition, and about one-half of people age 80 and over have more than one disability and need assistance. Curiously, health-care costs decrease as a person ages because the oldest of old—those 85 and over—are fittest and tend to die rapidly of pneumonia or multiple-organ failure (Angier, 1995, B5).

Senility, involving serious memory loss, confusion, and loss of the ability to reason, is not a natural consequence of aging. In fact, such disorders occur in at most 20 percent of 80-year-olds, whereas only 10 percent of elderly Americans show mild loss of memory. The symptoms of senility may derive from other causes, including a reaction to drugs. However, about 2.5 million Americans do suffer from neurological diseases, particularly Alzheimer's, an incurable disease of the brain.

Few of the elderly are incapacitated to the point of being relegated to nursing homes. In 2007, 39 percent of the elderly—65 and older—considered their health as excellent or very good, compared to to 64.8 percent of persons aged 18 to 64 who said so. During that same year, 53.6 percent of older persons lived with a spouse. Many more men than women live with their spouses: approximately 73 percent of older men and only 42 percent of older women aged 65 to 74. The reason for this is that men die at younger ages than women. Moreover, about 31 percent, or 11.2 million of noninstitutionalized older persons live alone: The proportion breaks down into 8.3 million women and 2.9 million men. One-half of women 75 and older, in fact, lived alone in 2008. At the same time, almost 471,000 grandparents 65 years old and older had primary responsibility for their grandchildren (U.S. Department of Health and Human Services, Administration on Aging).

As noted, only a minority of the elderly live in nursing homes: In 2006, only 1.6 million, representing 4.5 percent of the over-65-year-old population did. However, this proportion increases with age: For those 85 and over, the percentage rises to 17.0 percent. An additional 5 percent of the elderly live in some type of senior housing with supportive services available.

Work and Retirement. Although in the past the elderly continued to be employed, sometimes until they died, in 2009 approximately 60 percent of Americans 55 to 64 years old were in the labor force, and more than 16 percent of those 65 to 69 years old (Table 3). Interestingly, although labor force participation of persons 65 and older had been decreasing steadily, beginning in the 1990s such participation began going up—the Labor Department calls it the "graying of the workforce." This graying is projected to continue, at least until

Box 1 The Silver Century

Within a year or two, and for the first time in history, there will be more people over 60 than toddlers under 5 in the world. Throughout recorded history, people aged 65 and over have made up, at most, 2 to 3 percent of most societies. Today, this age group makes up 15 percent of the inhabitants of wealthy nations. The defining demographic trend of this century, then, will be the increase in the proportion of the world's elderly persons.

What will this trend mean? Three situations are already visible. First, by the 2020s, there will be a bulge in retirement when the last baby boomers leave the workforce. This will mean that a large number of elderly and very elderly (65+ and 85+) will need to be supported by a smaller and smaller proportion of the young still in the workforce. The smaller proportion of young workers is a result of the widespread fall in fertility rates in industrial countries in which women are not having enough children to replace the people who die. This is especially true in continental Europe and Japan, (in Japan, the number of persons 100 years and over doubled in 5 years, setting a record for the 33rd straight year as the world's longest-living nation), but even in the United States births only just equal deaths. Therefore, when the baby boomers retire, the size of the labor force will plummet. Finally, with life expectancy rising, people are spending much more time in retirement (again, Japan's life expectancy as of 2007 is the longest in the world: 86 years for women and 78.3 for men). In the United States, 22.6 percent of men are still in the workforce at 65 (as of 2009), while in Europe only 4 percent are. Consequently, the large number of older people will have to be supported for a longer period of time by fewer younger workers. The welfare state systems in Europe and America's Social Security system provide near-universal coverage for the retired, paid for by the current workers—who, as we saw, are a diminishing number.

Even some of the developing nations face similar problems. China, Iran, Brazil, and Turkey will be below replacement rate within 15 years. In China, thanks to the one-child policy, the fertility rate has decreased from six or seven children per woman in the 1960s, to below replacement rate. When the Red Guard generation reaches retirement age in around 2015, the working-age population will be too small to allow the continuous growth of China's economy.

Economists believe that there is a decade-long window of opportunity in which governments can forestall the collapse of systems that support the elderly. The negative impact of the retiring baby boomers will not be felt for another 10 years. At this time, governments will have to convince their citizens to postpone their retirements. This will not be easy. The idea of retirement is fairly recent—for most of history, people worked almost until they died—but it is a very popular idea. Workers began to retire as soon as they could afford to do so, even before social benefits were available, and they like retirement even more now that they live longer and more leisure activities are open to them. Governments will have to change the structure of pensions and benefits to make it more attractive to continue working longer. One thing is certain: A workplace revolution is coming. In the 1970s and 1980s, a large number of women entered the labor force. The next 25 years will bring in a large number of "older" workers, perhaps on a part-time basis. Such a future holds many positives: Staying in the labor force can provide elderly workers with a more stimulating environment, companionship, and a bit of extra money (Cairncross, 2004, 3, 4). This revolution may have started already: The crisis of the economy that began in 2007 and that is still affecting many people has forced a number of retirees to reenter the workforce. Of course, many were not able to do so because of the high rate of unemployment, but whether because of cuts in government services, or losses in the stock market, declines in the value of housing, or victimization by fraudulent financial investors, these elderly felt the need to continue working.

2016. The participation rate for women of this age group has risen even more dramatically, by 147 percent between 1977 and 2007. In addition, 21 percent of workers over 65 were self-employed in 1999, compared to only 7 percent of younger workers (Bureau of Labor Statistics, **http://stats.bls.gov/cps/cpsaat3/pdf.**)

One reason for the initial decline in employment for men is that industrial and postindustrial economies need highly skilled and educated workers, which places the elderly at a disadvantage with younger workers—their skills tend to be obsolete. Ageism also promotes the idea that older workers are not as productive as younger ones. In reality, although the elderly experience a decline in perception and reaction speed, they perform as well as if not better than younger workers. The elderly tend to be consistent in their output, change jobs less frequently, have fewer accidents, and have a lower absenteeism rate than younger workers (Giniger, Dispenzieri, & Eisenberg, 1983). The Age Discrimination Act of 1967 protects elderly workers to a certain extent, especially the amendment prohibiting forced retirement

TABLE 3   Employment Status of the Civilian Noninstitutional Population by Age and Sex, 2008. Annual Averages.
(Numbers in thousands)

Age	Civilian non-institutional population	Civilian labor force						Not in labor force
		Total	Percent of population	Employed		Unemployed		
				Total	Percent of population	Total	Percent of labor force	
Women								
16 years and over	120,675	71,767	59.5	67,876	56.2	3,891	5.4	48,908
16 to 19 years	8,415	3,385	40.2	2,837	33.7	549	16.2	5,030
16 to 17 years	4,508	1,314	29.2	1,063	23.6	251	19.1	3,194
18 to 19 years	3,907	2,071	53.0	1,774	45.4	297	14.3	1,836
20 to 24 years	10,160	7,109	70.0	6,484	63.8	625	8.8	3,050
25 to 54 years	63,574	48,195	75.8	45,965	72.3	2,229	4.6	15,379
25 to 34 years	19,994	15,030	75.2	14,200	71.0	830	5.5	4,964
25 to 29 years	10,363	7,862	75.9	7,397	71.4	466	5.9	2,501
30 to 34 years	9,631	7,168	74.4	6,803	70.6	365	5.1	2,463
35 to 44 years	21,132	16,089	76.1	15,360	72.7	730	4.5	5,043
35 to 39 years	10,395	7,814	75.2	7,437	71.5	377	4.8	2,581
40 to 44 years	10,737	8,275	77.1	7,922	73.8	353	4.3	2,462
45 to 54 years	22,448	17,075	76.1	16,406	73.1	669	3.9	5,372
45 to 49 years	11,536	8,908	77.2	8,565	74.2	343	3.9	2,628
50 to 54 years	10,912	8,167	74.8	7,841	71.9	326	4.0	2,744
55 to 64 years	17,367	10,270	59.1	9,893	57.0	377	3.7	7,097
55 to 59 years	9,515	6,445	67.7	6,199	65.2	246	3.8	3,070
60 to 64 years	7,852	3,825	48.7	3,694	47.0	132	3.4	4,027
65 years and over	21,160	2,808	13.3	2,697	12.7	111	3.9	18,352
65 to 69 years	5,995	1,585	26.4	1,528	25.5	57	3.6	4,410
70 to 74 years	4,728	676	14.3	644	13.6	32	4.7	4,052
75 years and over	10,437	547	5.2	525	5.0	22	4.0	9,890

Source: Current Population Survey, U.S. Dept of Labor, U.S. Bureau of Labor Statistics.

before the age of 70. The recent recession, however, has forced a number of people either to remain in the labor force for a longer time or to take early retirement—that is, at age 62—because having lost their job, they could not expect to get another one at their age when so many younger people were similarly unemployed.

Individuals are not all alike in their readiness to retire. For some, retirement may indeed be welcome; for others, it may cause feelings of uselessness and of being dispensable, leading to depression, and in acute cases, to a wish for early death. The higher the social status of the worker, the higher the job satisfaction and the less likelihood of early retirement (Atchley,

Blend Images/Alamy

The elderly do not have to stop being productive. Helping children with schoolwork is beneficial for both the retired person, who can still feel useful, and for the child, who will obtain a less stereotypical view of an older person.

1982). After retirement, higher-status workers also tend to continue to be involved in their professions. The bottom line, however, is the amount of income during retirement: If that is adequate, most persons choose to retire.

Finances. Although many elderly people—particularly women and minorities—find themselves living in straitened circumstances, the majority do not live in poverty. In 2008, the median household income of persons 65 and over was $29,744. However, it was only $17,359 for male householders living alone and only $13,775 for female householders living alone. Of course, wealth is apportioned very unequally in this age group. For instance, households containing families headed by a person 65 and older reported a median income in 2008 of $44,188. Still, some 3.4 million of the elderly 65 and over lived in poverty, with a poverty rate of 9.7 percent.

Not only in the United States but also in other wealthy countries, the elderly live quite well, according to a study of pensioners that showed their disposable income is 80 percent of the income of working people in their later years of work. In some countries, retirees have even more disposable income than younger working people. In Germany, for instance, the overall income of persons over 60 is 25 percent higher than that of younger Germans (*The Economist*, 2004, 6).

In 2008, 40 percent of the income of the elderly consisted of Social Security payments. Twenty percent of married elderly couples and about 41 percent of unmarried elderly persons relied on Social Security for 90 percent of their income. Fifty-five percent of those age 65 and over received income from assets, 35.4 percent received income from pensions and annuities, and 20.4 percent received income from earnings (**http://goliath.ecnext.com/ coms2/gi-0198-686656/Income-of-the-elderly-population.html**). For those in the highest income fifth, however, Social Security accounted for only approximately 20 percent. For too many Americans, then, the "golden years" may be bleak.

Interestingly, but not surprisingly, class divisions are most distinct in old age, in the sense that the wealthier elderly are so much better off than the poorer ones in length of life and enjoyment of good health and the good life. In most countries, people in the top social class live around five years longer than those in the bottom class (in Britain, the difference is 15 years). There are differences in life expectancy, especially in healthy life expectancy. For one thing, the poor elderly tend to live in neighborhoods that are crime-ridden and unfriendly, leading to their isolation and loneliness. For another, the elderly poor generally lack much education and did not spend their working life in the professions. This condition appears to lower their ability to remember things and solve puzzles: People with university degrees do better at age 75 at those activities than people with little education in their 50s. Mortality rates for white American men with the highest levels of education were about 10 percent lower than for white men with the least education, and the difference in the period 1990–1997 rose to 70 percent (*The Economist,* 2004, 7). Those with little education also tend to live unhealthier lives: They smoke, are overweight, and do not exercise.

The economic downturn of 2007–2010 also had a negative impact on the elderly, particularly those financially weak, and especially those who live in rural areas. Many such areas, in fact, have been experiencing a loss of population and, with it, services that the elderly need, such as medical care and even transportation. A recent article on the elderly in rural America notes how difficult it is for many of them. They are mostly widowed and live alone; they are in frail health, but medical services are far, in larger cities; and they have difficulty driving, yet have no other way of reaching necessities. The article mentions as an example one widow who lives on a farm alone. When she fell and broke her hip, it took her a long time to drag herself to the house, and then, instead of calling 911, she called her daughter in another town to come and feed the horses (Johnson, 2009)!

Finally, the perception of where one is in the pecking order (the stratification system of the society) is also important. Those who rank themselves as being low in status and not in control of their lives suffer worse health than those who rank themselves higher and in control of their lives.

Widowhood. Loneliness and other negative consequences follow the death of a spouse, particularly of a husband, for it seems that men adjust to widowhood a little better than women (however, there are five times more widows than widowers). Men tend to remarry more often, are members of more organizations, know more people from their preretirement years, are more likely to own and drive a car, and have higher incomes than women. However, elderly widowers fare worse than women: They are much more likely to die from a number of causes, from heart attacks to suicide, than elderly women.

Death and Dying. Historically, death has been accepted as a normal part of human existence. Lack of knowledge regarding hygiene and disease prevention coupled with subsistence economies resulted in very high death rates in both hunting–gathering and agricultural societies. It was not until the industrial societies were well established that death rates plummeted. With the ability of societies to control death—to a certain extent, of course—came a change in attitude toward it. When death was common and was within the experience of everyone, it was considered an ordinary event. As it became rarer, it tended to become associated with old age because, barring wars and accidents, it was mostly the old who died. Today, death is considered an out-of-the-ordinary event if it occurs at any time in the life cycle except in old age. As a result, it has acquired an aura of unnaturalness. And because religious beliefs that explained life and death as part of a divine plan have declined in importance in modern societies, the acceptance with which former generations greeted death has given way to the expectation that the miracles of modern medicine will bring us immortality. Death is no longer the natural capping of life; it is to be avoided at all costs and is considered separate, an antithesis to life.

This attitude toward death is reinforced by the fact that death has been removed from public life. People typically no longer die at home, in full view of family and friends; instead, they die in hospitals and nursing homes, and even there, dying patients are isolated from those expected to recuperate. Coupled with the fact that many elderly people are isolated from the rest of society to begin with, the result is that the population at large has seldom faced death, in the sense of seeing a person die.

Despite this strong avoidance of death, the elderly seem less afraid of it than younger people, particularly if their health is such that they see little chance of a normal lifestyle in their future. The elderly are socialized into accepting death because they are more likely to see it in their spouses and peers. As an increasing number of Americans join the ranks of the elderly, the idea of death is likely to lose some of its sting. It is already more acceptable to speak about death, and many of the elderly make it clear that they do not want to have their lives prolonged artificially if it means suffering or isolation rather than an improvement in the quality of life. During the past two decades, institutions called hospices—which do not attempt to cure but rather care for the dying—have sprung up to attempt to help the dying in the difficult period preceding death.

Women: Differentiation According to Gender

It is clear to all that the human race comes in two genders, male and female, and that both are needed if that race is to continue to exist. Yet it seems that a state of war is being waged between men and women all over the globe, producing neither winners nor losers, but much conflict. In developed countries, a high incidence of rape, various varieties of sexual harassment, domestic violence directed at women, and many other types of discrimination are the order of the day. In developing nations, especially where political conflicts are raging, women are the victims of horror stories: They are denied education and the simplest human rights, rape on massive levels is used against them as a weapon of war, and they are still considered chattel or property of men. To what do we owe this enmity between the sexes?

Societies assign unequal statuses to various segments of their population. Women (and children) have usually had an inferior status in most societies of the world, particularly where the family form has remained stubbornly patriarchal. One can understand why children should be somewhat subordinate to adults: They are physically weak and lack life experience and knowledge. But why women? What really differentiates men and women? Is it true that "Women are from Venus, Men are from Mars," as a best-selling book would have it? Why is rape so prevalent a crime, even in our society, when sexual mores are so relaxed that there is no stigma attached to sex among consenting adults?

Biological Facts

One is born either **male or female**; maleness and femaleness, then, are *biological* terms, descriptive of biological facts. **Masculine and feminine,** on the other hand, are adjectives reflecting *social* conditions, that is, descriptive of how males and females are expected to behave in a given society, and how they come to feel about themselves and each other. The first is a **sex status,** ascribed and not subject to change except in extraordinary circumstances; the second is a **gender role,** achieved and, thus, subject to change according to place and time. The first lies within the realm of biology, the second within that of culture, but both are subject to social interpretations and influences and can be detached from one another only for the sake of analysis. In reality, biology and culture are deeply intertwined.

The biological differences between men and women may be roughly divided into those that are of an anatomical nature, those that are of a genetic nature, and those that are of a hormonal nature. **Anatomical differences** are the most obvious, for they consist of the physical structure and appearance of the two sexes. These differences include height, weight, distribution of body fat and hair, and musculature. Such traits are called the **secondary sex characteristics,** and they may be measured on a continuum: that is, not every woman is shorter, lighter, more rounded, less hairy, and less muscular than a man, just as not every man is taller, heavier, more angular, more hairy, and more muscular than a woman. In fact, the most important anatomical difference lies in the distinct reproductive systems of males and females. The reproductive system of women allows them to become pregnant and give birth. The reproductive system of men allows them to impregnate women.

Pregnancy and nursing force women to be unable periodically to perform certain economic and social functions, whereas the role of men in reproduction ends with impregnation. These facts have profound social consequences.

Genetic differences become apparent when analyzing the **sex chromosomes,** which contain the genes that determine heredity in all living creatures. All humans inherit two sex chromosomes, one from the mother and one from the father. Females inherit two X-chromosomes (XX), and males inherit one X chromosome and one Y chromosome (XY). A male is born when an ovum (egg) bearing the X-chromosome is fertilized by a sperm bearing a Y-chromosome (each month a female produces one ovum throughout her fertile years, which contains an X-chromosome; a male produces sperm, half of which is made up of X-chromosomes inherited from his mother and the other half of Y-chromosomes inherited from his father). Whether chromosomal differences influence the personalities, abilities, and behaviors of males and females has not yet been scientifically established.

Hormonal differences begin to be felt at about three months after fertilization and are responsible for the differentiation into the two genders. Up to this time, the fetus is sexually undifferentiated: It may become either a male or a female. Hormones are chemicals that are secreted into the bloodstream by glands located in the body. The function of hormones is to stimulate some chemical processes and inhibit others. The hormones involved in the development of sex characteristics are estrogen and progesterone, produced by the ovaries in females, and testosterone and androgens produced by the testes in males. Both males and females produce male and female sex hormones, but the proportion in which they are produced varies by gender. The fetus with the XY chromosomal formation begins to secrete testosterone, which has the function of inhibiting the development of female characteristics; hence, the fetus will be born a male. At puberty, it is again the sex hormones that determine the development of secondary sex characteristics—they induce the growth of beards in males and breasts in females. Hormones, then, are influential in physical development. They also affect human behavior. Animal experiments have shown that an increase of testosterone, even in females, produces an increase in aggressive behavior and sex drive. Research into the hormone oxytocin, present in humans and other mammals, shows that it is responsible for feelings of satisfaction and goodwill toward others. It also stimulates the sensations of sexual arousal and climax, ensures that new mothers nurture their young, and that the uterus contracts during childbirth. Researchers are going so far as to say that the hormone is an excellent candidate for involvement in the formation of social bonds, and they liken it to a bridge between anatomy and behavior (Angier, 1991).

Other researchers also attribute the differences between men and women to hormonal causes, especially to the infusion of hormones at the proper moment—before birth, and especially at puberty—which influences the brain to behave in a gender-specific way—males with more aggression, females with more nurturance. These conclusions are based on animal experiments that show that females injected with the equivalent of the hormone testosterone—or even female siblings who develop beside a male fetus in the womb—invariably exhibit more aggressiveness, acting more like males. Nonetheless, there is no conclusive evidence that hormonal differences explain differences in the behavior of the two sexes. Even where correlations between the level of testosterone and aggressive behavior exist, it is impossible to show a cause-and-effect relationship. At most, it may be said that there is an association between the two (Hoyenga & Hoyenga, 1979, 139).

Studies in medicine also point to evidence that male and female brains function differently. Researchers have discovered, for instance, that in women such functions as language are more evenly divided between the left and right halves of the brain, whereas in men they are much more localized in the left half.

Cultural Differences

The differences in behavior between the two sexes are obviously not due strictly to biological influences. Culture plays a significant part, although less so than was at first believed by social scientists and feminists. For instance, a well-known study by researchers Money and Erhardt (1972) involved a pair of identical twin males, one of whom, in a tragic accident, was totally castrated during circumcision. The parents of the twins were subsequently convinced to raise this twin as a female. Other than surgically constructing a vagina, nothing was done to the twin until puberty except that the parents treated "her" as a little girl: the mother let her hair grow long, adorned her with hair ribbons, and dressed her in frilly clothes. According to the researchers, soon the little girl was behaving as little girls are expected to behave in our society: She was neater than her brother, she was more willing to help with housework, and she requested dolls and a dollhouse as Christmas presents. Even though the twin was, biologically, a male, "she" acted as a female does in American society. However, it was observed that she tended to be a leader in games with peers and was rather a tomboy.

The story, however, does not end with "... and she lived happily ever after." In fact, a follow-up study paints a totally different picture. New research shows that, far from being satisfied with her assigned gender, the girl/boy rejected the female identity and at 14 years of age chose to live as a man, undergoing extensive reconstructive surgery to attempt to attain a semblance of the male genitals he had lost. "Despite everyone telling him constantly that he was a girl, and despite his being treated with female hormones, his brain knew he was a male. It refused to take on what it was being told" (Angier, 1997, A10). The recollections of the adult girl/boy (identified only as "John") and his parents were that he had never accepted a feminine identity. On the contrary, he had torn off the dresses in which his parents had dressed him, had refused dolls, had sought out male friends, had imitated his father shaving rather than his mother putting on makeup, and had even tried to urinate standing up. His attempts to engage in feminine behavior were made only to obtain parental approval. He became especially unhappy when, at age 12, he was given female hormones and began growing breasts. At age 14 he threatened suicide, being friendless and thoroughly unhappy. When told by his father what had happened to him as an infant, "John" was relieved to hear it: "For the first time everything made sense, and I understood who and what I was" (Angier, 1997, A10). In short, what had been considered a classic case illustrating the importance of nurture and socialization on gender identification was turned on its head.

Nonetheless, the impact of culture cannot be discounted. If the behavior of the two sexes differed strictly on the basis of biology, then in all societies of the world, and in all instances, men and women would behave distinctly in the same ways. But they do not. Cross-cultural evidence indicates how deeply nurture can affect behavior. A classic study by anthropologist Margaret Mead (1935), who based her findings on an analysis of three preliterate tribes of New Guinea, revealed that men can act the way people think women do and vice versa. For instance, in one of the societies Mead studied, both men and women were gentle, emotionally responsive, noncompetitive, and lacking in aggression. In addition, both men and women were responsible for the care of children. In another tribe, however, both men and women had personality types that could be characterized as masculine; that is, both men and women were aggressive and violent. Women disliked anything connected with motherhood, such as pregnancy, nursing, and caring for their children. They were especially obnoxious to their daughters. Finally, in the third tribe, Mead found profound differences in the behavior of men and women. Contrary to expectations, however, each sex behaved in a manner that Americans would consider the opposite of how men and women "ought" to behave: women were domineering and aggressive and were the economic providers in the household. Men were passive, took care of the children, engaged in gossip, and liked to adorn themselves. Mead concluded from her analysis that sex roles vary in different societies; that is, a person born either a male or a female does not necessarily and always act in ways determined by his or her biological makeup. However, Mead never proclaimed the reversibility of sex roles and, in fact, tried to correct the mistaken assumptions—that females can be made to act exactly like males and vice versa—that a number of commentators made about her conclusions. She also found, and reported in her book, *Male and Female* (1949), that the seven cultures she studied exhibited homicidal violence, headhunting, plotting, and fighting, all on the part of males. In short, to conclude that culture is solely responsible for gender roles is equally shortsighted.

Another cross-cultural comparison of six societies also showed that in all of them boys were more aggressive and violent than girls, and girls were more nurturing and emotionally responsive, especially to children (Whiting, 1963). Findings such as this substantiate long-standing conclusions that fighting and leadership are associated predominantly with males and that males are more prone to aggressiveness, sexual attack, promiscuity, homosexuality, voyeurism, and other forms of aggressive sexual activity (Ford & Beach, 1951; Murdock, 1957). The conclusions regarding the greater aggressiveness of males seem to be so overwhelming that a well-known anthropologist was moved to state categorically: "In every known society, homicidal violence, whether spontaneous and outlawed or organized and sanctioned for military

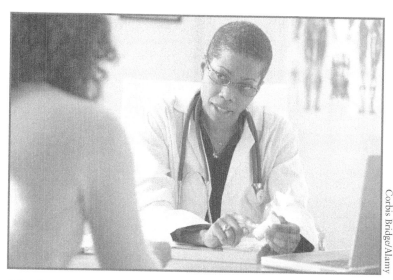

Although we are used to seeing women as nurses, of late women have entered professions that were formerly the almost exclusive province of men.

purposes, is committed overwhelmingly by men" (Konner, 1988, 34). This view is supported by the work of sociologist Steven Goldberg in *The Inevitability of Patriarchy* (1977), in which he maintains that according to his research: (a) patriarchy is a universal characteristic of societies; (b) roles performed by males are given higher status than those performed by females; and (c) men are dominant in male–female relationships (Goldberg, 1989, 16–18).

What conclusions can be drawn from these conflicting facts? Do men and women behave differently because they are biologically different? Or is it rather that they are socialized to accept different roles? In short, what makes us men or women? Nature or nurture? As usual, the issue cannot be answered simplistically. Biological differences between the sexes surely exist, in some areas to a significant extent. The concern, however, is the social significance that these differences acquire in human societies.

Sex and Gender Differentiated

Although *sex* and *gender* are used interchangeably in common parlance, in the social sciences the two terms need to be differentiated. *Sex* refers to a person's biological identity, whereas *gender* refers to the socially learned behaviors and cultural expectations that attach to males and females. Sex merely marks us as male or female and determines whether we have a reproductive system that enables us to bear children or one that provides some of the material necessary to conceive them. As we have seen, this biological fact is not sufficient to ensure that we become men and women. Femininity—being a woman—and masculinity—being a man—are cultural concepts. Therefore, they differ from society to society, they are associated with specific historical eras and geographical settings, and they are learned and interpreted differently even by members of the same society. That is why some women and men, having acquired a sexual identity that does not correspond to their physical sex, attempt to change the latter by surgical and medical means.

The Cultural Construction of Gender

We saw earlier that culture provides us with a script according to which we essentially organize our lives. We learn this script so well that we—at least, most of us—become absolutely convinced that the way we do things in our society is the right and only way to do them. We accept a set of assumptions that we seldom bother to examine, and we come to believe that they are the "truth" that should guide and direct our lives. We, therefore, often cringe at the way things are done in other societies.

Traditional Gender Roles

We live out our lives by fulfilling a variety of roles. Among the most important of such roles are **gender roles.** The traditional gender roles assigned to males and females in our society, as well as in most others, are the **instrumental role** for males and the **expressive role** for females. The instrumental role stresses rationality, competitiveness, aggression, and goal orientation. The expressive role emphasizes nurturing, emotion, and peace-making. Such traditional divisions of roles assume that there is a polarity between male and female roles, with behavior divided in two, as it were, and between opposite poles: emotion and nurturance at one end, reason and aggressiveness at the other. In reality, of course, there is a great deal of variety within each gender, and there are countless similarities in the roles of men and women (and the same roles may be filled by either men or women when the need arises or is perceived as arising).

Because they give birth to the young who depend for their survival on them, women have developed emotions and skills consonant with nurturing and caregiving. These have extended to other family members in need of care, such as the elderly or disabled. When societies were predominantly agricultural, women did a share of work outside the house alongside the men, in addition to tasks inside the house. But when economies began to depend on industry, men became the chief breadwinners outside the home. This occurred mostly in the middle classes, in which women were able to stay at home, expanding the expressive role. The notion then emerged that women were expected to sacrifice their personal goals and desires in favor of those of others. Working-class women incorporated all these roles—they had to work outside the home, at menial or industrial jobs, and fulfill the caretaker functions at home. This traditional division of roles crystallized during the industrial age, when men began to perform their instrumental role through their work outside the home.

In general terms, traditional roles, both masculine and feminine, have been upheld as the expected cultural models throughout the societies of the world, becoming stereotyped in the process. In our society, when people refer to the "typical" roles of men and women, they mean those that, in the past, were characteristic of a white, middle-class family. The stereotypes for other groups vary somewhat.

Gender Scripts

Gender roles, like all roles, are based on cultural scripts. The masculine script in our society has several variations. The traditional script includes distancing oneself from anything feminine ("sissy") and being occupationally and financially successful. Those who cannot achieve success through legitimate means may embrace some subcultural ways, including violence and physical aggression, and/or adopting a "cool" pose consisting of a manner of dress and posture that bespeaks fearlessness and emotional detachment. This pose is used as a survival mechanism in a society perceived as hostile and discriminatory. Another masculine script is one in which the expectation is for the man to be self-reliant and confident to the point of being "tough" (a John Wayne type of person). A fairly popular script focuses on adventure, sometimes accompanied by violence and a need to humiliate an opponent. This script expects men to excel in contact sports, never to walk away from a fight, and to kill and maim the enemy (do what must be done) in war. Finally, an optional script that has been emerging of late is one in which the "new" male is emotionally sensitive and expressive and values an egalitarian relationship with women.

Feminine scripts are based on the expectation that a woman, in addition to being nurturant, will be attractive in looks, not overly competitive, a listener rather than a talker, and one capable of adapting to various circumstances. The script provides that a woman not show her intelligence but rather support, facilitate, and cheer on from the sidelines her husband's (or man's) accomplishments. She is considered lucky to have a man in her life, and his care, as well as any needs of their children, are to come before her own needs. Again, the script may differ somewhat for women in other ethnic groups, but it always includes primary responsibility for child care.

In recent years the traditional feminine script has been pushed to the back, while the script of "professional" or "working woman" has emerged (see Table 4 for the occupations of contemporary women). Often, women try to combine the traditional script with the working woman script, producing the "superwoman" script. This script is very difficult to achieve and maintain, and it causes much role strain. A lesser number of women appear to follow a "contented single" script, in which a working woman seems satisfied with a lifestyle that does not include a relationship with a man, although it may involve the creation of a family (perhaps in a lesbian relationship). Finally, we should mention a theme that is woven through all the cultural scripts for women, and that is the division of women into "good girl/slut."

TABLE 4 20 Leading Occupations of Employed Women. 2009 Annual Averages (employment in thousands).

Occupation	Total Employed Women	Total Employed (Men and Women)	Percent Women	Women's Median Weekly Earnings
Total, 16 years and older (all employed women)	66,208	139,877	47.4	$657
Secretaries and administrative assistants	3,074	3,176	96.8	619
Registered nurses	2,612	2,839	92.0	1,035
Elementary and middle school teachers	2,343	2,862	81.9	891
Cashiers	2,273	3,056	74.4	361
Nursing, psychiatric, and home health aides	1,770	2,002	88.5	430
Retail salespersons	1,650	3,182	51.9	443
First-line supervisors/managers of retail sales workers	1,459	3,311	44.1	597
Waiters and waitresses	1,434	2,005	71.6	363
Maids and housekeeping cleaners	1,282	1,428	89.8	371
Customer service representatives	1,263	1,862	67.9	587
Childcare workers	1,228	1,292	95.1	364
Bookkeeping, accounting, and auditing clerks	1,205	1,306	92.3	627
Receptionists and information clerks	1,168	1,277	91.5	516
First-line supervisors/managers of office and administrative support	1,163	1,632	71.3	705
Managers, all others	1,106	3,249	34.1	1,037
Accountants and auditors	1,084	1,754	61.8	902
Teacher assistants	921	1,006	91.6	474
Cooks	831	2004	41.5	371
Office clerks, general	821	1,002	82.0	594
Personal and home care aides	789	926	85.2	406

Source: U.S. Department of Labor, Bureau of Labor Statistics, Annual Averages 2009.

Even elementary school children are aware of this distinction attributed to females who are either sexually conservative or sexually active.

As is obvious, gender scripts are perceived as being opposite and mutually exclusive: Women are one thing, men something else. In reality, as was already noted, men and women differ only slightly in the traits they display. A good portion of these traits overlap, and this is true of both physical traits (such as height, for instance) and behavioral traits (such as aggressiveness). Moreover, there are more differences within each gender group than between the two genders. The only exception to this pattern of overlapping traits seems to be dominance.

Box 2 Women and Science

Despite the pervasive scripts and the traditional roles women are expected to play in most societies of the world, many of them, today and throughout history, have overcome these obstacles. In addition to rulers known for their wisdom or shrewdness (Cleopatra, the female pharaoh Hatshepsut, Queens Elizabeth I and II, in addition to more modern prime ministers, such as Indira Gandhi and Golda Meir), many women have excelled in fields in which men predominate. Today, a substantial number of women are earning doctoral degrees in science and engineering and are working in such professions as architecture and construction, not to mention medical research. A number have even received Nobel prizes in science:

Marie S. Curie, Nobel Prize Winner in Physics, 1903, and in Chemistry, 1911

Irene Curie (Marie's daughter), Chemistry, 1935

Grety Radnitz Cori, Biochemistry, 1947

Maria Goeppert Mayer, Physics, 1963
Dorothy Crowfoot Hodgkin, Chemistry, 1964
Rosalyn Sussman Yalow, Medicine, 1977
Barbara McClintock, Medicine, 1983
Rita Levi-Montalcini, Medicine, 1986
Gertrude Elion, Medicine, 1988
Christiane Nüsslein-Volhard, Medicine, 1995
Linda B. Buck, 2004, Physiology and Medicine
Francoise Barre-Sinoujssi, 2008, Physiology and Medicine
Elizabeth H. Blackburn, 2009, Physiology and Medicine
Carol W. Greider, 2009, Physiology and Medicine
Ada Yonath, 2009, Chemistry
Elinor Ostrom, 2009, Economics

Source: http://www.nobelprize.org/nobel_prizes/lists/woment/html. (Accessed December 18, 2009).

Male Dominance

Male dominance is a fact of life in the majority of the world's societies. In our own case, despite our belief that we are an egalitarian society, a group of little boys will invariably take over playground equipment in a situation of mixed-gender play, unless prohibited to do so by an adult (Franklin, 1988, 30). The many sexual harassment situations on jobs and in the military are another indication of such dominance. On an institutional level, a realistic look is sufficient to illustrate the clear prevalence of men in the political, economic, social, and even religious arenas. There has never been a female president of the United States, and strong personality and interest in politics by a first lady have generally brought her nothing but criticism.

In the 111th Congress, there are 17 women in the Senate (out of 100 senators), and 74 women in the House of Representatives (out of 435 representatives). In administrative and managerial positions, women's share increased from 38 percent in the mid-1980s to 51 percent in 2008, the highest proportion in Western Europe and other developed nations (Women's Bureau, 2008). As for wage parity, it has never been achieved. In 2008, women earned approximately 77 percent of what men earned. Median weekly earnings of female full-time wage and salary workers were $638 in 2008 compared to $798 for their male counterparts. African-American and Hispanic women earned 63 cents and 53 cents, respectively, for every dollar that a white male earned. Women and men under 25 had fairly similar earnings, but women's earnings were much lower than men's in older age groups: Women 25 and over made less than 80 percent of what men in the same age group earned. Much more detailed data may be found at the U.S. Department of Labor, Bureau of Labor Statistics (2009).

Despite the preceding, things are definitely beginning to change. In some other societies, the changes have been rapid and dramatic. For instance, South Korea had been one of the most patriarchal societies of the world. Wives who did not produce male heirs were mistreated and abused. Prayers were said in households that girl children would die. But when the government instituted an industrial revolution in the 1970s, many young women came to the cities, went to college, entered the workforce, first as manual workers, then as white-collar workers. Large numbers entered the professions. Today, preference for male babies no longer exists—in fact, women can register their children in their own names. The same processes are occurring in India and China, as they are becoming industrial economies in which physical labor is no longer very necessary, and thinking and communicating are dominant skills, in which women excel to the same extent as men (Rosin, 2010).

What about the United States? Although the preference for male babies was never as strong here as in other societies, certainly male dominance was apparent. Now, however, fertility clinics are reporting that there is a definite preference for girl babies, which seems to be an indication that women feel empowered. Even though most of the elite and powerful positions in the society are still held by men, and even though child care and house care is still mainly in the hands of women, college-educated women expect to work outside the home, possibly earn more than their husbands, perhaps even have stay-at-home husbands. Working-class women, who have always had to work outside the home, now can bring in a higher income than the men in their lives: They can have employment as nurses, home health aides, in child care, in food preparation, and so on, while working-class men have difficulty getting jobs in construction and manufacturing, as these industries have faded. Thirty years ago, women contributed only 2 or 3 percent to the family income, whereas today the typical working wife brings in 42.2 percent of the household income, and 4 in 10 mothers are the primary breadwinners in their families (Rosin, 2010, 70). In an article entitled "The End of Men," the author, quoting a number of statistics and research, concludes that a role reversal is indeed going on, perhaps because a modern, postindustrial society is better suited to women!

Theories of Gender Role Development

Why and how do gender roles emerge in a society? How do they become so deeply embedded in the culture that they are eventually incorporated into our very personalities and behavior? Such questions cannot be answered with any degree of certainty. We can only speculate by referring to a number of theories that have been used in an attempt to answer them.

Structural Functionalist Theory. The **structural functionalist theory** is one of the most dominant ones in sociology. It assumes that those elements retained in a social system are ones that aid in the survival of that system. The development of the instrumental and expressive roles in the family institution is a kind of specialization that occurs within all small groups. Such specialization is *functional* because it meets social needs as well as institutional needs. A strong family needs someone to make important decisions and someone to foster the emotional well-being of members. Because of the close bond between mother and child, the expressive role is more consonant with a woman's nature; the male acquires the instrumental role by default.

The critique that may be made of this theory is that it assumes that male dominance and female subordination are natural and inevitable, based on biological makeup. We have seen, however, that research does not prove the absolute truth of this assumption.

Conflict Theory. Conflict theory is the other of the two most popular sociological theories. This theory assumes that power and privilege are based on the resources that an individual possesses. In turn, power is the ability to influence or control the lives of others, and it also derives from the economic resources that an individual can muster. Frederick Engels, Karl Marx's coauthor, maintained in his book, *The Origins of the Family, Private Property and the State* (1884/1902), that male dominance in the family was the result of the male's control over the family's economic resources. He also insisted that the concept of patriarchy developed in tandem with that of property, because if property were to be inherited, it became important for a man to know that the children born to his wife were indeed his own. In this sense, simple societies were much more egalitarian because there was no need to worry about who was going to inherit what—there was precious little surplus to leave anyone. A more recent interpretation of the theory holds that those individuals who have a higher income, educational attainment, and occupational status have the greater power, even in a relationship such as marriage. And because most men tend to marry women who are younger, less well educated, and who earn less money, they naturally become the more powerful partner.

Conflict theory has its shortcomings, also. There seems to be too much emphasis on economics and too little concern over other facets of relationships, such as sex, love, and companionship, as well as traditional societal expectations that would force women into a more submissive stance vis-à-vis men. In particular, gender roles and stereotypes, which have a tremendous impact on behavior, are ignored.

Feminist Theory. **Feminist theory** has borrowed much of the framework of conflict theory, especially the fact that women are underrepresented in positions of power in the society at large, a reflection of the lack of power women have within the family. Feminists also point out the existence of the wage differential between men and women, of prevalent gender discrimination in hiring and promotion, of sexual harassment in the workplace, of the frequency of divorce and out-of-wedlock births, which have led to the phenomenon of the "feminization of poverty" and of violence as a means of controlling the behavior of family members.

As is true of conflict theory, feminist theory is also criticized for its emphasis on the negative side of male–female relationships, while paying scant attention to the positives of such relationships: companionship, affection and love, sexual satisfaction, and intimacy. Feminism as a social movement has also been accused of not doing enough for certain groups of women: minorities, the poor, those in traditional women's jobs, stay-at-home mothers, rural residents, and single welfare mothers. Feminists are seen as representing mainly white, highly educated women, interested in such issues as abortion, gay rights, and political equality, while the average woman must contend with child care and economic survival.

Theories of Gender Socialization

Another group of theories focuses on the way cultural ideas about gender become part of an individual's personality and behavior patterns. Among the most influential theories are the social learning theory, the cognitive developmental theory, and the identification theory. A more ample discussion of the theories of gender socialization may be found on the Internet.

The Social Learning Theory. The **social learning theory** is based on the behaviorist notion that learning consists of observation, imitation, and reinforcement. In this view, children observe all kinds of behavior on the part of parents, peers, and others. They imitate some of this behavior: If they receive positive reinforcement for it—if parents seem delighted, or their friends approve, or teachers give them good grades—they continue this behavior. If the reinforcement is negative—parents scold them, friends laugh at them, teachers discipline them—they discontinue the behavior. Gender roles are learned in the same way. If a little girl puts on her mother's dress and primps in front of a mirror, and her mother smiles and says she looks pretty, the little girl assumes that females are supposed to dress up and look pretty. If a little boy does the same, and his father scowls and tells him that boys do not wear dresses unless they are sissies, then the boy realizes that his behavior is not proper for his gender.

Socialization into gender roles begins early. Parents respond to male and female infants differently, speaking more often to their daughters, whom they also touch more frequently and treat more delicately. The kinds of toys and games parents choose, the kinds of clothing they select for their children, the way they themselves behave and what they say directly about gender, even the jobs they hold—whether they are traditional for each gender or not, all offer subtle messages to their children regarding what is appropriate behavior for each gender.

Indeed, children observe and imitate the behavior of their parents, their siblings and peers, and characters encountered in the mass media. And they continue behavior that is rewarded. But not always, and not entirely. First, they do not imitate the same-sexed parent alone but both parents. Second, they are not merely passive entities but react to the messages they receive.

Cognitive Development Theory. According to the **cognitive development theory**, children learn gender roles according to which stage of cognitive development they have reached at any point. Cognitive development, in turn, is the way information is processed by individuals at different stages of physical maturation (Piaget, 1950, 1954; Kohlberg, 1969). For instance, even though children at 2 years of age may have noticed that there are two genders, they are not sure to which one they belong, nor whether it is a permanent or a temporary condition (they may think that it depends on wearing dresses or having long hair). It is not until children are 6 or 7 years old that they realize the reality of gender and its permanent nature. At this point, they proceed to select behavior befitting their gender, preferring to play with same-sexed playmates and sex-typed toys. They see gender as being rigidly defined; it is not until they are more mature that they perceive gender as more flexible and gender roles as somewhat overlapping (Vogel et al., 1991, 605).

Children do not reach their ideas about gender roles without much input from the culture. With help from the numerous agents of socialization—parents, siblings, peers, teachers, the media—they construct what sociologists call *gender schema,* or a set of traits that are perceived as being central to a particular gender (Bem, 1981, 1983, 1985). These vary according to age: at first, they are quite concrete—only girls wear ribbons in their hair, only boys play hockey, for instance. With maturity, the schemas grow more abstract: Men do not display emotions, women do not make the important decisions. Whether these perceptions are correct or incorrect, they contribute to the individual's gender identity. Newer theories attempt to combine social learning theory and cognitive development theory, or at least to point out the weaknesses in each. For instance, the social learning theory ignores the fact that different groups raise their children in different ways. The cognitive development theory, on the other hand, assumes that the child is passive and neglects to consider that the child can figure out gender roles on his or her own (Carroll, 2009, 97).

Identification Theory. Building on Freudian ideas, sociologist Nancy Chodorow maintains that children of both genders initially identify and develop strong attachments to their primary caretaker, who is generally the mother (Chodorow, 1978). For girls, the problem later is the issue of separation from the mother, which may lead, during the teenage years, to hostility and feelings of competition with her. For boys, the issue is to make a dramatic identification shift from identification with the mother to identification with the father. This shift usually occurs by the age of 6 or 7. In fact, in both agricultural and traditional, craft-based societies, at this age boys begin to leave the mother, going out with the father to farm or learn a skill. To detach successfully from identifying with the mother, boys must reject activities associated with women. Hence, in traditional societies there are *rites of passage* designed specifically to mark a young man's passage from childhood to adulthood and from boyhood to manhood. These changes are then reinforced by membership in exclusively male organizations. In our own society, although the change in identification does not occur so dramatically, there is a general turning away from the feminine role on the part of young boys: They organize "boys-only clubs," as well as enjoying camping and fishing trips in male-only company. Moreover, in contemporary societies it is more difficult to make this switch in identity because fathers are often absent for most of the day and do not offer a ready model. As a result, the young male often accepts a stereotypical gender role, one offered by peers and the media and often not corresponding to reality. This leads the young male to be anxious about whether he is fulfilling his role adequately and to overcompensate by trying to fill a rigid mold of the masculine role. This is one explanation for the "macho" image that some young males, particularly those whose status on the cultural totem pole is low, attempt to present to the world, as for instance, by joining gangs.

Agents of Gender Socialization

It should be clear that those most directly involved in creating gender identities for individuals are those closest to them. Therefore, parents, siblings, extended family members, peers, teachers, and today especially, the mass media play the most significant roles in this activity. These are the same agents who socialize each new generation.

The Media. The media have probably become more influential than any of the other socializing agents in maintaining gender stereotypes. In particular, it is television that has the impact because children spend more time watching it than they do interacting with parents, siblings and other family members, teachers, and friends. (With the advent of texting on smartphones, more children may be engaged in this activity than in watching TV. But television and computer games still represent a large percentage of children's entertainment.) In fact, the average child will have watched more hours of television by high school graduation than she will have spent in class! Television has tremendous educational value—children can be exposed to a great variety of skills, speech patterns and vocabulary, factual information, and emotions. At the same time, the medium is perceived as being authoritative, and children are not sophisticated enough to distinguish reality from fantasy. Fictional accounts of life, as represented in many of the situation comedies, are taken at face value by children, which is unfortunate because they hardly ever reflect reality. Women, especially, are almost universally presented in highly professional occupations—doctors, lawyers, newspaper reporters—although they are seldom shown actually working. Moreover, they are always beautiful and thin, seldom lose their tempers, and never lose their jobs, even when they are assertive with bosses. Despite documentaries and news items focusing on gender inequality, family violence, and sexual assaults, most prime-time shows still show men more frequently than women and in more authoritative positions, thus persevering in the traditional gender role stereotype.

Even when factual news stories are reported, they tend to be more frequently about men, and when they deal with women, they include such information as the woman's marital status, her age, her physical attributes, and often what she is wearing—information that would never appear with regard to a man.

In Sum. Newspapers and magazines also repeat the gender stereotypes. In the past, every daily paper had a section dedicated to women, which dealt with issues thought to be important to women—new recipes for feeding the family thriftily and cosmetics to keep the wife and mother looking good. Today, they no longer call the section "for women," but they present the same material in the guise of "food" or "fashion." Some magazines are clearly addressed to either men or women; *Playboy, Penthouse, Sports Illustrated, Gentlemen's Quarterly*, and others, are directed at men. *Vogue* and myriad other fashion magazines and *Good Housekeeping* and tens of other magazines dedicated to food preparation and other facets of housekeeping are intended strictly for female consumption.

We have been making the point that gender stereotypes are alive and well. Because we do acknowledge the very real differences between men and women, however, we might wonder whether it matters that gender roles are stereotyped. Unfortunately, there are consequences for individuals, families, and the society at large, a fact supported by polls showing that many people feel men in the United States enjoy a better quality of life than women. Although gender roles have undergone a dramatic change—from a hierarchical arrangement in which one sex was subordinated to the other to an androgynous arrangement in which both sexes fill both the instrumental and the expressive roles—gender expectations still limit a woman's lifestyle choices. Despite the fact that about 60 percent of women of working age are in the workforce, it is still expected that a woman's most important role is that of wife and mother. Women who choose a single lifestyle are often criticized as radicals who are undermining "family values." Yet in today's economy, it is necessary for all adults to work, so that most women must combine marriage, motherhood, and a career—or simply a job.

Indeed, combining outside work and the care of children and family is a difficult enterprise. Even where spouses are willing to take on a fair share of tasks, it is hard to divide one's time in such a way that everything and everybody are satisfied. Although research shows that men are spending more time in child-care and nurturing activities, in most cases housework is still the woman's responsibility, with men taking on automobile maintenance and lawn-mowing duties. In short, despite a greater flexibility in gender roles, gender stereotypes continue to constrain both men and women. For women, the constraints—in addition to the sheer difficulty of managing several roles at once—take the form of low self-esteem and a high incidence of mental illness. Women suffer double the rate of major depression as men (CDC/NCHS, National Health and Nutrition Examination Survey, 2008). The high ratio may be an indication that women are more likely to seek help for this condition than men, but it may also be an indication that the unequal power in marital relationships and inequalities in other areas of their life—as well as the subtle and obvious humiliations and harassment to which most women are subjected at some points in their lives—seriously affect women's mental health.

Another example of women's feelings of inadequacy is the efforts a large majority of them expend to constantly improve their appearance. Despite the advances women have made in aiming for and achieving careers, delaying marriage and motherhood, and having

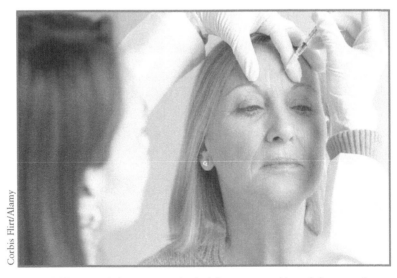

Corbis Flirt/Alamy

Women in Western societies are expected to look forever young, thin, and glamorous. As a result, cosmetic surgery is flourishing—anything from Botox injections to liposuction—but it sometimes has very negative results, including death.

more egalitarian marriages, they seem to have internalized conformist cultural expectations of beauty and femininity. Every women's magazine (including those written for teenage girls) has article after article about perfecting the size of her thighs, abs, and glutes, and beyond diet and exercise, when to undergo plastic surgery. Cosmetic surgery, once the province of the rich and the old, is now suggested to women at the appearance of their first wrinkle—that is, in their 30s. Some women have even been known to undergo toe-shortening or pinky-toe removal for the sake of fitting into high-heeled, pointy shoes. Collagen, botox, and implants into various parts of the anatomy are the order of the day, and the so-called reality TV shows are reinforcing women's preoccupation with looks, subjecting contestants to extensive surgery in a relentless pursuit of physical perfection. This attitude is hardly what the feminists of the 1960s meant when they complained about the narrow roles prescribed for women and decried in Betty Friedan's book, *The Feminine Mystique*. Nor is it strictly the fault of men, although women undertake these procedures mainly to please or appeal to men.

In fact, men, too, experience difficulty with gender stereotyping. Not all men are comfortable fulfilling the instrumental role, especially when that role requires assertiveness or even aggressiveness. Moreover, the role of breadwinner is not easy, particularly in times of economic downturn or for individuals who lack marketable skills. Partly as a result of this difficulty, we see many men walking away from their families or being delinquent in supporting their children. Or they substitute the role of breadwinner for one of "macho man," fathering a number of children for whom they do not care and behaving in a deviant manner that eventually leads to prison.

Should We Change?

Because of these reasons, it seems logical to attempt to change the stereotypes surrounding gender roles. Such changes, however, appear impossibly difficult to attain. Students of gender have suggested that *androgynous* roles, combining the expressive and instrumental roles in the same individual, would be ideal. An androgynous individual could pick and choose among feminine and masculine traits (or emotions or behaviors); he or she could be more flexible in a relationship and could feel more "complete" and satisfied, in the sense of not being obligated to behave one way or another because of limitations superimposed by one's gender. Some researchers, however, have denied that androgyny leads to greater self-confidence and satisfaction. Rather, they believe that assuming the instrumental role on the part of both men and women leads to higher rates of self-esteem, flexibility, and mental health. Masculine-oriented persons appear to experience a lesser incidence of stress, anxiety, depression, neuroticism, conflicts in work and achievement, and general dissatisfaction with their lives than do feminine-oriented individuals (Basow, 1992). Obviously, the problem of changing stereotypes, or changing the gender roles based on them, will not be solved easily or rapidly, but as noted earlier, they are definitely coming.

Sexuality

Although we agree that we are all sexual beings because of the biological imperative to reproduce the species, we are less in agreement with the statement that there are many ways of being sexual. These ways are elements of our cultural learning. In other words, it is our particular culture that tells us how, with whom, under what circumstances, and where it is proper to have sex. In most Western societies—in fact, in most societies of the world—a heterosexual, patriarchal pattern has been the most common cultural script.

Homosexual Behavior

Although homosexuality has been known to exist throughout history, it had been forced to live underground in most societies throughout history. Only recently has our society, and many others, accepted homosexuality as a right and prohibited discrimination against individuals who practice it. Homosexuals have transformed their status rapidly and dramatically. When World War II began, gay people in America had no legal rights, no organizations, a handful of private thinkers, and no public advocates. Today, the situation is much different. Homosexuals are out in the open and have a number of organizations that work to secure their rights and prevent discrimination. Before World War II, the societal attitude was that heterosexual sex (that between men and women) was the only "normal" form of sexual expression. Homosexual expression was stigmatized, and the majority of Americans practiced homophobia, meaning that they feared and dreaded being associated with homosexuality, and often acted on their hatred of homosexuals with violence. This attitude still exists, but homosexuals, who prefer to be referred to as "gays" when male and as "lesbians" when female, have become advocates for their rights as a minority group. As such, they have become not only visible but also politically active and have succeeded in convincing a large portion of Americans that heterosexuality need not be the only form of sexual expression (Kaiser, 1997).

There is no agreement among scholars why some people are heterosexual, others are homosexual, and still others are bisexual. The general consensus is that we are born with a sexual orientation that impels us to search out the opposite sex, the same sex, or both sexes. This orientation, however, may be culturally changed or suppressed. In the past, homosexuality was considered deviant behavior, even mental illness. In 1974, however, the American Psychiatric Association officially took it off the mental illness list. Moreover, scientists are finding that homosexual behavior is not limited to humans: The most recent research has shown that same-sex sexual activity has been observed "in more than 450 different species of animals, from flamingos to bison to beetles to guppies to warthogs" (Mooallem, 2010, 31).

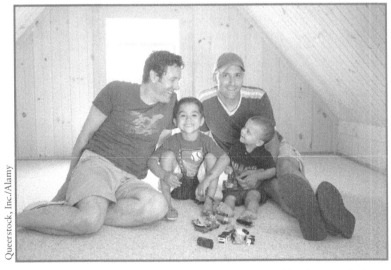

Homosexuality, once considered a crime, is increasingly accepted by Western societies. Consequently, a family consisting of two daddies and their children—either adopted, or fathered by one and carried by a surrogate mother—is no longer a rarity.

What proportion of the population is homosexual has remained questionable. First, not everyone admits to it in surveys. Second, some homosexual behavior is only episodic in nature—perhaps in the form of teenage experimentation. Kinsey, Pomeroy, and Martin (1948) had reported that about 10 percent of the population was homosexual, but a group of contemporary social scientists has developed more accurate samples, and they conclude that about 2.8 percent of men think of themselves as homosexual, and only 1.4 percent of women do (Laumann et al., 1994). More recent estimates are that approximately 8.8 million persons are gay, lesbian, and bisexual, or about 4 percent of 18- to 45-year-olds who identify themselves as gay or bisexuals (Gates, 2006).

Although greater tolerance toward this lifestyle currently exists among the public at large, instances of "gay bashing" still occur, and homophobia is a prevalent attitude among many Americans. The majority still refers to homosexuality as abnormal, immoral, sinful, sick, and wrong. Nonetheless, as a result of the active engagement of gay and lesbian groups who invoked the civil rights legislation to maintain that they have the right to marry, a number of states have granted such couples some legal rights. Massachusetts, Connecticut, Iowa, Vermont, and Washington, D.C., are the only states (and Federal District) that actually allow gays and lesbians to marry, but New Jersey allows same-sex civil unions, Oregon and New Hampshire allow domestic partnerships with the same rights, benefits, privileges and immunities as married couples have. California, which offered such marriages for several months, reinstated the ban on them after a voter initiative contradicted the California Supreme Court.

It seems, however, that the courts and legislatures are ahead of the American people in their acceptance of the homosexual lifestyle. In fact, when in 1973 the National Opinion Research Center at the University of Chicago surveyed the opinions of people regarding same-sex relations, 73 percent described them as always wrong and 8 percent as almost always wrong. By 2006, 56 percent called them always wrong and 5 percent almost always wrong. The most recent survey conducted in August of 2009 found that 49 percent still say that homosexual behavior is morally wrong, and 9 percent say it is morally acceptable. In addition, 35 percent say it is not a moral issue. And even those who oppose same-sex marriage (53 percent) are much more in favor of civil unions (30 percent).

Explanatory Theories of Homosexuality

No theory has successfully explained the causes of homosexuality. Psychoanalytic theories suggest that homosexuality is caused by a specific family configuration, namely, a dominating mother and a weak father or a rejecting mother and an absent father. However, these theories fail to explain why many in such families do not become homosexual and, vice versa, why children in some closely knit and loving families do.

Learning theories maintain that homosexuality, like other elements of socialization, is learned through such processes as imitation or rewards and punishments. These theories, too, do not take into account that homosexuals embrace this lifestyle despite punishment, and that heterosexual parents may produce homosexual children and homosexual parents may produce heterosexual children.

Biological theories attribute homosexuality either to inherited genes or to sex hormones. Geneticists have found higher rates of homosexuality among identical twins as compared to fraternal twins, thus leading them to believe that a shared recessive gene may be a causal factor. Scientists have also suggested that hormones affect future sexual orientation prenatally, inasmuch as they found that rates of homosexuality and bisexuality were "clumped" in specific families (Pillard & Weinrich, 1986). One neuroscientist examined the brain tissue of a number of homosexual men and heterosexual men and women. The tissue came from the hypothalamus—a zone in the center of the brain that regulates a number of essential body functions, including the sex drive. The finding emerged that, in heterosexual men, the specific area is three times as large as in homosexual men and heterosexual women. However, the scientist did not conclude that homosexuality depends on this cause, and his sample was very small (Suplee, 1991).

Nonetheless, it does appear that homosexuality is heritable, that is, that there is a genetic component to it, despite the difficulty of supplying cause and effect. In fact, because gay men have only one-fifth as many children as heterosexual men (from relations with women or in vitro fertilization), a gene for homosexuality should soon disappear, according to evolutionary theory. Inasmuch as it has not disappeared, researchers have set forth a number of speculations. One is that homosexuality may be a by-product of a gene that persists because it enhances fertility in other family members. Studies have found that gay men have more relatives than heterosexual men, especially on their mother's side (Wade, 2007, D6). Another clue to the origin of homosexuality is birth order. According to another study, it appears that having older brothers increases the chances that a man will be gay. This theory is based on the speculation that some event in the womb produces some type of antibodies to successive male pregnancies. According to this study, approximately 15 percent of gay men can attribute their homosexuality to the birth order, and with each older brother, the odds of same-sex attraction increases by 33 percent (Wade, 2007, D6).

The conclusion of other researchers in this area suggests that sexual orientation is probably arrived at through a combination of factors. There may be biological causes—for instance, sex hormones that could be influencing the brain in the prenatal and early neonatal phases of development. There may also be cultural factors that strengthen hormonal predispositions. Some women, for example, may be attracted to a lesbian lifestyle because they are drawn to the more emotional and expressive way women love.

Box 3   Acquiring a Homosexual Identity

During the socialization process, children assume that they will play the roles consonant with their gender. By adolescence, however, some individuals begin to see that their fantasies and actual behavior do not agree with the heterosexual model. They note their disinterest in persons of the opposite sex or in activities that are perceived as characteristic of their biological gender. The result is that they experience feelings of confusion and turmoil.

At some point during or after late adolescence, most homosexuals accept their identity and begin to present themselves to others with that label. However, they are selective in their presentation. They may, for instance, be known to friends and relatives, or in the local homosexual community, but keep their sexual identity hidden on the job. This situation used to be almost universal but has changed in the past decade, as even persons in government and the church have "come out." One researcher summarized these stages in a model that includes sensitization (before puberty, when future homosexuals begin to be aware of feeling "different"); identity confusion (in adolescence); identity assumption (accepting and "coming out"); and commitment (the decision to accept homosexuality as a way of life; Troidén, 1988).

Gays and lesbians appear to differ in their sexual behavior in the same way that men and women do. Differences appear to be due to gender more than to sexual orientation. Lesbians tend to have monogamous relationships just as heterosexual women do; they tend to equate love and sex; they are less sexually aroused by visual stimuli; they are not likely to objectify sex as a commodity; they are not very interested in sex with strangers or in public places; they look for long-term relationships; and they are less interested in sexual experimentation. All these characteristics are true of heterosexual women as well. Gays, on the other hand, are more promiscuous, just as heterosexual males are; they tend to separate love and emotional intimacy and sex; they are interested in pornography and are excited by visual stimuli; they are likely to objectify sex as a consumer product; they are not opposed to sex with strangers or in public places, often cruising for sexual partners in such locations; and they like sexual variety and experimentation. Finally, such industries as prostitution, pornography, topless bars, escort services, and adult bookstores tend to be supported by both heterosexual and homosexual males, rather than by women of either sexual orientation (Goode, 1990).

Bisexuality

Another form of sexual expression is bisexuality, or a person's attraction to both men and women (some researchers prefer the term *ambisexuality*). The percentages of people who define themselves as bisexuals have remained small; Kinsey's surveys (1953) indicated that 16 percent of single men and 9 percent of single women in their thirties could be termed bisexual. Later surveys (Knudson, 1990; Hite, 1981) both showed that approximately 6 percent of adults defined themselves as being bisexual, although Hite's survey concerned only male respondents.

Again, perspectives on bisexuality differ. On the one hand, some scientists maintain, as Kinsey did, that sexuality exists on a continuum and is not an either/or behavior. In this view, bisexuality represents a combination of heterosexuality and homosexuality. Other scientists have insisted that heterosexuals, homosexuals, and bisexuals form separate categories, basing their arguments on the facts that sex drive, production of testosterone, and certain psychological and social traits differ among the categories.

Regarding the causes of bisexuality, no specific or general theory has been proposed. In the largest study of bisexuality attempted, the findings were inconclusive: Most men and women had no homosexual experiences before adulthood and seemed to drift into relationships with both men and women, almost casually. However, the reasons for entering into various relationships with either same-sexed or other-sexed individuals differed according to gender. Women who defined themselves as bisexual noted that their emotional needs are sometimes filled by men and at other times by women, whereas bisexual men sometimes rationalize their bisexuality as a need for variety in their sex lives (Blumstein & Schwartz, 1977).

Sexually Transmitted Diseases

An unfortunate consequence of all types of sex, but particularly of unprotected, promiscuous sex, is sexually transmitted diseases (STDs). STDs are defined as diseases transmitted from one person to another through sexual contact, including oral–genital contact, anal intercourse, and oral–anal contact. STDs include chlamydia, gonorrhea, syphilis, AIDS, and about 30 others. These communicable diseases are very common because the viruses and bacteria that cause them have become increasingly resistant to drugs and because looser sexual mores have led people to engage in sex at earlier ages and with multiple partners. STDs affect people of all ages and all social classes. Untreated, they are very dangerous, leading to infertility and, in the worst cases, death. However, most may be cured if caught early enough, and all are preventable when proper information is available and care and responsibility for one's actions is taken. Unfortunately, it seems that many people do not take such responsibility. The Centers for Disease Control (CDC) report that although approximately 700,000 cases of gonorrhea occur every year in the United States, the disease is becoming resistant to the antibiotics with which it has been traditionally treated. Should the bacterium become resistant to the new type of antibiotics as well, it would lead to a severe crisis.

Twenty years ago the nation became conscious of a scourge that afflicted homosexual males (and later drug addicts who shared needles): the emergence of the human immunodeficiency virus (HIV), the virus that causes autoimmunodeficiency syndrome (AIDS). Since then, AIDS has become a leading cause of death for some populations and is the fifth leading cause of death among all Americans between the ages of 25 and 44. More than 583,000 Americans with AIDS have died in the United States, including adolescents and children under 15, and the disease has become a major killer in many other societies, especially those in Africa. The number of people living with AIDS in 34 states of the United States as of 2007 is estimated at more than 571,378, of whom 2,736 are children. More than one million persons live with HIV and AIDS, a fifth of whom are not aware that they are infected. When it became clear how HIV was spread, the government and a number of health organizations initiated a strongly worded campaign among homosexuals and drug addicts with the aim of prevention and protection. For gays, it urged the absolute necessity of having safe sex, that is, sex protected by condoms.

For a while, the fear of becoming HIV infected had the desired effect: As horror stories emerged of young gay men dying horrible deaths as a result of AIDS, more and more of them abandoned unprotected sex with men they had in the past picked up in bars, in adult bookstores, or in spas catering to gays. As a result, and because of new treatments and education efforts, AIDS-related deaths had declined by 42 percent between 1996 and 1997 and by another 20 percent between 1997 and 1998. Unfortunately, although the trend was slowing for the gay male population, it was increasing among women whose partners were bisexuals or drug abusers and for minorities.

New treatments can prolong the lives of AIDS victims and keep at bay the emergence of AIDS among the HIV infected. However, they have also had a negative effect. Some gay men, in fact, have acquired a false sense of security and are increasingly becoming careless, again engaging in high-risk sexual behavior. In particular, it is the generation of younger gays, who have not personally seen the devastation of disease and death that AIDS causes, who are the most reckless.

Internationally, about 33.4 million people are estimated to be living with HIV/AIDS in 2008, of whom almost half are women and approximately 2.3 million are children (2003). In 2008, AIDS had caused the deaths of approximately 2 million people, including 2.6 million adults and 380,000 children. In some nations, the disease is leaving millions of children orphans and is causing major catastrophes for new generations.

The Chapter in Brief

The elderly in the United States suffer from loss of status, income, and prestige, even though they are an ever-increasing proportion of the population. Because of the speed of technological change in modern industrial societies, many young persons are better informed and have more skills than the old, at least in certain areas. As a result, the old are devalued. In addition, the elderly suffer from declining health and vigor and so deviate from the ideal norms that prevail in a society that extols youth, beauty, and fitness. Many of the elderly have financial difficulties in addition to health problems; this is especially true of elderly women and members of minority groups. Discrimination against the elderly has been obvious in the area of employment, where the cards are stacked against anyone over age 40. In addition, many employers enforce the retirement age of 65 or earlier, which forces some employees to disengage before they are ready. Disengagement is supposed to be a mutual process by which the elderly give up social and occupational roles voluntarily so that these roles may be filled by younger persons. Other theoretical frameworks within which the elderly are studied include the modernization, interactionist, subculture, activity, exchange, and age stratification theories.

Many of the myths about the elderly are patently untrue. Not all are senile or miserable or lonely; only a minority have serious health problems; they are not all poor, nor do they all hate retirement. Most live independent lives. Many do face widowhood and the consequent loneliness of bereavement, and when their physical and mental health wane, they may face institutionalization. None of these are pleasant conclusions to life; however, inasmuch as the elderly are a growing segment of society, it is likely that the negative attitudes toward them will be somewhat reversed.

The fact that humanity exists in two sexes has brought it much conflict. In the war between the sexes, women appear to be the losers. From a biological point of view, the two sexes are needed for the species to reproduce: The function of males is to deposit sperm in the reproductive organs of females; the function of females is to carry the resulting embryo—and then the fetus—until it emerges as a fully formed human infant. Both parents can then nurture it until it can exist independently. Throughout history, these different biological functions have resulted in societies treating the two sexes differently and unequally.

Differences between men and women are of an anatomical, genetic, and hormonal nature. These differences certainly have effects on the behavior of men and women. Some of these differences seem to indicate that females are more social, are more suggestible, have lower self-esteem—at least beginning with adolescence—and are less achievement-oriented than males, who are judged to be more aggressive and assertive and to have more analytical minds. There is also evidence that females are superior in verbal ability and seem inclined to nurture infants and children (the expressive role), whereas males excel in spatial and quantitative abilities, facilitating the instrumental role. What remains unclear is whether these traits are inborn or a result of differences in socialization experiences.

Even though we are born either male or female, we must become socialized into sex roles. Such socialization begins in the cradle: Girl and boy babies are treated differently. Researchers theorize that socialization into sex roles occurs in the context of the functionalist and conflict theories through such processes as social learning, the cognitive developmental model, and identification. As to the agents of gender socialization, they are the family, the peer group, the school, and the mass media.

The fact that women have been treated unequally in most societies has had consequences on their lives. Traditional gender roles have been permeated by a sexist ideology that justifies the inequality between the sexes.

The obvious effect of sexism is that many options have been closed to women, who have been relegated for centuries to the roles of wives and mothers and little else. Sociocultural changes in contemporary postindustrial societies have opened more avenues for women. However, the entrance of so many women into the workforce and the consequent displacement of marriage and family have left many women puzzled and confused. It remains difficult for many women to reconcile their aspirations for personal achievement with their desire for a traditional family life. As a result, both men's and women's gender roles still remain far from clear-cut.

In acquiring the sexual portion of personality, not everyone is drawn to heterosexuality. Some individuals are drawn to members of their own gender, becoming homosexuals. Still others are attracted to both sexes, sometimes establishing a paired relationship with one gender after some experimentation, or otherwise remaining bisexual throughout their lives. Scientists have not established a definite cause for these behaviors.

A negative effect of unprotected or promiscuous sex is sexually transmitted diseases (STDs), the most dangerous of which is AIDS. This disease has killed many gay men and intravenous drug users and, increasingly, many women and children. It is also a scourge in developing nations, particularly in Africa.

Terms to Remember

activity theory In the study of the elderly, the theory that the key to successful aging is to replace former roles with new ones.

ageism An ideology that asserts the superiority of the young over the old. Used to justify discrimination against the elderly in political, economic, and social areas.

anatomical differences The differences in physical structure and appearance between the two sexes. The most important anatomical difference lies in the distinct reproductive systems of males and females.

cognitive development theory A theory that includes the idea that children learn gender roles according to which stage of cognitive development they have reached. Cognitive development is the way information is processed by individuals at different stages of physical maturation.

conflict perspective A theory that assumes that power and privilege are based on the resources an individual possesses.

disengagement theory A theory of aging that posits that the elderly withdraw from their former social and occupational roles so that these may be filled by the young. This should occur by mutual consent.

exchange theory In the study of the elderly, the theory that the disadvantaged position of the elderly in American society is due to their lack of the social and material resources that would make them valuable in interactions with the young.

expressive role Emphasizes nurturing, emotion, and peacemaking.

feminist theory A theory that has borrowed much of the framework of conflict theory, especially the fact that women are underrepresented in positions of power in the society at large, a reflection of the lack of power women have within the family.

gender roles Traditionally, the **instrumental** role is assigned to males and the **expressive** role is assigned to females.

genetic Pertaining to genes, which determine heredity in all living creatures.

hormones Chemicals that are secreted into the bloodstream by glands located in the body, whose functions are to stimulate some chemical processes and inhibit others.

instrumental role Stresses rationality, competitiveness, aggression, and goal orientation.

male or female Biological terms, descriptive of biological facts. They refer to a **sex status**, ascribed and not subject to change except in extraordinary circumstances.

masculine and feminine Reflect **social** conditions, describing how males and females are expected to behave in a given society and how they come to feel about themselves. They are **gender roles**, achieved and, thus, subject to change according to place and time.

modernization theory In the study of the elderly, the theory that the status of older people declines as the society in which they live becomes more modern and industrial.

secondary sex characteristics Include height, weight, distribution of body fat and hair, and musculature.

sex chromosomes Contain the genes that determine heredity in all living creatures.

sex status An ascribed condition referring to the biological terms male or female.

social learning theory A theory based on the behaviorist notion that learning consists of observation, imitation, and reinforcement.

structural functionalist theory One of the most dominant theories in sociology, which assumes that those elements are retained in a social system that aid in the survival of that system.

Suggested Readings

Carroll, Janelle. 2009. *Sexuality Now: Embracing Diversity*. 3rd ed. New York: Wadsworth. A well-written, easy-to-read text on a subject that is often buried in jargon.

Dychtwald, Ken. 2000. *Age Power: How the 21st Century Will Be Ruled by the New Old*. New York: Putnam. A gerontologist takes a look at the elderly and speculates about their future social patterns.

Epstein, Cynthia Fuchs, Carroll Seron, Bonnie Oglensky, and Robert Saute. 1999. *The Part-Time Paradox: Time Norms, Professional Life, Family and Gender*. New York: Routledge. A discussion of the conflicts inherent in the lives of women who work, the tension between the demands of career and family, and suggestions of how to solve some of these conflicts with part-time work.

Faludi, Susan. 1999. *Stiffed: The Betrayal of the American Man*. New York: William Morrow. A feminist author maintains that even though American men remain the dominant sex, they feel increasingly misunderstood and unappreciated.

Faludi, Susan. 2008 reprint. *The Terror Dream: Myth and Misogyny in an Insecure America*. New York: Picador. This book is outrageous and amusing, and certainly thought-provoking.

Quadagno, Jill. 2010. *Aging and the Life Course: An Introduction to Social Gerontology*. New York: McGraw-Hill. An overview of the aged and of the process of aging from the point of view of sociology.

Stoller, Eleanor Palo, and Rose Campbell Gibson. 2000. *Worlds of Difference: Inequality in the Aging Experience*. 2nd ed. Thousand Oaks, CA: Pine Forge Press. The experience of growing old according to a diverse number of people differing in race, class, and gender. An anthology written from a sociological perspective, showing a variety of norms and social structures on the road to aging.

Strauch, Barbara. 2010. *The Secret Life of the Grown-up Brain: The Surprising Talents of the Middle-Aged Mind*. Good news for the aging: Their minds might be getting slower, but they are also getting better.

Westheimer, Ruth K., and Sanford Lopater. 2004. *Human Sexuality*. Baltimore: Lippincott Williams & Wilkins. As the title suggests, this is a textbook on human sexuality and deals with the entire spectrum of this subject in clear and understandable language. The well-known Dr. Westheimer answers letters and queries on a variety of sexual issues.

Population, Urbanization, and Environment

From Chapter 11 of *Contemporary Society: An Introduction to Social Science*, Thirteenth Edition.
John A. Perry, Erna K. Perry. Copyright © 2012 by Pearson Education, Inc. All rights reserved.

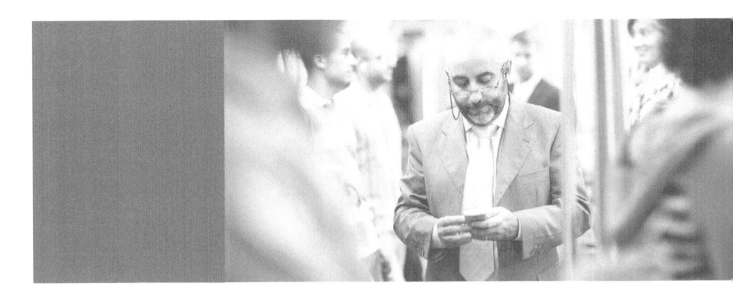

Population, Urbanization, and Environment

IN THIS CHAPTER, YOU WILL LEARN

- *about the importance of the discipline of demography and its various concepts;*
- *about the types of changes that occur within populations and their effects on societies;*
- *of the dangers of overpopulation;*
- *the meaning and effects of urbanization;*
- *about the characteristics of American cities;*
- *the difference between the process called urbanization and the attitude of urbanism, which has become predominant globally;*
- *about the emergence of suburbanization and metropolitanization;*
- *the nature of the urban crisis;*
- *about the discipline of ecology; and*
- *that humans have damaging effects on the various ecosystems, including on the global ecosystem.*

The principal sociocultural change that followed each technological revolution was a dramatic increase in population. After the Industrial Revolution, in addition, population growth was accompanied by a rise in the number of cities and ultimately an urban way of life that now pervades all industrial societies. In turn, large populations, the industrial system, and an urbanized lifestyle have wreaked havoc on the planet's environment. They have pushed the human species into acting in ways that are contrary to the ways in which they behaved when small groups of them roamed the vastness of the earth.

The triple trends that follow the process of modernization in societies around the world include a dramatic increase in population, a rush by rural residents to the cities, and the consequent damage that urban overcrowding, as well as the industrial system, do to the natural environment. China, for instance already has more than a billion people, many of whom are crowding into environmentally damaged cities.

All living things follow an instinctive urge to reproduce themselves. This urge is given the weight of a divine commandment in Western societies by the Biblical injunction to be fruitful and multiply. Non-Western societies are similarly affected by the need to procreate, judging from the seriously overpopulated world for which gloom and doom are periodically prophesied. In reality, if people were distributed evenly over the surface of the earth, there would only be about 55 people per square mile. The real problem, then, is **population density**, which varies from zero in some uninhabited regions of Antarctica to approximately 77,000 people per square mile on the island of Manhattan. In the United States, there are counties in the Great Plains region with fewer than 6 persons per square mile.

The distribution of people is a very vital issue because the welfare of a society often depends on such characteristics of its people as birthrates, death rates, sex ratios, age groups, marriage incidence, divorce frequency, and mobility. The gathering and interpretation of statistics in these areas are done by the discipline of **demography**, which is the scientific study of how births, deaths, and migration affect the composition, size, and distribution of populations.

Population density can be measured in a variety of ways. Looking at continents, 76 percent of the human population lives in Eurasia, 9 percent in North America, 10 percent in Africa, and 5 percent in South America and the Pacific islands. Looking at political units, 22 percent of all humans reside in the People's Republic of China, 15 percent live in India, 6.5 percent in the former Soviet Union, and 5.5 percent in remaining countries of the world. Maps showing the population density and the distribution and concentration of population throughout the United States may be found at **mysearchlab.com**.

Demographic Processes: Dynamics of Population Change

The chief source of information for demographers is the census, a sort of head count describing the composition and distribution of people according to their origins, skills, and activities, in addition to their location. In the United States, an elaborate census is conducted every 10 years (as prescribed by Article I of the Constitution). The accuracy of the census is important because not only are the seats in the House of Representatives apportioned according to the population of each state but also a number of federal entitlement programs are similarly allocated on the basis of census results. An example of the kinds of data the Bureau of the Census collects is provided by a rapid perusal of its "USA Statistics in Brief" in Table 1. These figures change every year as a result of three factors: the number of births, the number of deaths, and the number of people who move into a location or move out of it. Demographers refer to these factors as the birthrate, the death rate, and migration.

Birthrates

The crude **birthrate** is defined as the number of live births per 1,000 people during one year. (The actual formula that demographers use to obtain the crude birthrate is the number of live births in a given year, divided by the total population of a country and multiplied by 1,000.) A more accurate concept is **fertility** rate, which is "the number of births that 1,000 women

TABLE 1 Demographic Indicators for United States

	2009	2015	2025
Population			
Midyear population (in thousands)	307,212	325,540	357,452
Growth rate (percent)	1	1	0.9
Fertility			
Total fertility rate (births per woman)	2.1	2.1	2.1
Crude birth rate (per 1,000 population)	14	14	13
Births (in thousands)	4249	4470	4726
Mortality			
Life expectancy at birth (years)	78	79	80
Infant mortality rate (per 1,000 births)	6	6	5
Under 5 mortality rate (per 1,000 births)	8	7	5
Crude death rate (per 1,000 population)	8	8	9
Deaths (in thousands)	2574	2728	3088
Migration			
Net migration rate (per 1,000 population)	4	4	4
Net number of migrants (in thousands)	1327	1387	1576

Source: U.S. Census Bureau, International Data Base

would have in their lifetime if, at each year of age, they experienced the birthrates occurring in the specified year." **Fecundity** rates represent the biological potential for reproduction (how many births per 1,000 women of that age group could occur). At the height of the baby boom years, 1947, the crude birthrate in the United States was about 27 per 1,000. In 2009, the crude birthrate was 13.82, conspicuously lower than the post–World War II high and very low compared to a nation such as Afghanistan, with a birthrate of 53.4 per 1,000, or Uganda, with a rate of 51.1, but higher than the rate of Japan (8.7), Greece (9.5), or Italy (9.7).

Birthrates do not generally correspond to population density. In fact, densely populated areas such as Western Europe and Japan have low birthrates, as we saw earlier, whereas sparsely settled regions such as Arabia and interior Africa have very high birthrates. From the perspective of economics, high birthrates occur in the less industrialized and less urbanized countries of the world, the so-called underdeveloped nations. Conversely, highly industrialized and urbanized nations tend to have the lowest birthrates. Therefore, birthrates are recognized as the best single socioeconomic variable differentiating developed from underdeveloped nations. This distribution of birthrates is comparatively new: Between 1840 and 1930, the population of Europe grew from 194 million to 463 million, approximately double the rate for the world as a whole.

Death Rates

The crude **death rate**, also called **mortality rate**, is the number of deaths per 1,000 people of a given population per year. On a worldwide basis, death rates are highest in tropical Africa, whereas urban, industrial nations have low death rates in addition to low birthrates. However, some less urban and industrial nations, such as Thailand, Turkey, and Ecuador, also exhibit low death rates, even though their birthrates are moderate or high. The reason for this disparity is that the percentage of young people is higher in developing countries than it is in developed countries. Still, in 2009 the death rate in the United States was 8.38 per 1,000, whereas in Sierra Leone it was 20.62 per 1,000 (CIA World Factbook, 2009).

Death can result from a number of causes: traffic accidents, suicide, disease, or starvation. The great leveler of death rates has been Western medical technology, which in this century has reached almost every corner of the world. It has dramatically decreased death rates everywhere, even in locations where they had remained stubbornly high. Decreasing death rates, in fact, are a major cause of excessive population growth in Third World nations.

A truer measure of the quality of life in a society, or in a segment of a society, is the infant mortality rate. The **infant mortality** rate reflects the number of deaths among infants under 1 year of age for every 1,000 live births. In developing countries, that rate tends to be over 30, whereas in developed nations it tends to be under 20. In 2009, the infant mortality rate in the United States was 6.26 per 1,000, and 18 nations reported even lower infant mortality rates. By contrast, the infant mortality rate in Sierra Leone in 2004 was 154.95, in Angola it was 180.21, and in Niger 122.66. In the United States, the rate varies greatly according to social class and race: Infant mortality among the poor and minorities has been twice as high as that among the well-to-do in the last several decades. In fact, as of 2005 the infant mortality rate in Mississippi rose to 11.4, and among African Americans in that state it increased to 17 per thousand births. This means that 65 more babies died in 2005 than in 2004 (Eckholm, 2007, p. 1; CIA Factbook, 2009).

Infant mortality has some impact on **life expectancy**, which is the average number of years a person of a certain age can expect to live. In developing nations the average life expectancy is 64.4 years, but it may be much lower: It is 42.18 in Niger, 36.79 in Angola, and 40.88 in Ethiopia. In the United States, life expectancy has gone from 40 years at the turn of the preceding century to 77.43 for persons born between 1995 and 2000. Even Americans currently 65 to 75 years old can expect to live about 20 years longer. But again, not all categories of Americans have such prospects: At birth, life expectancy was about 6 years higher for white persons than for black persons. At age 65, white persons still were expected to live 2 years longer than black persons (Table 2). However, for persons who lived to age 85, life expectancy is slightly higher among black persons than among white persons (CDC, 2006, Table 27). The differences between genders are most likely genetic in nature; the differences between races are probably caused by variations in lifestyles resulting from social class, or perhaps black persons who live until 85 are healthier than white persons. (Most of the gains in the last 150 years in life expectancy have come from reductions in the deaths of infants and women in childbirth.)

Migration

Between 1880 and 1910, more than 28 million Europeans moved from that continent to the United States. Their movement is defined as international migration—movement of people from one country to another. In migration, **push factors** encourage people to leave one geographic area for another and **pull factors** attract people to a new area. For instance, in 1840 the potato famine was the push that made people leave Ireland, and the employment opportunities in the United States were the pull that attracted the Irish to come here. Today, similar push-and-pull factors are acting on Mexicans and Southeast Asians in their efforts to immigrate into the United States.

Immigration

We are a nation of immigrants. Immigration peaked in the first two decades of the twentieth century and did not begin to climb again until 1965, with legislation that eliminated ethnic bias and loosened quotas. Since 1980, an average of 570,000 people a year have come to these shores, not including the approximately 3 million illegal aliens who are in the country. The Immigration Reform and Control Act of 1986 was supposed to lessen the flood of undocumented aliens across U.S. borders because it prescribed high fines for employers who hired them. In reality, the illegal border crossings increased (Parrillo, 1990, 536). The Census Bureau calculates that legal and illegal aliens accounted for one-fourth to one-third of the country's population growth in the 1980s. In addition, the places of origin of the immigrants differ from those of previous waves. How to deal with immigration and the fate of illegal aliens have been controversial issues in the United States, ones the current administration and Congress are going to have to deal with in the near future.

Internal Migration

Between 1910 and 1955, millions of poor whites and blacks left the economically ailing South of the United States for the industrial jobs in the North. They were engaging in internal migration. Today, it is the South and the West that are growing in population, whereas the Midwest and Northeast are losing population. Internal migration does not affect the size of a nation's population; it affects the populations of regions and local communities. Internal migration has been very important in the history of the United States. We are a mobile country whose citizens willingly follow the siren song of better opportunity, whether it leads west, north, south, or east. Reversals, then, are common. Since 1980, nearly 100,000 more African Americans have moved into the South than have moved out, reversing an 80-year tide of migration. Most of

TABLE 2　Resident Population Projections by Race, Hispanic-Origin Status, and Age: 2010 and 2015

Age group	Total		White alone		Black alone		American Indian and Alaska Native alone		Asian alone		Native Hawaiian, Other Pacific Islander alone		Two or more races		Hispanic origin[1]		White alone, not of Hispanic origin	
	2010	2015	2010	2015	2010	2015	2010	2015	2010	2015	2010	2015	2010	2015	2010	2015	2010	2015
Total	310,233	325,540	246,630	256,306	39,909	42,137	3,188	3,472	14,415	16,527	592	662	5,499	6,435	49,726	57,711	200,853	203,208
Under 5 years	21,100	22,076	15,944	16,563	3,034	3,191	286	311	943	1,004	53	56	840	951	5,053	5,622	11,375	11,487
16 years and over	243,639	255,864	196,026	203,643	30,201	32,171	2,343	2,547	11,466	13,267	435	489	3,168	3,747	34,372	40,202	164,202	166,441
18 years and over	235,016	247,434	189,473	197,229	28,844	30,940	2,237	2,446	11,095	12,861	416	470	2,950	3,487	32,576	38,192	159,295	161,868
16 to 64 years	203,410	209,027	161,100	163,478	26,783	28,059	2,108	2,232	10,132	11,437	397	436	2,890	3,384	31,515	36,416	131,959	129,819
55 years and over	76,504	87,381	65,147	73,437	7,258	8,698	531	671	2,877	3,706	87	114	604	755	6,136	8,104	59,421	65,888
65 years and over	40,229	46,837	34,926	40,164	3,418	4,111	235	314	1,333	1,831	39	53	278	363	2,858	3,786	32,243	36,623
75 years and over	18,766	19,870	16,613	17,368	1,442	1,594	87	111	500	645	14	18	110	133	1,173	1,479	15,509	15,978
85 years and over	5,751	6,292	5,189	5,632	397	445	20	26	113	149	3	4	29	36	305	418	4,902	5,238
Median age (yrs.)	36.9	37.1	38.4	38.6	31.7	32.8	29.9	31.1	36.0	37.5	30.5	32.0	19.9	20.2	27.5	27.8	41.3	42.1

In thousands (310,233 represents 310,233,000), except as indicated. As ot July 1. Projections are based on assumptions about future births, deaths, and net international migration. More information on methodology and assumptions is available at <http://www.census.gov/population/www/projections/methodstatement.html> For definition of median, see Guide Io Tabular Presentation]

– Represents or rounds to zero.　[1] Persons of Hispanic origin may be any race.

Source: U.S. Census Bureau. "2006 National Population Projections." released August 2008: <http://www.census.gov/population/www/projections/2008projections.html>.

them are moving to the South for new jobs, for a better quality of life, or to renew family ties. Although most migration is driven by economic opportunity, the South has become more hospitable to African Americans in the sense that laws on civil rights, voter registration, and school desegregation and laws against discrimination on the job have created a much more tolerable atmosphere for black families (Weiss, 1989, Y29).

The Midwest, too, is experiencing something of a rebound, although Americans continue to favor the West and the South as places to live: As of 2006, the 50 fastest-growing metropolitan areas were distributed between two regions—23 in the West and 25 in the South (U.S. Bureau of the Census, Current Population Reports, 2006). The population of the United States is concentrated as follows: 113,317,879 live in the South, 71,568,081 live in the West, 66,836,911 live in the Midwest, and 55,283,679 live in the Northeast. The most populous states in the nation are California (36-plus million people), Texas (24-plus million), and New York (19.5 million). Sociologists and demographers had predicted that the coastal states would come to hold a greater proportion of the nation's population. The reason for this situation is economic: The coastal states account for the largest percentage of the real growth in wages and partnership income. The industrial heartland of the United States traditionally had been in the region around the Great Lakes because industry needed the transportation provided by the waterways, and the region was also rich in coal and iron ore. However, the rise of the information economy has moved population following jobs to the rim states of Massachusetts and New Jersey in the East and the Silicon Valley (from San Francisco to San Jose) in the West.

Characteristics and Composition of a Population

Demographers calculate not only a population's size—which is affected by birthrates, death rates, and migration rates—but also a number of other characteristics, the most important of which are the sex ratio, the marriage rate, and the age structure.

Sex Ratio

The **sex ratio** indicates how many males there are in a population in any single year per 100 females. More boys than girls are conceived and born (124 are conceived, 105 are born), but the ratio of males to females in the United States is 96.7 males for 100 females. The reasons for the greater number of females are to be found in the higher rates of miscarriage of male fetuses and males' susceptibility to disease, accidents, and violence. This is particularly true in wartime, but even in normal times women outnumber men beginning at about age 25 through old age. In relatively advanced countries, there are about 105 females for every 100 males. In Third World countries, however, the opposite is true: Although 5 or 6 percent more boys than girls are born, in India there are only 92.9 females for every 100 males, in China there are 93.8 females for every 100 males, and in Afghanistan there are 94.5 females for every 100 males. These conditions are due to high rates of female infanticide and the general negligence—if not outright murder—of female children, whom the cultures of these nations do not value to the same extent as males. It is reported that at least 60 million females in Asia are missing and feared dead, and around the world more than 100 million females are missing, victims only of their gender.

Because the sex ratio is fairly distributed even in the United States, the marriage rate is high (because each individual has the possibility of obtaining a mate). In addition, the marriage rate is positively related to the birthrate: The baby boom occurred after World War II, when soldiers came home, married, and had families. Beginning in the 1960s, late marriages, divorces, and increasing numbers of unmarried adults decreased our birthrates to their present low.

Age Structure

The age structure of a society influences it in a variety of ways (see Figures 1–2). A society whose members are concentrated in the age group 20–65 has a large labor force and few nonproductive dependents. On the other hand, if members are concentrated in the under-20, or the over-65 age group, the society has a large number of nonproductive individuals, which the government has to help support. A population with a large number of young people will also tend to have high birthrates, a situation occurring at present in developing countries. Naturally, a population with a high number of elderly people has a high death rate.

Population Pyramid Summary for United States

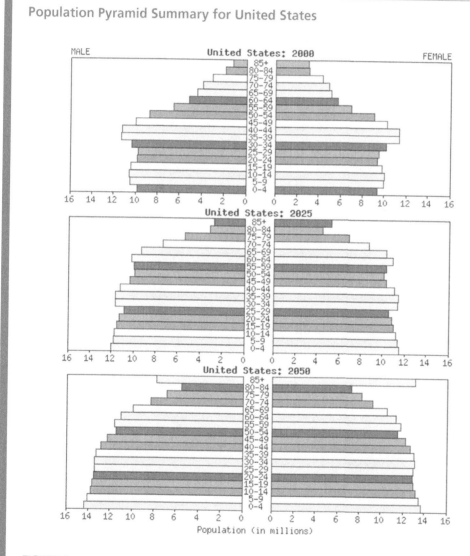

FIGURE 1
Source: U.S. Census Bureau, International Data Base

Population Pyramid Summary for China

FIGURE 2
Extract data from IDB Online Aggregation.
Source: U.S. Census Bureau, International Data Base

The age and sex composition of a population can be shown graphically by what is called a **population pyramid.** Each bar in such a graph represents a **birth cohort,** or all the people born in a specific time period. In a developing country, the pyramid has a truly pyramidal shape because its bottom is constituted by the largest birth cohort—the population consisting of those under 20. The top consists of a small proportion of those over 65. In a developed country, the declines in both the birthrate and the death rate make for a structure with a wide

Population Pyramid Summary for India

India: 2000

Male   Female

India: 2025

India: 2050

Population (in millions)

FIGURE 3

Extract data from IDB Online Aggregation.

Source: U.S. Census Bureau, International Data Base

middle and a rather narrow base and top. As Figures 1, 2 and 3 indicate, the United States, China, and India will experience a progressively higher number of elderly in the future, but China and India will continue to have a large contingent of young people.

The population pyramid is a useful tool for social planning. Obviously, in a society in which the majority of the population is under 20, there will be a need for maternity wards in hospitals, schools, and child care services. One whose members are predominantly old will need additional nursing homes, health care geared to the aged, provisions for pensions and Social Security, and so on.

Some demographers maintain that the widening gap between the age cohorts in different parts of the world is a time bomb (Bell, 1987, 15–16). The proportion of young people under 15 years in all of Africa is between 40 and 50 percent of the population; in almost all of Latin America it is about 40 percent of the population; in most of Asia, it is between 30 and 40 percent; whereas in the United States and Canada it is about 22 percent. What this means is that in the next 20 years there will be more than a doubling of the rates of entry into the labor forces of the nations with large percentages of young people. This will create conditions of unemployment and underemployment, which will add to the political instability of those nations. In addition, because of the huge increases in the number of women of child-bearing age in the next several decades—caused, in turn, by the young age structure of the population at the world level—a population momentum will result in a doubling of world population by 2050 to about 9.2 billion people, an increase of better than 50 percent over 1999.

One of the values of demography as a scientific discipline is its predictive function, for it is to the advantage of society to be aware of future trends and prepare for them. In the United States, the Census Bureau not only collects data reflecting the present but also attempts to

Box 1 Americans as the Census Bureau Sees Us

Every decade the Census Bureau counts the heads of Americans, just so we know how many we are. However, counting heads is the least of what the Bureau does: Its surveys also tell us, probably in more detail than we care to know, everything about us. How tall we are, how fat we are, how many pounds of sugar we eat yearly, how much television we watch, how many times we marry, how much education we have . . . and on and on to infinity.

Well, then, what do we look like? We are the fattest inhabitants of the planet, spending about eight-and-a-half hours a day watching TV, using computers, listening to the radio, or reading. Adolescents and adults spend more than 64 days a year watching TV, and a little more than a week using the Internet. In 2009, 74 percent of Americans 18 years old and older used the Internet, 60 percent used broadband connections at home, 55 percent of adults connected to the Internet wirelessly through WiFi or handheld devices such as a Smartphone.

We are taller than preceding generations: Although 24 percent of Americans in their seventies are shorter than 5 foot 6, only 10 percent of persons in their twenties are no taller than that. We are losing manufacturing jobs: They decreased in every job category except for pharmaceuticals. Jobs in textile mills fell by 42 percent, and the fastest-growing job is that of home health aide. We do produce one element in huge quantities: Solid waste is produced at a rate of 4.4 pounds per person per day, up from 3.7 pounds a decade ago.

We are wealthier than past generations: In 2005, more than half of American households owned stocks and mutual funds. Those people had a median household income of $65,000. The younger generation wants to copy this lifestyle: 75 percent of college freshmen state that their primary objective in attending college is to be financially very well off, whereas in the 1970s,

79 percent said their goal was to develop a meaningful philosophy of life. Unfortunately, the economic downturn that began in 2007 and continues in the present may have put a stop to their financial goals. Nonetheless, we are producing more women doctors: 27 percent of doctors were women in 2005, whereas in 1980 only 12 percent were. And 42,000 men and 41,000 women earned professional degrees in 2004, whereas in 1970 only 2,000 women and 33,000 men earned such degrees.

Some facts about us are negative. Around 45 million of us have no health insurance, and with medical costs rising, they can only pray that their health remains good or that the health reform legislation that passed in 2010 will cover them. Technology has made it possible for our leisure time to be private, and this trend will continue: We will read less and watch less broadcast television, but will spend more time using the Internet and watching cable and satellite television. This privatization of entertainment—you don't have to go to the theater or to the movies but can get it all while remaining alone in your living room—may lead to a lack of social contact, and social isolation is not good for humans, the social animals.

On the other hand, our national divorce rate that had made us the most divorcing people on earth for several decades has decreased: as of 2009 the rate was 3.4 per 1,000 people. This was the lowest since 1970 (with the exception of Nevada, which still claims a rate of 6.4 per 1,000—but this is a decline from 11.4 in 1990).

These and many more facts may be learned from the Census Bureau, and now we need not wait for the decennial count. The bureau will issue demographic and social data for areas with populations of over 65,000 every year in the American Community Survey (ACS) of the U.S. Census Bureau, Public Information Office.

make projections about the future. The Census Bureau has been projecting that the population of the United States by 2050 would stand at a high of approximately 420 million. The United Nations has also predicted that the United States will continue to increase in population during the first half of the twenty-first century. The reasons are twofold: one, the large number of immigrants who continue to arrive; and two, the higher fertility rate we display, which is unique among the developed nations. This will put the United States in a position of being the only developed country among the world's most populous nations with a tremendous impact on the world (Crossette, 2001, A5). In fact, because of their habits of high consumption, Americans use up more than one-third of the world's energy and material resources, even though they are less than 6 percent of the world's population. However, China is fast approaching a high level of development and consumption, and so it may usurp U.S. dominance.

Population around the World

The media often refer to a "crisis" of population, by which they mean that the number of people in the world has been increasing *geometrically* (that is, it has been doubling: 2, 4, 8, 16, 32, etc.) at ever shorter intervals of time. At present, world population is doubling every 35 years, so that every year there are about 74 million more births than deaths. In contrast, from 1 AD to the middle of the eighteenth century, the birthrate doubled only every 500 years.

Malthus and Marx

The increasingly shorter intervals at which population doubles have created the problem of overpopulation. Two centuries ago, some thinkers had already begun to realize that the earth would become overpopulated and lack sufficient resources unless birthrates were curbed. The best known of these thinkers was Thomas Malthus, who published his treatise, *An Essay on the Principles of Population*, in 1798. In it, Malthus asserted that whereas under favorable circumstances populations grow by geometric progression, the food supply increases by arithmetic progression—1, 2, 3, 4, 5, and so on. Therefore, eventually the food supply would become exhausted, causing increases in the death rate through starvation. Although he was quite pessimistic about the possibility of reversing this trend, Malthus suggested the use of preventive checks to control fertility. Later marriage and enforced celibacy were the checks he favored, neither one a particularly realistic alternative. The gloom of the Malthusian prophecy has been tempered by great advances in technology, agriculture, and methods of birth control. Nonetheless, the prophecy still has relevance, particularly for the developing nations in which, largely as a result of lower death rates, population growth does indeed outpace food production.

Karl Marx disagreed with Malthus about the causes of overpopulation. Inasmuch as he tended to attribute all the evils of society to the unequal distribution of resources, he maintained that the real issue was underproduction and limited employment opportunities, all failures of the capitalist system. If the society were well ordered, an increase in population would mean an increase in production and, thus, in wealth. But because of the way in which property was held in capitalist societies, workers remained poor and competed for the few jobs available. As a solution, Marx proposed a radical restructuring of society, particularly a more equitable distribution of food, housing, and the other necessities of life. The ideas of these two social commentators in today's context are examined on a number of Web sites noted on **mysearchlab.com**.

Demographic Transition

Demographers have calculated that if the current rate of population growth continues unabated, in a few centuries the population of the world will reach such a level that each person will have only one square foot of land area at his or her disposal. Of course, no one could live in such a minuscule space, but the calculations give dramatic evidence of the nightmarish possibilities. So do the following figures: The world gains 141 new human beings each minute, 10,000 each hour, 203,000 each day, and approximately 74 million each year! Every three years, the new additions to world population equal the total population of the United States. A world population of 6.1 billion people was reached by mid-2000 (the 5 billion mark was passed in 1987), and by 2150 the world population is expected to top 9 billion (Figure 4). Finally, nearly 50 percent of the world's population was born in the last 25 years.

However, most population experts expect that the growth rate will remain constant but will level out at some point between 8 billion and 15 billion people. This leveling off will take place if people attain zero population growth (a situation in which people only replace themselves) worldwide or if the demographic transition theory continues to function (see following discussion).

As noted, for most of human history the rates of population growth were barely sufficient for people to replace themselves. A high birthrate was necessary to compensate for the extremely high death rate. In addition, famine, disease, and wars periodically decimated many of the world's populations.

The Industrial Revolution, with its many technological innovations, changed all that. In the West, populations began to explode around the middle of the eighteenth century, but despite Malthus's warnings the uncontrolled growth failed to frighten people, who thought

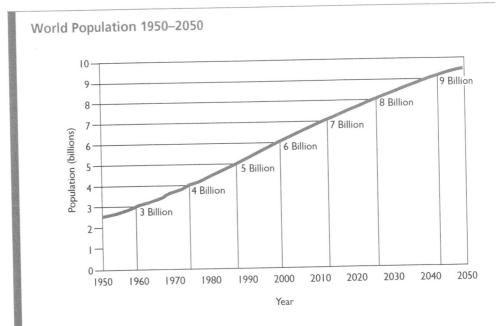

FIGURE 4
Source: U.S. Census Bureau, International Data Base, August 2006 version.

that technology would keep progressing and, thus, always ensure an adequate food supply. Population growth this time around was also accompanied by an increase in the standard of living. This correlation was interpreted as meaning that rapid growth was actually needed for economic expansion. After all, if there are more people, more products are consumed and more people are needed in the workforce to produce still more articles for consumption. In reality, rapid population growth erases any gains derived from improvements in agricultural and industrial technology.

In the past 200 years, the Western world has undergone what demographers call a *demographic transition.* Essentially, this means that Western societies have gone from high mortality and fertility rates to low mortality and fertility rates. Population grew rapidly for a time, and death rates dropped before birthrates did. Soon, however, birthrates were also falling off, and the population growth rate began to stabilize at a relatively low level.

In the belief that this transition represents a general pattern, demographers have pieced together a conceptual model of population growth. According to the model, societies pass through three basic stages of population growth. In the first stage, birthrates and death rates are both high, leading to a balance achieved through cycles of growth and decline. In the second stage, death rates decline but birthrates remain high, leading to unchecked population growth. In the third stage, birthrates decline, leading to stabilization of population. The model allows for shifts in population growth following unusual events, such as wars and depressions.

In applying the model, it may be seen that tropical Africa, tropical South America, and the eastern and middle sections of Asia are currently in the first stage. Parts of North Africa, the temperate part of South America, India, the People's Republic of China, and several other Third World nations are in the second stage. The United States, Australia, New Zealand, Japan, Canada, the United Kingdom, and northern and western Europe are all in the third stage.

Richard Lord/The Image Works

The highest rates of population growth occur in the poorest regions of the world. In many societies of Asia, Africa, and Arabia, women typically have between five and eight children. Here is an extended three-generation family with seven children.

Zero Population Growth

As of the 1970s, the industrial world (the United States, Europe, Japan, Australia) began to display extremely low population growth rates. In the United States, the fertility rate had declined for the first time below the replacement level or between 2.08 and 2.04. In the year 2009, the fertility rate in the United States stood at 2.05. (The replacement level is 2.1, the 2 representing the rate if each person merely reproduced himself or herself, and the 0.1 representing the people who remain childless.) Demographers refer to this phenomenon as **zero population growth**. This lower rate can be best appreciated by recalling that as recently as 1961 the American rate was well over 3.6 children per family. However, although the United States is a zero-population-growth (ZPG) society, the actual number of births has increased since 1970. The reason for this is that women born during the baby boom years following World War II have been in their child-bearing years from approximately 1970 into the 1990s. But although the absolute number of births may be higher, the number of births per woman is no higher than the ZPG.

In almost achieving ZPG, the United States is following the lead set by other urban, industrial nations. Conditions in cities, where most people are concentrated in these nations, do not lend themselves to large families. Housing is scarce, industrial jobs are not open to children, and it is expensive to educate and provide health protection for many children. Thus, urban families, regardless of religion and culture, tend to curb their fertility. Ireland, France, and Italy, for instance, are all Roman Catholic nations whose religion forbids birth control, yet the birthrate in these nations is among the lowest in the world and is declining. The average fertility rate in Western Europe is 1.6, and in Japan and South Korea it is 1.5.

Despite the optimism that may be engendered by the demographic transition model and the fact that a number of societies have attained zero population growth, the danger of overpopulation cannot be ignored. The human race is multiplying very rapidly, which has prompted the United Nations and the Population Reference Bureau to point out that the most rapid expansion is occurring in poor, underdeveloped nations, where food, housing, sanitation, and economic opportunities are already in short supply. If present trends continue, zero growth worldwide can be expected to occur no sooner than by the year 2040 (Table 3).

Population Policies

As mentioned, the rich nations of the world are experiencing slow rates of population growth, whereas many of the developing nations have a very low standard of living (including abject poverty and periodic famines) and rapidly increasing population growth. To counteract these factors, a number of nations have had to implement policies to try to control either growth or lack of growth of their populations. In the West, the low birthrates have prompted pro-natalists (those in favor of an increase in birthrates) to maintain that there is a danger that Western values, chiefly political democracy, may not survive. Others fear that economic prosperity may be undermined. Vital, productive, and creative societies may become passive and conservative. This would slow technological innovation, and a small workforce would have difficulty paying for the Social Security and health benefits for an older, retired population (Wattenberg & Zinsmeister, 1986; Cherlin, 1987).

On the other side of this spectrum have been nations such as China, India, Bangladesh, and Singapore, whose governments have imposed various methods of population control on their citizens. Some states in India, with the encouragement of the central government, forced men to be sterilized after having fathered their second child. Fines and imprisonment were the punishment for refusal. The program met with so much opposition that it effectively toppled the government of Prime Minister Indira Gandhi in 1977. Currently, even though it has a

TABLE 3   World's 20 Most Populous Countries: 2010

Rank	Country	Population
	World	6,817,246,761
1.	China	1,330,141,295
2.	India	1,173,108,018
3.	United States	310,232,863
4.	Indonesia	242,968,342
5.	Brazil	201,103,330
6.	Pakistan	177,276,594
7.	Banaladesh	158,065,841
8.	Nigeria	152,217,341
9.	Russia	139,390,205
10.	Japan	126,804,433
11.	Mexico	112,468,855
12.	Philippines	99,900,177
13.	Vietnam	89,571,130
14.	Ethiopia	88,013,491
15.	Germany	82,282,988
16.	Egypt	80,471,869
17.	Turkey	77,804,122
18.	Congo, Dem. Rep.	70,916,439
19.	Iran	67,037,517
20.	Thailand	66,404,688

Source: U.S. Census Bureau, International Data Base

fertility rate of 4.7 children per woman and will become the most populous nation in the world by approximately 2045, India is back to a voluntary population control program. Bangladesh was similarly unsuccessful with its forced sterilization program, and though it offers economic incentives to encourage sterilization, its fertility rate is a very high 6.3 children per woman. Singapore, which used both rewards and punishment in its goal to establish a two-child family, was so successful that it has had to reverse itself and is encouraging people to have three or more children if they can afford to. China, which tried to use the reward-and-punishment combination, has initially had less success. The Chinese government launched a one-child-per-family campaign, offering substantial rewards to couples who produce only one child: salary bonuses, free schooling, priority medical care, admission to the best schools, and preference in employment. Conversely, those who have more than one child must pay all costs for each additional child, are taxed 10 percent of their income, and are denied promotion. From 1979 to 1986, this method worked so well that China's birthrate was cut in half. But since 1986, the rate has begun to increase again, partly because some Chinese are willing to pay the fines to have more children and partly because the Chinese government was being criticized for encouraging abortions even late in pregnancy (some parents even engaged in female infanticide in their quest for their one male child). The result is that, having entered the 1990s with more than 1 billion people, China's population will double by approximately 2025. India, however, will overtake China in total population by 2037. A population of more than 2 billion people strains the economy of any society, and particularly one that has made gains only of late and with great difficulty.

Findings published by the independent Population Crisis Committee indicate that population policies in Asia have been unsuccessful in slowing growth, and continued population growth is contributing to an intensifying crisis in ecological and human resources. They add that it is unlikely that China and India will be able to stabilize growth until well into this century, by which time they may have added more than 1.5 billion people to the world (Crossette, 1992). Almost 98 percent of the world's population growth occurs in the poorest and less developed regions of the world that can least afford to support a large population. In many of these societies, where women have an average of 3.4 children, fertility rates are the highest (about 6.5), contraception use is the lowest (15 percent of married women), infant mortality rates are among the highest, life expectancy is among the lowest, as is the yearly gross domestic product (GDP) per capita—$1,130 (For the latest data, consult the Population Reference Bureau on the Internet.) However, in 2007 the average number of children per woman worldwide declined from 5.0 (1950) to 2.7, although in sub-Saharan Africa the average remained at 5.5 (**http://www.prb.org/Publications/Datasheets/2007/2007wpds.aspx**). Worldwide contraception use also increased to 62 percent from less than 10 percent in the 1960s.

Why do birthrates remain high in the less developed countries? First, because of diffusion, advances in medicine and technology have filtered into industrializing nations, reducing the death rate while the birthrate remains high. Because industrialization has been superimposed on the society, there has been no time to develop the value of small families, as happened in the industrial nations. Consequently, there is a cultural lag between material and nonmaterial culture. As they have been for thousands of years, children are valuable in agrarian societies: They offer hands to work the earth and constitute a kind of old-age insurance for parents who cannot count on pensions or Social Security. Moreover, gender inequality is prevalent in such societies, and a man's ability to have many children is a symbol of his manliness. In many countries of Latin America, even though women may want to curb their fertility and do understand how to use contraceptives, their men will not allow them to do so. In rural Africa, on the other hand, lack of education and ignorance of how conception takes place or of effective forms of birth control contributes to the high birthrate, as do high infant mortality rates and death rates of children (parents have many children in the hope that at least some will survive).

The Urban Society

Around the globe, the movement toward the cities continues unabated. In developing countries, every day brings thousands of rural residents to the large urban centers in search of jobs in an effort to avoid a life of backbreaking work with few rewards. Many never find the promised land and are condemned to live in makeshift shacks, eking out a livelihood by their wits. In the developed nations, some cities have remained vital, but not without exhibiting certain phenomena—a high crime rate, for instance, makes life in them less than ideal. In the United States, which is already a preeminently urban society, many cities are, or have been, in some form of crisis situation. Cities that were once centers of industry and commerce have lost population and business to the suburbs. With the consequent lower tax revenues, these cities cannot offer the services that middle-class residents demand. Consequently, they tend to become home to the poor and the recently arrived. The transition to an information society has deprived some cities of their essential role, as jobs have been lost and not recuperated. Many job holders are suburbanites who do not remain in the city outside work hours. City streets become deserted after six o'clock. In short, although cities have been meccas to people all over the world, in some situations they reach a point at which they decline and die.

Urbanization

As was mentioned earlier, one of the most significant effects of the sociocultural changes leading to modernization has been the extensive urbanization of societies. **Urbanization** is the population trend in which cities and their suburbs grow at the expense of rural areas. Industrial nations become urbanized because factories and plants are established in the center of populated areas so that a ready labor pool will be available. In turn, industry attracts labor from surrounding areas, resulting in the growth of cities. A larger population requires additional services; hence, it acts as a magnet to more commercial enterprises. An industrial economy can support densely populated areas, whereas in rural areas the land must be used for agriculture rather than to accommodate people and commerce.

Urbanization, however, does not account for all city growth. As a result of increased birthrates, decreased death rates, or immigration from abroad, cities may grow without a parallel decrease in rural population. Or they may grow because of overall population increase in both rural and urban areas. This has been the case in developing nations, where the death rates have been cut by improved hygiene and medical findings, but values regarding the control of births have not caught up. Urbanization is pervasive in the United States: 82 percent of the population is urban.

The Industrial Revolution and the Growth of Cities

The shift from rural to urban living began with the Industrial Revolution in Great Britain. Factories located in cities attracted a large number of people who could no longer make a living on the land. Science and technology had improved agricultural methods. New iron and steel plows, reapers, threshers, harvesters, tractors, and combines did much of the work once done by humans. Crop rotation, chemical fertilizers, irrigation, and insect and disease control increased yields per acre without necessitating additional human labor.

The continued improvements in agricultural methods, then, led directly to a decline in the rural population. In the United States, for instance, the average farm worker in 1820 produced enough food to feed four people. By 1950, one worker produced enough for 15.5 people; by 1969, enough for 47 people; and today enough for 50 people. Such superefficiency in food production has resulted in the disappearance of the small farmer, forcing many young farmers to abandon the rural way of life in favor of city life. At the same time, commercial agriculture creates a demand for agricultural machinery, which is produced in urban centers, adding still more to the trend toward urbanization. Urbanization, then, has been the hallmark of all industrial and industrializing nations.

In 2007, approximately 50 percent of people worldwide lived in urban areas, a percentage that is estimated to grow to 60 percent by 2030 (United Nations, 2007). This represents quite a difference from 1900, when 86.4 percent were rural dwellers and only 13.6 percent lived in cities (Palen, 2006). Urbanization as a population movement is continuing: In the United States, approximately 80 percent of people live in urban areas. The fastest rate of urbanization is claimed by Africa, but 70 percent of the population of Latin America will also live in urban areas in the twenty-first century. Moreover, these areas are becoming larger and larger: At the beginning of the twentieth century there were only four cities with a population of over 2 million, but there were 87 such cities by 1990, and today cities and their surrounding areas have grown to tremendous sizes. Note the changes to urban living in the various countries of the world at a Web site noted on **mysearchlab.com.**

Urbanism

Industrial societies have been undergoing an urban transition whose ultimate effect is urbanism as a way of life. In contrast to urbanization, which is an ongoing process, **urbanism** is a condition, a set of attitudes, a quality, or a way of life distinct from the rural. It refers to the fact that the traditional rural values of predominantly agricultural societies have been replaced by urban values. Moreover, these urban values are spread through the mass media globally, so that all industrial nations are beginning to look and think alike.

The transition from rural to urban residence has forced people to make adjustments that have had profound effects on personality and on social organization. The nuclear form of the family, the lack of a support network represented by the extended family and friends and neighbors, separation from the ties of the primary group, all led to an increase in individual freedom of action. But freedom of action in anonymous circumstances can result in behavior that is considered deviant or antisocial. The individual becomes a victim of anomie and alienation. In practical terms, a decrease in informal controls by the primary group necessitates an increase in formal controls by secondary groups such as government agencies, the police, and the courts. So the urban resident pays the price for freedom from primary group interference by increasing bureaucratization and an impersonal lifestyle. In the early decades of the century, social scientists felt that life in the big city was conducive to social disorganization and led to a decline of community because in the city there is no agreement on a multiplicity of norms.

American Cities

The extent of urbanization in the United States is clear when a few statistics are considered. When the first census was taken in 1790, 95 percent of the people lived in rural areas and only 5 percent lived in cities. By 1987, only 2 percent of the population lived on farms, and by 2008, 17 percent were described as rural residents and 80 percent as urban residents. In short, the urban trend introduced by the Industrial Revolution imported from Britain had caused an astonishingly large number of people to be brought together in cities, effecting tremendous social, economic, and political changes.

The growth and dominance of the industrial metropolis continued into the 1950s. Since then, a countermovement, sometimes referred to as urban decentralization, has been taking place (Edmonston & Guterbock, 1984). This movement includes suburbanization, the growth of megalopolis or regional cities, and the loss of population from central cities in the Northeast and Midwest in favor of the West and the Sunbelt.

Suburbia

As stated, from the middle of the nineteenth century until well into the 1950s, the population trend was toward urban areas. Since then, the trend has been toward suburbanization and metropolitanization, movements out and away from the central city but not back toward the rural areas. The most significant growth occurred in the **suburbs,** small communities on the outskirts of the central city and somewhat dependent on it. Residents of suburbs now outnumber residents of the central city.

The movement to the suburbs has had a variety of causes. First, cities expanded so rapidly that industry and business encroached on residential areas, forcing people to move ever farther from the city center. Second, a general increase in the standard of living permitted people to build larger and more comfortable homes on land that was cheaper than land in the city. People also began to want to escape the dirt, crime, and noise of the city. Finally, the widespread use of the automobile for transportation made it possible for people to reach jobs that were far from home.

The Impact of the Consumer Culture on the Growth of Suburbia

Following World War II, a combination of factors had brought in a consumer culture, which has since come to dominate American culture. The essence of the consumer culture is a focus on acquisition of material objects made possible by affluence, mobility, and leisure. For instance, the automobile, mass-produced and, thus, cheap enough to be available to a majority of people, led to the growth of the highway system on which the automobile could move freely and rapidly. In turn, highways were especially responsible for the spread of suburbanization to the extent that it became a pervasive national phenomenon. At the same time, other facets of social change became apparent and were reinforced by suburbanization.

As the cities had done before them, the suburbs spawned their own lifestyle, revolving around the absence of the father for long portions of the day, the necessity for a private vehicle, and the chauffeuring of children to various activities. In addition, trips to the shopping center or suburban mall had become the focus of recreation for suburbanites. The booming economy permitted one family member—usually the husband and father—to be the sole breadwinner, leaving the wife and mother to do the chauffering and shopping chores.

Shopping malls are a consequence of suburbanization and the decline of city centers. They offer a place to gather, chat, eat, visit a doctor, and sometimes attend religious services, in addition to shopping. Many other countries have copied the idea of such malls, as evidenced by this one in Dubai.

Originally, the suburbs attracted young married couples who were planning fairly large families—the baby boom parents of the years following World War II. The postwar economy increased individual incomes and made mortgage money available, so that for the first time home ownership became a dream a majority could fulfill. Most of the early suburbanites were between 25 and 45 years old, with children ranging in age from infancy to the teens. They were predominantly white, middle-income, high school graduates, politically conservative, and morally "proper." From these beginnings developed the stereotype of the suburbs as "bedroom" communities of almost identical homes.

Suburbia and Social Class

Today, the heterogeneity of the city is also found in the suburbs. With increasing rates of divorce, single-parent homes are to be found in the suburbs as frequently as in the city. Thus, the generalizations that urban residents used to make about the suburbs have been largely proved wrong. In addition, whereas originally suburbanization was a movement of white persons of middle-class or upper-middle-class background, leading to a high degree of racial segregation, minorities have also flocked to the suburbs since the 1970s. It appears that suburbanization is solely a function of social class: Middle-class blacks are moving from cities to suburbs much as their white counterparts did a decade or two earlier. In fact, so many of the more affluent minorities are leaving urban centers that some sociologists fear that urban deterioration cannot help but increase because those who are leaving are predominantly the middle and solid working class (DeWitt, 1994, A12). Suburbanization has become a movement defined by social class primarily because of the problems that are perceived to exist in central cities: crime, poor schools, unsafe neighborhoods, and so on.

Social class has repercussions on suburbs in other ways, too. For a variety of reasons, including a downturn in the economy, more suburban households saw real declines in median household income from 1979 to 1989 and again from 2008 on, rather than income growth. The net result has been that working-class suburbs have suffered, much as central cities have, while affluent suburbs have grown and prospered. This income gap between suburbs adds to a situation in which people of different incomes live isolated from one another (Minerbrook, 1992).

At first, suburbs depended on the central city for shopping and for commercial, cultural, and recreational activities. Later, city and suburbs became interdependent, with the suburbs providing the labor force for business and industry that were still housed in the city. Increasingly, however, the suburbs are becoming independent of the city. Business and industry have relocated in the suburbs and are housed in large shopping malls and professional complexes. Both jobs and facilities are now locally available to the suburban resident. Suburbs have mushroomed at the expense of the central city, which lost an important tax base when people, commerce, and industry moved away. Without tax money, the city cannot provide important facilities, forcing more people, commerce, and industry to move out. The central city is then left with a run-down transportation system, outmoded physical facilities, inadequate police protection, and poor schools. Only those who cannot afford to move out remain.

The economic crisis of the past decade has pushed some lower-income persons to buy or rent on the fringes of suburban areas, while the middle-class residents of these areas return to more urban centers, in a process called demographic inversion. Read more about this by googling the term.

Metropolitanization and Megalopolis

Some suburbs have grown so large that they have become towns and cities in their own right. These small cities, smaller suburbs, and the central city around which they are clustered make up the ecological city, or the metropolitan area. The U.S. Bureau of the Census uses "metropolitan areas," a collective term, as the basis for measuring units of population. The **Standard Metropolitan Statistical Area (SMSA)** consists of one or more counties containing at least one city of over 50,000 people or two cities totaling that number. Metropolitan areas with populations of 1 million or more are designated as Consolidated Metropolitan Statistical Areas (CMSAs). The Micropolitan Statistical Area comprises one urban cluster of 10,000 but less than 50,000 people. The term *Core Based Statistical Area* (CBSA), coined in 2000, refers collectively to metropolitan and micropolitan statistical areas. As of 2006, there were 17 CMSAs in the United States, 366 metropolitan statistical areas, and 560 micropolitan statistical areas, the largest ones being New York, Long Island, and northern New Jersey, with a population of 21 million, and Los Angeles, Riverside, and Anaheim with over 16 million. So thoroughly urban are these areas that it is easier to refer to them as regions of the country rather than cities (Table 4).

The principal criterion for a definition of metropolitan area is that it has a "contained" economy. This means that it is an area where a majority of people live, work, earn, and spend. As of the first decade of the twenty-first century, the metropolitan statistical areas and the micropolitan statistical areas in the United States constituted about 80 percent of the nation's population, or almost all of the nonrural portion of the country. This pattern of **metropolitanization** represents a return to the dominance of metropolitan areas, which began in the second decade of the past century.

The growth of metropolitan areas has meant a large concentration of people in comparatively small areas. This trend damages central cities and creates problems in local governments because each municipality, county, township, city, and village within the metropolitan area maintains its own government. In this bureaucratic maze, agencies and officials of neighboring governments are often at odds with one another, resulting in a waste of money and resources. Urban specialists have long favored some form of metropolitan government, but federal studies have concluded that nothing short of a broad regional government will relieve the chaotic situation of metropolitan areas.

Megalopolis

The large number of metropolitan areas is leading to a new phenomenon in the United States as well as in other industrial nations, that of urban sprawl known by the term *megalopolis*. In a **megalopolis**, one metropolitan area is joined to another without interruption. One such complex is the Great Lakes chain, beginning in Buffalo and continuing solidly to Milwaukee and farther west. By the year 2000, an estimated 40 million people were housed in this complex alone. Another megalopolis, the Boston–Washington complex, contains around 80 million people, while a third rapidly growing megalopolis is the one extending from San Diego to the San Francisco Bay area. On a global level, there are megalopolises in Japan, Great Britain, northwestern Europe, northern Italy, Brazil, and now even in China. Urban sociologists point out that a megalopolis is not just an overgrown metropolitan area but rather a system of cities distributed along "a major axis of traffic and communication" (Gottman, 1978, 56). Megalopolises are interdependent because they share not only the physical infrastructure—highways, railways, waterways, telephone lines, pipelines, water supply, and sewage systems—but also the flow of traffic, the movement of people and goods, and the flow of cables, telephone calls

TABLE 4   50 Largest Metropolitan Statistical Areas in 2008

Metropolitan statistical area	Total Change[a]	Natural increase			Net migration			Percent change
		Total	Births	Deaths	Total	International	Domestic migration	
Atlanta-Sandy Springs-Marietta, GA	1,128	405	640	235	599	189	410	26.6
Austin-Round Rock,TX	403	139	196	57	270	62	208	32.2
Baltimore-Towson, MD	114	92	285	194	−3	33	−35	4.5
Birmingham-Hoover, AL	66	33	124	91	33	9	23	6.3
Boston-Cambridge-Quincy, MA-NH	131	173	464	292	−85	172	−256	3.0
Buffalo-Niagara Falls, NY	−46	6	105	100	−46	10	−56	−3.9
Charlotte-Gastonia-Concord, NC-SC	371	109	196	87	266	44	224	27.9
Chicago-Naperville-Joliet, IL-IN-WI	471	593	1,165	572	−120	401	−521	5.2
Cincinnati-Middletown, OH-KY-IN	145	98	245	146	−1	18	−19	7.2
Cleveland-Elyria-Mentor, OH	−60	45	220	175	−104	26	−130	−2.8
Columbus, OH	160	108	213	106	57	31	26	9.9
Dallas-Fort Worth-Arlington, TX	1,138	543	817	274	574	304	269	22.1
Denver-Aurora, CO[b]	327	194	309	115	137	97	41	15.0
Detroit-Warren-Livonia, MI	−27	169	487	318	−238	95	−332	−0.6
Hartford-West Hartford-East Hartford, CT	42	31	113	83	17	28	−11	3.6
Houston-Sugar Land-Baytown, TX	1.013	486	740	252	468	277	191	21.5
Indianapolis-Carmel, IN	190	104	208	104	86	22	64	12.5
Jacksonville, FL	190	60	145	85	135	12	123	17.0
Kansas City, MO-KS	166	115	240	126	54	30	24	9.0
Las Vegas-Paradise, NV	490	117	216	99	380	SB	312	35.6
Los Angeles-Long Beach-Santa Ana, CA	507	983	1,621	637	−420	847	−1,267	4.1
Louisville/Jefferson County, KY-IN	82	43	134	91	41	12	29	7.1
Memphis, TN-MS-AR	81	74	162	88	11	13	−2	6.7
Miami-Fort Lauderdale-Pompano Beach, FL	407	178	573	395	217	439		8.1
Milwaukee-Waukesha-West Allis, WI	49	72	178	106	−50	25	−74	3.2
Minneapolis-St. Paul-Bloomington, MN-WI	261	221	378	156	53	75	−23	8.8
Nashville-Davidson—Murfreesboro—Franklin, TN	239	80	172	92	139	26	112	18.2
New Orleans-Metairie-Kenner, LA	−182	43	139	96	−298	11	−309	−13.9
New York-Northern New Jersey-Long Island, NY-NJ-PA	683	955	2,120	1,166	−687	1,145	−1,833	3.7
Oklahoma City, OK	111	64	146	82	52	21	32	10.1

Metropolitan statistical area	Number (1,000)							
	Total Change[a]	Natural increase			Net migration			Percent change
		Total	Births	Deaths	Total	International	Domestic migration	
Orlando-Kissimmee, FL	410	103	219	116	312	75	237	24.9
Philadelphia-Camden-Wilmington, PA-NJ-DE-MD	151	185	626	441	−12	100	−112	2.7
Phoenix-Mesa-Scottsdale, AZ	1,030	319	532	213	717	175	542	31.7
Pittsburgh, PA	−80	−26	205	232	−42	16	−58	−3.3
Portland-Vancouver-Beaverton, OR-WA	280	116	238	122	175	71	103	14.5
Providence-New Bedford-Fall River, RI-MA	14	37	158	122	−16	31	−47	0.9
Raleigh-Cary, NC	292	81	123	42	207	35	172	36.6
Richmond, VA	129	47	128	81	87	13	74	11.7
Riverside-San Bernardino-Ontario, CA	861	301	512	211	573	100	472	26.5
Sacramento—Arden Arcade—Roseville, CA	313	117	236	119	204	66	138	17.4
St. Louis, MO-IL[c]	118	96	303	207	−14	28	−41	4.4
Salt Lake City, UT	147	122	168	46	8	41	−33	15.2
San Antonio, TX	320	141	251	110	187	31	156	18.7
San Diego-Carlsbad-San Marcos, CA	187	213	376	163	−10	104	−114	6.7
San Francisco-Oakland-Fremont, CA	151	220	462	241	−93	260	−353	3.7
San Jose-Sunnyvale-Santa Clara, CA	83	154	229	75	−65	169	−234	4.8
Seattle-Tacoma-Bellevue, WA	301	172	347	175	130	108	21	9.9
Tampa-St. Petersburg-Clearwater, FL	338	20	257	237	328	62	266	14.1
Virginia Beach-Norfolk-Newport News, VA-NC	81	96	197	101	−10	−1	−9	5.2
Washington-Arlington-Alexandria, DC-VA-MD-WV	562	387	637	250	138	256	−118	11.7

[Covers period April 1, 2000, to July 1, 2008 (1,128 represents 1,128,000). Covers metropolitan statistical areas as defined by the U.S. Office of Management and Budget as of November 2007. All geographic boundaries for 2000 to 2008 population estimates are defined as of January 1, 2008. Minus sign (–) indicates decrease or outmigration]
[a] Total population change includes residual. This residual represents the change in population that cannot be attributed to any specific demographic component of change. See "State & County terms & definitions" al <http://www.census.gov/popest/topics/terms/states.html>.
[b] Broomfield County, CO, was formed from parts of Adams, Boulder, Jefferson, and Weld Counties, CO, on November 15, 2001, and is coextensive with Broomfield city. For purposes of defining and presenting data for metropolitan statistical areas, Broomfield city is treated as if it were a county at the time of the 2000 census.
[c] The portion of Sullivan city in Crawford County, Missouri, is legally part of the St. Louis, MO-IL MSA. Data shown here do not include this area.

Source: U.S. Census Bureau, "Table 10—Cumulative Estimates of the Components of Population Change for Metropolitan and Micropolitan Statistical Areas: April 1, 2000 to July 1, 2008 (CBSA-est2008-10)" (published 19 March 2009): <http://www.census.gov/population/www/estimates/CBSA-est2008-comp-chg.html>.

and mail. At the same time, the megalopolis may remain exceedingly varied, containing cities, towns, villages, suburbs, with their diverse populations also differentiated by social class and ethnicity, so that the regions resemble a mosaic. Descriptions and a listing of the largest metropolitan areas may be found on the Internet.

The Urban Crisis

It has been well publicized by the media that American cities are in trouble. The crisis of the cities has two components. First, suburbanization left the cities struggling to provide all the necessary services, and the departure of many upper-middle-class families, in addition to businesses and industries, resulted in a loss of more tax revenues. Second, there has been a shift in the regions of the country that are experiencing growth. The older, larger cities in the northeastern and north-central areas of the country are losing population as industrial jobs are becoming scarcer, while southern and southwestern cities, many of them new, are growing faster than the national average. The city of Detroit, Michigan, having lost population and jobs, has begun to tear down abandoned housing, turning the city back into an agricultural area. Because cities have tended to grow rapidly, very little planning has gone into their physical shape, and their social structure has also given rise to problems. The large concentration of people in cities requires buildings that are close together and many stories high. Without proper planning, this necessity can lead to ugliness, to lack of green and open spaces, to an "asphalt jungle" look. Modern city planners are much more aware of the need to pay special attention to a pleasing appearance, so that the cities of the future will probably be much more attractive than those of the past.

Slums and Ghettos

One consequence of the flight to suburbia has been an enlargement of areas called slums and ghettos. A slum is an area that has changed from what it was before but has not yet attained a new form. Residents of slums tend to be new immigrants, either from abroad or from rural areas of the country. They stay in the old, often decaying areas of the city because they are unskilled and can work only at menial jobs. Many exist on welfare, are victims of discrimination and segregation, and are unfamiliar with the cultural and physical aspects of the rest of the city.

Following the influx of African Americans from the rural South during and after World War II, most central areas of cities became ghettos. Ghettos are similar to slums in their origins, conditions, and problems, but they tend to contain a particular racial or ethnic group. Often, residents are members of the working poor (people who are chronically unemployed or underemployed), mothers with dependent children, the elderly, and the disabled. Slums are present globally, in every country. An overview of some of them may be found on the Internet.

Population Drain

The problematic aspects of cities cause a constant movement of population out of cities, but generally, when one segment moves out, another moves in. At least, that had been the pattern up to the late 1950s, when people began leaving cities for the suburbs. The decline in the heavy industry that had been a mainstay of the Great Lakes region's economy also contributed to the exodus away from the large cities of that region. Population loss leaves cities with a budget deficit and the unhappy need to raise taxes on housing and commercial property, which risks alienating more homeowners and driving out more businesses and jobs, or to cut spending and reduce services and risk making the city even less desirable (Levine, 1991, A9).

Attempts to Reclaim the City

Many cities have been fighting back vigorously to regain their former status. For one thing, cities still offer many desirable activities and jobs and so attract a substantial number of people. Many young professionals prefer to live in the central districts, near jobs and entertainment. Even married couples with children find real estate in cities to be more within their means than in the suburbs. Many instances of "gentrification," or the reclaiming of decaying neighborhoods by middle-class, professional families, are being noted. Gentrification, however, has also encountered criticism because the former residents of the gentrified neighborhoods are moved from housing they could afford into even worse areas.

Urban Renewal

The same criticism was raised when the government tried to resolve the plight of the cities through programs of urban renewal. Urban slums had been a reality in industrial societies ever since the Industrial Revolution brought rural people into the cities. There was always at least one group of people who, for a variety of reasons, could not find work and, thus, were condemned to live on the fringes of society, with government help. Following World War II, however, the government, in addition to simply helping the urban poor, began to provide loans to cities for building low-cost housing and later for slum clearance and public housing.

Unfortunately, these programs never worked. Slum clearance resulted in moving the urban poor from one neighborhood to another, with no benefit to the residents, only to those involved in the clearance and construction businesses. Public housing had equally little success. There is some stigma attached to living in public housing, and residents have no reason to display any pride of ownership. Therefore, the property, already shoddily built without consideration of people's wants and needs, is soon subject to acts of vandalism and wanton destruction.

The government has also tried to offer subsidies to people with insufficient incomes so that they may compete in the private housing market. These attempts have met with little success. Owners of rental property discriminate against families with many children or those with women as heads of households or in which the father is disabled. There is the fear of neighborhoods being overrun by an "undesirable" element. Suburbs and small towns have effectively kept out public housing or federally subsidized low-rent housing for the same reasons.

Urban renewal is an ineffective remedy for the crisis of the cities. If the same people continue to live in renovated buildings, the benefits accrue to them but not to the city because they continue to be unable to pay higher taxes. On the other hand, if slum areas are cleared in favor of new, expensive housing, commercial buildings, or shopping centers, benefits accrue to the city because these structures provide a good tax base but not to the former residents, who are displaced. However, the city is then able to attract middle- and upper-class residents and even shoppers from the suburbs. People come to the newly refurbished theaters and restaurants, and jobs can be created for city residents.

The Future of Cities

The fate of cities in the twenty-first century is uncertain. In the United States, cities contain the worst social problems that face society: crime, poverty, racial conflicts, pollution. At the same time, the larger the metropolitan area, the better are the opportunities for employment, recreation, and education. Some urban thinkers are convinced that cities can be revitalized because they serve the most important human function: They offer a place for coming together (Whyte, 1989). Others are less optimistic, particularly in view of the fact that urbanization

TABLE 5 Largest Cities in 2010

World rank	City	Country	City population	Metro population
1	Karachi	Pakistan	15,500,000	18,000.000
2	Shanghai	China	14,900,000	19,200,000
3	Mumbai (Bombay)	India	13,900,000	21,200,000
4	Beijing	China	12,460,000	17,550,000
5	Delhi	India	12,100,000	16,713,000
6	Buenos Aires	Argentina	11,655,000	12,924,000
7	Manila Metro	Philippines	11,560,000	13,503,000
8	Seoul	South Korea	11,153,000	24,472,000
9	Sao Paulo	Brazil	11,038,000	19,890,000
10	Moscow	Russia	10,524,000	14,800,000
11	Jakarta	Indonesia	10,100,000	24,100,000
12	Istanbul	Turkey	9,560,000	12,600,000
13	Bangkok	Thailand	9,100,000	11,970,000
14	Mexico City	Mexico	8,841,000	21,163,000
15	Tokyo	Japan	8,663,000	31,036,000
16	Tehran	Iran	8,430,000	13,450,000
17	New York City	USA	8,364,000	20,090,000
18	Kinshasa	Congo D.R.	8,200,000	10,100,000
19	Dhaka	Bangladesh	7,940,000	12,797,000
20	Lagos	Nigeria	7,938,000	9,123,000

Note: Metro population figures for China are often those of their prefectures.

Source: http://www.citymayors.com/statistics/largest-cities-mayor-1.html © The City Mayors Foundation. Reprinted by permission.

is an ongoing process, and the sheer numbers of people who will be urban residents in the twenty-first century are staggering (Table 5). In addition to all the problems that plague American cities, the environmental pollution in some of these cities is beginning to affect the residents' health. It seems imperative that governments plan a survival strategy for cities, but the road is strewn with obstacles and high costs.

The Natural Environment

Populations and the physical and social structures they erect exist within the framework of a natural environment. This natural environment has been progressively damaged precisely because of the growth of population and the disregard in which people have held their habitat. In Asia, overpopulation has led to land degradation by overuse, water supplies are constantly under strain, and agriculture is handicapped by soil and water depletion.

On a global scale, unabated expansion of population would soak up the world's capital and prevent the poorer nations from investing in technological development that might limit continued population growth. Environmentalists, therefore, paint apocalyptic pictures of the future. If the worst occurs, countless millions would become environmental refugees, swamping the nations that tried to conserve their soil, water and forests. The great-grandchildren of today's young people would have to share the planet with only a ragged cohort of adaptable species dominated by rats, cockroaches, weeds, and microbes. The world in which they survived would consist largely of deserts, patches of tropical forests, eroded mountains, dead coral reefs, and barren oceans, all buffeted by extremes of weather (Linden, 1992, 64). This list of catastrophes does not even include the additional danger represented by global warming.

What a world to live in and to leave to our descendants as their inheritance! And the ways to prevent this scenario from becoming reality, in the experts' opinion, is to "cut human propagation in half, so the world's numbers do not exceed 8 billion by midcentury" (Linden, 1992, 64) and to prevent the kinds of human activity that promote the rise in global temperature.

The World We Live In

The natural environment is the total complex of natural conditions and resources that occur in specific areas. It consists of such elements as landforms, climate, natural vegetation, soils, native animal life, underground and surface waters, and mineral resources. These elements do not remain static but vary from time to time and are different in different areas of the world.

There is a reciprocal relationship between the environment and people and their cultures. The environment affects almost every facet of people's lives, shaping their traditions and institutions; in turn, it is affected by people, often negatively. However, this relationship is not simple and direct. People can live differently in similar environments and even differently at different times in the same environment. And the same type of physical environment may be used in different ways by people who perceive land use differently.

The Ecosystem

The very technology that allowed people to limit the death rate, prompted spurts in population, and crowded large numbers into cities where there were industrial jobs is now endangering human life on earth by ignoring or despoiling the natural environment. Neglect of the environment is not new; however, the early humans saw themselves as insignificant inhabitants of a natural world to which they were related and on which they were dependent. Even though some of their actions damaged the environment, they acted out of ignorance. The complex technology that produces myriad articles for easing human life today has inspired in contemporary humans the notion that they are in control of the world and perhaps of the universe. Thus, the humble attitudes of our primitive ancestors, who tried to appease the spirits of plants and animals they thought responsible for their existence and welfare, have been replaced by confidence that nothing is impossible to humans. This arrogant attitude is a threat to the ecosystem.

The **ecosystem** is the way living things interact and interrelate among each other and their environment. The interaction maintains a balance that permits life to continue. People, land, animals, vegetation, atmosphere, and social processes are so interdependent that even slight alterations in one affect the others. The photosynthetic activity of green plants (that is, the fact that they take in carbon dioxide and give off oxygen) allows human life and produces the oxygen needed for the machinery of the industrial system. Without plants and animals and the microorganisms that live in them, there would be no pure water in lakes and rivers. Without certain processes that take place within the earth, there would be no food crops, oil, or coal. The ecosystem is, in short, the biological capital of humans: Human productivity depends on it, and the most advanced technology will be useless if it is destroyed. Learn more about the ecosystems of our world by browsing the Internet.

Ecology

The ecosystem, that delicately balanced, interdependent system consisting of living beings, nature, and the earth they inhabit, has been the focus of attention in recent years as more people have begun to show concern about the environment. The discipline of **ecology**, which studies the interrelationships in nature, has been in the forefront in the effort to make people aware of what is happening to where they live.

In ecological terms, there are various levels of ecosystems. A particular swamp or river is a local ecosystem; an ocean is a regional ecosystem; the planet Earth is a global ecosystem. An ecosystem is easily made unstable: Unforeseen events often disturb its balance. Floods and droughts change the soil, as do gradual climatic changes, population explosions, and the disappearance of particular species. However, the tendency of any ecosystem is to return to a balance. Each species of life has its niche in the physical environment, somewhat in the same way that each individual occupies a status in the social environment. The niche occupied by humans in the various ecosystems is different from that of other species because humans can affect and alter their environment, rather than waiting to adapt to it through evolution. Because humans have developed culture and social structure, they can act in a variety of ways toward the physical environment: They can cultivate trees or cut them down, clean rivers or pollute them, build roads and houses or leave the land alone. Other species must wait for nature to take its course, for they are limited in their behavior. Thus, humans have not only a great advantage over other living species but also a responsibility to organize themselves to remain in harmony with their environment. In this they have not been very successful.

We should note here that the idea of equilibrium is not universally accepted. A number of ecologists are revising the long-held balance theory following an accumulation of evidence to the effect that the real constant in nature is eternal turmoil: "Change and turmoil, more than constancy and balance, is the rule" (Stevens, 1990, B5–B6). Although the change in thinking has not yet produced a current new theory to replace the old one, the developing conviction that nature is ruled more by flux and disturbance is becoming the dominant idea. Those scientists who are not quite ready to abandon the notion of equilibrium in ecosystems agree that although there may be great disturbances and fluctuations in small populations within small ecosystems, these fluctuations may not appear as important if the larger picture is considered. Thus, they bring in the importance of scales of time and space. However, the consensus seems to favor an ecology of constant change and disruption, particularly following studies of naturally occurring external factors—such as climate and weather—that dislocate ecosystems.

Disruption of Ecosystems

The harmony of the global ecosystem is disturbed by overpopulation, environmental pollution, and environmental depletion. Overpopulation puts stress on the ecosystem because of an increase in birthrates without a consequent increase in death rates. Environmental pollution refers to the degradation of air, land, and water, as well as the physical aspects of the environment (eye and noise pollution). A terribly damaging event to the ecosystem of the Gulf of Mexico and the beach communities of Louisiana, Mississippi, Alabama, and Florida occurred in the spring of 2010. An oil rig belonging to the British Petroleum Corporation drilling in the Gulf exploded, spilling millions of barrels of oil. The damage done to this ecosystem, to its flora and fauna, to the workers whose life depended on it, will not be overcome for years. *Environmental depletion* is the term used to mean that natural resources are decreasing in proportion to increased demand for them (as in the case of energy).

Environmental Pollution

Pollution is the result of human actions, that is, human tampering with the environment that has harmful consequences. Pollutants are sometimes unforeseen and unwanted by-products of human activities or the residue of products made by humans, used, and thrown away. The central point is that as a society, we want to consume more, which means we must produce more, and which ultimately means we create more waste.

Pollution may be of the air, water, or land and may also involve our senses, such as seeing and hearing. Every year, about 140 million tons of pollutants are released into the air as by-products of burning fossil fuels (oil, natural gas, coal). The automobile is the heaviest polluter, accounting for about 80 percent of air pollution. Among the worst effects of pollution are acid rain, caused by sulfur dioxide emissions from coal-burning plants, and depletion of ozone, a form of oxygen normally found in the upper atmosphere, where it absorbs the ultraviolet radiation of the sun. Acid rain kills fish in lakes, reduces crop yields, and damages buildings. The decrease of ozone does harm to human eyes, throats, and lungs. A reduced ozone layer may result in a vastly changed climate on earth, the destruction of some animal and plant life, a greater incidence of skin cancers, and possibly damage of a genetic nature to both plants and animals, including humans.

In addition, carbon dioxide emissions resulting from the burning of fossil fuels (oil and coal) have grown dramatically in the past century. These emissions are contributing factors to climate change, specifically to rising temperatures that are thought to result in extreme weather patterns and in turn to the spread of infectious diseases. Unfortunately, the United States is the largest contributor to total carbon dioxide emissions in the world, though China may soon surpass us (United Nations, 2007 World Population Data Sheet).

Through the cleaning of the bilges of tankers alone, an estimated 22 million barrels of oil are dumped annually into the oceans. There have been several accidents in which oil has spilled

Ulrich Mueller/Shutterstock

Although this is a mountain of scrap metal, which can be recycled, our landfills are full of similar mountains of garbage, which are a consequence of our conspicuous consumption, and are creating problems of disposal.

and wrought terrible damage to the environment. One was an oil tanker, the Exxon Valdez, that ran aground in 1989 in Alaska's Prince William Sound, spilling more than 10 million gallons of crude oil on 1,000 miles of beach. A pristine environment was spoiled to such an extent that even today, 16 years later, scientists have discovered clumps of gooey oil, and oil still oozes from the beaches (Marsh, 2010).

Another accident was the explosion in the Gulf of Mexico of an oil-drilling rig. The explosion caused the oil to gush into the Gulf in huge plumes that spilled thousands, perhaps millions, of barrels of oil into the water. The explosion killed 11 workers, and the spill had been resistant to stopping. The damage done to wetlands, beaches, birds, fish, marine life, not to mention the people who make their living by fishing and other marine industries, has been overwhelming. The harm, unfortunately, to people and the environment, may not be repaired for decades, if ever.

Other kinds of water pollution are due to organic sewage, overfertilization of water by excess nutrients, water-borne bacteria or viruses, and organic chemicals such as insecticides, pesticides, and detergents that are toxic to aquatic life. Chemicals of all sorts can change the ecosystem of a body of water, killing fish and creating unpleasant tastes in the water supply. This is happening with the dispersants used to minimize the effects of the oil spill in the Gulf of Mexico.

The earth's soil is being polluted in a number of locations by pesticides, herbicides, chemical wastes, radioactive fallout, and garbage. Some of these pollutants are also harmful to humans, yet increasing amounts of them must be used to control certain pests, as these become resistant to the chemicals; residues of the chemicals tend to remain in the soil for a long time—sometimes years after the chemicals have been banned.

Prolonged exposure to intense noise not only damages human hearing but can also increase irritability and prevent sleep. A noise level of 80 decibels is annoying to most people, yet the noise level in a third-floor apartment adjacent to a freeway is about 87 decibels. Decaying property, smog, noxious odors, and inhibited visibility all take away from people's enjoyment of the environment.

Environmental Depletion.   The air, water, and land can be cleaned up, but once a resource is depleted, it is gone forever. Then an alternative source must be found. No nation in the world is completely self-sufficient in terms of its natural resources. Even the United States has to import large amounts of mica, bauxite, tin, and iron ore that are used annually in this country. Of course, the resource of most concern is oil because our consumption of energy has been rising rapidly since the turn of the century. The United States uses more energy than other countries. Americans spend more on automobiles than on food. Demand for electrical power has also constantly increased, tripling between the 1940s and the 1970s. Some experts maintain that nuclear sources are our only hope for the future, but others point out that these sources have severe limitations. Their safety is dubious, and they pose potential hazards.

The Greenhouse Effect.   Finally, the so-called greenhouse effect is causing concern. Essentially, the greenhouse effect refers to the heating of the earth's atmosphere by burning coal, wood, and oil, which produces carbon dioxide, nitrous oxides, chlorofluorocarbons, and methane. These gases accumulate in the **biosphere** and act as an insulating barrier, retaining heat from the earth that should be returning to space. Thus, the earth becomes hotter because the insulating barrier traps heat as do the glass panels in a greenhouse. The effects of such a warming trend could be catastrophic, but it is still possible to counteract these damaging effects if governments become serious about legislating changes in consumption and conservation of resources, reducing the combustion of fuels, and finding alternative sources of power.

Although talk of "global warming" had been heard for decades, it was not until early 2007 that scientists presented the world with a detailed portrait of the effects of climate change driven by human activity. The greenhouse gases that have been building up in the atmosphere have already produced changes from the poles to the tropics, from the melting of the polar ice caps to the desertification of former temperate climates. Scientists are predicting that the earth's climate and ecosystems face inevitable and profound changes: increasing droughts in southern Europe and the Middle East, in sub-Saharan Africa, and in the American Southwest and Mexico. On the other hand, flooding will endanger low-lying islands and river deltas of southern Asia. In fact, a rise of only three to five degrees Fahrenheit could lead to the inundation of coasts and islands inhabited by hundreds of millions of people. The worst effect of these climate changes is that the poorest countries would bear the brunt of them. Some regions would receive more rainfall and a longer growing season, but regions that are already suffering from inclement weather, a scarcity of resources, and coastal hazards would be affected very negatively. Such nations, and even the poor in wealthier nations, are least equipped to adjust to climate change (see the United Nations' Intergovernmental Panel on Climate Change).

Doomsayers have never been very popular, and in the past humanity seems to have always found escape from its own destruction in the emergence of new sources of food and energy. In fact, economists have argued that an accepted tenet of economic theory, limits to growth, may be misguided because whenever prices rise in reaction to scarcity, they stimulate human ingenuity to improve, invent, and find alternatives. However, the example of cultures that have disappeared is instructive: An island in the Pacific, Easter Island, shows indications of having once harbored a flourishing culture. By the time the Europeans landed there in the early eighteenth century, however, the few thousand inhabitants lived in extremely primitive conditions. It seems that a swelling population led to stripping trees on the island, so that eventually there were no building materials for housing or fishing boats. The people were forced to live in caves, and clans made war on each other to acquire the dwindling resources. In time, the victorious clans enslaved and finally cannibalized the vanquished, and a once-proud culture was reduced to a barbaric struggle for survival (Linden, 1992, 65).

The current report makes very clear that unless governments and individuals make a concerted effort to rein in greenhouse gas emissions, the earth will be three to seven degrees warmer by the next century. Warmer oceans make for more intense hurricanes, precipitation has decreased over the subtropics and tropics and increased in other parts of the Northern and Southern Hemispheres, and heavy precipitation has become more frequent in areas where it was not characteristic. These phenomena will continue and, if unchecked, will produce an earth different, but not better, than the one we know now. By googling the term "pollution," you will be able to find pages of information, including facts and statistics.

To summarize, the human species is faced with a threat to its physical and mental well-being, with an ecological imbalance and the consequent disappearance of entire species of animals and plants, and with a hazard to world peace because of the imbalance in the standard of living between the developed and the developing nations. Environmental problems, however, have a low priority for political leaders and the public in general. Yet, because of the complexities involved, any solution to these problems must involve governmental action. It is probable that some cultural values must be changed before people learn to appreciate their environment to a greater extent than is true at present.

The Chapter in Brief

Population density varies dramatically, with two-thirds of humanity concentrated in the area that runs through the southern half of Japan, the plains and hills of eastern China, the coasts and Ganges River plain of India, and the industrial districts of Europe as well as those of the United States. Birthrates and death rates are calculated on the basis of how many births and deaths occur in a given year per 1,000 people. High birthrates are characteristic of the less industrialized and less urbanized nations. This fact has engendered the demographic transition model, which holds that societies pass through three basic stages of population growth. Stabilization occurs in the third stage, in which birthrates decline. Lowering a population's birthrate is a cultural, and not a technical, matter.

The United States reached zero population growth in 1972, but the birthrate could go up again at any time. However, urban industrial nations curb and stabilize their populations because it is so difficult to have large families in such societies. The rapid growth of population, or population explosion, was predicted 200 years ago by Thomas Robert Malthus, who warned that overpopulation would become a threat to humanity because populations grow by geometric progression while food production increases arithmetically, at a much slower rate. The Malthusian prophecy has little relevance for the developed nations, but it may be applied to the developing nations, where population increase does pose serious problems.

The mechanization of agriculture and the factory system have led many people to move from the land to the city, where the jobs are. The movement of people from rural areas to cities is called urbanization. Of course, cities predate the rise of industry, but even the cities of antiquity tended to rise around rivers where the soil was fertile and where transportation was possible, leading to trade and commerce. Urbanization in the industrial era is different, however, in that it is a universal trend that is forever stamping entire societies as urban in nature. Life in cities has given rise to a lifestyle and tradition that, spread through the mass media, are becoming dominant in the national culture. Secondary relationships, formal organizations, and the institutions of the economy, government, and education have been strengthened, at the expense of primary relationships and the institutions of the family and religion.

In the United States, a further development in urbanization has been the trend toward suburbanization. Suburbs grew when people began to escape urban problems and as a result of the popularity of the automobile and the consumer culture, but today suburbs resemble cities. However, cities have suffered from the movement because they lack a sufficient tax base and cannot provide services to the remaining residents. Metropolitanization, or cities and suburbs that have grown large and in certain locations follow each other without interruption for great distances, is another current problem. Large metropolitan areas, also called megalopolises, have unique problems, such as the need for an expanded governmental bureaucracy. Although such programs as urban renewal and gentrification have attempted to remedy the plight of the inner cities, these areas are still plagued with problems, basically because they remain the home of those who cannot afford to move out of them.

Overpopulation, together with urban and industrial lifestyles, has engendered problems that threaten the environment. First, natural resources are finite and cannot support the dramatic increases in population. Second, our careless disregard for the environment threatens to destroy it because of the way it is being polluted. In particular, it is the accumulation of greenhouse gases in the atmosphere, a side effect of automobile emissions and other industrial processes, that are endangering the planet by creating global warming. We are already seeing these effects, from the melting of the polar ice caps to the creation of deserts, from extreme droughts to tragic floods, from severe hurricanes to disappearing ecosystems. Moreover, the people who are most at risk from these phenomena are the ones least likely to be able to prevent them or adjust to them: They are the poor of the world. Humans are only one element in the global ecosystem; however, their arrogance is such that they believe themselves to be at the center of creation. A change in cultural values and government action will probably be necessary before the pollution of the air, land, and water, as well as the wasting of natural resources, will be reversed.

Terms to Remember

biosphere   A thin film of air, water, and soil surrounding the earth.

birth cohort   All the people born in a specific time period.

birthrate   The number of births per 1,000 persons in a specific population per year.

death rate   The number of deaths per 1,000 persons in a specific population per year. Same as mortality rate.

demography   The study of the growth or decline of populations, their distribution throughout the world, and their composition.

ecology   The study of the relationship between living organisms and their environments.

ecosystem   A contained system of living and nonliving entities, and the manner in which they interact and maintain a balance that permits life to continue.

fecundity   The biological potential for producing offspring.

fertility rate   The average number of births per 1,000 women between the ages of 15 and 44, or during women's reproductive years.

infant mortality   The rate that reflects the number of deaths among infants under one year of age for every 1,000 live births.

life expectancy   The average number of years that a person at a given age can expect to live.

megalopolis   A complex in which one metropolitan area follows another without interruption. Also called urban sprawl.

metropolitanization   The tendency of suburbs, small cities, and surrounding rural areas to cluster around a central city and be considered as a single unit.

mortality rate   The number of deaths in a population per year.

pollution   The degradation of air, land, and water as well as the esthetic aspects of the environment.

population density   The ratio of people to a land area.

population pyramid   A graphic expression of the age and sex distribution of a given population.

pull factors   Factors that attract people to immigrate to a new area.

push factors   Factors that impel people to emigrate from one area to another.

sex ratio   Ratio of the number of males in a population in any single year per 100 females.

Standard Metropolitan Statistical Area (SMSA)   Term used by the U.S. Bureau of the Census to designate units of population consisting of a county or counties that include a city of 50,000 or more people. Metropolitan areas containing one million or more people are called Consolidated Metropolitan Statistical Areas (CMSAs).

suburbs   Smaller communities on the outskirts of central cities and somewhat dependent on them.

urbanism   A condition, a set of attitudes, a quality, or a way of life distinct from the rural.

urbanization   A population trend in which cities grow at the expense of rural areas.

zero population growth   A condition in which each person replaces himself or herself only (replacement level of 2.1); thus, the birthrate and the death rate are the same.

Suggested Readings

Anderson, Elijah. 1992. *StreetWise: Race, Class, and Change in an Urban Community*. Chicago: University of Chicago Press. A participant observation study that follows residents who are being displaced by gentrification, as well as those who come into the newly gentrified neighborhood.

Brown, Lester R. 2000. *State of the World: A Worldwatch Institute Report on Progress Toward a Sustainable Society*. New York: W. W. Norton. A collection of essays dealing with environmental issues on a global level.

Commoner, Barry. 1990. *Making Peace with the Planet*. New York: Pantheon. An early activist in the pro-earth movement speaks about the necessity of reconciling our needs for technological progress with protection of the environment.

Dunham-Jones, Ellen and June Williamson. 2008. *Retrofitting Suburbia: Urban Design Solutions for Redesigning Suburbs*. New York: Wiley. A series of case studies showing how suburbs have been made more livable.

Eade, John. 1996. *Living the Global City: Globalization as Local Process*. New York: Routledge. An examination of the way the new global economies, and all they portend, affect the everyday lives of ordinary people.

Feagin, Joe R. and Robert Parker. 1990. *Building American Cities: The Urban Real Estate Game*. Englewood Cliffs, NJ: Prentice Hall. A paperback whose theme is the effect of wealth and power and the development and decline of American cities.

Phillips, E. Barbara. 1996. *City Lights: Urban-Suburban Life in a Global Society*, 2nd ed. New York: Oxford University Press. An analysis of the major challenges facing American cities as they await the arrival of the global society.

Suzuki, David. 2007. *The Sacred Balance: Rediscovering Our Place in Nature*. Vancouver, BC: Greystone Books. A well-written account of the effects of humans on our planet and what the future holds in view of the radical changes that are occurring.

UN-Habitat. 2009. *Planning Sustainable Cities: Global Report on Human Settlements: 2009*. New York: UN-Habitat Core Team. Urban planning systems for a new century.

Weeks, John R. 1998. *Population: An Introduction to Concepts and Issues*, 7th ed. Belmont, CA. Wadsworth. A textbook in population studies, including examinations of issues in the United States and in the world.

Government: The Institution and the Theories and Ideologies That Underlie It

IN THIS CHAPTER, YOU WILL LEARN

- the reason for the emergence of the institution of government;
- the purpose and functions of government;
- the importance of legitimacy and authority in the exercise of political power, as well as the types of authority;
- the differences between the state and government;
- the definition of a nation–state;
- that social movements, governments, and economic behavior are based on ideologies;
- the differences between autocratic and democratic ideologies;
- about the dominant totalitarian ideology of the right and the social movement it spawned;
- about the dominant totalitarian ideology of the left and the social movements that followed; and
- the principles of the democratic ideology and of its subideologies of capitalism and democratic socialism.

Government is never very far from our thoughts. How could it be otherwise? We cannot drive a car, vote, or have a drink if we are underage without a government agency's okay. We cannot decide that we will not attend school if we are under 16: A government agency will send truant officers to find us and bring us into the classroom. We cannot play our stereo full blast because if a neighbor complains, an agency of government will

From Chapter 15 of *Contemporary Society: An Introduction to Social Science*, Thirteenth Edition. John A. Perry, Erna K. Perry. Copyright © 2012 by Pearson Education, Inc. All rights reserved.

make us turn it down or haul us off to jail for disturbing the peace. We cannot build any kind of house we want, even on our own lot: A government agency will first ensure that certain zoning regulations are satisfied. And these are just minor examples of government interference. Government decides who is a citizen, who can vote or work in the country, who is to obtain unemployment compensation or disability pensions. Government wants to know if a child is born, and who dies, as well as where, and how death takes place. In short, government is everywhere; it touches our lives in a million ways, reaching into our very kitchens and bedrooms. Why do we let it? Why do we need it? What is government, anyway?

The Institution of Government

Remember that pivotal institutions revolve around important human needs. One fundamental prerequisite of humans as biological organisms is a daily supply of water and food and some covering and shelter from the elements. Just as important and urgent is the need to be able to live in a sufficiently orderly environment, protected from outside enemies. In small groups, these needs are satisfied simply and without much conflict. When small groups of individuals become hundreds, matters become more complex. That is, when food is grown and not simply gathered, when objects are manufactured not simply found—in short, when clans or tribes settle into a permanent lifestyle—then a process must be instituted for making important decisions for the benefit of the group. This process consists of organizational patterns of behavior that eventually crystallize into the institutions of the economy and government. In turn, these patterns and their organization are shaped and buttressed by the ideologies prevalent in each society.

The U.S. Capitol building is one of the symbols of our government.

Government and Politics

The decision of who gets what of a society's rewards, and why they get it, is inherent in the institution of the economy. The implementation of the economic decisions and of all decisions that affect the society is left up to the institution of government. The two institutions are deeply intertwined. They consist of a number of patterns and traditions for getting things done. They also include people, a body of representatives with the authority and sufficient power to see to it that decisions made for the society are carried out, respected, and obeyed.

In most modern societies, the source of ultimate power is the state because it has a monopoly on the use of force within its borders. The state, however, is an abstract concept; the real day-to-day exercise of power is done by the government, which consists of a number of individuals who hold power in the name of the state. The process by which some people or groups acquire and maintain power is called **politics.**

Government, the institution, may be defined as the pattern of statuses and roles that a society develops to fulfill the need for order within and the need for defense against threats from without. It includes a system of norms, values, laws, and general patterns of behavior that legitimize the acquisition and exercise of power. The institution also determines the relationship of the government to the members of society. It is important to remember that, in essence, to govern means to control, and government can also be defined as the legitimate use of force to control human behavior within specific territorial boundaries.

The Purpose of Government

Societies need government because a group way of life requires a certain degree of social order. There are some things people must do and others they must refrain from doing to prevent chaos and maintain relative peace. In small societies, the family institution is sufficient to maintain social control over its members by exercising moral control. Moral control, which is essentially cultural learning, lies within the individual, having been internalized through socialization.

When societies grow large and complex, other institutions—religion, education, and government—must take over some of the functions of maintaining social order by exercising social control. Social control is the process by which a group induces or forces the individual to behave in a designated way by enforcing taboos, mores, and folkways. In large, complex societies, moral control and social control must be supplemented by political control. Political control is social control exerted by forces outside the individual, such as laws and agencies in charge of punishing those who violate laws.

The Functions of Government

The most important function of government is to implement political control. This involves maintaining order, settling disputes, and coordinating the activities of members of society. In addition, government must protect citizens from external threats. It does this by creating and maintaining armies, by providing such armies with weapons, and by securing strategic military installations. In some societies, the military institution itself acts as the government. In most, however, civilians are in charge of the government, and the military is subordinate to it.

The government is also in charge of planning and maintaining those facilities and activities that involve large portions of the population. Government agencies regulate the economy, build highways, are in charge of traffic regulation, fund schools, maintain national parks and museums, help run some hospitals, provide some health care, and so on. Government also subsidizes activities that are valued by the society but the private sector does not pursue, such as the arts. The preceding functions are *manifest,* or deliberate.

The unintended, or *latent*, functions of government have often included a great deal of repression. In the United States, however, governmental repression has been minimal. Latent functions here have included the formation of party machines, which were common in the past, as well as the alleged existence of power elites that act to maintain the status quo, including a system of social stratification. Even in nations that consider themselves classless, administrative and managerial elites have come into existence. The relationship between political power and socioeconomic status is entrenched everywhere.

Political Power: Legitimacy and Authority

Power is central to the political process because whoever exerts political control in a society must have power to do so. **Power** is a difficult concept to define. The early sociologist Max Weber defined it as "the probability that one actor within a social relationship will be in a position to carry out his own will despite resistance" (Weber, 1957, 152). Power is a significant factor in all kinds of social interaction. Parents have power over their children, professors have a certain degree of power over students, employers have power over employees, and so on. People have greater or lesser amounts of power according to the statuses they occupy in society and the roles they fill.

Power relationships are always somewhat reciprocal. That is, the child has some power over the parent: He or she can throw a temper tantrum or refuse to eat until the parent gives in. An employee can "take home" office supplies, or products, or pad expense accounts. A student can flatter the instructor to improve chances of a passing or above-average grade. In short, there are ways of sabotaging the power-holding individual in most interactions.

Power can be asserted in a number of ways. One way is to promise a reward in return for compliance. Another is to coerce, or threaten with punishment, the individual who does not comply. Finally, power can be asserted through influence, by being able to manipulate information or to have an effect on values, attitudes, and feelings. Television commentators and popular authors have power over many people because their statements are accepted as authoritative by a large public. Political leaders have a similar effect.

Legitimacy

Political power is power exercised by the state through its government. The reason the state can wield power is that people accept its authority. When power is held by an individual or group that is not acceptable to the members of society, that power is considered illegal and illegitimate. This kind of power is coercion, as when an armed thug demands the wallet of an unarmed victim.

Authority

For power to be legitimate, it must have authority. **Authority** is power over, or control of, individuals that is socially accepted as right and proper. A police officer who holds a gun to a suspect while trying to make an arrest is not displaying coercive power because it is the right of the officer to do so, inherent in the authority vested in his or her status. A private citizen engaged in the same activity, on the other hand, is committing a crime, because the citizen has no authority to hold a gun to anyone (except in self-defense). In other words, authority is the legitimate possession of power.

A government must have legitimate authority to be accepted. That is, citizens must believe "that the existing political institutions are the most appropriate ones for the society"

(Lipset, 1963, 64). No political system, not even one born of violence and functioning through force, can survive for very long without legitimacy. When people question the legitimacy of their government, the situation is called a **crisis of legitimacy** and is usually resolved with the overthrow of the government. The 1989 democracy movement in China exemplified a crisis of legitimacy, but the Chinese government was able to crush it. Today, people in a number of Arab nations are questioning the legitimacy of their ruling elites.

Types of Legitimate Authority

How does an individual or group or a government acquire authority? In other words, how does power become legitimized? In a classic thesis, German sociologist Max Weber maintained that the sources of authority lie in tradition, the law, and charisma (Weber, 1957, 324–369).

Traditional Authority. The oldest type of power that people know is authority that depends on tradition. The legitimization of power in **traditional authority** depends on the past. The authority of a person or group is accepted because "it has always been so." The religious authority of churches and the political authority of the government rest heavily on traditional sources.

Traditional authority tends to prevail in relatively homogeneous, nontechnological societies because citizens have similar group identification, sharing most of the same values, beliefs, and attitudes. However, even in heterogeneous and highly technological societies there are traditional sources of authority. The Constitution of the United States, as an example, is accepted by most Americans as an almost sacred document that forms the basis of the governmental system. Legislation that runs counter to the letter of the Constitution is considered illegitimate.

Legal-Rational Authority. **Legal-rational authority** is based on rules that are arrived at in a rational manner. Systems based on legal-rational authority are organized in a bureaucratic fashion because this pattern of social organization limits the exercise of power. In a bureaucracy, power resides in a social position and role rather than in a specific individual. In addition, this pattern of organization defines and specifies the exact amount of power that each role entails. Authority is based on obedience to the "**rule of law,**" rather than on loyalty to any given individual or group.

Legal-rational authority appears in complex, multigroup societies. In such societies, members are heterogeneous and belong to many subcultures. These societies usually experience rapid social change, resulting in a lack of uniformity in values, attitudes, and beliefs. Legal-rational authority is accepted because societal members are convinced that those who hold authority are using rational methods for the benefit of all. Social change, moreover, is reflected in frequent modifications to the law.

Charismatic Authority. One type of authority does not rest on tradition, reason, or the law. Rather, **charismatic authority** derives from the personality of an exceptional leader. Such authority may appear in a society that has a traditional base or in one that has a legal-rational base. Charismatic leaders seem to possess special characteristics that are described as magnetic, fascinating, and extraordinary by their followers. Such leaders as Mao Zedong, Adolf Hitler, Martin Luther King, and Fidel Castro have been described as charismatic. Presidents John F. Kennedy and Barack Obama have also been referred to as charismatic, but within the democratic system of government the charisma they display is different than the authority of authoritarian leaders.

Charismatic authority does not encourage stable social organization nor a stable political system. It has no system of rules, either traditional or rational, with which to guide behavior. In fact, it resists attempts at routinization or bureaucratization. Stability can be established only if the system based on the charismatic authority of a leader evolves into one of the other two systems of authority.

World History Archive/Newscom

Nazism was a totalitarian ideology of the right that owed much of its appeal to the charismatic personality of Adolf Hitler, who promised the German people a return to a former greatness—at a time when they were suffering economic difficulties and humiliations due to their defeat in World War I.

The State

Most societies today are nation states. The term state is frequently misunderstood and confused with the term *government*. Government, as the preceding discussion has shown, is the institution that develops as a consequence of the need to maintain social order in a society. Government, however, is a process that also includes the people who exercise political power in a society. The **state** is the abstract embodiment, or the symbol, of the political institution. Government provides political control through its political processes, through the laws it establishes and implements, and through the work of its agencies. The state is the formal representation of government. The functions of the state are carried out by the government. Government is the working, active arm of the state. Individuals and groups that make up the government, together with the laws they pass and the procedures they establish, change with time and with each administration, but the state goes on.

In some societies, it is easy to differentiate between the state and its government because the offices of the head of state and the head of government are held by two different persons. For instance, in Great Britain the queen is the head of state, whereas the prime minister is the head of government. Many other parliamentary democracies have a president as head of state and a prime minister as head of the government. In the United States, however, both offices are inherent in the position of president.

The state differs from all other institutions in two essential ways. First, membership in the state is compulsory for all living within its territorial limits, with the exception of those who are designated as aliens or temporary visitors. Second, the state differs from all other aspects of social organization in that its political control is complete. The state, and the state alone, can seize a citizen's property, can deprive a person of freedom by imprisonment, or, as a last resort, can take a citizen's life as punishment for a capital crime.

In a parliamentary system such as that of Great Britain, the head of state and the head of the government are embodied in two separate persons. The queen is the head of state, and the prime minister is the head of government.

These two conditions of the state are necessary if the state is to exercise effective, organized political control. If individuals could resign from the state, they would be relieved of all obligation to obey its laws. Moreover, because the state has the duty of enforcing certain patterns of behavior on all persons within its boundaries, the state's government must have the authority to use whatever sanctions are necessary to achieve this purpose. The state must possess sovereignty, or the supreme political power, which derives from its capacity to monopolize the use of force within its borders. A state's sovereignty is recognized both by its own citizens and by other states.

The basic components of the state are territory, population, government, and sovereignty. Within its territory, through its government, on the basis of its sovereignty, and for the benefit of its people, the state performs certain functions and deals with other states.

The state, in other words, is defined in terms of the size and complexity of the society in which it is found. It emerges in societies with large populations containing high numbers of composite groups, social classes, and associations. It is a means of governing such societies in that the state brings together under common rule many kinds of people. State societies are seldom ethnically homogeneous, and they usually display inequalities in the distribution of wealth and of economic functions. The existence of a state is a mark of a society's complexity of organization.

The state emerged or was established in many places, in many historic eras, and under many conditions. Throughout history there have existed city–states (some still exist today), empire states, theocratic states, tribal states, nation–states, centralized states, and decentralized states, autocratic, oligarchic, and democratic states, as well as states stratified by social class or by social estate. Despite its various forms and diverse origins, their common feature has been their emergence as an institutional solution to the problem of governing large and complex groups of people. And the historical trend has been to reduce the number of state forms to one predominant one, namely, the nation–state. This has occurred chiefly by means of cultural diffusion from Europe to other parts of the world, where the form was drafted on and combined with native systems of political rule.

Theoretical Views of the State

The fundamental reason for the emergence of government and its symbol, the state, as has been noted repeatedly, is the maintenance of social order. Theorists who see life from a functionalist perspective naturally accept the idea that the institution originated to perform this specific function. One of the older expressions of this idea may be found in the writings of Thomas Hobbes (1588–1679), an English philosopher, who speculated that the state emerged as a result of a "social contract" made by the people to end their existence in a "state of nature," in which life was "solitary, poor, nasty, brutish, and short." Modern social thinkers of the functionalist school perceive the state as an institution that is working quite well in maintaining law and order.

In addition, the state acts as an arbitrator in conflicts among individuals, as planner with the official goal of providing the greatest good for the greatest number, and to maintain relations with other states. Thus the state allocates scarce resources, regulates the economy, funds new research, protects those unable to work, looks out for the environment, and generally provides for the needs of the members of society. It also makes trade agreements, political alliances, or war with other states. All these functions require a centralized source of authority.

Theorists who view life from a conflict perspective maintain that the state emerged to protect the rights of a privileged few. The conflict view derives from the works of Jean-Jacques Rousseau (1712–1778), who disagreed with Hobbes, believing instead that before the emergence of the state, people lived as "noble savages" in peace and harmony. It was when the idea of private property developed that people began to fight among themselves and then had to resort to a central authority—the state—to restore peace. This central authority was not impartial but rather served the interests of the upper classes and kept the majority poor and oppressed.

These ideas were taken up by Karl Marx, who thought that all but the most primitive societies consisted of at least two classes. Of these, one dominated and exploited the others by means of social institutions. The state came to be an instrument in the service of the ruling classes. Marx concluded that the state would cease to exist only when the last stage of the evolution of societies was reached. In the classless societies that would follow communism, the state would "wither away" because in such societies there would no longer be any need to safeguard the interests of any one group.

As always, both the functionalist and the conflict perspectives show only one version of reality. It may be argued that the state maintains the status quo and with it some instances of social inequality. It may be equally argued that large, complex, heterogeneous societies cannot function without a central body with the authority to make certain vital decisions for the society.

The Nation–State

The continuous growth in size and complexity of societies led people to seek political organization first in clans based on kinship, later in tribes that were collections of clans, and finally in city–states. Around the fifteenth century, city–states gradually began to emerge as nation–states.

The **nation** is a culture group residing within the territory of the political state. A group of people are considered a nation if (1) they are permanent residents of a defined territory, (2) they exhibit some form of government, (3) they have a common culture, and (4) they declare themselves to be, and are considered by others to be, sovereign. When a group becomes a nation, older loyalties to family or tribe must be subordinated to the new political order, and a common literature, history, and a sense of a common future develop. A nation comes to have a "we" as against "them" feeling; that is, it develops a sense of unity so strong that, despite a lack of cultural uniformity, people consider themselves as separate from all others (who are then designated as "foreigners"). Historically, nationhood seems to have come first to the English, who, taking advantage of the dissolution of the medieval order, were able to achieve a sense of themselves as a separate and self-conscious people, although they retained a number of the institutions from the preceding social order. Few other nations were able to achieve this consciousness of themselves as a nation. Although the United States originally had a self-concept of nationhood based on its English character-istics, today its preoccupation with ethnicity has given rise to doubts regarding its identity (Greenfield, 1992). A number of other nation–states have problems in this area: Canada with its French-speaking minority, which does not want to give up its language or culture; Israel with its Arab minority, which does not want to give up its territory; and China with Tibet, which does not want to give up its sovereignty. Yugoslavia, which has emerged from a civil war in which several ethnic groups were pitted against one another, has been divided into several nations. The former country represents the dark side of nationhood in the sense that older tribal loyalties have never really been abandoned. They were merely hidden during the communist period, when nationhood was superimposed on peoples who considered themselves distinct.

The development of national states has been of vital importance in the modern world. Principally, the loyalties and beliefs of nationalism have been motivating forces in the organi-zation of complex, technological societies in the urban-industrial period. They have also been important forces in establishing and maintaining international antagonisms as a result of the ideology behind the nation–state, which is nationalism.

Nationalism

Nationalism may be defined as a set of beliefs about the superiority and difference of one's own nation and a defense of its interests above all others. It implies that the individual identifies with the nation, its culture, its interests, and its goals. Nationalism is ethnocentrism that cuts across all other loyalties to stress loyalty to the national group.

Historically, nationalism is a new movement. It first appeared in the second half of the eighteenth century. Before then, in the aftermath of the feudal era, all the Western world was relatively unified in culture and religion. The rulers of most Western nations constituted an international society of governing classes because of frequent intermarriages and kinship relations. The events following World War I, particularly the appearance of a number of communist and fascist regimes, effectively destroyed this unity. The new regimes stressed nationalism because they felt that a drive for national supremacy would strengthen them internally. Their goal was to create a monolithic state whose people had only one allegiance to the government and one overwhelming feeling of patriotism.

The classical liberals of that time, moreover, believed that the nation–state was the natural unit of self-government in human society. They thought that once the vast empires that had dominated the Western world disappeared, people, no longer oppressed by them, would live in harmony with one another, without need for wars or conflict. Marxists were even confident that modernization and the spread of socialism would eventually get rid of nationalism, and that it ultimately would have the same role as ethnic cooking: a quaint reminder of a past cultural tradition. But they were all wrong, as nationalism and the feelings of nationhood proved to be powerful forces all through the twentieth century, giving rise to wars and atrocities even into the new century.

In the United States, a strong sense of national identity emerged, at first as a result of a common ethnicity in terms of language and culture. Later, it was reinforced by a sense of "specialness," as people came to believe that the nation had a historical mission to be the model for other nations of the globe. In other words, the idea of nationhood was combined in the United States with some of the ideals of the Enlightenment period regarding the aim of universal civilization. However, the United States has not become the first universal nation; on the contrary, we have been for the past several decades experiencing a sharpening of more narrowly ethnic feelings that sometimes result in our questioning our national identity. Many of us have become hyphenated Americans, a fact that has some commentators stating that a national allegiance that depends on subscribing to abstract principles is insufficient to maintain nationhood.

The Ideologies Behind the Nation–State

The former Yugoslavia, now divided into its many component parts, had been in the news throughout the 1990s. The news reports told incessantly of war and starvation, of atrocities and refugees, of war criminal trials, of people thrown out of their ancestral homes and people taking over the ancestral homes of others. And yet, a few years ago, Yugoslavia was a unified country, a nation, whose people lived in reasonable harmony with one another. It is true that they were made up of a number of different ethnic and religious groups, but this did not seem to stop them from trading, interacting, and marrying each other.

What happened to break up their cohesion, to turn former friends into bitter enemies, to split families, pitting brother against brother? In a word, it all started with an ideology.

For nearly 50 years following the end of World War II, the ideology had been one of unity. Those same people who today proclaim themselves to be proud Slovenians, Serbs, Croatians, Bosnians, and Montenegrins, with deep wounds and profound hatreds for one another, were compelled by a communist dictator, General Tito, to bury the past and consider themselves one nation. That ideology was forced on them, but it worked. When communism unraveled all around them, however, a new ideology was needed to cement the nation. Such an ideology was found by revisiting the past; but, rather than unity, it led to the breakup of the nation.

Ideology is a system of beliefs, or doctrines, that provide a basis for collective action (Mannheim, 1936). Ideologies tend to develop around a central value, such as equality or racial purity. Those espousing a particular ideology claim to speak for major social groups in society: Marxists for the working class, feminists for all women. Some ideologies defend or rationalize the status quo; others criticize it and exhort people to change it. All followers of an ideology maintain that only they give the true picture of what the world is really like. As a result, ideologies are the underpinnings of all social movements and eventually of governments.

The Role of Ideology

First, ideologies explain why things are the way they are. Second, they reinforce the feelings of participants, clarifying them and making them a part of a program for action. Third, they direct members to behave in such a way that the desired change will be obtained. And finally, they educate people, justifying their actions.

Despite their important functions, ideologies often distort the truth. They also have a tendency to make of their followers "true believers," that is, supporters who are blindly loyal to them. In turn, the kind of fanaticism blind loyalty evokes does not respect the truth.

Ideologies tend to arise during periods of crisis and among those segments of society to whom the dominant world view has become unacceptable (Shils, 1968, 66–76). When groups of people begin to feel exploited or neglected, or if their status is being threatened by social change, or if their needs and desires are being thwarted in an existing order, they turn to a new or newly rediscovered ideology in which they see hope for a better future. In fact, ideologies are embodiments of ideas in action. Thus, they are meaningless outside social movements, some of which eventually become governments. Ideologies need to be organized and disseminated, and this is done by harnessing people into action.

Political Ideology

Ideologies vary in scope from comprehensive to partial. Totalitarian ideologies, for instance, insist that public authority control all the meaningful areas of life, whereas democratic ideologies limit themselves to a more restricted sphere.

Ideologies are abstract. That is, they do not necessarily reflect reality but are a model derived from the author's perceptions of reality.

Ideologies are reductionist, in that they set forth general and simple explanations and goals that are easily understandable. Although ideologies are meant to result in action, they do not always precede action. Sometimes, actions come first and then an ideology is formed to justify them.

Finally, although a number of ideologies guide human lives, it is the political ideology with its economic repercussions that affects the social lives of people most directly. Political scientist Robert Lane describes the nature and functions of political ideology in the following terms: Political ideology refers to concepts that: (1) deal with the questions: Who will be the rulers? How will the rulers be selected? By what principles will they govern? (2) constitute an argument; that is, they are intended to persuade and to counter opposing views; (3) integrally affect some of the major values of life; (4) embrace a program for the defense or reform or abolition of important social institutions; (5) are, in part, rationalization of group interest but not necessarily the interest of all groups espousing them; (6) are normative, ethical, moral in tone and content; (7) are (inevitably) torn from their context in a broader belief system and share the structural and stylistic properties of that system (Lane, 1962, 14–15).

One of the most important functions of ideology is to make the governors acceptable to the governed. In his book on the nature of government, Robert MacIver asserted that it is not force but the myth complex of society that makes people accept others as their rulers (MacIver, 1947, 17). This myth complex, which is the author's term for ideology, lends government a justification without which no prince or parliament, no tyrant or dictator could ever rule. Any government needs legitimate authority to continue to exist. And the underlying fabric of authority is ideology.

In pluralistic, heterogeneous societies, people tend to hold conflicting ideologies. In theory, the individual can pick and choose from among a number of such ideologies. In reality, most people are socialized into accepting the prevailing ideology, so that only a few even realize that a multiplicity of ideologies are available. In societies in which only one official ideology is allowed to exist, those who hold conflicting ideologies are persecuted as enemies of the state.

The foremost contemporary political ideologies that govern the lives of societies are divided into the autocratic (totalitarian, or dictatorial and authoritarian) and the democratic. The first group includes fascism, Nazism, and Soviet and other variants of communism; the second group includes democratic capitalism and democratic socialism.

Autocratic Ideologies

The basis of all **autocratic** ideologies is the belief that government should be in the hands of one individual—or group of individuals—with supreme power over the people of the society. Throughout history many forms of autocratic governments have existed: primitive kingships, despotism, tyranny, and absolutist monarchies such as those of czarist Russia. Military dictatorships and other forms of temporary or emergency rule are also autocratic in nature. The distinguishing feature of autocratic regimes is that the ruler does not have to account to anyone for any actions. The ruler makes all decisions without being subject to any law. In effect, the ruler is the law, and the people are subjects in the true sense of the word: They have no political rights at all.

Authoritarianism

In modern times, traditional autocracy has been replaced by ideologies of the right and of the left that we call either authoritarian or totalitarian. **Authoritarianism** is autocratic in the political arena but leaves a measure of choice up to the individual as long as the latter does not interfere with the rule of the leader or the party elite. Many nations throughout the world, though they define themselves as democratic or socialist, are really authoritarian regimes.

Totalitarianism

Totalitarian regimes differ in major ways both from the modern authoritarian systems and from the autocracies of the past. For one thing, they control the individual in all aspects of life, social and religious as well as political. For another, they are based on modern technology

Morteza Nikoubazl/Reuters/Landov

In an authoritarian society, even people's hairstyles are subject to control. Here, a barbershop in Iran with a poster of hairstyles allowed for men.

and mass legitimation (Friedrich & Brzezinski, 1966, 4). The word *totalitarian* came into existence when what were thought to be short-lived dictatorships of the left and right became permanent regimes. **Totalitarian** regimes have many aspects in common: (1) Their official ideology expresses a revolt against present society and idealistic hopes for a future society of perfect men and women; (2) they maintain a single party that functions as the organization through which the ideology is fostered and kept alive; (3) the state has an all-pervasive secret police and totally controls the mass media; (4) the state has a monopolistic control of arms, which means that force is concentrated in its hands; and (5) the economy is centrally planned and controlled. These features of totalitarian ideology have enabled many totalitarian states to exert total control over the lives of individuals. Such an attempt was never made by the older autocracies, nor is it made by the contemporary authoritarian regimes that are not totalitarian (Friedrich et al., 1969, 126; Gregor, 1968, 20–21).

The destinies of political systems that have evolved from totalitarian ideologies—fascism, national socialism (Nazism), communism (Soviet, Chinese, Cuban, North Korean)—have all been different. World War II put an end to fascism and Nazism, which have reappeared only sporadically in various nations. Communism continued to prosper for much of the twentieth century but has in the last few years dramatically collapsed in its major stronghold, the Soviet Union and its satellites. It is still hanging on in Cuba, North Korea, and much more tenuously in China and a few other nations. (In China communism is losing its hold, as the embrace of a market economy has proved more capable of producing the consumer goods all people seem to crave; but the Communist Party still maintains control of the government.) Communist movements, in the form of guerrilla warfare, have appeared in Central and South America (i.e., the Shining Path movement in Peru) and in various nations of Africa.

Totalitarianism of the Right: Fascism and Nazism

Fascism and Nazism, which no contemporary society admits to following, exemplified totalitarian regimes of the right that flourished in the first half of the twentieth century. Fascism emerged in Italy under the leadership of Benito Mussolini after World War I (a fascist government came to power in 1922). In 1933, a similar movement appeared in Germany, where it acquired the name of national socialism, or **Nazism**. Eventually, the movement crossed over into Asia, where it was embraced by Japan. It also took hold in the Western Hemisphere: Argentina established a fascist dictatorship under General Juan Peron in 1943 that lasted until the middle 1950s. In addition, fascism, in its various national transformations, appeared in Spain as the Falange party and in France, Romania, Hungary, and other nations under a variety of names.

Although there are differences between fascism and Nazism, the two movements have enough similarities that the latter can be considered merely a subtype of the former. Principally, they are identified by two different leaders: Benito Mussolini with fascism and Adolf Hitler with Nazism.

The principal elements of **fascism** included a distrust of reason, the denial of basic human equality, a code of behavior based on violence and distortion of truth, government by the elite, totalitarianism (that is, total control exerted by the government), racism, imperialism, and opposition to international law and order (Ebenstein, 1973). The ideology had fanatical and dogmatic overtones and presented issues that could not be discussed critically but must be accepted on faith. For instance, race was an issue for the Germans, and the infallibility of a leader was one for the Italians. Fascists also rejected the Judeo-Christian-Greek concept of equality. The fascist ideal is the concept of inequality, in the sense that some persons were considered superior to others: men to women, soldiers to civilians, party members to nonparty members, one's own nation to other nations, the strong to the weak, and the victors in war to the vanquished. Fascists considered it a fallacy that people were capable of self-government; rather, they preferred to believe that only a small minority of the population, qualified by birth, education, or social standing, were able to understand and do what was best for the whole society. It followed that in a fascist system, the government consisted of a self-appointed elite and was not dependent on popular consent, free elections, a free press, or an opposition.

Fascism was totalitarian in all social relations; in its objective, which was to control all phases of human life from birth to death; and in its means, because fascists were willing to use any form of coercion, from verbal threats to mass murder, to attain their goals. With the defeat of the Axis powers during World War II, the most virulent forms of fascism and Nazism were wiped out. Nonetheless, the ideology crops up sporadically in a number of social movements.

Totalitarianism of the Left: Communism

Communism, an economic and political system whose goals are total government control of the economy and total income redistribution with the ultimate aim of a classless society, is based on one of the most misunderstood and feared ideologies. And yet its avowed goal—the establishment of an egalitarian society—has been the ideal of some of the world's best minds and hearts through the centuries. Communism as it is known today originated in the conditions following the social changes brought about by the Industrial Revolution. The ideology sprang up as a reaction to the hunger, disease, poverty, and lack of medical care that were the daily realities of urban industrial masses in the nineteenth century. These conditions had been observed and lamented by many social thinkers and critics. Karl Marx proposed his own version of utopia, communism, which soon fired the imagination of vast numbers of followers.

The Marxist Foundation: Materialism. The basis of Marx's thought, as already noted, was the idea that people's conditions—in fact, all relationships in life—rested on an economic base. Culture, law, government, religion, esthetics, philosophy, and so on, were actually superstructures erected on economic foundations in every society. The economic base was so strong that it determined not only the superstructure but also the way people thought and behaved. As an example, in all societies, those who own property (or the means of production in industrial societies) determine the course of events in that society. Those who lack property are subject to, or at least directed by, others. This state of affairs, said Marx, began when the right to private property was asserted and will not stop until property is possessed by all.

Marx also stressed that change in societies (as in all facets of life) was constant and that it proceeded through struggle. In societies that were at the capitalist stage of development (as most Western societies were at the time of his writing), the struggle was between the bourgeoisie—the entrepreneurs who owned the means of production—and the proletariat—the industrial workers. There was little doubt in Marx's mind that the struggle would eventually be won by the proletariat.

Historical Prediction: The Dialectic. Marx arrived at this prediction through a basic tool of analysis called the dialectic (hence, the Marxist position is sometimes referred to as dialectical materialism). The dialectic as a method of inquiry is of Greek origin. It is basically a method of question and answer in which a position is stated (thesis) and then criticized until the opposite position is arrived at (antithesis). Finally, a middle position between the two opposites is attained (synthesis), and the process begins anew.

Marx used the dialectic method to interpret history. He maintained that because change in the economic system is reflected in the entire superstructure of society, it is possible to predict the course of history by noting economic changes and the course of the economy by noting historical patterns. The latter include a struggle between the old and the new in which the new always wins. Thus, feudalism overcame slavery, capitalism overcame feudalism, and socialism—and eventually communism—would inevitably overcome capitalism. Ultimately, Marx went on, the bourgeoisie would be destroyed and its place taken by the proletariat. This condition would occur in a stage called communism, which, however, would not be attained without violent revolution. The struggle was already apparent to Marx; he said he could see in capitalism the seed of its own destruction. Marx was quite specific about where the revolution would occur. He predicted that the most likely place would be Germany, from which it would spread to other highly industrialized nations, gradually reaching the less industrial ones. This prediction by Marx, as well as many others, was wrong; the revolution occurred in Russia, at the time one of the least industrialized nations of Europe.

Another prognostication that did not materialize was the predicted deterioration of the working class in capitalist economies. Trade unions and the welfare state combined to secure the well-being of workers, who consequently did not overthrow the bourgeoisie. Capitalism demonstrated that it could change to meet certain challenges, refuting Marx's certainty that it would never change and was, therefore, doomed to fail.

Finally, Marx underestimated the power of nationalism. He addressed the workers of the world, urging them to throw off their chains. But the workers of the world felt themselves to be primarily German, Russian, French, or Italian and only secondarily members of the proletariat. When World War I broke out, the workers of each nation flocked to the defense of their country against the advice of communist ideologues, who repeated Marx's warnings that national sentiment was only part of the superstructure by which the bourgeoisie reinforced their dominance over the proletariat.

Despite the failure of many of his predictions, Marx's ideology has taken root in a large number of nations. For most of the twentieth century, almost half the world lived under regimes that considered themselves Marxist and were anticipating the imminent fall of capitalism. Surprisingly, most of these nations, contrary to being the industrial monsters prophesied by Marx, were economically underdeveloped.

© Michael Reynolds/epa CORBIS

Mao Zedong would be very surprised to find a Ferrari dealership in today's China, ostensibly still a communist country.

Box 1   Communism and the USSR

The initial thrust toward revolution and the establishment of a communist regime came from a Russian disciple of Marx, Vladimir Ilyich Ulyanov, better known as Lenin (1870–1924). Lenin proceeded to rationalize the reasons for the continuing existence of capitalism (imperialism provided additional markets, as well as raw materials and cheap labor) and concentrated on ensuring that revolution would occur. He organized a small group of revolutionaries dedicated to the goal of overthrowing the postczarist provisional government in Russia (the czarist regime had been previously overthrown). They finally succeeded in 1917, and a Europe that was exhausted from World War I allowed the revolutionary regime to become entrenched. Lenin became obsessed with maintaining the revolution and for this reason felt that revolution elsewhere had to be postponed. He urged workers around the world to consider Russia their own country, representing their hopes and defending their interests. This internationalism, although ostensibly remaining constant, gave way during World War II, when nationalism was reawakened in people who once more came to the defense of their own countries. (For that matter, the Soviet Union itself was an amalgam of about 150 different nationality groups who obviously did not feel allegiance to the values and traditions of Great Russia despite the attempts of the Communist Party to impose a uniform culture on the people. In fact, as soon as communism lost its hold, the various nationalities began to clamor for independence.)

Although Lenin, and subsequently his successor Stalin, tried to turn the Marxist ideology into political practice, the latter differed quite dramatically from the former. There was only one political party—the Communist Party—and one leader of that party, so that decision making became virtually unilateral and dictatorial. One of Stalin's decisions was to industrialize the country rapidly, and for that purpose forced agricultural collectivization was instituted. Consumer goods had to give way to heavy industry. Farmers and workers were expected to work as hard as they could and produce as much as they could, but the state paid them as little as possible so that more could be accumulated for capital investment. Needless to say, people do not respond positively to hardships when no rewards are in sight, particularly when failure or disobedience is punished severely.

The economic system shaped by Marxist–Leninist thought is characterized by rigidly centralized planning. Such a scheme is in total contrast to the capitalist pattern, in which each entrepreneur decides what to produce and where to invest. Central planning, designed to be more efficient than the capitalist model, in reality proved to be inefficient. It lent itself to abuse and corruption and to the development of a vast bureaucracy that contributed to making life miserable for the average citizen. Nonetheless, despite the disruption caused by purges and the severe losses of life and property in World War II, the Soviet Union, before its breakup, had become the second-largest producing nation in the world, with a higher coal and steel production than that of the United States. That may be one reason why some of the developing nations had elected for a time to follow Marxist–Leninist economic models.

At its most repressive, communism remained dogmatic in its intent to abolish private property and nationalize the means of production everywhere. It continued to preach the necessity of class warfare, the dictatorship of the proletariat, and the concentration of power in a tightly structured party. Where it survives, it still maintains that it is reaching for that ultimate goal, the classless society.

Box 2 Communism in China

Chinese communism has also undergone a traumatic experience. When Mao Zedong, the communist leader, triumphed over the corrupt rightist Nationalist Chinese government, he inherited a vast, populous country, whose people for the most part were dirt-poor survival farmers. The Communist Party instituted a number of campaigns of ideological brainwashing in which intellectuals, artists, property and manufacturing plant owners, and middle-class persons, generally, were described as "capitalist-roaders." They were either executed, imprisoned, or sent to far-off rural areas to be "reeducated." Despite these cruel methods intended to rid the society of the bourgeoisie, the Chinese communists succeeded in feeding, clothing, providing health care, and educating the formerly starving masses of Chinese. In addition, the communists virtually stamped out graft, prostitution, and drug addiction, problems that had been endemic during the period preceding the communist takeover, partly as a result of foreign (including American) exploitation. The communists redistributed property, giving people hope and confidence that their lives would hold a better future. At the same time, abuses occurred, especially during the Cultural Revolution, as people existed in an atmosphere of rigid dogmatism, acquiescing in the personality cult of Mao and living in the fear that saying something politically suspect might send them to jail.

After the death of Mao and with the coming to power of Deng Xiaoping, the bleak egalitarian poverty of the Maoist period seemed to have drawn to a close. The new leader, in fact, abolished communes, encouraged trade with the West and a Western style of entrepreneurship, and opened the door to Western ideas, enabling the Chinese people to taste the joys of consumerism. Washing machines, television sets, and disco dancing became realities for some and seemed to become attainable for many as the average income more than doubled and tripled during the last 20 years.

The economic reforms have engendered success after success. Visitors to China are amazed at the improvements in living standards and the growing optimism of the people, as well as the construction boom and the apparent high standard of living. Political reform, however, has not followed economic reform, and decisions continue to be made by the ruling elite with no accountability to the people. Nonetheless, the changes in present-day China are astounding. The gross domestic product (GDP) representing the real growth rate of the economy, was 8.4 percent in 2009. This is a tremendous figure, compared to the American growth rate which hovers around 3 percent and has been lowered considerably in the last recession. It has allowed the Chinese economy to be the largest after the United States. The Chinese unemployment rate is only 4.3 percent, and only 2.8 percent of the population lives below the poverty line (CIA, 2010).

Despite the Communist ideology subscribed to by the government, China has developed a stratum of wealthy individuals beyond the wildest dreams of the Maoist generation. According to *Forbes* magazine's lists of the world's wealthiest people, China has close to 20 billionaires, the 400 richest Chinese are worth a combined total of $38 billion, and the children of this elite group are sent not to study Communist ideology but such skills and experiences as golf, ballet, private music lessons, horseback riding, ice-skating, skiing, and so on. Even their attitudes toward sex have changed: Whereas even 5 years ago books and magazines with sexual content were heavily censored and banned, today soft-core pornography is being published and popular Web sites publish erotic photos and materials. These changes are being attributed to urbanization, greater mobility permitted by the market economy, and the popularity of the World Wide Web. It is a small wonder that a number of commentators are beginning to proclaim that the twenty-first century will be the Chinese century.

Democratic Ideologies: Democracy

Although many nations refer to themselves as "people's democracies," it takes more than a self-imposed name to be a democracy. **Democracy** is an ideology, a philosophy, a theory, and a political system. In the Western view, democracy is a way of life containing elements that define the relations of the individual to society and government. These elements may be summarized as follows: (1) rational empiricism, (2) emphasis on the individual, (3) instrumental nature of the state, (4) voluntarism, (5) the law behind the law, (6) emphasis on means, (7) discussion and consent in human relations, and (8) basic equality of all human beings (Ebenstein, 1973).

In more familiar terms, the democratic ideology stresses the value of the individual. The individual is the basic unit of a democratic society, and both the values and processes of the political system revolve around him or her. Moreover, the individual is considered to be a person with a separate identity and worth, whereas autocratic systems value individuals only as members of a larger social whole.

Another central tenet of democracy is the principle that all persons are born free, that they are not subject to the rule of others, and that consequently the only legitimate basis for rule is people's consent to be ruled. This principle is founded on the ideas of John Locke and Jean-Jacques Rousseau regarding the social contract. According to these philosophers, the social contract was a mutual agreement entered into by people who empowered an entity, later called the state, to protect them by enacting and enforcing a number of laws. The state and its government are dependent on consent and contract; essentially, it is the trustee of the people, and its power derives from their consent. It exists at the pleasure of the people and has no authority or purpose except as assigned by the people.

Citizen participation and an environment in which diversity and opposition are allowed to flourish are also elements of democracy. The first is facilitated by an educated citizenry, and the second is important because free and unique individuals will necessarily exhibit ideas and interests that clash. The important point is that in a democracy, conflicts are resolved through the political process.

The preceding principles are to be found in what is called the "classic" democratic ideology. Of course, democracy as a political system suffers in the translation from the ideology on which it is based. Many modern societies, particularly those in the Western tradition, have embraced some of the democratic ideals and combined them with specific economic ideologies. Two of the best known are **democratic capitalism** and **democratic socialism.**

Democratic Capitalism

Capitalism developed as an explanation of and a rationalization for the industrial system and some of the new attitudes that system required. Nevertheless, capitalism is more than an economic system and is inextricably bound up with democracy, particularly in the United States. Some political scientists refer to capitalism as a subideology, a blend of political and economic ideas that are mutually reinforcing (Ebenstein, 1973, 219).

The ideas of classical capitalism were expressed by Scottish philosopher Adam Smith in his famous treatise, *The Wealth of Nations* (1776), whose central features included a belief in private ownership of property with no limitation on its accumulation, the existence of a profit motive, the dynamics of a free market, and the presence of competition. These conditions had to operate in an atmosphere of freedom from government interference: Individual entrepreneurs must be free to innovate, workers must be free to seek higher wages, and investors must be free to look for the highest returns. Government was to keep its hands off the economy (laissez-faire), tending instead to its basic functions of keeping peace and defending the nation.

The private ownership of property (or the means of production in an industrial economy) was considered beneficial in two ways. First, ownership of many assets means having power over individuals who have fewer assets, so it is preferable that such power be diffused among individual property owners rather than being concentrated in the state, where it may lead to abuse. Second, it was believed that progress, in the sense of economic growth for the benefit of the entire society, would be attained more easily if each individual used personal incentive to get ahead, including the incentive to make a profit.

Smith maintained, further, that the free market system worked smoothly, as if an "invisible hand" were directing it. In more recent times, the market system has been called planning by inducement, to differentiate it from planning by direction, a method used in the centralized economies of both fascist and communist systems. In the latter, the government tells people what and how much to produce. In the market system, no one tells producers what and how much to produce; they decide on their own according to factors of supply and demand. Ultimately, then, the free market results in consumer sovereignty: Consumers create demand, and producers satisfy this demand by supplying the required products.

Classical capitalism also stressed the importance of competition. It was thought that entrepreneurs would offer the best merchandise at the cheapest price to make more sales (and so more profit). In modern capitalism, competition has been diluted because of the existence of private or state monopolies.

The profit motive, another central point in classical capitalism, was certainly not a new invention. However, more opportunity for profit exists in a capitalist economy because capitalism guarantees freedom of trade and occupation, freedom to own property, and freedom to make contracts. At the same time that it offers all these opportunities, capitalism also allows for loss. Bankruptcies and failure are part of the system, and every year some enterprises have huge losses (typically, 4 out of 10 corporations report net losses yearly, and of 10 businesses begun in any one year, 6 fail that same year).

Classical capitalism has undergone many transformations, and today's capitalist economies are called mixed economies, particularly because a certain amount of government intervention has become mandatory. Although most property is still held privately, the government regulates the economy through taxation and legislation and even controls a certain amount of manufacturing and distribution. Primarily, the government ensures that the economic game is played fairly and the losers are not totally destroyed.

Socialism

Socialism, which like democracy is a philosophy and a political system in addition to being an ideology, is capable of coexisting with capitalism. Socialism is also subject to a vast variety of definitions, has throughout history reflected a large number of visions, and has assumed a multiplicity of roles. In general, socialism refers to an economic concept, but democratic socialism is an ideology that rests on both economic and political assumptions.

Democratic Socialism

A socialist economy within a democratic political system is called democratic socialism. Great Britain and the Scandinavian countries are the most prominent examples of democratic socialism, although they have departed in degrees from a socialistic ideology in the last few decades. These societies, also called welfare states, did not use revolutionary means to come to power. Rather, they prefer to work within a democratic system, generally parliamentary in nature, which uses the electoral system to obtain representation in the government. Economic policies in these societies are carried out by those who are elected to public office.

The most fundamental assumption underlying democratic socialism is that "participation in political decision making should be extended to economic decision making" (Sargent, 1969, 97). This assumption is what makes the system democratic because it states that voters should be able to control their economic condition, as they do their political condition, through the government they elect. In all other respects, democratic socialism accepts and supports the democratic ideology, both in theory and in practice.

Democratic socialism assumes that the state and its government are the necessary instruments through which people can achieve and maintain their objectives. The state must lead the society in the following objectives: holding most property in the name of the people (i.e., publicly), especially all major industries, utilities, and transportation; limiting the accumulation of private property; and regulating the economy.

Socialists also believe that direct planning of the economy can prevent depressions; that wealth should be distributed so that there is only a small income differential among people; that a comprehensive welfare state would eradicate special privileges and create more equal opportunities for all; and that the working class is the backbone of the society.

One of the greatest appeals of democratic socialism is its concern with humanitarian issues. Socialists accuse capitalists of failing to solve fundamental problems in society—poverty, disease, inequality—primarily because they are too preoccupied with profits. They maintain that only when the economic system is controlled by the people will solutions be found. Unfortunately, the means of solving the problems are sometimes as bad as the problems themselves. In socialist countries, the individual is provided with a considerable amount of economic security. There is a comprehensive health-care program, and food and housing are available to those too old or too sick to work. At the same time, the system spawns a large, complicated bureaucracy that is not directly answerable to the people and is often not responsive to them. In this sense, democratic socialism faces the same challenges as capitalism.

Democratic socialists argue that by ensuring everyone of economic security, they are making liberty possible for everyone. Democratic capitalists argue that only when property is held privately are people free to compete for rewards. Despite its commendable goals, socialism has been suffering a long period of ideological stagnation and electoral defeat.

Many societies that had in the past embraced communism and socialism as their socioeconomic ideologies are today straying from them. Having found a strictly centralized, planned economy difficult to manipulate, these societies have adopted, although some still to a limited degree, the profit motive and price setting through the instrument of a market system. In fact, both communism and socialism seem to be drawing toward capitalism in many respects, while the latter, because of growing government regulation, is beginning to acquire some aspects of socialism.

The Chapter in Brief

The institution of government arises from humanity's need for social order. When social control can no longer be administered within the family because of the size and complexity of a society, some kind of body with the authority to make decisions binding on the society becomes essential.

To be acceptable to members of society, government must have authority. Authority may have a basis in tradition, in reason and the law, or in the charisma of a leader. Authority may be defined as legitimate power. Power is the ability of one person or group to influence the behavior of another person or group in a desired direction. Force or the threat of force underlies power.

Government is process, but the state is the formal abstract structure representing government. Its elements are territory, population, government, and sovereignty. The state's chief aim is to impose organized political control over its citizens, and it can do so because it has a monopoly over the legitimate use of force within its territory.

The organization of societies into nation–states is a comparatively recent event in history. A central government that oversees a particular territory in which people have similar characteristics develops a sense of unity and nationhood. Nationalism is the ideology behind the nation–state; it may be defined as a set of beliefs about the superiority of one's own nation and a defense of its interests above all others.

Ideologies—which underlie social movements and forms of government—are systems of ideas that are rational, intelligible, and organized into a logical pattern of thought. The political systems of societies are all built on ideological structures, and the most important function of ideologies is to make the governors acceptable to the governed.

Political ideologies fall into either the autocratic or the democratic camp. The basis of autocratic ideologies is the belief that government should be in the hands of one or more individuals who have supreme power and are above the law. In modern times, traditional autocracies have been replaced by totalitarian regimes that offer prescriptions for a lifestyle with implications in all facets of life. Fascism and Nazism are two such totalitarian ideologies of the right.

A totalitarian ideology of the left that enjoyed wide popularity in the twentieth century, but now seems to be on the wane, is communism. Its main thrust is the establishment of an egalitarian society. Its founder was Karl Marx, who based the ideology on materialism, or the notion that people's conditions and beliefs were determined by economic relationships. Although Marx was accurate and perspicacious on many points, he was also wrong on a number of them: where the revolution would occur, how nationalistic workers would be, and the course of capitalism.

Democracy is the ideology most directly opposed to autocracy. Its primary concerns are the individual and his or her rights. It postulates that individuals are by nature rational, moral, equal, free, and endowed with certain rights. As a result, in its political system, the state and its government are considered mere instruments and act as trustees of delegated power. Capitalism is a subideology in the area of the economy. Its central features include the private ownership of property, the existence of a profit motive, the dynamics of a free market, and the presence of competition. Today's capitalistic economies are usually called mixed economies because of the government controls and regulations that have become mandatory.

Democratic socialism assumes that participation in political decision making should be extended to economic decision making. Additional assumptions are that major national industries should be publicly held, the profit motive and excessive competition are against the public good, higher priority should be given to public needs than to private wants, extensive national planning would avoid the production of frivolous goods and services in favor of necessities, only a small income differential should exist, and a comprehensive welfare state should eradicate special privileges.

Terms to Remember

authority   Power over, or control of, individuals that is socially accepted as right and proper.

authoritarianism   A type of autocracy (see below) in which power is held by an absolute monarch, dictator, or small elite. Power is limited to the political sphere.

autocracy   An ideology directly opposed to democracy, in which government rests in the hands of one individual or group who holds supreme power over the people.

charismatic authority   According to Max Weber, a type of authority based on the leadership of a person with charisma. A charismatic leader is thought to possess special gifts of a magnetic, fascinating, and extraordinary nature.

communism   A political and economic ideology whose ultimate goal is total government control of the economy and total income redistribution, leading to the creation of a classless society.

democracy   An ideology, philosophy, theory, and political system assuming the basic value of the individual, as well as his or her rationality, morality, equality, and possession of specific rights.

democratic capitalism   A blend of political and economic ideology whose tenets include the private ownership of property, the profit motive, a free market economy, and competition. The function of government in this system is to ensure that the economic game is played fairly.

democratic socialism   A blend of political and economic ideology whose chief assumption is that participation in political decision making should be extended to economic decision making. The function of the government in this system is to control and guide the economy for the benefit of the voters who elected it.

fascism   A totalitarian ideology of the right that became prominent in various nations beginning in Italy under Benito Mussolini.

government   A pivotal institution arising out of the need to maintain order, control, organize, protect, and defend the people of a society. Government is the acting arm of the state; it includes a political process in which a body of representatives is endowed with authority and power to make and carry out decisions for the society and see to it that order is maintained and laws are obeyed.

ideology A system of ideas, values, beliefs, and attitudes that a society or groups within a society share and accept as true.

legal-rational authority According to Weber, a type of authority accepted by members of society because it is based on rational methods and laws and is exerted for their benefit.

nation A culture group residing within the territory of a political state.

nationalism The ideology behind the nation–state. A set of beliefs about the superiority of one's own nation and a defense of its interest above all others.

Nazism The German version of fascism that flourished under the leadership of Adolf Hitler.

politics The people and processes that make up and direct the government of the state, its policies, and its actions.

power The probability that one individual in a social relationship will carry out his or her own will despite resistance. The ability of one person or group to direct the behavior of another person or group in a desired direction, under the ultimate, though not always obvious, threat of force.

rule of law A constitutional principle holding that those in public authority derive, maintain, and exercise their powers on the basis of specific laws, and not on the basis of their personal power.

state The abstract embodiment, or the symbol, of the political institution or government.

totalitarianism A type of autocracy of the left or of the right, characterized by a totalist ideology, a single party, a government-controlled secret police, and a monopoly over mass communications, weapons, and the economy by the ruling elite.

traditional authority According to Weber, authority that is based on reverence for tradition.

Suggested Readings

Busky, Donald F. 2000. *Democratic Socialism: A Global Survey*. New York: Praeger Publishers. An in-depth, well-referenced, and up-to-date analysis of the history of social democratic parties and governments worldwide from their beginnings in the nineteenth century to the present.

deTocqueville, Alexis. 1969 [orig. 1834–1840]. *Democracy in America*. Garden City, NY: Doubleday/Anchor. A classic examination of the new political system and the new society of the United States as viewed by an aristocratic Frenchman on a journey in the 1830s. His insights are as sharp now as when he wrote them.

Kershaw, Ian and Moshe Lewin, eds. 2004. *Stalinism and Nazism: Dictatorships in Comparison*. New York: Cambridge University Press. Two historians who specialize in Nazism and Stalinism summarize the research on those political movements. In addition, they provide new perspectives on these two dictatorships of the modern era: the cult of personality, the war machine, and the changed attitudes in postwar Germany and Russia.

Lieberthal, Kenneth. 1995. *Governing China: From Revolution through Reform*. New York: W. W. Norton. An overview of the changes undergone by this ancient nation, with a focus on the continuity from imperial times through the communist revolution and beyond.

Lind, Michael. 1995. *The Next American Nation*. New York: The Free Press. Subtitled "The New Nationalism and the Fourth American Revolution," this book proclaims to be the manifesto of American liberal nationalism, which the author defines as a prescription for prosperity and justice based on a "cultural fusion and genetic amalgamation . . . for Americans of all races."

Malia, Martin. 1994. *The Soviet Tragedy: A History of Socialism in Russia, 1917–1991*. New York: The Free Press. See also: Pipes, Richard. 1994. *Russia under the Bolshevik Regime*. New York: Knopf.

These two books offer analyses and interpretations of the ideology of communism as it was lived in Soviet Russia, that is, from the Russian Revolution to the dismantling of the Soviet system.

Service, Robert. 2007. *Comrades! A History of World Communism*. Cambridge, MA: Harvard University Press. A survey of the varieties of Communist ideologies and regimes, illustrating the patterns that make up totalitarianism. A controversial, but engaging introduction to this important modern movement.

Taha, Abir. 2005. *Nietzsche, Prophet of Nazism: The Cult of the Superman*. New York: AuthorHouse. A philosophical look at the roots of Nazism with discussions relative to the belief in Aryanism, a doctrine of racial superiority.

The Government of the United States of America

IN THIS CHAPTER, YOU WILL LEARN

- *the historical sequence in the establishment of American political institutions;*
- *about the implications of the executive branch;*
- *the weaknesses of the legislative branch;*
- *the functions of the judicial branch; and*
- *the importance of limited government.*

We hold these truths to be self-evident, that all men are created equal, that they are endowed by their Creator with certain inalienable Rights, that among these are Life, Liberty and the pursuit of Happiness.

We the People of the United States, in Order to form a more perfect Union, establish Justice, insure domestic Tranquility, provide for the common Defence, promote the general Welfare, and secure the Blessings of Liberty to ourselves and our Posterity, do ordain and establish this Constitution for the United States of America.

Every American schoolchild is familiar with at least some of these words. They have become the myths with which we clothe parts of our history. Their sound evokes an emotional response, just like the American flag waving on the Fourth of July. The words, of course, are part of the documents we hold sacred, the Declaration of Independence and the Constitution of the United States. As familiar as they are to us, the posterity mentioned in the preamble to the Constitution, few of us are likely to have thought much about what such documents mean, and especially what they meant then, when they were written. For indeed they were spectacular for their times, and the political system that was spawned by the ideology behind them, cumbersome and inefficient as it may be, has served American society quite well for more than 200 years. That is a record few societies have been able to equal.

From Chapter 16 of *Contemporary Society: An Introduction to Social Science,* Thirteenth Edition. John A. Perry, Erna K. Perry. Copyright © 2012 by Pearson Education, Inc. All rights reserved.

The emergence of the United States as a nation goes back to 1776, at the time of the Declaration of Independence. Until that time, as is well known, the settled territories of the New World had been merely colonies of Great Britain. Claiming a "long train of abuses and usurpations," and accusing the king of Great Britain of absolute despotism, the representatives of the colonists resolved to "dissolve the bonds which have connected them with another, and to assume, among the powers of the earth, the separate and equal station to which the Laws of Nature and of Nature's God entitle them." In other words, the decision was made to establish a separate, sovereign nation–state. This did not happen until the 13 independent states were joined into a union, when the Articles of Confederation were ratified by all the states in 1781. The U.S. government itself began to function only when the Constitution was ratified by a sufficient number of states in 1788 and George Washington was inaugurated as the first president the following year (see Figure 1 for the differences between government under the Articles of Confederation and government under the U.S. Constitution).

A Comparison Between Federalism and Confederation

Government under the Articles of Confederation
1781–1788

Central Government

State

State

The People

The People

The Confederation was a union of states—the central government received authority from the states and had no direct authority over the people

Government under the U.S. Constitution:
(Federal System) 1789–present

The Constitution of the United States of America

National Government

The People

The States

FIGURE 1   The federal union is a union of *people,* that is, both the national government and state governments receive authority from the people (through their vote) and exercise direct authority over them through legislation.

Most of the principles by which we still govern ourselves were outlined at the Constitutional Convention of 1787.

The Constitutional Convention

With the exception of political parties, all the political institutions of the United States were conceived and delineated at the Constitutional Convention of 1787. As the colonies had just fought a war to free themselves from dependence on a British monarch, it was understood by all the delegates that the government to be established would be republican in nature and based on popular support. However, although these ideas struck a positive chord in many people, there was much suspicion and cynicism among the delegates about the validity of this new ideology. Could it be translated into a political instrument that would not disintegrate into mob rule?

The delegates were also dissatisfied with the weak central government that had existed under the Articles of Confederation—the first document drawn up after the Declaration of Independence—which envisioned a loose confederation of independent states. At that time, the colonists had no vision of a unified nation. They thought that each of the 13 states was too different from its neighbors and that the huge continent still to be settled did not lend itself to unity. They were fearful that a republic that covered such a vast geographic area could not survive. During the Revolutionary War, each state assumed the powers of a sovereign nation and jealously guarded its independence. The Articles of Confederation did establish a central government, but it was a very weak one and, in the long run, unworkable. The failures of the Articles of Confederation led many citizens to insist that a new constitution was needed.

What Is a Constitution?

The object of every revolution is to institute a new political order. After the American Revolution, it became apparent that a new agreement was needed between the governors and the governed that would reflect the new values, interests, and beliefs of the community.

To most people, the word *constitution* suggests a specific written document drawn up in the past to guide political procedures. However, a constitution need not exist in a written form. The term, and especially its adjective, *constitutional,* has a particular meaning and a strict connotation. The term is reserved to describe a government that is subject to **limitations** and that operates in accordance with general rules rather than arbitrarily. In other words, the existence of a constitution places a system of effective restraints on political power.

The idea of a written constitution became popular during the revolutionary struggles that accompanied the formation of many nation–states. Today, most of the so-called developed nations have written constitutions. Ironically, Great Britain, where many of the ideas of **constitutional government** originated, does not have a written constitution. The principles and concepts of its constitution are contained in ordinary laws and statutes, as well as in the Magna Carta, the great charter outlining certain liberties due British subjects.

Constitutions establish a framework for government. They limit the power of the government by stating the bounds of its authority. They provide specific procedures for governmental action—and, by implication, forbid other actions. The governed are guaranteed protection against possibly arbitrary actions of the governors. The ultimate authority is vested in the law: The law is supreme over governors and governed alike.

Box 1   The Constitutional Convention

In writing the Declaration of Independence, Thomas Jefferson was influenced by the English philosopher John Locke. Locke, in his *Second Treatise on Government,* maintained that it was absurd for people to continue being ruled by the "divine right" of kings, or hereditary aristocracies that were not subject to control by the people. He suggested that legitimate government could be established only by the people themselves, and that such government could exist only by their consent.

In their resolution to develop a system of government that would represent the common good of each person and the interest of each state, the representatives of the 13 states may be considered true revolutionaries. The signers of the Constitution have been accused of plotting to preserve the interests of their (high) social class. They were, after all, wealthy landowners and professionals, as well as merchants and budding industrialists, and their privileged status in society was beginning to be challenged by the new economic system imported from Britain, industrialism. Some of them may have felt that a strong central government would stop the grumbling of the small farmers and the new industrial workers flocking to the cities. And certainly not all were convinced of the desirability of a government based on the consent of the governed (democracy) rather than one based on the rule of a landed, wealthy elite (aristocracy).

Some historians have claimed that merchants and businessmen, who constituted an ascending social class in the colonies at that time (in the 1780s), wanted a strong national government so that industry and trade would be promoted, private property would be protected, and the public debt—of which they were the creditors—would be paid off (Current et al., 1983, 170). Other historians have maintained that the motives of the framers were much less mercenary; but even if their motives were not monolithic, it is indeed true that, as a class, the framers were the wealthiest and would have had a greater concern for maintaining the status quo than the general population.

Although greater equality and popular participation in government, the main principles of democracy, were not what the leaders of the American Revolution had in mind, the winds of change were in the air, the Revolution having set loose some egalitarian and democratizing tendencies that it was too late to inhibit. Whether or not the convention was called primarily to preserve power or the status quo, the need for a written constitution that would lay the foundation for a new, workable type of government was soon established. This Constitution was rapidly approved by almost all the states, and suffrage on the issue was widely held. It appears that constitutional principles were accepted by the general population, including small farmers and artisans, and the minutes of the convention do not point to any maneuverings for maintaining the status quo. Again, there is no doubt that some representatives were committed to protecting the rights of a wealthy minority, but the chief concern of the large number of those present was for a government that would survive and be functional while serving the interests of all groups in the society.

The so-called rule of law is an important principle of constitutionality. (It is in direct opposition to the "rule of men" that prevails in most autocratic regimes.) This principle holds that those in public authority derive, maintain, and exercise their powers on the basis of laws specifically drawn up and not on the basis of a leader's will. Consequently, every act of an elected or appointed official is carried out under the authority of the law and is subject to the judgment of appropriate legal authorities.

The Constitution of the United States

The Constitution that underlies the American political system similarly imposes restraints on the government. The four major constitutional principles of American government, for instance, are (1) federalism, (2) separation of power and checks and balances, (3) judicial supremacy, and (4) limited government. Federalism ensures a dispersal of power because it is a system in which state governments retain supremacy in certain constitutionally specified areas (states' rights), and the national government retains supremacy in others. Political power is also dispersed by its separation into three branches: the legislative, the executive, and the judicial. The Constitution establishes a judiciary system that is topped by the U.S. Supreme Court. The latter constitutes a further restraint on political power because it functions as the final authority in interpreting the meaning of the Constitution. Finally, political power is limited by the fact that the Constitution grants individuals some rights and liberties that are outside the control of the government.

Federalism

One of the most important contributions of the Constitution to American government—as well as a peculiarly American invention—has been the system we call federalism. This system is contrasted with a **unitary** form, in which political power is centralized in a national government, and with the **confederate** form, in which political power belongs ultimately to the governments of the individual states. **Federalism** may be defined as a system of distributing political power between a central national government and the governments of the geographic regions into which the nation is divided—in the case of the United States, individual states. The power of each is supreme in its own area. The allocation of power is outlined in the Constitution and may be altered only by a constitutional amendment, a process in which both the national government and the individual states are equally involved (see the constitutional limits and obligations outlined in Box 2).

In theory, at least, the state governments in a federal system are not subordinate to the central government. They are sovereign in certain areas of jurisdiction and share sovereignty, power, and responsibility for decision making with the central government in many other areas. The Tenth Amendment to the Constitution delineates the powers allocated to the national government and to the states. It specifies that those powers not delegated specifically to the U.S. government by the Constitution, and not prohibited by it, are **residual or reserved powers** for the states or the people.

The United States, in reality, has a great many governments. Not only is there a national (central) government, but there are also governments in each of the 50 states and, in addition, thousands of smaller governmental units within the states, such as counties, cities, towns and townships, special districts, and school districts. All these governments have a special relationship to each other. State governments can create, change, or abolish the smaller governments of counties, cities, towns, and special districts. State governments, then, are more independent and more powerful than the smaller governments and together with the national government form the basis of the federal system.

Box 2 Constitutional Limits and Obligations

Both the national government and the state governments are subject to certain restraints mandated by the Constitution. These limits are necessary for federalism to work. For instance, states are prohibited from:

- making treaties with foreign governments;
- coining money, issuing bills of credit, or making anything but gold and silver coin a tender in payment of debts; or
- authorizing a private person to interfere with the shipping and commerce of other nations.

Without the consent of Congress, states cannot:

- tax imports or exports;
- tax foreign ships;
- keep troops or ships in time of peace (except for the National Guard);
- enter into alliances or compacts with other states or foreign nations that would increase the political power in the states, which might interfere with the supremacy of the national government; or
- engage in war, unless invaded or in such danger as to make any delay perilous (and, the invasion of one state is equivalent to an invasion of the whole United States).

The national government, on the other hand, guarantees to each state:

- a republican form of government;
- protection against domestic insurrection; and
- that it will refrain from exercising its powers in such a way as to interfere with the state's ability to perform its responsibilities (today, such protection derives from the political process; that is, from the fact that representatives elected from the states participate in the decisions of Congress, thus protecting states' rights and interests).

States also have certain obligations to one another that the Constitution spells out:

- *Full Faith and Credit:* Article IV of the Constitution requires that each state recognize (give full faith and credit) the public records, public acts, and civil judicial proceedings of every other state. This means that if you marry in one state, you are considered married in every state, and if you have a driver's license in one state you can drive in every other state (although if you decide to reside in a different state, eventually you will have to obtain a license in the state of your residence).
- *Extradition:* Because most criminal law is state law, most crimes perpetrated are committed against the state, not the national government. Nonetheless, states are charged by the Constitution to return a person who has committed a crime in another state to that state for trial or imprisonment. This provision prevents criminals from simply escaping to neighboring states to avoid prosecution.
- *Privileges and Immunities:* The Constitution requires each state to provide all privileges and immunities offered to its own residents to all citizens who happen to be in that state. This provision was meant to prevent states from discriminating against persons from other states: If you travel to New York State and you are from Nevada, you still pay the same sales tax as New York State residents, and the police are obliged to offer protection to you. (But there are exceptions: Only residents of a particular state can vote in that state's elections, and students attending schools in a state in which they do not permanently reside pay higher tuition at that state's universities.)

How Federalism Has Worked

The federal system has worked particularly well in countries of a large size, with considerable regional differences, and with a number of different racial and ethnic groups. The heterogeneity of such a country makes a unitary form of government impractical. And the federal system has a number of advantages. Under a federal system, government is closer to the people. It is possible for many to become personally involved in the numerous agencies of local governments. Also, administrative functions are decentralized because the national government shares with the state governments the responsibility for the implementation and direction of many programs (the Interstate Highway System is one example). In addition, the states act as proving grounds, where both legislation and legislators may be tried for effectiveness without involving the entire nation.

Of course, federalism also has its disadvantages. Chief among these is the existence of a complex bureaucracy with numerous agencies quibbling and squabbling about the extent of their authority and their share of resources. A further problem is the inequality with which some programs that have been made the responsibility of the states are administered by the different states. Not only does each state place different values on various programs and carry them out accordingly, but often how well a program is carried out depends on the resources of the state. Education and welfare programs are particularly dependent on the resources of the individual states. A predominantly rural, sparsely populated state allocates fewer funds to welfare and education than a large industrial state.

The nature of federalism and the way power has been allocated between the national government and the individual states has undergone a variety of changes during our history. In addition, because this allocation is not very clearly outlined in the Constitution, the Supreme Court has had to intervene on a number of occasions and so has had a hand in defining the federal system.

Trend toward Centralization

Partially to repair such inequities, the tendency has been for the national government to assume more and more of the responsibilities previously assigned to the states. To many, this tendency represents a usurpation of power, and they clamor for the restoration of states' rights. To others, the tendency is unavoidable and represents a welcome helping hand. Problems emerging from the urbanization and industrialization of the nation, such as overcrowding, unemployment, crime, pollution—to mention just the most visible ones—simply cannot be solved by state governments. Not only have most state governments until recently been dominated by rural elements opposed to city interests, but they also lack the financial resources and the professional expertise to solve such gigantic problems.

The federal government, on the other hand, has both huge resources and many departments whose staffs are trained in specific areas of health, education, policing, transportation, social welfare, and housing. And the president and Congress cannot turn deaf ears to the states' needs, because citizens of the states are the ones who vote them into office.

In many instances, the federal government has had to impose federal controls because of the inefficiency with which the states were meeting their obligations. An example is civil rights legislation. This legislation was imposed by the federal government on the states, through several acts of Congress, to compel the states to accept the Supreme Court's 1954 decision that racial segregation in the schools was unconstitutional. Another area in which the states lagged was consumer protection. This lag prompted the federal government to pass legislation making its own agencies responsible for maintaining standards of meat inspection, automobile safety, truth in packaging and lending, and many other areas, including water and air quality.

The Impact of the Federal Government

The federal government has its greatest impact on state and local governments in the funds it makes available through numerous **grant-in-aid** programs. These grants originally consisted of public land, but now they are in the form of cash. Today, federal grants help build and maintain highways, airports, hospitals, libraries, health programs, the Social Security system, public education, vocational education, public housing, crime control, and welfare. The purpose of these grants is to equalize the services that rich and poor states are able to provide for their residents. These grants have also revitalized some state programs, especially where funds are shared in some proportion between state and federal governments.

The system of grants, however, has been criticized. In granting aid, the federal government has the right to specify in detail how and for what purpose local governments can use federal funds. It has been proposed that a better way of sharing revenues would be for the

The Government of the United States of America

One of the areas in which federalism has been successful is the interstate highway system: the federal government provides funding for its construction and maintenance, as do the governments of individual states.

federal government to return a given percentage of the revenues it collects in taxes to the states. Revenue sharing on a small scale was started in the early 1970s. This system also has problems, however, particularly in allocation and control. These problems may damage some segments of a state's population, most probably the urban poor.

Despite the trend toward centralization, there is cooperation among all levels of government. Local, state, and federal agencies cooperate in an almost endless number of activities. Examples of such cooperation may be found in the Social Security system, the Selective Service, the National Guard, and so on. The federal government has also experimented with trying to solve problems on a regional level. One such experiment, and a successful one, is the Tennessee Valley Authority (TVA), which develops the resources in the area of the Tennessee River basin. Because it seems to be the most workable system for a large, heterogeneous nation faced with many problems, such cooperative federalism is likely to continue to exist.

A turn toward conservatism in the U.S. political arena began in the 1990s. This trend included exhortations by a number of political leaders to return more power to the states. Of course, power carries with it the responsibility for the economic well-being of the states, which would revert to their citizens. Republican legislators resumed arguing the "states' rights" position, citing the Tenth Amendment to the Constitution as the instrument that limits the national government to its appropriate role in American society.

Separation of Powers

The principle of **separation of powers** is prescribed by the Constitution and provides for the legislative, executive, and judicial functions to be divided among three separate branches of government. That is, one branch formulates and enacts laws, another sees that the laws are carried out, and a third determines whether the laws are in agreement with the Constitution.

The principle of separation of powers was not new to the writers of the Constitution. It had been expressed by a number of thinkers of the time, particularly John Locke and Charles Montesquieu. These thinkers maintained that it was too tempting for frail human nature to allow too much power to accumulate in one body of government. In particular, persons entrusted to make laws should not also be allowed to execute them.

The three branches cannot be absolutely separate. Legislators are not the only ones who make laws, the president is not the only one who executes them, and the courts are not the only ones who pass judgment. If this were not the case, the government could not act at all: The president might refuse to enforce a law passed by Congress, Congress might refuse to accept the pronouncement of the Court, and the system would be deadlocked. Consequently, another principle, that of **checks and balances,** was incorporated to ensure that the three governmental branches can check on and balance one another. A degree of independence for each is assured by some processes, whereas a great deal of interdependence is assured by others. For example, the president's powers relating to Congress are limited, in that the president cannot remove any members of Congress or shorten or lengthen their terms of office. In turn, the powers of Congress are limited in relation to the executive branch, in that Congress cannot remove a president from office except by impeachment, a difficult and unpleasant process. The judicial branch is independent of the other two in that appointment to the Supreme Court is for life. Also, Supreme Court pronouncements on constitutional principles are binding on both the president and Congress. However, the Court is dependent on the other two branches in that appointments to it are made by the president with the advice and consent of the Senate.

In short, the principle of separation of powers does not really separate powers so much as it provides that they be shared, for each branch is involved directly with the workings of the other two. In such a situation, responsibility for public policy is difficult to pinpoint. For a comparison of the American system of separation of powers and the British parliamentary system, in which responsibility is concentrated, see Figure 2.

How Checks and Balances Work

Each decision-making body of the government is brought to office by a different constituency. The president is elected by all the citizens of the nation who meet certain requirements. House members are elected by the voters of congressional districts. Senate members are elected by the voters of individual states. And members of the Supreme Court are appointed by the president with Senate approval. The lengths of terms of office are also different for the three branches, and they do not coincide with one another. Consequently, it is impossible to renew the entire government at any one time.

Each of the three bodies has the ability to check on the decisions of the others. Congress is divided into two houses (a condition called bicameralism), each of which has absolute veto power over the other. Bills cannot become law without the approval of both the House and the Senate. Congress is granted legislative or law-making powers, but the president is supposed to recommend and initiate legislation. Although the president has the power to veto proposed legislation, this veto can be overridden by a two-thirds majority of both houses of Congress. It is congressional legislation that allocates power to the executive branch. Although the president is given power in military and foreign affairs, the approval of two-thirds of the Senate is necessary for the signing of treaties. Finally, presidential programs depend on Congress for funds.

Once they are installed on the bench, Supreme Court members are quite independent. Appointment, however, is made by the president with the advice and consent of the Senate. Congress, in addition, may vary the number of justices and exert a degree of control over the cases heard by the Court. The justices are also subject to impeachment. In turn, the Court can

A Comparison of the American System of Separation of Powers and the British Parliamentary System

The American System of Separation of Powers

The British Parliamentary System of Concentration of Responsibility

FIGURE 2

invalidate both presidential actions and congressional legislation that are deemed contrary to the Constitution. This last power, called judicial review, is not specifically authorized by the Constitution but is now interpreted as being implied by it.

Criticism of the Separation of Powers

Criticisms of the system of separation of powers range from the fact that it is cumbersome, unwieldy, and slow to the fact that diffusion and fragmentation of authority make it easy to "pass the buck." These characteristics, moreover, lead to a tendency to maintain the status quo because changes occur so slowly and painfully. There is also a certain degree of governmental powerlessness in instances when legislation is opposed by important private-interest groups. Sometimes the system seems to be confused and lack purpose. On the other hand, the system does provide more stability than many parliamentary systems, in which the legislative branch is the most important and a government crisis can cause the parliament to call for new elections.

The Presidency: The Executive Branch

The office of the presidency emerged from the Constitutional Convention only after much discussion. At that time, there existed no models on which to pattern the presidency. Most contemporary governments were unacceptable to the recently independent Americans. The old Greek and Roman republics offered models of multiple leadership in committee-like organizations. But these, too, were feared by the representatives as tending to paralyze action. What finally took shape as the office of the chief executive included the following features: (1) there was to be only one chief executive; (2) the executive was ensured a four-year term that could be terminated only by death or impeachment; (3) the electoral base for the presidency would be independent of Congress; and (4) the executive was to be provided with certain constitutional powers independent of Congress, the electors, the people, and the states.

The Nature of the Presidency

Many points were left unanswered and undefined by the delegates at the Constitutional Convention. Consequently, the office has continued to evolve and take shape with each individual president. Although it has been said that the power of the office depends more on the president's capacities as a persuader than on real authority, presidential impact on the population of the United States is considerable. It is also generally felt that the office has grown in strength and prestige to a greater extent than the other two branches of government. As a result of involvement in Vietnam, which began as a presidential action without the consent of Congress, and other actions that have been interpreted as excesses of presidential privilege, a movement to curb presidential power emerges occasionally.

Traditionally, much has depended on the personality of the president. Individual presidents seem to mold the office to fit their perception of it. There have been presidents who believed that they had no authority outside that specifically granted them by the Constitution. There have been others who believed that the president could do anything to fulfill the needs of the nation, unless it was specifically forbidden by the Constitution or by the laws of the country. Others still have taken what is commonly called a caretaker's role: They have considered their job to be a purely administrative one. As a rule, history has tended to honor the active, dynamic presidents who have become actual political leaders of the nation. (See the following list of all the American presidents and their party affiliations).

In his roles as head of state and chief diplomat, a U.S. president must present a powerful as well as a glamorous image to the world. Here, among pomp and circumstance, the first couple entertain the Indian Prime Minister and his wife.

American Presidents, 1789–2008

Name	Party	Birth/Death	Term
1. George Washington	Federalist	1732–1799	1789–1797
2. John Adams	Federalist	1735–1826	1797–1801
3. Thomas Jefferson	Democratic-Republican	1743–1826	1801–1809
4. James Madison	Democratic-Republican	1741–1836	1809–1817
5. James Monroe	Democratic-Republican	1748–1831	1817–1825
6. John Quincy Adams	Democratic-Republican	1767–1848	1825–1829
7. Andrew Jackson	Democrat	1767–1845	1829–1837
8. Martin Van Buren	Democrat	1782–1862	1837–1841
9. William Henry Harrison	Whig	1773–1841	1841
10. John Tyler	Whig	1790–1862	1841–1845
11. James K. Polk	Democrat	1795–1849	1845–1849
12. Zachary Taylor	Whig	1784–1850	1849–1850
13. Millard Fillmore	Whig	1800–1874	1850–1853
14. Franklin Pierce	Democrat	1804–1869	1853–1857
15. James Buchanan	Democrat	1791–1868	1857–1861
16. Abraham Lincoln	Republican	1809–1865	1861–1865
17. Andrew Johnson	Democrat	1808–1875	1865–1869
18. Ulysses S. Grant	Republican	1822–1885	1869–1877
19. Rutherford B. Hayes	Republican	1822–1893	1877–1881

4. **Chief Diplomat or Foreign Policy Maker.** This is probably the president's most important role. The president is the official channel of communication between the United States and foreign nations, even though appointments to diplomatic posts and the signing of treaties require congressional approval. The president is also Commander in Chief of the Armed Forces, although the Constitution grants Congress the power to raise armies and declare war. Thus, a president can react to a war situation speedily and without the prior approval of Congress. In the eyes of some critics, certain presidents have abused this power (by initiating or escalating conflicts in North Korea, Vietnam, Cambodia, Libya, Kosovo, Afghanistan, and Iraq). This role has been a major point of contention, which Congress attempted to solve in 1973 by passing the War Powers Resolution. Under this resolution, the president must consult with Congress in every possible instance before involving U.S. troops in hostilities; must notify Congress within 48 hours of having committed troops; and cannot hold troops in any foreign intervention for more than 60 days without congressional approval.

5. **Party Leader.** Upon being nominated a candidate for the presidency, the nominee assumes the title of leader of the party, even though involvement in party politics may have been minimal up to this point. This title is retained by the president, whose statements on party policy become authoritative. The president is instrumental in carrying out the party platform, and the national party organization is under close presidential supervision. However, state and local party organizations remain largely outside presidential control.

The numerous roles of the president force the chief executive to be a kind of jack-of-all-trades. As for the presidential role envisioned by the writers of the Constitution, it is obvious that their intent has been reversed. Whereas they had conceived the office as a device for minimizing personal power, in effect, the office tends to maximize it. One reason for this is simple: in time of crisis, when swift and effective leadership is called for, the cumbersome apparatus of Congress tends to be anything but dynamic.

Congress: The Legislative Branch

The major function of the legislative branch is to *enact legislation* binding on the entire nation. Because of its two-chamber structure, the interests of the members' states and districts, and legislation proposed by the executive branch, enacting legislation is a slow and painful process involving compromise and negotiation. For this process to be fair, input from a variety of interests must be taken into account. Thus, the second function of the legislative branch is to ensure a system of *representation*. The third function of the legislative branch is *oversight*, which means that it must supervise and investigate the manner in which the legislative bureaucracy is carrying out and implementing the laws Congress mandated.

The delegates to the Constitutional Convention wanted to make sure that the new system of government would include some sort of popular representative assembly. The difficulty lay in reaching an agreement on how best to protect the interests of the wealthy minority against the impulsiveness and excesses of the common people, who constituted the majority. Further, the delegates needed to reconcile equitably the interests of the heavily populated states with those of the sparsely populated ones. A compromise was finally struck in which the House of Representatives was to be the forum for the people of the entire nation and the Senate the forum of the states and of minorities.

As to how the people would actually be represented, two alternatives were open to the delegates. They could devise a system of representation based on geography, in which each legislator represented a group of persons living in the same area. Or they could follow the parliamentary system, in which the population was divided politically and each legislator represented a group of persons sharing the same political orientation and living in the same geographic area. The first alternative, which the delegates ultimately chose, is called the single-member constituency system. The second is called the proportional representation system.

Again, reality today is not what was envisioned by the founders. Conflicts between large and small states have not occurred, but a situation did arise in the Senate in which the more populated states were underrepresented while the sparsely populated states were widely over-represented. Whether the Senate truly represents minorities and whether the House of Representatives really represents the people on a national scale are also debatable issues.

The Issue of Representation

The Constitution leaves the manner of election of representatives to the individual states. The state legislatures chose to divide the states into congressional districts for elections. Because in the course of time these districts became populated by different numbers of people, rural districts tended to be overrepresented and urban and suburban districts tended to be underrepresented in the House. Beginning in 1962, however, reapportionment has been correcting this situation. Districts must now be reapportioned every 10 years, after the Census. However, the manner in which members of Congress are chosen prompts some scholars to contend that Congress represents not "the people" but "some people," namely local elites who tend to exert influence on national decision making. And as a general rule, members of Congress tend to be concerned not with the general public welfare but only with the welfare of those in their districts.

The issue of representation is further clouded by the apathy of congressional constituents, less than half of whom even know their congressional representative's name or how he or she votes on any given legislation. In the past, studies have shown that members of Congress did not seem to represent the feelings of most of their constituents, especially in the sphere of foreign relations and social welfare. The conclusion may be drawn that, except on the subject of civil rights, members of Congress are unaware of their constituents' preferences, and constituents are unaware of their representatives' voting behavior, even on major issues. It may be inferred, then, that only a politically active, interested minority of constituents is usually influential.

Because Congress is the body charged with making laws, it is only natural that its main function is to debate public issues. In the Senate, the relatively small number of members (100) permits a semblance of free debate, but the large number of representatives in the House does not. Thus, the **House Rules Committee** determines the specific time allotted for the debate of important legislation, and time is then divided equally between the two parties. Because of this function, the Rules Committee is very powerful. It determines whether motions and amendments may be made, and this power is sometimes extended to include decisions about the merits of certain legislation. Bargains may be struck between proponents of a bill and chairpersons of legislative committees to have certain objectionable items deleted from a bill before a rule is granted as to the procedure to be followed in the debate of proposed legislation. This situation, so accommodating to brokerage politics, has been somewhat improved with the adoption of a fixed set of procedural rules. Another improvement is that the membership of the committee has been enlarged to break its former control by Southern conservatives.

Congressional Committees

Debate is only one step in enacting legislation. Most of the tedious deliberations regarding the purpose of the legislation and how best to have it passed, the language in which to frame it, and other points of this nature are delegated to committees, which are, in effect, subgroups of Congress, or legislatures in miniature. They have the responsibility for controlling the flow of legislation. Also, they deal with proposals according to their subject matter, and each committee is eventually expected to develop expertise in its subject.

Seniority Rule. The most controversial characteristic of congressional organization, and one that particularly affects the allocation of members to committees, is **seniority rule.** According to this hallowed rule, the chair of each committee goes without question to the member of the majority party who has served longest on the committee. The only way to attain a chair, then, is to outlast one's colleagues on the committee, hope that one is reelected several times, and pray that one's party is the majority party. Criticism of seniority rule has been voiced, particularly by the liberal segment of Congress, because its members have been, in the past, consistently overlooked for committee chairs in favor of Southern Democrats or Midwest Republicans. These used to be reelected term after term because of effective partisan machines in their congressional districts, but the hold of the Southern Democrats was broken by the election in 1994 of many Republicans, making the Republican Party the majority party in Congress. The Democrats regained a number of seats in the 2006 elections and are currently in the majority in the Senate. The Republicans regained control of the House in the 2010 election.

Another function of congressional committees is to serve as sounding boards for the interest groups or lobbies, agencies, and occasionally private individuals who attempt to influence committee members. In this role, congressional committees become brokers among different interest and power groups. They sift the tremendous amount of information that comes in and stem some of the pressures for or against a given legislative proposal.

A committee chairperson can manipulate hearings so that certain opinions are never given a forum at all. This procedure, together with filibustering and certain decisions of the Rules Committee, was used for years by the Southern conservatives in command of key committees to thwart civil rights legislation.

The organization of Congress leads to a certain degree of ineffectiveness. The older members cling to old traditions and demand deference from the younger members, and various committees exert a powerful influence and can often make or break proposed legislation. Soon after their election, the new members of Congress come to think of themselves as members of an elite group, which tends to interfere with their relationship with the constituents who elected them but strengthens the bonds with their fellow Congress members. Indeed, members of Congress do form quite an exclusive club, legislating for more than 300 million people. (See an organizational chart of the Senate in the 112th Congress in Figure 3 and a profile of the membership of the 112th Congress in Box 3.) Incoming members soon realize that if they do not abide by the rituals and traditions, their attempts at legislation will get nowhere. Thus, what emerges is brokerage politics, in which new members accommodate certain older key members and in exchange are nominated to important committees or are granted other favors.

The Subordinate Role of Congress

Critics have long said that the House responds 20 or 30 years after social problems arise, if at all. Younger members of Congress have been making renewed efforts to break away from outdated customs and irrelevant traditions and to restore initiative and a progressive outlook to the legislative body.

Although the Constitution gave Congress the potential for power, the role of Congress, especially in the fields of foreign relations and military affairs, has been a subordinate one. Most policy proposals tend to originate in the executive branch and from military and industrial pressure groups. As a result, the function of Congress has been one of acting on these

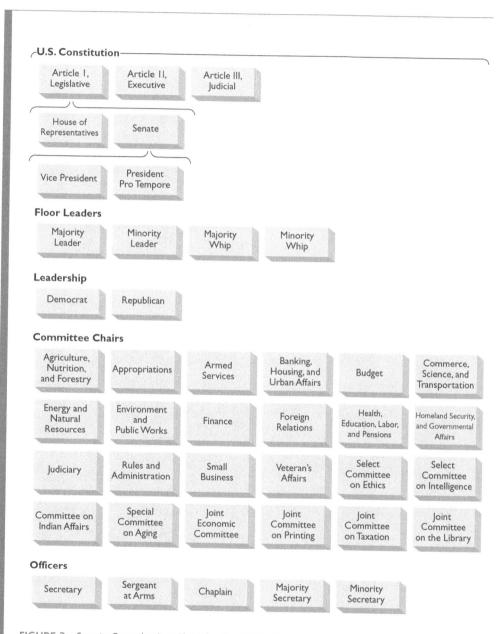

FIGURE 3 Senate Organization Chart for the 112th Congress.
Source: http://www.senate.gov/pagelayout/reference/e_one_on_teasers/org_chart.htm. Accessed 5/18/2007.

How a Bill Becomes Law

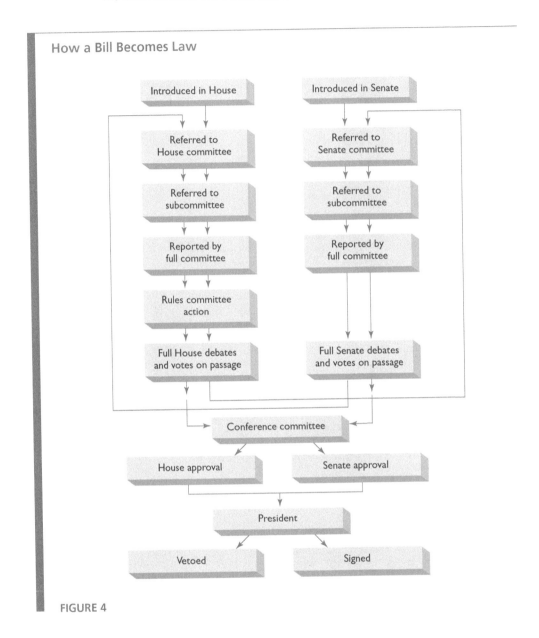

FIGURE 4

proposals, deliberating on their advantages and disadvantages, and finally accepting, rejecting, or modifying the proposed legislation. Figure 4 above illustrates how a bill becomes a law.

The very structure of Congress does not lend itself to effectiveness and efficiency. Swift action is constantly impeded and thwarted by the committee system and by pressures from opposing interest groups and different constituencies. Inertia in the legislative process is further encouraged by lack of adequate staffs that could help members of Congress make intelligent decisions on the issues that come before them. Another obstacle to effective action is the

Box 3 Membership of the 112th Congress: A Profile

Congress is composed of 540 individuals from the 50 states, as well as the District of Columbia, Puerto Rico, Guam, the U.S. Virgin Islands, and American Samoa.[1] This count assumes that no seat is temporarily vacant. The following is a profile of the 112th Congress.

Currently, in the House of Representatives, there are 199 Democrats (including five Delegates and the Resident Commissioner), 241 Republicans, and one vacant seat. The Senate has 51 Democrats, two Independents, who have aligned themselves with the Democrats, and 47 Republicans.

The average age of members of the House is 56.7, of the Senate is 62.2 years, at the convening of the 112th Congress; The U.S. Constitution requires Representatives to be at least 25 years old when they take office. The youngest Representative, as well as youngest member of Congress, is Aaron Schock (R-IL), 29. The oldest Representative is Ralph Hall (R-TX), 87.

Senators must be at least 30 years old when they take office. The youngest Senator is Senator Mike Lee (R-UT), who is 39. The oldest Senator is Frank Lautenberg (D-NJ) who is 87. The overwhelming majority of members have a college education: 99 percent of Senators and 92 percent of House Members. The dominant professions of members are public service/politics, business, medicine, and law. Protestants collectively constitute the majority religious affiliation of members (57 percent). Roman Catholics account for 29 percent of members, whereas numerous other affiliations are also represented.

The average length of service in the House, at the beginning of the Congress, is about 10 years (4.9 terms); in the Senate, 11.4 years (1.9 terms).

A record number of 92 women serve in the 112th Congress: 75 in the House, 17 in the Senate. There are 44 black or African-American members in the House, including 2 Delegates, and 1 black Senator. There are 31 Hispanic or Latino Members serving: 30 in the House, including the Resident Commissioner, and 1 in the Senate. 13 members (12 Representatives, and 1 Senator) are Asian, Indian American (Asian), or Native Hawaiian/other Pacific Islander. There is 1 American Indian (Native American), who serves in the House.

Foreign Born

Eight Representatives and one Senator were born outside the United States. Their places of birth include Cuba, Taiwan, Japan, Pakistan, Peru, and Canada.

Source: Congressional Research Service; CQ Roll Call Member Profiles.

fact that Congress cannot be, at the same time, responsive to the national interest and to the diverse interests of its constituents. Finally, because congressional members who displease their constituents or their seniors either fail to be reelected or have their projects defeated, the tendency against rocking the boat is strong. All these factors have in the course of time allowed Congress to be accused of no longer initiating laws but being content merely to approve or veto laws originating mainly in the White House.

The Supreme Court: The Judicial Branch

The Supreme Court was designed to represent a final bulwark against majority tyranny. It was also intended as a check on the representational aspect of Congress and on the independent aspect of the presidency. To that purpose, the Constitution has been interpreted as granting the Supreme Court the power of judicial review.

Judicial review is the ability to judge whether a specific presidential or congressional act or a given piece of state legislation conforms to the spirit and letter of the Constitution. In essence, it is the power to declare laws unconstitutional. This power, which is not explicit in the Constitution, has been criticized on the ground that it is inconsistent with democratic principles. It has been said that it gives undue power to the Supreme Court, whose members are not popularly elected and whose terms are for life (Table 1).

TABLE 1 Chief Justices of the Supreme Court of the United States, 1789–2007

Name	State App't From	Appointed by President	Judical Oath Taken	Date Service Terminated
Jay, John	New York	Washington	October 19, 1789	June 29, 1795
Rutledge, John	South Carolina	Washington	August 12, 1795	December 15, 1795
Ellsworth, Oliver	Connecticut	Washington	March 8, 1796	December 15, 1800
Marshall, John	Virginia	Adams, John	February 4, 1801	July 6, 1835
Taney, Roger Brooke	Maryland	Jackson	March 28, 1836	October 12, 1864
Chase, Salmon Portland	Ohio	Lincoln	December 15, 1864	May 7, 1873
Waite, Morrison Remick	Ohio	Grant	March 4, 1874	March 23, 1888
Fuller, Melville Weston	Illinois	Cleveland	October 8, 1888	July 4, 1910
White, Edward Douglass	Louisiana	Taft	December 19,1910	May 19,1921
Taft, William Howard	Connecticut	Harding	July 11, 1921	February 3, 1930
Hughes, Charles Evans	New York	Hoover	February 24, 1930	June 30, 1941
Stone, Harlan Fiske	New York	Roosevelt, F.	July 3, 1941	April 22, 1946
Vinson, Fred Moore	Kentucky	Truman	June 24, 1946	September 8, 1953
Warren, Earl	California	Eisenhower	October 5, 1953	June 23,1969
Burger, Warren Earl	Virginia	Nixon	June 23, 1969	September 26, 1986
Rehnquist, William H.	Virginia	Reagan	September 26, 1986	September 3, 2005
Roberts, John G.,Jr	Maryland	Bush, G. W.	September 29, 2005	

Source: http://www.supremecourtus.gov/about/members.pdf. Accessed 5/18/07

The specifics of judicial review were not made clear by the framers of the Constitution. The current interpretation of the principle stems from the classic decision in *Marbury v. Madison,* in which Chief Justice John Marshall set forth the following guidelines:

1. The Constitution is the supreme law of the land, binding on all three branches of government.
2. It is the deliberate intent of the Constitution to create a government with limited powers.
3. Therefore, any act of the legislature, either national or state, that is in violation of the Constitution is void.
4. It is definitely within the province of the judicial branch to interpret the law.
5. If a law is repugnant to the Constitution, and the matter comes before a court, its judges are bound to declare the law void in deference to the supremacy of the Constitution.

Although the principle of judicial review is a feature lacking in most other democracies, it has become a very important factor in American political life. In essence, it may be said that some of the nation's most relevant policy decisions have been made not by Congress or the executive branch but by the Court. And indeed, many of the Court's decisions were made to protect certain minorities, just as the framers of the Constitution had intended. Other decisions, according to critics, have had a much more political agenda. Table 2 lists other influential cases decided by the Supreme Court.

TABLE 2 The Most Influential Supreme Court Cases

Marbury v. Madison (1803)	Established the principle of judicial review
McCullough v. Maryland (1819)	Strengthened the power of the federal government over state governments
Dred Scott v. Sanford (1857)	Held that slaves were property and could never become citizens
Plessy v. Ferguson (1896)	Set forth the "separate but equal" doctrine
Brown v. Topeka Board of Education (1954)	Abolished the "separate but equal" doctrine, banning segregation in public schools
Miranda v. Arizona (1966)	Held that arresting officers must inform suspects of their rights
Roe v. Wade (1973)	Decided that women, under the right of privacy, had the freedom to choose abortion during the first three months of pregnancy

The Court System

The Constitution provides only for the inclusion of a Supreme Court as part of the national government. Congress establishes "inferior" or lower courts as they become necessary. Because of the federal form of government, the judicial system that has developed in the United States is complex. It includes a set of judicial hierarchies for each state in addition to the federal judicial hierarchy. In effect, each citizen is subject to two court systems, although the nature of each specific case determines whether the state or federal courts have jurisdiction. The federal courts are used in cases arising from any controversy involving the Constitution, the statutes and treaties of the United States, and admiralty and maritime law. Federal courts also have jurisdiction in cases involving ambassadors and members of the diplomatic corps, conflicts between states, and any controversy in which the United States is a party.

State courts, although not inferior to federal courts, have jurisdiction in cases arising from state constitutions and state statutes, as well as out of the common law of their state. As noted, both federal and state courts are arranged hierarchically and parallel one another. In the federal system, the lowest level is composed of 94 District Courts, each with a bench of up to 24 judges. It is at this level that prosecution brought by the Department of Justice usually begins because District Courts have jurisdiction over all cases tried under the laws and Constitution of the United States. The next level up is represented by 12 Courts of Appeal, each having three to nine judges. At the top is the Supreme Court. At one time, the Supreme Court was the forum for airing conflicts among sovereigns. Today, however, most cases it hears are appeals from rulings of lower courts. Cases may be appealed—or the Supreme Court may exercise its power to review the ruling of another court—through a writ of certiorari. This is basically an order by the Supreme Court to review the decision of a lower court. It can be issued at the discretion of the Court and requires the agreement of any four justices.

Functions of the Judicial System

One of the primary functions of the judicial system is to resolve conflict. Courts and judges hear and rule on disputes that are brought before them; they do not initiate these proceedings on the decision of a judge that a wrong has been committed. In other words, they decide only actual cases or controversies between parties, and they do so in adversary proceedings. The adversary system puts certain constraints on judges and courts. Although the latter have considerable power, they cannot use that power unless they are called to declare themselves. That is, although they have the ultimate ability to rule on what exactly is the law, they must wait passively until one party sues another, or the prosecution files a complaint, or the police arrest a criminal, before they can take any action.

Courts and judges guard and protect the legal system and the political structure. In this function, they administer the law, thus ensuring through such procedures as punishment, awarding damages, issuing orders, and overseeing the machinery of the law that the various constitutions, legislative acts, treaties, and judicial decisions are respected in the society.

They guarantee the political structure in three ways: by interpreting state or federal constitutions through judicial review, by making decisions limiting legislative and executive excesses, and by maintaining themselves above and independent of political and interest group pressures. They are expected to act as neutral referees.

The Supreme Court. Judges and courts on occasion mold policy because their decisions may influence and control future legislation. Because many laws are general, much of a judge's work at any level of the judicial structure lies in interpreting and applying the law to specific cases. For example, what does automotive negligence mean, exactly? Do defective brakes on one Ford Motor Company car constitute negligence? In exercising the judicial power to interpret and apply statutes to specific cases, a judge does, in a certain way, assert law-making power. Thus, judges possess a degree of choice that may be as great as that of other legislative bodies. This element of choice is sometimes criticized as being a violation of the separation of powers. Some even believe that it may pull the judicial institution into the political arena.

Steve Petteway, Collection of the Supreme Court of the United States

The justices who sit on the U.S. Supreme Court represent a very important part of the American form of government. Their power lies mainly in the process of judicial review, which is essentially the power to declare any act passed by Congress, the president, or state legislature as unconstitutional.

In fact, especially in the case of the Supreme Court, critics maintain that despite the principle of judicial restraint which Justices profess to follow, the Supreme Court is actually too activist. By activism, critics mean that its decisions correspond quite closely with the dominant philosophy prevailing among the governing elite at any time, or that its decisions are made according to ideologies that have effects in the political arena. During the 1930s, when the philosophy of rugged individualism was popular, the Court reflected this conservative tone by handing down many decisions against President Roosevelt's attempts at social reforms. In the 1960s and 1970s, when the political climate was more liberal, Court decisions reflected this liberalism, as exemplified by decisions on legislation regarding civil rights, women's rights, abortion rights, and legislation protecting Americans with disabilities. Reflecting a more conservative time again, in the 2000 presidential election the Supreme Court played a determining role in the election of President George W. Bush. Currently, the Court has a majority of conservative Justices who, with their decisions, are reflecting a conservative agenda. For instance, the District of Columbia had passed a strict gun control law, but in a decision written by Justice Antonin Scalia in 2008, the Court vetoed it. And although Congress had passed the McCain–Feingold campaign finance bill, and President Bush had signed it into law, in 2010 the Court decided that corporations and labor unions have the right to spend unlimited funds to elect candidates of their choice, an item that the legislation had specifically forbidden.

That is why each administration hopes to appoint justices that will reflect its own agenda. Republican administrations appointed Chief Justice Roberts, as well as such conservative justices as Thomas, Alito, and Scalia. Democratic administrations appointed several other Justices who, they hoped, would toe a liberal line (but not all of them did). The current administration appointed the second and third women on the Court, Sonia Sotomayor and Elena Kagan. Activism on the part of the Court is generally considered unfortunate because the judges' neutrality and impartiality have long given the legal system the reputation of being a "system of laws, not of men."

Another criticism of the Supreme Court is that there is frequently a time lag between changes in philosophy and the decisions illustrating the changes. Often, this is a result of the justices' insulation from the facts of political life, which follows from their life terms on the bench. At other times, it is due to their relative independence of congressional and executive jurisdiction.

The nine justices who sit on the U.S. Supreme Court reflect further ties to the governing elites by their social backgrounds. Until the 1967 appointment of Justice Thurgood Marshall, no African American had ever served on the bench. There also were no women appointees until the 1981 appointment of Justice Sandra Day O'Connor. A quick biographical rundown, moreover, reveals that the majority have come from socially prominent, economically comfortable, and politically active families (however, this is not true of all Justices; a smaller number come from humbler backgrounds). Hence, the further criticism that some of the decisions handed down by the Court reflect the philosophical and moral sentiments of the American upper-middle class rather than of the majority of Americans.

The Importance of Limited Government

It was noted at the beginning of the chapter that one of the chief preoccupations of the framers of the Constitution was to establish a government whose power was limited. This principle of limited government was important to them because the history of the world was full of instances of powerful governments that oppressed the people they ruled. The principle continues to be fundamental to the American political system and bears stressing. Limited government is basic to constitutionalism because, in the democratic tradition, the purpose of a constitution is precisely to limit the power of government. The principle of limited government is expressed in the Constitution through the instruments discussed earlier: federalism, separation of powers, and judicial review.

Further limitations on government are embodied in the Bill of Rights and particularly in the First Amendment. This amendment guarantees the freedoms of speech, of the press, of assembly, and of religion against the exercise of arbitrary power. The Fourteenth Amendment forbids the states to deprive any individual of life, liberty, or property without due process of law. It also forbids them to deny equal protection of the law to anyone.

The purpose of limits on governmental power is not to weaken the government. A government must be able to deal effectively with threats from outside and challenges from within. At the same time, the founders of this nation and most people today recognize the importance of a national government that respects the rights of both states and individuals.

The rights guaranteed by the Bill of Rights have not been completely fulfilled. Perhaps they never will be. Whether or not the struggle for the fulfillment of these rights will continue depends on an informed and alert citizenry, eager to point out and correct any abuses.

The Chapter in Brief

The political system that developed in the United States following the Revolution was based on democratic ideology. One of the most important principles that resulted when the attempt was made to translate ideology into practice was the principle of limited government. This principle is carried out by several typically American institutions. The first and foremost of those is the Constitution, which prescribes that American government is a government subject to limitations and operating in accordance with general rules. The existence of a constitution imposes restraints on the power of government and allows the rule of law to prevail over individuals or groups with power. Essentially, the Constitution holds that those in public authority derive, exercise, and maintain their powers on the basis of laws.

The American Constitution imposes restraints on the power of government through the principles of federalism, the separation of powers, the system of checks and balances, and judicial supremacy. Federalism is a system that provides for the division of power between state governments and the national government. The separation of powers, establishing legislative, executive, and judicial branches, and the system of checks and balances are aimed at ensuring that power is not concentrated in any one area of the government. The judicial system and the principle of judicial review establish the final authority for interpretation of the Constitution. The Bill of Rights sets limits on political power by granting individuals certain rights and liberties.

Not all of these political provisions have worked as the framers of the Constitution intended. Federalism, for instance, has shifted toward centralization because in today's society many of the complex activities required of government cannot be performed by state and local governments. The executive branch has gained in power over the legislative branch, a fault perhaps of the ambiguity with which the Constitution describes the executive office. In addition, because the legislative branch is slow and cumbersome, presidents have found it expedient to arrogate to themselves powers that may not be properly theirs. This occurs particularly in times of crisis. The Supreme Court has a powerful tool at its disposal, namely, judicial review. Judicial review is the ability to rule on the constitutionality of laws originating either in the executive or in the legislative branch. The decisions of the Supreme Court have tended to reflect the current thinking of the government elite and of political activists. Nevertheless, the Constitution is flexible enough to permit change in any direction deemed favorable by the people.

Terms to Remember

checks and balances The method resulting from the principle of separation of powers in which each branch of government is directly and indirectly involved in the workings of the other branches.

confederate Type of government in which political power belongs to the governments of individual states.

constitutional government A government that is subject to limitations and operates in accordance with general rules rather than arbitrarily. The existence of a constitution places a system of effective restraints on political power.

federalism A form of government in which power is distributed between the central and regional units, each retaining sovereignty in specified spheres.

grant-in-aid Funds made available by the federal government to the individual states.

House Rules Committee The group with the power to determine the specific time allotted for the debate of important legislation. This is one of the most important committees in the House of Representatives.

judicial review The power exercised by the Supreme Court to invalidate presidential, congressional, and state legislative action that it deems contrary to the Constitution of the United States.

limitations A constitutional government is subject to them.

residual or reserved powers Powers reserved for the states or the people according to the Constitution of the United States.

seniority rule A principle strictly adhered to in Congress by which committee chairs and memberships are determined by years of service in Congress and on the particular committee.

separation of powers An arrangement prescribed by the Constitution in which three separate branches of government are entrusted with the legislative, executive, and judicial functions.

unitary A form of government in which political power is centralized.

Suggested Readings

Alter, Jonathan. 2010. *The Promise: President Obama, Year One.* New York: Simon and Schuster. A respected journalist and historian with access to the White House offers an interesting perspective on President Obama's first year in office.

Barber, James David. 1992. *The Presidential Character.* 4th ed. Englewood Cliffs, NJ: Prentice Hall. An interesting work that attempts to predict presidential performance.

Galderisi, Peter, Marni Ezra, and Michael Lyons, eds. 2001. *Congressional Primaries and the Politics of Representation.* Latham, MD: Rowman and Littlefield. A selection of readings on the subject of congressional primary elections.

O'Brien, David M. 1990. *Storm Center.* 2nd ed. New York: Norton. The role of the Supreme Court in American politics.

Neustadt, Richard E. 1990. *Presidential Power and the Modern President.* New York: Free Press. An influential book whose theme is that what constitutes presidential power is the power of persuasion.

Samuel, Terence. 2010. *The Upper House: A Journey Behind the Closed Doors of the U.S. Senate.* New York: Palgrave Macmillan. A window on the U.S. Senate, showing candid portraits of the senators, as well as their sometimes bizarre customs and folkways.

Shesol, Jeff. 2010. *Supreme Power: Franklin Roosevelt vs. the Supreme Court.* New York: W. W. Norton. How President Roosevelt packed the Court to pass some of the legislation that helped overcome the problems of the Great Depression. This historical account has relevance today.

Sinclair, Barbara. 1997. *Unorthodox Lawmaking: New Legislative Processes in the U.S. Congress.* Washington, DC: Congressional Quarterly Press. An analysis, presented in great detail, of the American legislative process.

Walker, David B. 1995. *The Rebirth of Federalism.* Chatham, NJ: Chatham House. A historical review of American federalism and an analysis of its present-day condition.

The Economy: Concepts and History

IN THIS CHAPTER, YOU WILL LEARN

- *the purpose and functions of the economy as an institution;*
- *the concepts that economists use in describing economies;*
- *the historical development of Western economies;*
- *the nature and features of the American economy in its historical framework;*
- *the characteristics of the corporate hierarchy; and*
- *about the development of a global economic system.*

At one time, not so long ago, to mention GM, or RCA, or US Steel, was to use symbols of vast economic wealth and power. These were the "giant corporations" that had made the United States the most affluent country in the world, as well as a leader in political and cultural values, the country whom all others respected or envied, loved or hated, but at any rate wanted to emulate. Today, some of these giants have been dwarfed or do not exist, and others, with such names as Microsoft, AOL, Yahoo, Google, and Apple, have taken their place. What happened in such a short span of time is, quite simply, that one economic era was passing and another was dawning. In the preceding era, the manufacture of a vast array of products was what made the country—and its citizens—rich. The United States was very good at this: We made machines that turned out so many things so quickly that their cost came down, and almost everyone could buy them. But while we were basking in our success, and before we realized what was happening, others were learning to produce just as efficiently and more cheaply. Moreover, manufacturing itself is no longer as wealth producing as it had once been. We have entered a period characterized by the use and manipulation of data, or information, to create new products. The emerging economy has

From Chapter 18 of *Contemporary Society: An Introduction to Social Science,* Thirteenth Edition. John A. Perry, Erna K. Perry. Copyright © 2012 by Pearson Education, Inc. All rights reserved.

Work in today's postindustrial society differs dramatically from work in the past. Sectors of our economy have shifted to the degree that we are now predominantly a service economy with professionals and other workers using technological know-how.

been described as one of fashion, that is, as fickle and changeable in the products it creates and sells as the latest skirt length or tie width. To understand the changes we are facing and to which we must adapt—as well as the threats and downturns to which the economy is subject—it is imperative to know exactly what an economy is, what it does, and how it has developed historically.

The Economic Institution

Some elements essential to human survival are freely available: the air we breathe, for instance, or the water we drink (though even those two resources may be difficult to obtain in their unpolluted form in some areas). On the other hand, food, shelter, and protective coverings have been scarce resources in most societies. In some geographic locations, these resources are more abundant than in others, but everywhere an effort must be made to accumulate an adequate supply for survival. We have seen in the discussion of institutions that a primary responsibility of each society is to bring needs and resources together, that is, to solve a universal need in the best possible way. The patterns of behavior that have emerged in the course of time to help people obtain the scarce resources needed for survival make up the institution of the economy, one of the *five pivotal human institutions* (the other four being: the family, religion, education, and government). The economy, then, is in essence a blueprint for a system of behavior through which people adapt to their environment by making decisions and choices aimed at satisfying their needs and combating the problem of scarcity.

The first decision people in a society must make concerns the need for *production*. Production may mean hunting an animal and bringing it back to camp, sowing and harvesting a field, turning a bolt on an assembly line, or entering data into a computer. The point is that societies must motivate their members to perform those tasks so that they may eat, cover themselves, and have a safe place in which to be protected from the elements.

The next decision concerns the necessity of distributing what has been produced. *Distribution* is easy in a society that has no surplus: Whatever is produced is immediately distributed and consumed. If there is a surplus, however, the question, "Who gets what, and how?" becomes more difficult. Some individuals always accumulate more of the surplus than others. This gives them an extra edge—it makes them stronger, healthier, or wealthier—than others, and this advantage is multiplied when the excess is passed on to their children. Eventually, the result is a stratified society in which the methods of distribution include barter, gifts, dowries, monetary systems, wages, investments, and so on.

The final issue in the economy is *consumption*. Consumption, again, presents no problems in simple societies. In more complex societies, however, people develop desires for things that are not needed strictly for survival. They want more variety in food, more colorful clothing, more comfortable or luxurious housing. In industrial societies, moreover, consumption is encouraged because it makes the economy grow; however, on occasion, consumption must be limited because a certain resource is temporarily scarce (as when gasoline had to be rationed in the United States in the 1970s).

The study of the structure, functions, and general working of the economy belongs to the social science discipline of economics. Economists, as well as sociologists and psychologists, analyze the economy because the institution consists of the interactions of people in pursuit of a livelihood and because it is interdependent with other institutions. In particular, social scientists examine the various types of economic systems: the size, functions, and power of the formal organizations in which economic activities go on; occupations, work, and leisure, as these affect people; and similar issues.

Economic Decision Making

The basic questions that every economic system must decide may be summarized as follows:

1. Which commodities should be produced, and in what quantities?
2. How should these commodities be produced with greatest efficiency?
3. For whom should these commodities be produced (how should they be distributed)?

Different societies solve these economic questions in different ways. In some, the questions are solved by relying entirely on *custom and tradition*. Specific crops are grown or articles manufactured because it has always been done this way. In others, decisions are made by *command*. A ruler or body of representatives orders that such and such crops will be grown or such and such articles will be made. These rulings may also be based on tradition, or they may be made for reasons of personal aggrandizement or even because they are perceived to be (or alleged to be) beneficial to the people. Finally, in some societies, answers to these questions are decided according to the working of a *market* that depends on supply and demand, on prices, profits, and losses.

Very few economies today are based entirely on only one of the systems described. Most are a mixture of two or even all three of them. In the American economy, for instance, both private and public (governmental) organizations exercise economic control. Moreover, supply and demand never function in a clear-cut way. There are ways of creating demand and limiting supply to keep prices artificially high. Both the market and the command system are used to make economic decisions in Western industrial societies.

Basic Elements of the Economy

The goods and services that are produced in each society derive from the resources that are found naturally in that society. (Of course, when barter and trade come into being, resources may be imported from and exchanged with other societies.) **Resources** are defined as everything that is needed for the production of goods and services. Resources include material objects as well as the human energy used in producing goods and services. Material objects may be found in nature or may be made by people. The human energy expended in making products is called **labor,** and natural resources, such as land, minerals, and water, are called **land** by economists. Finally, material objects made by humans, such as machinery, factories, shoes, and computers, are known as **capital.**

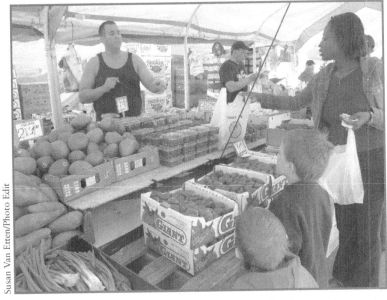

Susan Van Etten/Photo Edit

We call our economy a market system, a term derived from a real marketplace where people still buy and sell, despite the availability of supermarkets and shopping malls.

Factors of Production

Labor, land, and capital, in addition to *entrepreneurship*, are the basic elements that must be combined in the production of goods and services. They are referred to as the **factors of production**. For example, when building a house, people are driven by the spirit of entrepreneurship to use human energy (labor) to put a structure on a lot (land) using both natural material objects (wood, stone) and human-made material objects (nails, hammers, bricks, etc.). In economic terms, the result is a good that one can use or that one can sell or trade for another good.

In addition to these basic factors of production, *technology*, *time*, and *efficiency* play important parts in production. The more skill and knowledge (technology) a society has, the more effective is its production of goods and services. Time is an economic resource that is scarce and precious: If production is to be effective, in fact, it must occur within reasonable time limits. Efficiency is also an important factor in production because it is a way of obtaining the highest output from a given combination of resources in the least amount of time.

Resources are versatile. They can be put to many different uses. Land can be used to grow crops or for building factories, apartments, or shopping centers. Labor can be used to harvest crops or to develop complex data systems or to teach. But resources are finite. They can be used up or destroyed and cannot always be replaced. Societies must, therefore, conserve their resources and try to replace those used up in production.

Economic Choices and Opportunity Costs

Because resources are scarce, versatile, and finite, people in each society find that they must make certain choices. The classic economic choice has been the one commonly referred to as between guns and butter, meaning that a society must choose between producing weapons for defense and growing food to feed its people. Almost every action illustrates this type of choice: Even the fact that a student is reading this chapter rather than jogging or talking on his or her cellphone demonstrates that, to obtain a good grade in social science, the student is willing to sacrifice doing other, presumably more pleasant, things. This sacrifice is called the **opportunity cost**.

Of course, in analyzing the economy we are not interested in personal opportunity costs. We are interested in the concept because we can then put a value on the resources needed to produce something, and so make rational choices. In some respects, economics can be defined as the study of how to allocate scarce resources to attain the greatest satisfaction for the greatest number of people. A society must decide whether to use land, labor, and capital in a specific amount of dollars to build a nuclear attack submarine (and so be able to defend the country from hostile enemies) or to build housing, or railroads, or highways, or any of a thousand other alternatives. Even an affluent society that can do many things at the same time has to make these choices at some point. Everything we do as individuals, and everything a society does, involves an opportunity cost.

Limits to Output: The Production Possibilities Frontier

Economic systems are geared toward increasing output, but output has limits. Resources and technology are the variables that affect the absolute production possibilities of a society. A society that has more factors of production can produce more goods and services. A society that has more technology (the knowledge of how to use resources) can achieve the same goal.

Both resources and technology are fixed, however, so production possibilities are ultimately limited: There is just so much that can be produced at any given time. This is just as well because people want a great variety of goods and services, so it makes little sense to concentrate on producing a large amount of one product. It is only important for people to realize that the more resources and technology are used in producing one product, the less resources and technology will be available for producing another. Economists maintain, therefore, that every society is faced with a **production-possibility frontier,** and they chart production possibilities on a graph as production-possibility schedules. These schedules illustrate how much of each commodity can be produced when available resources are split among the number of commodities desired.

Specialization of Labor

The economic conditions that we experience today are the results of conditions that arose around 10,000 years ago, when the first agricultural revolution transformed groups of hunters and gatherers into settled food producers. When people began to tend crops that had been planted and to care for animals that had been domesticated, they discovered that they could create surpluses. That is, they could produce more than they required for their immediate survival. This meant that not everyone was needed to work the land. The end result was *specialization of labor.*

Specialization is effective and efficient. It means that some people can devote themselves to tasks other than food production and that some become strictly consumers of products that others make. Because people have different talents, specialization gives each the opportunity to do what he or she does best.

Not only is work specialized in contemporary industrial societies, but it also proceeds according to a division of labor. This means that each worker repeats a single action, without necessarily knowing what the finished product will look like. Again, division of labor adds to the efficiency and rapidity with which a product can be manufactured. However, the method decreases workers' sense of control over their jobs, their independence, and the feeling of accomplishment that usually accompanies a job well done. In industrial systems, workers no longer make things; rather, they sell their labor to factory owners and become part of an anonymous "labor force." In the new economic era that is emerging, specialization may lose some of its importance, as the new processes require a less regimented, more creative worker.

Trade, Barter, and Money

If one specializes in making a particular product, it makes sense to trade it for a product that someone else makes and that one needs. In the past, trading was literally done in marketplaces. Today, the term is also used figuratively, especially in the context of the economy. In fact, the American economy is called a "market system" because groups of people specialize in producing specific objects and voluntarily exchange them according to contracts agreeable to both parties.

At one time, all economic systems depended on barter or on the direct exchange of goods. Barter, however, is cumbersome and awkward. This is where the concept of money comes in. **Money** is a medium of exchange. It makes it possible for one individual to sell a product to another individual who wants it, obtain money for it, and use the money to buy another product from a third individual who has it for sale.

Contemporary Economic Systems: How Choices Are Made

Economic institutions are both cultural and social systems. They are social systems because people hold specific statuses and play the roles corresponding to those statuses. They are cultural systems because patterns of behavior, values, and expectations emerge around a system of production. These patterns are then made legitimate by a philosophy or ideology that the people accept as valid. In the modern industrial societies of the world, the three economic patterns of behavior and the legitimizing ideologies that underlie them are capitalism, socialism, and communism. (Of the three, only capitalism seems to hold its own, as communism has been largely abandoned, and socialism has acquired a more capitalistic face.)

The economic system of a society is determined largely by that society's concept of property. **Property** is defined as the rights that an owner has to an object, as compared with the rights of those who are not owners of that object. The concept of property arises because resources are scarce, and it is profitable to own some of them. In most societies, ownership of property takes one of three forms: communal, private, or public. In the *communal* form of ownership, property belongs to a community. Any member of the community may use it but may not own it. In the *private* form of ownership, property belongs to individuals. Unless an individual gives permission, his or her property may not be used by others. In the *public* form of ownership, the state or an officially recognized political authority owns property in the name of the people. Generally, schools, highways, parks, and public transportation systems are publicly owned.

Although the manner in which property is owned determines the economic system of a society, none is limited strictly to one form. All societies recognize some private ownership, and some public ownership is essential to all. It is the extent to which one or the other form is recognized that differentiates one system from another.

All three economic systems—communism, socialism, and capitalism—lie at different points on an ideal continuum. What accounts for their differences is the extent to which the government intervenes in the economy. In modified capitalism, government interferes least, although intervention is increasing. In democratic socialism, government interferes in essential industries. In communism, government determines all economic action. The economies of modern societies are matters of degree rather than kind.

Western Economies in Historical Perspective

The economies of the Western world are mostly modified capitalist, mixed-market economies. Their roots go back to a momentous transformation that occurred in Western Europe as it was emerging from the Middle Ages. The transformation revolved around the transition from a chiefly agricultural to a chiefly industrial mode of production. This transformation was marked by conflict because fundamental changes had to occur in the class structure and in the values and beliefs of societies. In agrarian societies, for instance, wealth, power, and status had belonged to landowners. In feudal Europe, this class was the landed aristocracy; in pre–Civil War America, it was the plantation owners and other large landholders. When industry became the chief mode of production, the status and power shifted to those who controlled industrial and financial capital.

The Birth of Capitalism

Industrialization brought in its wake a middle class (or bourgeoisie), whose values and beliefs facilitated the accumulation of capital and its continued reinvestment. In particular, the idea of the value of the individual human being and of personal fulfillment had to take hold. These ideas were in opposition to those prevalent in the preceding feudal era, in which the importance of the individual was downplayed, and happiness was not even an issue: At best, it was thought that people might attain it after death rather than in this life. In the new industrial system, the individual had to learn that it was okay to aspire to a better social status, wealth, and prestige, and that these could be acquired through hard work. Thus, the profit motive and the work ethic were given positive social value.

This transformation of values and beliefs was occurring at the same time that certain religious ideas, put in motion by the Protestant Reformation, were also circulating in Europe. The new religious doctrines extolled hard work, thrift, and denial of sensual pleasures and, thus, seemed to go hand in hand with some of the notions of capitalism. The relationship between the new religious ideas and the emergence of capitalism was analyzed by Max Weber in his classic work, *The Protestant Ethic and the Spirit of Capitalism* (1904–1905/1958). The doctrines appealed especially to the emerging merchant classes in England and Holland, who came to be called Puritans. The Puritans were convinced that their way of life was particularly pleasing to God; thus, they became especially receptive to the new economic system, capitalism, and eventually brought it with them to the New World.

As industrialism required a reorganization of values, so **capitalism** at first required a rearrangement of concepts about the function of an economy. Instead of gold and silver, which landowners used as an exchange medium, the basis of wealth became ownership of the factors of production: land, labor, and capital, as well as the spirit of entrepreneurship. In addition, the factors of production were abstracted, dehumanized, treated as objects, and bought and sold in the marketplace. In particular, labor, which once was given to a landowner in exchange for food, shelter, and protection, could now be sold in exchange for wages to the highest bidder. Wealth shifted from landowners to those who owned or controlled the means of production—those who had machines, tools, and materials. These new owners were the merchant middle classes. And the latter were employing free citizens, rather than serfs or vassals, to do the labor needed for production.

The new economic system greatly increased the production of goods and services, putting them within reach of many more societal members. The once poor and powerless, but sheltered and protected, serfs and apprentices became a working class (in Marxian terms, the proletariat). In exchange for wages, they gave up individual responsibility for their work, which became the responsibility of the employer.

During the nineteenth century, capitalism in Western societies was organized as a factory production system in which factories were owned by a few powerful individuals and families. Toward the end of the century, however, this system began to decline and to be replaced by **finance** and **industrial capitalism.**

Aspects of Industrial Capitalism

Up to the middle of the nineteenth century, the predominant form of business organization had been the company, owned and managed by a single owner or a partnership. Although some of these companies operated on a large scale, a great proportion of their profits had to be reinvested in the company, keeping the amount of cash disposable for growth at a minimum. These business organizations prevalent during the early part of industrialism were concerned mainly with manufacturing, mining, and transportation, all forms of industrial capitalism.

Today, of the millions of businesses in the United States, two-thirds are still sole proprietorships. A sole proprietorship is the simplest form of business organization, having the advantage that the owner is in sole and total control of the enterprise. However, this form of business organization has a number of disadvantages: The owner has unlimited liability for any debts the business incurs; it is difficult to raise sufficient money to make the business a big success; and when the owner dies or retires, the enterprise goes out of business. It is symptomatic of these disadvantages that three of every five new businesses go bankrupt before their third year of operation.

Partnerships, a slightly more complex form of business organization, involve two or more individuals, who agree to contribute some of their own resources to an enterprise in return for a share of the profits or losses. The advantage is that more money can be raised, but decision making is usually more difficult, and each partner is liable for all the debts and claims against the partnership. This form of business organization is the least common in the United States, making up less than 10 percent of all firms and accounting for less than 5 percent of all firm sales.

The Corporate Form of Industrial Organization

During the final years of the nineteenth century, a change was made in the direction of finance capitalism. *Finance capitalism* is characterized by these conditions: Investment banks and insurance companies dominate industry, large aggregates of capital are formed, ownership becomes separate from management, and the holding company appears.

Building railroads was a form of industrial capitalism that not only enriched the owners, but also expanded the country, allowing people to move into places that had been isolated previously.

The foremost product of finance capitalism is the **corporation,** a form of enterprise typically organized for large-scale production. To raise the huge sums of money needed for expansion, the owners of a company offer to sell stocks or bonds. **Stocks** are shares of ownership of the corporations. **Bonds** are promises to repay a loan with a set rate of interest. The buyers of shares or bonds become in effect the coowners of the new organization. They may have as much or more power than the original owners, depending on the percentage of shares they own. Management and responsibility for operations are now carried out by executive managers hired by a centralized board of directors. The latter are elected at the annual stockholders' meetings, at which each share of stock corresponds to one vote.

The separation of ownership from management was designed to ensure that the profit motive does not become the prime concern of the managers, who are really salaried employees of the corporation. Their functions are to pursue the welfare of the corporation; the real owners—the shareholders—are, in effect, absentee owners.

The corporation is designated by the government as a legal entity. As such, it can acquire resources, own assets, manufacture and sell goods, extend credit or incur debts, sue and be sued, and perform other similar functions—all distinct from its owners, the shareholders. The *limited liability clause* ensures that the shareholders lose only their investment and are liable for nothing else if the corporation becomes bankrupt.

The corporation has become by far the most effective form of business organization because of its ability to raise capital. By pooling the savings of thousands of households, corporations acquire large sums of capital to buy raw materials and machinery and to pay for production. The shareholders also have advantages: They need not be concerned with managing the enterprise, investments may be spread among a number of corporations, and they can be easily disposed of.

Corporations are stable in the sense that they are not subject to death or disease of the owners in the same way sole proprietorships or partnerships are. An ill or inefficient manager is simply replaced. This "immortality" allows long-range planning and growth to take place. Corporations also offer certain tax advantages because the rate of taxation is different for corporations than for individuals. The government offers corporations many tax advantages and breaks, so much so that this government largesse has been characterized as "corporate welfare" (Barlett & Steele, 1998, 36–40). Hoping to create jobs, the federal government offers many incentives, from tax abatements to price supports, from lucrative government contracts to outright grants. The same is true of state and local governments, which practically bribe corporations to locate in their geographic areas.

The very success of the corporate form of organization has led to some abuse. In the late nineteenth century, when corporations were coming into their own, they fueled economic expansion at great costs to small businesses. Monopolies and trusts came to replace the small entrepreneur and became the most powerful segment of the economy. In a **monopoly,** one firm produces the entire market supply of a specific product; **trusts** are mergers of corporations for the purpose of cornering a market. The early "captains of industry" (also remembered, perhaps more accurately, as the "robber barons") built huge industrial empires: Rockefeller in oil, Carnegie in steel, Armour and Swift in meat packing, Vanderbilt and Stanford in railroads, Morgan in banking, and Henry Ford in automobiles. So powerful were the heads of these empires that Henry Ford could single-handedly decide to raise the price of his car and, in addition, to make all Model Ts in black only. When told by his managers that people complained about the lack of choice in colors, he is reported to have said, "I don't care what you give them as long as it is black." The end result was that these corporations acquired such market power that they were able to set prices at will and totally destroy competition. Eventually, the power of monopolies and trusts grew to such an extent that reformers began to perceive them as social problems to be eradicated. Reformers began to talk of "trust-busting," or breaking up the enormous concentrations of economic power, and finally the government stepped in. Regulatory legislation was passed in the form of the Sherman Antitrust Act of 1890, prohibiting monopolistic activities in restraint of trade, and later the Federal Trade Commission Act of 1914 was passed, prohibiting unfair competition.

At present, corporations represent about 20 percent of all businesses, but corporate sales represent almost 90 percent of all business revenues. This high industrial concentration is called **oligopoly.** The pros and cons of oligopoly continue to be debated among economists and in the media. On the one hand, those who defend the large size and power of the corporations argue that modern technological and scientific advances require sophisticated machinery and teams of specialized personnel to operate it. The tremendous outlays of capital necessary to finance such projects are available only from large corporations, which can afford pilot plants and sales campaigns and are better able to absorb failures. On the other hand, critics maintain that large size and great power make it impossible for smaller firms to compete, leading to high prices, price fixing, and monopoly. An even greater danger may be the political power that large corporations wield as a result of the creation of interest groups and political action committees (PACs), which may be able to alter the political decision-making process for their own benefit.

Corporations are powerful not only because some have been allowed to grow to gigantic proportions but also because they can own stock in other corporations, giving them an inordinate amount of control. Executive officers in one corporation are frequently members of the board of directors of other corporations, a condition called *interlocking directorates,* which also can lead to abuse. The small investor who owns a hundred or so shares in a corporation is virtually powerless in corporate affairs. On the other hand, a well-paid top manager of a corporation can afford to purchase large blocks of stock. Owning even less than 1 percent of a corporation the size of General Motors may in effect allow such a shareholder to be in control of millions of dollars. In addition, some corporations are able to engage in unethical behavior that is profitable to top administrators and financially detrimental to their employees and shareholders. An example in the last decade of the twentieth century was provided by Enron, a corporation whose business dealings had to be investigated by Congress.

The power of the corporations does not go unchallenged, nor is it monolithic. Business cycles and unforeseen events can alter the powerful status of a corporation. Government intervention and consumer lobbying have similar effects. The government, for instance, had instituted an antitrust suit against the Microsoft Corporation and tried to determine whether it was a monopoly. Rival manufacturers had accused Microsoft of using its market power to bully them to shield its monopoly in operating system software from the challenge of other Internet software. Shifts of the economy away from manufacturing, as well as global competition, have of late eroded the power of many corporate giants, but others have risen to take their place. In addition, the recession that struck in 2008 had such a dismal effect on the automobile industry that the federal government had to bail out General Motors and Chrysler, once powerful corporations that were about to go bankrupt.

From Competition to Advertising

The oligopolistic nature of corporations has also changed the classical capitalist idea that the consumer is king in a free market, in which many producers compete for the consumer's business by offering high quality at low prices. When a small number of corporations have a lion's share of the market, there is little need for competition. Instead, to increase their profits, corporations spend large sums of money for advertising, hoping to sway the consumer into buying essentially the same products as the ones their competitors offer.

Advertising creates an artificial demand for products for which there is no real need. Anyone who has strolled through the malls of American cities is aware of the myriad products displayed for sale in stores, many of which fill no conceivable need. Advertising ensures that a desire for those products is created nonetheless. The public is saturated with advertising until it becomes convinced that the new product is indispensable. Another ploy used by manufacturing corporations to increase their profits is planned obsolescence, which means that products are deliberately built shoddily so that they must be replaced more often.

Advertising has been immensely successful as a method of increasing consumption—so much so that it has become a profitable industry in its own right. People in capitalist societies are willing to spend much more money on the often frivolous goods they are convinced they need than on taxes, which would allow the government to provide much-needed public services. It is a situation that has prompted some economists critical of these facets of capitalism to describe life in capitalist societies as offering private affluence but public squalor. They say that, for instance, fine automobiles are available to those who can afford them, but mass transit systems for those who cannot pay for private automobiles are sorely inadequate. However, this is only one side of the story: Government is generally ineffective in providing well for public needs, and the capitalist ideology has convinced most people that individual effort will bring them personal affluence; thus, they are less concerned about public needs.

Diversification and Multinationalism

Whether it is good or bad, ethical or unethical, the fact is that most corporations have attempted to become even larger. Two ways in which they have been doing so is through diversification and multinationalism. *Diversification* is a corporation's acquisition of controlling shares in other corporations, often in totally different industries. A cosmetics company may also own a company—or a controlling share of a company—that produces movies and another that manufactures drugs. Diversification is a result of mergers and takeovers, some of which occur without the approval of the company being acquired. This procedure has been criticized because it results in the growth of a corporation without having to produce anything.

Multinationalism refers to the fact that instead of merely exporting their products to foreign lands, some corporations move the production process itself into other countries. Moving the industrial process abroad is successful for corporations because labor is cheaper than in the United States and markets are vastly expanded. Therefore, profits increase. But both American workers and ultimately the host nations are suspicious of **multinational corporations,** whose profits are often greater than the national budgets of the host nations. Such profits and the fact that the corporations virtually control thousands of jobs give them excessive power, casting them in the light of exploiters. On the other hand, it has been shown that direct foreign investment raises demand for American goods and services and creates jobs and wealth at home. Such direct investment more than doubled in the years 1992 to 1995, as most of the world competed for American capital to finance their own economies. Even Japan, which had steadfastly refused to open its market to America, has had to relent because

Japanese consumers want to eat at McDonald's, buy at Toys 'R' Us, and shop at the Gap. It seems, then, that despite the feeling that multinationalism is a form of economic colonialism, many products of American business are very popular. American corporations have become models for many countries that send their students to learn business methods and management skills at American universities (Myerson, 1995, E1, E14).

A side effect of multinationalism that worries Americans is the fact that a growing number of developing nations have become proficient in mass production at much lower wages than American workers demand. For instance, U.S. wages are several times higher than Taiwan's or South Korea's and about seven times higher than Mexico's. Even cheaper are labor costs in China, which is becoming a major producer of consumer goods. Because so many U.S. companies are having their products manufactured overseas and also because they cannot compete with the products of foreign companies, American companies are laying off workers altogether or replacing them with lower-paid, part-time employees for whom they need not pay benefits.

The Nature of Work in the Industrial Society

In all societies, except the very simplest ones, obtaining the necessities for survival has meant that individuals have had to work. Workers are employed in one of three sectors of the economy. The **primary sector** deals with the extraction and processing of raw materials and includes such activities as agriculture, fishing, mining, and forestry. In the mid-nineteenth century, two-thirds of the American labor force was employed in the primary sector. Today, only 3 percent are.

The **secondary sector** is concerned with manufacturing and constructing, or turning raw materials into finished products, such as producing automobiles, building homes, or packaging foods. The United States was very accomplished in this sector, deriving most of its wealth from work in it. Our large corporations in fact were instrumental in this sector, producing cars, washing machines, electronics, and so on.

The **tertiary sector,** in which 80 percent of the American labor force is involved, involves services, such as repairing automobiles, remodeling homes, providing education, or healing the sick members of a society.

The *quaternary sector* involves intellectual activities in government, culture, scientific research, higher education, and information technology.

Some economists would add a *quinary sector,* which would include individuals at the highest level of decision making—top executives, officials in government, university presidents, top scientific researchers, and prominent leaders in health and the media.

Shifting Sectors

Historically, a dramatic switch has occurred when societies have become industrialized. In the first stages of industrialization, the large majority of workers are employed in the primary sector. As an example, in the early years of this country, almost 95 percent of workers were employed in agriculture. It took that many people to provide enough food for the nation. By 1900, only 38 percent of the workforce was in farming. Today, only approximately 2 percent is still engaged in farming. Farming is now so efficient that very few people are needed to grow enough food for the whole population and for export.

As industrialization progresses, employment shifts from one sector to the next. From the turn of the century until the middle of it, the secondary sector showed a steady increase—from 35.8 percent in 1900 to 40.3 percent in 1950. As of 1950, the secondary sector has been declining—from 40.3 to 30 percent in 1982 and to below 20 percent as of 1997. The tertiary sector, on the other hand, has seen a spectacular spurt in growth—from 26.6 percent in 1900 to 62.1 percent in 1975 and 78 percent of GDP as of 2006 (Glushko & Saxenian, 2006). Obviously, in this latest stage of industrialization, the great majority of workers are employed in the tertiary sector of the economy. In contrast, blue-collar workers employed in the primary and secondary sectors shrunk from 37.6 percent in 1900 to 4.5 percent in 1975 and 13 percent in 2002. As the United States loses more of its manufacturing jobs to foreign countries, unemployment in these sectors is becoming endemic and very problematic, as we will see later in this chapter.

Professionalization

The shift into the tertiary sector has resulted in important changes in the occupational structure. More people are becoming professionals, managers, or technicians, and there is less need for unskilled or semiskilled occupations. Consequently, there have been changes in the stratification system, causing chronic unemployment for the segment of the population that is unable to attain professionalization.

Professions are more than specialized occupations. They require both theoretical knowledge and training in an art or a science. A carpenter needs training, but a physician needs to possess a body of theoretical knowledge in addition to training. Because of their long years of specialization, professionals are able to exert a great degree of autonomy over what they do. Professionals also establish associations that regulate the credentials of their members and maintain certain codes of behavior and ethics.

Professions have consistently increased in prestige and are the highest-paid occupations in the tertiary sector. As a result, there has been a tendency to professionalize any occupation that lends itself to it. Professionalization has not been very successful in the first two sectors of the economy, but it has been very successful among the white-collar workers of the tertiary sector.

The Corporate Bureaucracy

Industrial production involves a complex machine technology, an executive and administrative bureaucracy including a white-collar labor force, and the wielders of the machines themselves, the blue-collar labor force. The goals of a pure bureaucracy however, can differ from the way a bureaucracy works in reality. At the height of the industrial era, the corporate bureaucracy was a pyramid consisting of the following divisions.

The Executive

A chief executive officer (CEO) must be able to break all emotional bonds that might stand in the way of a career and must have personality traits that include self-discipline, ability to submit to authority, emotional and intellectual "cool," the capacity to sublimate immediate goals for future benefits, and an unusual amount of ambition and desire for success. In addition, such a person has to possess an element of ruthlessness to overcome possible obstacles, must have a great deal of self-confidence, and must be able to make rapid decisions that are adhered to, for better or for worse.

Although the CEO must keep one finger in every pot of the organization, there are three general functions that every executive must fulfill: (1) establish organizational policy, (2) see that favorable relations exist between the organization and outside forces, and (3) be in charge of the operation and organization of the industrial plant.

Anxiety. Much has been made of the strains suffered by executives in their roles as corporate leaders, and the proverbial executive ulcer appears in countless jokes. Some of the difficulty encountered by executives on the way up may be due to the inability to adjust from the role of a subordinate with drive and ambition to that of ultimate decision maker and leader. In addition, such an executive may be the object of envy and feel the burden of responsibility for the welfare of the organization.

On the other hand, top executives are extremely well remunerated for their efforts (Table 1). The difference between the average worker's salary and that of the average CEO is continually increasing: In 1960, it was a multiple of 41; in 1991, it was 93 (Kinsley, 1991, 41). From 1990 to 2003, CEO pay rose by 313 percent, and corporate profits rose by 128 percent. In 2008, chief executives of large companies made 319 times the average worker's annual pay. This averaged to an annual total compensation of $10.9 million, whereas the median income for these CEOs was $8.1 million. The median pay for full-time workers, on the other hand, was $37,544 in 2008.

In the 1990s, the executives did make their companies profitable, creating one of history's greatest bull markets and so enriching their shareholders. During those heady days, it was not unusual for some CEOs to earn $100 million in a year. Beginning in 2000, however, the economy slowed and stocks fell, some drastically. While shareholders lost an average 12 percent of their portfolios, chief executives received an average 22 percent raise in salary and bonuses. Even following the recession that began in 2007–2008, CEOS suffered very little in terms of losing income. On the other hand, a number of investment banks and insurance giants failed and had to be bailed out by the federal government, resulting in the loss of jobs for a large number of workers, and a burden for taxpayers.

TABLE 1   Executive Pay Watch: Trends in CEO Pay

2009 Average CEO Pay at S&P 500 Companies

Salary	$1,041,012
Bonus	$203,714
Stock Awards	$2,630,574
Option Awards	$2,284,595
Non-Equity Incentive Plan Compensation	$1,790,703
Pension and Deferred Compensation Earnings	$1,060,867
All Other Compensation	$235,232
Total	$9,246,697

Source: AFL-CIO. Analysis of pay data from 292 companies provided by salary.com.

The generosity with which American CEOs are rewarded has created a lot of controversy, especially as the global economy spawns an increasing number of mergers between American and foreign companies. Some economists perceive American-style pay as a mechanism for jump-starting economic performance. Other economists view the high salaries and perks, especially in comparison to those paid by other nations, as leading to increasing greed and excess.

The American form of management has both advantages and disadvantages. The high salaries and perks tend to isolate the CEO from subordinates, and even from the public at large, leading to some wrong decisions. The American automobile industry, for instance, lost a large amount of world market share, mainly to the Japanese, because it kept producing automobiles that the public no longer wanted. On the other hand, greed is a tremendous motivating force and may spur CEOs to extraordinary performance

Between the position of corporate managers and that of the industrial workers who actually produce the goods, we find the vast limbo of the middle section of the industrial bureaucracy, consisting of executive vice presidents, specialists, office workers, and supervisors. This rung of the hierarchy is proving to be the most obsolete in the new economic era and will probably be gradually phased out.

Industrial Workers

The last group in the corporate bureaucracy of the industrial system consists of those who actually turn the wheels of the system, the industrial, or blue-collar, workers. This class of workers evolved in an interesting way, and they are currently at a critical stage of development. Trends point to the necessity of their transformation into a more skilled, automated, responsible, and creative workforce.

Before the changes introduced by industrialization, most people in Western societies lived and worked on farms. It was a subsistence type of livelihood, except for the landowners, who could afford education and interests that went beyond sheer physical labor. Of course, societies also needed craftspeople and artisans: individuals who could make shoes, sew clothing, make furniture, and work in stone and metals. These individuals had a loftier position in the stratification system than the peasants who worked the soil, and the more talented acquired fame as what we would now call artists. By the tenth century, such individuals were organizing themselves into a variety of **guilds** (kinds of labor unions), of which the merchant and craft guilds had mostly economic objectives. Craft guilds were occupational associations established by the artisans in specific fields. The guilds restricted membership, requiring an apprenticeship period before an artisan could become a journeyman. In turn, the journeyman had to produce a "masterpiece" before he could be judged a master craftsman. In the guild system, an apprentice was taken into his master's home and clothed and fed along with the master's family. Though apprentices may have been exploited and may have gone hungry (depending on the master's personality and circumstances), they were made to feel protected, and all their needs were provided for.

In the early stages of industrialization, work was done in the home, with merchants providing the raw material and paying for the finished product. This system was called the *cottage* or *putting-out system*. Although there was pressure to produce more, the workers remained basically in control of how and when to work, establishing their own hours and employing members of their family or apprentices as helpers. In addition, they were free to cultivate plots of land for additional revenue. In both the guild and the cottage systems, individual artisans produced the whole product and later an entire facet of the production process. They could see what they were making and could feel pride in a job well done.

The Factory System

The factory system, the next step in the progress of industry, changed all that. Workers were herded into a central building together with tens or hundreds of others. They were told exactly how much to produce in a specific amount of time, when to come to work, when to go home. The hours were long (a 12- or 14-hour day was not unusual), the environment was unpleasant—lacking in the most primitive hygiene facilities—and the pay was minimal. The entire family, dragged from a rural locale to the dirty and crowded city, found that it had to run the machines to eke out a meager livelihood.

Most important, however, was the change in how a worker produced goods. No longer responsible for the whole article, each worker now repeated the same routine action endlessly all day, often without really understanding its relation to the finished product.

The relationship between employee and employer also underwent a drastic change. The employer was now among the owners of the means of production, the "bourgeoisie" in Marxist terms, and the employee was a member of the "proletariat," or industrial workers. The employer felt no moral obligation or responsibility toward the employees and in a business slump had no qualms about firing or laying off workers. They were no more than names in a payroll ledger, unlike the apprentices to a master craftsman of former times. Working conditions in factories began to be characterized by impersonality and anonymity, features that persist to the present.

Conditions in the urban centers, meanwhile, were appalling. Workers could no longer supplement their livelihood by hunting or growing things. The owners and managers of industry were able to amass fortunes in those early days of capitalism, unhampered by government regulations, but not much of this wealth trickled down to the workers. The workers' wages always seemed to lag behind prices, forcing them to live in substandard conditions. They had no medical care, even for the numerous industrial accidents that occurred in the unsafe factories of the day. The worst trauma of all was the complete lack of security that workers experienced. The capitalistic system was unstable and subject to deep business cycles, and workers never knew when they would be laid off.

Inevitably, workers realized that they must organize, that no individual or chance circumstance would eliminate the hardships and injustices of their condition. Their only salvation lay in unity of purpose. However, it was not until the twentieth century that the goal of organized and peaceful industrial relations was reached.

The American Labor Movement

The labor movement in the United States had made only sporadic attempts at organization before the Civil War. The establishment of national labor organizations occurred in the period following the Civil War and up to Roosevelt's New Deal during the Great Depression. It was a difficult struggle: The effort to join together nationally for the purpose of collective bargaining had many obstacles to overcome.

In the United States, workers had been a scarce commodity, but increasing mechanization was displacing artisans and skilled workers. The growing concentration of industry

Box 1 Methods of Production: Craft, Mass, and Lean

Labor productivity in the United States had been on a steady upward move from the time the Industrial Revolution gained a foothold in the New World. For instance, in America's most important industry, the automobile industry, the first cars were produced by the craft method; that is, each car was made to order. With this method, factories were turning out only a few hundred cars a year, costs were high and did not decrease when volume increased, consistency and reliability were unequal, and the small craft shops could not afford the systematic research that would lead to technological advances. More important, with this method only the very wealthy could afford cars.

Mass production all but banished the craft method. This technique revolved around the idea of complete interchangeability of parts and the ease of fitting parts to each other. To speed up the process on the assembly line, Henry Ford assigned each worker only one task, which the worker performed while standing next to a moving line. Ford also designed machine tools that would perform only one task, thus avoiding the need to readjust tools to do a variety of tasks. In this way, Ford could use untrained, inexpensive labor, instead of the high-cost, highly skilled labor needed for the craft method. He also hired large numbers of "rework men," whose job it was to patch up defective cars. Because the latter were untrained and unmotivated, Ford had to increase the numbers of industrial, manufacturing, and product engineers. But while Ford and the founder of General Motors, William Durant, succeeded very well with their mass-production technique in the factory, they never managed to organize efficiently the bloated engineering, manufacturing, and marketing complex. This feat was accomplished by later General Motors presidents, but on the basis of creating specialized and decentralized departments, each of which knew little about the functioning of the others. There was a complete division of labor, in other words.

The new system of "lean" production that Americans began to embrace in the 1980s derives from the experience of the Japanese. Following World War II. Japanese labor unions succeeded in winning an agreement in which employees were guaranteed lifetime employment and a pay scale based on seniority instead of job function. In return, employees agreed to be flexible in the work assignments they accepted and committed to helping the company find new and more efficient production methods. In this situation, the system worked out by Toyota has become a model for all of Japan's lean production method. The scores of engineering and production specialists used by the mass-production method were never used by the Japanese. Instead, they trained workers to do the specialists' work. Workers were organized into teams, each with its own leader, and were told to decide together how best to perform the necessary operations, thus foregoing the need for a supervisor. Slowly, additional responsibilities were added to the teams, and each worker could stop the assembly line if a problem appeared that the worker could not resolve. Moreover, each error had to be traced back to its cause, and a solution had to be devised so that it would never recur. The result is that whereas in mass-production plants, 25 percent of total work hours and 20 percent of plant area are dedicated to fixing errors that occur on the assembly line, Toyota's assembly plants have virtually no rework areas and perform almost no rework. Yields approach 100 percent, and the line almost never stops.

There are many more steps in the system of lean production—as well as in the way suppliers are used, and especially in the relationship of manufacturer and consumer—but in a nutshell, the goals of lean production are these: (1) whereas mass producers set limited goals—a certain number of defects, a maximum level of inventories—lean producers set their goals on perfection—zero defects, zero inventories, and continually declining costs; (2) lean production's main objective is to push responsibility far down the organizational ladder; and (3) the career path in lean production leads to a broadening of professional skills applied in a team setting instead of an attempt to climb upward in a rigid hierarchy with growing proficiency in a narrow area of specialization.

It appears that lean production combines the best features of craft production and mass production: the ability to reduce costs per unit, improve quality and respond rapidly to consumers' wishes while providing employees with challenging work. Although lean production has not been quickly or painlessly adopted, "it will supplant mass production and the remaining outposts of craft production in all areas of industrial endeavor and become the standard global production system of the 21st century. As a result, the world will be a different and better place" (Womack, Jones, & Roos, 1990, 38).

and the separation of ownership from the management of industry in the growth of the corporation produced feelings of anonymity and destroyed feelings of loyalty. The consequent depersonalization led to an indifferent attitude on the part of all concerned. The American labor force was a heterogeneous lot, representing different ethnic, cultural, religious, and racial backgrounds that were usually mutually incompatible and suspicious of each other.

In addition, American workers were not keenly aware of their status as a social class. They believed the ideology of unlimited opportunity and viewed their status as transitional, only a step in their ascent to riches and power. Thus, they were unwilling to organize into a group they thought they would soon abandon. Finally, the federal system of government stood in the way of effective organization: If workers organized in one state, the industry involved would move to another. The mood of the day was inimical to labor, too. The heroes of the day were the captains of industry, whose rags-to-riches stories fascinated the public.

Despite these obstacles, in 1869 workers organized themselves into the Knights of Labor and later, in 1886, into the American Federation of Labor (AFL). Under the leadership of Samuel Gompers, the AFL grew, and by 1920 four of the five million unionized workers were members of the AFL. In its early days, the AFL was interested principally in organizing skilled workers, so most of its member unions were craft unions. In a craft, or *horizontal*, union, each skill is organized into a separate entity. The workers in the building industry, for instance, are divided into carpenters, plumbers, bricklayers, and painters, and each group has its own union. The opposite form of union organization is represented by the United Mine Workers, who belong to an industrial, or *vertical*, union. In this form, all the workers are organized into one union, regardless of the tasks they perform in their industry. One labor leader committed to the industrial type of union who has come down in history as a hero of labor was the president of the United Auto Workers, Walter Reuther.

Although initially the government supported the opposition of business to unionization, eventually laws were passed that were interpreted as an admission on the part of government that workers had the right to organize and join unions. During the presidency of Franklin

AP Photo/Charlie Riedel

The factory system in the United States today is quite different from what it was in the past (note the clean facility, the female worker, the fact that she wears gloves), but the assembly line is still its chief method of production.

Delano Roosevelt, one of the worst periods of economic activity in the history of the United States, unionization was encouraged because it was thought that it would give workers additional purchasing power—through higher wages—and, thus, stimulate the stagnant economy. Legal sanctions for worker organization were also provided by the National Industrial Recovery Act of 1933, which prohibited employers from interfering with the process of unionization. This legislation was superseded by the Wagner Act of a few years later. The provisions for the protection of the workers encompassed in the Wagner Act were closely followed by the Social Security Act of 1935. This last piece of legislation was a clear attempt on the part of the government to alleviate the insecurity associated with the lot of the industrial worker, and it signaled an attitude of concern for public welfare.

Collective Bargaining

The most fundamental function that the union performs for the worker is collective bargaining. This process has become an accepted institution in our society. Although conflicts between labor and management crop up periodically, most solutions take place within the framework of collective bargaining. Some aspects of collective bargaining are employed every day, as workers air their complaints through what are called grievance procedures. These procedures generally involve the services of a shop steward or chairperson elected by the workers, who is given a degree of immunity from layoffs to remain loyal to the workers. The presence of the shop steward has done much to alleviate the problem of powerful and authoritarian supervisors and bosses and helps explain the tremendous unionization that has occurred in the mass-production industries.

Collective bargaining was also embraced by many white-collar workers such as teachers and workers in public jobs—that is, persons who work for states, counties, and local governments. As a result of collective bargaining, these occupations ensured that employees received fair remuneration and such benefits as health insurance and pensions (employees contributed to both but were helped by their employers). At present, a number of states that have been experiencing a shortfall in their budgets have decided to eliminate collective bargaining, leaving their employees without the right to bargain. Legislation to that effect has already been passed in several Midwestern states, but employees are fighting back with protests and lawsuits.

The Labor Movement Today

Like other sectors of society, organized labor is not free from strife and problems. It suffers from the same ailments as big business and big government. Its leadership has at times been corrupt, seeking power and financial perks at the expense of the workers it represents. Consequently, the government has had to take steps and intervene in its affairs.

In 2009 around 12.3 percent of employed wage and salary workers—about 15.3 million persons—belonged to or were represented by unions. The great majority belonged to those affiliated with the AFL-CIO, such as the Teamsters, the United Auto Workers, the Communications Workers, and so on. The rest belonged to independent unions not affiliated with the AFL-CIO, such as the National Education Association, the Nurses' Union, and the United Mine Workers (Table 2). Workers in the public sector have a high rate of unionization, whereas those in agriculture, finance, insurance, real estate, and service industries have low rates. More men than women belong to unions because they tend to work in industries with high unionization. For the same reason, more blacks than whites are unionized and more urban residents than rural residents. Finally, union members earn more: In 2009, unionized, full-time, wage and salary workers had usual median weekly earnings of $908, against a median of $710 for nonunionized workers (**http://www.bls.gov/news.release/union2.nr0.htm**).

Decline of Unionism

The degree of unionization in the private sector has declined since 1965, while union growth in the public sector has increased. After reaching a membership of almost 25 percent of the total workforce in the mid-1950s, union membership has declined to the current 12 percent.

TABLE 2 Union Affiliation of Employed Wage and Salary Workers by Occupation and Industry (Numbers in thousands)

	2009				
		Members of unions[a]		Represented by unions[b]	
Occupation and industry	Total employed	Total	Percent of employed	Total	Percent of employed
OCCUPATION					
Management, professional, and related occupations	44,845	6,027	13.4	6,821	15.2
Management, business, and financial operations occupations	16,978	822	4.8	997	5.9
Management occupations	11,548	473	4.1	585	5.1
Business and financial operations occupations	5,430	348	6.4	412	7.6
Professional and related occupations	27,867	5,206	18.7	5,824	20.9
Computer and mathematical occupations	3,306	175	5.3	207	6.3
Architecture and engineering occupations	2,512	194	7.7	228	9.1
Life, physical, and social science occupations	1,220	122	10.0	141	11.6
Community and social services occupations	2,269	366	16.1	396	17.5
Legal occupations	1,335	79	5.9	97	7.3
Education, training, and library occupations	8,318	3,172	38.1	3,503	42.1
Arts, design, entertainment, sports, and media occupations	1,840	136	7.4	157	8.5
Healthcare practitioner and technical occupations	7,067	962	13.6	1,096	15.5
Service occupations	22,364	2,588	11.6	2,830	12.7
Healthcare support occupations	3,159	317	10.0	353	11.2
Protective service occupations	3,120	1,111	35.6	1,180	37.8
Food preparation and serving related occupations	7,621	334	4.4	389	5.1
Building and grounds cleaning and maintenance occupations	4,592	521	11.3	570	12.4
Personal care and service occupations	3,873	306	7.9	338	8.7

(Continued)

TABLE 2 *(Continued)*

| Occupation and industry | Total employed | 2009 | | | |
| | | Members of unions[a] | | Represented by unions[b] | |
		Total	Percent of employed	Total	Percent of employed
Sales and office occupations	30,998	2,231	7.2	2,499	8.1
Sales and related occupations	13,331	411	3.1	480	3.6
Office and administrative support occupations	17,667	1,820	10.3	2,019	11.4
Natural resources, construction, and maintenance occupations	11,231	1,989	17.7	2,088	18.6
Farming, fishing, and forestry occupations	880	24	2.8	26	2.9
Construction and extraction occupations	5,820	1,220	21.0	1,269	21.8
Installation, maintenance, and repair occupations	4,531	744	16.4	793	17.5
Production, transportation, and material moving occupations	15,052	2,492	16.6	2,666	17.7
Production occupations	7,309	1,082	14.8	1,164	15.9
Transportation and material moving occupations	7,742	1,410	18.2	1,502	19.4
INDUSTRY					
Private sector	103,357	7,431	7.2	8,226	8.0
Agriculture and related industries	1,045	12	1.1	14	1.4
Nonagricultural industries	102,312	7,419	7.3	8,212	8.0
Mining, quarrying, and oil and gas extraction	662	57	8.6	63	9.5
Construction	6,613	958	14.5	993	15.0
Manufacturing	13,454	1,470	10.9	1,595	11.9
Durable goods	8,438	907	10.8	985	11.7
Nondurable goods	5,016	562	11.2	610	12.2
Wholesale and retail trade	17,851	937	5.3	1,032	5.8
Wholesale trade	3,386	167	4.9	185	5.5
Retail trade	14,465	770	5.3	847	5.9
Transportation and utilities	5,162	1,144	22.2	1,210	23.4
Transportation and warehousing	4,256	908	21.3	960	22.6
Utilities	906	237	26.1	249	27.5
Information[c]	2,790	280	10.0	312	11.2
Publishing, except Internet	633	34	5.3	41	6.5
Motion pictures and sound recording industries	331	42	12.8	43	13.0
Broadcasting, except Internet	534	25	4.7	30	5.5
Telecommunications	1,088	174	16.0	192	17.7

Occupation and industry	Total employed	Members of unions[a]		Represented by unions[b]	
		2009			
		Total	Percent of employed	Total	Percent of employed
Financial activities	8,236	150	1.8	193	2.3
Finance and insurance	6,199	88	1.4	120	1.9
Finance	4,043	56	1.4	73	1.8
Insurance	2,155	32	1.5	48	2.2
Real estate and rental and leasing	2,037	61	3.0	73	3.6
Professional and business services	11,325	256	2.3	314	2.8
Professional and technical services	6,915	78	1.1	107	1.5
Management, administrative, and waste services	4,410	178	4.0	207	4.7
Education and health services	19,269	1,655	8.6	1,912	9.9
Educational services	3,816	494	12.9	580	15.2
Health care and social assistance	15,454	1,161	7.5	1,332	8.6
Leisure and hospitality	11,352	349	3.1	407	3.6
Arts, entertainment, and recreation	2,143	138	6.4	152	7.1
Accommodation and food services	9,209	211	2.3	255	2.8
Accommodation	1,390	108	7.8	115	8.3
Food services and drinking places	7,819	103	1.3	140	1.8
Other services[c]	5,598	164	2.9	182	3.2
Other services, except private households	4,775	147	3.1	163	3.4
Public sector	21,133	7,896	37.4	8,677	41.1
Federal government	3,594	1,005	28.0	1,192	33.2
State government	6,294	2,025	32.2	2,222	35.3
Local government	11,244	4,867	43.3	5,263	46.8

[a] Data refer to members of a labor union or an employee association similar to a union.
[b] Data refer to both union members and workers who report no union affiliation but whose jobs are covered by a union or an employee association contract.
[c] Includes other industries, not shown separately.

Note: Effective with January 2009 data, industries reflect the introduction of the 2007 Census industry classification system into the Current Population Survey. This industry classification system is derived from the 2007 North American Industry Classification System. No historical data have been revised. Data refer to the sole or principal job of full-and part-time wage and salary workers. All self-employed workers are excluded, both those with incorporated businesses as well as those with unincorporated businesses. Updated population controls are introduced annually with the release of January data.

Source: U.S. Bureau of Labor Statistics.

There are a number of reasons for this decline. Although mass production, heavy industry, transportation, public utilities, and construction remain heavily unionized, jobs in this sector of the economy are declining, as we saw at the beginning of this discussion. Domestic output has been changing from manufactured goods, industries that were heavily unionized, to services, which were sparsely unionized. Professional, technical, and white-collar workers, besides identifying with management, usually benefit from the same wage increases as their blue-collar counterparts. In the trade and service industries, employees are too diffused in location for effective unionization, and professional and technical workers are inclined to join professional associations instead of labor unions. In addition, a substantial increase in the labor force within the past several decades has consisted of women, part-time workers, and young people. These groups are difficult to unionize because they tend to change jobs fairly frequently. In addition, consumer demand has favored foreign-manufactured goods, which are cheaper, and foreign competition in industries such as automobiles and steel has further reduced the unionized workforce.

The leadership of organized labor may be a further factor in the decline of labor unions. There are fewer dedicated individuals and more bureaucrats who display a greater interest in running the organization than in recruiting new members. A number of labor leaders gave all organized labor a bad name by their ties to organized crime. Finally, it may be that part of the reason for the unions' decline is their success: Unions were able to gain sizable wage advantages over nonunion workers. Hence, they prompted many employers to use nonunion labor or to move plants to regions of the United States that were not heavily unionized (such as the South and Southwest) and abroad. In short, their success in raising wages may have ultimately affected the employment opportunities in the union sector as against the nonunion sector. That may explain instances in which workers themselves voted to remain nonunionized.

American Labor and the Global Economy

The American workforce faces great challenges. The transition into the tertiary sector was supposed to move the economy from dirty, heavy industry to clean, well-lit offices. Not all workers, however, made this transition smoothly. Of all new jobs created in the past decade, 88 percent were in the service industries. Wages in this sector have been well below average manufacturing wages. At the same time, unskilled workers, particularly those lacking even a high school diploma, experience high unemployment, even though that rate has been fairly low compared to rates in other countries. In reality, there are vast differences among workers in different types of jobs, in different industries, and in different regions of the country. The pay of the least-skilled workers has stagnated or actually declined, whereas workers with more education and skills have enjoyed increased earnings. This is creating a widening gap in incomes and is effectively killing the "American dream," or the ability of working-class people to enter the middle class and a comfortable standard of living (Table 3). There are a number of reasons for this income gap.

Productivity is the amount, in dollars, that a worker produces in a given hour. The worker could be using computers, or complex machinery, or a hammer and wrench, or a telephone, or one's brain and hands. A worker can be working alone or in a team or on an assembly line. The important thing is that to flourish, an economy needs to have rising productivity. Technological innovations produced such rising productivity from about the end of the nineteenth century to about the 1970s. In tandem with productivity, the pay of American workers rose, so that they could afford private housing, more than one vehicle per family, and a college education for their

TABLE 3 Union Affiliation of Employed Wage and Salary Workers by Selected Characteristics (Numbers in thousands)

| Characteristic | 2009 | | | | |
| | Total employed | Members of unions[a] | | Represented by unions[b] | |
		Total	Percent of employed	Total	Percent of employed
AGE AND SEX					
Total, 16 years and over	124,490	15,327	12.3	16,904	13.6
16 to 24 years	17,173	813	4.7	941	5.5
25 years and over	107,317	14,514	13.5	15,962	14.9
25 to 34 years	28,067	2,942	10.5	3,262	11.6
35 to 44 years	28,066	3,669	13.1	4,035	14.4
45 to 54 years	29,054	4,551	15.7	4,994	17.2
55 to 64 years	17,599	2,926	16.6	3,186	18.1
65 years and over	4,530	425	9.4	485	10.7
Men, 16 years and over	63,539	8,441	13.3	9,176	14.4
16 to 24 years	8,555	493	5.8	560	6.5
25 years and over	54,984	7,947	14.5	8,616	15.7
25 to 34 years	14,952	1,633	10.9	1,786	11.9
35 to 44 years	14,679	2,077	14.1	2,250	15.3
45 to 54 years	14,421	2,492	17.3	2,693	18.7
55 to 64 years	8,647	1,536	17.8	1,654	19.1
65 years and over	2,285	211	9.2	233	10.2
Women, 16 years and over	60,951	6,887	11.3	7,727	12.7
16 to 24 years	8,619	320	3.7	381	4.4
25 years and over	52,333	6,567	12.5	7,346	14.0
25 to 34 years	13,116	1,309	10.0	1,476	11.3
35 to 44 years	13,387	1,593	11.9	1,785	13.3
45 to 54 years	14,633	2,060	14.1	2,302	15.7
55 to 64 years	8,952	1,390	15.5	1,532	17.1
65 years and over	2,245	215	9.6	252	11.2
RACE, HISPANIC OR LATINO ETHNICITY, AND SEX					
White, 16 years and over	101,581	12,330	12.1	13,595	13.4
Men	52,691	6,918	13.1	7,512	14.3
Women	48,889	5,412	11.1	6,083	12.4
Black or African American, 16 years and over	14,127	1,966	13.9	2,172	15.4
Men	6,257	964	15.4	1,046	16.7

(Continued)

TABLE 3 *(Continued)*

	2009				
Characteristic	Total employed	Members of unions[a]		Represented by unions[b]	
		Total	Percent of employed	Total	Percent of employed
Women	7,870	1,002	12.7	1,126	14.3
Asian, 16 years and over	5,847	664	11.4	730	12.5
Men	3,075	332	10.8	370	12.0
Women	2,772	333	12.0	361	13.0
Hispanic or Latino ethnicity, 16 years and over	18,034	1,841	10.2	2,036	11.3
Men	10,518	1,108	10.5	1,199	11.4
Women	7,515	733	9.7	836	11.1
FULL- OR PART-TIME STATUS[c]					
Full-time workers	99,820	13,602	13.6	14,960	15.0
Part-time workers	24,431	1,698	7.0	1,913	7.8

[a] Data refer to members of a labor union or an employee association similar to a union.
[b] Data refer to both union members and workers who report no union affiliation but whose jobs are covered by a union or an employee association contract.
[c] The distinction between full- and part-time workers is based on hours usually worked. These data will not sum to totals because full- or part-time status on the principal job is not identifiable for a small number of multiple jobholders.

Note: Estimates for the above race groups (white, black or African American, and Asian) do not sum to totals because data are not presented for all races. Persons whose ethnicity is identified as Hispanic or Latino may be of any race. Data refer to the sole or principal job of full- and part-time wage and salary workers. All self-employed workers are excluded, both those with incorporated businesses as well as those with unincorporated businesses. Updated population controls are introduced annually with the release of January data.

Source: U.S. Bureau of Labor Statistics (http://www.bls.gov/cps/cpsaat40.pdf)

children. In the 1970s, however, productivity began to decline. Where the annual productivity growth rate had been 3.2 percent in the period 1948–1966, it had declined to 1.2 percent in the period 1990–1997. The slowing of labor productivity was a worldwide phenomenon, but it had been greater in the United States than in other industrialized countries. It has been one factor in the stagnation of American paychecks.

In addition, America's accustomed role as the world's economic leader was seriously threatened by competition from Europe and Asia in the 1980s. The United States had for years indulged in excessive consumption and low national savings, as well as decreased productivity. Many American plants were old and inefficient. If corporations were to rebuild these plants, it would be at a tremendous cost. Coupled with the expense of employing only organized labor, the cost would prevent these corporations from competing in a world market.

American corporations solved these challenges in two ways. First, they used some surgical procedures, such as reengineering their work. They cut costs by laying off employees or used cheaper labor by employing part-time or temporary workers. They adopted new technologies and management styles. Many shifted their way of doing business to be more in step with the emerging high technologies. Second, they sought potential markets in new places. Often this included moving manufacturing abroad, or *global sourcing*. Global sourcing allows the creation of world capital markets, meaning that companies can build plants anywhere in the world, wherever it is cheapest or where the workers are the best skilled. Over the last several decades, the capital investments of American firms abroad grew by a much higher percentage than their domestic investments. Foreign operation of American-owned firms accounted for more than $1 trillion in sales per year. Profits earned by American firms in the United States dropped by 21 percent between 1989 and 1990, but the overseas profits of American-owned firms surged by 15 percent. In other words, American firms had discovered that they could make higher profits by producing their goods abroad, using cheap and more skilled labor than American workers, and selling products directly on the world market.

Today, the American economy and the economies of other nations are linked by a number of so-called flows. One is the *goods and services flow*, also called trade flow, by which is meant that the United States exports goods and services to other nations and imports goods and services from other nations. *Capital and labor flow*, also called resource flow, means that American firms establish production facilities in foreign countries, and foreign firms establish production facilities in the United States. At the same time, labor also flows, in that many workers immigrate into the United States every year, and some American workers move to other countries to work. *Information and technology flows* refer to the fact that the United States transmits information to other countries and receives information from other countries regarding products, prices, investment opportunities, interest rates, etc. Similarly, technology created in the United States is used in other countries, and American firms use technology developed abroad. Finally, in *financial flows*, money is transferred between the United States and other countries for such purposes as paying for imports, buying assets, paying interest on debt, and providing for foreign aid.

As noted, the extent of these flows has greatly increased in the past several decades. Such an increase in the volume of international trade has been more significant for other countries, but the United States has also profited from the growth of exports and imports, allowing the nation to remain the world's leading trading nation. An overview of international trade includes the facts that as of 2009, we had a trade deficit in goods and services of 380.7 billion, imports were $1,933.7 billion, and exports were $1,553.1 billion (**http://www.census.gov/indicator/ www/ustrade.html**). We import some of the same goods that we export, that is, automobiles, computers, chemicals, telecommunications equipment, and semiconductors. The import and export of goods and services occurs with other industrial nations rather than with developing nations, and our most important trading partner is Canada.

International trade and an open economy allow the United States to specialize, that is, to focus on industries whose products are exportable and away from industries whose products can be imported. This kind of specialization on an international scale increases the productivity of the nation and, thus, its standard of living. Despite this reality, neither governments nor individuals or special-interest groups are always in favor of free trade.

Governments have traditionally imposed a variety of protective tariffs, import quotas, licensing requirements, and export subsidies in attempts to impede imports and boost exports. Governments impose these barriers to free trade usually in response to political pressures by domestic industries, which are temporarily hurt by free trade. Protectionism plays well with some segments of the labor force and industry, but economists maintain that consumers and the entire nation are better served when trade remains unimpeded.

The trend around the world has been toward a decrease in protective tariffs and other impediments. Many nations have entered into agreements to reduce trade barriers. Among the most important ones are the General Agreement on Tariffs and Trade (GATT) and the World Trade Organization (WTO), both of which have been positive forces in liberalizing world trade. The WTO, however, has been a source of controversy in that critics are worried that the rules established to expand international trade and investment will lead firms to evade national laws, especially those that protect workers and the environment.

Another way that nations have sought to reduce protectionism has been through the creation of regional free-trade zones, or trade blocs. One of the most effective has been the European Union (EU), comprising 25 European nations, which has achieved greater productivity, output, and faster economic growth for the members. Another is the North American Free Trade Agreement (NAFTA), a trading bloc formed by the United States, Canada, and Mexico, according to which most trade barriers were to be eliminated by 2008. Although critics of NAFTA were fearful that American workers would lose their jobs as firms relocated in Mexico to take advantage of lower wages and weaker environmental

Box 2 Globalism and Its Foes

The 1990s saw phenomenal growth in the spread of capitalism around the globe. Former communist and socialist economies abandoned command forms or nationalization of industries to pursue the free market and engage in free trade. Generally referred to as "globalism" or "globalization," the movement has found a welcome in many economies and cultures of nations around the world. Although economists and politicians have sung globalization's praises, however, ordinary people here and abroad have looked at the movement with a much more critical eye. This criticism came to public attention when it erupted in violence at such events as a meeting of the World Trade Organization (WTO), a meeting of the World Bank and the International Monetary Fund (IMF), and at one of the meetings of leaders of the Group of Eight in Genoa.

Who are the violent protesters, and what do they want? As to who they are, no one could have predicted in the past that this unusual combination of groups would ever agree on anything. The protesters, in fact, consist of religious groups who complain that the poorest nations of the world are excessively burdened with international debt and should obtain debt forgiveness. They protest against the World Bank and the IMF because these institutions are the leading lenders to those countries.

Another group of protesters are environmentalists, who complain that the spread of free-market capitalism is damaging the environment and contributing to the greenhouse effect. They also believe that the poor nations are being depleted of their natural resources. They are protesting against the World Bank for funding projects that contribute to environmental degradation and against the IMF for offering some governments aid if they decrease their spending on protecting the environment.

A third group of protesters are students, who are concerned with the poor working conditions in overseas factories producing articles for American companies. They accuse the World Bank and the IMF of standing behind the interests of corporations rather than of workers and of forcing companies in developing countries to accept investment by multinational corporations.

Organized labor is also part of these protesting groups. The AFL-CIO, the United Steelworkers of America, and the Teamsters all claim that global trade will have a negative impact on workers in wealthy, industrial societies. They demand stricter trade and labor standards to be enforced around the globe. They want the WTO to change certain trade rules and the IMF to stop encouraging poor nations to develop export-oriented industries at the expense of American labor.

Finally, a number of ad hoc coalitions, such as Global Exchange, 50 Years is Enough, and the Ruckus Society, insist that globalization works against native cultures, increasing social injustice and poverty. They protest against the World Bank and the IMF because they see these institutions as the chief instruments of capitalist expansion, working in tandem with the big corporations (Kahn, 2000, A5).

It is too early to know whether this motley crew of protesters will succeed as a social movement or disperse after a few instances of headline grabbing. What is becoming clearer, however, is that many people around the globe perceive the United States as an imperialistic power. Perhaps they admire the successes of capitalism and the free market economy, and perhaps they envy them. Americans believe they are spreading democracy and human rights around the world, but many in the world believe they are spreading economic and cultural domination.

regulations, in effect the employment rate had risen in the United States until the recessionary period, and it is generally felt that the standard of living has improved in all three countries.

After a painful transitional period, the American economy seemed to regain its edge worldwide. The 1990s saw full employment and a rising stock market. Profitability returned to the old corporations, and myriad new, highly lucrative companies were created in the new high technology field. Beginning in 2000, however, the economy slowed, and in 2008 we were in a full recession and very high unemployment rates, conditions from which we have still not recovered. In fact, the events of the past three years of the decade have been so tragic in terms of our economy that they have soured a large proportion of Americans, who no longer believe in the American dream. Some of the reasons for the economic meltdown and the difficulty of pulling out of it.

The Chapter in Brief

To sustain life, people need a constant supply of food, sufficient shelter, and clothing for protection from the elements. These goods are scarce and require effort to obtain. The institution of the economy consists of the patterns of behavior that revolve around obtaining the scarce resources necessary for survival.

Essentially, societal members must decide what to produce, how to distribute and exchange what is produced, and in what manner to consume it. These decisions are made either by relying on custom and tradition, by the command of a leader or group of leaders, or by the functioning of a market dependent on supply and demand and on prices, profits, and losses. Most modern economies use a variety of these methods in decision making. Resources include labor, land, capital, entrepreneurship, and technology. Resources are versatile but finite; they must be conserved.

Modern industrial economies are characterized by (1) large amounts of capital; (2) extreme specialization and division of labor, which are methods for producing more goods with less effort; and (3) the use of money as the chief medium of exchange. Economic systems are both social and cultural systems legitimized by an ideology accepted by most people as valid. Capitalism, socialism (in both democratic and nondemocratic forms), and communism are the three ideologies underlying most of the modern industrial economies.

The corporation is a form of business enterprise that originated in the middle of the nineteenth century and provided the economy with a tremendous boost. Essentially, this form of business organization makes great sums of money available with diminished risks for individuals. The corporation has made finance capitalism—characterized by the dominance of investment banks and insurance companies, by tremendous aggregates of capital, by separation of ownership from management, and by holding companies—become prevalent.

The trend has been toward ever-greater concentrations of economic power, called oligopoly, in the hands of corporations, some of which are highly diversified and multinational. Although the concentration of power leads to the formation of powerful pressure groups and to unfair competition with smaller firms, it also provides the sophisticated machinery and specialized personnel required for modern technological and scientific advances.

The corporation has given rise to a bureaucracy of managers and white-collar workers, who have become a definite force in the social life of the nation and around whom a fictional mythology and scientific research have developed. Corporate CEOs are extremely well remunerated, and some have engaged in forms of white-collar crime. It is felt that a reorganization of the corporate form of management is essential.

The remaining rung on the industrial ladder belongs to the blue-collar workers who run the machines and the assembly lines to turn out the finished products of industry. Their destinies have been traditionally separate from the rest of the industrial personnel.

The American economy, in which a modified version of capitalism called a mixed market prevails, is characterized by a workforce that is employed largely in the tertiary sector. That is, it supplies services instead of extracting raw materials (the primary sector) or turning them into finished products (the secondary sector). This shift in sectors has resulted in changes in the occupational structure of the society as well as in the stratification system. The changes consist of a trend toward professionalization of jobs that can be upgraded, whereas the unskilled or under-educated become the permanently unemployed or underemployed.

Organization of labor in the United States began in the late nineteenth century and did not flourish again until the passage of legislation acknowledging government's responsibility for the welfare of workers. The labor movement saw a further reawakening during the tenure of President Franklin Roosevelt, who encouraged unionization in the belief that it would give workers increased purchasing power, which in turn would stimulate the economy.

Today, organized labor is experiencing declining growth, partly as a result of the decline of the secondary sector and the growth of the tertiary sector, whose workers have traditionally avoided unionization, and partly because of other factors. American labor is now competing with better-educated, better-trained, and more disciplined foreign labor, just as the American economy is challenged by sharp competition from abroad.

Beginning in the 1970s, productivity in the United States began to decline. In addition, American industrial machinery and plants were old. Declining productivity results in a stagnating economy. To counteract this and other factors, American firms reengineered their work, cut costs by laying off employees or using part-time workers, and began to move manufacturing abroad, engaging in global sourcing. This method became so successful that we have effectively moved toward a global type of economy, in which goods and services, capital and labor, information and technology, and finances flow from the United States to other nations and back again.

International trade has been very profitable for all involved, especially for the industrial nations. International trade and an open economy allow the United States to specialize, focusing on specific products, and, thus, increase productivity. However, many segments of the population believe that open international trade allows American jobs to go abroad, and consequently, they pressure the government to impede it. The government does this by imposing various tariffs and other trade barriers. Economists have shown that protectionism is detrimental in the long run, so governments have done away with most trade barriers. Instead, nations have entered into agreements such as GATT and WTO, both of which have additionally liberalized trade barriers. In addition, nations have tried to reduce protectionism by creating regional free-trade zones, such as the European Union and the North American Free Trade Agreement (NAFTA). These trading blocs have been successful despite fears that they would hurt American workers. There are vocal critics, however, who claim that economic globalism leads to exploitation of workers and weakened environmental regulations.

The American economy reached a pinnacle during the 1990s with bubbles in the real estate market and trading practices in the investment banking industry making many people very wealthy. Unfortunately, these bubbles burst toward the end of 2007, and we have entered a period of high unemployment rates and sky-high deficits.

Terms to Remember

bonds Promises to repay a loan with a set rate of interest.

capital All material objects made by humans. One of the factors of production.

capitalism An economic system in which property belongs to private individuals; production is engaged in for a profit motive; and prices, wages, and profits are regulated by supply and demand, as well as competition. The welfare of the individual is the chief concern.

corporation A form of enterprise organized for large-scale productions.

factors of production   Labor, land, capital, entrepreneurship, time and technology, or the basic elements that are combined in the production of goods and services.

finance capitalism   Capitalism associated with a later stage of industrialism in which business organizations are characterized by (1) dominance of investment banks and insurance companies, (2) large aggregates of capital, (3) ownership separate from management, (4) appearance of the holding company, and (5) appearance of the corporation.

guilds   Kinds of labor unions that were common during the middle ages.

industrial capitalism   Capitalism associated with an early stage of industrialism in which business organizations were concerned mainly with manufacturing, mining, and transportation.

labor   A human resource. One of the factors of production.

land   Natural material things such as land, minerals, water. Another of the factors of production.

money   The preeminent medium of exchange.

monopoly   A situation in which one firm produces the entire market supply of a specific product.

multinational corporations   Corporations that extend production to foreign nations at great profit to themselves (because labor is cheap and markets are expanded) but at the risk of being perceived as threats to the hosts.

oligopoly   A condition of high industrial concentration in which a small number of corporations dominate an entire industry, effectively preventing price competition.

opportunity cost   The sacrifice involved in making an economic choice.

partnership   A more complex form of business organization than a sole proprietorship that involves two or more individuals.

productivity   The amount in dollars that a worker produces in a given hour.

primary sector of the economy   Deals with the extraction and processing of raw materials (agriculture, fishing, mining, and forestry).

production-possibility limits   The optimum amount of production that a society can attain. Each society faces a production-possibility frontier beyond which it cannot produce.

property   The rights that an owner has to an object as compared with the rights of those who are not owners of that object.

resources   Everything that is needed for the production of goods and services.

secondary sector of the economy   Is concerned with manufacturing and constructing, turning raw materials into finished products.

stocks   Shares of ownership in a corporation.

tertiary sector of the economy   Involves services—repairing, remodeling, educating, healing, etc.,

trusts   Mergers of corporations for the purpose of cornering a market.

Suggested Readings

Appleby, Joyce. 2010. *The Relentless Revolution: A History of Capitalism.* New York: W. W. Norton. A new account of the most modern of economic systems, focusing on the way the system is constantly changing, revolutionizing the structure of society from within.

Barlett, Donald L., and James B. Steele. 1992. *America: What Went Wrong?* Kansas City, MO: Andrews & McMeel. Two Pulitzer Prize–winning journalists turn their investigative lens to the economic effects the past generation of presidents and members of Congress have had on the nation. The authors conclude that the latter have been changing the American economy, by design and default, to favor the privileged, the powerful, and the influential at the expense of everyone else.

Friedman, Thomas L. 2005. *The World Is Flat: A Brief History of the Twenty-First Century.* New York: Farrar, Strauss and Giroux. The award-winning *New York Times* columnist explains the convergence of technology and events that has led to globalization. The world is flat because manufacturing and services can flow from one country to the next, allowing people of different countries to create wealth for their societies. A clear narrative that includes successes as well as failures and discontents that globalization evokes.

Galbraith, John Kenneth. 1992. *The Culture of Contentment*. New York: Houghton Mifflin. An influential liberal economist critiques the state of the American economy in the 1980s, blaming much of the trouble on the nonintervention—or selective intervention—of the government so that public needs are neglected at the expense of benefits accruing to the few. The author concludes that we have unleashed capitalism only to have it succumb to its own self-destructive tendencies.

Levitt, Steven D., and Stephen J. Dubner. 2005. *Freakonomics*. New York: William Morrow/HarperCollins. Neither a conventional economics book nor a run-of-the-mill social science book, but a new and different way of looking at everyday matters.

Levy, Frank. 1999. *The New Dollars and Dreams*. New York: Russell Sage Foundation. This book is an update of a 1987 book. The author analyzes the performance of the American economy since World War II, when steadily rising living standards were a fact. He then explains what has happened since the 1970s, in which productivity slowed and incomes began to stagnate, and what happened in the 1990s to prompt an economic recovery.

Luttwak, Edward. 1999. *Turbo-Capitalism: Winners and Losers in the Global Economy*. New York: HarperCollins. The author characterizes the state of today's American economy as turbocharged, that is, overheated by the abolition of anticompetition laws and regulations, by the technological innovations brought on by the computer revolution, and by privatization and removal of most import barriers. Although turbo-capitalism is superior to the communist and socialist economic formulations, it has some corrosive effects on society.

Porter, Michael E., 1998. *The Competitive Advantage of Nations*. New York: The Free Press. The author has examined 10 economies and shows that productivity is central to a nation's competitive market position.

There are also a number of articles of interest:

Austen, Ben. 2009. "End of the Road: After Detroit, the Wreck of an American Dream." *Harper's Magazine*. August.

Brill, Steven. 2010. "What's a Bailed-Out Banker Worth?" *The New York Times Magazine*. January 3, pp. 32–49.

Cohen, Patricia. 2007. "In Economics Departments, a Growing Will to Debate Fundamental Assumptions." Web site of the U.S. Department of Commerce with information about the state of the economy.

References

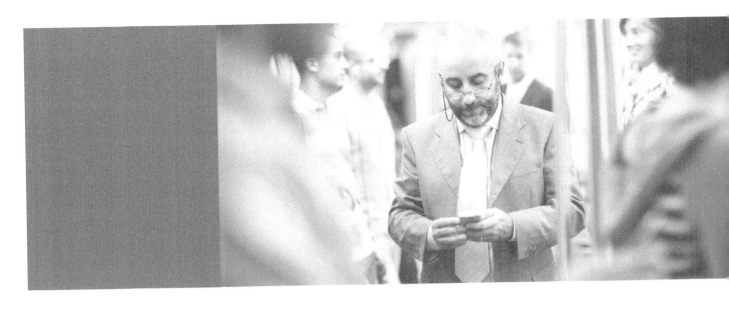

References

Abbott, Charles, and Christopher Doering. 2009. "One in Seven Americans Short of Food." *Reuters,* November 16.

Abramson, Jill. 1998. "The Business of Persuasion Thrives in Nation's Capital." *The New York Times,* September 29, pp. 1–22, 23.

Adorno, T. W., Else Frenkel-Brunswik, Daniel J. Levinson, and R. Nevitt Sanford. 1950. *The Authoritarian Personality.* New York: Harper & Brothers.

Alba, Richard D. 1990. *Ethnic Identity: The Transformation of White America.* New Haven, CT: Yale University Press.

Albrecht, Stan L. 1980. "Reactions and Adjustments to Divorce: Differences in the Experiences of Males and Females." *Family Relations,* January, pp. 59–68.

Alexander, Herbert E. 1980. *Financing Politics: Money, Elections, and Political Reform.* Washington, DC: Congressional Quarterly Press.

Allman, William. 1994. "A Family Legacy for Lucy." *U.S. News & World Report,* April 11, p. 55.

Allport, Gordon. 1954. *The Nature of Prejudice.* Reading, MA: Addison-Wesley.

American Anthropological Association. 1996. "Statement on Race." *American Association of Physical Anthropologists (AJPA)* 101, pp. 569–570. Now available at *http://www.aaanet.org.*

American Religious Identification Survey (ARIS). 2001. Graduate Center Survey of Religion in America. Complements U.S. Census. October.

Americans for Divorce Reform. *http://www.divorcereform@usanet.*

Andrews, P. 1993. "Fossil Evidence on Human Origins and Dispersal." In Russell L. Ciochon and John G. Fleagle, *The Human Evolution Source Book.* Englewood Cliffs, NJ: Prentice Hall, pp. 3–11.

Angier, Natalie. 1991. "A Potent Peptide Prompts an Urge to Cuddle." *The New York Times,* January 22, pp. B5, B8.

Angier, Natalie. 1995. "If You Are Really Ancient, You May Be Better Off." *The New York Times,* June 11, pp. 1 & 5E.

Angier, Natalie. 1997. "Sexual Identity Not Pliable After All, Report Says." *The New York Times,* March 14, 1997, pp. 1, A10.

Archdeacon, Thomas J. 1983. *Becoming American: An Ethnic History.* New York: Free Press.

Atchley, Robert C. 1982. "Retirement: Leaving the World of Work." *Annals,* 464, November, pp. 120–131.

Barlett, Donald L., and James B. Steele. 1998. "Corporate Welfare." *Time.* November 9, pp. 36–40.

Barna Research Group. 2004. "Beliefs: Heaven and Hell." *http://www.barna.org/FlexPage. aspx?Page=Topic&TopicID=3.* Accessed 7/13/04.

Basow, Susan. 1992. *Gender Stereotypes and Roles.* 3rd ed. Belmont, CA: Brooks/Cole.

Baylor Institute for Studies of Religion. 2006. *American Piety in the 21st Century.* September.

BBC News. 2007. "'Altruistic' Brain Region Found." *http://newsvote.bbc.uk/mpapps/pagetools/print/news/ bbc.co.uk/1/hi/health/6278907.stm.*

Bearak, Barry. 1998. "Caste Hate, and Murder, Outlast India's Reforms." *The New York Times,* September 19, p. A3.

Becker, Howard S. 1963. *Outsiders: Studies in the Sociology of Deviance.* New York: Free Press.

Bell, Daniel. 1987. "The World and the United States in 2013." *Daedalus* 116(3): 1–31.

Bellah, Robert N. 1970. *Beyond Belief.* New York: Harper & Row.

Bellah, Robert N., Richard Madsen, William M. Sullivan, Ann Swidler, and Steven M. Tipton. 1985. *Habits of the Heart.* Los Angeles: University of California Press.

Belsky, Jay, and Laurence D. Steinberg. 1978. "The Effects of Day Care: A Critical Review." *Child Development* 49: 929–949.

Bem, Sandra L. 1981. "Gender Schema Theory: A Cognitive Account of Sex Typing." *Psychological Review* 88: 354–364.

Bem, Sandra L. 1983. "Gender Schema Theory and Its Implications for Child Development." *Signs* 8: 598–616.

Bem, Sandra L. 1985. "Androgyny and Gender Schema Theory: A Conceptual and Empirical Integration." In T. B. Sonderegger, ed., *Nebraska Symposium on Motivations: Psychology of Gender.* Lincoln: University of Nebraska Press.

Besharov, Douglas, and Peter Germanis. 2001. *Rethinking WIC: An Evaluation of the Women, Infants, and Children Program.* Washington, DC: AEI Press.

Bierman, Jeffrey A. 1990. "The Effect of Television Sports Media on Black Male Youth." *Sociological Inquiry* 60 (Fall): 413, 427.

Bilefsky, Dan. 2008. "Old Custom Fades in Albania: Woman as Man of the Family." *The New York Times,* June 25, pp A1–A12.

Blake, Judith, and Kingsley Davis. 1964. "Norms, Values, and Sanctions." In Robert E. L. Faris, ed., *Handbook of Modern Sociology.* Chicago: Rand McNally, p. 456.

Blau, Peter M., and Otis Dudley Duncan. 1967. *The American Occupational Structure.* New York: Wiley.

Blau, Peter M., and Marshall W. Meyer. 1971. *Bureaucracy in Modern Society.* New York: Random House.

Blood, Robert O., Jr., and Donald M. Wolfe. 1960. *Husbands and Wives: The Dynamics of Married Living.* Glencoe, IL: Free Press.

Blumer, Herbert. 1946/1969. "Collective Behavior." In Alfred McClung Lee, ed., *Principles of Sociology.* New York: Harper & Row.

Blumer, Herbert. 1951. "Social Movements." In Alfred McClung Lee, ed., *Principles of Sociology.* New York: Barnes & Noble.

Blumstein, P. W., and Pepper Schwartz. 1977. "Bisexuality: Some Social Psychological Issues." *Journal of Social Issues* 33(2): 30–45.

Bonner, Raymond, and Ford Fassenden. 2000. "Absence of Executions: A Special Report. States With No Death Penalty Share Lower Homicide Rates." *The New York Times,* September 22, p. A1.

Boswell, John. 1989. *The Kindness of Strangers.* New York: Pantheon.

Bowles, Samuel, and Herbert Gintis. 1976. *Schooling in Capitalist America: Educational Reform and the Contradictions of Economic Life.* New York: Basic Books.

Bradsher, Keith. 1995a. "America's Opportunity Gap." *The New York Times,* June 4, Section 4, p. 4.

Bradsher, Keith. 1995b. "Low Ranking for Poor American Children." *The New York Times,* August 14, p. A7.

Bramlett, Matthew D., and William D. Mosher. 2002. "Cohabitation, Marriage, Divorce and Remarriage in the United States." National Center for Health Statistics. *Vital and Health Statistics* 23(22): 23.

Branigin, William. 1992. "North vs. South at the U.S." *The Washington Post National Weekly Edition,* December 14–20, pp. 10–11.

Broad, William J., 2003. "In a Lab on Long Island, a Visit to the Big Bang." *The New York Times,* January 14, p. D4.

Broderick, Carlfried B. 1993. *Understanding Family Process: Basics of Family Systems Theory.* Thousand Oaks, CA: Sage.

Brody, Jane E. 1983. "Divorce's Stress Exacts Long Term Health Toll." *The New York Times,* December 13, p. C1.

Bronner, Ethan. 1998. "Winds of Change Rustle University of Chicago." *The New York Times,* December 28, pp. 1, 18.

Brooks, David. 2010. "The Tea Party Teens." *The New York Times,* January 5, p. A17.

Brown, Patricia Leigh. 2009. "Invisible Immigrants, Old and Left With 'Nobody to Talk To'." *The New York Times,* August 30, p. A1.

Browne, Malcolm W. 1992. "2 Skulls in China: Evidence of Early Humans Outside of Africa?" *The New York Times,* June 4, p. A7.

Bumiller, Elisabeth. 2010. "In Camouflage or Afghan Veil, A Fragile Bond." *The New York Times,* May 30, pp. 1–10.

Bumpass, Larry, and Hsien-Hen Lu. 2000. "Trends in Cohabitation and Implications for Children's Family Contexts." Unpublished manuscript, Center for Demography, University of Wisconsin, Madison, WI.

Bumpass, Larry, and James A. Sweet. 1995. "The Changing Character of Stepfamilies: Implications of Cohabitations and Nonmarital Childbearing." *Demography* 32(3): 425–436.

Bureau of Economic Analysis. 2010. *http:// www.bea. gov/national/xls/gdplev.xls.*

Bureau of Justice Statistics/Capital Punishment/ Summary findings, 2004. *http://www.ojp.usdoj.gov/bjs/cp.htm.*

Bureau of Justice Statistics Publications. 2005. *Family Violence.* NCJ207846. June.

Bureau of Labor Statistics. 2006. *http://stats.bls.gov/cpsaatab.htm.*

Bureau of Labor Statistics. 2009. "Women in the Labor Force: A Databook, 2009 Edition." Report 1018. September.

Butterfield, Fox. 2004. "With Longer Sentences, Cost of Fighting Crime Is Higher." *The New York Times,* May 3, p. A18.

Cairncross, Frances. 2004. "Forever Young." *The Economist,* March 27, pp. 3–4.

Caplow, Theodore. 1968. *Two Against One: Coalitions in Triads.* Englewood Cliffs, NJ: Prentice Hall.

Carey, Benedict, 2004. "Addicted to Mother's Love: It's Biology, Stupid." *The New York Times,* June 29, p. D.7.

Carey, Benedict. 2007. "Do You Believe in Magic?" *The New York Times,* January 23, pp. D1, D6.

Carey, Benedict. 2010. "Families' Every Hug and Fuss, Taped, Analyzed and Archived." *The New York Times,* May 23, pp. 1–17.

Carroll, Janelle. 2009. *Sexuality Now: Embracing Diversity.* 3rd ed. New York: Wadsworth, p. 97.

Carroll, Sean B. 2005. *Endless Forms Most Beautiful.* New York: Norton.

Catalano, Shannan. 2007. "Intimate Partner Violence in the United States." U.S. Department of Justice, Bureau of Justice Statistics. Available at *http://www.ojp.usdoj.gov/bjs/intimate/ipy.htm.*

Cave, Damien. 2010. "Baby Boomers Are Backing Arizona's Tough New Law While Young People Are Rejecting It." *The New York Times,* May 18, pp. A17–A17.

CDC/NCHS, National Health and Nutrition Examination Survey, 2008. *http://www.cdc.gov/nchs/nhanes.htm.*

Center on Budget and Policy Priorities. 2006. "The Number of Uninsured Americans Is at an All-Time High." August 29. *http://www.cbpp.org/8-29-06health.htm.*

Centers for Disease Control and Prevention (CDC). 2007. "A Glance at the HIV/AIDS Epidemic." Revised June 2007. *http://www.cdc.gov/hiv/resources/factsheet/ataglance.htm#3.*

Centers for Disease Control and Prevention, Fastats, December 2009.

Chen, M. Keith. 2007. "Prison Conditions: Gently Does It." *The Economist,* July 26.

Cherlin, Andrew J. 1981. *Marriage, Divorce, Remarriage.* Boston: Harvard University Press.

Cherlin, Andrew J. 1987. "Don't Fear the 'Depopulation' Bomb." *Christian Science Monitor,* January 5, p. 16.

Child Trends Research Brief. 2009. "Children in Poverty: Trends, Consequences, and Policy Options." April.

Chodorow, Nancy. 1978. *The Reproduction of Mothering.* Berkeley: University of California Press.

Chua, Amy. 2009. "Where is U.S. Policy Headed?" *The New York Times,* October 22 (*www.nytimes.com/crossroads*).

CIA. 2007. *http://www.cia.gov/library/publications/the-world-factbook.*

CIA. 2010. *http://www.cia.gov/library/publications/the-world-factbook.*

Cloward, Richard A., and Lloyd E. Ohlin. 1960. *Delinquency and Opportunity: A Theory of Delinquent Gangs.* New York: Free Press.

CNNMoney.com. 2006. "CEO Paycheck: $24,000 a Day." June 21 (by Jeanne Sahadi, CNNMoney senior writer).

Cohen, Albert K. 1955. *Delinquent Boys: The Culture of the Gang.* New York: Free Press.

Cohen, Patricia. 2004. "Forget Lonely. Life Is Healthy at the Top." *The New York Times,* May 15, p. A17.

Cohn, Werner. 1958. "The Politics of American Jews." In Marshall Sklare, ed., *The Jews: Social Patterns of an American Group.* Glencoe, IL: Free Press.

Coleman, James S. 1966. *Equality of Educational Opportunity.* Washington, DC: U.S. Government Printing Office.

Coleman, James S. 1981. *High School Achievement: Public, Catholic, and Private Schools Compared.* New York: Basic Books.

College Board Research, Educational Testing Service. 2001. *http://www.etc.org/research/newpubs.htm.* Accessed 8/15/04.

Collins, Randall. 1979. *The Credential Society: An Historical Sociology of Education and Stratification.* New York: Academic Press.

Conant, Jennet, and Pat Wingert. 1987. "You'd Better Sit Down, Kids." *Newsweek,* August 24, p. 58.

Cooley, Charles Horton. 1909/1910. *Social Organization, A Study of the Larger Mind.* New York: Scribner's.

Cooley, Charles Horton. 1909/1964. *Human Nature and the Social Order.* New York: Schocken, p. 152.

Cowley, Geoffrey. 1998. "Wilson's World." *Newsweek,* June 22, pp. 59–61.

Creveld, Martin van. 2007. *The Changing Face of War: Lessons of Combat from the Marne to Iraq.* New York: Ballantine Books.

Crossette, Barbara. 1992. "Population Policy in Asia is Faulted." *The New York Times,* September 16, p. A7.

Crossette, Barbara. 2001. "Against a Trend, U.S. Population Will Bloom, U.N. Says." *The New York Times,* February 28, pp. A1, A5.

Dahl, Robert A. 1956. *A Preface to Democratic Theory.* Chicago: University of Chicago Press.

Dahl, Robert A. 1967. *Pluralist Democracy in the United States.* Chicago: Rand McNally, p. 24.

Dahl, Robert A., and Charles E. Lindblom. 1976. *Politics, Economics, and Welfare.* Chicago: University of Chicago Press.

Davidson, James D. 2004. "American Catholics and American Catholicism: An Inventory of Facts, Trends and Influences: *http://www.be.edu/bc.org/research/rap/church-in-america/davidson.html.*

Davis, Kingsley. 1947. *Final Note on a Case of Extreme Isolation.* New York: John Wiley.

Davis, Kingsley, and Wilbert Moore. 1945. "Some Principles of Stratification." *American Sociological Review* 10: 242–249.

DeParle, Jason, and Robert M. Gebeloff. 2010. "Living on Nothing but Food Stamps." *The New York Times,* January 3, pp. 1–18.

DeWitt, Karen. 1994. "Wave of Suburban Growth Is Being Fed by Minorities." *The New York Times,* August 15, pp. 1, 12.

Dillon, Sam. 2009. "Study Finds High Rate of Imprisonment Among Dropouts." *The New York Times,* October 8. p. A12.

Domestic Violence Statistics. American Bar Association, Commission on Domestic Violence. Survey of Recent Statistics. *http://www.abanet.org/domviol/statistics. html.* Accessed 10/20/2007.

Donnerstein, Ed, Ron Slaby, and Leonard Eron. 1993. "The Mass Media and Youth Aggression." *Violence and Youth.* Washington, DC: American Psychology Association.

Dowd, James J. 1980a. "Exchange Rates and Old People." *Journal of Gerontology* 35: 596–602.

Dowd, James J. 1980b. *Stratification among the Aged.* Monterey, CA: Brooks/Cole.

Dreifus, Claudia. 1998. "Tracing Evolution of Cosmos from Its Simplest Elements." *The New York Times,* April 28, p. B15.

Dunn, Judy, and Robert Plomin. 1990. *Separate Lives: Why Siblings Are So Different.* New York: Basic Books.

Durkheim, Emile. 1897/1951/1966. *Le suicide: Etude de Sociologie.* J. A. Spaulding and George Simpson, transl. New York: Free Press.

Durkheim, Emile. 1912/1947. *The Elementary Forms of Religious Life.* Reprinted Edition. New York: Free Press.

Dye, Thomas R., and L. Harmon Zeigler. 1984. *The Irony of Democracy: An Uncommon Introduction to American Politics.* Monterey, CA: Brooks/Cole.

Dye, Thomas R., and L. Harmon Zeigler. 1993. *The Irony of Democracy: An Uncommon Introduction to American Politics,* 9th ed. Belmont, CA: Wadsworth.

Eakin, Emily. 2001. "Tilling History with Biology's Tools." *The New York Times,* February 10, pp. A15–17.

Eaton, Joe, and M.B. Pell. February 24, 2010. "Lobbyists Swarm Capitol to Influence Health Reform." *http:// www.publicintegrity.org/articles/entry/1953.*

Ebenstein, William. 1973. *Today's Isms.* 7th ed. Englewood Cliffs, NJ: Prentice Hall.

Eckholm, Erik. 2007a. "Childhood Poverty Is Found to Portend High Adult Costs." *The New York Times,* January 25, p. A15.

Eckholm, Erik. 2007b. "In Turnabout, Infant Deaths Climb in South." *The New York Times,* April 22, pp. 1–20.

Economist, The. 2004. "Forever Young: A Survey of Retirement." March 27, pp. 3–18.

Edmonston, Barry, and Thomas M. Guterbock. 1984. "Is Suburbanization Slowing Down? Recent Trends in Population Deconcentration in U.S. Metropolitan Areas." *Social Forces* 62(4): 9005–9025.

Edsall, Thomas B. 2007. "Party Boy: Why the GOP's Future Belongs to Rudy." *The New Republic,* May 21, pp. 26–32.

"Educational Attainment by Race and Hispanic Origin: 1970–2009." *The 2011 Statistical Abstract, Education.*

Egan, Timothy. 1998. "From Adolescent Angst to Shooting Up Schools." *The New York Times,* June 14, pp. 1, 20.

Ehrenreich, Barbara. 1989. *Fear of Falling: The Inner Life of the Middle Class.* New York: Pantheon.

Elkind, David. 1981. *The Hurried Child: Growing Up Too Fast Too Soon.* Reading, MA: Addison-Wesley.

Engels, Frederick. 1902 (First published 1884). *The Origin of the Family, Private Property and the State.* Ernest Untermann, transl. Chicago: C. H. Kerr & Company.

Ericksen, Julia A. 1999. *Kiss and Tell: Surveying Sex in the Twentieth Century.* Cambridge, MA: Harvard University Press.

Erikson, Erik H. 1963. *Childhood and Society.* New York: W. W. Norton.

Erikson, Erik H. 1968. *Identity, Youth and Crisis.* New York: W. W. Norton.

Erikson, Kai T. 1964. "Notes on the Sociology of Deviance." In Howard Becker, ed. *The Other Side: Perspectives on Deviance,* New York: Free Press.

Etzioni, Amitai. 1975. *A Comparative Analysis of Complex Organizations,* rev. ed. New York: Free Press.

Ewing, Charles P. 1995. *Kids Who Kill.* New York: Avon.

Family Violence Prevention Fund: Action Center. 2009. *http://www.endabuse.org/content/action_center/ detail/754.*

Fearon, James D., and David D. Laitin. 2002. "Ethnicity, Insurgency and Civil War." *American Political Science Review* 97(1), 75–90.

Ferguson, Thomas, and Joel Rogers. 1986. *Right Turn: The Decline of the Democrats and the Future of American Politics.* New York: Hill and Wang.

Fisher, Claude. 1984. *The Urban Experience.* New York: Harcourt Brace Jovanovich.

Flanigan, William H., and Nancy Zingale. 1998. *Political Behavior of the American Electorate.* 9th ed. Washington, DC: Congressional Quarterly Press.

Fogel, Robert William, and Stanley L. Engerman. 1974. *Time on the Cross.* Boston, Little, Brown and Company. Reissued 1995.

Ford, Clelland S., and Frank A. Beach. 1951. *Patterns of Sexual Behavior.* New York: Harper & Row.

Franklin, Clyde W. II. 1988. *Men and Society.* Chicago: Nelson Hall.

Fratkin, Elliot. 1997. *Aarial Pastoralists of Kenya.* New York: Prentice Hall.

Frazier, Franklin E. 1966. *The Negro Family in the United States.* Chicago: University of Chicago Press.

Friedrich, Carl J., and Zbigniew Brzezinski. 1966. *Totalitarian Dictatorship and Autocracy.* New York: Praeger.

Friedrich, Carl J., Michael Curtis, and Benjamin R. Barber. 1969. *Totalitarianism in Perspective: Three Views.* New York: Praeger.

Frieze, I., J. Parsons, P. Johnson, D. N. Ruble, and G. Zellman, eds. 1978. *Women and Sex Roles.* New York: Norton.

Frieze, I., and S. J. Ramsey. 1976. "Nonverbal Maintenance of Traditional Sex Roles." *Journal of Social Issues* 32: 133–141.

Fry, Richard, and D'Vera Cohn. 2010. "New Economics of Marriage: The Rise of Wives." Pew Research Center Publications. *http://pewresearch.org/pubs/1466/economics-marriage-rise-of-wives.* Accessed 01/19/2010.

Fukuyama, Francis. 1999. *The Great Disruption: Human Nature and the Reconstitution of Social Orders.* New York: Free Press.

Gallup/CNN/USA Today Poll, September 8–10, 2000. *The New York Times,* October 29, p. 5.

Gallup Poll, May and October 2003.

Gallup Poll, 2006. "Estimating Americans' Worship Behavior." January 3.

Gans, Herbert J. 1962/1982. *The Urban Villagers: Group and Class in the Life of Italian-Americans.* New York: Free Press.

Gates, Gary J. 2006. "Same Sex Couples and the Gay, Lesbian, Bisexual Population: New Estimates from the American Community Survey." The Williams Institute. UCLA School of Law. October. Retrieved from http://escholarship.org/uc/item/8h08t0zf.

Gee, Henry. 2002. "Touma'A: Face of the Deep." *Nature,* 115, pp. 195–199.

Gelles, Richard J., Murray A. Straus, and Suzanne K. Steinmetz. 2006. *Behind Closed Doors: Violence in the American Family.* New Brunswick, NJ: Transaction Publishers.

Gerth, H. H., and C. Wright Mills, eds. 1946. *From Max Weber: Essays in Sociology.* New York: Oxford University.

Gilligan, Carol. 1982. *In a Different Voice: Psychological Theory and Women's Development.* Cambridge, MA: Harvard University Press.

Gilmer, Todd P., and Richard G. Kronick. 2009. "Hard Times and Health Insurance: How Many Americans will be Uninsured by 2010?" Published online 28 May on the *Health Affairs* Web site.

Giniger, Seymour, Angelo Dispenzieri, and Joseph Eisenberg. 1983. "Age, Experience, and Performance on Speed and Skill Jobs in an Applied Setting." *Journal of Applied Psychology* 68: 469–475.

Gladwell, Malcolm. 1998. "Do Parents Matter?" *The New Yorker,* August 17, pp. 54–64.

Gladwell, Malcolm. 2006. "Here's Why." *The New Yorker,* April 10, p. 80–82.

Glaeser, Edward L. 2005. "Inequality." Harvard Institute for Economic Research. July.

Gleick, Elizabeth. 1995. "Rich Justice, Poor Justice." *Time,* June 19, p. 42.

Glock, Charles Y., and Rodney Stark. 1965. *Religion and Society in Tension.* Chicago: Rand McNally.

Glueck, Sheldon, and Eleanor Glueck. 1956. *Physique and Delinquency.* New York: Harper & Row.

Glushko, Bob, and Anno Saxenian. 2006. "The Information and Services Economy." University of California at Berkeley, School of Information. Fall.

Goffman, Erving. 1961. *Asylums: Essays on the Social Situation of Mental Patients and Other Inmates.* Garden City, NY: Anchor.

Goldberg Steven. 1977. *The Inevitability of Patriarchy.* London: Temple Smith.

Goldberg, Steven. 1989. "The Theory of Patriarchy: A Final Summation." *International Journal of Sociology and Social Policy* 9(1): 16–18.

Goldman, Ari L. 1991. "Portrait of Religion in U.S. Holds Dozens of Surprises." *The New York Times,* April 10, pp. 1, A11.

Goleman, Daniel. 1989. "Sad Legacy of Abuse." *The New York Times,* January 24, pp. A1, A22.

Goleman, Daniel. 1992. "New Storm Brews on Whether Crime Has Roots in Genes." *The New York Times,* September 15, B5, B8.

Goleman, Daniel. 2006. *Social Intelligence.* New York: Bantam.

Goode, E. 1990. *Deviant Behavior.* 3rd ed. Upper Saddle River, NJ: Prentice Hall.

Goode, Erica. 2001. "With Fears Fading, More Gays Spurn Old Preventive Message." *The New York Times,* August 19, pp. 1, 30.

Goode, William J. 1963. *World Revolution and Family Patterns.* New York: Free Press.

Goodheart, Adam. 2004. "Change of Heart." *AARP,* May/June, pp. 37–41, 75.

Goodman, Walter, 1992. "Seeking Traces of the First Americans." *The New York Times,* October 20, p. B4.

Gottman, J. M. 1978. "Megalopolitan Systems Around the World." In L. S. Bourne and J. W. Simmonds, eds., *Systems of Cities: Readings on Structure, Growth, and Policy.* New York: Oxford University Press.

Graham, John. 2004. "How Long Do Stars Usually Live?" *Scientific American,* March 29. *www.sciam.com/article.* Accessed 6/5/04.

Greenfield, Liah. 1992. *Nationalism: Five Roads to Modernity*. Cambridge, MA: Harvard University Press.

Gregor, A. James. 1968. *Contemporary Radical Ideologies*. New York: Random House.

Grusky, David B., and Robert M. Hauser. 1984. "Comparative Social Mobility Revisited: Models of Convergence and Divergence in 16 Countries." *American Sociological Review,* 49: 19–38.

Gutman, Herbert G. 1976. *The Black Family in Slavery and Freedom, 1750–1925*. New York: Pantheon Books.

Hall, Trish. 1991. "Breaking Up Is Becoming Harder to Do." *The New York Times,* March 14, pp. B1–B4.

Harlow, Harry. 1966. "Learning to Love." *American Scientist* 54: 224–272.

Harris, Fred. 1986. *America's Democracy: The Ideal and the Reality,* 3rd ed. Glenview, IL: Scott, Foresman.

Harris, Judith Rich. 1999. *The Nurture Assumption.* New York: Touchstone.

Harris Poll #59, October 15, 2003. Taylor, Humphrey, "While Most Americans Believe in God, Only 36% Attend a Religious Service Once a Month or More Often." *http://www.harrisinteractive.com/harrispoll/index.* Accessed 8/12/04.

Harrison, Algea O., et al. 1990. "Family Ecologies of Ethnic Minority Children." *Child Development* 61: 347–362

Harvey, David. 1973. *Social Justice and the City.* Baltimore: Johns Hopkins University Press.

Harvey, David. 1984. *The Limits to Capital.* Chicago: University of Chicago Press.

Harvey, David. 1985. *Consciousness and the Urban Experience.* Baltimore: Johns Hopkins University Press.

Hauser, Robert M., and David L. Featherman. 1977. *The Process of Stratification: Trends and Analysis.* New York: Academic Press.

Haviland, William A. 1995. *Anthropology.* 7th ed. New York: Harcourt Brace College Publishers.

Hayden, Thomas. 2002. "A Theory Evolves." *U.S. News & World Report,* July 29, pp. 43–50.

Hayden, Thomas. 2004. "Jawboning Evolution." *U.S. News & World Report,* April 5, p. 72.

Headland, Thomas, and Lawrence Reid. 1989. "Hunter Gatherers and Their Neighbors from Prehistory to the Present." *Current Anthropology* 30: 43–66.

Herberg, Will. 1960. *Protestant, Catholic, Jew.* Garden City, NY: Doubleday (Anchor Books).

Herbert, Bob. 1999. "Addicted to Violence." *The New York Times,* April 22, p. A31.

Herbert, Wray. 1982. "Sources of Temperament: Bashful at Birth?" *Science News,* January 16, p. 36.

Hertz, Tom. 2006. "Understanding Mobility in America." *Center for American Progress,* April 26.

Hetherington, E. Mavis, and John Kelly. 2002. *For Better or for Worse: Divorce Reconsidered.* New York: Norton.

Hite, Shere. 1981. *The Hite Report on Male Sexuality.* New York: Knopf.

Hofstadter, Richard. 1954. *The American Political Tradition.* New York: Vintage.

Holzer, Harry J., Peter Edelman, and Paul Offner. 2006. *Reconnecting Disadvantaged Young Men.* Washington, DC. *http://www.urban.org/url.cfm?ID=900956.*

Hoover, Kenneth, and Todd Donovan. 1995. *The Elements of Social Scientific Thinking.* 6th ed. New York: St. Martin's Press.

Horn, Jack C., and Jeff Meer. 1987. "The Vintage Years." *Psychology Today,* 21(5): 76–90.

Horn, Joseph M., Robert Plomin, and Ray Rosenman. 1976. "Heritability of Personality Traits in Adult Male Twins." *Behavior Genetics,* January, pp. 17–30.

Hoyenga, K. B., and K. Hoyenga. 1979. *The Question of Sex Differences: Psychological, Cultural, and Biological Issues.* Boston: Little, Brown.

Human Development Report. 2006. "Beyond Scarcity: Power, Poverty, and the Global Water Crisis." New York: United Nations Development Programme.

Hunt, Morton, and Bernice Hunt. 1980. "Another World, Another Life" In *Family in Transition,* Arlene Skolnick and Jerome H. Skolnick, eds. Boston: Little, Brown.

Hurley, Dan. 2004. "On Crime as Science (A Neighbor at a Time)." *The New York Times,* January 6, pp. D1, D2.

Irving, Carl. 1990. "Sociologist Refutes Midlife Crisis." *The (Cleveland) Plain Dealer,* October 25, p. 11E.

Jacquet, Constant H., and Alice M. Jones. 1991. *Yearbook of American and Canadian Churches.* Nashville, TN: Abingdon Press.

Jencks, Christopher. 1979. *Who Gets Ahead? The Determinants of Economic Success in America.* New York: Basic Books.

Jencks, Christopher. 1994. *Homeless.* Cambridge, MA: Harvard University Press.

Jencks, Christopher, Marshall Smith, Henry Acland, Mary Jo Bane, David Cohen, Herbert Gintis, Barbara Heyns, and Stephan Michelson. 1972. *Inequality.* New York: Basic Books.

Johnson, Kirk. 2009. "For Rural Elderly, Times Are Distinctly Harder." *The New York Times,* December 10. See also: nytimes.com/national, "Old and on the Farm."

Jolly, Clifford J., and Randall White. 1995. *Physical Anthropology and Archaelogy.* 5th ed. New York: McGraw-Hill.

Juel-Nielson, Neils. 1980. *Individual and Environment: Monozygotic Twins Reared Apart.* New York: International Universities Press.

Kahn, Joseph. 2000. "Globalism Unites a Many-Striped Multitude of Foes." *The New York Times,* April 15, p. A5.

Kaiser, Charles, 1997. *The Gay Metropolis.* Boston: Houghton Mifflin, Introduction.

Keller, Helen. 1903. *The Story of My Life.* New York: Doubleday, Page & Co., p. 24.

Keller, Susanne. 1963. *Beyond the Ruling Class.* New York: Random House.

Kennedy, Ruby Jo Reeves. 1944. "Single or Triple Melting Pot? Intermarriage Trends in New Haven, 1870–1940." *American Journal of Sociology* 49: 331–339.

Kerckhoff, Alan C., Richard T. Campbell, and Idee Winfield-Laird. 1985. "Social Mobility in Great Britain and the United States." *American Journal of Sociology* 91: 281–308.

Kershaw, Sarah. 2008. "In Studies of Virtual Twins, Nature Wins Again." *The New York Times,* September 3.

Killian, Lewis M. 1964. "Social Movements." In Robert E. Faris, ed., *Handbook of Modern Sociology.* Chicago: Rand McNally.

Kinsey, Alfred C., Wardell B. Pomeroy, and Charles E. Martin. 1948. *Sexual Behavior in the Human Male.* Philadelphia: Saunders.

Kinsey, Alfred C., Wardell Pomeroy, Charles E. Martin, and Paul Gebhard. 1953. *Sexual Behavior in the Human Female.* Philadelphia: Saunders.

Kinsley, Michael. 1991. "TRB." *The New Republic,* January 21, pp. 4, 41.

Kishiyama, Mark M., et al. 2009. "Socioeconomic Disparities Affect Prefrontal Function in Children." *Journal of Cognitive Neuroscience* 1(6): 1106–1115.

Knudson, M. 1990. "Hear America Swinging?" *Baltimore Sun,* February 19, pp. 1A, 7A.

Kohlberg, Lawrence. 1963. "The Development of Children's Orientation Toward a Moral Order: I. Sequence in the Development of Moral Thought." *Human Development* 6: 11–33.

Kohlberg, Lawrence. 1969. "Stage and Sequence: The Cognitive-Developmental Approach to Socialization." In D. A. Gloslin, ed., *Handbook of Socialization Theory and Research.* Chicago: Rand McNally, pp. 347–480.

Kohlberg, Lawrence. 1981. *The Philosophy of Moral Development: Moral Stages and the Idea of Justice.* New York, Harper & Row.

Kohn, Melvin. 1977. *Class and Conformity: A Study in Values.* 2nd ed. Homewood, IL: Dorsey Press.

Kolata, Gina. 1998. "Scientists Brace for Changes in Path of Human Evolution." *The New York Times,* March 21, pp. 1–12.

Konner, Melvin. 1988. "The Aggressors." *The New York Times Magazine,* August 14, pp. 33–34.

Kornblum, William, and T. M. Williams. 1978. "Life-Style, Leisure, and Community Life," in D. Steet and Associates, eds., *Handbook of Contemporary Urban Life.* San Francisco: Jossey-Bass.

Kosmin, B., Mayer Egon, and A. Keyser. 2001. *American Religious Identification Survey.* New York: The Graduate Center of the City University of New York. (October).

Kozma, Anna-Liza. 1997. "Gender Foretells Arguments' Results: Women Lose." *The (Cleveland) Plain Dealer* (originally from the *Chicago Tribune*), March 4, p. 4E.

Kristof, Nicholas. 1991. "China. The End of the Golden Road." *The New York Times Magazine,* December 1, pp. 53, 87.

Kron, Josh. 2010. "For Rwandan Students, Ethnic Tensions Lurk." *The New York Times,* May 16.

Krugman, Paul. 2006. "Wages, Wealth and Politics." *The New York Times,* August 18, p. A19.

Krugman, Paul. 2007. "Gilded Once More." *The New York Times,* April 27, p. 20.

Krugman, Paul. 2011. "Degrees and Dollars." *The New York Times,* March 7, p. A19.

Lane, Robert E. 1962. *Political Ideology: Why the American Common Man Believes What He Does.* New York: Free Press.

Lasswell, Harold, and Abraham Kaplan. 1950. *Power and Society.* New Haven, CT: Yale University Press.

Laumann, Edward O., John H. Gagnon, Robert T. Michael, and Stuart Michaels. 1994. *The Social Organization of Sexuality: Sexual Practices in the United States.* Chicago: University of Chicago Press.

Lehmann-Haupt, Christopher. 1996. "How Did Man Get So Bad? By Looking to the Apes." *The New York Times,* October 10, p. B6.

Lemonick, Michael D. 1994. "One Less Missing Link." *Time,* October 3, pp. 68–69.

Lenski, Gerhard. 1966. *Power and Privilege: A Theory of Social Stratification.* New York: McGraw-Hill.

Lenski, Gerhard. 1970/1987. *Human Societies.* New York: McGraw-Hill.

Leonhardt, David. 2001. "For the Boss, Happy Days Are Still Here." *The New York Times,* April 1, Section 3, pp. 1, 8.

Lévi-Strauss, Claude. 1971. "The Family." In *Family in Transition,* Arlene S. Skolnick and Jerome H. Skolnick, eds. Boston: Little, Brown.

Levine, Richard. 1991. "Economic Troubles and Service Cuts Reduce the Lure of New York City." *The New York Times,* April 1, p. A9.

Levy, Frank, and Richard J. Murnane. 2004. *The New Division of Labor.* Princeton, NJ: Princeton University Press.

Lewin, Tamar. 2001. "Study Says Little Has Changed in Views on Working Mothers." *The New York Times,* September 10, p. A20.

Lewin, Tamar. 2006. "At Colleges, Women Are Leaving Men in the Dust." *The New York Times,* July 9, pp. 1, 19.

Lewin, Tamar. 2010. "After Years of Falling, Teen Pregnancy Rate Rises." *The New York Times,* January 27, p. A16.

Liazos, Alexander. 1972. "The Poverty of the Sociology of Deviance: Nuts, Sluts, and Perverts." *Social Problems* 20: 103–120.

Linden, Eugene. 1992. "Too Many People." *Time,* Fall (Special Issue), p. 64.

Lino, Mark. 1999. "Expenditures on Children by Families: 1998 Annual Report." Washington, DC: U.S. Department of Agriculture, Center for Nutrition Policy and Promotion.

Lipset, Seymour Martin. 1963. *Political Man.* Garden City, NY: Doubleday.

Lipset, Seymour Martin. 1976. "Equality and Inequality." In Robert K. Merton and Robert Nisbet, eds. *Contemporary Social Problems.* 4th ed. New York: Harcourt Brace Jovanovich.

Lipset, Seymour Martin, and Reinhard Bendix. 1959. *Social Mobility in Industrial Society.* Berkeley: University of California Press.

Lofland, John. 1981. "Collective Behavior: The Elementary Forms." In N. Rosenberg and R. H. Turner, eds., *Social Psychology: Sociological Perspectives.* New York: Basic.

Lofland, John. 1985. *Protest: Studies of Collective Behavior and Social Movements.* New Brunswick, NJ: Transaction.

Lofland, Lyn. 1973. *A World of Strangers.* New York: Basic.

Lombroso, Cesare. 1911. *Crime: Its Causes and Remedies.* Boston: Little, Brown.

Lowi, Theodore J. 1979. *The End of Liberalism: Ideology, Policy and the Crisis of Public Authority.* 2nd ed. New York: Norton.

Luepnitz, Deborah. 1979. "Which Aspects of Divorce Affect Children?" *The Family Coordinator* 28 (January), pp. 79–85.

Lyall, Sarah. 2004. "Britain Cracks Down on Nasties Like the 'Neighbor from Hell.' " *The New York Times,* April 2, pp. 1, A6.

MacIver, Robert. 1947. *The Web of Government.* New York: Macmillan.

Mangels, John. 2009. "Cleveland Researchers Say Fossil Find Overturns Thinking on Human Evolution." *The Plain Dealer,* October 1.

Mannheim, Karl. 1936. *Ideology and Utopia.* New York: Harcourt Brace.

Marantz Henig, Robin. 2009. "Understanding the Anxious Mind." *The New York Times,* September 29.

Marquardt, Elizabeth. 2006. *Between Two Worlds: The Inner Lives of Children of Divorce.* New York: Three Rivers Press.

Marsh, Bill. 2010. "Even With a Cleanup, Spilled Oil Stays With Us." *The New York Times,* June 5, Week in Review.

Martin, Steven. 2006. "Trends in Marital Dissolution by Women's Education in the United States." *Demographic Research,* 13 December. *http://www.demographicresearch.org.* Accessed 7/11/07.

Marx, Gary T. 1967. *Protest and Prejudice.* New York: Harper & Row.

Marx, Karl, and Friedrich Engels. 1964. *On Religion.* New York: Schocken Books.

Maslow, Abraham. 1968. *Toward a Psychology of Being.* 2nd ed. New York: Van Nostrand.

Mauss, Armand L. 1975. *Social Problems of Social Movements.* Philadelphia: Lippincott.

McCready, William C., and Andrew M. Greeley. 1976. *The Ultimate Values of the American Population.* Beverly Hills, CA: Sage Publications.

McElvaine, Robert S. 2000. *Eve's Seed: Biology, the Sexes and the Course of History.* New York: McGraw-Hill.

McGoldrick, Monica, and Betty Carter, eds. 1988. *The Changing Family Life Cycle: A Framework for Family Therapy.* New York: Gardner Press.

McGuire, Meredith B. 1987. *Religion: The Social Context.* 2nd ed. Belmont, CA: Wadsworth.

McNeil, Donald G. Jr. 2004. "When Real Food Isn't an Option." *The New York Times,* May 23, Section 4, pp. 1, 12.

McPherson, Miller, Lynn Smith-Lovin, and Matthew E. Brashears, 2006. "Social Isolation in America: Changes in Core Discussion Networks over Two Decades." *American Sociological Review* 71(3), June, pp. 353–374.

McWhorter, John. 2001. "Against Reparations." *The New Republic,* July 23, pp. 32–38.

Mead, Margaret. 1935. *Sex and Temperament in Three Primitive Societies.* Magnolia, MA: Peter Smith.

Mead, Margaret. 1949/1970. *Male and Female.* London: Penguin Books.

Mehrabian, A. 1971. "Verbal and Nonverbal Interaction of Strangers in a Waiting Situation." *Journal of Experimental Research in Personality* 5: 127–138.

Merton, Robert K. 1938. "Social Structure and Anomie." *American Sociological Review* 3: 672–682.

Merton, Robert K. 1968. *Social Theory and Social Structure.* 2nd ed. New York: Free Press.

Mills, C. Wright. (1956) 1958. *The Power Elite.* New York: Oxford University Press.

Minerbrook, Scott. 1992. "A Tale of Two Suburbias." *U.S. News & World Report.* November 9, pp. 32, 40.

Mitchell, Alison. 1998. "A New Form of Lobbying Puts Public Face on Private Interest." *The New York Times,* September 30, A1–A14.

Moffet, Robert K., and Jack F. Scherer. 1976. *Dealing with Divorce.* Boston: Little, Brown.

Money, John, and Anke Erhardt. 1972. *Man and Woman, Boy and Girl.* Baltimore: Johns Hopkins University Press.

Mooallem, Jon. 2010. "The Love That Dare Not Squawk its Name." *The New York Times Magazine,* April 4, 2010, pp. 26–35, 44–46.

Murdock, George Peter. 1945. "The Common Denominator of Cultures." In Ralph Linton, ed., *The Science of Man in the World Crisis.* New York: Columbia University Press, pp. 123–142.

Murdock, George Peter. 1957. "World Ethnographic Sample." *American Anthropologist* 59: 664–687.

Murdock, George Peter. 1949/1965. *Social Structure.* New York: Free Press.

Murray, Christopher J. L., Sandeep C. Kulkarni, Catherine Michaud, Niels Tomijima, Maria T. Bulzacchelli, Terrell J. Iandiorio, and Majid Ezzati. 2006. "Eight Americas: Investigating Mortality Disparities Across Races, Counties, and Race-Counties in the United States." *PLoS Med* 3(9): e260. DOI: 10.1371/journal. pmed.0030260. (September 12).

Myers, David. 2004. *Psychology.* 7th ed. New York: W. H. Freeman & Co.

Myerson, Allen R. 1995. "American Money Makes the Whole World Sing." *The New York Times,* December 17, pp. E1, E14.

Nagourney, Adam. 2006. "Internet Injects Sweeping Change into U.S. Politics." *The New York Times,* April 2, pp. 1, 17.

Narayan, Shoba. 1998. "Lessons from an Arranged Marriage." *New Woman,* January.

NASA/Goddard Space Flight Center. "New Image of Infant Universe Reveals Era of First Stars, Age of Cosmos, and More." February 2, 2003. *http://www.gsfc. nasa.gov/topstory/2003/0206mapresults.html.*

Nash, Madeleine J. 1993. "How Did Life Begin?" *Time,* October 11, pp. 69–74.

National Center for Health Statistics. 2006. Vital Statistics. *http://www.cdc.gov/nchs/vitalstats.htm.* Accessed: 6/12/07.

National Clearinghouse on Child Abuse and Neglect. 2004. "Child Abuse and Neglect Fatalities: Statistics and Interventions." *http://nccanch.acf.hhs.gov.* Accessed 12/11/04.

National Law Center for Homelessness and Poverty (NLCHPI), 2004. "2004 Appropriations Fail to Keep Pace with Increasing Homelessness." January 23.

Neergard, Lauran. 2006. "Where You Live Linked to Life Expectancy." *Houston Chronicle. http://www.houstonchronicle.com/section:national news.htm.*

NielsenWire. 2009. "The Three Screen Report: Americans Watch More TV Than Ever; Web and Mobile Video Up Too." May 20.

Nisbet, Robert A. 1970. *The Social Bond.* New York: Knopf.

O'Dea, Thomas F. 1966. *The Sociology of Religion.* Englewood Cliffs, NJ: Prentice Hall.

O'Dea, Thomas F., and Janet O'Dea Aviad. 1983. *The Sociology of Religion,* 2nd ed. Englewood Cliffs, NJ: Prentice Hall.

Owen, D. R. 1972. "The 47 XYY Male: A Review." *Psychological Bulletin* 78, 209–233.

Palen, J. John. 2006. *The Urban World.* 6th ed. New York: McGraw-Hill.

Palen, J. John. 2008. *The Urban World.* 8th ed. Paradigm Publishers.

Palmore, Erdman. 1977. "Facts on Aging." *Gerontologist* 17: 315–320.

Park, Robert Ezra. 1967. "The Urban Community as a Spatial Pattern and a Moral Order." In R. H. Turner, ed., *Robert E. Park on Social Control and Collective Behavior.* Chicago: University of Chicago Press.

Parker-Pope, Tara. 2010. "The Science of a Happy Marriage." *The New York Times,* May 11, pp. D1–D6.

Parrillo, Vincent N. 1990. *Strangers to These Shores.* 3rd ed. New York: Macmillan.

Patterson, Gerald R. 1980. "Children Who Steal." In *Understanding Crime: Current Theory and Research.* Travis Hirschi and Michael Gottfredson, eds. Beverly Hills, CA: Sage.

Patterson, Orlando. 2006. "A Poverty of the Mind." *The New York Times,* March 26, p. 13.

Pear, Robert. 1993. "Poverty in U.S. Grew Faster Than Population Last Year." *The New York Times,* October 5, p. 10.

Pear, Robert. 1998. "Number on Welfare Dips Below 10 Million." *The New York Times,* January 21, p. 12.

Pew Forum Resources. 2006. *Religion and World Affairs. http://pewforum.org/worldaffairs.* Accessed 5/9/2007.

Pew Global Attitudes Project. 2002. "What the World Thinks in 2002." December 4. *http://www.people-press. org.* Accessed 6/6/04.

Pew Research Center for the People and the Press. 2004. "GOP The Religion-Friendly Party . . ." *Survey Reports.* Released August 24, 2004. Accessed 9/15/2007.

Pew Research Center for the People and the Press. 2005. "GOP Makes Gains Among the Working Class, While Democrats Hold onto the Union Vote." August 2.

Pew Research Center for the People and the Press. 2007. Survey Reports. "Summary of Findings: Public Knowledge of Current Affairs . . ." April 15. *http://people-press.org/reports/print/php3?PageID=1137.* Accessed 5/23/2007.

Pew Research Center for the People and the Press. 2008. "Inside the Middle Class: Bad Times Hit the Good Life." April 9. *http://pewsocialtrends.org/pubs/706-middle-class-poll.* April 9. Accessed 11/14/09.

The Pew Forum on Religion & Public Life. 2008. "The U.S. Religious Landscape Survey." February 25. *http:// pewforum.org/Datasets/Deataset-ownload.aspx*

Pew Research Center Publications. 2009a. "Dissecting the 2008 Electorate: Most Diverse in U.S. History." April 30. Accessed 03/02/10.

Pew Research Center for the People and the Press. 2009b. "Majority Continues to Support Civil Unions. Most Still Oppose Same-Sex Marriage." *http://people-press.org/report/553/same-sex-marriage*. Accessed 12/16/09.

Phillips, Kevin. 1990. *The Politics of Rich and Poor: Wealth and the American Electorate in the Reagan Aftermath*. New York: Random House.

Piaget, Jean. 1950. *The Psychology of Intelligence*. London: Routledge & Kegan Paul.

Piaget, Jean. 1954. *The Construction of Reality in the Child*. New York: Basic Books.

Piketty, Thomas, and Emmanuel Saez. 2006. "The Evolution of Top Incomes: A Historical and International Perspective." National Bureau of Economic Research. January. *http://www.nber.org/papers/*(W11955).

Pillard, R. C., and J. D. Weinrich. 1986. "Evidence of Familial Nature of Male Homosexuality." *Archives of General Psychiatry* 43: 808–812.

Pilon, Mary. 2010. "What's a Degree Really Worth?" *The Wall Street Journal*. Digital Network. February 02. *http://www.online.wsj.com/article/SB10001424*.

Piven, Frances Fox, and Richard A. Cloward. 1995. "Collective Protest: A Critique of Resource-Mobilization Theory." In Stanford M. Lyman, ed., *Social Movements*. New York: New York Unversity Press.

Police Executive Research Forum. 2006. "Violent Crime in America: 24 Months of Alarming Trends." October. *http://www.policeforum.org*.

Pope, Justin. 2004. "Study Finds More College Students But Not More Graduates." *Plain Dealer*, May 27, A6.

Popenoe, David. 1995. *Sociology*. Englewood Cliffs, NJ: Prentice Hall.

Population Reference Bureau. 2001. *2001 World Population Data Sheet*. Washington, DC: U.S. Government Printing Office.

Population Reference Bureau. 2007. *World Population Highlights*. Population Bulletin 62, no. 3 (2007). September.

Population Reference Bureau. 2010. *2010 World Population Highlights: Key Findings From PRB's 2010 World Population Data Sheet*. Population Bulletin 65, no. 2 (2010).

Preston, Julia. 2010. "Illegal Immigrant Students Protest at McCain Office." *The New York Times*, May 18, p. A17.

Prewitt, Kenneth, Sidney Verba, and Robert H. Salisbury. 1987. *An Introduction to American Government*. 5th ed. New York: Harper & Row.

Putnam, Robert D. 2000. *Bowling Alone: The Collapse and Revival of American Community*. New York: Simon and Schuster.

Qian, Zhenchao. 1998. "Changes in Assortive Mating: The Impact of Age and Education, 1970–1990." *Demography* 35(3): 279–292.

Quirk, Matthew. 2007. "The Mexican Connection." *The Atlantic*, April, p. 26.

Radelet, Michael L., and Ronald L. Akers, 1996. "Deterrence and the Death Penalty: The Views of the Experts." *Journal of Criminal Law and Criminology*, 87: 1–16.

Raudenbush, Stephen, and Felton Earls. 1997. "Neighborhoods and Violent Crime: A Multilevel Study of Collective Efficacy." *Science*, August 15, pp. 918–924.

Reich, Robert B. 1991. "Up the Workers." *The New Republic*, May 13, pp. 21–25

Relethford, John H. 2000. *The Human Species*. Mountainview, CA: Mayfield Publishing.

Rincon, Paul. 2 Jan 2004. BBC Online. 31 Mar 2004. *http://news.bbc.co.uk/1/hi/sci/tech/3361925.stm*.

Roberts, Sam. 2007. "51% of Women Are Now Living Without Spouse." *The New York Times*, January 16, p. A15.

Robinson, Randall. 2001. *The Debt: What America Owes to Blacks*. New York: Dutton/ Plume.

Rodriguez, Gregory. 1998. "Minority Leader." *The New Republic*, October 19, pp. 21–24.

Rodriguez, Gregory. 2003. "Mongrel America." *The Atlantic Monthly*, Vol. 291, No. 1, Jan./Feb.

Rogers, Carl R. 1961. *On Becoming a Person*. Boston: Houghton Mifflin.

Rosenthal, Elizabeth. 2009. "An Amazon Culture Withers as Food Dries Up." *The New York Times*, July 25, pp. A1-A6.

Rosin, Hanna. 2010. "The End of Men." *The Atlantic*. July/August, pp. 56–72.

Rymer, R. 1993. *Genie: An Abused Child's Flight from Silence*. New York: HarperCollins.

Safilios-Rothschild, Constantina. 1967. "A Comparison of Power Structure and Marital Satisfaction in Urban Greek and French Families." *Journal of Marriage and the Family* 30: 527–531.

Safire, William. 1995. "News About Jews: The Dwindling Percentage." *The New York Times*, July 17, p. A11.

Salisbury, Robert H. 1969. "An Exchange Theory of Interest Groups." *Midwest Journal of Political Science* 13(February): 1–32.

Sampson, R. J., S. W. Raudenbush, and F. Earls. 1997. "Neighborhoods and Violent Crime: A Multilevel Study of Collective Efficacy." *Science*, August 15, pp. 918–924.

Samuelson, Robert J. 2001. "Indifferent to Inequality?" *Newsweek*, May 7, p. 45.

Sapir, Edward. 1949. *Selected Writings of Edward Sapir in Language, Culture, and Personality*, David G. Mandelbaum, ed. Berkeley: University of California Press.

References

Sapir, Edward. 1960. *Culture, Language and Personality: Selected Essays*. Berkeley: University of California Press.

Sapolsky, R. M., and L. J. Share. 2004. "A Pacific Culture Among Wild Baboons: Its Emergence and Transmission." *PLoSBiol*2(4): e106.DOI:10.1371/journal,pbio.0020106.

Sargent, Lyman T. 1969. *Contemporary Political Ideologies*. Homewood, IL: Dorsey.

Scanzoni, John H., and Maximiliane Szinovacz. 1980. *Family Decision Making: A Developmental Sex Role Model*. Beverly Hills, CA: Sage.

Schattschneider, E. E. 1942. *Party Government*. New York: Farrar & Rinehart, p. 1.

Schrof, Joanne M. 1994. "A Lens on Matrimony." *U.S. News & World Report,* February 21, pp. 66–69.*The New York Times,* January 25, pp. A1, A16.

Schwartz, John. 2007. "Of Gay Sheep, Modern Science and the Perils of Bad Publicity." *The New York Times,* January 25, p. A8.

Semple, Kirk. 2009. "Bhutanese Refugees Forge a Life in the Bronx." *The New York Times,* September 25, pp. A21–23.

Sengupta, Somini. 2001. "How Many Poor Children Is Too Many?" *The New York Times,* July 8, p. WK3.

Shea, Christopher. 2005. "Econophysics." *The New York Times,* December 11, p. B12.

Sheldon, William H. 1940. *The Varieties of Human Physique*. New York: Harper.

Sheldon, William H., et al. 1949. *Varieties of Delinquent Youth*. New York: Harper & Row.

Shils, Edward. 1961. "Mass Society and Its Culture." In N. Jacobs, ed., *Culture for the Millions*. New York: Van Nostrand Reinhold.

Shils, Edward. 1968. "The Concept of Ideology." In David L. Sills, ed. *The International Encyclopedia of the Social Sciences*. New York: Macmillan and Free Press.

Shorto, Russell. 1997. "Belief by the Numbers." *The New York Times Magazine,* December 7, pp. 60–61.

Shreeve, Jamie. 2009. "Oldest Skeleton of Human Ancestor Found." *National Geographic Magazine,* October 1.

Shute, Nancy. 2001. "Where We Come From." *U.S. News & World Report.* January 29, pp. 34–41.

Simmel, Georg. (1905) 1956. *Conflict and the Web of Group Affiliation*. Kurt H. Wolff, transl. Glencoe, IL: Free Press.

Simpson, George E., and J. Milton Yinger. 1972. *Racial and Cultural Minorities: An Analysis of Prejudice and Discrimination*. 4th ed. New York: Harper & Row. (See also: 1985, 5th ed. New York: Plenum Press).

Slackman, Michael. 2009. "Purge of Iranian Universities Feared." *The New York Times,* September 1.

Smith, Adam. 1976. *The Wealth of Nations*. Chicago: University of Chicago Press.

Smith, Douglas A., and Patrick R. Gartin. 1989. "Specifying Specific Deterrence: The Influence of Arrest on Future Criminal Activity." *American Sociological Review* 54(1): 94–105.

Smith, Rupert. 2007. *The Utility of Force in the Modern World*. New York: Alfred A. Knopf.

Smits, Paul, and Vincent Kane. 2009. "Homelessness and Our Nation's Veterans." Power Point presentation at National Coalition for Homeless Veterans, June 10. *www.nchv.org/news_article.cfm?id=632.*

Snarey, John. 1987. "A Question of Morality." *Psychology Today,* June, pp. 6–8.

Sondermann, Fred A., William C. Olson, and David S. McLellan. 1970. *The Theory and Practice of International Relations*. 3rd ed. Englewood Cliffs, NJ: Prentice Hall.

Sowell, Thomas. 1983. *The Economics and Politics of Race: An International Perspective*. New York: Morrow.

Spencer, Herbert. 1873. *Descriptive Sociology*. Vol. I, New York: Appleton.

Spitz, Rene A. 1964. "Hospitalism." In Rose L. Coser, ed., *The Family: Its Structure and Functions*. New York: St. Martin's Press, pp. 399–425. Originally appeared in *The Psychoanalytic Study of the Child,* 1945, Vol. 1. New York: International Universities Press.

Stanley, S. M., Whitton, S. W., and Markham, H. J. 2004. "Maybe I do: Interpersonal Commitment and Premarital or Nonmarital Cohabitation." *Journal of Family Issues,* Vol. 25, pp. 496–519.

Stark, Rodney. 1985. *Sociology*. Belmont, CA: Wadsworth.

Stark, Rodney, and W. S. Bainbridge. 1985. *The Future of Religion: Secularization, Revival, and Cult Formation*. Berkeley: University of California Press.

Starrels, Marjorie. 1992. "Attitude Similarity Between Mothers and Children Regarding Maternal Employment," *Journal of Marriage and the Family* 54: 91–103.

Stein, Rob. 2010. "Rise in Teenage Pregnancy Rate Spurs New Debate On Arresting It." *The Washington Post.* *http://www.washingtonpost.com/wp-dyn/content/article/2010/01/25/AR2010012503957_p.* Accessed 02/07/2010.

Steinberg, Laurence, and Susan Silverberg. 1987. "Marital Satisfaction in Middle Stages of Family Life Cycle." *Journal of Marriage and the Family* 49 (4): 751–760.

Steinfels, Peter. 1998. "A Contrarian Sociologist of Religion Changes His Mind: Modernity Does Not Necessarily Lead to a Decline in Religion." *The New York Times,* September 5, p. 11.

Stephan, James E., Rosenbaum, Janet E., Person, and Ann E. 2010. "Beyond One Size Fits All College Dreams." *American Educator,* Fall 2010, pp. 2–11.

Stevens, William K. 1990, "New Eye on Nature: The Real Constant is Eternal Turmoil." *The New York Times,* July 31, pp. B5, B6.

References

Stoessinger, John G. 1975. *The Might of Nations: World Politics in Our Time.* 5th ed. New York: Random House.

Stolberg, Sheryl Gay. 1999. "Birth Rate at New Low as Teenage Pregnancy Declines." *The New York Times,* April 29, p. A22.

Stolberg, Sheryl Gay. 2001. "Researchers Find a Link Between Behavioral Problems and Time in Child Care." *The New York Times,* April 19, p. A18.

Strayhorn, Joseph M., and Jillian C. Strayhorn. 2009. "Religiosity and Teen Birth Rate in the United States." *Reproductive Health,* Vol. 6, No. 14. September.

Subramanian, Sribala. 1995. "The Story in Our Genes." *Time,* January 16, pp. 54–55.

Suplee, C. 1991. "Brain May Determine Sexuality." *The Washington Post,* August 30, pp. A1, A13.

Surowiecki, James. 2004. *The Wisdom of Crowds.* Doubleday.

Surowiecki, James. 2005. *The Wisdom of Crowds.* New York: Anchor.

Sutherland, Edwin H. 1949, 1961. *White Collar Crime.* New York: Dryden.

Suttles, Gerald. 1970. *The Social Order of the Slum.* Chicago: University of Chicago Press.

Szinovacz, Maximiliane E. 1987. "Family Power." In *Handbook of Marriage and the Family.* New York: Plenum, pp. 652–693.

Tierney, John. 2007. "The Voices in My Head Say 'Buy It!' Why Argue?" *The New York Times,* January 16, Science Section.

Tilley, Charles. 2006. *Why?* Princeton, NJ: Princeton University Press.

Thurow, Lester C. 1999. "Building Wealth." *The Atlantic Monthly,* June, pp. 57–69.

Tönnies, Ferdinand. (1887) 1957. *Community and Society.* New York: Harper Torchbooks.

Trigaux, Robert. 2006. "CEO Pay Eclipses Ridiculous." *St. Petersburg Times,* April 24, p. 1D.

Troidén, Richard R. 1988. *Gay and Lesbian Identity: A Sociological Analysis.* New York: General Hall, pp. 42–58.

Trumbull, Mark. 2009. "Poverty Is Up, But How Much? Census Tells Two Stories." *The Christian Science Monitor.* October 20.

Turnbull, Colin. 1973. *The Mountain People.* New York: Simon & Schuster.

United Nations. 2007. "Population and Vital Statistics Report." Series A. Vol. LIX, No. 1. Department of Economic and Social Affairs. January 1, Table 3, p. 16.

United States Department of Labor, Bureau of Labor Statistics. Employment Situation Summary. Current Empoyment Statistics. 2011.

U.S. Census Bureau. 2003. Economic and Statistics Administration. U.S. Census Press Release, December 18.

U.S. Census Bureau. 2004. Historical Income Tables–Income Equality. Table IE–1. *http://www.census.gov/hhes/income/histinc/ei1.html.* Accessed 7/8/07.

U.S. Census Bureau. 2006. "Percent of the Total Population Who Are 65 Years and Over." 2006 Population Estimates, July.

U.S. Census Bureau. 2007a. Current Population Reports. "Domestic Net Migration in the United States: 2000 to 2004." Issued April 2006.

U.S. Census Bureau. 2008. "Income, Poverty, and Health Insurance Coverage in the United States: 2008." Press Release, September 10, 2009, p. 9. *http://www.census.gov/Press-Release/www/releases/archives/income_wealth/014227i.html.*

U.S. Census Bureau. 2009. "American's Families and Living Arrangements." Current Population Survey, March.

U.S. Census Bureau. 2005–2009. "Selected Social Characteristics in the United States: 2005–2009." American Factfinder.

U.S. Census Bureau. 2009. "Educational Attainment by Race and Hispanic Origin: 1970–2009." The 2011 Statistical Abstract. Education.

U.S. Conference of Mayors, 2006. "Hunger and Homelessness Remains a Critical Issue for Families; Leading Causes Cited Are Unemployment, Mental Illness, and Lack of Affordable Housing." *http:www.usmayors.org/USCM/home.asp.*

U.S. Department of Education. 2006. "A Test of Leadership: Charting the Future of U.S. Higher Education." A Report of the Commission Appointed by Secretary of Education Margaret Spellings. Washington, DC. September.

U.S. Department of Education. 2009. "The Nation's Report Card: Trends in Academic Progress in Reading and Mathematics 2008." April.

U.S. Department of Health and Human Services, Administration for Children and Families. *http://www.nccic.org/index.html.* Last updated June 28, 2006.

U.S. Department of Health and Human Services. Administration for Children and Families. Chapter 3, Child Maltreatment, 2007.

U.S. Department of Health and Human Services, Administration on Aging. "Profile of Older Americans: 2000," p. 10. *http://www.aoa.gov/aoa/stats/profile/default.htm.* Accessed 8/11/2001.

U.S. Department of Health and Human Services, Administration on Aging. "Life Expectancy by Age Group & Race in Years, 1997." Facts and Figures: Statistics on Minority Aging in the U.S.—The Many Faces of Aging. *http://www.aoa.gov/minorityaccess/stats.html.* Accessed 8/27/2001.

U.S. Department of Justice, Bureau of Justice Statistics, 2001a. *Criminal Offenders Statistics,* "Lifetime Likelihood of Going to State or Federal Prison."

References

U.S. Department of Justice, Bureau of Justice Statistics, 2001b. *Criminal Offenders Statistics.* "Recidivism."

U.S. Department of Labor. 2000. *Highlights of Women's Earnings in 2005.* May. Report 943, p. 1. *http://www. dol.gov/wb/factsheets/qf-laborforce-06.htm.*

Veblen, Thorstein. (1899) 1953. *The Theory of the Leisure Class.* New York: The New American Library.

Verba, Sidney, Kay Schlozman, and Henry Brady. 1995. *Voice and Equality.* Cambridge, MA: Harvard University Press.

Viotti, Paul R., and Mark V. Kauppi. 1987. *International Relations Theory.* New York: Macmillan.

Vogel, Dena Ann, Margaret A. Lake, Suzanne Evans, and Katherine Hildebrandt Karraker. 1991. "Children and Adults' Sex-Stereotyped Perceptions of Infants." *Sex Roles* 24: 605.

Wade, Nicholas. 1997. "Neanderthal DNA Sheds New Light on Human Origins." *The New York Times,* July 11, pp. 1, A14.

Wade, Nicholas. 2000. "DNA Tests Cast Doubt on Link Between Neanderthals and Modern Man." *The New York Times,* March 29, p. A16.

Wade, Nicholas. 2002. "Insight Into Human-Chimp Differences." *The New York Times,* April 12, p. A18.

Wade, Nicholas. 2003. "Why Humans and Their Fur Parted Ways." *The New York Times,* August 19, pp. D1, D4.

Wade, Nicholas. 2007. "Pas de Deux of Sexuality Is Written in the Genes." *The New York Times,* April 10, pp. D1, D6.

Wade, Nicholas. 2010a. "Human Culture, an Evolutionary Force." *The New York Times,* March 2, pp. D1–D4.

Wade, Nicholas. 2010b. "In Tibetans, Signals of Fast Evolution." *The New York Times,* July 2, p. A7.

Wagley, Charles, and Marvin Harris. 1958. *Minorities in the New World.* New York: Columbia.

Wallerstein, Judith. 1989. "Children after Divorce." *The New York Times Magazine,* January 22, pp. 19–44.

Wallerstein, Judith, and Sandra Blakeslee. 1989. *Second Chances.* New York: Ticknor & Fields.

Wallerstein, Judith S., and Joan B. Kelly. 1983. "The Effects of Parental Divorce: Experiences of the Child in Later Years." In Arlene S. Skolnick and Jerome H. Skolnick, eds., *Family in Transition.* Boston: Little, Brown.

Wallis, Claudia. 1987. "Is Day Care Bad for Babies?" *Time* (June 22), p. 63.

Wartik, Nancy. 2004. "Hard-Wired for Prejudice? Experts Examine Human Response to Outsiders." *The New York Times,* April 20, p. D5.

Wattenberg, Ben J., and Karl Zinsmeister. 1986. "The Birth Dearth: The Geopolitical Consequences." *Public Opinion* 8 (December/January): 6–13.

Wattenberg, Martin P. 1994. *The Decline of American Political Parties.* Cambridge, MA: Harvard University Press.

Weber, Max. 1925/1947. *Theory of Social and Economic Organization.* A. L. Henderson and Talcott Parsons, transl. New York: Free Press.

Weber, Max. 1957. *The Theory of Social and Economic Organization.* New York: Free Press.

Weber, Max. 1904–5/1958. *The Protestant Ethic and the Spirit of Capitalism.* New York: Charles Scribner's Sons.

Weishaus, Sylvia, and Dorothy Field. 1988. "A Half Century of Marriage: Continuity or Change?" *Journal of Marriage and the Family* 50(August), pp. 763–774.

Weiss, Kenneth R. 1989. "80–Year Tide of Migration by Blacks Out of the South Has Turned Around." *The New York Times,* June 1, p. Y29.

Weitzman, Lenore J. 1985. *The Divorce Revolution: The Unexpected Social and Economic Consequences for Women and Children in America.* New York: Free Press.

White, E. B. 1949. *Here Is New York.* New York: Harper & Row, pp. 27–30.

Whiting, B. 1963. *Six Cultures: Studies in Child Rearing.* London: Wiley.

Whorf, Benjamin. 1956. *Language, Thought and Reality.* New York: Wiley.

Whyte, William H. 1989. *Cities.* New York: Doubleday.

Wilford, John Noble. 1992. "Jawbone Offers Clues in Search for 'Missing Link.' " *The New York Times,* March 17, p. B5.

Wilford, John Noble. 1993. "Old Tablet from Turkish Site Shows Early Spread of Culture." *The New York Times,* November 9, p. B7.

Wilford, John Noble. 1997. "New Clues Show Where People Made the Great Leap to Agriculture." *The New York Times,* November 18, pp. B9, B12.

Wilford, John Noble. 1998a. "Ancestral Humans Could Speak, Anthropologists' Finding Suggests." *The New York Times,* April 28, pp. 1, 17.

Wilford, John Noble. 1998b. "Look Who's Talking. Don't Bother Listening." *The New York Times,* May 3, Section 4, p. 4.

Wilford, John Noble. 1999. "Discovery Suggests Man Is a Bit Neanderthal." *The New York Times,* April 25, pp. 1, 21.

Wilford, John Noble. 2000. "Skulls in Caucasus Linked to Early Humans in Africa." *The New York Times,* May 12, pp. 1, A28.

Wilford, John Noble. 2001. "The Family of Man Grows a Little Larger." *The New York Times,* March 25, p. 3.

Wilford, John Noble. 2003. "New Clue on Which Came First, Tools or Better Diets." *The New York Times,* October 21, Section F, 3.

Wilford, John Noble. 2004a. "Fossils Found in Spain Seen as Last Link to Great Apes." *The New York Times,* November 19, p. A8.

Wilford, John Noble. 2004b. "Less Jaw, Big Brain: Evolution Milestone Laid to Gene Flaw." *The New York Times,* March 25, pp. 1, A18.

Wilford, John Noble. 2007a. "Fossils Reveal Clues on Human Ancestor." *The New York Times,* September 20.

Wilford, John Noble. 2007b. "Lost in a Million-Year Gap, Solid Clue to Human Origins." *The New York Times,* September 18, p. D1, 4.

Wilford, John Noble. 2009. "Fossil Skeleton Predates Lucy." *The New York Times,* October 1.

Wilford, John Noble. 2010. "In Syria, a Prologue for Cities." *The New York Times,* April 6. pp. D1–D4)

Williams, Robin, Jr. 1970. *American Society: A Sociological Interpretation.* 3rd ed. New York: Knopf.

Wilkinson Microwave Anisotropy Probe (MAP), October 29, 2010.

Wilson, Edward O. 1980. *Sociobiology,* abridged ed. New York: Belknap Press.

Wilson, Edward O. 1998. "Back from Chaos." *The Atlantic Monthly,* March, pp. 41–62.

Wilson, Edward O. 1999. *Consilience: The Unity of Knowledge.* New York: Vintage.

Wilson, James Q., and George L. Kelling. 1982. "Broken Windows." *Atlantic Monthly,* March, pp. 29–38.

Wilson, William Julius. 1978. *The Declining Significance of Race.* Chicago: University of Chicago Press.

Wilson, William Julius. 1987. *The Truly Disadvantaged: The Inner City, the Underclass, and Public Policy.* Chicago: University of Chicago Press.

Wirth, Louis. 1938. "Urbanism as a Way of Life." *American Journal of Sociology* 44: 1–44.

Wolfe, Alan. 1998. "The Homosexual Exception." *The New York Times Magazine,* February 8, pp. 46–47.

Wolin, Sheldon S. 1980. "Foreword." In *Democratic Elitism: A Critique,* Peter Bachrach, ed. Lanham, MD: University Press of America.

Womack, James P., Daniel T. Jones, and Daniel Roos. 1990. "How Lean Production Can Change the World." *The New York Times Magazine,* September 23, pp. 20–23, 34–38.

Women's Bureau, U.S. Department of Labor, Bureau of Labor Statistics, Employment and Earnings. November 2005. *http://www.dol.gov/wb/stats/main.htm.* Accessed 8/8/07.

World Development Indicators. 2004. World Bank Group. *http://worldbank.org/data/wdi2004/index.htm.* Accessed 9/12/07.

World Development Report, 2000–2001. Press Conference on 2001 World Indicators. April 29, 2001. *http://www.worldbank.org/ndr/2001/overview.html.*

World Development Indicators, 2010. *www.worldbank.org/data.*

World Resources. 1996–1997. *The Urban Environment.* New York: Oxford University Press.

Wrangham, Richard, and Dale Peterson. 1996. *Demonic Males: Apes and the Origins of Human Violence.* New York: Houghton Mifflin.

Yardley, Jim. 2006. "First Comes the Car, Then the $10,000 License Plate." *The New York Times,* July 6, p. A4.

Yetman, Norman R. 1985. *Majority and Minority: The Dynamics of Race and Ethnicity in American Life.* Boston: Allyn & Bacon.

Yetman Norman R., and C. Hoy Steele, eds. 1971. *Majority and Minority.* Boston: Allyn & Bacon.

Zeller, Tom. 2000. "Calculating One Kind of Middle Class." *The New York Times,* October 29, p. 5.

Zernike, Kate. 2000. "Gap Widens Again on Tests Given to Blacks and Whites." *The New York Times,* August 25, p. A14.

gender roles
  cognitive development theory, 230
Generativity, 117
Geometric progression, 253
Gerontologist, 240, 366
Global poverty, 181
Global village, 185
Good health, 32, 212
Gottfredson, Michael, 366
Government
  American Indian care and, 317
Grandparents
  supportive, 215
Grasslands, 53
Greenhouse effect, 272, 352
Group size, 81
Group therapy, 106, 132
group(s), 10
Guam, 317
Guilds, 340
Gun control, 321
gypsies, 66, 191

H
hair color, 98
Harlem, 84
Harper's Magazine, 190, 356
Hawaiians, 32
Health care
  Centers for Disease Control and Prevention (CDC), 360
  health insurance, coverage, 369
Hell's Angels, 69
Henry, William A., 310
High-income countries, 182
Hispanics, 169, 189
Hitler, Adolf, 281-282
homeless persons, 174
Homosexual behavior, 234-235
Homosexuals
  attitudes toward, 238
Hoover, Herbert, 311
Horticultural societies, 86
Household income, 167-168, 201, 218, 252
Human immunodeficiency virus
  Human immunodeficiency virus (HIV), 237
Hutus, 191
Hypertension, 130, 215

I
id, 105, 132, 172
Ideal culture, 64
Ideal type, 83
illegal aliens, 207, 246
Imitation, 100, 229
Immigration and Nationality Act, 206
Impotence, 130
In vitro fertilization, 236
Income inequality, 180
Industrializing Nations, 258-259
Infant mortality rate, 244-245
Infants/newborns
  mortality rate, 244-245
Infertility, medical/high-tech solutions to
  in vitro fertilization, 236
In-groups, 85
institutional racism, 194
Institutionalized means, 134
Intellectual activities, 337
Intergenerational mobility, 178
Interlocking directorates, 335
Intermarriages, 286
Interracial marriage, 190

J
Japan
  World War II, 256, 289-290
Jewish Americans, 205
Jung, Carl, 106
Juvenile delinquency, 138

K
Kagan, Jerome, 113
Kohlberg, Lawrence, 108
Kosovo, 312
Krugman, Paul, 57

L
Labeling, 135-138
labeling theory, 135-138
Labor force
  sexual harassment in, 229
  significance of, 193, 371
Labor unions, 321, 340
Land degradation, 268
Larceny-theft, 138
Latchkey children, 116
Latin Americans, 207
Least Industrialized Nations, 291
Lesbian community, 11
Lesbians and gay men
  in the military, 67
Liberia, 181
Life course, 120, 240
Limits to growth, 273
Lincoln, Abraham, 310
Lombroso, Cesare, 128
Los Angeles riots, 199
Louisiana, 270, 318
Lower-middle class, 168
Low-income countries, 182

M
Malaria, 181
Malthus, Thomas, 253
Maltreatment, 369
Manila, 268
marital partners, 79
Marital satisfaction, 367
Marriage
  civil unions, 235, 367
  interracial, 190
  midlife, 117
  satisfaction in, 367-368
  widowhood and, 238
Marriage, communication in
  coercion, 88
  scapegoating, 191
Marriage, rituals in
  engagement, 235
Maslow, Abraham H., 118
Master status, 78, 136, 161
Matrimony, 368
Mayer, Egon, 364
Medical technology, 245
Megalopolis, 260
Megalopolises, 263
Melting pot, 188, 364
Memory loss, 215
men and boys, 109
Mental disorders, 130-132
Mental health and aging
  Alzheimer's, 215
Miami, 189, 264
Michaels, Stuart, 364
Microsoft Corporation, 162, 335
Middle age, 107
Middle-aged families
  marital satisfaction in, 367
military service
  economic problems, 168
  suicide in, 117
  upward mobility in, 183
Modeling, 60
Modernization theory, 212
Monarchies, 288
Money laundering, 139
Moore, Wilbert, 361
Multiple partners, 237

N
National Center for Health Statistics, 359
National Crime Victimization Survey, 140
National Crime Victimization Survey (NCVS), 140
National Party, 312
NCVS, 140
Negative sanctions, 63
Negro, 362
Net migration rate, 244
Net worth, 162
Nevada, 252, 304
Newborns, 109
Niger, 182, 245
Nonmaterial culture, 59-60, 258

Normative organizations, 92
Normlessness, 133
North Korea, 181, 289, 312

O
Operant conditioning, 106
Out-groups, 85

P
Pacific Islanders, 198
PACs, 335
pass laws, 62
Pastoral societies, 86
Personal fulfillment, 332
Phenotype, 32
Piaget, Jean, 108
Piaget, Jean, theory of cognitive, 108
Pine Ridge Reservation, 197
Pituitary gland, 114
Planned obsolescence, 336
Plea bargaining, 145
Pluralistic society, 204
Political Action Committees, 335
Political Action Committees (PACs), 335
political activity, 197
Political attitudes, 201
Political process, 280, 304
Political state, 285
population increases, 53
Population momentum, 252
Population Reference Bureau, 256, 367
Positive sanctions, 63
Postconventional level, 109
Postindustrial societies, 50, 77, 164, 212
Posttraumatic stress disorder, 106, 175
Posttraumatic stress disorder (PTSD), 175
Poverty
  elderly in, 213-214
  eliminating, 180
poverty, and crime, 4
Poverty rate, 169-170, 197-198, 218
Power elite, 365
Power elites, 280
Prenatal care, 130
Preoperational stage, 108
Primary aging, 215
Primary groups, 64, 73, 115, 135
Primatology, 11
Property crimes, 139-141
Proportional representation, 313
Protestant Reformation, 332
Psychological disorders, 132
Psychological theories, 132-133
Psychosexual stages, 106-107
Puritans, 332

Q
Quantitative approach, 10
Quantitative research, 10

R
race and ethnicity
  median family income, 198
Racial inequality, 209
Real culture, 64
Recidivism rates, 5
reparations, 365
Replacement level, 256
Republican Party, definition, 311
Republican Party, who votes for, 311
Republicans, 176, 314
Research designs, 19
research methods
  dependent variables, 9
Residential patterns
  of segregation, 189
Resource-mobilization theory, 367
Retreatism, 149
Rites of passage, 230
Ritualism, 149
Rogers, Joel, 361
Role confusion, 94, 107
Roman Catholics, 68, 317
Roosevelt, Franklin, 323, 354
Roosevelt, Franklin D., 323, 354

S